MARKETS IN THE MAKING

Markets in the Making: Rethinking Competition, Goods, and Innovation

Michel Callon

TRANSLATED BY OLIVIA CUSTER

EDITED BY MARTHA POON

ZONE BOOKS
633 Vanderbilt Street, Brooklyn, New York 11218

Originally published in France as *L'Emprise des marchés: Comprendre leur fonctionnement pour pouvoir les changer* © 2017 Éditions la Découverte

Cet ouvrage a bénéficié du soutien des Programmes d'aide à la publication de l'Institut français. The publisher would also like to thank the French Ministry of Culture for assistance with this translation.

Printed in the United States of America.
Distributed by Princeton University Press,
Princeton, New Jersey, and Woodstock, United Kingdom

Library of Congress Cataloging-in-Publication Data
Names: Callon, Michel, author. | Poon, Martha, editor.
Title: Markets in the making : rethinking competition, goods, and innovation / Michel Callon ; translated by Olivia Custer ; edited by Martha Poon.
Other titles: Emprise des marchés. English
Description: Brooklyn, New York : Zone Books, [2021] | Series: Near futures | Includes bibliographical references and index. | Summary: "If you're convinced you know what a market is, think again. As product designers and entrepreneurs soon discover, stable commercial transactions are more enigmatic than economic theory makes them out to be. Slicing through blunt theories of supply and demand, Michel Callon presents a rigorously researched but counterintuitive model of how everyday market activity get produced, at scale." —Provided by publisher.
Identifiers: LCCN 2021010740 (print) | LCCN 2021010741 (ebook) | ISBN 9781942130574 (hardback) | ISBN 9781942130581 (ebook)
Subjects: LCSH: Markets. | Marketing. | Capitalism. | Consumer goods. | Commercial products.
Classification: LCC HF5471 .C3513 2021 (print) | LCC HF5471 (ebook) | DDC 330.12/2—dc23
LC record available at https://lccn.loc.gov/2021010740
LC ebook record available at https://lccn.loc.gov/2021010741

CONTENTS

Preface to the English Edition

This book is the culmination of a research career I began in the 1970s, which, over the course of many years, led me to ask questions about the meaning of the word "market." The word itself does not seem complicated, yet its significance remained a mystery to me for a long time.

I am aware that my feelings are not shared by the majority. Many are convinced they know what a market is because they are told they live in market economies. Others trust in experts who have been writing on the topic over the course of several centuries. One of the objectives of this book is to persuade the reader that we need to reexamine our most deeply held convictions.

The feeling of false familiarity is not the only obstacle to fully understanding how markets are formed and how they transform. With so many challenges to the future of our societies, whether it be climate change, ecological damage, human rights, growing inequality, or geopolitical confrontations, it can feel like markets are of secondary importance. Circumstances conspire to edge markets out of our attention and dissuade us from deepening our exploration of what they can do or make happen (in French, *faire-faire*).

This book takes a gamble in the opposite direction. It takes seriously the famous affirmation of economist and anthropologist Karl Polanyi when he evokes the possible role of markets in the future: "The end of market society means in no way the absence of markets. These continue, in various fashions, to ensure the freedom of the consumer, to indicate the shifting of demand, to influence producers' income, and to serve as an instrument of accountancy, while ceasing altogether to be an organ of economic self-regulation."[1]

To my ear, Polanyi's message rings crystal clear. He refuses to treat markets as either straightforward instruments that should be regulated or as harmful institutions that we should be rid of. According to him, we should neither fight markets nor consider them mere instruments. Instead, he invites us to preserve the strengths of markets, with their capacity to contribute to realizing collective and individual well-being, while at the same time ensuring the preservation of values that are deemed to be essential. In his words, "Civic liberties, private enterprise and wage-system fused into a pattern of life which favored moral freedom and independence of mind.... We must try to maintain by all means in our power these high values inherited from the market-economy which collapsed."[2]

Polanyi is correct. In economic life, commercial practices will remain essential because there is no substitute; they play a role no other institution is able to hold. To advance this claim, I have pursued a simple strategy. I take up the basic query that imposed itself on me at the beginning of my research career and has preoccupied me ever since: "What is a market?"

In every study I have ever undertaken, the market has been there, like a weighty, but indecipherable shadow. Everywhere and nowhere, I could feel its presence, even if I could never grasp it. The dissatisfaction I experienced had nothing to do with dogmatic considerations or disciplinary loyalty. No matter what I read, I found no definitions that coincided with my empirical observations. The discomfort was unleashed during the first study I ever did on the development of an electric vehicle.

It is amusing to remember that at the end of the nineteenth century, a world record for speed was set by a vehicle called "La Jamais Contente" (The Never Happy), powered by a 750-kilogram lead battery. Less remembered are the generously financed projects, launched in several countries in the 1970s, notably in France, to give electric vehicles a second chance.

The Club of Rome's report put ecological questions and growth on the agenda of the highest circles of administration and power. By 1971, a minister of the environment was named in France for the first time. In the domain of industry, the objective was to bring forth solutions to the problems posed by pollution and the risk of exhausting combustible fossil fuel resources. A call for concerted action was issued by the state to overturn scientific and technical barriers standing in the way of alternative viable markets. Collaborations were organized between all of the stakeholders, from university researchers to consumer representatives, industry leaders, technical centers, government ministers, and so on. Efforts to develop an alternative to thermal engines centered on several types of fuel cells whose remarkable performance had already been demonstrated in space. Back then, we were already speaking of a hydrogen economy powered by nuclear electricity.

I received funding that assured me freedom and autonomy for three years and became what we would now call an embedded researcher. I was granted unlimited access to archives and the possibility of collaborating with teams of researchers and engineers working on the project. Progressive and modernizing French technocrats felt that including a sociologist and general engineer, one with additional training in economics, would surely boost the program! This is how I found myself at the heart of the reactor where social structures are transformed, in a kind of crucible where the ingredients that form what we call society are melted down and reformed, all while being pounded by often violent controversies between groups who saw the future differently. Through it all, I was surrounded by markets, either those that existed or those that were slated to exist.

I noticed that an economist colleague of similar training who did not have my access to the field of action was relying on standard tools to analyze and predict whether the transition from thermal to electric cars would eventually occur. He took into account all of the available variables and ended up with the conclusion that he was unable to make a serious prediction about anything. What completely escaped him were the observations I made in my daily environment: the profound uncertainty when knotting together economic, social, technical, political, and social concerns, as well as the multiple temporal horizons of the projects underway.

In the moment, many clever people announced what the market logic was and where things were going. Yet from where I stood, all I could see was a chaotic construction site, sciences in the making, commercial practices in the making, from which structured markets might one day emerge, but only if circumstances proved favorable. Very quickly, I further understood that distinguishing between *markets in the making* and *made markets* makes no sense. There are only *markets in the making* that are being transformed more or less intensively. Whether in my work on the treatments developed for rare diseases or on innovation in services, every one of the studies I have carried out reconfirms this original finding.

The bottom line is that economics, sociology, and anthropology all share the objective of moving themselves as far away as possible from operating markets in order to simplify their representation in theory. This means that researchers today continue to face the same challenge, the same confusion as I did. This book seeks to give firm guidance on how to dissolve the tension between academic theories and what is happening in the field.

What can we hope for by plunging ourselves into the effervescence of commercial practices instead of seeing them in vague outlines from the great distance imposed by abstraction? In other words, what is the value added by coming down into the empirical weeds? At the conceptual level, my approach will not only give us a more realistic understanding of how markets work, but it will open our eyes to everything that permits a functioning market to be formed, established, maintained, and transformed. Having looked more closely, we will discover that the concepts of competition, goods, and innovation need to be significantly reworked.

A second result, the most important, in my opinion, is to dissociate two big terms that get confused with one another: "markets" and "capitalism." The notion of "market agencement" presented in this book allows for this conceptual disintrication because it closely observes the substance and materiality of market practices. The confusion that prevails today dissipates the diversity of forms in market organizations. The tricky dissociation I will make in the book is now much easier to defend, since recent works, such as those by Katharina Pistor,[3] or older ones such as those by historians of accounting techniques or credit practices, make it possible to better characterize market arrangements that are specifically capitalist, distinguishing them from those that are not.

There remain a number of difficulties in the approach I am proposing. Although I will make the strong case that we must make the conceptual adjustments outlined above, carrying out the empirical research to support these changes is no light task. The materials most accessible to me come from current economic forms; thus, these examples are privileged. I have tried to develop the generality of the concept but acknowledge that more work needs to be done.

Another set of difficulties relates to politics. A central notion in my work is "matters of concern." The framings described in this book that lead to commercial transactions are also arrangements that shape behaviors. The behavioral effect incites and nourishes movements of resistance that level critiques. As I will emphasize, researchers need to treat these movements carefully and give them their place in the analysis. As I will argue, critique is not external to the market, but is rather its dynamic heartbeat: it generates the motion that keeps markets fresh and alive. This does not imply that researchers should be dispassionate observers. In the final chapter of the book, I will make the case that it is altogether laudable for academics to participate in generating and expressing matters of concern.

The first version of this book was published in France in 2017. The translation was no smooth ride, since the original text alternated between theoretical developments (which I recognize were somewhat arduous) and more vivid descriptions to illustrate how the analysis might work. I would like to thank Olivia Custer for having conveyed these movements in tone and style without ever sacrificing the coherence of the whole.

Translation is a difficult and risky art form. It frequently requires transposing and reformulating ideas for audiences with different experiences and disciplinary backgrounds. This interpretive work was done with remarkable patience by Martha Poon, to whom I express my profound gratitude. Over the course of our exchange, entire passages were rewritten to the point where it crossed my mind that a second edition might be issued in French by translating backward from the English one. I will be saving my energies instead for a second volume, which will explore the process of constructing what might be called a "good" market agencement.

Let me close by profoundly acknowledging Michel Feher, who believed in this book and unambivalently supported its translation.

— *Michel Callon, 2020*

The Enigma of the Market

La coutume, en faisant un livre, c'est de commencer
Par un petit préambule et en voilà un.
—Marivaux, *Le paysan parvenu*

FROM THE STREETS OF LONDON...

"Dolls that THINK together, dolls that LAUGH together, dolls that CRY together, dolls that DRINK together. NOT sixty—I'll give you your bus fare home if it helps you. NOT fifty, NOT forty, THIRTY-FIVE IS CHEAP, NOT thirty-two fifty, 'ere, an' to CLEAR 'EM, I won't even charge you thirty. HALF THAT [BANG] FIFTEEN POUND THE PAIR."[1]

The streets of London, mid-1980s. Science and technology studies scholar Trevor Pinch is there to try to understand the mechanisms of an activity almost as old as human societies. The British call it "pitching." How do you convince a random person lost in thought—it could be you, it could be me—to develop a sudden enthusiasm for perfumes with unfamiliar names or an avid interest in Chinese porcelain seen a million times before? How do you get them to be attracted to ordinary bath towels, to feel a sudden emotion at the sight of banal kitchen utensils, or to be drawn by compositions of freshly cut flowers? In short, the activity involves producing *cupido emptrix*, the passion, the fever to acquire, in this passerby. Not only to interest them, attract their attention, divert them from their trajectory, persuade them that all this is good for them, that they need it, that they are in a state of lack, but above all (because at that point, the outcome might be theft, barter, or gift) to convince them to shell out cash. If that does not happen, the pitcher will have pitched in vain.

The seller's ultimate objective, his holy grail, is to lead a stranger to engage in a market transaction. Whether this challenge is taken up by the pitchers on the streets of London or the engineers and sales representatives of Renault, Fiat, Samsung, Apple, or the French telecom company Orange does not make any difference: the nature of the solutions they must invent are the same. What is true for the street vendor is even truer for high-tech companies that have to create demand for products no one had yet dared to imagine. The questions a street seller must answer every morning are the same ones that any multinational company has to face daily. The former merely does so with a great economy of means, counting only on himself, like a magician with nothing in his hands, nothing in his pockets. As Pinch understood perfectly, street sales make more easily visible what complex modern organizations tend instead to render opaque and difficult to decipher.

The pitcher experiments, observes, interprets, and transforms his practices. He has to make a living off this work and live by its daily repetitions. If the quality of his observations leaves something to be desired, if the lessons he draws from the experiments he attempts turn out to be irrelevant, if the actions he decides on are inappropriate, he faces failure and finds himself at a loss, helpless in front of a crowd that evaporates in an instant. Pitching is a full-fledged trade and it needs to be learned. There are, indeed, training courses for beginners. Neophytes start by learning by heart a spiel drilled into them by an elder. They also train at organizing the material space in which they will operate. They practice the scenario they will follow. Experienced pitchers can be spotted by their capacity to adapt, their talent for improvising, but above all, by their way of structuring the action, which, as Pinch describes, runs through four successive stages.

The first stage aims at constituting an audience, or, better, an interested public. Pitchers speak of "building the edge," alluding to a Cockney expression that plays on words to refer to the English expression "hedge and ditch," designating the practice of limiting a terrain by hedges and ditches in order to ensure one has a hold on it. Once this is accomplished, the anonymous flow of a lonely crowd gives way instead to an agglutination, a limited space occupied by those who have been diverted and grouped together, set aside from the current, extracted from the continuous flux. This space, which is circumscribed by a sort of invisible border, porous, but not too porous, will become the pitcher's field for maneuvering. Creating the *clinamen*, the diversion that allows for a first coalescing, is neither obvious nor natural. As Pinch observes, inducing the first person to stop is a delicate venture.

Multiple strategies are elaborated to facilitate this first diversion, the first stepping aside. The pitcher can, for instance, call on an accomplice to stand ostentatiously in front of the stall, or he can sacrifice goods, giving them away to those just passing by, who then play the part of a fixation abscess. Once the first potential clients have been stopped in their blind rush, they must not be lost, since they will serve as bait, or *réclame*, to use a French word from falconry that refers to the lure that induces the bird of prey to return, but equally refers to an advertisement. "Closer to me, closer to heaven, " says the hawker. Humor plays a crucial role in the whole process, capturing and fixing attention. And price figures early on in this process of catching people's attention because, as Pinch underlines, the customer's mind must be prepared. No tricks or false hopes. No pretense that any favors are being done. "Look at the prices, you'll never believe them. They're the lowest ever seen." The stakes are established immediately: not only is one there to buy, one is there to buy not goods, but a price.

This is therefore the first point the street seller must make, and since what is for sale has not been mentioned yet, he explains why it is so inexpensive. "These jewels belong to a guy who took off for Spain with my wife; since he's taking care of my wife, I've decided to take care of his things." The scene grows more crowded. Henceforth the seller, his assistants, and the customers are no longer alone. New characters have invited themselves in: the seller's wife, her lover, and the jewels, which the seller—who can blame him?—has decided to get rid of, since he cannot get rid of the lover. When it comes to clothes for sale whose price needs to be justified, the pitcher invokes the London department store that went bankrupt and was forced to sell off luxury items at bargain prices. Each good is thus inscribed in a story that explains why it is a good deal—and the story does not matter much because no one quite believes it. When in the market in Sarcelles it is said, with a little smile, that the pair of Ray-Bans or the Hermès scarf being sold at rock-bottom prices fell off the truck, highlighting in a striking phrase that the good's career is complicated, that it followed an exceptional path, is it not that career that, making it unique, determines its value? The good, even if it looks like a thousand others, even if it is only one copy, is actually different because of this history, which has led it to this particular stall on this particular day. It has been made particular, or, as I would put it, *singularized*. Extracted from the anonymous crowd by the twists of a plot, it, in turn, contributes to extracting from the anonymous flow those particular customers whose attention is caught and who begin to take an interest in this particular good, rather than any other.

Price is proof of this singularity, sometimes the only proof: "Look at this garment. It's not even worth thirty pence, not even twenty pence. When I tell you the price, it will knock you over!" This dress, which looks like so many other dresses, is made different by the simple fact that it is offered at a different price. The pitcher turns things around, going against the grain of everything that is generally said about markets. It is not the case that there is the dress, on the one hand, with its intrinsic properties (color, style, and so on), and the price on the other, external to the dress and determining its value. The price is attached to the dress; it is one of its qualities. The dress is red, has a plunging neckline, and is not…expensive. The customer did not get interested in *a* dress but in *that* dress, the one that is not expensive. And that is no doubt the reason he let himself be roped in, the low price of the dress being a result of its singular story, a story he does not yet know, but that he guesses between the lines of the pitcher's speech. No dress is quite like any other; this unique character helps put the customer and the dress in a singular relationship to one another, a singularity that hails the gawker, saying, "This one's for you." Throughout the warm-up that leads to the transaction, the·singularity of this relation will be maintained and developed by the third actor in this event: the pitcher.

After the first framing operation and the constitution of a gathering in which each person expects to get a personal deal and already knows they will have to pay to make good on the deal, the second step can begin. Speeches are one thing: they can convince, excite curiosity, pave the way for a positive decision. But then there are also the things themselves. A relation is not just a matter of intelligence, reason, and calculation. It supposes a physical attachment. To get the customer to shell out money, he must be touched deep down, and for him to be touched, the simplest thing is to invite him to…touch, test, feel, stroke, so that all his senses are solicited and solicit him to ensure that the good enters his life, to become an integral part of himself, to transform and constitute his new identity. The customer must be affected. The pitchers in the streets of London call this the "flash" and, they add, "Flash means cash." The pitcher strokes the necklaces and earrings, offers a whiff of perfume to a lady whose age makes one surmise she has smelled and inhaled many others over the course of her existence; he invites an onlooker to manipulate the towels, crease the materials so they reveal their softness to the onlooker's expert fingers; he demonstrates the exquisite delicacy of the china by placing behind it a candle that the customer discerns through the transparency of the material. The goods' qualities (or at least some of them, since some must be hidden in order to put others forward) are made evident, palpable, graspable, and thus add to the promise of rock-bottom prices, the first quality around which the others gravitate.

The better to showcase, put forth, or make explicit the qualities of their wares, pitchers attend to the presentation, playing with different dispositions, piling up towels on this side so as to make obvious how soft and supple the fabric is or composing on that side pyramids of bracelets that set off one another's value, just as a book's value is drawn from the collection it belongs to, from which it is detached with an exlibris proudly underlining the connection. Singularity is formed from comparisons and the groupings that are suggested and materialized on the seller's stall. To insist on the importance of the material demonstration of qualities, pitchers claim that "what cannot speak cannot lie." It is not enough to state the facts. Rather, just as in laboratory research, facts must be shown, demonstrated, tried through an experiment that tests the properties and reactions of the substances or entities involved. The vendor may thus efface himself behind the mixer that "does everything by itself," and he proves it by showing it. Or throws the plates in the air to show off how robust they are.

Henceforth, these goods have been rendered desirable, their qualities have been demonstrated over the course of a series of trials that involve the body and the five senses of the customer and have in the end (perhaps) affected him so strongly that he no longer can contemplate breaking the links already established between himself and some of these goods. He agrees to pay to obtain them. All that is left is for the price, which none but the vendor knows, to be affixed.

The formulation of a price, that is to say, the determination of a number that the customer knows at this stage to be the lowest found in the market (the market thus appears in the background, a décor to highlight and contextualize the action), is set by going down the price ladder, step by step. Hawkers refer to this descending movement during which prices are broken one after another as "ramping." First, prices as set by competitors are announced, either by the pitcher, by a customer, or by a carefully primed accomplice. The pitcher also brings in the prices quoted in catalogs he shows or passes around. Remember the twin dolls at the beginning of this prologue and the final price—fifteen pounds for the pair—that the pitcher reached after having gone through all the prices that would have been reasonable, but that he swept aside. Each time a price is announced, the pitcher hits the table in front of him with a large stick that looks like a baseball bat. When he reaches the price he has chosen, the bang is even louder than the previous ones, putting an end to the batting process. Prices are knocked down, literally as well as figuratively. Each time a new and lower price is announced, the pitcher asks who is interested. Hands are raised. More and more hands go up as the beating (produced by the blows) and the beat (as in a musical beat) of the prices progress. In order to transform the interest (evidenced by raised hands) into a firm commitment (consenting to pay and paying), the pitcher announces a new lowering, which further heats up the crowd. The beating and the beat ring out like a military march that brooks no retreat and pushes the gawker to pull bills from his pocket as though that were an inevitable gesture, the logical conclusion of a gradual and collective commitment. Turning back would be to abandon one's word or to contradict oneself. Having agreed to a higher price, he can only accept to pay a lower price.

The customer feels compelled to buy. It is hard to find an adequate expression for this process, an expression that captures its intimate logic. The pitcher holds out the bag into which he has placed the clothes or the china, or even the dolls, with their tinned laughter. An onlooker grabs it, and it is passed from hand to hand until it reaches the person whose hand had been up throughout the price batting. Did he decide, or was he made to decide by the *dispositif*—the staging and the devices?[2] Obviously it was both. Were he to go back on his word, he would lose face; he does not want to go back on his word. The deal is sealed, in the bag. The will to buy belongs to him, but it belongs just as much to the assembled crowd that passes the bag along until it reaches him or to the showman and his demonstrations, his know-how [*savoir faire*], and his knowing how to induce [*savoir faire faire*]. It is clear how impoverished the usual representation of the transaction is when it presents this transaction in terms of a supply and a demand, elaborated and constituted independently of one another, external to one another, simply meeting in such a way as to produce an agreement.

How insufficient is the idea that the price measures a value, when it in fact participates in the constitution of value? (I will return to this point at length because I know it may be hard to grasp.) We all remember the syllogism our philosophy teachers presented with a sly smile: everything that is rare is expensive, a cheap horse is rare, so a cheap horse is expensive. But what if the economy of markets actually rests entirely on that syllogism, which seems lame only to those who have understood nothing of the ways markets function? Transforming a dress, twin dolls, or a china plate into a unique and singular piece destined for that particular customer or setting up a device that makes the meetings between each of these goods and a client extracted from the anonymous crowd into a unique event, is that not to create a rarity, an extreme rarity? And when that singularity, when the uniqueness, is largely (although obviously not only) the price, a price below what can even be imagined, the miracle happens: what is cheap is dear to me. The pitcher knows what all merchants the world over know, but that those who theorize about markets sometimes forget. The price is on sale, no more, but no less, than the china's delicacy, the fabric's softness, or the dolls' performances. The formulation of the price, the ramping that runs all the other market prices before our eyes, is an attempt to make the good as dear as possible in both senses of the term: cherished and expensive.

The pitcher's commercial activity does not end with this first purchase. For the activity to be profitable, other clients must come forward while the logic of singularization that produces the aforementioned rarity is preserved. This is the fourth step. The vendor faces a daunting dilemma: how to reconcile a mass market—he must reach a certain sales volume to hope for a profit—with goods and transactions that he so successfully singularized? To refer to the solution they devised, street sellers speak of "twirling the edge."

This twirling allows the pitcher to catch the attention of those who are still on the far side of the border between the general public and those onlookers who are already interested. It aims to recruit new customers, to push farther into the clustering of people and to transform them into customers. This requires competence, know-how, and a specific type of work. The whirlwind of the sale chalks up sales so as to increase the quantity of goods sold without compromising the singular dimension of each transaction. The pitcher shows us the most fundamental of strategies, the one that includes all the others. He moves about through the proxy of assistants. While he takes care of one buyer, he shouts, "Over there!" to his assistant, pointing to an onlooker who seems ready to join the audience assembled around his stall. The assistant flits among the gawkers, twirling to induce them to join the ongoing demonstration. Meanwhile, the pitcher, ready to welcome the newcomer, must not lose those he has already begun to ease toward a commercial transaction.

The twirling of the sale makes it clear that there are not, on the one hand, personalized markets, and on the other hand, anonymous mass markets where everything is alike and simply adds up to create sale volumes. Mass markets should always be perceived as juxtapositions of a myriad of bilateral transactions. The challenge facing all those who live by commercial transactions and give life to markets is to produce the mass from singularization without losing the latter in the process.

This reveals market dynamics clearly. A supply is not a given, preconstituted block that faces an equally set block, that of a demand. Supply and demand emerge and express themselves over the course of a continuous process. They are constantly in motion. They are inscribed in a space, delimited by the borders of the audience traced out by the vendor; they unfurl over time, the time that unfolds through the eddies of the sale. These eddies give a form to the deployment of the sale that can overcome the apparent contradiction between quality and quantity, between, on the one hand, bilateral transactions and the singularization they require and, on the other hand, their aggregation and massification. The clients were not already there, defined as such, waiting to respond to the pitcher's call. Their number is not a given. Working simultaneously on the clustered crowd and conquering new clients by twirling: this is the program for any seller worthy of the name.

Over the course of the quest for the transaction, the importance of the material framework becomes clear. The pitcher, set up behind his stall and raised on a stage that gives him an overview, sees everything; he supervises the sale space. He dominates the battalions of pedestrians flowing by, and he identifies, a bit like profilers at the entrance of nightclubs, those whose pace slackens or whose head turns; he sees the hand go up and the commitments of potential buyers; he delegates to his assistant the mechanics of the transaction and money collection, but he also sends him to the front to attract those pedestrians who are hesitating. With his loudspeaker, he imposes his speech and masters the sonic space. He sets up his word as the dominant discourse, relaying and amplifying customer questions and the answers provided.

This is how one sells what, to a hurried observer, may look like hundreds, thousands, or millions of copies of the same object, but that from the point of view of the sellers and, let it be added, the buyers, is a succession: a multitude of separate transactions, each distinct and different, are juxtaposed in time and space. The fiction of supply and demand curves crossing in the single plane of a sheet of paper, collapsing time and space, does not hold up in front of the reality of the devices required to produce this intersection—I should say these many intersections—by deploying, unfolding, both *space* and *time*.

...TO THE STRIP IN LAS VEGAS

The bilateral transaction is at the very core of markets, their ways of functioning, and their developments. The constantly renewed challenge to which markets find practical solutions is to singularize, ensure payment, and multiply the number of transactions. The solutions imagined by street hawkers have general value. The four steps Pinch describes, which are recognized by the sellers themselves (building the edge, flashing, ramping and batting, twirling the edge) can be found in every sector of market activity. To be convinced of that, one need only take off for Las Vegas and its topography of addiction.

Gone are the pitcher's china cups and dolls afflicted with pathological empathy. Here is Las Vegas, shimmering like a mirage in the middle of the desert, with its casinos, its rooms in which slot machines unfurl as far as the eye can see, lined up next to one another, all alike to untrained eyes, but to untrained eyes only. Let us listen to anthropologist Natasha Schüll, who surveyed those game rooms for months, followed and interviewed dozens of gamblers, from the occasional gambler to those who lose body and soul to it, met the architects who designed these sites so as to trap the customers, the computer scientists who assemble microprocessors and write the algorithms that get better and better at capturing gamblers and their money. It is a game of cat and mouse in which the mouse knows it is a mouse and is happy to be one, and the cat is a cat that knows it is a cat and sees in the mouse nothing other than prey that should be captured under other cats' very whiskers.[3]

What do Pinch's London and Schüll's Las Vegas have in common? At first glance, nothing, or almost nothing, except that money is exchanged for good or services. One is a primal scene, the other modernity in its tackiest, most cynical, most elaborate, and as some people denounce, most amoral version. Yet there is no qualitative leap between the two. The same obsessions dominate on both sides of the Atlantic: deflect, capture, attach, make pay by singularizing goods and, with them, those who will be their beneficiaries, and then multiply bilateral transactions to build up sales volume. The street sellers in London help us understand Las Vegas; Las Vegas helps us understand both the street sellers and capitalist markets.

First step. What Las Vegas, its casinos, and its slot machines attempt to deflect is not the flow of pedestrians hurrying toward their daily occupations. If one took a bird's-eye perspective, one would see the masses rushing to travel agencies, checking out tour operators, buying cheap plane tickets on flights specially chartered by Las Vegas casinos that offer them slash-priced rooms; one would see crowds, hypnotized by the Strip's lights, in procession from the whole world toward gambling's Mecca, letting themselves be swallowed by the majestic entrances to Caesars Palace, Excalibur, or Paris Las Vegas, letting themselves be carried along through the labyrinths that lead them to the slot machine rooms, allowing themselves to be caught by one of them in order to take possession of the place that has been saved for them, specially designed for them. Here they are now, finally crossing the threshold to heaven...or hell. Here they are now in the "zone," as gamblers call the space around the machine, cut off from the rest of the world, a space that becomes their habitat, their ecological niche. Building the edge. The mouse is now within reach of the cat's claws, already consenting, open to being played with by the cat through the slot machines. The machine's virtual rollers slide over each other in a digital-mechanical din; the ruthless face-off, the dance, can start. The choreography of this dance has been practiced hundreds and thousands of times. The space has been rarified, folded back on itself. All that is left is a singular point, the point of contact between two agencies, the one that plays and the one that makes play.

Molly is in the "zone." She's fed up with turning in circles, dragging her existence like a ball chained to her ankle from one slot machine to another. She draws a map. She starts in the top left-hand corner of a sheet of paper with the MGM Grand, the casino where she works. A little lower to the right she draws the 7-Eleven, the gas station where she refuels and where, when she's filled her tank, she plays the slot machine lined up there like a reminder, just to relax a little and take the edge off her impatience. A little lower down, the Palace Station crops up, her neighborhood casino, where she gambles in the evenings and on weekends. Next comes the supermarket where she shops on weekends and gambles for a handful of minutes, just so as not to lose the touch. Then her clumsy fingers, more accustomed to pushing the button that allows her to sever contact with the world than to hold a pen, draw the clinic from which she gets the medication for her anxiety. Finally, in the bottom left-hand corner, the last step before the loop closes back on itself and another circuit begins through the same steps, is the building where she goes to Gamblers Anonymous meetings every Wednesday evening. Molly then traces the path, or one should say the bumpy route, that connects all these sites. Finally she finishes the map by drawing herself in the middle of the space she has delimited, sitting in front of a slot machine. No exit—she doesn't want one; what she wants is an absolutely closed-off space, the space of compulsive consumption in which she gives herself over to what she knows is a vice and that she struggles to fight with molecules and collective expiation practices. As we will see, the casinos have calculated that a gambler who pursues her path, from remission to relapse, is more profitable than one who lets out all the blood in a single session. Casinos prod users they way a cat prods a mouse with its paw to ensure the latter is still alive. When it becomes clear the user has somewhat revived, the casino brings out its claws. From this perspective, therapy is not necessarily an antidote to addiction; it is one of its essential components, financed by the casinos. One goes back and forth between one and the other the way one can go from mall to mall, run from one errand to the next, or go into debt from one loan to another while giving oneself breaks, allowing oneself the pleasure of a cup of coffee while sitting at a terrace to catch one's breath for a few minutes before diving back into the crowd that is going in circles, rushing, and from which one is extracted for a moment, but only for a moment.

The capture of a gambler who delights in staying in the "zone," a sort of black hole where forces are reversed and keep her prisoner, has been calculated precisely. Organizing the tracking and the catch requires sophisticated devices: a group of human and nonhuman beaters far more complex than the hawker's assistant, but carrying out the same tasks. Once attracted into the "zone," the customer has to be kept there so that she doesn't escape, at least while she can still be used. When they describe this capture, gamblers talk about being hooked, caught, harpooned, bewitched, or about becoming junkies. As in the streets of London, the capture is effected by gaining hold of bodies and minds. There, to touch the customer, to attach him, he had to be allowed to touch the cloth, encouraged to finger it. Here, the task is a little more complicated: one does not fall in love with a slot machine as one does with a smiling doll or a piece of lingerie whose crazy story and silky texture get the better of you. To ensure the hold and to make it as active as wished require more preparatory work, studies, behavioral observations, brain imagery. It requires starting from the observation that all slot machine experts now share as though it were obvious, although there is nothing self-evident about it. What Molly, like all her fellow gamblers, is looking for is not only or even mostly the pleasure of the bet, the frisson that runs up her spine for the few seconds before the virtual rollers come to a stop. None of that is what she desperately seeks. Rather, she is looking for escape, for being able to cut herself off from the rest of the world, detach from her life and her environment. "You who enter here, abandon all hope." As Molly puts it, "No exit, no escape."

Once gamblers are in the "zone," once their territory has been circumscribed and the borders traced out, the gambler has to be kept, has to be attached to the machine; in other words, things must be managed so that she becomes attached to it. The flashing—a little more complicated than in London with china and cloth that can be touched. Here there is none of that. But for a good engineer, a good psychologist, a good architect-designer, a good computer scientist, no challenge is too daunting. It is worth rising to this one. What needs to be done especially is to carefully define the profiles of a good candidate for addiction in order to attract and attach her and then to take care of everything from the music to the smells, to compose an atmosphere that provides a bubble for the gambler, providing all the nourishment she might require and protecting her from the rest of the world. Carefully eliminate every perturbation, any parasites. Casino design professionals think of everything. For instance, it often happens that a gambler does not hold up to the pressure and succumbs to a heart attack. What has to happen at that point—and many studies, as well as lucrative contracts for those researchers who landed them, were required to figure out how to set this up—is for the unconscious guest to be whisked away immediately without upsetting other players. Cameras, control centers, nurses, stretchers and defibrillators that can be reached within seconds, dexterity at eliminating the body without a sound. And it works. You can watch it on the screens: the other gamblers do not notice a thing. Lost in their machines, it is as if they have been disconnected from everything around them. Like the one who fell beside them, they are cut off from their environment; unlike him, they are lucky enough to be able to continue.

The observation systems for behavior and the great amount of accumulated data make it possible to singularize the attachment; it is made to measure. One can figure out the pain threshold for a particular gambler, whose name one might not know, but to whom the facial recognition software has assigned a number in order to be able to track him. When the threshold beyond which he may not be able to withstand the pressure is reached, the algorithms pull back, the sequences of gains and losses are recalculated to bring down the pressure without thereby giving up on siphoning off the bank accounts. The state of equilibrium, what ensures the most regular and systematic withdrawals, is achieved in full with the customer's complete cooperation when the user who cannot calculate anything any longer gives himself over to the machine and, rather than regularly pushing the button that sets off the rollers' infernal cycle, delegates that last action by opting for autoplay. This abandonment is even more impressive with the poker games. The machine has learned the gambler's favorite strategies, the risks they like to take, the rate of their gains, and it becomes such a good substitute, such a faithful lieutenant, that the gambler does not even have to play anymore to enjoy the benefits of the anesthesia the game provides. The machine plays against itself, the gambler being so deactivated, so cut off from everything, that there is no source of greater pleasure for him than these automatic plays. To reach this abandon, the relationship and the service had to be personalized. "Tell me how you play, and I promise to play in your stead as you would have liked to play," says the machine. "I know, better than even you do, what you like and what binds you to me. I will relieve you even of the burden of playing. Relax. Enjoy life—enjoy your life! I have your back, I am thinking of you constantly. I know, for instance, that you have natural needs to satisfy. Take the time to get a meal at the casino restaurant where you can win free games. Take the time for a bathroom break." The gambler, however, is not always credulous. There are limits to trust. What if the machine went off the rails? What if it were slyly disguising its treachery, taking advantage of these interruptions to change its mind and accelerate the player's bankruptcy? Some gamblers, fearing such betrayal (they do not fear losing all their money, but they do fear not being able to go on playing at their own rhythm and for as long as possible before they're broke for good), pull on several pairs of pants or diapers in order to be able to pee as much as they need to without taking their eyes off the machine as it plays in their stead and takes all their money.

By way of the machine, the casino has attached the customer, pinned him down, holding him in its claws. All that is left is to get him to pay. Let us not, however, imagine for a second that the sequence of affixing a price and its payment begins after the harpooning, the way a ransom is requested after the hostage is captured. To imagine that prices are external to the processes of attachment and singularization would be to understand nothing about market mechanisms. As in London, the price is a quality, or rather an essential component, of the service. In Las Vegas, that is so much the case that it is by affixing the price and getting the gambler to pay it that attachment is obtained, that the deal is sealed. The pleasure that payment produces, that the repeated pressing of the button provides, attaches the gambler, somewhat as in a psychoanalytic cure, the money given over to the therapist ensuring that one is attached to him; the transfer of money paves the way for affective transfer. What a pleasure to be able to pay to forget, to not owe anyone anything, to wipe oneself out. Ah, *cupido emptrix*, when you have a hold on us, it is a powerful one. Slot machine designers and computer experts have understood that so well that they offer the gambler the sequences of gains and losses that provide maximal pleasure for him. These sequences and relative volumes, activated by pressing on a button, are part of the game. To formulate the price is to formulate the good. Read for its economic significance, what Schüll's discomforting ethnography demonstrates is that in machine gambling, the price is one of the good's qualities, no more, no less. Price is both the supply and the demand; it is not the result of a meeting, a confrontation, between preconstituted supplies and demands.

The hawker's problem of capturing the attention of passing traffic is but one kind of challenge. Casinos further face the problem of constantly increasing the number of visitors flocking to Las Vegas so they can multiply bilateral transactions and grow sales revenue. What is the point of managing to get crowds of onlookers to come from the other end of the world if one fails to capture them as they cover the last few yards that separate them from open slot machines? In order to manage this capture, casinos design devices that combine the traditional and tested know-how that pitchers and their assistants have with high-tech tools. Twirling the edge? As in London, street beaters harpoon anonymous onlookers, seduce them with attractive propositions, and take them on, as soon as they hit the Strip, so as to lead them to the machine. To boost revenues, however, the best strategy is to establish and maintain a state of addiction; one must not let slip between one's fingers someone who has already come, who has tried a game of poker and left traces and a profile (here is how I play and react) in one of the centers of big data, someone to whom the machine can offer the games he likes and his favorite sequences as soon as he is within range of screens. One day it will be possible to reach him at home through an app. Each gambler is a person whom the casino addresses and to whom it sends its propositions. There is no contradiction between quantity and quality; quantity is not antithetical to a bespoke service and the singularization of goods and agents. Datafication makes this even more obvious.

You might think it a strange idea to open a book devoted to the markets, and more precisely to the most recent and complex types of markets, with street vendors, who seem of another age. Isn't it even stranger to establish a parallel between that primitive form of commerce and the gambling industry, which so skillfully deploys the glitzy resources of modern technology? By bringing together these two very extreme situations, I want to suggest the problems that have to be solved have not changed: the point is to tie supplies and demands together around goods whose characteristics are constantly evolving, the only aim being to set up a transaction that takes place in exchange for payment.

Market activities always face the same questions: Who is ready to pay, how much, and for what? But what does change between situations are the mechanisms of solving these problems.

This book sets out a hypothesis, namely, that when confronted with the enigma of the market, actors constantly invent new devices that are repeatedly modified and transformed. But these changes are not random or arbitrary. In order to be successful (sometimes), commercial activities must be organized (*agencées*) in a certain way. One cannot rely on chance to lead a man wandering down the street without a care or rushing toward an important business meeting to take a sudden interest in a pair of dolls he did not know existed a few minutes earlier or to fight to be able to take advantage of the exceptional opportunity given to him to be one of the lucky few to have a chance to acquire this rare good. It is not by chance that you lead a homemaker to take an avid interest in laundry detergent that promises the most dazzling white, an adolescent to go broke for flavored vaping products, or a senior executive to no longer be able to disconnect from screens he used to do very well without. None of these results could be obtained without the design and implementation of rigorously structured *agencements*.[4] This book is devoted to exploring and analyzing those structures. Before getting to the heart of the matter, however, we need to rid ourselves of a number of mistaken assumptions and common notions—such as the concepts of supply and demand—that contribute to obscuring, rather than illuminating the enigma of the market.

CHAPTER ONE

From Interface Markets
to Market Agencements

WHAT IS A MARKET?

As we begin this investigation, it is important that my readers and I agree on the limitations of existing discourses and the need to explore new modes of understanding the thing we call a "market." The purpose of this introductory chapter is to establish such an agreement so that we can move on to the novel answers that I would like to propose.

What, then, is a market?

In 1994, Alan Greenspan, then president of the Federal Reserve, believing he knew, said this: "There's nothing involved in Federal regulation which makes it superior to market regulation." A few years later, he pursued this line of reasoning even further: "Bank loan officers, in my experience, know far more about the risks and workings of their counterparties than do bank regulators."[1] Only the obtuse do not change their minds, however. By 2008, as the financial crisis was devastating Western economies, this same man, Alan Greenspan, was called to a hearing by the US House of Representatives. By this point, he was almost a mere citizen. He repented. He did not feel responsible for what was happening; he did not seem to regret having made bad decisions. What seemed to hurt him the most was that he had thought he had known what markets were, what they did, and how to regulate them, whereas he had to come to realize that he knew almost nothing about how they work:

I made a mistake in presuming that the self-interest of organizations, specifically banks and others, were such that they were best capable of protecting their own shareholders and their equity in the firms.... So the problem here is something which looked to be a very solid edifice, and, indeed, a critical pillar to market competition and free markets, did break down. And I think that, as I said, shocked me. I still do not fully understand why it happened and, obviously, to the extent that I figure out where it happened and why, I will change my views. If the facts change, I will change.... What I am saying to you is, yes, I found a flaw [in my ideology], I don't know how significant or permanent it is, but I have been very distressed by that fact.[2]

When influential experts such as Alan Greenspan begin to doubt their theories and admit that they do not really know what markets are or how they work, it is time for some reflection.[3] One of the principal difficulties to overcome is that the descriptions that attempt to account for market activity are so enormously diverse. Nevertheless, it seems feasible to me that we pull out a few elements from the array of existing descriptions that link them together in a coherent manner. These common elements form an implicit model that gives the word "market" its most common meaning. As a result, whoever uses the word "market," either in ordinary conversation or for elaborating analytic theories, adopts this common meaning, which is largely shared, but rarely discussed. I call this distilled model of markets the "interface market." In contrast, I will propose an alternative model, which I have named the "agencement model."[4] It is my sincere hope that from now on, whenever theorists speak of markets or the market, they will begin to invoke the agencement model in place of the far less realistic interface model.

This introductory chapter is dedicated to presenting the two models side by side to show their commonalities and their differences. I will abstain from discussing any other economic forms or their respective merits and will focus my attention exclusively on the notion of a market so as to better specify the object to which the word is supposed to refer.[5] I will also avoid conflating the terms "market economy" and "capitalism," as is too often done.[6] I begin from the hypothesis that there have existed, there exist, and there could exist market forms that are not capitalist. The notion of market agencement should make it easier to decouple these terms.

THE INTERFACE MARKET MODEL

Anyone hoping for a ready-to-use definition of a market will be discouraged by a systematic study of the academic or general literature. The problem is not a dearth of answers and definitions; it is their great abundance and the frequent contradictions.

The diversity can easily be explained if one allows that individual experiences of the market are not reducible to one another. Who would claim that a single definition encompasses what an Egyptian peasant feels as he discusses the price of a bale of cotton with a trader from Cairo, *and* does justice to the diverging work of famous and recognized economists such as Milton Friedman, Friedrich Hayek, Oliver Williamson, or Richard Nelson, *and* takes into account Monsanto's maneuvers as it uses all available means to eliminate traditional agriculture? And yet who would dare contest that in referring to the market, each of the agents contributes to a series of questions that are shared and over which they are divided, but that the notion of a market helps to articulate? Everybody talks about the market. Everybody is pointing to different practices and different issues. However, each in their own way recognizes the existence of common stakes, even if some strive to elaborate theoretical models while others seek only to understand concrete practices.

To identify the common elements among the current concepts of markets, the only possible strategy is to follow the advice of Colette Depeyre and Hervé Dumez, who suggest we investigate the different uses of the word as a point of departure. In my study, I will pay equal attention to people who engage in markets and to professionals who study from the outside how markets work.[7] Although informatic tools exist that can scour the literature in bulk, the enterprise I will undertake can be executed without such an investment. One way to simplify the work without losing sight of the final objective is to follow a selection of specialists who have consecrated part of their energy to this work. There are economists, sociologists, and anthropologists who have in effect dedicated sustained efforts to pass from local, empirical observations to a stylized, abstracted, and generalizable account of markets. It is by reconstituting their strategies of abstraction and by verifying what is largely shared in the end that we should be able to sort out some common elements in the existing literature that define what I have called the interface model.

The most common, oldest, and most constant meaning of the word "market" refers to sites, generally public sites, covered or outdoors, where all sorts of merchants exhibit and sell foodstuffs and common household items. There are many examples of this form of market: the one in Chichicastenango that Simone de Beauvoir refers to in *The Mandarins*; the one in Lima that the economist Roger Guesnerie visits in his essential book on market economy;[8] the fairs in Champagne that, in the Middles Ages, with their currencies and charters, organized long-term European trade; flea markets; fish markets; a market in Marseille where Cuvier is said to have discovered the principles of his natural history; the Tsukiji market in Tokyo, which I used to visit in the early morning whenever I was in Japan, always dazzled by the streaming colors; the labyrinths of the souk in Sefrou that Clifford Geertz described so well;[9] the markets of Provence depicted by Michèle de La Pradelle and that appear in Gilbert Bécaud's songs.[10] It would be tempting to extend the list—why not Wall Street or the Matif?[11]—and to start an inventory of the places where, since high antiquity, merchants and clients have met in person in order to render and preserve the singularity of each marketplace.

The simple fact that the same word, "market," is used to describe places and activities that are so different, across such different times and places, is an invitation to move beyond the specificities of each case and to bring out the common traits. The idea is to reach an underlying representation that captures the essential through successive abstractions. It is worth noting that the work of abstraction is not limited to specialists. Common thinking deploys expressions such as "the market of ideas," "the dating market," "putting oneself on the job market," and so on. However, it is mostly experts, those who have chosen to study markets professionally, who have taken the most significant steps toward abstract representation. They have, in fact, followed the strategy of academic thinking. Whatever their claimed disciplinary affiliation, experts have sought to find common features of markets, shared across various configurations, in order to catch the unity of a given reality beyond contingencies and particular circumstances.[12]

When economist Roger Guesnerie left the market he visited in Lima in the 1970s, he resolved almost reluctantly to erase from the picture he drew of commercial relations "the ponchos, the chiseled faces of old Indians chewing coca, the cries of children around the mother carrying the youngest on her back in the traditional way," noting that he had observed these things at one of the famous barter markets of the Andes, where goods were exchanged for goods and not money. He had a twinge of regret as he took on the task of distancing himself from what he saw, as any scientist worthy of the name must.[13] Guesnerie is not alone in having done this because every discipline imposes the same method. When Mark Granovetter analyzed the labor market in sociology, he endeavored to gradually reveal the underlying structure beyond events and observable encounters, tracing the networks of social relations and their morphology in order to give an account of the conditions in which transactions take place—in this case, hiring.[14] I could give many other references that would all show this movement of abstraction.[15] As I will show, this strategy of abstraction unfolds in three directions, thereby construing an overall coherence that permits one to speak of the construction of a model.

First, the strategy emphasizes the idea of an abstract space in which relationships are themselves abstractions: they are established by encounters between agents defined as sellers and agents defined as buyers. The movement then insists that these relations are governed by mechanisms of competition. Finally, for these relationships to endure and for the market to be stabilized, it is judged necessary that rules, conventions, or, more largely, institutions come into existence.

In my reading, these elements are common to the majority of scholarly representations of the market. They constitute a shared basis, a sort of greatest common denominator or core from which more sophisticated analyses (such as those offered by neoclassical economics or social-network sociology) are developed, particularly within economics and sociology. This stripped-back model, now widely taken for granted and rarely discussed, is a starting point from which, by gradually enriching it, everyone can elaborate their own conception of markets and their functioning. I propose to name this model the "interface market." To identify the common constitutive elements, I will mobilize work that was mostly done by economists of different schools who were among the first to make explicit the categories that are largely adopted by everyone who is interested in discussing market activities and that are practically naturalized—think competition, supply and demand, or market structure. As we will see, establishing a common model will prove to be useful for highlighting, by contrast, the characteristics of my alternative model of market agencements.

FIRST ABSTRACTION: SELLERS, BUYERS, AND PLATFORM GOODS

Consider the work of economist Maurice Allais, which has greatly contributed to how we can think through the stakes of modeling and abstraction. For him, "the market" (note the definite article, which introduces a word that refers to a general category of things or beings) presents itself as a situation in which "groups of buyers and sellers are in continuous business relations and effect transactions spread over all sorts of products."[16] Put forward in his *Cours d'économie générale*, this definition corresponds to minimal abstraction. It preserves the buyers and sellers of marketplaces (without yet speaking of supply and demand); it assigns a central role to the establishing of relations between buyers and sellers and to the ensuing transactions.

In order to reach this first level of abstraction, the material sites that allow and provide the framework for markets have to be erased so that it becomes possible to focus only on the goods and the agents prepared to engage in transactions. Nothing is left of Lima, Chichicastenango, Tsukiji, or Marseille, the stalls or the instruments that allow for weighing and counting, the labyrinth of alleyways guiding customers' wanderings, or the conversations between agents that lead to a possible agreement. What is foregrounded is the crowd of buyers and sellers, without geolocalizations, bereft of ponchos and chiseled faces. With no identity other than their role in the transaction, they are plunged into a dematerialized space.

What is more, the existence of a population of buyers and a population of sellers implies that goods have already been developed to provoke the establishment of commercial transactions.[17] In the interface model, goods play a foundational role in the constitution and the setting in motion of these two populations by creating conditions for them to meet. Goods are, or can be, defined by the qualities (or attributes) that are attached to them and that determine their profile. The description of those qualities might be subject to debate. However, beyond the inevitable conflicts of interpretation they generate, goods constitute identifiable and stabilized things, localizable in time and space. Their existence is a given; they are already there, available. Regardless of how one describes agents, their skills, and their motivations and however one analyzes the structure of each of the populations (networks or separate atoms), what characterizes goods from an economic point of view is that they connect and coordinate these two populations of agents, the buyers and the sellers, while also maintaining their own autonomy.

To characterize this conception, we need only turn toward recent developments in neoclassical economics that propose the notion of platform goods to describe the growing role that goods play, a role that is no longer solely limited to configuring relationships between populations of buyers and sellers. The simplest and best-known example of such goods is the free newspaper. The daily handed to subway commuters each morning as they go to work is financed by advertising inserted in the pages. The newspaper, as a good, puts three different "groups" of agents into relation: the advertising agencies who buy space, the users of public transportation who glance at the ads as they read the papers, and the company that conceives the newspaper, putting it together and distributing it. Using the term "platform" to designate such goods underscores that their function is to articulate several separate populations of agents. Economists have coined the term "multisided markets" to designate this type of market organization.[18] As defined by economists, these platform goods and their multisided markets have become more numerous. Initially developed to describe credit card markets, the model is now applied to mobile phones and video games. This proliferation is evidently linked to the growth of digital technology and what some are calling "datafication."[19]

Paradoxically, the notion of platform goods perfectly accounts for the role played by all goods as we analyzed them earlier through the interface model, even though it was not initially imagined for these cases. The concept applies particularly well to more usual configurations in which there are only two distinct populations of agents—that is, two sides in the market. In all multisided markets as defined by economists, the principal function of goods is to articulate expectations, propositions, and requests that are external to the goods themselves. This is what makes it appropriate to redescribe goods as platforms. A platform good maintains the separation between several populations of agents while ensuring that they are put into relation with one another. Considering all goods as platforms when referring to multisided markets (including two-sided markets) is quite useful for capturing one of the essential characteristics of the common vision of markets that I am examining in this section.

This point is worth repeating. To call all shoes "platform shoes" captures one of the essential characteristics of the interface market model, even if multisided market analysts wouldn't do this themselves! Whether we're speaking of shoes, books, automobiles, vegetables, free newspapers, Google and its ad exchanges, or bank cards, the only important thing is the capacity of these goods to put agents in relation to one another and to provoke encounters likely to end in a commercial transaction. In every case, the goods are taken as a given. Nothing is said, nothing has to be said, about the process that sets up the situation, a process that is considered to happen outside the market that, when successfully concluded, ends in the establishment of a market. This conceptualization is the shared minimal definition of markets that I am attempting to show. It is based on the following triptych: supply, demand, and goods offered. It therefore focuses on the relations that organize markets and on their structures.

A last remark. The notion of the platform is evidently polysemic. It has become a catch-all buzzword. In economics, a platform is generally defined as an intermediary that creates a market and/or assembles a group of users to facilitate economic or social exchange. In my way of thinking about objects, it is not illogical, therefore, to extend this same word, "platform," to describe the role of goods as they are conceived in the interface market model, which also, in their own way, must bring agents together. If we follow this general and largely accepted definition, we would naturally also consider software companies such as Amazon, Uber, or Meetic to be platforms, since these enterprises act to bring together, to match, to marry. But as we will see in Chapter 4, which is devoted to how encounters are organized within market agencements, these two meanings must be disentangled.

SECOND ABSTRACTION: COMPETITION

The first abstraction says nothing precise about how markets are set in motion and says nothing about what impels their dynamism and their extension. The second strategy of abstraction in the interface model strives to achieve a higher level of generality by revealing what is common to concrete markets, despite their diversity: it adds that as a particular form of economic organization, *the* market is synonymous with competition.

Competition is the motor that sets the machine in motion and structures its functioning. Whether one opens an economics textbook, a treatise of economic sociology, or a work of anthropology, whether one listens to a high-ranked civil servant or a company boss, a union official or a judge charged with ruling on market compliance with regulations, one almost inevitably encounters the question of competition. This observation holds from Adam Smith, who saw in competition "the force which tends to equate market and natural prices,"[20] all the way to the most recent developments in economic theory. The study of markets has constantly revolved around the analysis of modalities of competition between agents and around the relation between competition and cooperation. With his pithy formulation, Fernand Braudel perfectly summarized what is taken to be an obvious, shared understanding on the subject, despite varying conceptions of the market: *the market is competition.* Almost two centuries ago, Antoine-Augustin Cournot had expressed it in just as striking a manner: "What economists understand by market is not a place where acquisitions and sales are made, but a whole territory whose parts are linked by relations of free competition."[21] If Cournot's definition has stayed on people's minds, it is because it brings together in a single sentence both elements of the abstraction: the one that dematerializes the space and sets up the scene as one where supplies and demands confront each other (the first abstraction) and the one that makes competition the mainspring of this confrontation.[22]

"Competition" does not have a single meaning. The best-known and widely spread conception is that of so-called neoclassical economics. Let us turn once again to Allais, who gives a simple, concrete definition: "Competition corresponds to a market situation in which each seller sells to the buyer who accepts the highest price and each buyer buys from the seller who offers the lowest price."[23] This situation is a reference point for what has been called "pure" and "perfect" competition. As the definition implies, prices serve here as coordinating mechanisms: they constitute the criteria for agents' decisions, and their perpetual adjustment ensures the existence of a viable equilibrium. Allais emphasizes that such a configuration is only rarely found in reality, but he desists from saying never. Imperfection rules in this lowly world, and the degrees of its intensity depend on circumstances. Indeed, numerous and powerful are the forces that are opposed to competition and tend to institute situations of monopoly. Allais provides a few examples: too few agents; consumers' attachments to habits and insufficient information about products (he says brands too often mask this insufficiency); industrial concentration, aided by technical progress; pushing to expand factory size, as well as horizontal or vertical integration, which both in turn lead to the constitution of monopolies;[24] the financial power of certain agents (giving them the power to wait, analyze markets, practice dumping, and so on); the political power of certain agents; the importance of the state as a buyer.

Observable configurations fall somewhere between the opposite poles of perfect competition and perfect monopoly in an in-between ruled by what is customarily called "imperfect" competition.[25] The history of recent developments in neoclassical economics revolves around the analysis of mechanisms of imperfect competition (and in particular of the factors identified by Allais) and of the tools, notably mathematical ones (such as game theory) that make it possible to give an account of these mechanisms and to indicate how their (supposedly) negative effects might be mitigated. As all economics students learn, this normative demand is linked to the hypothesis that the allocation of resources is considered optimal, or according to the less optimistic, efficient, when it is satisfied.

In my inquiry, I do not intend to privilege the neoclassical conception of competition in any way. Whatever its theoretical value may be, it provides only one among several visions of the concrete forms competition can take. (I will discuss this in greater detail in Chapter 8, where I examine the case of financial markets and the economy of climate change.)

One could easily illustrate the existence of many other analyses of competition. They frequently start from the notion of pure and perfect competition elaborated (and imposed as the reference model) by neoclassical economics. Many then go on to highlight the model's lack of realism, showing that in reality, imperfections dominate. Some scholars consider that imperfections are due to social networks that frame relationships between agents, thereby constraining their behavior.[26] Some locate imperfection in the unequal distribution of capital and the relations of domination this produces. To yet others, it is the institutional regulations or conventions that narrowly define the modalities of competition.[27]

Lastly, I would like to point to the fairly widespread vision proposed by the evolutionary economists, who have contributed in an original manner to the analysis of the role of technical progress and innovation in the dynamic of economic activities. They, too, consider competition to be the principal motor of economic activities. However, instead of putting agents and prices at the center of the competitive device, they consider the confrontation between a wider range of forces. They take into account agents and the supplies and demands they are supposed to express or to trigger, but they also consider that behind those entities, doing battle with one another, hybridizing, spreading, or disappearing, are technologies, skills, rules of the game, routines, know-how, and capacities for innovation that are simply using human agents or goods as vectors. The analogy with sociobiology, sometimes explicit, is obvious: socio-biology indeed asserts that genes at war with one another use human organ-isms in order to materialize their advantage. This conception of competition, as well as the processes of mutation and selection it implies, has the virtue of attributing an essential role to both agents and objects. According to the usual conceptions of competition, products are seen as passive objects whose role is simply to make possible the encounter between supplies and demands; in evolutionary economics, goods play a more active role in the dynamic of com-petition through their constant transformation. Goods and their technological trajectories orient, frame, and stimulate commercial activity.

In an economy characterized by the rampant proliferation of products whose number, ephemeral character, perpetual renewal, and infinite differen-tiation provoke gridlock and congestion, it is not absurd to describe a market as a process of mutation and selection between goods fighting for their own survival, where agents are left to adapt as intelligently as possible to the logic that organizes these variations.[28]

In any case, regardless of the definition of the competition that is chosen, the structure proposed by the first abstraction remains untouched: the uni-verse of goods is left outside the universe of agents, whoever they may be.

Likewise for the role of innovation, which is viewed as a response to steep competition that would end in ruinous consequences for the loser if it were to continue for too long. By innovating, companies are supposed to reduce com-petition, or at least attenuate its most devastating consequences. In the inter-face market model, innovation is impelled by competition. This hypothesis leads to a principal interest in synergies that can be deployed by companies to assure themselves control over this competitive advantage: investments conse-crated to in-house research and development, patenting, technology purchases, subcontracting contracts, start-up acquisitions, mergers, or even participation in cooperative networks such as academic research.

Since Joseph Schumpeter, one of the first scholars interested in this topic, one of the most often asked questions within the interface market model is about the impact of competition on innovation. The concrete activities devoted to the design and qualification of goods are considered to be on the fringes of the market per se. This work, which is at the heart of the market dynamics, is never mentioned or discussed in the literature. It is mentioned only to assess its cost or chances of success. As we will see later on, in the market agencement model, the role of competition is entirely the inverse. Competition cannot exist outside of innovation strategies.

THIRD ABSTRACTION: INSTITUTIONS

The market cannot be reduced to one-off and random encounters. It must also organize and ensure multiple and repeated transactions. These words are largely synonymous with and summed up by Allais's expression "continuous relations," which points toward the idea that there are stable structures in place that guarantee the organized recurrence of transactions. The third abstraction, which renders explicit the conditions that ensure stability, brings about the notion of institutions. This idea was notably developed and enriched by (neo)institutionalist currents of thought. As elegantly summarized by economists Benjamin Coriat and Olivier Weinstein, "The market exists insofar as *sustainable structures* are set up that frame *multiple* and *repeated* transactions in such a way that, beyond the accomplishment of each particular transaction, a relative continuity in the nature of relations between economic agents is ensured."[29]

It would be no exaggeration to point out that the vast majority of those interested in markets adopt this point of view. All viable markets require rules, private or public conventions, and laws or regulations that are shared and apply to all participants. The market, experts have concluded, is an institution.[30]

Money is one of the central elements of this institutional apparatus. Rules accompany its creation, circulation, and uses, as well as the organizations that take charge of its elaboration and monitor its applications.[31] Nevertheless, the idea of necessary recourse to monetary payments has been left out of the analysis. Some authors used to consider barter, a practice of exchange without monetary compensation, to be at the heart of the notion of the market. According to them, it is irrelevant whether or not a payment with money takes place: money is introduced just to facilitate commercial exchanges when the number of agents (buyers and sellers) and the number of goods circulating grow beyond a certain threshold and the complexity of the organization of relations is such that barter becomes impracticable and inefficient on a large scale. Since for them the function of money is purely instrumental, they consider its use to have no effect on the nature and unfolding of the transactions. This conception of money, which has long been endorsed by the majority of economists interested in markets, is no longer tenable because there is no serious ethnographic research to support it. Scholars should be restricting the term "market" to economic organizations in which transfers of property between sellers and buyers are effected against monetary payment because it is quite impossible to prove the historical solidity of the hypothesis according to which monetary payment progressively replaced barter. As a matter of fact, money probably did not appear as a simple technical tool exclusively designed to facilitate exchanges and cope with complexity. Recent interventions in economic anthropology incite us to give up the tempting, but vain quest for origins and to focus instead on existing arrangements and the mechanisms of their transformation and to abandon the hope of being able to validate a genealogy according to which barter (or debt) is money's ancestor.[32]

Moreover, and this point is extremely important in my view, in making recourse to money as a central element in what is named a market, most specialists actually jettison the notion of exchange and its implicit association with solidarity: to speak of market exchange is nothing short of confusing.[33] This is why I propose that we acknowledge money as an essential element of the interface model.

As for rules, another form of institution, the number and content vary from expert to expert. All agree, however, that commercial institutions must ensure that once a transaction is realized, buyer and seller are clear of obligations: "Production and exchange could not have developed without a legal regime that puts in place a sufficiently efficient barrier against the risk of spoliation."[34] This requires that property rights be defined and that the conditions of their transfer be strictly overseen and guaranteed.[35] Beyond these rules (deemed *constitutive*), one can imagine many other rules (considered *regulative*) that frame, for instance, competition, product certification, or the determination of working periods.[36]

A final point merits attention. Increasing generalization is aided by the introduction of supply and demand, two notions that seem obvious to the point of being naturalized. Buyers and sellers, who are the only observables in marketplaces, are replaced by the forces of supply and demand they are taken to formulate, even though they rarely do formulate them. In the end, after these are aggregated, the abstraction speaks only of global supply and demand. Schumpeter noted that this movement of abstraction, which seems so simple and obvious (that is, the assumption that a purchase results from the encounter between one demand and one offer), was slowly constituted through numerous efforts spread out over more than a century. Once adopted, the two complementary notions of global supply and demand can be quantified and represented in charts. They enter into common expressions such as "decline in demand," "surplus supply," or the "crossed elasticity of demand." The entities further become manipulable and can be the object of political strategies and targeted policies. Thus, we speak of sustaining demand, increasing supply, or growing parts of the market that favor competition and innovation.

This third set of abstractions is essential. Complementing and amplifying the realism of the two preceding abstractions, it permits us to speak in a coherent fashion of the market as a general entity while at the same time leaving the door open to a wide variety of descriptions that depend upon the precise manner in which the institutional frameworks are defined.

The triple movement of abstraction outlined above leads to a minimal description of market activities and organizations that I've proposed we call the interface model of the market. The reference, often implicit, to this model (*n* populations of agents, goods that act as platforms, competing agents, and rules to shape, coordinate, and regulate their behaviors) can be found across academic disciplines and even in ordinary parlance. Everything around us unfolds as if the ordinary meaning of the word "market" should be conflated with this model. Rendered so unproblematic, the word is frequently taken up in more complex theoretical constructions as if its meaning can be taken for granted. Among the most influential thinkers and writers, rare are the individuals who would openly endorse this minimal definition, having never fully discussed it.

Douglass North, in his 1977 article "Markets and Other Allocation Systems in History," commenting on Polanyi's thesis in *The Great Transformation*, acknowledges the importance of examining the organizational forms that support economic activities. But in contrast to Polanyi, who merely describes the diversity of forms, he explains it by introducing the hypothesis of universal economic behavior in humans: all human agents will pursue maximal gains by managing transaction costs. This straightforward explanation must nevertheless rely on the minimal definition of markets. Without saying so explicitly, North takes in Polanyi's own definition of a market while taking the opportunity to make it very specific and restrictive: markets are institutions that make prices. North adds, in passing, that such markets can exist only under certain poorly understood conditions that must include the following features: a number of significant buyers and sellers, a set of (clearly defined) goods, agreement on the medium of exchange, and enforcement of property rights. That is all he says. Even though North is among the rare economists taking an interest in the specific nature of markets as organizational forms, he is nevertheless content to cement in place a minimal definition taken from standard economic thinking that fixates upon autonomous offers of supply and demand, well-stabilized goods, and prices that supposedly fluctuate upon the confrontation of supply and demand.

Harrison White, one of the founders of the new economic sociology and of network analysis, confirms this: "A market is a social arena in which buyers and sellers meet. But for buyers and sellers to exist, a product has to exist and someone has to produce it."[37] Viviana Zelizer, an American sociologist with profound influence in economic anthropology, concurs: "Markets are sets of social relations in which actors transfer goods and services."[38] These three authors, who could not be more different from one another (and I could quote many others), share the same motif—that of the interface market—as they weave, embroider, and stretch their respective theoretical webs. Likewise, this model has served and continues to serve as the implicit and quasi-unique reference in public policy circles that seek to regulate market competition.

Far from me is it to say that all those who have studied markets up to now are in error. As the rest of this book unfolds, I will constantly make reference to their work. But as we will see in the next section, this conception of the market, the market interface model, gives an incomplete and too narrow view of market organizations. This is why I prefer to resort to the market agencement model that I am now presenting. This shift is all the more timely with the increased commodification of living beings and the explosion of digital technology, where the interface market model has become an obstacle to the analysis of novel market activities.

The ambition of this book is to change the specific traits of markets that come to mind when we discuss market activities, such that we effectively have a new meaning to associate with the word "market" when it is used in shorthand to refer to market activities.

TOWARD THE MODEL OF MARKET AGENCEMENTS

To isolate the lacunas that the agencement model must fill, the simplest strategy is to establish a list of the contributions and limits of the interface model it is designed to replace. Let's begin by pulling out the fundamental contributions that cannot be jettisoned.

The first contribution relates to the distinction that the interface market introduces between agents and goods. To establish a market, it is necessary to divide the constitutive entities into two great groups—the subjects (the agents) who participate directly or indirectly in initiating and executing transactions and the objects (the goods in all their various forms) upon which the transactions occur; or, translated into the language of Western law, which guarantees this separation, the persons and the other things. Without this great divide, the transaction is not possible.

The second contribution is that the transaction consists of a transfer, or if we prefer, a commutation, of property rights. As a consequence, these must be defined in a sufficiently precise manner, must be defended, and are susceptible to contestation. The third contribution is to note that relationships of competition develop between the different agents. Using all legal means at their disposal, the game is to garner control over the establishment of new transactions.

Lastly, the fourth contribution concerns the proper qualification of commercial transactions. The idea that this can be assimilated with exchange is abandoned, and with it the expression "market exchange." A commercial transaction simply consists of monetary payment, after which the agents are quits.

The different contributions of the interface market, contributions that I take up in turn, should not mask their true insufficiencies, which I will present in a synthetic manner, one by one, in the lines that follow: a) they do not take into account the material composition of market activities; b) they bracket out the coconstructive process of creating supply and demand, which leads to underestimating the crucial role played by bilateral transactions and the initiation of these transactions; c) they create unrealism through the concepts of aggregated supply and demand and bring about difficulties in comprehending the actual mechanisms for establishing prices; d) they create a total impasse on the complex processes that result in a separation between agents and goods; e) the hypothesis that goods are platforms precludes us from recognizing they are processes; f) and lastly, they imply a description of agents that underestimates their diversity, heterogeneity, and plasticity.

The agencement model has been conceived to integrate all of these contributions and also to respond to their insufficiencies. But before diving into its detailed analysis, it is useful to show in broad strokes how it reworks some of the hypotheses of the interface market and thus provides a different perspective from most existing analyses.

KEY ROLE OF THE MATERIAL COMPONENT

The material component plays an essential part in commercial activities. This assertion is in stark contrast not only with the model of interface markets, but also with the economic or sociological analyses that have up to now built on it. Rules, conventions, norms, and values, the nature of laws, the forms of social-relationship networks are, as we noted, so many variables, alongside those of need, the calculation of interests, the search for distinctiveness, and the desire for imitation that analysts invoke to give an account both of the ways markets function and of the diversity of their forms of organization.[39] In principle, nothing prevents us from including material devices in the definition and description of institutions, but it is a fact that this option is only rarely chosen.[40] For a social sciences expert, whether an economist, a sociologist, or an anthropologist, institutions, psychological wellsprings, or cultural values are often "realities without bodies."[41]

We cannot be satisfied with such bracketing. Max Weber's observation should be taken seriously as that of one of the rare authors to have long ago suggested the active role of the material component in the organization and accomplishment of transactions. According to Weber, the material component is not there simply to serve as a backdrop for interactions that are reducible to pure social relations; it does not simply furnish resources to these relations. "It is the physical assemblages that allow the emergence and accomplishments of one of the distinctive characteristics of commercial activities: bargaining."[42] This formulation is precious because we find in it not only notions such as emergence and material *assemblages*, to which we will return throughout this book, but also the clearest and most direct possible affirmation that these material assemblages contribute to formatting commercial transactions.

Despite its accuracy, the Weberian intuition was long ignored, even if as influential an author as Polanyi does not forget to mention the physical sites in the description he gives of the elements of a market. It came back into force only very recently, in the early 2000s, with work, inspired by science and technology studies[43] that turned toward concrete markets, aiming to bring out the importance, for their functioning, of things—and therefore of products and procedures—as well as the active role of knowledge, know-how, tools, instruments, or devices.[44] This new approach, largely unknown, introduced a major discontinuity with previous analyses. One of the main ambitions of this book is to show how interesting and fecund it is.

THE STRATEGIC PURPOSE OF MARKET AGENCEMENTS

The interface market model evokes the creation of relationships between supplies and demands connected around goods; it describes the transfer of property rights; it refers to competitive behavior and monetary payments. It does not, however, explain how these different actions end up connecting to one another and organizing in such a way as to regularly and successfully produce the observed result: commercial transactions are realized.

Most analysts have understood that in order to account for this constantly renewed miracle, the picture needs to be fleshed out, and more complete models have to be put forward, ones that include in their description the forces that explain why and how this collective-oriented action can emerge. But there are not many answers. Either one considers that it is the agents who, impelled by the calculation of their interests, by their needs, or by any other force or motivation, set markets in motion and keep them animated. Or one imagines that these actions undertaken by agents are fashioned and oriented by norms, rules, systems of social relations or domination, or structures such as the division of labor that channel them toward establishing commercial transactions.

The notion of agencement, that is to say, a heterogeneous assemblage, putting the accent as it does on the role played by material devices, makes it possible to avoid choosing one or the other of these two solutions. Markets consist of arrangements that play a double role. They contribute to imposing guiding frameworks on individual actions and provide them with motives while channeling collective action toward the conclusion of commercial transactions. Fairs, supermarkets, meeting or matching algorithms, production technologies, calculation and management tools, metrological instruments, advertising campaigns, formulas for establishing prices, brands, the innumerable means for provoking attachments are all devices (which we will explore throughout this book) that format and orient behavior and interactions in an even stronger way than do the supposed human interest or the sole ascendency of rules, norms, laws, or customs or systems of social relations. Market agencements do not exclude any of these forces. Rather, they situate them within the entire set of material and textual devices (including legal coding) that structure and prompt commercial activities.[45]

One can thus characterize market agencements through their strategic purpose, which is to organize and promote the establishment of bilateral transactions. We will need no fewer than five chapters to explain how they manage this.

COMPETITION IS THE STRUGGLE TO ESTABLISH BILATERAL TRANSACTIONS...

In the market agencement model, what is at stake in competition is establishing transactions. Establishing each new bilateral transaction—one particular seller, one particular good, one particular buyer—is competition's one and only goal.

It may be a radically new transaction, or it may be the renewal of a transaction that has already taken place. Even if buyer and seller seem to have preserved the same identity, and even if the good in question seems very similar to the one that was on offer earlier, it is a different event. The new bilateral transaction is different from the previous ones and cannot, under any circumstances, be considered identical to it or considered to be a mere repetition. The time and place have changed, and with them, in a more or less superficial way, more or less profound, yet real, the identities of the buyer and seller and the qualities of the transferred goods have changed, as well. No transaction is quite like any other. Each must be conquered, and it is precisely for this new conquest that there is competition.

In the classical representation of monopoly, a company confiscates the entire supply by having exclusivity over the good, thereby rendering customers captive. Monopoly signifies the absence of competition. In market agencements, under their bilateral form (that is, this buyer, this seller, and this singularized good at this place and at this time),[46] monopoly is on the contrary the ultimate expression of the competitive struggle. The more a company is able to sideline the agents who might threaten the series of its bilateral monopolies, the more it is able to singularize each of the goods it offers to each of its clients, the more its competitive power is increased.

This is not a new way of looking at things. It has already been brilliantly illustrated by authors such as Joan Robinson and Edward Chamberlin in the first decades of the twentieth century. In his masterful history of economic analysis, Joseph Schumpeter offers this comment on these two authors: they "allow monopoly to 'swallow up the competitive analysis'—every firm being a monopolist, that is, a single seller of its own product."[47] Whereas in the traditional conception, monopoly and competition are opposites, according to these two authors, monopoly is the strategy that expresses the logic of competition in its purest form.[48] The search for monopoly by all available means—this is what drives competition.[49] And the most radical way to reach it is to impose the singularization not of the good, but of the bilateral transaction itself, in other words, of the trio made up of the one who offers, the one who demands, and the good. In market agencements, perfect competition, which one might call *competitive monopolism*, has nothing to do with that of neoclassical economics. Its only goal is to make bilateral transactions proliferate, and what is at stake is control of that proliferation.

THE PROLIFERATION OF TRANSACTIONS REQUIRES INNOVATION

Innovation is inextricably linked to commercial activity, since the latter consists in establishing bilateral transactions, and each successful transaction rests on its singularization, that is to say, on a specific qualification, however tenuous it may be, and in certain cases, it can be reduced to a mere difference in price of the good sold and bought. If a company does not innovate, it (gradually) excludes itself from commercial activity. In market agencement, innovation is not an exceptional or occasional strategy that agents develop to escape competition or alleviate its rigor. Competition does not stimulate innovation any more than it paralyzes it.[50] Innovation is the essence of competition. The greater the singularization, that is to say, the greater the scope of the innovation, the more intense is the competition; the weaker it is, that is to say, the more innovation is minor or superficial, the more moderate the competition.[51] Competition can even effectively disappear when singularization tends toward the imperceptible. If one were not afraid of paradoxical formulations, one might say that in the market agencement model, pure and perfect competition as it is usually described in economics textbooks (a large number of agents offering and seeking the same product) corresponds to a complete extinction of competition and to the long-term collapse of market agencement itself.[52]

In certain forms of commercial organization, the rhythm and depth of innovations, by which I mean the proliferation of bilateral transactions, grow spectacularly. This is referred to as a regime of intensive innovation, which is becoming the rule in activities in the computationally driven tech sector.[53] This is why the agencement model cannot be shunted aside. In the following chapters, I will put forward numerous examples showing how my model permits us to realistically analyze the way in which merchant activities are linked to the massive mobilization of digital technologies, while the interface model finds itself maladapted to these cases. The personalization and individualization of services, or the made to order (sometimes called "mass customization"), underscores the realism of my concept of competition. The seeming paradox, which is completely comprehensible once we retool our intellectual model, is that singularization strategies, essentially a qualitative pursuit, are the basis of growth, which is expressed quantitatively.

Singularization's central role in commercial transactions is assimilated, in the model, into the concept of innovation. Without innovation, there is no competition, and as a consequence, there is no market activity. And since innovation strategies are diverse, so, too, are the forms of competition.[54]

To show that innovation plays just as important a role in slower markets, which seem more traditional and quite different from tech markets, let's consider the French case of AMAPs, an acronym that translates to "associations for the maintenance of peasant agriculture" (Associations pour le maintien d'une agriculture paysanne).[55] According to the leaders of the movement, the goal of these associations is not to eliminate the market, but rather to invent new forms of commercial activities. However, as in any market agencement, a threat lurks. There is the danger of producers or consumers switching to other transactions, implying other partners and other goods. For example, the consumer can change producer within the AMAP or turn elsewhere, or the producer might decide to commercialize part of his production in a different way. Within the association, attachments are obtained by organized coprofiling of products, consumers, and producers—that is, by the singularization of each new bilateral transaction. Yet as in any market agencement, attachments can be undone at any moment. Members of the association, whether producers or consumers, can change partners not only within the AMAP, but also by looking for partners outside the AMAP. This is why as a collective market agencement designer, the AMAP relentlessly strives to keep members active and extend membership. It succeeds by constantly reshaping devices of singularization.

This is the reason why AMAPs create frequently revised charters that define and guarantee the qualities of the marketable products (freshness, origin, availability); they introduce new agents; they construct tables detailing delivery sites and frequency, as well as production calendars; they establish rules for decision making; they clarify general principles that define the goals of organized collective action—for example, supporting a new form of agriculture, developing healthy and sustainable foods, and so on.[56] The association is an agencement that aims to link a group of producers and a group of consumers around duly qualified goods.

Although they are often likened to very primitive and almost futureless forms of commercial organizations, AMAPs are sites where innovation that is collectively controlled and decided is central and combines all of the technical, organizational, and social dimensions one usually aims to pry apart. If perchance the goods on offer by an AMAP are not sufficiently singular and convincing, the AMAP will disappear. Indeed, this often happens.

Without innovation, there are no market agencements of any nature whatsoever. As we will see throughout this book, the rule brooks no exceptions.

PROCESS GOODS

If the coprofiling of singular supplies and demands around goods that are themselves singular constitutes the strategic problem that markets must continuously resolve, then it is unrealistic to assume two preexisting blocks of supplies and demands that are independent from one another and that are linked through goods acting as unifying platforms whose origin is considered unproblematic. In other words, if the singularity of a good must be established for each and every transaction, then supply, demand, and the qualities of products do not drive market activity, but are the result achieved by endless activities that constitute and reconstitute an active market agencement.

As goods are transformed throughout the process of design, production, and commercialization, so are the supplies and demands for them. Goods, supplies, and demands are not separate sets; they are intimately connected, caught up in bundles of evolving relationships that ensure otherwise incomprehensible adjustment and adequation. This process can be called *qualification*, which aims at ensuring the coproduction of goods' characteristics, as well as those of the buyers and sellers, into the activity I refer to as coprofiling. The qualification of goods does not precede the establishment of markets; these activities are at its heart.

The process of qualification is a central feature of all commercial activities, although it has only recently become visible and been laid claim to, because it is becoming hugely amplified in sectors such as the health care, electronic commerce, and service industries. To illustrate, let us take the example of a recognizable mass-market product whose market architecture is reminiscent of an interface market: a model of car with hundreds of thousands sold. A car first exists on a drawing board or in a 3-D digital representation, then as a set of specifications, then as a series of plans and diagrams in a design department, then as a model on a platform, under the as yet vague guise of a concept car, then as a prototype image on glossy paper with its technical annexes, then as a floor model in showrooms put into words by the explanations and rhetoric of the salespeople, then as an object of tests and comparisons in consumer magazines. (An entirely novel set of sequences will need to be added to this account to include autonomous vehicles, which, for example, require lengthy trials in urban situations.)

After the transaction is concluded, after the car has been purchased and rolls off the lot, it continues to be requalified, to live a life that was not necessarily programmed: it becomes an object of social distinction; it is leased or resold as a secondhand vehicle (which its previous owner may have anticipated by taking care of it and choosing a highly rated model); it is reduced to a wreck whose components are recycled as materials or as spare parts; or it is remanufactured in certain developing countries before leading a second commercial life; or it may eventually be requalified as a classic car.

The successive requalifications of the product and its concurrent transformations start in design departments or research centers, continue in normalization or certification services, and persist once the transaction has taken place. Each moment of requalification can mobilize a large number of agents. Yet the agents can also be concentrated in one site—for instance, in a marketing department, in which case, a very limited number of agents may be involved. The point is that goods are qualified as a result of some kind of collective and collaborative activity, and the form taken at one moment of commercial transaction is only one of the many forms they will take over the course of their careers. Over the course of this book, I will give numerous examples to illustrate the general nature of this phenomenon.

I hope it is becoming clear why a product must be considered a process. Products are made up of a series of actions, a succession of operations that transform and displace them, passing them from hand to hand through a series of metamorphoses that work out forms judged attractive by economic agents who pay to enjoy their benefits.[57] Over the course of these metamorphoses, the qualities of products vary. The career of a product has no other purpose than to be transformed into a good, that is, a thing that is sought after, researched, desired, and deserving of being purchased. Marketing, broadly redefined as the concern for getting a product to market, pulls together every single one of the operations that lead to its being involved in a singular commercial transaction. To reduce marketing to superficial operations that aim to make a good desirable to people who have no need for it (Alain Souchon, in his beautiful song, "Foule sentimentale" talks of "desires inflicted on us") while ignoring the material practices of design and production, is at best a tautology. At worst, it is a sign of completely underestimating the relentless processes by which goods are qualified. My observation applies equally to the AMAP and to chemical or pharmaceutical industries. A product, as Chamberlin underlines, is an economic variable like any other.[58]

PROLIFERATING AGENTS, PLASTIC IDENTITIES, AND NETWORKING

Unlike the platform good in the interface model, the process good articulates supplies and demands. If it did not, it would not warrant the name "market good." This articulation, however, is an action that involves a series of modifications and adaptations that connect design, production, and circulation activities to one another. The action must mobilize multiple agents to collectively engage in the creation, manufacturing, sale, and use of these products.

Understood in this broadened vision, the list of agents enrolled in commercial activity stretches well beyond the usual roles imagined by the notions of supply and demand in the interface market model. It includes, for instance, researchers, some of whom work in university laboratories, others in industrial research centers, engineers, civil servants and experts in competition policy, and bankers prompted to invest in new lines of activity; it involves users or consumers (individual or collective), governmental agencies, lawyers, professional associations, unions, and even certification bodies. These multiple agents, who vary from sector to sector, are likely to be involved at one moment or another, in one capacity or another, in the qualification or requalification of a good where the only horizon of their action is the potential commercialization of that good. Agents generally come from state spheres as much as from civil society, and indeed, there is no reason to draw a categorical distinction between the two. All of the various activities whose objective is to find a market for goods should be included in the market.

It does not therefore make sense to refer to two intertwined populations, or even to two independent populations of buyers and sellers. The essential notion here is networks. Not the familiar social networks linking agents whose identities are stabilized, but networks that, as we will see, cross all the different populations involved in commercial activities. Within these networks, goods, agents, and material infrastructures are caught up in the same dynamic, where they are subject to being transformed while coevolving.[59] Along these networks, the qualities of products and the identities of people are reworked until they get adjusted to one another.

To put it in a nutshell, while the interface market model, which describes markets as organizations structured around groups of agents and platform goods, has neither thickness nor depth, the image of commercial activities that prevails in the market agencement model is temporal and longitudinal.[60]

This requalification has important consequences for the relations between markets and societies. Max Weber speaks of "consociation" to designate the form of social relations instituted by markets.[61] A particular form of socialization, consociation results from the instauration of competition, which is the simplest modality of coordination that leads an actor to take another into account. According to Weber, the market generates social relations, or, if you prefer, sociability, through competition. Weber thus breaks with the classical point of view articulated by Adam Smith: "Two greyhounds, in running down the same hare, have sometimes the appearance of acting in some sort of concert. Each turns her [the hare being hunted] toward his companion, or endeavors to intercept her when his companion turns her toward himself. This, however, is not the effect of any contract, but of the accidental concurrence of their passions in the same object at that particular time."[62] Yet contrary to what Smith imagined, effective competition does not require isolated agents with only the contingent convergence of their desires connecting them. But neither is consociation reducible to a simple coordination. As Weber would have it, competition is born of collective work, constantly renewed and necessary to the establishment of bilateral transactions.[63] The coproduction of supplies, demands, and goods—which has to somehow handle the concerns and contestations it provokes—is at the heart of the commercial dynamic. It implies establishing collaborative relations, organizing negotiations, setting decisional processes into motion, structuring and reconfiguring networks. It does not work through rarifying relations; it organizes their proliferation.

Market activities engender social relations, but not just any social relations. They also manufacture impersonal relations, but not exclusively. One of this book's objectives is to further characterize this double process.

CHAPTER SUMMARIES: UNDERSTANDING MARKETS AS FRAMINGS

Now that the major traits that distinguish market agencements from other possible conceptions of the market have been identified (that is, the interface market), we can turn to analyzing the way they function. How does collective action lead to the production of bilateral transactions? How does it renew and extend them?

To answer these questions, I will now introduce the notion of *framing* (*cadrage*) which refers to the devices that orient and structure action toward its strategic goal.[64] In the case of market agencements, I suggest marking out five framings. I will devote one chapter to each framing, each of which corresponds to a different operation that, when combined with the others, prepares and formats commercial transactions. Distinguishing five types of framings does not imply these are naturally distinct sites or a chronological development. These framings are, as we will see, multisited and open to back-and-forth. What follows is a brief overview of the rest of the book.

The agencement model begins by empirically observing that for the market transaction to take place, there must first be a split between the goods that will be the object of a market transaction at some moment of their existence and the agencies capable of evaluating and appreciating the goods that will pass through their hands at another point in time. It may seem counterintuitive, but the entities capable of evaluating a good at first are not the potential future buyers. They are in fact the groups involved in creating it and acting as provisional and tentative spokespeople for them. What it entails for agents to be split from the good is to do work to create the conditions for the good to be widely evaluated and eventually requalified. The examples to come will help to clarify this unusual starting point.

Introducing this split between goods and their evaluation, which appears most clearly at the moment of transaction itself, is the result of many stages of work, beginning at the moment of the good's conception. Chapters 2 and 3 present two framings that organize this separation. The first framing has the function of formatting the entities designed to be marketed. To designate this little-studied process, I invoke a neologism, *market-oriented passiva(c)tion*, which a) detaches the good and liberates it from all those who participated in its elaboration and profiling, b) renders it apt to provoke courses of actions and to contribute to their realization (that is, imbues it with uses), c) ensures that its behavior is at least to a certain extent controllable and predictable, and d) organizes the attribution and transfer of property rights.[65] It is worth noting that the investments necessary for market-oriented passiva(c)tion are all the greater, more expensive, and more complex as the entities that must be transformed into commercial goods are close to the living world or include living beings.

The successive transformations through which the future good passes coincide with it being evaluated. The evaluations, which feed and orient the qualification process, suppose a second series of framings that will ensure that the agencies formatted to carry out these evaluation operations are getting the job done. The evaluating agencies, which can be individuals or collective entities such as a consumer group or company, must have the equipment at their disposal without which they cannot do their work. This includes know-how, manuals, comparative guides, accounting tools, management instruments, cost-benefit analysis methods, data, algorithms, and so on.

If what I am describing as yet sounds obscure, just remember that the model of interface markets forgoes taking all the formatting I am describing into account. It simply presumes that pass(act)ivated goods and agencies that evaluate them are available, ready made, and lie outside the analysis of markets. Yet, as my research, along with that of others, shows, in concrete markets, making goods pass(act)ive and populating the marketplace with evaluating agencies directly contributes to spurring commercial activity.[66] Making this happen requires mobilizing considerable material, legal, and discursive means to ensure that throughout the conception, production, and commercialization process, the objects involved will indeed do what they are supposed to do and that the different agents involved have the tools and instruments they need to evaluate the goods at their disposal. (As an example, think of the controversy around the safety of self-driving vehicles.) That is to say, at each point in the qualification process, agents should be able to envision how sellers and buyers will value the good and consequently decide how it might be transformed.

It is not, however, enough for the goods to be made pass(act)ive and for a set of agencies to be given the capacity to evaluate and transform them. It is also necessary that certain agencies agree to pay to acquire the goods they are being offered. Two extra series of framings contribute to this result. The first framing orchestrates encounters between process goods as their form successively changes and the different agencies involved in their qualification-singularization. These encounters can happen at any stage of the good's career. The second framing organizes the attachment of the goods to potential buyers in such a way as to obtain the latter's willingness to pay.

Chapter 4 will present the devices required to orchestrate all of these encounters. These devices have technical-material components such as matching algorithms, trade shows and fairs, congresses and conferences, corner stores and malls, window displays, directories, supermarket carts, internet sites and their web interfaces, and more. They also have textual and audiovisual components (advertising messages, clips, brochures) and human components (intermediaries, consultants, technology-transfer agencies, salespeople, influencers, customer service, and so on).

Market devices aim to capture potential customers' attention and to make them deviate from their original trajectories, just like the street sellers calling out on the sidewalk in London. This is not enough, however. Imagine a framing of encounters that awakens curiosity, fires up desire, excites the passions, amplifies and transforms these into interest, and yet ultimately fails to obtain the willingness to pay. Payment can be obtained only if the good ends up attached to the client and the client to the good. That is to say, the process of singularization must go so far as to make the good and the agent reciprocally constitutive of one another. This is the aim of the fourth series of framings, which will be presented in Chapter 5. Carrying out the labor of incorporation, which has more to do with affect than it does with interests, uses, or needs, requires even more devices.

Once the process of attachment is well under way, the final step is to transform the ongoing attachment into a willingness to pay while at the same time setting the price of the good that is the object of the transaction. In market agencements, establishing the price is not mechanically determined by a confrontation between two blocks, supply and demand. It is the result of the particular activities, analyzed in Chapter 6, that constitute what I have called "price formulation." Price formulation is based on both qualitative and quantitative operations. It connects the particular conditions of the transaction to more general evaluations, such that the price becomes a variable that qualifies the good and contributes to its singularization. These activities require appropriate devices that draw on the skills and know-how of a great number of actors who mobilize research tools and sophisticated calculations. They are at the heart of the power relations enacted by commercial practices.

The five framings entail engaging with, investing in, and implementing an array of devices that structure the various activities that will lead to the proliferation of bilateral transactions. It all comes down to a series of goal-oriented actions—a) rendering goods pass(act)ive; b) activating agencies capable of evaluating and transforming these goods; c) organizing their encounter; d) ensuring the attachment of the goods to the agencies; e) obtaining consent to pay; and f) setting a price and compelling payment–actions that combine and interweave with one another, with possible feedback loops and iterations.

Market agencements are constantly dealing with forces that provoke them to reformulate and reformat themselves. This constant *reagencing* can ultimately even put their strategic goal into question.[67] Analysis of how agencements function is therefore not distinct from analysis of their transformations.

The dramatic expansion of market agencements today is examined in Chapter 7, which also explores the different trajectories they are liable to follow and dwells on the way they combine market and nonmarket activities.

Chapter 8, which concludes the book, introduces the question of political engineering to the analysis of market agencements. One of the expected benefits of the method followed here, and in fact its only justification, is indeed that it offers new perspectives on the following question: Can one organize market activities not so that they embody an ideal invented by experts in the quiet of their consulting companies' offices, but rather so that they also respond to the demands of a precise set of specifications that, following a debate, establish objectives and their priorities?

The answer to this question will require a subsequent book. First, however, a problem has to be solved. Imagine that specifications for a market have been defined and approved. Is it realistic to imagine that one can move from ideas directly to concrete devices without the project falling apart and drifting again and again? It is one thing to put propositions on the table, to formulate orientations. Implementing them is something else altogether. The final chapter examines specific examples—financial markets, the economies of climate change and genetically modified plants—to figure out the strategy that should be followed and to show how, at some points, ideas can impinge upon framings (for example, theoretical models or intuitions, expectations, legal considerations) and thus can be shown to act on the architecture of market agencements and their functioning.

The notion of market agencement I have developed provides a general framework for the description of market activities. The model makes it possible to grasp the unity of the market order while maintaining the diversity of its possible configurations. There is no other theoretical formulation that I know of that takes into account all five of the framings presented here or the way they are articulated with one another. The objective of this book is to fill this lacuna. To this end, I will rely equally on work carried out by social scientists and by professionals in commercial activities, whoever they may be. My only and basic goal is better analyzing market practices and how they cause matters of concern. At this stage, I will not propose any agencements as correctives in an uneasy world. I will instead simply consider a number of useful studies that, despite their diversity and sometimes their opposition to one another, contain potential contributions toward the gradual exploration of a model that none of them explicitly envisage, but that taken together, they suggest. At stake is the possibility of properly understanding markets so as to better identify the means of transforming them.

As we reach the end of this introductory chapter, it is my hope that the reader will be convinced to join me in this adventure. Before getting on board, you should know that in order to demonstrate the generality of the model, the cases presented have been chosen from a wide variety of sectors. For obvious reasons, for the length of the journey, I will accord a special place to the technologies and know-how developed by the companies that populate Silicon Valley, some of which have imposed their way on the world at large. They achieve these ends by conceiving of tools, equipment, devices, and infrastructures that reinforce and render even more performant the framings of market agencements—which explains their success, all while rendering them more noticeable. As a consequence, markets are now easier to analyze and debate.

CHAPTER TWO

The Process of Making Goods Mobile and Alienable

No commercial activity is possible unless a deep and durable dissymmetry has been established. On the one hand, there are the different agents involved in preparing and realizing commercial transactions; on the other hand, there are the goods destined to become merchandise. This distinction largely overlaps with the distinction between people and things that is foundational for Western law—without it, no market could exist. The great divide between entities to which rights and obligations apply and entities that are bearers of rights and obligations to each other authorizes the transfer of property rights in exchange for monetary payment; thus, this divide underlies the appropriation of goods by agents.[1] The appropriation may apply to the thing itself, conceived as an indivisible entity by Roman law. It may also apply to duly specified rights corresponding to particular uses and bringing out certain qualities of the thing, as in Anglo-Saxon law.[2]

The distinction can appear indisputable because it is taken as substantive. Things are incapable of intentional actions and can be defined by their passivity: they are ready to become goods that are exchanged. This simple and obvious criterion allows for a first sorting, for instance, between a car (the thing) and its owner (the person, the physical or legal entity), or between the prototype (the thing) and the engineer (the person) who designs it. Indeed, other than in a metaphorical sense, who would dare claim that the car or the model can own their owner or their designer or use them to develop their own programs of action?

Yet this distinction is becoming less and less clear, or to put it another way, more and more difficult to establish and impose. The connected cars being brought to market by some companies are blurring boundaries. Heavy investments in both legal work and technology are required to establish and enforce, in this case, a clear separation between drivers and their car. With the increasing role played by artificial intelligence, these situations are multiplying. This is why this book adopts an altogether different position. I recognize the fundamental importance of the great divide, yet I refuse to consider it as self-evident. Based on countless studies by my colleagues and me on the relationships between people and things, we famously concluded that the distinction and asymmetry between entities destined to become commodities and the entities qualified as agents are not givens. What we showed, through detailed empirical studies, is that agents and goods get separated out and endowed with rights and responsibilities through a consequential set of processes. These processes can be long, often costly, and are made up of a multitude of trials to overcome and problems to be solved. The result is always fragile and temporary.

Economic or sociological studies that implicitly refer to what I have called interface markets have one main virtue: they, too, underline the foundational and structuring character of the distinction in markets. Once the necessity of the asymmetry has been posited, however, the principal limit of these kinds of studies is that they lose interest in the processes and in the instabilities that affect these processes. Although the existence of process is not denied, the numerous costly and uncertain activities associated with it are considered to be outside the market and thought not to interfere with its functioning.

Market agencement makes this process the central question—and that is why it is here that I begin. The activities involved in design, manufacture, and commercialization that lead to the constitution of an always fragile and problematic disentangling of people and things are not dismissed as being external to market activities. They are instead at the center of what it means to establish a market. These activities develop according to two complementary logics. On the one hand, there is everything that corresponds to what I will call the *market-oriented passiva(c)tion* of goods. On the other hand, there is the whole set of mechanisms that establish agents capable of evaluating, calculating, deciding, or implementing courses of action, as we will see later, in Chapter 3.

My specific aim in this chapter is to understand how the activity of a thing can be directed and controlled while being rendered mobile and alienable. It is devoted to the analysis of the puzzling processes that can transform an entity of any kind into a good that can become a commodity. In order to move forward in exploring this enigma, I start from anthropological work that advances our understanding of these mechanisms. It is worth noting that economic anthropology does not always break with some of the fundamental hypotheses of interface markets, notably, the thesis of which is that that the world of goods and the world of agents can be described separately. Despite those limits, if appropriately reworked, some of the analytical tools developed by this discipline will prove useful. Consequently, as I make reference to older works of anthropology, the reader should not assume that I fully endorse the analyses proposed. First of all, because the problems anthropologists once dealt with were different from mine, but more importantly, because as with any good scientific work, the most important part is the methods and concepts they provide. In what follows, I am most interested in discovering useful methods and concepts.[3]

In the first part of the chapter, I present the main concepts that make it possible to follow the process of passiva(c)tion of goods. In a second part, I will then apply the proposed analysis to categories of goods reputed to resist merchandization, such as so-called fictitious commodities, or, among others, living beings. Finally, I insist on some of the concerns that the market-oriented passiva(c)tion process may generate.

I. The Process of Market Passiva(c)tion

SPACES OF CIRCULATION AND THE CAREERS OF GOODS

In interface markets, although they may have been difficult to define, the goods are given, and their properties are stable.

However simple and convincing it is, this perspective is untenable. It chooses to ignore that some entities are being denied the right and the possibility of becoming commodities, sometimes after enduring controversies, and conversely, to ignore the fact that well-established commodities might be violently contested.[4] It also disregards that other things reach the state of goods only at the end of long processes, over the course of which they transform and change status multiple times. In one interaction, they are goods; in another, they are gifts for relatives, until they end up, after several avatars, in huge dumps, from whence they are recycled and sold as spare parts to interested industries. It is difficult to settle for analyzing the ways markets function as though these transformations, these perpetual changes in status, did not exist. They cannot simply be taken for granted.

SPACES OF CIRCULATION

In economic anthropology, one of the first solutions imagined to explain how the status of a commercial good is acquired was to introduce the notion of the space (or sphere) of circulation. Strongly inspired by Karl Marx and Marcel Mauss, this body of work is closely linked to the notions of systems of exchange and cultural systems. In general, these studies took a comparative approach and probed the differences between Western and non-Western societies.

In Marx's analysis, there exists a sort of structural abyss between Western capitalist society and other economies that either preceded it or developed in other parts of the world. In the Western economy, everything may become a commodity when there is a prospect of profit and accumulation (work and land are no exception), while other economies were perceived to contain the expansion of the market sphere. Drawing on the opposition between gift and commodity, Mauss contributed to exploring this discontinuity, this radical opposition between capitalist and noncapitalist economies. He showed that it depended on the existence of fundamentally different systems of exchange and therefore of sociability. For decades, exploring different regimes of the circulation of goods, those characterized as commercial and those characterized as noncommercial, was one of economic anthropology's favorite themes.[5]

One of the most impactful theses was developed by Paul Bohannan in his 1955 study of the circulation of different types of goods in West Africa.[6] According to Bohannan, the goods exchanged among the Tiv in Nigeria can be classified in three large categories, which correspond to distinct spheres of exchange. One sphere concerns subsistence goods; another, goods that constitute the wealth of their holders (bracelets, herds, slaves); the third is made up of marriageable women. Exchanges are possible within each sphere, or, if you prefer, between the goods that belong to the same category. Exchanges are very difficult or even forbidden between distinct spheres; this is particularly the case insofar as no unified currency generally exists. Other studies have empirically attempted to confirm the existence of spheres of exchange in a great number of societies. Goods, depending on the category to which they belong, are destined to circulate in spaces that are separate from one another.

These observations were originally made in non-Western societies, but have since been extended to the West, notably to underline the existence of commercial and noncommercial spheres between which circulation is made difficult. For example, Maurice Bloch and Jonathan Parry consider the family a site that has been protected from the invasion of the market, at least up to a certain era.[7] One could also cite work that aligns with the analyses of Karl Polanyi, Marshall Sahlins, or Marcel Mauss and insists upon the existence of spaces and goods that resist commodification for moral, political, or even economic reasons. The things that escape the market will vary, depending on historical eras and societies. Some contemporary societies, for instance, show great hesitation in allowing blood, organs, or fundamental scientific knowledge to enter the market sphere. When exchange appears to be the only possible option, other than pure gift or predation,[8] they will only enter into commercial exchange depending upon the spaces of circulation in which they take place.

These different analyses share a single hypothesis. They all rest on the idea that it is always possible, in principle, at least, to shield certain goods from commodification by including them in systems of social relations and institutional frameworks that forbid it. It bears repeating that the distinction is not between entities that are *naturally* passive and would be inevitably destined, whatever one did, to become commodities at some point, and entities that are *naturally* active (agents) and would seize them for profit, but rather between spaces that are *socially* constituted and impose their rules on circulation. This idea of spaces of circulation and specific exchange systems that confer a certain status on things is a first step in the direction of process goods. To become a commodity, the thing must be torn out of the world to which it is attached and displaced in order to then be reassigned to a new world. Certain moves, certain transitions from one sphere to another, from one space to another, are made impossible or very costly. Thus, certain goods or certain beings are not exchangeable. They must be kept, and they are kept. To take another example of which economists are fond, in contemporary societies, children who are unhappy with their parents, even if they wanted to, would have real difficulty in getting rid of them and exchanging them for better fathers or mothers or selling them to whomever would be willing to buy them. In a country such as France, the commercialization of children (and indeed also of parents) is taboo: one can adopt them, but one cannot buy them.

The idea of spheres of circulation shows that there is nothing in a thing that prevents it from becoming a commodity, or, on the contrary, destines it to do so. However, this idea is far from satisfactory. The arbitrary nature of things is replaced with more arbitrariness: someone from the society or culture is responsible for this sorting. In speaking of binarism, Jane Guyer has given a good summary of these limits.[9] According to her, evoking the existence of specialized spheres of exchange assumes that one could establish clear and definite distinctions between them, as well as between the goods involved, distinctions that always end up opposing two terms of a pair, market relations and community relations. Moreover, adds Guyer, such a vision seriously misunderstands the network of exchanges and transactions that any collective maintains with the outside world.

The binarism is useful because it protects thought from naturalism. However, it also introduces an equally difficult problem. How are these separations produced? Although such exclusions are often empirically observable, binarism fails to raise the important question of the mechanisms that organize this distribution, ensure its continued existence, or, on the contrary, more or less sporadically cast them in doubt. If and when they exist, how are these spheres instituted, sustained, transformed? Binarism ultimately endows these structures with a deus ex machina (social environment, institutions, social norms, culture, or the sacred), a constraining force that is recorded, but not explained. Where does this force come from? How is one to account for the fact that it fades out at certain moments, only to return later in a new form? The market-nonmarket binarism imposes structural constraints, which are generally imputed to culture or values, that it never explains or analyzes.

FROM SPHERES TO TRAJECTORIES: A MATTER OF CAREERS

One way to escape is to not focus on the spheres themselves, but on the objects or goods that refuse to circulate in the spheres that are supposed to keep them captive. Guyer, revisiting the terrain Bohannan explored, notes that conversions between spheres are more frequent than one thinks, that they happen at any moment in any place, and that it is difficult to sustain that these spaces of circulation are sealed off from one another. If one moves to Western societies, it is impossible not to notice that an entity such as blood seems to resist commodity status under certain circumstances. Blood endlessly transforms as it circulates. In some places, it is a noncommercial entity, and elsewhere in the same society, under the form of plasma or transformed blood products, it is a market commodity.[10]

Drawing on this observation, Arjun Appadurai and his colleagues applied the notion of "career" to things. The term is usually used to describe the trajectory of human beings moving (more or less voluntarily) from one position to another.[11] These authors tell us that if one simply brackets the agents between whose hands a thing passes and the social spaces they are supposed to travel through, if one observes the states things occupy as though one were a physicist following the traces of particles in a bubble chamber, it becomes manifest that the zigzagging trajectories of things cross supposedly impermeable borders.

Written in 1988, *The Social Life of Things* is full of examples borrowed from different societies and eras. The story of how relics develop is particularly instructive. A fragment of a human body transforms into a relic only at the end of a long route that often starts with thefts and pillage. Being forcibly taken institutes and attests to its value and ends with the organization of more or less illicit markets. What might one say of those masks or statues, sacred objects within the African societies that produce them, that first circulate in closed circuits, only to end their career, after multiple adventures, exhibited in the display cases of North American museums or in a halo of light in the dark rooms of the Quai Branly Museum in Paris and are then reproduced in glossy art books that gush endlessly about their magical powers? And what of those statues blasted out by Daesh that show up in private collections before being bought up, *morale oblige*, by museums that will, sooner or later, be ordered to return them to their countries of origin? The Aristotelian world of spheres and circular orbits has gone haywire; goods follow unpredictable trajectories. The closed world that turns on itself gives way to infinite space and open trajectories.

These are general mechanisms that do not apply exclusively to the most culturally sensitive objects. To be convinced that all things have complex trajectories, one need only think of trash and the sorting and recycling operations to which it has given rise. After it is consigned to the correctly marked bin, the newspaper or magazine you bought and perhaps read finds itself in a circuit in which it changes status several times; it may be ultimately consigned as worthless waste, or, on the contrary, it may be transformed into a potentially valuable material that reenters commercial circuits or the circuits of a circular economy. Some waste is even transformed into authentic works of art, such as compressed car wrecks taken from dumps, which were first exhibited by César in 1960 at the Musée d'Art Moderne de la Ville de Paris. The old fridge you put out on the sidewalk to be picked up as trash might be of interest to someone who needs one to tide them over. A friend of mine, a connoisseur in hand-knotted rugs who lives in a wealthy suburb, has collected magnificent specimens that their owners, no doubt unaware of their value (or secretly generous), put out on the street.

The career of radioactive substances provides the most spectacular and controversial example of trajectories. Some, intermediate or highly active, are destined to be forgotten, ending up as ultimate waste in underground shafts, locked into the clay of the Champagne region for several hundred thousand years. Others, such as those used as fuels, are considered potentially valuable material, recycled to start a new life in nuclear plants specially designed to reprocess them. Geographer Romain Garcier has followed the trajectories of these different substances, whose classifications and destinies are constantly evolving.[12] Some are sent to Siberia without hope of return, while others come back transformed in order to participate in generating energy. Things are never at rest. The more that innovations multiply, the more they proliferate, the more cumbersome they become, and the more often they are ordered to change place, to transform, to hide away, without being able to disappear completely. The ultimate radioactive waste that has to be buried once and for all continues to trouble local residents' sleep. Things are not attached to social spaces that define their status as the planets of the solar system are set in their orbits. When you follow a good, you see it constantly change state: one moment, it is a commercial good, the next, a present offered to anonymous recipients or a scrap thrown into a waste site, then once again inserted into a market cycle, sometimes diverted, stolen, as relics once were and radioactive materials still are, before entering a sacred sphere where, as Annette Weiner and Maurice Godelier tell it, they come to rest, at least for a while.[13] The plutonium that may be buried five hundred meters down in Bure, a small village in the east of France, could, due to its long-term radioactivity, reach that improbable status, buried for eternity in impregnable galleries.

Things are not the only entities that are subject to these incessant metamorphoses. It is no coincidence that Appadurai appeals to notions such as career or biography. He could just as well have opted for curriculum vitae, which applies indifferently to the life of a university professor or a piece of plutonium. Professors sometimes provide classes for which they are paid. At other moments, they offer services for free to nonprofit associations. Eventually, they, too, must be retired, even if they are not compressed and buried just yet! The existence of things and people can be described, narrated, converted into stories; the discourses of which they are the heroes contribute to shaping their careers.

Imagine for a moment that you could back away to a distant viewpoint and contemplate the circulation of the goods that surround us, those that make up ordinary life. Imagine you were then attentive to the trajectories they follow and the transformations to which they are subjected over the course of their circulation. You would quickly be convinced that things have something to do with manufacturing their own destiny, for they are not susceptible to the same transformations, nor are the same careers open to them, depending on whether they are human fragments, plastic bottles, richly embroidered cloth, pieces of plutonium, or a painting. If the careers of a relic, a piece of textile, an aluminum can, a car, or a work of art are so different, it is because they depend, at least in part, on the qualities and characteristics accumulated by these objects along the way. Their history and their material matter.

The essential contribution of economic anthropology is to underline the unstable and shaky status of goods: they are not destined to turn in circles, like caged animals. Its other merit is to suggest that the lives of goods are not totally independent of their progressively acquired qualities and, notably, their material qualities, just as human beings' careers are not completely independent of their dispositions. Bohannan invites us to shift our way of looking so as to focus on things and their circulation. Appadurai and his colleagues go further. They shatter the spheres and introduce greater realism in the description of the trajectories. At the same time, they have indirectly staged the role materiality plays as it interferes in the dynamic of displacements and changes of status.

DISENTANGLING THINGS FROM A DENSITY OF ASSOCIATIONS

Considering the career of things constitutes a decisive step forward. It shows that goods are not eventually destined to be objects of market transactions by virtue of a social logic that is beyond them or because of the space in which they move. Rather, they are participants in market transactions only at certain moments, and the possibility of being framed as commodities is constantly under threat by forces that push them to branch off and lead them to change status and state. This analysis, and the outcome it leads to, are crucial. However, they do not reach inside the mechanisms of these transformations or further our understanding of them. Some explanations are eliminated, but the question remains: Which forces rip things out in one state and dissolve them in another?

The importance of this question has not escaped some of the anthropologists or sociologists who have extended the work of Appadurai and colleagues. Starting from the idea that changes in status do not fall from the sky and that things do not move forward on their own, they have focused their attention on the processes that accompany changes of state, those processes that mold things, profile them, and set them into motion. How do things get displaced, adjusted, modified?

An important step forward was taken by Annette Weiner when she turned her attention to the existence of inalienable possessions, that is to say, entities that resist, in some circumstances, all forms of exchange and circulation. To explain certain objects' capacity to come to a standstill, she proposes the idea of "social density." As she puts it, the greater the social density of an object, the harder it is to set it into motion. Rather than moving from hand to hand, it stays attached to the person who owns it. According to her, and reformulated in my own vocabulary, this density is the result of a set of associations that, when they are strong, numerous, and durable, weigh the thing down. In the end, these associations condemn it to a form of immobility, thereby imposing a stable status. Weiner thus talks about the narrow connection made between the thing and the person in whose possession it is, its past history, and the resulting attachments, of the secret that surrounds its existence and renders it sometimes elusive, and so on. There are many possible connections of many types. If nothing is done to organize and facilitate its disentangling, the thing ends up being a stakeholder in the person or group of people to which it has been attached. Dense objects move slowly. Conversely, objects whose density is lower are likely to be put into circulation.

Weiner gives the example of the coats worn by Maori women. These coats are attached to the lineage and transcend the people who wear them. One could easily transpose this to contemporary societies. The careers of certain entities have them so entangled with the people who possess them that separation can only be difficult, violent, and painful. Connections have been woven; the associations established have progressively become very intense. The density has grown constantly: "I cannot shed this; it will break my heart...."

The point I am interested in is the one Weiner adds. The density that measures the tendency to immobility (or mobility) is not a property intrinsic to things, since it depends on the associations or connections through which they have gradually been constituted. Relying upon this, I would conclude that if children cannot exchange and sell their parents, it is because the attachments are numerous and strong and oppose separation. Similarly, if certain elements of scientific knowledge sometimes resist those who would sell them, it is because they constitute only an addition to a larger set of results with which, according to some, they remain irrevocably associated, so that detaching them is impossible. If the commercialization of human tissue provokes indignation, it is because it is not easy to separate it from those from whom it has been drawn and who consider it an integral and inalienable part of their identity. It would not add much intelligibility to say—and on this point I part ways with Weiner—that these resistances are cultural, that they depend on values or moral convictions. If children and their parents are intensely attached to one another, if scientific texts are so strongly connected to all those that preceded them, if cells have a hard time being detached from bodies, it is because throughout these entangled existences, connections have been woven that, like warp and weft, combine these elements to produce a single piece of seamless fabric; inroads into it can be made only by tearing it. What I take from Weiner is a very simple, but fundamental point: that it is essential to pay attention to the connections, to how these are established or undone, to consider their strength and not their supposed origins.

The density of associations and attachments, which are not external to things but constitute their very matter and substance, much as successive layers built up by a 3-D printer gradually shape an object, can vary continuously, depending on the connections that are made or unmade, depending on time and interactions. These variations explain how changes of states can be produced in ways that are not necessarily sudden or dramatic. The simple mechanism of relative densities moves us away from the market-nonmarket binarism that Guyer rightly criticizes and the scenography that Appadurai reimagines, a scenography that, although it abandons the existence of borders between sealed-off spaces, does endorse the hypothesis that there is an exclusive opposition between the different possible states.[14] The notion of density allows one to understand why the changes are not necessarily brutal. What counts is not so much the existence of separate and distinct states, but the gradual process whereby density is transformed. A thing detaches, sometimes slowly, sometimes rapidly. It can then enter an exchange and, if it detaches even more and in a particular way, become a candidate for commodification.

Describing density as merely "social" runs the risk of allowing it to be forgotten that the material properties of objects count as much as those usually described as social. The successive layers mentioned earlier are obviously both social and material. (A 3-D printer manufactures composite materials!) It is easy to break free from this opposition by speaking of sociotechnical density (or more simply, of just density), which includes any kind of ties. In fact, Weiner observes that a thing will enter more or less easily into a type of exchange or mobility, depending on whether it is more or less hard, divisible or unbreakable, perishable or immutable, heavy or light, changing with time, reproducible, vulnerable, fragile, easily lost—all properties that have to do with certain arrangements of atoms and molecules. The social nature of density is unquestionable if, and only if, one understands the term "social" (*socius*, association) in the sense given to it by Bruno Latour. He uses the term in a way that allowed him to change the very meaning of the word "society" by showing that it is the associations and connections that count—all the associations and all the connections, whatever their nature.[15]

Some anthropologists intuited this in their studies devoted to societies far removed from us in both time and space. In his work devoted to Indonesian society, Webb Keane follows the career of a piece of fabric that moves from being a banner proudly flown, to the vehicle for insulting a hereditary enemy, to the means of appeasing an irritated client, or, again, into a metaphor for poverty. As he notes, this versatility and the significations it authorizes depend directly on the material characteristics of the thing, which lends itself, as one can so fittingly say, to these successive reinterpretations, each interpretation intersecting with its material qualities.[16] It therefore makes no sense, according to him, and we can only agree on this point, to separate what belongs to the order of the social or the cultural, which would explain why the changes in state and status are possible, and what belongs to the order of the material and of functionalities. Yes, associations are at the heart of things themselves, of their being and their destiny, but they are neither social, nor symbolic, nor material, nor physical, but all of these at the same time. The thing constitutes a nexus of connections and associations, and on condition that one does not distinguish a priori among these associations, those that are social and those that are not, one can even assert that it is only that. It is transformed and requalified depending on the associations into which it enters.

For a good to be able to travel from one site to another, it must be transferable, that is to say, movable. If its density is too great, if the elements it associates are too narrowly and too definitively tied to one another, the transfer becomes problematic. It is at this point, the point at which things are about to be (re)formatted in order to be able to circulate, that it is useful to introduce the notion of *disentanglement* proposed by Nicholas Thomas.[17]

The Volkswagen Golf I have just acquired, whether I bought it or it was given to me, would be of no use to me without the network of highways, garages, gas stations, without those oil companies that fight to preserve their monopolies on the Iraqi oil rigs and have no compunction spewing the carbon that lay under the earth for millennia into the atmosphere, without insurance companies, without driving associations, driving schools, traffic rules or police to enforce them. This environment is what Gilbert Simondon suggests calling the *associated milieu*, and all goods require one. A completely disentangled good, one for which all the associations that constitute it had been undone, could no longer function.[18] The good would no longer exist and would simply disappear.

The associated milieu, whose characteristics narrowly depend on the particular object, is made necessary by the object itself, whose conditions of existence it ensures in return. The associated milieu is not limited to a simple technological infrastructure.[19] It is more like a nourishing milieu. Without that milieu, the Golf I bought would be condemned to immobility and would be of no use to me. The usage rights that Volkswagen sells me can be effective only if the associated milieu that authorizes the corresponding actions is available and can be mobilized at any moment. Buying a car that one cannot drive is, of course, conceivable, but it is not likely that the market for such a good would have a sustainable future.

This analysis is not limited to so-called material objects. It can be extended to all services. The caregiver who comes to my house to take care of my little girl can do their job only if the elements they need are available: bottles and milk, creams and nipples, music to soothe and put to sleep, the changing table for diapering, all of these are to hand, as is the Wi-Fi that will help them pass time until I get home. In short, if I make available the associated milieu that allows the caregiver to use the appropriate skills and do the job, the requested service can be provided. With adequate training and preparation, this person can easily move between families, on condition the apartments are properly equipped. Service can travel, just like the Golf. The caregiver's skills in action, which are themselves framed, are available to me at a preagreed time slot. If I need to take my baby to be looked after by a student living in a sparely appointed studio apartment, I will need to make arrangements to supply the associated milieu, as well, one that would be easily mobilized at my house, but to which this young person may not have access. If I am attached to this person, having total faith in their qualities, I will have to take on this complex problem, which will lead me to furnish the missing elements myself. It is a bit as though the buyer of the Golf had to participate in setting up a garage near their house to be sure of being able to take advantage of its services or as though they were being asked to design the traffic rules and enforce them. This analysis applies to any prestation. Lisa Gitelman's work shows that while Edison could record sound on tinfoil, the sound itself could be subject to a commercial transaction only if there were devices in homes to play it back.[20] The same applies to digital data: without an appropriate associated milieu to "read" them, they remain as mysterious as the silicon in which they are inscribed.

Without its associated milieu, a good or service is nothing. And yet it can travel from one agent to another because it can be separated from its milieu. The car depends on the networks that fuel it and the administrations that regulate its uses, yet it remains distinct from them, which is what allows it to exist as a transferable good that can engage in the describable activities in which it participates. The principal task of the collective that conceives the good, individualizes it, and then transfers it to its user is to dissociate the good appropriately from its milieu while ensuring they remain complementary.

All those who work to design and manufacture the vehicle must manage the feat of offering a good that can function *autonomously*, even as this functioning requires a milieu on which they generally cannot have much influence, at least in the short run. The technical architecture of my Golf can be read as a compromise between these contradictory requirements, autonomy and heteronomy, independence and dependence, with a tank that ensures fuel until the next refill, tires that adhere to the road enough, but not too much, so that movement and trips are possible, a steering wheel and a steering system that transfer control of the itinerary to me, and so on. The fuel tank, the tires, the steering wheel—these interfaces ensure the autonomy of the vehicle while cementing, as heteronomy requires, the relations it must maintain with its milieu so that this autonomy persists, is renewable, and is there for me to enjoy. When strikes lead to dry gas pumps or inaccessible highways, when the road infrastructure falls into disrepair, the automobile cannot conceal the fact that it is also a heteromobile.

To be successful, the disentanglement of the good that is called on to circulate must make it possible for an equilibrium to be reached, an always fragile and delicate equilibrium between autonomy and heteronomy. Only under this condition can the good be transferred and change hands. The problems to be solved in order to achieve this are always specific. They depend on the good or service.

FRAMING REENTANGLEMENT: PASSIVA(C)TION

The career of a good begins with its judicious disentanglement, establishing a viable compromise between autonomy and heteronomy. This process is a required and obligatory passage point. For it to pursue its career, however, it must further insert itself into the life of its addressee.

There is no lack of words for giving an account of this *reentanglement*. "Use," "need," "will to distinguish oneself," "cupidity," "desire"—these are just some of the notions frequently invoked for designating the mechanisms that draw goods and those they are destined for to one another. When nothing as yet indicates whether it will be a commodity, rather than a gift, one can also appeal to the obligation to accept and receive, a sense of friendship or of solidarity.

However relevant they may seem, these explanations have a serious drawback: they cut corners. Why not begin by sticking to what can be observed, rather than trying to identify motives or forces that are always hard to grasp? For a good, the reentanglement involves being engaged in courses of action that it has contributed to provoking or soliciting and that mingle its existence with that of its intended recipient. The courses of action may be multiple, and it would be unrealistic to establish an inventory of explanations, since one would have to list all the verbs in the English language. Any observation of one's surroundings will show this diversity and its constant renewal. Collecting, moving around, communicating, caring for, cultivating oneself, playing, distinguishing oneself, feeding oneself, tending to one's baby, mourning a relative, remembering loved ones: these are a few of the courses that goods arouse and into which they can reorient action, taking part and offering their contribution. The advantage of this open perspective is that it includes any of the preceding notions (need, desire, and so on) and is deliberately receptive to new descriptions. Moreover, it applies both to material goods and to services deemed immaterial, which can be described as particular courses of action. Finally, it is consistent with the most recent scholarly developments concerning the ways in which objects participate in collective life.[21]

Let us take the case of a photocopy machine. It invites certain courses of action that it solicits, promises, and allows and in which it participates.[22] Via its perfectly designed interfaces (screens displaying instructions or icons and technical affordances that invite users to undertake some kind of action, such as opening the lid, putting the document to copy at the right place, or refilling the paper compartment), it suggests certain operations and excludes others. It creates differences; it produces effects. While presenting itself as a simple instrument whose purpose is to produce copies, it *acts* and *makes act* according to certain modalities that characterize it as a copy machine.

To describe this capacity that objects have to orient human action, Madeleine Akrich introduced the notion of the "script," designating a set of actions suggested by material devices. As she put it, "Technical objects define a framework of action together with the actors and the space in which they are supposed to act."[23] There are scripts in the simplest of objects around us. A speed bump indicates to the driver to slow down: "In a world where it can happen that children can come running out of school and cross the street without looking out for traffic." The speed bump's script is both technical (not slowing down means breaking axles) and moral (taking care of children).

What is true of photocopiers or speed bumps is also true of any entity that is destined to be mobilized in any course of action, whether it is a car, a food processor, food, or medicine. A transgenic plant fights off undesirable parasites, secretes therapeutic substances, and resists weed killers: it has direct effects upon its environment—it acts. It also makes act both by inducing farmers to beware of its dissemination and by alleviating their workload; by pushing government to launch multidisciplinary research projects on public-health risks; by moving ecologists to undertake political protests; and by encouraging consumers to buy it by being regularly available and of predictable quality. The same goes for cyanobacteria, which naturally absorb carbon dioxide in the wild for their own development and which are reframed and reprogrammed to transform this greenhouse gas into fuel in a controlled and predictable manner, or for retroviruses, which naturally carry serious pathologies that are neutralized while preserving the viruses' capacity to transfer molecules to tumors and destroy them.

As these examples show, these different entities have been subjected to a formatting that channels their capacity to elicit courses of action and to participate in them efficiently.

Indeed, scripts do not describe all programs of possible actions a priori. They necessarily leave room for the unexpected, for improvisation, for novel courses of action, for diversions produced by the interactions in which objects are mobilized. Entities that have been taught through successive reformatting and reframing to engage in determined courses of action can at any moment reclaim the initiative, act in unexpected ways, and pull their intended recipients into uncontrollable adventures. As we will see further on, situations involving living beings are especially prone to this eventuality. For example, biological vectors used to transport molecules to specific targets can miss them, and chemical substances can create toxic side effects. Objects connected through communication networks are also more prone to slipping off script.

Reentanglement is part of the process that transforms a thing into a "usable" good that is able to take part in some course of action within the buyer's world. To work, reentanglement must be framed, and the frame must be complex and well conceived. The balance is subtle—too much autonomy, and the good will becomes uncontrollably independent; too little autonomy will unduly restrict the scope of potential actions. As all drivers know, a car does not settle for being a passive tool for moving from point A to point B. It can suggest the races between rival gangs that delighted Hollywood studios in the sixties; it can transform a quiet family man into a madman ready to destroy everything in his path. And if connected to an autonomous driving system, it can reduce passengers to powerless robots.

Objects, goods, entities that have been ably disentangled to act autonomously, sometimes take such a pleasure in their autonomy that they overflow the frameworks designed for them, pushing action down unknown and unpredictable paths that may turn out to be undesirable.[24] The tension between autonomous action and independence applies to all goods that have been profiled to elicit people's interest. Some are closer to one pole than the other, but all are subject to it to some degree. If the contradiction is not handled efficiently, it endangers their circulation and, of course, their (possible) aptitude for becoming commodities.

The set of specifications for entities destined to pass from hand to hand responds, therefore, to a triple requirement. First, the candidate thing must enjoy sufficient independence to be disentangled from its conceiver-producers and thus be able to circulate from place to place. "(Relative) autonomy" is the term for this property, which implies, among other things, that the thing not be condemned to immobility by too high a density. Second, the thing must be capable of acting and making act in such a way as to interest an acquirer. However—third requirement—its aptitude for entering into courses of action has to be framed: the behavior of the thing has to be sufficiently predictable and controllable to avoid unexpected and unmanageable disturbances. Autonomy, capacity to contribute to courses of action, and predictability are the properties that, in variable modes, must be found in any good that aspires to change hands. Obtaining these properties usually requires operations to shape and transform, solving problems that depend on the things involved and are most acute when these are living beings or connected objects. For example, to anticipate and avoid risky and dangerous situations, a driverless car should allow passengers to monitor and master their environment and, if necessary, make decisions they deem appropriate.[25] I would like to suggest the name *passiva(c)-tion* for the strange process that leads an entity to be capable of living its own life, to be active, to act and make act, but not too much, and always in a specific manner within preestablished frameworks.[26]

Passiva(c)tion, considered as a continuous process, leads the good to enter the life of its addressee, to penetrate the intimate spaces of that life. The simple fact of participating in a course of action that cannot be reduced to any other course of action, not even a similar one, is a matter of what Simondon called "individuation." The good does not suddenly barge into the addressee's life. Both evolve together—we are gradually tangled up with it. This is why I will refer to *singularization*. The driver, such and such a driver, such and such a car, and their associated milieus are in permanent symbiosis and develop a unique story. The skeptics who zealously denounce consumerist society may mock this driver, and yet this driver, who moons over his sparkling new customized Golf, a few hundred thousand apparently identical copies of which are in daily circulation on the road and that he nevertheless considers unique, is a far better philosopher than all those who hold him in contempt.

NONMARKET-ORIENTED PASSIVA(C)TION: KEEPING WHILE GIVING

Consider a successful passiva(c)tion. The good has been profiled to change hands. It is capable of participating in courses of action and thus escapes the fatal destiny of the numerous innovations that interest no one. It is neither too active nor too unpredictable; it acts and makes act in an orderly fashion, following the programs that have been imagined for it, without too much deviation. Yet having been made transferable, the good is not quite ready to be transformed into a commodity. It remains for it to be detached from the entity that puts it into circulation.

To account for the detachment process that allows for property rights to be switched, I need to return to the work in economic anthropology. Ever since the seminal work of Mauss and Malinowski and their reevaluation by Sahlins, one of the major concerns of economic anthropology has been the relationship between gift and market transactions. The answer given depends on the type of question posed. Some have been interested in analyzing the different forms of economies and associated social relations when each of these types of good circulates, while others have been focused on the issue of domination. Yet others have probed the deep meaning of these categories. My objective is not to take part in those debates, let alone to take sides. As I have written previously here, what interests me in this multifarious and often contradictory literature is the analytical tools it proposes in order to describe the modalities of disentanglement and entanglement or to express the movement of detachment and reattachment in words. It happens that authors such as Thomas, Weiner, and Godelier developed concepts that turn out to be valuable for my own project, even if they are engaged in different theoretical projects. The simplest strategy to reveal the mechanisms of detachment is to consider the goods that remain attached to a person or lineage. These goods are characterized, as we say, by a high density that condemns them to immobility. Over the course of time, numerous strong attachments have been woven such that the goods have become part of the people who hold them. In the Western world, inheritance refers to this type of configuration. In popular understanding, what can be inherited (*un héritage*) is what an individual owns, what he has. In French law, the old idea of a *bien inné* (innate good), a good that "cannot be separated from the person's very existence,"[27] gives a pretty good idea of this form of relationship. Attached goods constitute extended bodies for their owners, variable over time, and yet coherent in such a way as to ensure at least temporary indivisibility. They participate in the constitution of the owner's identity.

Such an attachment can be obtained and sanctioned by a thousand different devices. Weiner, who studies Oceanic societies and revisits Malinowski's work, refers to a jumble of rites, origin myths, genealogies, and their connections to the gods. In Western societies, the law plays a central role, sustained by many material and narrative devices that make explicit, guarantee, and certify possession and the associations that constitute possession. Such goods can be described as inalienable. They cannot be ceded or detached; one cannot *dispossess* oneself of them because that would be to make one a stranger to oneself. Maurice Godelier, prolonging and enriching Weiner's analyses, adds that this is how the sphere of the sacred is constituted.

Weiner goes further. She makes a genuine discovery by showing that there exist certain goods that, while inalienable, can nevertheless be alienated. Translation: they can be kept, even as they are given to another. They pass into B's hands while remaining in A's possession (keeping while giving).

Godelier illustrates this strange and paradoxical practice through the example of the Baruya, where women are circulated through marriage. As he tells it, the practice is based on the direct exchange of two women between two men and two lineages, the sister of each becoming the other's wife. Each family remains obliged to the other throughout its lifetime; both share the yield of their fields and their salt, which serves as money. They mutually invite each other; they clear land together for new gardens. The obligation persists despite the fact that B has given his own sister in marriage to A, whose sister he married, because the woman that was given was not really separated or completely disjoined from the one who did the giving. In the Baruya community, women have a double status: they are both entities that circulate and family members who continue to belong to the lineage from which they issue.[28]

Let us summarize: in keeping while giving, a) the good changes hands while continuing to be attached to Person A who puts it into circulation; b) the good does not cease to belong to A while being in B's possession, and then in C's, and so on; c) the good carries something of A with it—let us say that A is present in the good and acts in it as a restoring force.

All those who have at some point taken an interest in property rights will inevitably recognize these practices as illustrations, not explicit, but direct, of the bundle-of-rights theory. In this way of conceiving property, different rights are attached to a thing. One of the most accomplished formulations of this theory is given by Elinor Ostrom. According to her, a property right includes rights of access, withdrawal, management, exclusion, and alienation. One can thus distinguish between owners (for instance, communal) who do not have alienation rights and owners who have all the rights and can therefore enter into commercial transactions.[29] The list of rights can be extended and detailed, but the essential thing, for my purposes here, is the simple separation between, on the one hand, the right of use and, on the other hand, the right to alienate, to separate, to detach, to no longer be present in the thing. The very existence of "keeping while giving" practices proves this separation is possible and shows its relevance in understanding why inalienable goods can be put into circulation and pass from hand to hand. Once reformulated in the terms of Western legal theory (A keeps the right of alienation and transfers use rights to B), this practice of dismembering property seems not only conceivable, but is actually not unusual, as the following illustrations show.[30]

If I keep the bare property rights to an apartment for myself, contrary to what is usually done for fiscal reasons, while giving a usufruct to a friend, I would say that the thing (the apartment) remains in my possession while being useable by a third party.[31]

Scientific activity provides another illustration. The law that states the proportional relation between force and acceleration remains attached to Newton, while all are free to use it. When I apply it to a new situation, I have the usufruct, but I know full well that it remains, as grammar indicates, Newton's law, a law that is firmly attached to its discoverer. A law that has not been discovered and that therefore cannot be attributed to anyone is like an apartment that no one can identify and localize and that therefore no one can use. The law without "its" Newton disappears; Newton without "his" law is no longer Newton.

The famous Brennus Shield that the French Rugby Federation bestows each year for a one-year period on the captain of the winning team of the French championship provides another example. The club keeps it for a year and then returns it to the federation, to which it continues to belong, which then puts it back in circulation the following year. The shield, which the rugbymen nickname *la planche* (the board), remains in federation's possession while having toured France several times since its creation in 1892.

Disentangling (to allow circulation) without detaching (to maintain possession) requires a great deal of know-how, ingeniousness, and skill. In so-called modern societies, the law, as we have just seen, obviously plays an essential and irreplaceable role, both by offering an analytic framework (for the possible dismembering of property rights) and by providing for and imposing constraints (sanctions). And yet on its own, it cannot ensure that all the conditions for "keeping while giving" be satisfied. Without proofs and material markers to support it in the event of challenges or litigation, the law is insufficient.

Mauss's *The Gift* is a convenient place to start to introduce this point. Picking up on *hau*, a key notion of Maori law that can be understood, according to him, as the spirit or soul of the person who gives, Mauss insists on the presence of the giver in the thing; this presence is not superficial, not simply inscribed in the thing like a signature or a reference. The *hau* is the giver in the given thing; it marks that the thing is still in the giver's possession and that it cannot be definitively detached from him.

Mauss's interpretation has given rise to many critical commentaries that, except for Lévi-Strauss's, do not question the idea that something of the giver remains in the given thing.[32] But how does this presence manifest itself? As Godelier quite rightly observes, however one makes sense of the notion of *hau*, it would be a mistake to consider that it is a pure phenomenon of belief and imagination. This is not so. For the mechanism of disentanglement without detachment to function properly, A *really* must be present in the good. This requires specific devices, necessarily material, that have been constantly invented, tested, transformed, and transmitted over the course of time.

Viviana Zelizer has studied these devices extensively. She observes that the most common strategy for maintaining the attachment of a thing that circulates is *earmarking*. Originally, this notion referred to the marks made by farmers on the ears of their herd animals to mark ownership. By means of this little mutilation, the (relatively) indelible presence of the farmer is conserved in the animal's flesh. The animal, however, is not hampered by this intervention, since the scarification does not prevent movement or even a possible change of hands. However, anyone who crosses a marked cow's path knows that they meet the animal's owner who really is there, in the animal, not distant, but present, actual.[33]

A banknote, designed to pass anonymously from one hand to another and to be easily detached from the last person to hold it, can be transformed into a gift that remains attached to the giver. The most standard practice, which at some point became a national sport in Italy, is to write a few words on the bill that will remind the receiver of the donor's name and affection. Any bill, at any time, can be diverted with a slight transformation—a little indelible ink will mark, materially modify, the thing and qualify it as a potential gift. Similarly, a first name engraved on a piece of jewelry can make certain that a donor is present at his loved one's side. Earmarking, says Zelizer, can be generalized to cover a set of practices that modify a thing to create a reminder of its attachment. Many different transformations can be imagined. The banknote, rather than being the medium for love notes, might be slipped into an envelope with a kind word. A coin, on which it is difficult to write anything, can be personalized through the choice of metal used. When a grandparent gives it to their grandchild, they transform the silver (the metal) into a mark that is all the more powerful if it is accompanied by an admonishment such as "Put it in the piggybank I gave you for Christmas."

Marking by engraving, marking by making sure the thing is accompanied by a few scribbled words or a well-crafted speech, marking by depositing something of oneself in the thing—numerous earmarking strategies can be imagined to ensure the effective presence in the thing of the person who put it into circulation and to whom it continues to belong, even in their absence.[34] Nonetheless, however intense the marking, this binding presence is never established once and for all. The envelope can be torn up, the bill with the scrawl or coin from the grandfather can be put into circulation, the piece of jewelry can be pawned. To keep possession, the force of law (or custom) is, as we have seen, often necessary. Truth be told, it is in fact the combination of both that ensures the attachment endures and is robust. The anecdote that follows gives an indication of how this works.

Zelizer tells the story of a rich widower who gave his mistress and her twin sister the equivalent of a million dollars, in cash or in kind, over more than seven years. Every ten days, Mrs. Conley came to receive money, or an object, that the millionaire's secretary would hand over to her personally. The tax authorities found out about this and had the millionaire condemned for tax evasion because they considered that the sums transferred in this manner were not gifts, but genuine payments for sexual services. Put in prison, the sisters appealed after the millionaire's death. And they won! The judges considered that the money and things that had changed hands were presents and that it was not a matter of paying for sexual services. The proof? The love notes that the millionaire slipped into the envelopes full of banknotes; the notes materially marked his presence. Irrefutable.

MARKET-ORIENTED PASSIVA(C)TION: DISENTANGLEMENT WITH DETACHMENT

The difference between *nonmarket-oriented* and *market-oriented* passiva(c)tion is a tenuous one. The former maintains attachment, whereas the latter ensures detachment. In one case, A retains possession; in the other, possession is transferred to B. Under these circumstances, in order to move from one regime to the other, would it be enough to attach property rights to the thing (for instance, the right to alienate, as it is defined in the bundles-of-rights theory), to attribute these rights to A, and then to give A the capacity for ceding them to B?

Granted, such arrangements are necessary, and we will examine the problems they pose in a coming section. Without them, no commercial transfer can be concluded. However, they are not sufficient in themselves to ensure such transfers. The law, which alone cannot provide an answer to the question of attachment, cannot solve the problem of detachment alone, either. Just as attachment does, detachment requires that a good be transformed so that it may be torn away from its prior owner. Thomas provides this intuition when he makes the case that "the alienation of a thing [object, person, or element of a person] is its dissociation from producers, former users, or prior context"[35] and insists on the material operations that produce this dissociation. The reality of the work involved in this detaching is never so clear as when it is a matter of making detachable a thing that has been previously attached to the person who puts it into circulation.

Consider an autographed letter written and signed by a famous person—Pasquale Paoli, for instance.[36] Suppose he gave it to a friend or an admirer. Paoli is, beyond any possible doubt, present in the letter: there is not a single upstroke or downstroke that does not recall the pen and the hand that held it. That presence is, of course, essential, but it does not ensure Paoli's presence in the sense defined above. As the American judges made clear when they ruled on Mrs. Conley and her sister's appeal, something more is needed—a mark, in that case, a mark of affection, saying that this is indeed something that carries with it the person who put it into circulation. A few words traced out on a sheet of vellum paper to go with the letter, if it is sent by mail, or a little speech full of feeling, if it was hand delivered by Paoli.[37] These very simple devices requalify the letter in such a way that it prolongs Paoli's person; it is part of him. And the words that surround the letter, whether written or spoken, add new associations, entangling it further, manifesting and explaining the attachment: "I give it to you for it to attest to my affection; I will be at your side through it, you will think of me."

Experience shows that even duly marked, the given thing can find another life and be transformed into a commodity. The mechanism is quite simple.

It requires either purely and simply erasing (or disqualifying) the material proof, textual or oral, that attests to the connections between the thing and the person who put it into circulation or transforming the attachments into mere references and traces. The first strategy, when it is possible, is the most immediate and inexpensive. All that is required is to get rid of the wrapping paper and the kind little note, as happens when people put things up for sale on the internet the day after Christmas. Stripping the thing does not require much effort or audacity, especially if the donor is not the sort to check what happened to his present. "What in the world did you do with the gaming console? I don't see it anymore!" The second strategy is subtler and more general. The hand-written letter is no longer a thing that puts its addressee in the presence of Paoli in person. It is transformed into a letter that, just like the accompanying note, is endowed with a new quality—namely, that of having been written by the very hand of a great person. The largely indelible associations (the upstrokes and the downstrokes) combine with other marks initially destined to ensure the presence of the person (the note accompanying the letter) in such a way as to redefine the thing, enrich it with new characteristics, and transform its qualification.[38] The presence is transformed into a reference materialized in traces that can be authenticated; the traces add a new property to the thing, rather than attesting that it is (still) possessed by its emitter. This is the result of the work of *demarking*.

Demarking, whereby marks are transformed into traces and references, requires the construction of a narrative that introduces a plot connecting different events in the life of the thing—in this case, the letter. Simultaneously, the thing, which will no doubt have been appraised, is transformed. Here, the letter is now escorted by documents, catalogs, certificates, graphologist reports, anecdotes about Paoli's life. The set of these textual, iconic, and audiovisual elements associated with the letter tell, narrate, and attest to the series of events inscribed in it, extending it and forming its new substance. The stories woven together on this occasion are very different from the discourses that accompanied the gift. Rather than attaching it to Paoli, they supplement the thing, adding new qualities to it. Remember Mrs. Conley and her judges—what would they have decided had she taken it into her mind to compose brochures and catalogs, including an index for the sweet notes, recounting the curriculum vitae of the jewels received and showing bundles of bills with their serial numbers? This very simple example allows us to grasp the relevance of the notions suggested by anthropologists. To explain how a thing is profiled to become a commodity or to switch over to a noncommercial regime, one needs to consider the series of associations, the successive operations of entanglement and disentanglement, the practices of earmarking and demarking. Either the thing says and repeats that it is one with the donor and that it remains attached to the donor even if it changes hands, or it circulates in such a way as to liberate itself from the person who puts it into circulation without their presence being preserved except as a traceable reference: it says and repeats that it is no longer in the possession of the one who has parted with it, even, or especially, if it preserves the mention of them having been there. In this second scenario, it has acquired a form of independence. Appropriately defined, property rights can effectively be attached to it.[39]

The problem that must be solved in cases where marked goods must be unmarked is not an exceptional one: the general rule, if there is one, is that objects always keep the imprint, in one form or another, of those through whose hands they pass.[40] At the heart of detachment, there is, then, the tension between marking, which proves presence, and the transformation of marks into references, which enriches the process of qualifying goods. This tension increases with the growing role of accumulated biographical references in the career of things that are engaged in market circuits and notably with the strategy of commercial brands (*marques*) that synthesize these references.[41] It culminates with the demand for traceability. A traceable good is one whose career and biography are established, attested, and made public. Each episode of its life, associating it to a particular agent or event, adds a new quality to it, facilitating the evaluation (examined in Chapter 3). A Camembert is a Camembert *from* Normandy, made with unpasteurized milk, *moulé à la louche*, according to the traditional technique; a university professor may have done doctoral work under the supervision of the famous Nobel laureate physicist Richard Feynman. Traceability, which must avoid the trap of marking, is extremely strategic: it not only establishes the qualities of the good—it also guarantees a well-managed passiva(c)tion insofar as the history of a being is taken as some guarantee of future behavior.[42]

The material work that ensures the transition from nonmarket-oriented passiva(c)tion to market-oriented (and vice versa) is gradual and progressive;

this explains why certain goods can have a hybrid status. Fair trade offers a good illustration. A package of coffee carries two stories. One story ensures the producer is present to the consumer with a message, amplified by ads and packaging, that says, "It is for you that he worked; show you are grateful"; the other story makes each connection into an event whose trace is preserved, all of which are thought to enrich the coffee's qualities.[43] Observation shows how many ways there are of fine-tuning these two stories: some goods give a very analytic and fact-based account of their biographies—for instance, through technical data sheets or in a description of the ingredients inscribed on the packaging, while others, on the contrary, make their life into an inexhaustible source of continuously changing qualities, as in the case of works of art when they are put up for auction. Well-drafted love letters are open to both interpretations and both destinies: Do not forget me! Be happy to have known me!

It is not easy to carry out the operations, often violent, that ensure the success of market-oriented passiva(c)tion. Seen from the point of view of those who work to establish market transactions, these operations, when they abort, can be experienced as failures when it comes to the confrontation between two opposing regimes: the one that strives to detach and the one that maintains attachment. A striking illustration of such a situation is given by Fred Myers's work on land transactions between Aboriginals and Westerners. When a newly arrived European acquires a piece of land in Australia, paying for it and registering the property transfer, the Aboriginals from whom the European thinks he is buying the land consider they are selling hot air. Indeed, despite the money he has received, he keeps that land, which is associated with a cosmological order about which the contract says nothing, but which imposes such weighty connections to the land that any complete and permanent detachment is impossible. Not only is the density of the land such that disentangling the connections so that it might become exchangeable is impossible within a normal contractual framework; the transaction was in any case bound to fail, since the contract did not provide a full inventory of associations.

If only those Europeans had more clearly understood that in some market transactions, you can keep the thing while selling it in the same way as gifts keep the presence of the donor. The difference is that the good to which the contract refers is not the same for both parties. A land with ancestors attached is not a land with detached ancestors. The dissonance is neither cognitive nor symbolic. It is really the outcome of the thing itself, considered as the outcome of a nexus of associations. Thinking that the deal is incomplete or that the Aboriginal will finally become reasonable is just denying the existence of two radically incompatible cosmologies. Had Westerners chosen not to dispossess natives by whatever means, they could have imagined law devices allowing compromises acceptable to both sides. Actually, such devices could exist, as proved by the bundle-of-rights theory.

I have chosen this case because the confrontation between two cosmologies is well articulated and extreme. But as we will see later in this chapter, similarly extreme situations are commonplace within societies that share common views on the nature of markets.

THE PROBLEM OF PROPERTY RIGHTS

Detaching the good for its possible reattachment elsewhere paves the way for the transfer of property rights against payment, without which there is no market transaction. In order to circulate, to pass from hand to hand, a good must be disentangled from its associated milieu while maintaining the relations that allow it to function. This double requirement, a source of tensions and contradictions, makes detachment tricky. It is notably difficult to identify Agent A, the entity that gets property rights and who will therefore be entitled to transfer them to Agent B.

These sorts of difficulties have an obvious origin. The associated milieus have to be carefully and conveniently designed and manufactured to make feasible the disentanglement of the good and their unbroken functioning. A Golf drives on a network of highways governed by traffic laws, an iPod a child has spent all his money on can't stream songs without iTunes, a babysitter arrives into a prepared environment that allows the caregiver to provide care. Providing the milieu requires work, inspiration, and a great deal of perspiration. Of course, those who develop commercial goods can find ways to free themselves, to a certain extent, from these complementary investments by playing on the qualities of the goods. For instance, a car designed to not require any cooling liquid could function without the infrastructure organized to make this liquid widely available. Yet no matter how ingenious the engineers who created such a car, it would still require the constitution of some associated milieu—some form of roadway—even a crude one, pared down to just a few elements. Without it, no passiva(c)tion is imaginable, no vehicle that is both autonomous and controllable can exist, and as a consequence, commodification is not possible. It is only in an arbitrary manner, always open to dispute, that rights are attributed exclusively to the developers and producers of the good in question. In fact, the entire set of agents who participated, in a necessarily coordinated way, in the constitution of that good and its associated milieu should be considered. Answers can be examined only on a case-by-case basis. And it appears that with the attempts to commercialize living beings and digital data, they are becoming increasingly debatable and complex. In many situations, to identify Agent A, the entity that gets property rights and who will therefore be entitled to transfer them to Agent B, is a long and hazardous journey. Identifying the rights that will be commuted is a first challenge. A second challenge is to determine who conceived of the good and to accept that they be the sole legitimate bearer of these rights. This deserves a word of explanation.

The history of property rights shows us that the controversies born of this paradox—dissociating those who develop the goods and those who develop the associated milieu—are enduring. Consider, for instance, the well-known late eighteenth-century debates around the birth of copyright law, which involved the attribution of authorship.[44] Who is the author of *The Barber of Seville* or *La religieuse*? How can paternity of a work be attributed to a single person, when it is easily shown that it was composed by borrowing and plagiarism? Along the same lines: Is it reasonable to consider that Newton is the author of the laws of gravitation and of the *Principia*, when it is obvious that if someone really has to be responsible, it can only be God himself, the God Newton admits to serving to as a technical assistant? There are associated milieus from which the works cannot be detached: in the first case, the crowd of anonymous people who contributed to the emergence of Figaro as a character; in the second case, God or nature. It requires a juridical fiction (or convention), plausible, but circumstantial, to decide that Beaumarchais and Diderot are the authors, forgetting those who prepared the ground, whereas Newton is only the discoverer, the wise explorer of a work whose paternity escapes him completely. Newton, Einstein, or Watson and Crick only elucidate laws they had no hand in constituting, whereas Edison, Diesel, or Craig Venter created objects that did not exist before them: the filament bulb for the first, an effective motor for the second, and synthesized DNA for the third.

In the case of scientific discovery, the entity is considered to be indiscernible from the associated milieu that completely absorbs it. Although we can name the scientists who made the discovery, no property right can be attached to their findings. The case of invention or creation turns out differently. The entity can become a good because it does not dissolve into its associated milieu, and it is therefore possible (thanks to such legal fictions as legal persons) to identify, from among the many who may have participated in the invention, the small number to whom property rights will be attributed. Depending on the goods, these fictions turn out to be more or less robust and more or less up to the task of garnering a double recognition: that the good was developed independently of its associated milieu and that those who develop it can be identified without ambiguity.

In the case of a car, it is somewhat easier to draw distinctions. There is a collection of human beings at a car company who, with the help of tools, instruments, and machines, bring the car from the drawing board to the shop floor, to prototyping platforms, to the production units, and finally to sales sites. There is also a set of actors who contribute to realizing the public and private infrastructures that allow the automobile to circulate and accomplish the actions for which it was conceived. The situation becomes more complicated, however, when it comes to introducing a new kind of vehicle into the existing milieu. The current milieu is not adapted to supporting a market for electric cars, which have different fueling and maintenance requirements than those with combustion engines. Think also of so-called "self-driving vehicles" and the heavily complex associated milieus they require. These vehicles may circulate only if the moral, technical, economic, legal, and town-planning concerns have been satisfactorily resolved.[45] Every radical innovation highlights the need to (re)build a world that will allow a novel good to exist and to develop unhindered.

With the development of digital technologies and biotechnologies, these different operations—the separation between the good and its associated milieu and the determination of the rights bearers—become more elusive. The legal conventions that justified them are under pressure and have to be reconsidered on a case-by-case basis. Each new good leads back to the following fundamental questions: What is its associated milieu? What are the forces that structure and organize it? How can the uses that can be attached to a good be identified and to which agents can their conception be attributed? In sum, marketing goods always leads to rehashing the debate that raged three centuries ago. There may be less talk of God, of the creator and his creation, but more of nature and its autoregulation mechanisms; there is less talk of literary works, but more on lines of code, or the syntax of computer languages, or the translation of the genome into genetic information. Despite these changes, the same questions persist. And if no satisfying answer is given, the market-oriented passiva(c)tion of goods, the one that detaches them, frames their courses of action, and organizes the transfer of property rights, is curtailed.

When a start-up cranks out lines of code to develop new applications or software as a service, when it encrypts confidential data to avoid being hacked, it is only one active element in a network of high-powered mathematicians, companies, or groups of software engineers whose productions it constantly draws on and that in return feed off what it produces and makes available. It must be added that the mesh of the milieu in which software services function is heightened by the success of the open-source movement.[46] In this case, each service provided and its associated milieu is the result of a collective and continuous process that makes it difficult to distinguish them, that scrambles both the attribution of property rights and their distribution among those who develop the good and those who develop the associated milieu. The legal convention that supposed a decoupling and a desynchronization of innovations (those that concern the goods and those that concern the associated milieu) then loses credibility and efficacy. That is no doubt why the commodification of these services has generated suggestions for changing or adapting property rights. There is notably a gradual sliding from the conception of property as an absolute right of a person to a thing to a conception of property as depending on a bundle of rights connecting the owner to other people through a complex set of social and legal relations that run through the asset.[47]

In my research on patents, the development of nonhuman beings such as animals, plants, or microorganisms as market goods has provided the ideal example on which to examine these issue of property rights in detail. Consider, for instance, the recent development of new "assisted" or "targeted" techniques of mutagenesis. These are increasingly used to mold the genetic profile of certain plants in order to make them able to withstand drought or certain herbicides, produce medical molecules, or facilitate their conservation. Whereas pure and simple transgenesis involves introducing a new gene in a plant, whose qualities are thus artificially transformed, assisted mutagenesis solicits the active and constant collaboration of Mother Nature. Mutagenesis is a phenomenon that occurs spontaneously when plants reproduce. However, the resulting mutations are infrequent and very random. Under these conditions, why not help nature by guiding the process, instead of entrusting everything to chance? This little boost requires knowledge and elaborate techniques, especially when it is a matter of localizing and identifying the genes involved in producing particular agronomic, organoleptic, or medicinal characteristics that have been judged of interest.

In what follows, I would like to consider a special case of a broccoli genetically modified to enhance its cancer-prevention properties. The lengthy and eventful story of its design is interesting and exemplary. This singular broccoli is the distant result of crossbreeding done in the 1980s between a cultivated broccoli and a wild broccoli from the south of Italy. Not only does it taste good—it also contains exceptional levels of glucoraphanin, a nutrient that develops antioxidant enzymes. In this particular case, before the cross was made, the broccoli genome had to be sequenced, and the genes responsible for the properties being sought had to be localized and identified. This cross could have happened in a natural way. Even if the probability of such an event is extremely low, it is not zero. What the breeder does is to take a possibility nature might produce and make it happen with certainty in a controlled fashion.

The contrast with pure and simple transgenesis is striking. In both cases, the developer of new seeds performs a gesture that is inscribed in a long lineage of prior investments, some of which go all the way back to the neolithic age, that have led the variety on which the breeder is working to its current state through repeated crossing and selecting. These investments flow from both human work and the work of nature. By introducing a foreign gene, radical transgenesis provokes a deep break in the course of this history. It detaches the plant from a past and a milieu in which nature played the main part, humans merely accompanying and orienting it. In its gentlest forms, assisted mutagenesis, in contrast, maintains and prolongs the entanglements from which novelty and diversity emerge without discombobulating the composition of the hybrid collectives, composed of human beings and natural entities, that piloted evolution to that point. To put it in an image, the elaboration of a new variety can in one case easily be attributed, at least in the main, to the scientists and engineers, whereas in the second, it is part of a natural history in which humans bear only a small portion of responsibility. To put it differently, with transgenesis, the plant is ripped out of its traditional associated milieu and is endowed with a new associated milieu manufactured in a lab and then controlled, insofar as possible, by the scientists and engineers; with assisted mutagenesis, the associated world, its modes of organization and its rules of functioning are preserved, at least in part, since the experts are only hastening the passiva(c)tion process. In the first case, it is not illegitimate to consider that the property rights can be attributed to the teams who did the work and, therefore, given the work contracts that cover this, to the companies that employ them: the associated milieu required by the transgenic plant is largely composed of the scientific and technical infrastructure (laboratories, field experiments, simulations, and so on) necessary for their conception, development, and monitoring and therefore does not depend too much on other agents, notably those who consider that the only legitimate option, both moral and technical, is to cooperate with Mother Nature. Transgenesis is a technique of passiva(c)tion that can be directly articulated with the commercial circuit and with bilateral commercial transactions. In the second case, the forces that contribute to the emergence of the new variety are distributed between the scientists and engineers, on the one hand, and nature, on the other, in such a way that it is problematic to separate what comes from whom in the creation of the new variety. Transgenesis draws heavily on human creativity, whereas assisted mutagenesis rests largely on nature's creativity.

Between these two extreme possibilities, there are a host of intermediary strategies that combine the intelligent cooperation of natural forces and human forces in variable proportions. In these circumstances, the difficulty of establishing who is the author of these transformations is such that the office charged with delivering patents cannot avoid debates worthy of the most eminent Scholastic tradition. Indeed, they have to determine the respective roles of natural determinism and human intervention, case by case, plant after plant. The problem raised is in fact that of distinguishing the forces that act on the good from the forces that act on its associated milieu. If you consider, for instance, that such and such a type of assisted mutation sets off "essentially" biological processes[48]—to pick up on the surprising terminology used in a 1998 European directive that sounds like unavowed reminiscences of the ancient philosophical theory according to which substances exist, that is to say, categories that precede all others—and, therefore, if it is mainly nature that produces *both* the good *and* its milieu, then it is presumed that it is nature that ensures the passiva(c)tion. The directive specifies that in this case, the production process cannot be patented; no property right can be attributed to the teams that produced this mutagenesis. If one decides, on the contrary, that the transformation is the result of a particularly ingenious technique (reaching beyond the operations of a traditional breeder who only organizes and channels the work of Mother Nature), appropriation becomes easier, since there is a creation by an industrious person of an original entity whose conception, as an autonomous and acting entity, can be dissociated from that of its associated milieu. This obviously applies to transgenesis that completely or almost completely breaks free from nature's work: the gene can therefore be patented. Thus qualified, the good more easily enters commercial transactions, since the presence of these new qualities guarantees the attribution of rights and their permutation.

Generalizing is easy. We can measure in this case how great a dilemma living beings set up, given the tension that they bring to the fore between passiva(c)tion and appropriation. This question is so complex that it is sometimes impossible to reach a clear and settled position, as shown by the recent twists in the anticancer broccoli saga. In March 2015, the Enlarged Board of Appeal of the European Patent Office ruled that plants stemming from essentially biological processes could be protected on condition that they fulfill the three requirements for obtaining a patent: novelty, inventiveness, and industrial applicability. In sum, in its ruling, the board says that the process cannot be subject to a patent, but that the plant that it produces (the asset) can be. This can seem a lame compromise, even though there are many arguments in its favor. One can, of course, consider that by accelerating and orienting nature's course, humans participate in the creation of an entity that might never have seen the light of day, given how low the probability of that particular mutation is. This observation is enough to justify attributing property rights. Problems persist, however. The new variety is torn out of the natural milieu that allowed it to emerge and that is thus severed from a part of its creative power, since that variety, at least for the time it is protected by a patent, can no longer intervene in the constitution of new species. As popular wisdom has it, it is robbing Peter (nature) to pay Paul (Monsanto). Or to put it another way, this comes down to inciting Paul to innovate, but discouraging Peter from doing the same. Who can evaluate the consequences of this decision, which can only be arbitrary, in terms of efficiency or social well-being?

I do not want to get into a discussion about patent law because I will return to this elsewhere.[49] What I am interested in here are the issues the patenting process must address, which tend to be forgotten. To deal with all these issues, which concern the modalities of commodification of living beings, one would have to reexamine some of the foundations of property law, one at a time. The distinction between discovery and innovation made sense at the end of the eighteenth century, when it was a matter of tracing the limit between what accrues to man and what accrues to God or nature. It does not anymore. This absurdity is nowhere as blatant as in the realm of biotechnologies, as well as digital technologies. In the process of conceiving new beings, human and non-human entities are in tight collaboration, and it seems difficult not to take that into account in allocating property rights. In fact, not only does patent law rest on an outdated metaphysics, it moreover claims its economic justification on the basis of a theory of innovation that is oblivious to all the studies conducted since the end of the 1970s, studies that show how unrealistic the models are that deny the open, collective, iterative, and gradual character of innovation processes, especially in the case of biotechnologies. In avoiding the reality of pas-siva(c)tion devices, patent offices are hanging on to solutions that fall short of the considerable stakes that emerge with the commodification of the living.

The urgent need to imagine new solutions is all the greater, given that the (debatable) legal arguments that push toward attributing property rights to the developers, by underestimating the part nature plays, increase the ontological uncertainties associated with the goods produced. The dilemma is striking: if nature's participation is taken to have been essential, it becomes difficult to attach private rights to the newcomer, but the confidence in the future behavior of the new good is great. What is called "nature" is the name given to a long story over the course of which each new event has been stringently evaluated, and that is why it is a credible guarantor. *A contrario*, if this participation is considered secondary, then the organism in question can be more easily appropriated, but the fact that it is considered completely artificial makes its passiva(c)tion uncertain. Framing it, controlling its behavior, monitoring collateral damages thus become categorical imperatives; this requires considerable investments from the one who elaborated the new organism and who, having decided to forgo the regulatory mechanisms of Mother Nature insofar as possible, can be held responsible for the effects produced, whether they be judged good or bad. When, in order to facilitate market-oriented passiva(c)tion, developers manipulate both the goods and their associated milieus, the latter constitute worlds that are (clandestinely) sold with the good without the slightest discussion. Under such conditions, it is not surprising that they provoke contestation and protests.

Services, given that they increasingly require the involvement of their (human) recipients, also provide a striking illustration of the tensions between passiva(c)tion and appropriation. There are interesting controversies around personal data, the information everyone leaves on networks. Some elements of this data are acquired before the transaction. Other data are produced during the transaction and define, in successive strokes, a taste profile, a profile that is built up as transactions are carried out. Can these data be considered passiva(c)ted goods, and if so, by whom can they be appropriated?

Consider for a moment to the case of Amazon. The databases the company has built up make it possible to establish that between such and such a date, I had a definite leaning toward a particular type of music, book, or household appliance. Amazon saves the complete series of such data. The data would not exist as a set that could lead to establishing profiles if this recording and saving and the controlled management of its dissemination, with all the costs and necessary technical operations, were not carefully organized. Amazon operates the passiva(c)tion of a part of "me" that, before it was passiva(c)ted by Amazon, did not exist. I bought CDs, books, and household appliances, but these choices were not the focus of any attention. Now that they exist, the data are worked on by Amazon, and they most certainly contribute in a silent, surreptitious way to objectivize me. They appear to have been carefully extracted and separated from me, disentangled from my person in order to give a picture of me. But who can say if this assertion is correct? Nobody. What is for certain is that through Amazon's computer and commercial strategy, these data start having their own independent life. Then they come back at me on the screen and force me to see in them a sort of reflection of a personality, mine, that had escaped me up until then. It is as if "I" were different from "me." They seek to give me an image of me, as mirrors are supposed to do, an image I was unable to see by myself that had escaped me up until then. And here is Amazon appropriating these data without even asking me! Granted, these data exist, and certainly exist in a state of passiva(c)tion, only because of Amazon's operations. Of course, they are not separable from the sociotechnical environment that participates in their elaboration. But this is precisely why, even if they are limited and restricted in this way, the question of the attribution of property rights might arise, and in an acute manner. In the same way that the plant obtained by mutagenesis is unquestionably the result of a close collaboration between nature and its human developers, I would claim that the data by which Amazon defines me and from which it benefits are the fruit of a joint action. And whatever my opinion on the realism and accuracy of these data, I have the right to share in the results. The production and elaboration of these data provide a striking example of a situation in which the goods (data) and their world—what is sometimes called the Amazon fulfillment network and includes my participation and contribution—are simultaneously reconfigured while remaining connected.

Must I accept that these data be detached from me, reduce me to mere information, when it contributes to building what can be seen by third parties as my identity? In these conditions, it is legitimate that "I" resist this unconsented passiva(c)tion and the reconfiguration it leads to and that "I" claim new rights to be recognized. These are indeed becoming central questions because there are more and more traces that one accounts for and that one takes into account. They are not necessarily limited to simple data extracted from client behavior. Replace Amazon with any biotech company interested in rare diseases and the consumer with any patient suffering from an incurable genetic disease, and you see that the cells he transmits to the company, which will (perhaps) allow the company to design a therapy adapted to his profile, are just as ambivalent as the data Amazon records.[50] The same problem always comes back, the problem of disentangling, its modalities, and the stakes associated with it. These appear so very problematically in the case of market-oriented passiva(c)tion when the process of detachment and reattachment is oriented toward preparing a market transaction and the transfer of property rights that it requires.

The reason I have devoted so many lines to property rights is that in the years to come, they are destined to play a central role in the commoditization process, particularly with the growing importance of so-called intellectual property. Their attribution is a decisive step in the process of passiva(c)tion and can't be properly understood without the notion of associated milieu that is at the heart of this first framing.

Before considering the other framings, I would like to demonstrate the fruitfulness of the concept of passiva(c)tion and of its grid of analysis by applying it to a number of goods that have deeply impacted, and still impact, the dynamics of market agencements. These cases will clearly demonstrate how the work of the market-oriented passiva(c)tion of goods functions, the difficulties involved, the trials that have to be overcome, the concerns generated, and the solutions that have to be imagined to assuage them. I am asking for the reader's patience. The increasingly complex process of the passiva(c)tion of these goods, and in particular, of money, cannot be explained in a few sentences.

II. Market-Oriented Passiva(c)tion Is a Never-Ending Odyssey: The Telling Example of Commodities Deemed Fictitious

Let us recap. Before it can engage in a commercial transaction, a candidate thing, whether an industrial product or a service, must first be disentangled from all those who have engaged in its successive transformations, starting from its conception and including the ways in which it has been marketed. The candidate good will have acquired a quality that can be called (relative) autonomy. This implies that the thing is not condemned to immobility by too great a density of ties. Second, the thing must be capable of acting and making act so that a buyer becomes interested: this is the condition for the candidate to become a commodity, which implies a successful coupling with its associated milieu. The aptitude for entering into courses of action—our third requirement—however, needs to be framed: a market good's behavior has to be (reasonably) predictable and controllable so as to avoid unexpected and unmanageable disarray. In order for a transfer of property to take place, the good must—fourth condition—have been detached from those who put it into circulation; this can be referred to as the good's "independence." Finally, last requirement, it has been made possible to attach property rights to the good and attribute them unambiguously and unobjectionably to a perfectly identifiable Agent A, who is then in a position to cede them to the Buyer B according to prespecified procedures.

Autonomy, the capacity to contribute to courses of action, the predictability of the courses of action elicited, as well as their manageability, and the possibility of attributing property rights to identified agents—these are the main *aptitudes* (or dispositions) with which things must be (gradually) endowed in order for them to acquire the status of commodities. Such faculties are neither natural nor innate. They are all acquired. And that is why one can legitimately speak of market-oriented passiva(c)tion as a task.[51]

Although the activities of market-oriented passiva(c)tion are everywhere, they are absent from economics and sociology textbooks. Given how much energy these activities consume, how many questions and problems they raise, this strange silence cannot endure, especially as more living entities enter into the market area and era. Yet although these activities are only now beginning to be seen and analyzed, they are not new. It might be that the history of markets is indistinguishable from the history of the multiple ventures launched throughout the ages in order to passiva(c)te things and bring them into the universe of market activities. In some cases, the difficulties lie in the passiva(c)tion activities themselves and the equilibrium they must reach in order for things to be autonomous and capable of action without being too resistant to control. In other cases, the main problems arise when the detachment of things has to be organized, when property rights have to be associated with them and their alienation made possible. For yet others, what turns out to be particularly hazardous is pulling all the parts of the process together.

In the following, I will present, albeit in a stylized and perhaps too schematic way, a few of the interminable odysseys through which goods seeking commoditization travel. In this exercise, my aim is not to reach historical truth (that is quite beyond me), but to bring to light the reality and the content of the task of market passiva(c)tion. I will appeal to the grid of analysis presented above to guide this investigation: it will help us understand how to obtain the capacities that determine a thing's aptitude for transforming into a commodity.

Which cases should I select? From a historical point of view, entities, such as land, work, and money have undoubtedly played and still play a central role in the expansion of market agencements. Many investments, particularly legal ones, were imposed and many battles were fought that led them to a certain kind of (relatively) durable and (relatively) stable passiva(c)tion, which is now irreversible. Let us be clear—retracing this historical process, even in an over-simplified way, is neither endorsing it nor legitimizing it. There is no *one best way*. Evolution, with all its *coups de force*, struggles, and violence, does not mean justice.

Polanyi, as we know, was particularly interested in these three cases of commodification. He chose them because he had clearly recognized the central role that these goods historically have played in the development and expansion of what he calls the market economy. And it was because he perceived the arbitrary and brutal nature of the commodification of these entities—land, human work, and money—that he invented the notion of fictitious goods. By using the term "fictitious," which became widely controversial, he most likely wanted to underline that from his point of view, these things were never meant to become commodities and at the same time to claim that current markets are consequently illegitimate and somehow not civilized.

But how can you decide if a good is fictitious? One answer might be that its commodification process has provoked violent reactions or acts of resistance. One could also imagine, by mobilizing the notion of density, that it cannot be easily dissociated from those who use it, cultivate it, and so on. Both of these criteria would be appropriate, provided, as we will see, that they are considered simultaneously. Yet Polanyi chooses another path, no doubt linked to the industrial economy that surrounds him and to the influence of Marx.

According to Polanyi, a commodity is fictitious if it was not produced in order to be sold in the market:

> The crucial point is this: labor, land, and money are essential elements of industry; they also must be organized in markets; in fact, these markets form an absolutely vital part of the economic system. But labor, land, and money are obviously not commodities.... None of them is produced for sale. The commodity description of labor, land, and money is entirely fictitious.
>
> Nevertheless, it is with the help of this fiction that the actual markets for labor, land, and money are organized.[52]

Polanyi forgoes all caution when he resorts to the adverb "obviously." A math teacher I once had frequently told us not to use the word in an oral exam because it inevitably attracts tricky questions from the examiners. Philippe Steiner's commentary confirms this. He quite rightly observes that by declaring certain commodities fictitious, Polanyi is privileging a particular definition of production, the one that corresponds to the industrial world and its machines.[53] In market agencements, however, there is no reason for such a restrictive definition.

In order to become a commodity, a thing must go through transformations, enter into the process of passiva(c)tion that accompanies the detaching and reattaching. There is no reason not to consider this very real process as a form of production in its own right. The relevant distinction is not between fiction and reality, but rather between the different gradients of resistance the goods show to passiva(c)tion. From that perspective, but from that perspective alone, Polanyi is not wrong. For the land that turns green in the spring to become a profitable investment; to rent the labor of the human being with whom I speak, exchange, or play and for whom I have affection; for the pocket money I give my children to transform into capital that brings in interest, I will have made many investments and overcome many obstacles!

To understand why such efforts have nevertheless been made to turn labor, land, and money into commodities, one need only note what they have in common: they are inexhaustible sources of actions. They suggest actions to which they make a decisive contribution. They are also the potential source of high profits, a common trait that explains their appeal when market agencements are more and more shaped by what is commonly called capitalism.

For those who strive, for whatever reason, to expand the scope of market transactions, the price to be paid is that the resistance of labor, land, and money to this process of commodification must be overcome. This is not an easy task. Resistance can come from people who oppose this movement and who are helped by the high densities of these entities. Yet frontal confrontation is not the only option. A wide range of strategies have been and could be envisaged, such as attempts to negotiate compromises or to insist that voices raised must be heard. In any case, however, the outcome depends on the dynamics of the power struggles, as discussed in Chapter 8.

Human beings have indeed a capacity for creativity and invention that largely surpasses that of all other known entities. They have a great aptitude for acting autonomously. However—and this is the dark side of the force—that aptitude is difficult to discipline, frame, and reduce to behavior that can at least partly be predicted and controlled. Moreover, it cannot be presumed that human beings have an aptitude for being appropriated and alienated.

Land, or at least some parcels of it, with appropriate, if costly investments, may also hold a huge potential for action: with a bit of construction, it can be lived on; with cultivation, it can nourish those who care for it; with exploration and excavation, it can participate in the production of materials and energy; maintained, it becomes a landscape; properly preserved, it captures greenhouse gases, protects from floods, and filters rain water. Parcels of land are relatively easy to discipline; in other words, they can become predictable. However—and this is their weak spot—they are dense, inclined to immobility, heteronomous, highly dependent on those who participate in the process of its valorization, and consequently resistant, both physically and socially, to alienation.

As for money, like the living beings to which it is often compared, it is capable of suggesting many courses of action and of participating in them in an independent and autonomous fashion. However, being difficult to master and discipline, it can easily lead to overflowings (*débordements*) and unpredictable catastrophes.

One can already sense that the commodification of human labor, land, and money is no easy task. The high potential for action of these entities is weakened when one attempts to master them or to ensure their autonomy.

HUMAN LABOR

Market agencements are the outcome of long and often violent evolutions that result in whatever configuration they might have at a given time and place. Modalities of passiva(c)tion of goods developed gradually. Multiple forms of arrangements have come to exist, some of which are able to assert their coherence and end up imposing their own temporalities and their own strategic orientations. (See Chapter 7.)

The progressive passiva(c)tion of labor is still in progress. Its history is tragic, full of noise and fury, violent actions, backtracking, and ephemeral victories that are quickly contested. Solutions and sociotechnical devices have been devised; some have disappeared, others have survived and spread, establishing compromises between opposing forces and sometimes reaching a balance that is always open to question. So-called human rights and especially social rights have been hard won and must constantly be reclaimed. Without the mobilization of intellectuals, without the ethical questions and the controversies that they have aroused at different times, these inventions and the material, police, and legal measures that accompany them would not have happened. Some of these rights are now widely available. This does not mean that they are the rule.

In this story, with multiple ramifications, it is possible to pick out at least two crucial stages. What is probably essential in this odyssey is the emergence of slavery, or more precisely, of various types of slavery, in different places and at different times. The statuses of slaves have been indeed highly variable over the course of history. In Rome, for instance, depending on the period, the causes of the enslavement of a human being could be unpaid debt or capture during a war, the slave status of the parents, and so on. In practice, the slave was considered a hybrid being between a thing, which could be sold, and a person to be cared for. He could enjoy variable rights, he could buy back his freedom, exercise professions as different as those of prostitute, secretary, accountant, preceptor, agricultural worker, or even manager of a joint business.[54] The diversity of his status depended on the state of the balance of power between slaves and free citizens, which included moral rules. (In some cases and at certain times, the master had, for example, the right of life and death over a slave, while in other circumstances, this right was taken away.)

Beyond the multifarious forms that slavery takes, it seems plausible that with it, a new possible qualification of the human being emerged, a human being who was put to work and could eventually, at some point, be sold or bought because he could work. Slavery, as one form of harnessing human labor, has not disappeared. As has been well documented, it still exists and even thrives in contemporary societies. Slavery has not faded into the past, even if illegal. When compared with solutions enforced by modern market agencements, it continues to offer an alternative form of the commodification of human work simply because it requires a less demanding associated milieu: a cellar, some Kalashnikovs, the possibility of scaring the person's family, no constraining regulation, and so on.[55]

The other stage in the commodification of human labor is the one that led to the notion of a labor force and to the different and evolving devices that allowed this entity to be activated and alienated. Authors such as Marx and Polanyi and the theorists of dispossession such as geographer David Harvey illustrate this long history of the transformation of human labor into a good able to be engaged in a commercial transaction when they underline the historical importance of enclosures, still of contemporary relevance in non-Western countries. These brutal acts are used to detach labor power by ripping it out of its milieu, the world that fosters it, and to transform it into an entity that can be attached to other worlds (for instance that of industrial production) under the condition of monetary compensation (such as a salary).

Attempts to requalify *human labor* as labor power (which must be produced and, Marx would add, reproduced), requires, as all processes of *commercial passiva(c)tion* do, huge material investments, often accompanied by violent actions. Labor power does not exist outside the devices that frame, format, and "free" it to make it into a commodity.

The most intimate human activities have not been spared by this process. For instance, multiple and sophisticated devices have been elaborated over centuries in order to ensure the commercial passiva(c)tion of sexual services: the shop window in Amsterdam erases all attachments—in particular, those that connect the showcased person to family members or the immediate environment. The little red light shows the person to be available for certain courses of action, sometimes explicitly suggested, and at the same time, it ignites desire in some passersby. Nothing can by nature escape market-oriented passiva(c)tion. The success of the process depends on the capacity of some agents to impose their own strategic visions. This capacity hinges on whatever contributes to ensuring a leading role in enacting adequate sociotechnical devices: law, police, or military interventions, machine design, management rules, expert knowledge, monetary resources, moral principles, religious prescriptions, the whole being seasoned with a grain of trickery and Machiavellianism. Anything goes if no one can oppose.[56]

From a descriptive standpoint, why should we insist on maintaining that labor power is a commodity distinct from all the others? Granted, it has certain particular characteristics, but nothing prevents it from being transformed into a commodity: although the particular difficulties may change in this case, the general process for achieving commodification does not. It involves producing, via successive transformations, framed autonomy and transferable entities (the service rendered), detaching in order to reattach. The human being is translated into work and the work into labor power. The service delivered can then be attributed to the latter and paid to the person who provides it. This requalification, which was in no way self-evident, now takes place as a matter of routine and on a large scale. By framing it in words shared with physics ("work," "power"), this qualification designates and enacts an entity that acts, and makes act and react, which must be kept up (trained), maintained, and framed by a set of devices that are material (machines, for example), institutional (hierarchy, for example), or textual (labor law, for example). The human being is "domesticated" and transformed. This domestication through successive requalifications is never completed. The design of devices that frame, orient, and mobilize labor power constantly evolve as an outcome of shifting power relationships and trials of strength.

In his study of the French textile industry in the eighteenth and nineteenth centuries, William Reddy describes the controversial process that, through successive stages, led industrial employers to manage work as a commodity. There were no self-evident answers to the questions they asked themselves. What does the entrepreneur buy? How can work be measured? The answers were imagined and imposed over time. There was no dearth of conflicts and struggles. Little by little, however, workers were forced to accept that their compensation would be linked to the variable effort they put in and that this would be measured by attributing a monetary value to the movement of a finger or the length of a lunch break.[57] Yves-Marie Abraham has shown how, since 1848, when the border between Mexico and the United States was drawn as it is today, Mexican labor has been progressively and enduringly domesticated by American firms.[58] First the workers were imported, reduced to a purely muscular labor force, cut off (disentangled and detached) from their home milieus, parked in uncomfortable camps; the *braceros* (those equated with mere arms) were easily commoditized. The second stage was that of the *maquiladoras*, American firms crossing the border in order to continue to take advantage of a workforce formatted as it was in the first period, but now courtesy of the Mexican state. Then came the time of illegal migration and workers without papers, a very efficient device for maintaining the earlier frameworks for managing the workforce, this time through the fear of being sent back to Mexico. The author's conclusion is beyond dispute. Despite an array of objections for moral reasons, convictions about equality, or simply human empathy, in the absence of interventions to stop the processes that produce it, human labor is not a fictitious commodity: appropriately formatted, it is a full-fledged commodity, very real, and very concrete.

Taylorization and the ways of shaping the workforce it imposed are an important chapter in this story. Laurent Thévenot provides us with a precise description of the range of activities, the technologies and knowledge, required to develop and produce the machinery that ensures both the autonomy of the workforce and its management. As he explains, "Taylor's handbook, therefore, contains a particularly large repertoire of form-giving instruments.... In it are to be found objects used in production on the shop floor, instruments, plans, conventions, scientific formulas, school precepts, ways of giving instructions which are close to military orders, methods of payment to be used in companies, principles, advice and examples to follow when deciding what action to take."[59]

These formatting operations, both difficult and costly, are often associated with production imperatives. We do not consider them to belong to market activity itself, whereas in fact they are situated at the very heart of it insofar as they facilitate the attribution and transfer of property rights. As one could expect, the planned economies of Eastern Bloc countries, when they were trying to directly quantify the labor value to measure the exchange value of goods, participated in this venture, the market passiva(c)tion of human labor. They contributed to conceiving precise ways of measuring the different elements of the work process. This led, in the end, to the concept of a unit of work, making it possible to evaluate workers' productivity and to distribute revenues according to this measure. Martha Lampland, who reconstituted the history of these practices and devices from the 1920s to the 1950s in Hungary, shows that these experiences played a part, without it ever being avowed, in the development of a science of human labor commoditization.[60]

Taylorization of the workforce establishes a compromise between the diverse requirements for market passiva(c)tion, a compromise that privileges the need to domesticate labor and operates to the detriment of the human aptitude for starting new courses of action. To respond to the criticism leveled against Taylorization and to move beyond its limits, industry invented new forms of organization that Luc Boltanski and Ève Chiapello have gathered under the suggestive rubric of the "new spirit of capitalism." These transformations, which it would be wrong to mistake for a simple process of work intensification, shift the point of equilibrium between, on the one hand, framing the workforce in such a way that it accomplishes certain (measurable) actions and, on the other hand, framing the workforce as a source of novel courses of action—that is, between the workforce that *does* and the workforce that *invents*. The passiva(c)tion process, by its very nature, is always torn between two contradictory requirements.[61] Organizing by "project groups," a mantra for experts in industrial organization, marks a new point of equilibrium between autonomy, initiative, and management and augurs new forms of resistance, overflowings that will in turn have to be taken into account by passiva(c)tion devices.[62]

Like any entity shaped to be passiva(c)ted, labor power requires an associated milieu that makes possible, promotes, and frames the enactment of its capacity to act. For each configuration, it would be quite easy to make a detailed inventory of these assemblages. The sociotechnical organization of work, law, unemployment, vocational training, educational system, infrastructures allowing mobility and transfer, are nothing but an indicative list of those elements.

LAND

The same analysis would allow us to follow the transformations and the requalifications of land, to trace the main stages of its commercial passiva(c)tion over the long term. It would become clear that a number of episodes, such as the advent of enclosures, are shared with the history of human labor and of labor power. Land's weak point is not its propensity to reject all forms of discipline: on the contrary, unfortunately, it tends to withstand the worst hardship in silence. Its weakness, rather, is its limited capacity for autonomy. Land does not move; it cannot be moved.

However, no battle is impossible to win. Just as some human beings were transformed willy-nilly into labor power, land has gradually become documents in the form of sheets of paper, light and easy to set into motion, that constitute property rights that are easy to attribute and easy to commute. There is nothing original or extraordinary about the procedure required to produce land commodities. Land is closed, confined, registered, transformed into plots on a map, qualified as a constructible zone, or agricultural land, or as participating in a space devoted to promising economic development. It can be the object of notarized deeds; it can be transferred, sold. With these new qualities, produced in a novel form, it becomes an entity that can engage in commercial transactions: it circulates from hand to hand, suggesting courses of action whose variety increases in proportion to the abundance of available qualifications. The devices that allow for it to be made into a commodity are as complex as, but no more fictitious than those that transform the human being into labor power or a merino sheep into lamb chops in a supermarket. This is no longer the same land, and yet it is still that land. Note, however, that the mechanisms operating here can be found everywhere; they aim at detaching an entity, translating and transforming it, stabilizing it and making it active—in short, at making it available for courses of action that it suggests and in which it participates.

Once it has been requalified by these passiva(c)tion devices, land, just like the human being, is different, and yet is still present as land. The metaphor that comes to my mind is transubstantiation, so well glossed in Luis Buñuel's *The Milky Way*. The rabbit is (indeed) in the rabbit pâté, but in a different form from the rabbit running in the fields; the fish is in the fish stick, but in a different form from what it is in the wild, in the depths of the ocean. Would one say of the rabbit in the pâté that it is more fictitious than the one in the fields? Would one say of the cod that I unfreeze in the microwave that it is more fictitious than the one Norwegian fishermen pull up off the coast of Newfoundland? Obviously not! The same goes for the two lands, the one in the land registry and the one that feeds the wild boar. Considered at different stages of the qualification and passiva(c)tion process, they are as fictitious and as real as one another. The material operations of translation and production that transform and displace can obviously be contested, and indeed are contested in much the same terms. This fish stick is awful! This pâté has no taste! The land described by this vile piece of paper, which the notary reads with a shaking voice in front of buyers who are total strangers to me, has nothing to do with the land that my ancestors handed down to me! The labor power you buy at slashed prices is an offense to human beings and their dignity! One would have to be deaf not to hear them and incredibly naïve to think that these denunciations or criticisms are enough to threaten the course of market passiva(c)tion.

MONEY AND ITS DERIVATIVES

Money, the third element of Polanyi's triptych of fictitious commodities, deserves particular attention. First, because its increasing commodification, corresponding to what is usually referred to as the financialization of the economy, has an expanding impact on people's lives and in particular on the growth of social inequalities.[63] Second, because analyzing the modalities of its market passiva(c)tion sheds interesting light on the subtle mechanisms of this general process. In this introduction to these matters, I do not mean to undertake the *n*th history or genealogy of money.[64] Instead, I aim to highlight that it constantly fluctuates between two modes of existence, that of a strictly framed and profiled technical instrument that enters into clearly defined and controlled courses of action and that of an entity that, even as it accomplishes the functions specified for it, can, as it passes from hand to hand, provoke new courses of action that are hard to control, stoking dreams of riches and power, inflaming speculation, nourishing behavior oriented by greed or—perhaps more rarely—altruism. The case of money is all the more interesting to consider because the problem of finding a balance between the order it allows for and the disorders it produces has been at the heart of incessant debates, so great is its capacity for activating passions.

Money's passiva(c)tion process is an amazing story. Each new move raises deep concerns and fuels heated debates and violent struggles. It acts as a magnifying lens making visible the trials any entity has to pass on the way to commoditization. Yet this particular angle of view has been overlooked. The issues that usually get discussed revolve around oppositions seen as structural, such as the one between token and material stuff or between state money and market money.[65] Others focus their analysis on the diversity of monies and their institutional hierarchies. By considering its commoditization/passiva(c)tion process, we get rid of these usual binarisms and classifications.

Before starting, I should emphasize that considering the process of the market passiva(c)tion of money as an object of study per se is the complete inverse from theses that assert that money *is* a commodity. For example, as it will be easy to notice, my analysis of money as commodity departs from the opposite assumptions of the Marxian tradition. For me, money becomes a commodity not because of something that would be its inherent value (such as labor value), but because it can be transformed into what is usually called credit, its price being the interest paid by the buyer to the seller. As I will document further, this requalification is the founding step in a long series of derivations that deepen and extend its never-ending commoditization process. To have an overall and updated view of this process, it will thus be necessary to pay particular attention to most recent and sophisticated financial products.

Let us start with the obvious. No entity is destined by its essence to play the role of what anthropologists (or economists) usually consider money. An indirect proof of this is given by the variety of things, materials, or objects that in different societies and different eras have been used: dolphin teeth, gold or silver coins, seashells, cigarettes, stamps, paper bills, and so on. And this diversity is increasing, rather than decreasing. When I go shopping, I carry in my bag coins, bills, my checkbook, my credit or debit cards, and also my mobile phone transformed into a means of payment; when I went for a walk in Rome in the 1970s, I always took with me stamps or sweets to sweeten the deal of any transaction. The list is endless.

Rather than defining money through its supposed characteristics, it is tempting, as has been the custom since Aristotle, to define it through the functions it fulfills.[66]

Four functions are generally recognized. First, money serves as a *means of payment*. It makes it possible to acquire a good and conclude the transfer of property rights. When I buy a bottle of olive oil at the supermarket, I pay for the right to put it in my shopping bag. As an ordinary economic agent, what I am experiencing is that money allows me to settle my purchases. The cashier thinks in the same terms when asking whether I will pay in cash, or by card, or by check. In a few seconds, I take on a debt, which I will pay off, either immediately if I pay cash or later if I use a Visa card. Likewise, when I pay back a mortgage, I make payments according to a schedule that has set the amounts and the timetable.

The second function usually ascribed to money is that of a *medium* that facilitates exchanges. It is said that without money, human beings would have to engage in complicated barter operations in order to obtain the necessities of life. If I need eggs, ham, pickles, and bread to make a sandwich, and money does not exist, I will be forced to find the people who have these ingredients or who are willing to procure them for me in exchange for the goods and services I possess. If everyone had to proceed in this way, the task would rapidly become very complex, and everyone would spend their time trying to find a partner willing to accept the exchange they seek. Money, or so the thinking goes, avoids these complications: as long as I am rich enough, I can acquire everything I need in a single visit to the neighborhood supermarket. It is a sort of lubricant that makes transactions in a complex society easier; it is a substitute for bartering,[67] which, on the contrary, would impede these transactions.

Despite the almost unanimous support for this way of understanding its function, its reality is far from obvious. Who actually goes through the checkout considering they are exchanging banknotes for leeks? The function of money as a means of exchange emerges only in exceptional circumstances, and even there, it operates in the opposite way from what is expected. Many authors in fact consider, with good reason, that barter does not precede money, but rather substitutes for it in case of need, and that it appeared, and is likely to appear, only after money did.[68] Barter takes over when money is missing or when it is incapable of fulfilling its other functions properly. The inverse is implausible because exchange, even in a simple form, requires cognitive skills well beyond human faculties. Exchange without money is possible only in particular situations where an existing currency is missing or creates more problems than it solves. In this case, the agents can rely on it mentally to carry out their calculations. It is in reference to these current situations that we can speak of money as a means of exchange: it is money that allows barter, and not barter that, because of its failures, paves the way for the emergence of money. In other situations, it seems better to stick to the first function, that of means of payment.

The third function usually attributed to money is that it can be used as a *store of value*. If I raise chickens and sell them at the end of the month for more than I need for my regular consumption, I can keep my gains in the form of money, which I will use later for new purchases. In this case, money acts as an asset that transports purchasing power from one period to another and/or from one point in space to another. For it to be able to play this role, it must be the case that in this other point of space-time, it maintains its function as a payment instrument.

Finally, in the fourth function usually mentioned, money is used as an *accounting unit*, providing a convenient and coherent means of affixing prices and hence of comparing the values of different goods that it makes commensurable. Instead of saying (as in a fictional system without money) that a pineapple is worth six pots of yogurt, which in turn are worth four liters of milk, I can say that their price is the same—seven euros—and I can begin complicated arithmetical operations.

Is it satisfying to stick to this instrumental definition of money and to the list of the four functions it fulfills? The answer is no. First, because the functions that make something into money in the usual sense given to this word have a history; they are not given once and for all; they constantly evolve.[69] Furthermore, and more importantly, this general (and purely instrumental) definition of money and its functions is not satisfactory because in reality, the properties that allow these functions to be performed exert irrepressible pressure on it to transform it, at a stroke, into a financial product, into a good that can be bought and sold against payment. A rapid detour to examine the qualities required for it to fulfill its different functions will make this point clearer.

Precious metals were often chosen to serve as money because of their material aptitude for accomplishing certain instrumental tasks. Having been extracted from the earth, duly transformed and conditioned, they are able to withstand the handovers and long circuits that commercial transactions sometimes require, and therefore they constitute an efficient means of exchange. In the form of coins, they can be added or divided, which makes them good candidates for the functions of accounting units and means of payment. Being resistant to corrosion and to the passage of time, they can be accumulated and stocked. Their purity can be controlled, and their properties are easily guaranteed. These properties prepare them to be used to store value. Granted, they have certain defects: they are unwieldy and heavy, specific equipment is required to measure their weight and control their composition, but all in all, they constitute loyal instruments.

The material characteristics that authorize the successful accomplishment of their instrumental functions as money facilitate the transformation of precious metals into commodities. This is the case, first because they provide material for manufacturing things such as utensils or jewelry.[70]

Anthropologists and economists are right to speak of "commodity money" when they refer to these types of money, which are easy to pass(act)ivate and to convert.

However, the aptitude of money to transform itself or to be transformed into a commodity is not limited to such simple recycling operations. If I have a hundred-gram piece of gold (accounting unit), I can choose to preserve it (store of value) and use it later as a means of payment that will allow me to acquire an "exchangeable" good (means of exchange) for this coin. I can also, however, be convinced to lend it to someone who is short on means of payment in return for an additional sum. I make my hundred grams of gold available to him, and he buys the use of it at a certain price, corresponding to what is called interest. The coin thereby acquires commodity status, not because it is gold, but because it has stable functions that interest my buyer: he will be able to mobilize it for specific courses of action (to buy a car, hoarding, or whatever). It has become an asset, or what in French bears the felicitous name "*un actif*." In this case, this asset is described as financial. The money (my gold coin) generates money (the interest paid by the borrower).

In order for this strange generation to take place, the money must have a new quality that is suggestively called "liquidity."[71] Liquidity (greater or smaller: there are "degrees of liquidity") measures its (greater or lesser) capacity to maintain and have a good chance of successfully accomplishing its functions. If the money (candidate for commodity status) could not be used as a means of payment at some later date and in some other place, if its value were not preserved, I doubt that my borrower would accept to shell out money (the interest he will pay me) to have the right to use it. Money, through its functions, allows certain actions (buying, selling, hoarding, and so on) to be accomplished. For it to transform into a commodity, it is necessary and sufficient that the capacity to undertake these actions be guaranteed over time and through space. It is not therefore fundamentally different from the Volkswagen Golf we were considering earlier. Just like the car, the money needs an associated milieu that makes its uses possible. To move about, the Golf requires, among other things, road infrastructures, the establishment of driving rules, a network of garages and gas stations, the recruitment of police officers, and more. The associated milieu that allows money to be liquid (and fungible), to circulate freely, to accomplish its instrumental functions at all times in all places, is no less complex in terms of equipment than the one that allows the Golf to move. Appropriate legislation and regulation, banking networks, emitting institutions, central banks, administrative authorities, civil and criminal legal codes, juridical institutions, the Serious Fraud Office (UK), or the Federal Trade Commission (USA) — these are some of the elements that must be assembled to provide money with the environment it needs in order to function. Therefore, not one of the four functions than can be eventually fulfilled by money can be described as an intrinsic property. This is the reason why the Aristotelian conception does not hold water: it forgets the necessity of an appropriate associated milieu. To act as money, an entity should be a finely tuned assemblage of material and institutional components. Money is neither a mere institution nor a mere material. It is an entanglement of both. Money without associated milieu is no longer money.[72]

Then we can push further the comparison between Golf and money. Imagine a country with little road infrastructure, made up of vast desert stretches crossed by impetuous and unpredictable rivers and without garages or mechanics with the know-how to provide rapid and efficient repairs to a car after an accident. We can be confident that in such an environment, the latest trendy Golf, stuffed with electronics, devilishly urban with its integrated GPS, low-profile tires, reduced ground clearance, backup radars useful for parking in the small, crowded streets of the capital city, would seem quite simply poorly adapted. Anyone who dreams of adventure, daring crossings of overflowing wadis and nights sleeping on a vehicle roof to guard against great cats, will not give a Golf even a second glance. He will skip the Volkswagen hatchback and make a beeline for the Land Rovers, for four-wheel drives able to withstand the hardest trials and most extreme conditions.

The same goes for money. Would it not make sense to draw a distinction between four-wheel drive or all-terrain currencies, apt at fulfilling some of what has been progressively counted as their basic functions in underequipped and threatening environments, and high-tech currencies that offer a diversified range of features and circulate smoothly in milieus that are heavily endowed with institutions and infrastructures of all sorts, such that they can fully exploit their qualities? It makes sense, then, to consider that there are, on the one hand, precious metals, not yet turned into coins, fulfilling their role as means of payment, reserves of worth, and so on more or less well (to be fair:

pretty well) in a rather hostile environment; and, on the other hand, there are electronically loaded currencies circulating at light speed, transforming back and forth between credits and assets, that owe it to their "hypercivilized" associated milieu that they preserve all the instrumental functions.

It would doubtless be easy to situate along this continuum running from all-terrain currencies to the high-tech ones a series of monies that establish variable compromises between aptitude for liquidity, on one side, and efficiency in their instrumental functions, on the other. The outcome would depend on how their material characteristics and their associated milieus are arranged, or using the terms I proposed above, depending on the balance they achieve between autonomy and independence. Banknotes are no doubt situated halfway between the extreme poles. They shift more easily and faster between one function and another than do masses of precious metal, thus demonstrating a greater aptitude for liquidity. In return, they require a better-equipped and richer-associated milieu: circulating faster than metals, they wear out faster (issuing institutions establish programs to renew them periodically); they travel less far because the creation of unified monetary zones (with currencies that serve as accounting units, such as the European Currency Unit, which then have to be transformed into legal tender such as the euro) is an expensive, endless project. Symmetrically, a banknote is less liquid, but less demanding in terms of associated milieu, than electronic money. The reader can pursue the analysis to decide how to assign positions to Old Master paintings or collector stamps. The conclusion would no doubt be, as it is for the authors of economics textbooks who love these sorts of examples: as a means of payment, a Rembrandt painting has serious disadvantages. For instance, even if I manage to transport it, I am not sure that my neighborhood car dealer will be open to accepting it without further discussion as payment for the four-wheel drive I wish to acquire. He would, however, recognize that as a store of value, the Rembrandt does a pretty good job and would furthermore observe that to fulfill both functions in the long term requires a highly specialized associated milieu whose constitution is perforce slow and costly (existence of a milieu of experts and amateurs, organization of auctions, and so on).[73] In other words, a wide range of hybrid currencies exist, torn between their instrumental functions and their status as commodities, just as in the car market, one finds an array of real fake urban four-wheel-drive vehicles not really up to the task of crossing riverbeds, but nonetheless capable of negotiating the rocky back roads in Corsica, of parking smoothly on Paris sidewalks, and of giving their drivers a panoramic view that serves to reassure.

The experts in monetary techniques have noted the existence of this tension and the extreme forms of currency to which it leads. As opposed to the aforementioned commodity currencies (such as precious metals), they speak of *fiat money* to designate the currencies with high liquidity and fungibility (banknotes, lines of credit, and so on): in order to function as an instrument of money, these monies indeed require institutions conceived so as to create the confidence that guarantees their continuity. It is possible to insist on the issue of confidence (the French expression is in fact *monnaie fiduciaire*, fiduciary currency), but we should then also talk about confidence in the case of the latest Golf: the buyer knows, without having to do complicated research, that he will be able to use it in the city and on the highway. That confidence originates in the very existence of an associated milieu adapted to the good's characteristics, whether it is a car or a currency.[74] The milieu should therefore be put under the spotlight. I will come back to the confidence issue in Chapter 5, devoted to *affectio mercatus*.

The reader will have understood that liquidity, its faculty of circulating without losing at least some its different functionalities, is not without connection with money's material characteristics, just as the car is technically different, depending on whether it aspires to be recognized as an off-road vehicle or as a simple city car.

Here is my hypothesis: the more that the material qualities of a currency render it (potentially) adept at accomplishing its four functions almost simultaneously and with the same efficiency, the more it is likely to become a commodity. However, it will also require a rich, complex, and diversified associated milieu for these capacities to be effectively exercised. Conversely, the more laborious that fulfilling of its functions is, the more it struggles to move from one function to another, the less it is liquid and the less its function as a currency instrument calls for a heavily equipped associated milieu, but the more it is difficult to transform into a commodity. On the one hand, light electronic currency, liquid and demanding, on the other, the heavy masses of precious metals, viscous and accommodating.

To make the connection with the repertoire of market passiva(c)tion, one further observation is necessary. The set of specifications for market passiva(c)tion indeed requires that transferable property rights be attributed. There again, even a rapid inspection shows that the qualities of the currency as it emerges from its interactions with its associated milieu count. Question: Who is the owner of the piece of precious metal that is offered to me in return for the good I wish to sell? The answer is problematic, given how much the trajectory and the biography of this piece of metal, including probable thefts and misappropriations, are likely to have been long and disrupted. It is hard to trace it from its extraction to this day when I am enjoined to accept it as a means of payment. Question: Who really owns the banknote that, given my reticence, my client decides to pull out of his briefcase? The answer is simpler and quicker: the "bearer" of the bill is reputed to be its owner, provided that an adequate associated milieu does exist. Attribution and commutation are even easier in the case of electronic money and particularly in the use of mobile phones, suitably reconfigured, as means of payment and transfers.[75] Holders of bank accounts can easily assert their property rights on the wealth they have amassed because their accounts are held by hardware and legal assemblages (lines of code, networks of inscriptions, computers, transmission infrastructures...that require more sophisticated competencies and tools to be cracked than any safe deposit box). If, however, perchance one chose Old Master paintings as currency, one would have to be in a position to gather rapidly and lug around a bunch of documents that ensured that it was indeed a Rembrandt and that guaranteed property rights. High liquidity, which, as we have seen, encourages commodification, also facilitates attribution and transfer of property rights.

This detour may have seemed a little long and tedious, but it was necessary to understand the inherent difficulties in transforming money into a commodity and the role that material properties play. Luckily, it leads to a simple proposition, which can be expressed as follows: the market passiva(c)tion of money requires an associated milieu that is all the more complex, heavily equipped, and costly as its properties make money fit to accomplish its different instrumental functions efficiently and effectively. The same movement that increases its performances as instrument money favors its transformation into a commodity. However, this transformation subjects its bearers to considerable risk unless the associated milieu required for it to continue to function as instrument money is conceived and set up with the greatest attention and professionalism. The history of money is at least in part the history of a long succession of necessarily imperfect solutions and arrangements imagined to handle this recurring tension.

Carried by technological innovations, money wants only to flow, to live its own life, to stray from the paths traced for it and the instrument roles assigned to it. Money, which is chosen and profiled to serve simultaneously as a store of value, means of payment, and accounting unit simply by virtue of its mobility, its divisibility, its immutability, the ease with which it can be accumulated, its traceability, and its liquidity, constantly suggests courses of action (those of commodities) for which it had not been necessarily programmed, but into which, with the complicity of its bearers, it shifts without further ado. Money stimulates sales by setting up the complementary roles of buyer and seller, it acquires sometimes a general value and gives legitimate access (as theft does not) to all sorts of good. Because it makes acquisition possible, money heats up minds, fans passions, greed, and usurious loans. It becomes even more active as it becomes an asset (*actif*) and provokes speculative fever.[76] Whereas one might want to confine it to the role of a technical instrument, it spills over into other roles. Whatever measures are taken, it always manages, somehow or other, to escape from the framework some would like to impose on it and to become the object of commercial transactions. Money, engaged in the process of commodification, flows, slips away, ebbs, insinuates itself, spreads, contracts, and dilates like quicksilver. Money is something to track down, to attempt to get hold of; one lends it, demanding that it return enlarged by its interest. It makes debts that are paid back, capital plus interest. It is invested to produce more than what was invested. It buys on credit and brings in the profits for playing a bull market. Money thus engenders money as a living being perpetuates itself endlessly, multiplying in its progeny. You thought it was here, and suddenly it is gone; now you see it, now you don't. Money is never as inclined to stray from its state of being a well-framed instrument (its function is to count, change, pay, and store value), to edge closer to the status of goods transferable in return for compensation of the monetary sort and to tip over into the sphere of commodification at the very moment when it best fulfills its instrumental functions. The properties of money make it into a permanent provocation. Although it was profiled to serve—that is, to initiate determined and controllable actions, by virtue of the very qualities conferred on it, it suddenly transforms irresistibly into the master and intrudes into the intimacy of those who seize it. There is nothing fictitious about these successive transformations, which make money into a full-blown commodity. Money makes those who possess it and who are possessed by it act almost unwittingly. It is not surprising that it should have become a central character in dramatic literature from Aristophanes's *Wasps* to Tom Wolfe's *Bonfire of the Vanities* or Émile Zola's *The Kill*. Money can, of course, bring about altruistic acts, but if Apuleius's ass were to return, it would attest that money generates more serious crimes than acts of generosity.

Over a long period and throughout many trials, it turned out that the coevolving transformations of monies and of their associated milieus, up to electronic currency, have gradually increased liquidity. This evolution, money's process of passiva(c)tion, has been viable only because it has been narrowly framed. Unless it is held in check, excess liquidity is a permanent threat that ends up bringing general devastation as it transforms into impetuous torrents. Conversely, insufficient liquidity paralyzes investments and risk taking. How can one take advantage of what money allows and suggests one does without being totally submerged? In answer to this nagging question, through numerous vicissitudes, controversies, conflicts, and trials, devices and solutions have been imagined, tested, and imposed over time and in different places. How far should one agree to go in the process of commodification of money and its transformation into an asset (*actif*)? This (fifth) function, hitherto less visible but now central, that of financial instrument born of the successful combination of the four prior ones, must itself be properly mastered. If it is not, it devastates everything. Liquidity always raises the question of the appropriate damming measures.

The most frequent strategies are to let monies proliferate while organizing their functional specialization and somehow limiting their aptitude for playing all roles at once. This strategy is all the easier to implement—because a given currency, even if it has appropriate and carefully profiled characteristics, is never perfectly versatile and can respond only very imperfectly and very partially to all the functions expected of it. There is no such thing as an all-purpose money.[77]

Any textbook on financial institutions will confirm this. At least three categories of distinct monetary masses are defined. The first, M1, whose stock evolves from day to day, corresponds to the money used in transactions: it includes available cash and instantaneously available deposits, such as checking accounts. The second, M2, includes M1 and the money that requires a managed conversion in order to be used in transactions, such as savings accounts. Finally M3, a third form of money (beyond M2), includes not only M1 and M2, but also financial instruments such as credit cards that allow for limited payments in a certain time period.[78] These different monetary masses and therefore types of money correspond to functional specialization.[79] In certain countries, these differences have been reinforced by regulation that forbids banks to engage in short-term speculation with their own funds or forces them to choose between managing assets and managing the deposits of means of payment.[80]

A simple way of controlling the tendency money has of slipping without warning from its role as an instrument to that of a commodity is to clamp down in a strict and permanent way on its instrumental qualities or to even go so far as to forbid some of them. For example, its aptitude to transform into a commodity can be compromised by making it less easily divisible, by forbidding it to be a universal means of payment, or by hampering its convertibility. Polanyi observed that both in traditional societies and in so-called modern societies, several material forms of money coexist, each being assigned exclusively to certain types of goods.[81] Archaeologists report that the Vikings who settled in southeastern England in the ninth century organized the coexistence of their own money, made of silver masses of differing weights, which was used in the countryside, and the native money, reserved for urban transactions, which was made of silver coins. In France, the *pièces jaunes*, small-denomination coins collected to finance a foundation serving the public good, or the silver coins put aside for grandchildren, attest to such ongoing practices. Similarly, within the private space of households, money that comes from the salaries of family members may be earmarked for certain specific uses: one portion of a spouse's paycheck may be allocated to the other as pocket money; the internship stipends paid to an adolescent whose parents cover his tuition or the unexpected thirteenth month earned by the young person who still lives with their parents may be reserved for household expenses.[82] Natasha Schüll tells the story of a gambler who, having received a large sum of money at the death of her young son—a death for which she felt partially responsible because her addiction prevented her from taking proper care of him—explained that she had no other option but to deplete it in casinos because she would not have wanted to take advantage of it herself.[83] Bruce Carruthers and Arthur Stinchcombe observe that just like households, organizations distribute their funds into categories, certain sums being more fungible—that is to say, usable more widely, than others. (For instance, they create strategic reserves or forbid access to them by higher rungs of the hierarchy.)[84] The money the Japanese state collects from betting on horse races goes to scientific research. Money's use is often related to the way it was acquired: dirty money requires laundering. As Viviana Zelizer puts it, the practices that frame and limit the instrumental functions of money lead to the constitution of special monies characterized by narrowly specialized uses.[85] The resulting restrictions, which can institute serious constraints, as in the case of so-called local currencies, have the effect of making the transformation of money into a commodity less likely. More generally, money, whether in the form of coins or bills, savings accounts or bank checks, credit cards or bills of exchange, can be assigned to different types of transactions. For example, by using its material properties, "plastic" money—plastic, indeed, but stuffed with electronics that give it the capacity to memorize, retrace, and add up transactions—can be reprogrammed, for example as credit cards or debit cards, depending on the various associated milieus in which it is made active. Privilege may be given to the credit function (store of value) or almost exclusively to the debit function (means of payment). These different orientations were all the easier to implement because the functions attributed to this hybrid, combining polymers and silicon, depend only on specific architectures of data flows that are designed before the cards can carry credit in place of debit.[86]

Local or private currencies such as LETS,[87] controlled by communities of their users, are generally characterized by strict regulation and even the complete outlawing of certain of their functions: bills are useable only as a means of payment within a strictly delimited collective; they cannot give rise to loans; there are rules about their convertibility to other currencies; unusable after a certain date, they cannot be used as a store of value. All sorts of configurations can be imagined.[88] The credit cards put into circulation by big distribution companies are private monies for the impecunious whose functions (payment, credit, obtaining cash) are strictly regulated.[89] The findings are unanimous. All-terrain currencies able to fulfill the four functions that have ended up being assigned to them in all places and at all times—all-purpose money, in other words—simply cannot exist. In each currency, there is a sleeping Rembrandt just waiting to be roused from its slumber!

Such measures of specialization, demarcation, territorialization, and interdiction localize money, fragment its uses, and decouple its functions. They thereby generate another opposition, which adds to the impression of splintering: that between private and public monies. This opposition has considerable effects. The former tend to limit or control money's propensity to transform into a commodity and activate financial strategies. The latter, on the contrary, facilitate this transformation by providing a vast circulation space and guaranteeing, through rules aimed at reducing the uncertainties associated with its use and by multiplying specialized monies and appropriated rules of conversion between them, that the four functions be correctly fulfilled and contribute to increased and supposedly well-framed liquidity.[90]

The different damming actions I have sketched explain why currencies are always multiple, each being called on to fulfill certain functions, rather than others. This observation holds not only for traditional societies, but equally and especially for those described as advanced. When a certain type of currency, for instance, that attached to the function of payment, is lacking, specialized monies very quickly will appear to compensate for its weaknesses, or counterfeit currency will fill the gap. The multiplication of monies and their regulation is the result of initiatives that in large measure escape government control, despite their massive involvement in monetary policy. Everywhere one can observe monies that are multiple, fragmented, specialized, hierarchized, and supported by user communities that are separate from one another. The recent development of so-called cryptocurrencies shows how certain technologies such as blockchains have forced central banks to react so as not to imperil their monetary sovereignty.[91] Those private monies raise, like the libra, the crucial question of their conversion, often surrounded with phenomena that bring about exclusion.[92] With my revenues as a (retired) academic, I regularly use M1, a little M2, and extremely rarely M3, to which I have only indirect and costly access. Local and specialized money confines its users within borders that are difficult to transgress. The Uzbek farmer who sells his cotton to state companies will have a hard time converting the money from his sales into dollars.

The proliferation of devices aimed at containing money's propensity to provoke financial activities leads to remarkable results that calm the concerns it raises. The problem, as some see it, is that containment durably weakens the money's efficacy. Speculation can be avoided by playing on the properties of a currency, but how far should one go in this exercise of self-defense? A currency that is allowed at least to a certain extent to transform into an asset (*actif*)—that is, to be active as a commodity, opens the way to courses of action, initiatives, and (ad)ventures that would otherwise be impossible. How is the right equilibrium to be found? How can money be authorized to be active, but not too active? This is not a new question. It has been the subject of erudite and moral reflection for centuries. Aristotle, the Church Fathers, and the successive commentators of the Koran, among others, warned against the damaging effects of this apparently crazy practice of making money into a sort of living being able to engender itself and multiply itself via interest rates; they tried to propose acceptable accommodations.

We are still facing the dilemma. Granted, money has such mobilizing force that it can produce nefarious and dangerous effects. However, it is also such a force in mobilizing and liberating energies that it would be a shame to neutralize its dynamism out of prudence or fear of risk. Like a wild animal whose outbursts or rampages are feared, but whose power one tries to use by taming it, money must be domesticated. However, that must be done in a subtle and appropriate way: neither too much nor too little. In short, what is at stake is preserving the faculty money has to make act beyond its strictly determined and now well-entrenched four technical functions without leaving the leeway for it to provoke (too much) disorder and chaos. Since there is no a priori recipe, this meticulous calibration between liquidity and viscosity has taken place through a long series of trial-and-error experiments; it has given rise to crises, controversies, and violent clashes, including those still happening before our very eyes.

Taming the beast—or, to put it in more graceful terms, controlling liquidity—takes time. It is ongoing, and there is no end in sight. It requires a series of technical and regulatory inventions that, through successive steps, liberate its mobilizing forces, its almost infinite capacity to incite and make act, while trying to contain them within acceptable limits in order to avoid excessively violent shocks and to maintain the possibility of its exercising its instrumental functions. Two episodes played a crucial role in this long-running story of the never-ending market passiva(c)tion of money. The first corresponds to the theological battles over interest payments: thanks to a great deal of rhetorical skill and the development of ingenious regulatory devices, these were eventually recognized, at least in certain social circles, as legitimate after having long been considered dangerous and potentially immoral.[93] Money now works for us, or rather for some of us. The second battle, still raging, is the one over what are now called financial instruments. Whereas the story about interest rates and their vicissitudes is widely known and documented, the one about these products of a very particular kind is still to be written. Given their contemporary importance, it is not superfluous to devote a few lines to them, because they give a compelling illustration of the logic and difficulties of the market passiva(c)tion of money. Furthermore they show the relevance of the notions I have proposed to giving an account of this process, which is central to the endless commodification of money.

Even though what are now called financial products or instruments seem to have a distant origin, it is only recently that they have been used systematically and that markets have been organized for them.[94] Take the case of stocks: it took a few centuries for them to behave like recognized entities that have stable and legitimate qualities and codified behavior and that can easily be detached and reattached. For instance, in France, many years went by before a space appeared for them to change hands legitimately and before the agents engaged in these transactions were authorized to leave the cafés in rue Quincampoix in Paris, to which they had been relegated and instead be admitted into what were considered honorable places. Stocks contaminated those through whose hands they passed. A genuine social prophylactic had to be set up in order to make them into commodities like any other. That required, for example, that lists of exchangeable stocks be established and imposed and that the identities of those people who could have access to the transaction be defined precisely. Alex Preda, in his history of financial markets, gives a minute description of the constitution of a world that progressively obtains the market passiva(c)tion of this strange good, this unpredictable vector for disorder and suspect passions—namely, a stock that is bought and sold and that can be promoted and accumulated. Before the passiva(c)tion was accomplished (it actually happened only at the beginning of the twentieth century, when, in 1905, accounting became compulsory for brokers on the New York Stock Exchange), and despite the huge efforts by professionals who follow stock prices, analyze the reasons for pricings, and offer tools to determine value and explain their evolution, the limit between the stock market and the casino is tenuous. Taming stocks ("*action*," as the French language judiciously chose to name this product, under-lining the need for serious regulation to prevent it acting in random directions) turned out to be difficult; it required a great deal of effort, ingeniousness, and material and institutional investments to manage things such that it neither returns to a wild state nor veers out of control.[95]

Derivatives, the regulation of which is far from complete and which have developed spectacularly in the last decades, turn out to be even more difficult to tame. To stigmatize their constant overflowings and their excessive capacity for provoking courses of action that run out of control, these are sometimes referred to as toxic products or junk bonds. Their commodification is hardly a walk in the park. To illustrate some of the difficulties encountered and the devices imagined in response, I will say a few words about the beginnings of the modern history of derivatives (forward contracts) and a few of the trials and tribulations through which they had to pass before invading and coloniz-ing financial markets.

A forward contract allows a seller to establish the sales price of a good before the transaction actually takes place. The seller can thus protect himself against a sudden large drop in prices. The trade-off is that if prices go up, in other words, if at the moment of the transaction they are higher than the price that had been established ahead of time, the seller is deprived of the benefit of the rise. This very simple tool allows for an adjustment between buyer and seller. It is particularly useful when the prices for the goods that are the object of the transaction (the underlying goods) are irregular and unpredictable. Such volatility can have multiple causes—for instance, weather, in the case of cereals such as wheat or corn, or the fluctuations in supply and demand, as in the case of certain metals, or raw materials, or financial products such as...foreign currencies and interest rates. The large-scale development of for-ward contracts began in the middle of the nineteenth century in the United States and concerned mostly agricultural products. It gradually extended to goods such as gold and silver, sugar or petroleum. It was only in the 1970s that forward contracts became common practice in financial markets.

The way this tool spread resembles all stories of innovation. It revolves around a number of actors and institutions defending opposite and often incompatible interests. It is made of negotiations and compromises that lead to the gradual transformation of the tool and its requalification.[96] Yuval Millo has traced the main moments of this evolution—that is, of the gradual passiva(c)-tion of an entity, the forward contract, whose disentanglement and reentanglement were made easier without that leading to its becoming out of control or becoming the source of unmanageable overflowings and disorders.[97]

The first step of this requalification process involved dissociating the contract from the obligation to deliver the underlying asset.[98] Indeed, at the very beginning, on the Chicago Stock Exchange, when a farmer sold his wheat on the futures market, he had to deliver it to his buyer at the moment and price established by the contract. By making the price of the futures contract and what underlies it converge, this clause avoided speculation and prevented the signing of futures contracts being equivalent to a simple game of chance. However, it also brought heavy constraints on the resale of the contract to a third party before its execution, since to be able to fulfill this obligation, the operators had to buy back or sell back the contracts they had sold or bought.

These drawbacks became more problematic when people started imagining future sales of—why not?—stocks or portfolios of stocks, or even indexes. Futures contracts can act as insurance against the fluctuations to which all these goods are exposed, but their handling raises considerable problems. First, in the case of deliverable financial assets such as stocks or stock portfolios, there were witching hours in the market when transactions were realized and considerable blocks of stocks had to change hands at the same moment. The next problem with the delivery clause was insurmountable because some underlying assets, such as benchmark interest rates, have no physical existence and are therefore difficult to...deliver! These difficulties can be avoided by eliminating the delivery clause, but the risk of incontrollable speculative swings is then amplified, since no reality principle can be brought to bear on the agents engaged in these transactions, at least in the short term. In the end, after epic battles between the various protagonists of the financial markets, the solution adopted for mastering these new goods was the creation of institutions such as the CFTC, the Commodity Futures Trading Commission,[99] whose job is to strictly regulate the transactions, one of the most important innovations being the distinction drawn between real assets and synthetic assets, a distinction whose purpose is to insure against the risks produced by derivatives. A degree of regulation is achieved by technical measures such as, among others, the creation of central counterparty clearinghouses and the institution of limits on the daily fluctuations of contracts.

By allowing the delivery of the underlying clause to be eliminated, these devices transformed the futures contract into a financial product that could be subject to successive transactions without obligations to buy back or resell, since the different holders were freed from the requirement to deliver what underlies it. In this case, the closure of the contract gives rise to a cash settlement corresponding to the difference in price between the price at the close of the contract and the value of the asset finally observed. Thus physically disentangled and detached from the "good" and its initial holder, but also from the underlying asset to be provided to the buyer (hectoliters of grains, blocks of stock, or…immaterial indexes), the contract becomes an autonomous entity that can easily be sold. Its passiva(c)tion has made progress. It can pass from hand to hand, it can be transferred seamlessly from one agent to another, rendering services to its successive holders.

The contract's increased autonomy obviously raises problems. As those who insisted on the delivery of the underlying asset as a key requirement had understood, one of the problems is the risk of unbridled speculation, despite all the precautions taken. An attached contract limits this risk, but prevents it from becoming a full-blown commodity; a detached contract facilitates that mutation, but encourages the behavior that makes the stock market seem like a casino. And the more derivatives and derivatives of derivatives there are, the more the risk increases. Innovative products raise more and more complicated problems for regulation and control. (Talk of "responsible financial products" relies on a euphemism that discreetly draws attention to, without acknowledging, the fact that often they are irresponsible.) As Hsin Hin Lim, an equity derivatives and structured finance lawyer in the City of London mischievously notes, "When I look at a derivative product the probabilities are not known. At least in a casino the odds are certain."[100] And in fact, the difference between the two sectors, the casinos and financial markets, is dwindling. What is amusing, and I will get back to this when I come to *affectio mercatus*, is that gambling activities followed a parallel path in their evolution. Intense investments were required for the passiva(c)tion of the strange goods they offer to progress; it worked so well that as we will see in Chapter 5, their commodification is no longer considered problematic. Attesting to the convergence of the sectors, certain hybrid products that combine gambling and finance are appearing in market activity. The development of betting exchanges (still forbidden by some countries, such as France), where one exchanges bets on ongoing competitions for monetary compensation, attests to this alignment. The more gambling activities are embedded in market activities, the harder it is to exclude financial speculation from them, even if they are difficult to regulate. The passiva(c)tion of financial products is a continuous process, and there seems to be no end in sight.

In the history of the passiva(c)tion of financial instruments, regulation and the creation of institutions charged with implementing and enforcing it have played and continue to play a key role, as do technological and material innovations (notably in software) that allow for product design, elaboration, qualification, conservation, tracing, and transacting.[101] Taken together, these actions have led to a considerable increase in the liquidity of assets, but also to more complex operations, a proliferation of products, and difficulties in avoiding sudden crises or untimely overflowings. What chief architect would be conceited enough to dare claim he fully understands and masters the sources and effects of liquidity?

Some may be surprised by my approach in these pages devoted to money and to the actions undertaken to promote its commodification and ensure control over it, more or less successfully. Why focus so much on money's properties, on its capacity to be disentangled, made independent (but not too independent), when there is a sort of soft consensus around the idea that with the development and omnipresence of *fiat monies*, money is first and foremost a symbol, a social convention whose regulation should fall to the purest will—for instance, the political will?

In a programmatic article published in 2006, anthropologist Bill Maurer reminds us that since Plato and Aristotle, the analysis of money has constantly oscillated between two opposing interpretations.[102] The first one insists on its symbolic dimension, the second on its material reality. Maurer, following Keane, invites us to get rid of this binarism. In the preceding lines, I have done nothing but implement this advice. The opposition between these two sides of the coin is no longer relevant and actually disappears as soon as one takes an interest, as I have done, in the process of commodification and the transformations it implies and brings about.

There is, however, nothing revolutionary about this perspective. Keynes laid the ground for it when he asserted that money does not have any intrinsic functions, but has, instead, properties that authorize certain courses of action. According to him, "money" is the name given to those entities that have an aptitude for doing or for making others do certain things, such as establishing prices or constituting reserves that can be used at a later date as means of payment. It suggests and authorizes certain courses of action, some of which have been progressively (at least partially) regulated and have become the functions expected of it and that it fulfills more or less efficiently, while others draw it in new directions by generating types of action that spill over the framework of usual functions and are harder to contain, such as those that lead it to play the role of a recognized asset. The same properties that make it an efficient servant push it toward its commodification. It nourishes speculation, speculation that is not in itself a bad thing, since it is a way to care for the future, but that can become so if it is not regulated by a painstakingly designed associated milieu. Servant, for sure, but not all that faithful!

Thanks to the constantly renewed work of passiva(c)tion and the regulations it institutes, the human being, land, and money have gradually been transformed into goods that can enter market transactions.[103] Particularly recalcitrant in the face of any attempts to make them simultaneously autonomous, active, independent, and controllable, these three groups of entities now play a strategic part in the development of market agencements, notably, those that can be characterized as capitalist. The history of their commodification, largely irreversible, shows constantly renewed trials of strength to open the way for making the most of their unique potential for action.

I hope the reader will have understood that I am not trying to justify these different processes. I am merely trying to identify what they have in common in order to better understand what commodification is. That said, passiva(c)tion, like any framing, raises concerns, resistance, and alternative projects, the content of which differs according to the goods involved. It is in these confrontations that moral claims are forged and expressed, implicitly or explicitly. As an analyst, I limit myself to pointing out the existence of the latter, displaying their content, and describing how they are or are not taken into account. Certain ethical issues are at the heart of passiva(c)tion. To invoke an overused term, this is the root of what we can call market critique.

THE PASSIVA(C)TION OF CERTAIN LIVING BEINGS

The difficulties raised by the market-oriented passiva(c)tion of nonhuman beings are just as great as those raised by the market-oriented passiva(c)tion of humans. The ongoing domestication of land and money have already proven striking illustrations.

The opposition between humans and nonhumans, however, is too simple to encompass all cases. Populations that are being commoditized are more different and more varied than is generally supposed, and the borders do not necessarily lie where one expects them. Nonhumans are neither easier nor more difficult to tame, to put to work, and to frame (*cadrer*) than humans. Some of them resist domestication, while others bend to it without effective resistance. On both sides, one can in fact observe a whole range of behavior. Among nonhumans it is, however, no doubt living beings that raise the most difficult problems, even if, as the chemical entity with which I will start proves, common nonhuman, nonliving entities can already cause considerable headaches.

Chemical industries throughout their existence and their enormous growth have confronted the difficulties of framing the entities with which they flood the market. Some steps of their market-oriented passiva(c)tion are not particularly problematic. Chemical engineering is preoccupied only with organizing the production of molecules or combinations of molecules with their nexus of associations, which are easily detached from everything that contributes to producing and qualifying them. What a distillation column collects is, as the name indications, successfully disentangled. The distillate, thanks to chemical knowledge and technology, can continue its career without its origins and its biography weighing directly on the actions that it will enable: whether it is extracted from oil shale or passed through the hands of engineers working for multinational companies does not have direct consequences on the services it is able to offer.

Although the detachment of these chemical beings, however complex it may be, is not out of reach, the same cannot be said of the task of managing their behavior once they exit the plants and begin their autonomous lives. Substances and chemical products are goods whose quasi-natural propensity is to react, to enter into new combinations, to catalyze, to migrate, to transform themselves or embed themselves, to pollute, and these actions are not entirely predictable or subject to discipline. The lead that the oil industry uses to improve fuel performance endlessly contaminates the planet, and plastic is colonizing the oceans. By making available substances that have duly been detached and are easy to alienate, but are still very active, the chemical industry constantly runs the risk of losing control over them, of no longer being able to ensure the delicate balance between autonomy, which remains within the framework set out for these substances, and recurrent slippages, which overflow the framework. This is no doubt why the chemical sector has such a hard time constructing a moral image for itself. The beings on which it works and that it puts into circulation are hard to educate properly.[104] Despite all the precautions taken or incompletely taken, they provoke disorder. This ambivalence is due to their very being, which is riven by uncertainties that can be considered ontological.

The commodification process becomes even more problematic as one moves from chemicals into the world of living beings. Indeed, if we consider only the careers of so-called inert entities and their instrumental uses, we would miss the new actions and novel outlets that have opened up around living entities. The living, whether human or nonhuman, has the huge advantage of being creative, good at multitasking, adaptive, evolving, even if, like money, it has the frightening drawback of being more difficult to maintain within a framework. The stakes are such that the coming decades may well become a time when the passiva(c)tion of the living processes becomes more intense. This is a necessary prelude to their commodification.

The living reproduces itself, develops, and evolves, permanent cellular regeneration being a condition for all these characteristics. How can one make such beings available without paralyzing their capacity to *make others act* and to provoke new courses of action, at least for a moment, in those who become attached to them? There is no reason to think that what has been possible for the human being cannot be achieved with less complicated living beings or even with assemblages of machines and human beings such as those offered by service providers.

Indeed, as far as animals are concerned, we are not starting from scratch. The most extreme and perhaps also the oldest form of their passiva(c)tion is the one that, by stripping or denying them of their condition as living beings, transforms them into food for humans. Over the course of time, this project has constantly become organized and more complex, forming a long chain of activities that take place in different sites and that mobilize a wide range of know-how, techniques, and organizations. Through successive stages, it leads a cow or a sheep frolicking in a green pasture or bored to tears in an industrial stable to lie quietly, in the form of leg of lamb, sirloin steak, or tripe *à la mode de Caen*, waiting for a client who will let himself be tempted enough to pull out his wallet before savoring them at home. The operations involved in disentangling are well known: begin by reducing the animal to a quasi-automaton in industrial stables that have openings organized for it to be able to contemplate the milieu from which it has been torn, calm it when taking it out of its factory, and then, sometimes using the services of an animal decoy, a sort of collaborating double agent in man's service to lead the way (and which will be spared in order for it to repeat this ignominious task), lead the animal to the truck, slaughter it, skin it, gut it, put aside the spinal column and "risky" offal to end up with half carcasses or quartered ones. Then the muscles must be separated to remove the membrane, superficial fat, and connected bones. Finally, the pieces must be put into groups based on types of muscle and vacuum packed. Thus requalified as meat ready to be cut, made into pieces, and perhaps put into plastic containers for retail sale, the animal is finally ready to enter into new courses of action, such as a thoughtfully organized birthday dinner for grandma, who will enthuse over how tender the roast beef is or how skilled the butcher. What is fascinating about this story, a long-running story that helped populate the planet with domestic animals, is that this process has evolved continuously, as though nothing were ever to be taken for granted. The contents of supply and demand are constantly reworked and readjusted, the same problem always requiring a solution: disentangling the good, detaching it, and profiling it so that it can easily enter into more and more singular courses of action.[105]

At the same time, in parallel to human beings, tamed and domesticated animals have been gradually put to task and transformed into workforce—for instance, to provide milk or as pack animals—that could be involved in market

THE PROCESS OF MAKING GOODS MOBILE AND ALIENABLE

135

transactions. Millions of horses and mules sold to the military died on the battlefield during the Great War.[106] It used to be that one rented the services of ox teams. Servicing by bulls is still for sale. More and more dogs trained to lead the blind will be sold, as will capuchin monkeys who can assist muscular dystrophy patients with daily tasks, thus entering into competition with human caregivers. When the very programming mechanisms of life are targeted, as is the case with biotechnologies that act on its most intimate dynamics, there seems to be no limit to the ways living beings can be put to work. There are, however, innumerable difficulties, since domestication and the controls it requires always raise daunting problems and often raise numerous objections.

A striking illustration of the complexity of these market-oriented passiva(c)tion processes is provided by the genetically modified organisms (GMOs) that are invading the food and health care industries (plants and seeds, therapeutic genes, tissues, cells and organs, and so on). For each of these beings, a compromise must be found; it is difficult to strike, since what makes them of interest is their capacity to act and react, while their commodification is possible only if these qualities are limited to some extent, domesticated, made predictable, and if the capacity inherent in life to overflow set frameworks can be brought under control.

There are numerous examples of this evolution and the devices it requires, if only to ensure that the sanitary and environmental effects of the commercialized products are under control.[107] I will simply mention the telling case of plant seeds. These are indeed living organisms in the very ordinary sense of the term, since they are capable of reproducing themselves. Reproduction generally brings modifications (either deliberately or spontaneously), and these modifications, even if they are very useful for selection operations, have the serious drawback that they sometimes make the seeds so unpredictable that their transformation into commodities becomes problematic. To get around this difficulty, the (regulatory) notion of plant variety was introduced.[108] A variety is defined by the homogeneity of the plants considered and by the stability of their characteristics over reproductive cycles. Obtaining these properties, which requires a lot of work and which is sanctioned by institutional recognition, provides a perfect illustration of the process involved in the passiva(c)tion of goods. Once they are put into circulation, the seeds continue to act, as indeed they must, since it is asked of them that they produce new harvests. Nothing attaches them any longer either to those who produced them or to the conditions of their production; they live their own existence autonomously while behaving predictably. They are available to enter market transactions. This device is all the more original and efficient because having been created and stabilized (that is to say, duly passiva(c)ted), the variety is made available to farmers who are authorized to engage it in crossbreeding and selection operations in order to give rise to new varieties that will in turn be passiva(c)ted. Life is thus given the chance to exercise its creative force in a slow and controlled way. At the same time, some of life's states are temporarily frozen so as to make it possible to establish temporarily stable market agencements.

Manufacturing such varieties is not simple. Considerable investments were required to obtain them and ensure their sustainability while leaving room for the creative process to begin anew. This has taken numerous experiments, both in laboratories and in open fields. It required developing regulations and then negotiating to have them accepted, setting up surveillance mechanisms and conservation arrangements. Persistence has paid off. These efforts have been crowned by the legally sanctioned certificate of plant variety protection (Certificat d'Obtention Végétale, COV). It defines and imposes plant qualities that allow them to be recognized as varieties and prepares them to become goods . . . ready for the market.

And yet even as it seemed that a durable solution had been found to the problem of plant passiva(c)tion, the delicate equilibrium on which it was based was upset by scientists and engineers. The living never cease to be a surprise. Until recently, the selectors, whether they started their work with known varieties or not, were not supposed to add anything to the abundant mechanisms through which nature crossbreeds and selects species. If they wanted to transform the seeds into commercial goods, their ambition and competence did not extend beyond organizing the process wisely, channeling it so as to ensure the stability of the species obtained. With the development of transgenic techniques, selectors no longer simply organize natural processes intelligently. They intervene directly in the genome in order to create plants that are, for example, able to repel the attacks of certain insects, resist the aggressions of powerful herbicides, withstand drought, or manufacture molecules with therapeutic uses. The entity thus transformed can make appear and make possible in a sudden rapid way unprecedented courses of action; therein lies its interest. The increased activation of the plant is, of course, an advantage, but it is also the source of weaknesses. The seed of a genetically modified plant, because it is the result of suspending the mechanisms of natural selection, represents a leap into the unknown. It becomes a suspicious object. Having been obtained by novel means, the new entity inevitably generates problems of control and mastery for which there are no ready-made solutions.[109] The uncertainty as to the consequences that may result for the environment and for health reach their zenith: the seed becomes the object of concern.

Passiva(c)tion, elegantly obtained in the case of varieties whose stability and homogeneity was almost certainly ensured, becomes a constantly renewed formidable challenge. It raises a whole host of novel problems that it is far from simple to solve: how can one ensure that the modifications that have been introduced on purpose, forcing nature, will not provoke unexpected effects and collateral damage? How can they be identified and prevented? At what point does experimentation give way to perfectly predictable and well-framed production? Can one even still assert that there is a clear demarcation between these two phases? Is it not the case that exploitation is actually experimentation on a large scale? Seed passiva(c)tion is not only a real scientific and technical conundrum; it is also becoming a serious political preoccupation. Seeds can sow doubt and concern. Passiva(c)tion activities, which used to be invisible and ignored, are now in the limelight and at the heart of market activities and public debates. Controversies are in full swing, and consensus is elusive. GMPs (genetically modified plants) are problem beings that will probably never grow out of their adolescent crisis.

What goes for plant genomes also goes for human genomes; what goes for plant transgenesis also goes for gene therapy. Take the case of a genetic disease called X-linked severe combined immunodeficiency (X-SCID), which results from the malfunction of a single gene. It condemns affected newborns to living in a maximally isolated sterile environment, an artificial bubble, in order to avoid infections—hence the name bubble boy disease. Having identified the responsible gene, researchers decided to replace it with a gene drug. The latter is inserted, outside the organism (*ex vivo*), into the patient's cells via a viral vector of the retrovirus type. This vector allows the gene to penetrate the cell and insert itself into the genome; the missing protein is thus produced in the children. Once this step has been accomplished, the corrected cells, which are the origin of the elements responsible for the immune system defenses (T lymphocytes), are reinjected into the patient. The first vector chosen for this task by Alain Fischer was a retrovirus that seemed to fit the bill perfectly. In trials, it turned out not to. Although it was efficient in most cases, reliably playing its part as a vector and simple transport mechanism, it induced leukemia in certain babies because it took the liberty of introducing itself near one of the genes that fosters cancers. It turned out that the virus more or less handles its job, but that like all living entities, it sometimes happens to do something other than what it is told to do, triggering unacceptable actions.

To regain control of the virus's passiva(c)tion, the scientific community decided to research and modify the vector so as to control it more efficiently and make it safer. The size of the new institute leading the fight against genetic diseases gives some sense of the order of magnitude of the work and investments that were required to manage to discipline these recalcitrant entities. It includes more than four hundred and fifty researchers who follow cohorts of patients (more than eighteen thousand) from childhood through adulthood, combining cutting-edge biological research and clinical procedures. In order to align the treatments and manage them so they can in fine be subject to commercial transactions, the vectors have to be selected and pass(act)ivated in such a way as to limit the range of actions possible for them to those of faithful, predictable conveyors that ensure that their package, the gene drug, arrives at the predicted site and that, once arrived, it does its job properly. This logistical requirement applies everywhere. It has been at the heart of medicine for a while, but it becomes ever more pressing and hard to satisfy when treatments, as is increasingly the case, rest on the alignment and the activation of long chains of living beings who have to continue to live their lives while also remaining within a set and predictable framework without untimely overflowing. Pass(act)ivating the retrovirus and the gene-drug requires, as is the case of any entity whose vocation is to become a commodity, their careful disentanglement. For instance, in certain therapeutic strategies, the chosen retrovirus is one that in its "wild" state is responsible for AIDS: its functions, therefore, had to be meticulously deactivated. These genetic or cellular therapies reveal the operations of disentanglement and reentanglement in a pure form, high-lighting the scale and scope of the problems that must be solved in order for the two operations to be successful.

The example of genetic therapies is particularly striking, but what is called biomedicine is rife with such situations and configurations. The therapies' targets are less and less local and discrete entities such as cells, or genes that are separate and (relatively) independent of one another and more and more complex biological processes, putting into play a multitude of entities and interactions (they are described as cascading reactions) whose malfunction is responsible for the pathology in question. The effects of the interventions imagined to deal with these are very difficult to anticipate. Adjusting them requires incessant back-and-forth between the lab and the hospital bed. It depends on the patient's personality and leads to singularizing constantly evolving treatments, treatments that never really move out of the experimental phase. The idea of ontological uncertainty that I evoked earlier applies perfectly to these treatments, just as it applies to transgenic plants or certain chemical molecules. Passiva(c)tion aims to make a profit from all of them while trying to manage them through a framework.

This example taken from medicine, more specifically, biomedicine, resonates with service activities. As Jean Gadrey showed, services can be described as systems that mobilize simultaneously and in varying proportions nonhuman entities (generally called technical entities, but that can be, as in medicine, nonhuman living beings such as retroviruses) and human beings in order to accomplish certain courses of action that, if the service proves of good quality, are successfully led to term.[110] The rental car offer allows me to go from Paris to Marseille to take care of my elderly ailing mother and to visit the Mucem museum; the offer of IT consulting allows a company to set up a cost-accounting system to track how its costs evolve; the offer of music streaming allows an adolescent to listen to his favorite singer and to revel in the pleasure of hearing his inimitable voice yet again. From this perspective, a service is not different from traditional material goods: if a user decides to buy a computer, a frozen pizza, or a subscription to Spotify, it is because each of these goods authorizes him to realize certain actions he prizes (surfing the internet, quelling his hunger, or letting himself stream his favorite songs). The only difference is that the good generally boils down to a material assemblage, whereas the service involves a complex arrangement combining human beings and technical entities. Services and the actions that they offer, promise, allow, and enable are harder to stabilize and control, notably because that requires making sure that the humans (or the nonhuman living beings in the case of biomedicine) involved do not take (too much) initiative.[111] Reducing the part of humans and/or Taylorizing their activities are the two most common strategies. These strategies cannot, however, solve all the passiva(c)tion problems for services because pushed to their extreme, they threaten quality and efficiency. Through gradual adjustments, service design must find a compromise between too much and too little discipline so as to tap living beings' capacities for improvising and adapting while protecting themselves from derailing, the acts of resistance or even sabotage, of which they are also capable.[112] Making an inventory of the different strategies deployed is one research aim for those interested in market agencements. It would no doubt show the growing importance of computer devices that enable controls without hampering initiative too much or that are designed to guide robots and their algorithms within frameworks.[113]

The scope and the nature of ontological uncertainties surrounding goods involved in commercial transactions are at the heart of concerns and problems that their framing provokes. Yet as we have already examined, we must never forget that other sources of concerns and questions connected to the attribution and transfer of property rights graft onto these uncertainties and complicate the picture. A passiva(c)ted and detached good does not automatically become a commodity. To claim commercial status, the passiva(c)tion must also be compatible with the attribution of property rights and their transfer.

SOME FINAL REMARKS ON OVERCOMING TRIALS OF STRENGTH IN PASSIVA(C)TION

The transformation of any sort of entity into a passiva(c)ted good is a long process that must fulfill a precise and demanding set of specifications. This process has not yet been given all the attention it deserves, no doubt because the structural model of the interface market so present in the implicit representations of commercial activities tends to suggest that it lies outside markets in the strict sense and that it interferes only very marginally with the way markets work.[114]

This chapter has taken a different point of view. All of these activities are at the heart of *market agencements* because the very possibility of commercial transactions depends on them. They take the form of a sequence of operations that constitute a series of mandatory steps. That is why it is relevant to talk of framing (*cadrage*) and to add that its success is never guaranteed.

A first way of showing the importance of a phenomenon is to give it a name. I suggested we speak of market *passiva(c)tion* to refer to the framing without which no market could exist. Having recognized its importance, the ambition of this chapter was to begin exploring this process by proposing first elements of analysis.

In anthropology, some studies have drawn attention to the mechanisms that by affecting and transforming the goods themselves prepare them to become commodities. From their perspective, the notion of *disentanglement* already appeared central. Any entity whatsoever is caught up in a web of sociotechnical associations, relations that constitute it, some of which must be undone for it to be put into circulation. If it is not to be condemned to endless wanderings, the entity must then reassociate with the one who takes hold of it. However, this double movement, without which a thing would be condemned to immobility, can take very different forms, depending on whether the anticipated outcome is a gift or a commercial transaction. In the first case, the presence of the one who puts it into circulation (and thus becomes its donor) is maintained, and the thing continues to be a part of him in some way, whereas in the second, the thing is rendered independent of the one who becomes its seller. I use the word "detachment" to refer to this particular mode of disentangling.

The possible reassociation of the good to an agent (its buyer) depends on its capacity to act and to make act, which enables it to be involved in courses of action undertaken by the buyer. However, this *reentanglement* will be successful only if the good's capacity to act is both real and framed. If this were not the case, the good would rapidly involve a number of agents not party to the (bilateral) transaction in unpredictable and uncontrolled ways; the latter could rapidly be led to contest the content or terms of the transaction. We can agree to call this particular mode of reassociating goods "reattachment"; we can, therefore, speak of processes of detachment and reattachment.

For the transformation to be successfully completed, the set of specifications that frame the transformation of things into commodities requires that a last step be taken: the permutation of property rights in return for monetary compensation. We saw that to identify those rights, to attribute them (first to the developers/producers), and then to transfer them, one has to be able to distinguish between the actions concerning the good and those aiming at its associated milieu. If the detachment is done according to this requirement—that is to say, if the interfaces are developed in such a way as to ensure the good's controlled dissociation from its milieu while maintaining relations between the two, then the good's passiva(c)tion is successful, and it can henceforth be sold and bought: in this case, one can speak of *market-oriented passiva(c)tion*.

The mere description of the sequence of operations necessary for market-oriented passiva(c)tion shows that this metamorphosis is far from straightforward. Its success can remain uncertain because of its complexity and the often massive and coordinated investments it requires. Not least among the difficulties is implementing the series of transformations and translations that make goods transferable, autonomous, predictable, detachable, followed by the possible support of property rights. Each case is singular, raises particular difficulties, and calls for specific solutions. Amazon's data, lands, money, and financial products, labor forces, the wild plant become certified variety—these do not go through the same transformations and do not require the same investments. Not only are the imagined solutions unique—they are also provisional, fragile, and always contestable. Each good offers solutions or resists in its own way.

I have compiled a table to indicate how certain categories of goods, over the course of the long story of their commercial domestication, revealed their relative aptitudes for transforming into commodities. I would ask the reader to indulge me by considering the following attempt at a schematic summary of what has been said in the preceding pages. This presentation, to be discussed and enriched, is simply provided to give some idea what such a table might look like. Bear in mind that the qualification of the different dispositions, as they appear in the table, can be read as a summary of the series of trials of strength each entity has overcome over its history.

	Disposition for acting by itself	Disposition for provoking courses of action	Disposition for being framed	Disposition for being detached	Disposition for being alienated
Chemical Entities	+ +	+ +	−	+ +	+ +
Human Labor	+	+ +	− −	−	−
Land	O	+ +	+	−	−
Money and Financial Products	+	+ +	− −	+ +	+ +
Nonhuman Living Beings	+	+ +	−	−	−

Sketch of a table: At the end of successive trials, things acquire dispositions from having been passiva(c)ted.

As with all of the framings we will review in the following chapters, market-oriented passiva(c)tion provokes resistances, alternative initiatives that act as so many forces pushing for the reorganization and reconfiguration of activities. We could easily give an inventory of these. I will come back to this in Chapter 7. For the moment, we can simply evoke as illustrations the innumerable conflicts, protests, and struggles provoked in the last century by the overflowings of the chemical industry.[115] Or in the same register, consider the objections to instituting a market for carbon emissions quotas, which, according to some, endorses the right to liberate (to disentangle) carbon buried in the earth's crust and then to detach it from those who liberated it, when it should have been left in the earth with no property rights attached to it at all. Or think of the many ongoing struggles generated by the passiva(c)tion of human labor. As for disentangling living beings other than humans, this has caused increasing worries, resulting in the recent evolution of the law and new constraints implied for the market-oriented passiva(c)tion of animals or plants. The distinction between domestic animals (such as cows, dogs, and cats), liminal animals (such as storks, squirrels, or voles), and wild animals (such as wolves or boars) might lead to the recognition of different rights, depending on how the animals participate in collective life and in particular on the relationships of dependence in which they hold us and we hold them.[116] Similarly, new conceptions of plant life invoke scientific authorities that highlight the complex networks and subtle interactions that plants develop among each other and that disentanglement practices imperil.[117] To touch one of these beings is to intervene in the web of connections it depends on and to activate the resistances they carry. These concerns amplify, as we have seen, with the conception of genetically modified plants and the break with their milieu that it provokes.[118] In all these cases, including the booming activities associated with datafication,[119] the question raised is the one so well identified by Thomas, namely, that of the possibility and viability, of disentanglement with detachment.

However, no doubt the most striking are the escalating worries connected to the increasing financialization of the economy—that is to say, the commodification of money. Money is accused of corrupting and depersonalizing human relationships. That is no doubt why there are more and more initiatives that aim to frame and fragment the instrumental functions of money so that it becomes neither too liquid nor too viscous. In the face of all the overflowings of money that is too liquid, real monetary insurgency is developing, to pick up on the suggestive expression through which Frédéric Lordon and André Orléan characterize the repeated insurrection of private money against state money.[120] The deindexation that affects exchange rates and makes exchanges more difficult, recourse to foreign currencies so as to escape national monetary constraints, freeing inflation, and debt restructuring are some of the strategies for effecting a greater separation between the means of payment and store-of-value functions. The attempts (often aborted!) to standardize financial products in order to introduce viscosity in speculative operations and the generalization of participatory financing platforms specializing in credits and loans should also be mentioned. These devices (would) contribute to multiplying the currencies whose functions and modes of circulation are or would be tightly regulated. The struggles have never been as intense and violent between specialized and universal currencies as in today's turbulent world.[121]

In conversations about those famous fictitious commodities, as in the realm of health care and the environment, where the controversies concerning commodification are particularly lively and intense, what is at stake is the crucial question of disentangling and of detachment. The answers do not preexist; they are not known ahead of time; they are generally multiple and contradictory and are decided after experiments and trials that test the solidity of connections and the will to undo or consolidate, them.

The clash at the heart of market agencements between forces mobilized to ensure the success of disentanglement and detachment and the forces opposed to that appears most clearly in the ecological controversies that, through the references they make to nature, provide repeated occasions to redefine the place of the market. For example, costly, complex investigations are undertaken in order to decide on reparations or compensation; over the course of investigations that become a sort of coming-of-age adventure, the actors discover how and why they were affected by the catastrophe that struck them. Let us follow Marion Fourcade in her remarkable comparative analysis of French and American oil spills.[122] At the end of their collective investigation following the spill of the *Amoco Cadiz* off the coasts of Brittany, residents reached a nonnegotiable conclusion. It is because they are attached to a nature, which is itself attached to them and from which they do not wish to detach, that the damage affects the whole of their world, a complex world in which every element depends on every other and in which it would be vain to attempt to separate the population of the shoreline from the nature that makes them live and that they make live. In the United States, the disentangling is easier because, as Fourcade shows concerning the spill from the *Exxon Valdez*, the disentangling is largely already realized and institutionalized—nature is separate from society and kept at a distance from the public; as a result, detachment becomes possible, even if it requires considerable effort. For the Americans, financial compensation can be legitimate reparation for the damage, whereas for the Bretons, the only imaginable reparation would be one that took as its task to weave back together the dense web of relations that the oil spill distended, those between their community and nature. Fourcade makes perfectly clear that on the French side, the collective investigation shows that the Bretons are profoundly attached to their environment and that no compensation can wash away the outrage. On the American side, with the help of economic science, people come to terms with the idea that the damage can be erased by monetary compensation, since the interests and the fate of the human communities can be detached from those of nature. Granted, in this example there is no *good* involved, only *harm*. However, when the question as to their transformation into commodities comes around, the same goes for goods and harms: what opposes their change of status is the refusal to advance in the project of detaching and reattaching. The Bretons refuse to link the oil spill to a list of identifiable effects that concern only them and for which they would ask for monetary compensation. What the investigation concluded was that the oil spill affects them *and* their associated milieu; it is not possible to distinguish between the two. One can, of course, invoke ethical or moral convictions or worldviews or ideologies to explain whether actors move into market action or refuse to do so. Doing so, however, leads to ignoring or minimizing the importance of the work in relation to which successfully refusing is only a result. If goods are processes, and not platforms, the work involved aims at manufacturing associations; its stakes are detachment and reattachment.

Different places, different times, similar problems. The debate over oil spills, even if different, echoes another debate, mentioned above, that took place in Australia. The question there, that of the commercializing of Aboriginal lands, was the following: Were the Aboriginals owners of the lands over which they moved, going from one place to another without settling or putting up fences? In the eyes of Western doctrines, the answer was obviously "no." The Aboriginals were not settled; they did not cultivate their lands, they did not divide them. The lands were, in a sense, empty entities, pure space-time. Legal experts speak in such cases of *terra nullius*; as is said of the wild boar that roams the scrubland, ignoring fences and barbed wire, it is *res nullius*, a thing without a master.

But why in the world did the Aboriginals not divide their lands? The answer has been given a thousand times. In their eyes, the world is different from what it has become for us. It cannot be reduced to a simple surface or a simple volume with almost geometrical characteristics. In their eyes, the world is only permanent creations and recreations. Populated with people, animals, plants, ritual sites, ancestors, constantly put into movement, living, as it were, it cannot be separated, disentangled, detached from humans. The land does not belong to agents. It is rather the people who belong to the land, engaged in relationships of crossed possession, and not in unilateral property relations.

As he recalls this story, John Law adds that one cannot reduce the tension to a mere opposition between diverging visions, for this position only reinforces the hypothesis that what exists is a single world, considered from several angles.[123] Law further states that whenever one talks of beliefs, conceptions, visions, even if it is to recognize their legitimacy, one is likewise granting that a unique outside world exists and that all people can do is change their way of looking at that world and interpreting it. I wholeheartedly agree with John Law's perspective, which invites us to reject this solution.

As we have begun to see, the process of market-oriented passiva(c)tion involves detailed material operations. The inquiries that passiva(c)tion provokes and the trials that it encounters demand real and continuous labor to format and frame. Depending on the forces that are present, these attempts can always lead in a number of different directions and will result in the establishment of outcomes that must be recognized as substantially different worlds.

If one wishes to act upon markets, the target is not world visions. The target is the devices that frame the markets.

CHAPTER THREE

Agencies and Their Qualculative Equipment

In this chapter, I will explore the following question: How do agents go about producing the judgments and making the calculations that allow them to introduce order into the universe of goods and to effectively participate in the passiva(c)tion process?[1]

Market passiva(c)tion and the transformations in goods it implies is not an end in itself. As the word "good" indicates, pass(act)ivated objects or things, qualified and requalified, must, in the end, have a value in the eyes of agents who must then decide whether or not to pay a price in order to gain their possession. However, for agents to be in a position to appreciate how the goods on offer can contribute to their own activities and to engage in the work of evaluation, they must have the skills that allow them to introduce an order into the universe of the goods that surrounds them.

As we saw in the preceding chapter, goods go through different stages of elaboration. A car begins its existence as a set of plans and ends it as a heap of scrap. Between those two moments, the car takes on a thousand different forms. It also meddles in the career of other goods with linked destinies. The universe of a good whose qualification is in the making is a chaotic web of changing relationships between entities that are themselves in flux. The complexity is on par with a website situated among billions of others in the World Wide Web or a species connected through millions of others to planet Earth. Wherever I go, whether I am wandering through my apartment, surfing the internet, or browsing in a mall, I stumble across beings that have been commoditized. If I were not in a position to make distinctions, if I were not helped to introduce a certain minimal order into all of this by separating images and sounds with my eyes and ears, by touching and stroking the material to appreciate the texture with my hands, by analyzing smells with my nose, and by classifying with my brain, then how could I contemplate attaching myself to any of them? All the possible differences lie in front of me. How can I grasp them, put them into words, make them exist, and share them? If I were not able to accomplish these elementary operations, the process of the passiva(c)tion of goods would come to a grinding halt. There would be nothing left but undifferentiated chaos.

Drawing from the solutions suggested by sociology and economics, I will introduce the idea of a *qualculative* agency as the active force of ordering the world of goods. A qualculative agency is a collective entity that has equipment and instruments at its disposal that will assist in the task of ordering by establishing lists, identifying similarities and differences, and producing comparisons and hierarchies between goods. This equipment, which combines both numerical calculations and qualitative appreciations (hence the neologism), is not akin to mere instrumentation, whose only use would be to amplify human capacities without modifying them. The equipment actively participates in the constitution of classifications and the shaping of rankings. It represents an active and productive force that contributes to goods' transformations over the entire course of passiva(c)tion by qualifying and requalifying them. That is why qualculative agencies can be described as distributed agencies, and not simply as capacities possessed by discrete individuals. Furthermore, as several detailed examples we will cover demonstrate, as a result of the wide variations in the qualculating power that different arrangements can provide, as well as differences in their implementation, there is a great inequality between qualculative agencies. The commercial world is profoundly marked by power relations and domination anchored in invisible infrastructures and expressed in the nature and characteristics of goods as they are framed. By qualculating for and with us, invisible infrastructures decide, in part, our differential relationships to the material world in which we live.

THERE ARE A MULTITUDE OF AGENTS WITH DIFFERENT EQUIPMENT

As we saw, the functioning of interface markets requires a structural divide between objectified goods endowed with their own properties and human agents who, on this objective basis, and because they are capable of judgment and calculation, can appreciate the goods' qualities. In interface markets, the agents are inherently equipped as human beings, ready to activate, that is to say, identify, the goods—to characterize them, classify them, compare them, and establish a hierarchy. There is no question of where agents come from and how they came to be where they are with the skills and powers of calculation they have. Strictly speaking, just as the model treats the process of passiva(c)-tion as external to commercial activity, it also externalizes how agents become formatted such that they are capable of evaluating and making decisions. The interface market is ostensibly established and developed in a world populated by agents with well-defined identities and competencies.

In the most extreme representations, the lack of consideration for the processes that produce agents leads to two simplifications. The first concerns the skills attributed to agents. These skills are essentially cognitive (they involve the capacity to classify and calculate), and in the most basic models, they are entirely embodied within the person. The second simplification is a strict limitation of the list of agents considered to be strategic in the description and functioning of commercial activities. The agents taken into account are sellers and clients whose positions may switch, as in the case of financial markets. The face-off between these two groups is taken to be the crucial event during which the qualities of goods are evaluated and decided.

This double simplification very quickly turns out to be untenable as soon as one takes an interest in agents operating in concrete markets. Not only are the types of agents involved in commercial activities numerous and profoundly different from one another—the roles they play are not limited to those of matching supply and demand. Furthermore, some agents are heavily endowed with specialized equipment without which they could not operate in the marketplace. The point for us here is therefore to reach a more realistic description of these complex processes.

I will begin by drawing upon a set of empirically grounded studies that have enriched an overly caricatured picture of how markets operate. Granted, these studies do not go so far as to challenge the basic hypothesis that there is a radical separation between the universe of platform goods and the universe of evaluating agents. They do, however, convincingly show that agents can only rarely be reduced to their bare somatic resources: they are always equipped with extrasomatic prostheses. Moreover, they also show that the list of agents who take part in the struggle for goods' qualification is generally long and includes heterogeneous agents with very different profiles. These two findings—that agents are always equipped and that agents are also differentiated—is the foundation of the notion of qualculative agency.

ENRICHING OUR DESCRIPTION OF AGENTS AND THEIR EQUIPMENT

Economists and sociologists have already largely abandoned the idea that agents, reduced to their own somatic and cognitive resources, are able to complete evaluation operations in a satisfying way.[2] Little by little, the *homo economicus* of yesterday's textbooks, that slightly autistic being preoccupied only with his own preferences or states of mind, is slowly moving off the spectrum.

Economists have been driven by a double realization. On the one hand, in recent studies, the image of an agent who simply observes prices, focuses inward, and pays only marginal attention to the actions of other agents in making decisions has given way to more complex representations. An economic agent's eyes are not only fixed on prices. They are open to the environment. Being a strategist himself, he tries to anticipate and take into account the strategies other agents are developing; sometimes he chooses straightforward confrontation, and in other cases, he prefers cooperation. He no longer hesitates to get involved in relations with others, the relations that game theory tries to describe. In a certain sense, *homo economicus* is becoming social. When he calculates, he takes other agents' calculations into account.

The other significant advance of so-called "orthodox" economic theory is to reconsider the role of information. The information that agents need to make decisions must be rendered explicit, be put into circulation, and made accessible. In order to make a decision, to undertake a purchase or put something up for sale, an agent needs to know and evaluate the good's characteristics. Sometimes he can do so directly, but very often, notably in the case of services, the evaluation can be made only once the transaction is completed.[3] In order to reduce the uncertainties surrounding transactions, a whole set of devices and procedures aimed at characterizing and guaranteeing the qualities of the good on offer and generally backed by governments has been imagined.

Among them, one can cite the most common ones, such as systems of "appellations contrôlées," the name for specific markers of geographic origin within France,[4] technical norms, legal classifications, labels, or certifications. That is why socioeconomic theories have given ever more importance to the different tools that make it possible to describe products' qualities and to ensure that the description is correct. Of course, there is no way of eliminating all possible uncertainties, especially since some of them constitute precisely the most interesting aspect of the good on offer. For instance, when I used to buy a ticket for the Easter bullfight in Nîmes, I had at my disposal all the information on the bulls' provenance, the past performances of the bullfighters, and the weather forecasts, which assured me that I would, indeed, attend an event called a bullfight. But I did not demand to know ahead of time whether Paquirri would earn two ears and the tail! With all sporting events, part of the pleasure of the show is in the uncertainty.[5]

The existence of such devices, the fact that they are more and more numerous and sophisticated and that they are used more and more systematically, underlines the limits of economic agents' competence. Left alone, a consumer would be incapable of doing what these various tools accomplish. It turns out that economic agents are dependent beings with handicaps and cognitive deficiencies.[6] Although people are perpetually engaged in a complex world of transactions, they are able to carry out only quasi-mechanical classification and ranking operations.

Thanks to economists, the list of instruments that assist agents is now fairly well known. (Sociologists have also made some contributions, to which I will return.) The list includes everything that enables information to be extracted and produced and everything involved in collecting, analyzing, combining, synthesizing, and circulating information. Besides the aforementioned labels, brands, standards, or appellations contrôlées, other devices include manuals, guides, specialized journals, catalogs, trade fairs, private or public demonstrations—everything that makes it possible to know a little more about the goods and to move ahead in making explicit what their qualities are. To these traditional devices, one should add the different electronic tools (databases, mathematical algorithms) to which agents delegate complex evaluation tasks and whose role is particularly important in markets such as financial markets. It is no longer possible to consider agents as isolated individuals. If one wants to give an account of the evaluation work they do, one has to include the entire range of extrasomatic resources to which they constantly appeal in order to put together a description of goods.

Other studies at the intersection between economics and cognitive science have further insisted on the intrinsically limited character of agents' rationality. Finding exhaustive and accessible information is no longer the problem. The issue is more fundamental and addresses the very nature of the calculations and evaluations of which the agents are capable, whatever the quality of their extrasomatic equipment. The activities of the human spirit, by their very nature, are embedded in procedures, routines, or rules of thumb that have been gradually elaborated over the course of history and that have proven their efficacy and relevance through successive rounds of trial and error. Something we can be pretty sure of—and this is already a lot—is that these routines work. They end up calculating and evaluating on the agents' behalf, and agents will follow them unthinkingly, dedicating whatever calculating faculties they may have, if any, to enriching these routines, rather than to challenging them.

Let's consider how projects are evaluated in a cutting-edge company that allocates significant research-and-development capacities to perfecting and qualifying new products. Since the beginning of the twentieth century, companies have striven to elaborate and formulate rules to guide their choices and nourish their decisions, whether by simply consulting experts to identify technical barriers or by exploring market possibilities. These rules, which are the result of informal practices (exchanges with colleagues, collecting sales data), have been progressively expanded, made both more explicit and more formal, leading to procedures and devices that are, today, excessively complex. In a pharmaceutical company, the definition of a research program goes through a series of evaluations, mobilizing a gigantic amount of commercial, medical, and financial data and appealing to battalions of experts and calculation instruments that compare, classify, and grade the molecules. These different devices continue to rely on implicit hypotheses that set their limits. Numerous studies show that the sterility afflicting a good part of the pharmaceutical industry for the moment can be traced precisely to its inability to break out of evaluation frameworks that privilege certain product profiles over other modes of qualification.[7]

One of the objectives of so-called behavioral economics is to analyze the different mechanisms that lead agents, whether individual or collective, not to question the behaviors they adopt and to remain in some way prisoners of their behavior. Behavioral economics stresses the empirical study of observable decision mechanisms and in particular the analysis of cognitive "biases."[8] One might say that neoclassical economics describes economic agents as they should be and deduces that from what equipment they must have. In contrast, behavioral economics describes them precisely as they are, with their inextricable mix of reason and emotion, cold calculation and burning passions, somatic and extrasomatic resources. This is why behavioral economics emphasizes the part that can be played by certain technical devices, which are designed to draw the agent back to reason and calculation when they engage in an activity that might deflect him from those virtues. For instance, a light or sound signal might warn a building occupant that he is moving to a different price grid for electricity and incite him to adapt his behavior to take advantage of this position. Thus conceived, material devices are not supposed to modify agents' cognitive processes: they are simply *nudging* them to make the right choice without changing their modes of reasoning.[9] They do, however, produce a new conception of the agent, of technology, and of the relation between the two. Technology is not considered as a mere extension of the human body and brain, an extension like a hammer used to drive in a nail that would amplify existing faculties and skills without altering them. Rather, the technology plays a specific, active role that only it can play. It goes to the heart of the action, deflects it, acts on its content, and (perhaps) subjects it to a transformation that is not only quantitative, but also qualitative. A nudge that reorients your behavior has nothing in common with a hammer driving in a nail.

Whether or not, thanks to the numerous informational devices that assist them, agents have at hand the relevant information, they can get carried away by their instincts, by their routines, or simply by courses of action in which they are caught up and that catch them. When this happens, a signal can remind them of what they end up forgetting, despite all their aids—namely, that more reasonable behavior is possible and that another course of action might be more in their favor. Despite prostheses, calculating capacities can fall by the wayside or be poorly directed unless awakened and redirected. Nudging is a continuation of advice; it is prescription by other means. You are nudged whenever your Apple Watch signals that you've been sitting too long, reminds you of a meeting, or informs you to start cooking for your dinner guests. Nudging invades daily life.

Sociology takes the opposite point of departure. Unlike most economists, sociologists consider that calculation is rare and awkward or even ineffective and impossible. A first way of relativizing the importance of calculation without denying the agent all capacity to choose is to underline the importance of values or norms that frame and regulate reasoning and behavior. There is no denying that agents confront lists of options or establish rankings to group these options and compare them to make hierarchies and express preferences. Yes, agents really do calculate. However, they are also equally constituted as calculated objects by other agents because the framework that delimits and organizes the operations they carry out partly escapes them. Do they really establish the lists they use? Do they really establish all the groups and rankings? Do they really define their preferences alone? Obviously not! In its most traditional versions, sociology considers individual calculation impossible, or rather, that it is mostly determined by *social* mechanisms that are beyond the agent's control. Agents are acted on more than they act. This is why so many sociologists prefer the term "agent," which is passive, to the term "actor," which is active. Choices are mostly influenced by an agent's class or networks or by the cultural models and the dispositions that have shaped the agent's behaviors.

Just as economic theory became progressively interested in the cognitive capacities of agents, going so far as to include the cognitive prostheses agents endow themselves with in the analysis, sociology has likewise striven to put together a more precise representation of the ways calculating skills are distributed between the agents and the world that surrounds them. The solutions of the two disciplines are somewhat different. Whereas economic theory often maintains a normative concern and considers that certain forms of market organization and decision formatting are more efficient or more desirable than others, sociology prefers to concentrate on the analysis of existing mechanisms and devices, thus focusing on the world as it is, and not as it should be.

A first set of studies from the sociological perspective converges with those of economists. The evaluations led by agents and the decisions that follow owe a great deal to cognitive prostheses that collect and analyze information in the agents' stead. For example, fine-wine markets and art markets have become canonical objects of study in economic sociology for their ability to magnify the use of prostheses in evaluating goods. In this context, we discover AOCs (appellations d'origine contrôlée), terroirs, fairs, specialized guides and journals, tasting clubs, critic groups, enlightened amateurs, salons, experts and catalogues raisonnés, training sessions, comparative tests, labels, and norms. Producers and consumers, sellers and clients, never find themselves face to face, limited to their own somatic resources, empty-handed, with nothing in their pockets. When it comes time to make a decision, a whole crowd of parties is present to assist, prompting agents on what they should think, say, and write, like Captain Daniel's ghost to Mrs. Muir.[10]

All of the assistance may not be physically present at the moment of a transaction, but the protagonists of commercial exchange have always read and heard, listened to, learned, and incorporated the analyses, advice, and rankings offered by multiple human and nonhuman assistants. Notably, they have in mind recommendations made by friends or family members with whom they share social media and in whom they trust. They are immersed in a social and cultural milieu that forged their categories and their references and in a world of devices that constantly produce and offer evaluations, make calculation tools available, and contribute to shaping their judgment and choices. The universe of prostheses offering help and support to agents patiently described by sociology and anthropology is much richer than the inventories drawn up by economists. Beyond material prostheses such as catalogs, tests, warnings, and so on, there are social prostheses such as social interactions or social media, all of which can be heavily technical. This suggests we should think in terms of sociocognitive prostheses in order to recognize all the equipment and assistance at the agent's disposal for calculating, judging, and reaching decisions, some of which ends up being incorporated into their very being.[11]

By complicating the description of agents and highlighting the importance of prostheses and incorporation mechanisms, as well as the contribution of social and cultural milieus, the types of studies I am drawing upon here have pushed beyond the stylized simplification of interface markets, with its tendency to limit the list of economic agents to the emblematic figures of the supplier-seller and the consumer-buyer. Take the nature of the firm, long regarded as a black box, a mere individual agent whose interests are expressed and defended by shareholders. Drawing on industrial history and organization studies, economists and sociologists have gradually opened the firm up, documenting the diversity of groups and interests that take part in defining the objectives and activities, as well as the diversity of their logics of action and forms of evaluation. These studies have come to recognize that industrial researchers, sales representatives, production engineers, consumers, financial and regulatory institutions, and government authorities, to name a few, do not necessarily share the same vision. Yet all of them strive to be involved in one way or another in decision making, even if they are not always able to impose their point of view.

As a way of describing companies and the mechanisms through which to evaluate their activities—and, hence the qualification of the goods they commercialize—studies have very convincingly demonstrated that there are inequalities in the struggle between shareholders and stakeholders to impose certain criteria. It often comes down to a sterile, head-on clash between those whose priority is profit and those who call for responsibility. Sociology has further contributed to this movement, not only by refining analysis of the different stakeholders involved in companies' lives, but especially, as we saw previously, by showing the infinite variety of the world of intermediaries and the devices that participate in the evaluation of goods.

Given the interest of evolutionary economics in innovation processes, it has provided the broadest opening to approaching and acknowledging the network of agents that intervene in formatting market transactions. All the actors who participate in the process of designing and commercializing new products, from academic research to the distribution circuits, via patent offices, banks and intermediate financiers, insurance and reinsurance companies, administrations and governments, user associations, or religious authorities, are by rights included in the analysis, since each takes part in one way or another, at one point or another, in the process of evaluating, qualifying, and selecting goods; this is the process that leads, in the end, to the singularization of exchanges. In certain sectors, such as health care, the innovation networks that bring all these agents together and coordinate their activities, grow and grow more complex in direct proportion to the intensity of the personalization in the treatments that are offered.

The analysis of market agencements can be based only on empirical investigations and observations. It capitalizes on the results accumulated by prior studies. First, it recognizes that the evaluation of process goods never operates on a single site, nor can it be narrowly located in time (that is, it is not confined to one marketing agency or to the ultimate site of the commercial transaction): the qualification of goods and their evaluation is a process that unfolds in space and time. Second, the analysis recognizes that the numerous agents involved in these evaluations have tools and equipment: they mobilize sociocognitive prostheses that differ from one agent to another, but are also likely to be somewhat standardized. Third, it takes into consideration the collective, organized, and conflictual aspect of the evaluation processes that fix the characteristics of the goods that become objects of market transactions.

Each of these three contributions is essential. Their principal limit is that they do not completely break with the model of interface markets, even if they do provide powerful backing for the introduction of market agencements as an alternative model. Granted, the acknowledgment of these points describes agents' skills in an infinitely more realistic way. Granted, a throng of new agents appears that no one had thought to take into account, which enlarges the perimeter of activities we consider commercial. What remains unchanged, however, is the idea that there is a radical and insurmountable separation between the world of the agents who classify, establish hierarchies, calculate, judge, and evaluate and the world of the goods that are the passive stakes of these operations. The interaction between the two universes is hard to think of and to analyze, given that the idea of the separation persists.

In contrast, the dynamic of market agencements is entirely structured around the interactions between agents and goods. The qualification and evaluation work conducted by agents transforms the goods and in return calls for further evaluation. Yes, goods do participate, in their own way, in their own classification and in the classification of agents! That has been shown by a considerable body of work on distributed cognition and action whose importance continues to escape economic sociology and economics. Unfortunately, the lessons from science and technology studies (STS) have yet to be widely understood. Sociotechnical prostheses do not simply provide tools for the action; insofar as they participate in it, they shape and structure it from the inside.

One way to reexpress the insights of STS is to introduce the notion of qualculative agency. To begin, I will say a word about the work of evaluation itself.

What is it made up of? And how do sociocognitive prostheses contribute to it?

FROM CALCULATION TO QUALCULATION

To show you the significance of qualculation, I must first review some basic ideas about calculation operations and their significance.[12] Conflating calculation with math will be the source of many misinterpretations of my model.

Calculating does not necessarily mean carrying out mathematical or even numerical operations. This observation is in line with common sense. I can point to numerous examples in which agents seek to obtain results through calculations that do not involve numbers. One speaks, for instance, of strategic calculation to explain a political or economic decision. In French, you might hear an adolescent use this expression to declare they have no interest in one of their mates: "Je ne le calcule pas," I do not take him into my calculations. This means there is no interest in the other person—they don't count. The expression "to calculate" in relation to a person means to judge someone to be a worthy friend. To refrain from "calculating" is to act as though they did not exist.

In its most generally accepted meaning, calculation designates the fundamental operation through which one evaluates and orders the world before embarking on an action. It begins when distinctions between things or states of the world are established; it continues through imagining courses of action associated with those things or states; and it reaches its (possible) end when the predictable consequences of these different courses of action are appraised.

My definition of calculation is deliberately wide, but not unique. I seek to avoid the oppositional distinction between judgment and calculation in conventional, but narrower definitions. To calculate is to identify entities, gather them in lists, group them in classes, then set up a hierarchy among these entities in each class, and then, possibly, but not necessarily, to introduce from this ordinal classification called ranking cardinal numbers (grades or scores) and, with them, possible quantitative relationships. For example, one might assert that such-and-such an entity is twice or half as interesting, efficient, or competitive as some other entity. The diversity of the forms of operations associated with each of these steps explains why calculation can fulfill the requirements for mathematical or algorithmic formulations, or it can be close to intuition, to a judgment based on authority, to a decision in an uncertain situation, or finally, it can be tantamount to giving up on deciding. With this definition and the sequence of different operations implied, the oppositional divide between qualitative judgment and numerical quantitative calculation disappears.[13] In order to underline the importance of this continuum between judgment and calculation, I have adopted a neologism suggested by sociologist Franck Cochoy: "qualculation" combines qualitative and quantitative dimensions in variable proportions.[14]

Qualculation has the huge advantage of dissipating the mysterious halo around the irruption of numbers in economic activities and in particular in commercial activities. There is no discontinuous leap from the universe of sensation to that of words and values and then to that of numbers. The movement leading to classification, ranking, ordinal numbers, then cardinal numbers is continuous. In fact, what close observation reveals is that the transition from one to the other is not made in one go. At each step, numbers and words are combined, all the more easily because figures and numbers are also words that, used as such, can have a plurality of meanings that are not abandoned when they are used as figures in ranking or comparing operations.

To confront the enigma of passing from qualitative to quantitative, anthropology has developed frames of analysis quite similar to the ones I am using. For instance, in her work on commercial relations in West Africa, Jane Guyer suggests distinguishing among three steps in the process of evaluating goods.[15] The first establishes a nominal scale, the second an ordinal scale, and the third a numerical scale.[16]

Guyer explains that an unnamed good cannot exist. The word or the set of words designating a good serve to differentiate it from other goods and to position it with respect to them. Naming is a form of distinction whose meanings are enriched by the usage of words and the semantic networks that connect them, more or less directly, to other words. Guyer refers to a nominal scale the way one speaks of a scale of colors, because the denomination of goods constitutes a primary form of evaluation, one that might be qualified as relational. Indeed, this is what economists draw attention to when they evoke the idea that goods are more or less substitutable, closer to or further from one another, and have values and therefore prices that are interdependent. According to economists, the notion of cross elasticity provides a precise measure of this interdependence.[17] Furthermore, nominal scales, like numerical and ordinal scales, have the advantage of being both objects that are made available to the agent and objects agents use and manipulate. This observation holds in any Western supermarket. If I hesitate between a package of pasta and a package of rice, whatever the similarities and differences I postulate between the two, I cannot completely abstract myself from a set of conventions, significations, relations, and discourses carried by language and the use of words. Furthermore, I am not the only one to raise the question of whether they can be substituted for one another or whether they differ: this is attested to by the decision the supermarket manager makes to put the two packages next to each other on the shelf. From the point of view of an anthropologist interested as much in the process of evaluation as in its result, it is crucial to recognize this double dimension of denomination. It is both individual and collective.

The work of evaluating cannot escape from the (gentle) tyranny of words and the relations they suggest. It is also dependent on operations that institute hierarchies that involve the implementation of what Guyer calls "ordinal scales," whose function is to institute a series of gradations between goods. These scales allow for the use of comparatives and superlatives. Guyer provides numerous examples throughout her book, showing how the value of goods can be categorized in relation to qualities such as religiosity, robustness, beauty, originality, or efficiency. What she observes in African societies can easily be transposed to Western societies, where ordinal scales abound and are permanently renewed, as the rise of indicators of all sorts attests.

Ordinal scales are precursors of cardinal numbers that bring us closer to the universe of figures and numeration systems, in sum, to what Guyer calls "numerical scales." These scales give a quantitative dimension to evaluation; they prepare the commercial transaction and the commensurability it implies. As Guyer confirms, there is no reason to oppose judgment and calculation, since one moves to the other in a gradual and inclusive way. And of course, it is meaningless to circumscribe any opposition between rational or so-called prerational mentalities. From the Ivy League schools and les Grandes Écoles, from Auvergne to West Africa, we all qualculate.

A "cognitive" vision of calculation, limited to operations involving identification, classification, ranking, and measure conveniently blurs the overly clear distinction between pure judgment and pure calculation. However, the material dimension of the calculation, and hence the link between evaluation activities and the processes whereby goods are transformed through singular-ization—that is, the very activities that are at the heart of commercial activities, would escape analysis. Linguist Émile Benveniste examined the vocabulary of counting in Latin sources, confirming that there is indeed an intimate link between calculating and judging or estimating.[18] Moreover, he also underlined a remarkable characteristic of this vocabulary: there is explicit reference to a material movement of detachment (cutting) and of reattachment (leading to a result). This accent on material displacement in calculation, which also appears in the notion of centers of calculation developed by Bruno Latour, helps us sketch a very general definition that feeds into the definition of *qualcul*.

Calculation is a three-step process that leads to the constitution of a space of calculation:

a) First, in order to be calculated, the entities under consideration must be identified and detached: a finite number of entities are displaced and disposed in a unique space. We have to imagine this space of calculation in a very broad sense: it is the "count" itself, but also by extension the surface onto which the entities to be calculated are displaced (literally or by proxy) and then compared and manipulated according to a common operational principle. It is import-ant to remember how varied these spaces of calculation can be. A bill, a chess-board, a factory, a negotiating screen, a trading floor, a software spreadsheet, a compensating clearinghouse, a computer disk, a supermarket shopping cart (*caddie*, in French) and the "caddytainer," a device on wheels with deep buck-ets for moving goods from storage to display shelves that we'll come back to in Chapter 6:[19] all of these spaces can be analyzed as spaces, but each one pro-vides a different form of calculation.

b) Once isolated, the entities under consideration (that is, "taken into account") have to be connected through associations made between them. That is to say, they are subject to manipulations and transformations, always in a very material sense. (Think of movements left or right, up or down, super-positions or juxtapositions.) These procedures can easily be recognized when a rule is applied in a mathematical sense or a mechanical calculator is used: as Charles Babbage described on his famous visit to a clearinghouse in the City in London, a calculation-based economy is precisely an economy of displace-ments. However, these displacements are also at work in less mechanical situ-ations. A financial arbitrageur materially associates two entities by displaying their results in the same window on his screen (for instance, an index and the corresponding derivative, or a company and its target in the case of a possible takeover). Insurers do this, too, when they construct actuarial tables and the associated charts, as do user groups when they make lists of products to compare their qualities.

c) A third movement is needed to get to the end of a calculation: extracting a result. The calculation has to bring out a new entity that makes it possible to establish a certain order among different configurations. In its simplest form, this result can be an alternative, or an ordered list that enables the ranking of choices, or a score or a sum that can be compared with other scores or sums. This entity is, in turn, the result of manipulations in the calculation space. To invoke the Latin *summa*, it *summarizes* the units taken into account. This entity is not new in the sense of coming out of nowhere: it is prefigured by the arrangements described above. However, it must be susceptible to being displaced, to leaving the calculation space and circulating in places such as guides, magazines, software, and so on, without transporting the calculation apparatus with it.

Without these material operations and the devices they require, no judgment, no calculation would be possible.[20] The configurations of qualculation are diverse. The order book for an electronic stock exchange is a qualculation space (literally in computer memory) where buy and sell orders get ordered according to a set of priority rules. Traders can observe the order book on their screens, explore its depths, and intervene in several ways. The execution price is qualculated by an algorithm. A supermarket can also be considered as a qualculation device. The products it presents are limited in number and have been extracted from their production and distribution contexts. Placed on different shelves, which are themselves situated in different sections of the store, supermarket products are associated, grouped, or dispersed in different ways. References and markings must allow consumers to classify products and make selections, choices (that are in part) qualculated by the intense activity of marketing professionals. To say that the supermarket is a qualculation space is not to say the space is homogeneous or that the qualculation is clear-cut and simple. The supermarket is in fact a space within which other qualculation devices abound: packaging, shopping lists, shopping carts allowing prior choices to be assessed at a glance, cash registers assigning numbers, and so on.[21] Different devices cohabit, fit together, are complementary to one another, or on the contrary, cancel each other out.

One of the main advantages of this definition is that it connects the material and cognitive dimensions of qualculation. In other words, because it creates a space that allows for cognitive operations, qualculation cannot be carried through to an endpoint without mobilizing tools and equipment. The skills that agents must mobilize (identifying entities, constituting lists, establishing classifications, making hierarchies, writing reports) require specific extrasomatic resources. The set of specifications that prostheses and equipment must satisfy is strictly determined by the nature and purpose of the qualculative operations.

Qualculation is first and foremost a material activity, even and especially when it is described as mental. This fact explains why evaluation operations cannot be dissociated from the process through which goods are qualified and requalified. Defined in this way, a process of evaluation does not remain external to the goods to which it is applied. The operations transform the goods. Each new qualculation, going through operations that identify, detach, put into relation, rank, and digitalize, requires a series of material and equipped operations based on dissociations, displacements, and reassociations. By that very fact, it modifies the entities on which it operates and restructures the spaces in which they move. This applies in a spectacular way to marketing activities, as we saw in the examples given to illustrate qualculation, but in an even more obvious and striking way, it applies to design and manufacture, and further downstream, to activities associated with usages. The process of transformation through evaluation acts on goods by reconfiguring the relations into which they enter and continues uninterrupted throughout the good's career. Some measure of the scope and depth of transformation can be found by comparing the qualities of a good when it initially emerges in a still inchoate form from an R&D lab and the qualities that disappear with it when it is finally incinerated as waste.

To offer a better grasp of the profound nature of the space-time described by his theory of relativity, Einstein imagined an experiment in which he rode a light wave. What could one learn and what could one see, he asked, if one were a proton, moving at the speed of light? Inspired by this thought experiment, one could decide to follow some cells from the moment they are manipulated in a petri dish by a researcher until their injection into a sick body. Those cells, after an itinerary from manipulation to manipulation, qualification to requalification, will allow a sick organ to regain some of its functions. Anyone given the chance to join these cells in their wanderings and reconfigurations would move with them from site to site, observing the evaluation operations different agents implement along the way. They would have a live experience of the successive transformations that result. Live observation makes clear why it is incorrect to restrict the term "production" to the manufacturing phase. A good is produced progressively, over its whole lifespan. It is production that transforms a cell, initially pluripotent, into a complex treatment dedicated to repairing the myocardium. What is true of a reprogrammed and reconfigured cell is equally true of any other good. Production of a car begins in a design department or in conception software; it continues on the platform on which the prototype is made, then in the manufacturing unit of factories, and finally in the dealer's showroom. Production involves pushing an entity forward, displacing it from site to site while transforming and requalifying it in order to finally reach the bilateral transaction.

The term "qualculation" does not merely refer to the different material and cognitive, quantitative and qualitative operations through which properly equipped agents evaluate goods. It also refers to the fact that the evaluation, through its practical modalities, transforms and requalifies goods, fully participating in the process of their production. To evaluate is to qualculate; to qualculate is to requalify; to requalify is to produce.

You now know enough about evaluation as qualculation for me to introduce the notion of a *qualculative agency*.

QUALCULATIVE AGENCIES

As I have just defined them, qualculations are materially cumbersome and involve complicated operations. Because of this complexity, the forces required to implement and discipline them go well beyond the capacities of a human brain or body. Instances of evaluation are made up of assemblages, collectives composed of technical elements, algorithms, cooperating human beings, procedures, and more. To mark this collective and heterogeneous dimension of qualculation, I choose to speak of "agencies" and not "agents." Although the two words have differing etymologies, because of their homophony, the former is often substituted for the latter in usual usage. Like agents, an agency acts—it acts in a structuring and structured way. Like agents, an agency is capable of reflection, analysis, and strategic behavior, and like agents, it collects and makes collections, institutes differences, compares, classifies. An agency is capable of all that and therefore of qualculating because it is composed of a slew of human and nonhuman entities, both textual and material, that are solicited, that take initiatives, that cooperate to make it act. In a sense, the agency acts in the name of agents. This is easier to understand when the agency designates an explicitly collective entity, such as a company, an administration, a union, or a user group. It is also the case, however, when the agency works on behalf of an individual agent, such as a consumer, a trader, or a sales representative, who, as we will see, is heavily equipped and never acts or thinks alone.

Each agency has capacities for qualculation, skills that are at least in part singular and original. This does not preclude that agencies may have some similar equipment or that there be family resemblances between them. Monsanto is as different as possible from Toyota, but from the point of view of an American pension fund that is looking for the best investment and that has adopted appropriate tools, comparisons between the two giant multinationals are possible and can be qualculated! A consumer in South Korea and one in Germany do not qualculate in exactly the same way, yet they mobilize a great number of similar sociocognitive prostheses. Some are shared and stable, others evolve over time and are subject to constant bricolage. To grasp the diversity of qualculative agencies, one must therefore start with an analysis of their equipment and look into the modalities of their design, implementation, and dissemination.

Before jumping into the colorful world of agencies and their constitutive prostheses, I would like to reinforce an essential point I have already raised. A qualculative agency does not confront entities that are external to itself (that is, the goods in their different states). In qualculating, agencies intervene directly, through their equipment, to fashion the reality they evaluate. In sum, the equipped qualculation participates in instituting a reality that it contributes to making exist, and it makes obsolete the stark opposition between a subject who evaluates and an evaluated object.

To make this point very clear, let us return to the one piece of equipment that has profoundly shaped modern commercial activities and is at the heart of the form of market economy that is called capitalism. Not all markets are capitalist—it should be clear by now that this hypothesis guides my investigations. But those that are can be identified by their qualculative tools, and in particular because they mobilize an accounting tool: double-entry bookkeeping. Tell me how you qualculate, and I will tell you how much of a capitalist you are.

Max Weber devoted a significant part of his energies to answering a simple question: Why did capitalism develop in the West at the turn of the seventeenth and eighteenth centuries? His answer invokes two main and complementary factors. The first is the Protestant ethic. The second, which later gave rise to numerous studies, but is less well known, involves the invention and especially the widespread diffusion and implementation of double-entry bookkeeping. Double-entry bookkeeping is an accounting tool that ensures that all realized operations are doubly registered, once as credit and once as debit. It allows one to follow the value of the assets an agent accumulates and to measure what are now called returns on investment. In sum, capitalism, in order to develop as we know it, needed a spirit to guide it and a tool of control to keep it on course. The spirit was provided by religion, the control by the Venetian banks of the fifteenth century. The spirit orients the action, the tool checks that the sought-after results are obtained and can influence the action, should that prove necessary.

This linkage of the spirit and the tools of capitalism, which Weber implicitly refuses, is very suggestive. Yet it is laden with ambiguities, compatible with two opposite interpretations, each of which claims to explain why the agent is pushed to accumulate capital in view of drawing the highest possible revenue from it. According to the first interpretation, control of the operations is in the agent's hands: he is the pilot and the only pilot. Double-entry bookkeeping provides the tool he needs to implement his programs and check that he reaches his objectives. The spirit of capitalism that animates agents has at its disposal an instrument that allows it to check its own direction. The second interpretation defends the opposite thesis. Double-entry bookkeeping, by the simple fact of being used, imposes a logical, qualculative coherence on agents that goes well beyond what they would be capable of if left to their own devices. Without double-entry bookkeeping, no agent would be in a position to become a capitalist, attentive to accumulation and returns on investment. In one case, the tool is completely controlled; in the other, it relentlessly dictates its law.

Until recently, it was not possible to move beyond this opposition and the endless controversies surrounding double-entry bookkeeping. There are those who, following in Werner Sombart's steps, consider it to be the moving force of capitalism and others who assert that without the help of a true entrepreneurial spirit, rooted in mentalities, a mere accounting tool could not have led to the rise of capitalism. It is not the double accounting that calculates, they add, but rather the human agent, the entrepreneur who uses it. In one case, the agent does what the tool prescribes; in the other, he conceives of the tools that improve what he wants to do.

Studies devoted to accounting techniques and management tools over the last few decades provide a way out of this sterile controversy by showing that both theses are as false as they are true. An entrepreneur who calculates his profits and measures the accumulation of his capital does not use double-entry bookkeeping in order to make a more precise, rapid, and exact calculation, the idea of which would have preexisted the tool itself. Nor does he let himself be blindly led by the tool. It is the duo made up of the entrepreneur and the double-entry bookkeeping that conceives of the calculation and executes it. One might even say that double-entry bookkeeping, by the mere fact of its availability, suggests the calculation to the entrepreneur, who, in return, accepts the invitation and asks double-entry bookkeeping to make the calculation it offers while being ready also to modify the tool if the latter does not prove entirely satisfactory.[22] The relations between the elements of this duo, the agent and the double-entry bookkeeping, are complex. Each element suggests and stimulates the other. Double-entry bookkeeping does not measure an accumulation of capital that developed without it and to which it gives the instruments it needs. Rather—Weber says it explicitly—it contributes to establishing or instituting the very accumulation it measures: "Capital accounting," without which there would be no talk of accumulation, "is the valuation and verification of opportunities for profit and of the success of profit-making activity by means of a valuation of the total assets (goods and money) of the enterprise at the beginning of a profit-making venture, and the comparison of this with a similar valuation of the assets still present and newly acquired, at the end of the process." Weber adds that this capital account does not observe practices, but rather establishes what he calls lucrative activities: "An economic 'enterprise' [*Unternehmen*] is autonomous action capable of orientation to capital accounting. This orientation takes place by means of 'calculation'; ex-ante calculation of the probable risks and chances of profit, ex-post calculation for the verification of the actual profit or loss resulting."[23]

A capital account orients the action and makes the agent a potential capitalist, who, by endorsing the tool, becomes an acting capitalist.

As Ève Chiapello emphasizes, in order even to speak of accumulation and returns on capital, one must have at one's disposal the very notion of capital, which we now recognize is the result of identifiable operations established and described by accounting institutions. One must also be able to grasp and measure how it increases as it circulates and goes through metamorphoses.[24] It is not an exaggeration to say that the categories that serve to think markets, to shape and frame commercial activity, are linked to the existence of the duo made up by human agents and accounting "tools." This is true both of capitalist markets and of what are called "alternative" markets. In one case, there are capital accounts, in the other, accounting techniques that make things such as surplus production explicit, whose use can then be discussed by the parties involved.

The duo of agents and their tools, or, if you prefer, tools and their agents, is like a pair of dancers who make each other dance as they dance themselves, leading or following depending on the moment, in such a way as to improvise and compose a choreography that, to the spectator, looks as though a single spirit has inspired it; in the same way, one speaks of the spirit of capitalism to refer to the partnership between the entrepreneur and his accounts. Take away either of the dancers, and the dance, like capitalism, vanishes like a dream.

This adjustment between two partners, an adjustment that ensures that they dance a tango as much as the tango makes them dance, is the result of a long history. The same goes for capitalism. As Peter Miller and later Ève Chiapello explain, notions such as capital, salary, profit, or return on investment, which serve as reference points for entrepreneurial (capitalist) action, were elaborated over long periods and in close interaction with the accounting practices that inform them. This story is now quite well known. Luca Pacioli, a student of Leon Battista Alberti's, presents double-entry bookkeeping in its canonical form in 1494. By registering operations twice, it connects different accounts (debit/credit; liability/asset), presenting each of them on two juxtaposed pages so that one can see them at a single glance. This presentation (called "bilateral") makes it possible to determine how much different lines of activity participate in profit making and to track how the profit evolves. It took time to unify and standardize this accounting tool. For a long time, the debit and credit accounts continued to be presented sequentially, rather than being juxtaposed. In the middle of the sixteenth century, Fugger, the famous banking family, had still not adopted the complete system. It would therefore be an exaggeration to claim that behavior as varied as maximizing profit or managing partnerships is a mechanical consequence of double-entry bookkeeping: double-entry bookkeeping becomes a universal technique only in the nineteenth century. As with any innovation, the adjustment process between tools and dispositions was a process drawn out through different variations, setbacks, or sudden advances, fought over by both pioneers and opponents. Capitalism took form with and through its accounting tools over the course of this mutual process of apprenticeship. Each one reshaped the other simultaneously.[25]

An agent who calculates his profits and the increase in his assets is an agent who is equipped. The key point to remember, however, is that the equipment is not composed of neutral instruments. Return on investment no more preexists in the agent's mind than it exists objectively outside the agent. Return on investment is instituted by the calculations of an equipped agent, and its being instituted owes as much to the agent as to the equipment.

This finding has a general value. Qualculative agencies, the name I give to these qualculating duos, contribute significantly to instituting the realities they qualculate.[26] Market shares, a juicy market sector such as those industrial activities described by employees of the Boston Consulting Group as "cash cows," only take shape, can only be manipulated, and can only orient action, even as they are also the object of action through the marketing tools or the BCG studies that bring them into existence.[27] If you change the equipment, commercial practices undergo a deep transformation. Operations such as establishing lists, filling in Excel spreadsheets, setting up macros to multiply and add lines or columns, keeping books of accounts—all these put elements of material support into play. Their structuring power, however, goes much further. These operations are connected to a set of activities that are part of logistics in the traditional sense of the term and without which qualculations would be impossible. Manipulations in accounting correspond to operations and notions such as stock and storage, inventory and counting, shelf placement, packaging, or bar codes.

SOME EXAMPLES OF DIVERSE AGENCIES AND THEIR EQUIPMENT

Qualculative agencies associated with the manufacturing, marketing, and consumer activities on the forefront of the commercial scene are highly visible. They should not, however, lead us to forget all the other agencies, those working in the shadows, those that interface markets tend to relegate to the margins, but that are nevertheless at the heart of market agencements. These agencies may belong to the world of design, or to the world of users, or to any one of the intermediary spheres that contribute to the uninterrupted chain of successive requalifications of goods.

In this section, I would like to give some idea of just how diverse qualculative agencies are. First, I want to show that agencies are everywhere, profiling and classifying. I also want to highlight a number of unexplored terrains. Despite the efforts that have been made to delve into the universe of qualculative agencies, many sites, including strategic ones, have not yet been sufficiently studied. The idea that *there is no one best way to qualculate* commercial transactions optimally should emerge as we move through the section. This result will be essential to refresh the analysis of market efficiency. (See Chapter 8.)

To underline the dissemination of qualculative agencies and both their proliferation and the extraordinary expansion of their equipment, the simplest is to follow *scoring* practices. As we have seen, once lists of entities are established, once they have been put into relation with one another and ranked, any process of qualification may lead to quantitative estimates that transform ordinal numbers into cardinal ones. For mouthfeel or astringency, such and such a wine comes out ahead of some other wine, the first, for instance, being in the nth position, whereas the second is in $n+2$. Once the ordinal scale is established, there are a thousand ways to transform it into a series of ratios or numerical relations. In commercial activities, whether they concern wine or cars, *ranking* and *scoring* attest to the presence and activity of qualculating agencies. To give a realistic picture of the place and role of qualculating agencies in market agencements, one can therefore start by looking for these words and their synonyms.

Investigating the practices they refer to is the starting point of research.

These words are everywhere. Open to a random page of a consumer review such as the French magazine *Que choisir* and you will find a series of tables that compare articles that are defined by a certain set of qualities in such a way as to end up with rankings and scores following classical scoring techniques. Leafing through these pages, you may learn that ham is evaluated according to the quality of the meat, its salt, additives, microbiology, and organoleptic characteristics. A little farther on, you are given no fewer than thirty criteria for the qualculation of a steam cleaner, from the rate of steam to their working range or their average life span. In both cases, the various products evaluated are given scores ranging from 6 to 14. Wandering through the offices of any company's marketing department or any financial institution, one will find a parade of matrices and tables comparing products according to some criterion or other, establishing hierarchies, giving out scores, and deducing from those what actions should be given priority.[28]

The following examples do not claim to be exhaustive. They simply aim to suggest and illustrate the omnipresence of qualculating agencies and how diverse their skills are over the course of the passiva(c)tion process. For the most part, these agencies relate to market agencements' areas that are upstream of commercial transactions. In a later section devoted to power relations, I will try to correct for this asymmetry by focusing on the agencies on the consumption side of the process.

IN RESEARCH AND DEVELOPMENT

When I started my research career, at the beginning of the 1970s, it was not easy to persuade French companies to accept being studied by a sociologist who promised nothing in return. May '68 was fresh in everyone's memory, and no one had forgotten that the social sciences had played an active role in what were then called "the events." Thanks to Lucien Karpik, then director of the Centre de sociologie de l'innovation, and on the recommendation of Pierre Laffitte, then director of the École des Mines, I had an opportunity to be integrated in a large French industrial group that was present on all continents and a leader in its field. My only mission was to understand how innovation projects were conceived and carried out. I was free to move around as I pleased—the doors were wide open. The only concession asked of me was that I introduce myself not as a sociologist, but as an engineer-sociologist. Within a few weeks everyone in fact forgot that I was a sociologist. That did not bother me at all, especially since I had a diploma as "Ingénieur des mines" and a masters and higher degree in economics in my pocket!

After a few months, having visited the groups' different centers and research labs and having interviewed dozens of those who worked in the research, production, and marketing departments, I had acquired a solid understanding of the innovation projects under way. I was just a young engineer who seemed to have been given a vague evaluation assignment by the management. Without a doubt, this is why the director of R&D asked me to test a tool that had been recommended to him by a consulting firm. To be applied, this very simple instrument required that a list of the research and innovation projects be established. I quickly realized that my role was not so much to identify the projects as to constitute them from a scattered group of operations among which I was to try to find some coherence. Once this list was obtained...and approved...the following step involved imagining a set of criteria through which projects could be grouped in homogeneous categories. I was not terribly imaginative in the criteria I suggested for classifying projects: aims (knowledge acquisition, development, product innovation, process innovation, and so on), forms of organization (one or several centers involved, subcontracting to outside organizations), budget, and more.

The next step was to situate the projects in a hierarchy, to produce hierarchies not only within each class, but also between classes. The consulting company, which had made an inventory of practices in use in the industrial world, suggested using qualiquantitative formulas; I shamelessly adopted and adapted them. These formulas, which link a certain number of parameters such as the cost of a project, its duration, number of researchers involved, market share anticipated, and so on, also included a scientific appreciation in the form of a score from 1 to 5 on the basis of a few subcriteria. I had been told that this score should be taken very seriously because the long-term quality of the group's R&D depended on it. I therefore spent hours with the scientific director, an eminent scientist, and some of his colleagues, "grading" the scientific quality of projects. After many hours of investigation and interviews, I had in hand a table that presented all of the projects and their different scores.

When I finished this task, I had a confused feeling, sharpened by a touch of guilty conscience, that the result was arbitrary, that the ranking was non-sense—as engineers like to say, believing only their lab instruments, which spit out numbers that do not react to the experimenter's mood swings. Start the procedure all over again with the same projects, and you will end up with a completely different result! What reassured me at the time was that deep down, I was convinced that all the tables I had filled in would end up abandoned in a cupboard to the gnawing criticism of mice. I was convinced that the various interests and power relations would continue to determine the decisions concerning the funding of the projects. What I did not immediately understand, but realized when a few months later the director of R&D invited me to an executive committee meeting, was that the famous scientific score that had required so much work was going to make it possible to save some projects that would otherwise have completely disappeared, so far did they appear to be from the market! Of course, the tool had not abolished influence relations—the meeting gave me a chance to see just how violent they could be—but it did participate in their reconfiguration. A scientific director who can show a score that guarantees a project's contribution to the long-term future and to the company's reputation has a far greater chance of making himself heard.

Once my assignment was finished, I did what I should have done before I started. I rushed to the (numerous) books and reports on selection tools for industrial innovation projects. I realized that my work fell within a wider move to design and formalize qualculation tools for research and innovation activities. Like the one I had helped to design and set up, scrupulously following the instructions I had been given, all these tools have analogous characteristics: they establish lists of projects, group them into classes, give them a score in order to be able, in the end, to constitute what was beginning to be called a portfolio of R&D activities. The techniques for constituting projects and the procedures for classifying and grading vary from one method to another. However, as was easily verified, in all cases, by participating in their characterization, evaluation, and hierarchical ranking, these tools contributed to shaping and transforming the research and innovation activities themselves. Of course, these qualculating activities did not appear out of nowhere. In one way or another, often implicitly, they already existed, but the equipment they had was different, and it therefore oriented and shaped the activities

AGENCIES AND THEIR QUALCULATIVE EQUIPMENT

differently. The qualculative agency has been transformed by the systematic use of formalized tools and their gradual transformations. The scientific score has become less important, and with this modification of the qualculation tool, R&D has been massively reoriented toward more short-term projects or projects with a closer connection to markets as they can be anticipated,[29] redefining the *profiling* of research and the ways in which goods that will get as far as the market are qualified. Change the qualculation tool, transform the qualculative agency, and you get different goods.

What is particularly interesting in the case of R&D is the inverse relation between the evanescent nature of the activities to be evaluated and the arsenal of tools and instruments implemented to evaluate them. When entities are harder to identify, collect, group into homogeneous classes, compare, and rank, the heavier and more complex the equipment becomes. To give an image in a slightly different vocabulary from the one I am using here: uncertainties about the qualities of a good do not discourage qualculation; on the contrary they make it ever more necessary and more sophisticated.

IN START-UPS

As the passiva(c)tion process grows longer, an increasing number of agencies intervene in the process, providing plenty of illustrations that the more uncertain a good is, the more it requires qualculation and sophisticated equipment. Since the beginning of the 1970s, for instance, formalized qualculation equipment has intruded into all the activities involved in designing and developing goods. Designing equipment has become more difficult and more problematic because the way these activities are organized has changed profoundly over the last two decades. Big companies, which used to prefer doing their research internally, tend now to outsource it. This change is particularly noticeable in the health sector. "Big Pharma" companies such as Pfizer, GlaxoSmithKline, Novartis, or Sanofi take over developing and commercializing promising molecules while delegating the conception of such molecules to contract research organizations or very innovative small companies, biotech start-ups, which they reserve the right to buy out.[30]

The choice to outsource research makes qualculations devilishly complicated. On the one hand, there are the start-ups that do the initial development of molecules and vectors while these are still very far from constituting medical treatments and will require numerous qualifications, requalifications, and transformations before they can be prescribed by a general practitioner or a hospital and be covered by medical insurers. On the other hand, there are the Big Pharmas, seeking new molecules and ready for the long uphill battle to gain approval for commercialization, even if it is extremely expensive, because in the current economic system, it can provide huge returns. However, before deciding to take the plunge, the Big Pharma company has to have answers to some simple questions: Is there a chance that these molecules will lead to a profitable therapy? Will it be possible to replace the test subjects with real patients? Will the researchers be able to hand this over to doctors? In other words, how can the molecules be evaluated—that is to say, how can their current qualities be defined while anticipating their future qualities? How can one undertake to evaluate a molecule whose chances of success are often meager and whose commercial potential, expressed in sales revenues, will be known only a decade later, once it has gone through a complete cycle of transformations?

Rather than imagine a theoretical and abstract answer to these questions, Liliana Doganova went to the field to investigate.[31] She discovered the central role played by what the natives call "business models," not to be confused with "business plans." The business plan comes later, after the business model, once the qualities of the goods that are candidates for commercialization have been determined more precisely and it becomes possible to do market surveys, analyze the competition, estimate sales, and so on. The molecule that is still in the lab state is too uncertain, too unpredictable, to submit to those sorts of exercises. Yet that is not a reason to give up or hand things over to simple judgment or mere intuition. Of course, we already know that purely numerical calculation is impossible. Frank Knight was right: when the event or the entity to be calculated has no precedent, when it is unique and moreover is in a transitory state, a numerical calculation on the basis of objective or subjective probabilities cannot be made.[32] However, as the business model proves, qualculation is conceivable.

The only way to get started is to dismiss the supposed uniqueness of the molecule being considered and to seek out its fellow creatures by exploring databases or searching available memories. As Doganova and Marie Eyquem-Renault tell us, there is no more violent obsession than the one that impels agencies to identify similar goods when they are dealing with novel, singular beings that may seem unique, but that never arrive alone and isolated in a brand new world. Compare! That is the injunction. And to succeed in that requires unbridled imagination, endless investigations, testing relationships, consulting huge databases, summoning consultants and experts who have been living among such molecules for years. When the investigation is concluded, while the singularity of the molecule in question has been preserved (since that is where its value lies), it is no longer alone. With a little elbowing, it has been pushed into classifications, networks of chemical, biological, social, regulatory, and financial relations, and it is inscribed in rankings. Its capacities have been clarified, and it begins to inhabit a familiar world populated by beings that are expected to treat identified pathologies more or less well. As a consequence of those abilities, through good times and bad, probabilities can be associated with these molecules in ways that are neither purely subjective (because they are the result of lengthy ordering labor) nor purely objective (this ordering is hypothetical), but that do lead to rankings, ordinal scales, and with a little insistence, cardinal scales! One can thus compare estimations and chances, getting around the problem Knight correctly identified. And from this emerges a first version of a business model, subject of course to requalculation, whose only aim is not to calculate yields or returns on investment, but to show that value can be created; the business model can qualculate molecules in order to say to what extent, appropriately pass(act)ivated, they will be in a position to attach themselves to a sick, suffering body. To show how generalized this tool is and that the qualculation made by Big Pharmas and biotechs is not out of the ordinary, Doganova observes that the practices through which the relations and evaluations are construed can be analyzed with the same notions anthropologist Jane Guyer put forward to describe African markets: naming, listing, classifying, comparing, establishing hierarchies, and finally attributing scores. *Nihil novum sub sole*—there's nothing new under the sun. It is not that nothing new ever happens—this molecule is unique—but more simply, that nothing is so new that it cannot be qualculated by properly equipped agencies. The water Heraclitus watched flow is never the same, but it is always water.

IN FINANCIAL MARKETS

The qualculation tools used to evaluate goods that still have a long way to go before reaching the client for whom they are destined reach their greatest level of sophistication in the tools associated with the boom of financial markets. One could devote an entire book to financial agencies. I will limit myself here to a few of those imagined to evaluate companies and through them the goods these companies offer their clients.

How should a company be evaluated? The question is not new, and the answers are not obvious. One could move straight to considering the goods it sells and evaluating them by trying, for instance, to show what these goods do to reduce health inequality, facilitate access to essential services, and so on. The tools necessary for that type of qualculation are not inexistent, but no long investigation is required to see that they do not play an essential role in evaluating companies. The equipment that is used most corresponds to the growing influence of a form of qualculation that originates in the vision of markets imposed by a cohort of economists during the 1980s, the most prominent of whom was Milton Friedman. According to Friedman, a company's aim is to maximize its financial value—that is to say, its value for shareholders, or, to put it another way, the price that investors are ready to pay at any given instant in order to acquire shares. The qualculation tool is financial markets themselves, where stocks are continuously appraised as they are traded. Trading floors are the main qualculative agencies, and they dominate those who would wish to institute other modes of qualculation. Friedman's solution finally became the universal standard, just as, after many vicissitudes, the standard meter bar did in its time.

The hold this model has developed is the result of obstinate efforts, of which Marion Fourcade and Rakesh Khurana have described the main steps.[33] They have shown how a profession (economists) maneuvered to take over business schools, train generations of managers, control the specialized publications, and get the ear of the political and economic elites. In the end, a vast qualculative device was set up aligning managers' interests with those of shareholders through incentives such as stock options, theoretical tools such as the theory of agency, and the promotion of takeover strategies, which create a genuine market for the control of firms. Generations of consultants went out and taught companies to recenter their activities on the center of their trade, to avoid situations of conglomerates like the plague, because they confuse shareholders, and to launch mergers and acquisitions or LBOs—leveraged buy-outs.[34] All this went with the introduction of accounting tools and evaluation methods that made it possible to qualculate the decisions to be made and hence to determine the qualities of goods that should be developed.

In an editorial in *Le Monde* dated April 23, 2013, written shortly before his death, Jérôme Haas, who fought his whole life to show that accounting norms should be subjected to debate, underlined the limits of these tools and the choices they insidiously impose: "Behind the technicality" of these tools, he writes, we should learn to see that "societal choices" exist, whether these are "preference for the present or awareness of the long term"—that there is a "diversity of socioeconomic models."[35] He reminds us of Weber's lesson: "Tell me how you qualculate, and I will tell you what world you live in." Perhaps the lesson should be reversed: "Tell me what world you want to live in, and I will tell you how to qualculate."

There is a long history of the emergence and development of stock markets that gradually found the appropriate qualculation tools, leading up to the moment when it became possible to institute financial markets as the main qualculative agencies of company values and indirectly of commercial goods. In his study of the history of stock market equipment, Alex Preda showed how important the introduction of the ticker was. As of the end of the nineteenth century, it created new forms of qualculation and new ways of making decisions in financial markets.[36] In its original form, the ticker is a very simple material device that receives information sent out by the financial markets and transcribes stock values in the form of continuous curves, which make it possible to follow their variations over time. For these recordings to be possible, a whole sociotechnical infrastructure had to be imagined, from noting prices, to transmitting them through the telegraph networks, to the reception by tickers distributed in different places accessible to interested professionals. With the ticker, the prices of stocks sold in one or more markets could be known and compared in far-flung places in real time. This encouraged new practices of arbitrage and speculation. Visualizing the continuous evolution of prices furthermore allowed the development of techniques of graphic analysis and opened the way for finance to be mathematized.[37] The ticker did not just provide information. It constructed data that, given its format, produced specific effects by suggesting certain interpretations and certain types of decisions. A curve's shape was, indeed, interpreted as the result of aggregating a multitude of individual behavior patterns. Hence, since it was about behavior, it could suggest the hypothesis that there are underlying regularities. It made sense, then, to talk about the behavior of curves and, for instance, to imagine that one could expect reversals after certain episodes of continuous rise or fall or to consider that the existence of plateaus depended on a sequence of prior events readable in the curves. The curves, so it was thought, are signs of the existence of collective patterns of behavior and give access to the laws that govern them.

This equipment has become ever more sophisticated. Tickers still exist, but they are now in digital form, and they trace the variations of numerous financial products. Calculating curves is standard practice with the development of big data and software technology. A whole series of data-crunching and data-processing tools have been added to the infrastructure. On the trading floor of a modern investment bank, there are also negotiating automata, telephones, price analysis software, and more. All this qualculation equipment carries categories, or worldviews, as one used to say, ways of apprehending reality and action, returns on experience that frame how companies and the goods they develop are evaluated. The equipment is collective and distributed. It would make no sense to try dissociate it or distinguish it from the traders, analysts, or investors who will decide whether to buy at this or that price on the basis of the qualculations performed. They are incorporated into one other like the soul and the brain. They are qualculative agencies.

These qualculative agencies do not restrict themselves to numerical calculations, even in financial markets rife with numbers, even in the era of triumphant computers. Take the case studied by Daniel Beunza and Raghu Garud of the financial analysts in the beginning of the 2000s during the internet bubble.[38] New businesses are appearing. They are strange beings, firms that do not (yet) have any profits and constitute difficult problems for all the experts whose job is precisely to evaluate companies' potential. What should one think of early stage Amazon? How can this start-up, which looks like no other, be described? How can one set a price for the shares it emits or the services it promises? This case is particularly interesting because it highlights the fact that where numbers, calculations of investment profitability, and dividend expectations reign, there is no other possible strategy than qualculation.

Beunza and Garud show that in the case of Amazon, the big problem for financial analysts and investors was to know how to evaluate a company that was without precedent and whose qualities were still being elaborated. What they discovered will not come as a surprise to the reader. Financial analysts qualculate the market in same way as the Yorubas described by Guyer. They try to get a perspective on the singularity of the companies they analyze, not to eliminate or deny it (you don't kill the goose of the golden eggs), but to move forward in their qualification. To that end, they set out in search of similar cases, family resemblances, as Wittgenstein would have said, in order to produce classifications (naming) and classes (ranking) as preludes to scoring and numbering.

When Amazon was created, it initially dealt only in books. The question was whether it should be seen as a company comparable to classic bookstores, but with more powerful technology, or whether it should be put in the big family of companies born with the internet and digital technologies, companies whose essential quality was to introduce and test radically new forms of production, distribution, and consumption. Depending on the analyst, depending on how they conducted their investigations, the ways they defined the relevant traits and constructed resemblances, Amazon was profiled differently, as were the services it was supposed to provide. And depending on those choices, depending on the events that took place and were interpreted and analyzed, different modalities of qualculation were privileged. It is clear that at this stage of the analysis of market agencements, it is not a matter of determining whether or not the evaluations were correct, but rather simply of observing the qualculative practices, their diversity, and the tests to which they gave rise. As Beunza and Garud show, analyzing Amazon involved the identification, manipulation, and processing of large amounts of data, as well as the construction of classificatory frameworks and their analysis. Beunza and Garud do not study the impact of these qualculations on Amazon's decisions, but I would guess there was plenty. (For example, in another case study, Alexandra Ouroussoff has shown how the evaluations produced by rating agencies can lead companies toward decisions that are considered to be low risk, privileging strategies of horizontal concentration or vertical integration that allow companies to show that they are in a good position to manage the competition.)[39]

Friedman's narrow focus on the market and the share values it is supposed to calculate ignores the thousands of diverging qualculations supported by agencies that often disagree with one another. It would have been futile for Friedman to invoke the transitory nature of this situation, for him to assert that the strength of the market lies in the fact that it always finds the true value in the end. The true value is like Minerva's owl. It arrives once the losses and profits have been taken and once all of the qualculations have been made. The markets, because they are market agencements, live only in the transitory and know only the torment of processes.

I will return to the functioning of financial markets in Chapter 8.

IN REINSURANCE

I encourage the reader to fill in the picture I am painting by wandering through market agencements and exploring the different profiling and scoring practices, those of banks who define and qualify loans as a function of the evaluation of potential borrowers (identification, classification, ranking, hierarchies, and so on), normalizing agencies, rating agencies, international institutions, and more. Qualculative agencies are everywhere, and everywhere they take each other on, attempting to have their qualculation methods and tools prevail.[40] Out of these confrontations, goods emerge, fragile and unstable, their qualities having been fixed at least temporarily. These are singular goods, rendered comparable even as they evolve to adjust to their respective intended recipients.

Before moving on to the analysis of the power relations between agencies, I would like simply to mention one type of qualculating agency that plays a central part in contemporary capitalist markets and that gives a striking illustration of the way market agencements function.

Until recently, the reinsurance industry had barely been studied empirically. We now have the study produced by Paula Jarzabkowski and her colleagues concerning insurance against what is nicely called "acts of God," those "natural" catastrophes that, like earthquakes, tornadoes, cyclones, floods or fires, strike unexpectedly: "Nescitis diem neque horam"—"You do not know the day or hour."[41] The problem with these exceptional catastrophes, which provoke damages worth billions of dollars, is that each of them is unique—each provokes new effects. Insurance concerning these events is a challenge to understanding and reason. The scope of the damages is such that not only can a single insurer not guarantee them, but even when a pool of insurers is constituted, reinsurers have to be found to insure the insurers.

Jarzabkowski and her colleagues examine reinsurance practices in detail, with particular attention to how premiums were established. The result is fascinating. The qualculation instruments combine very sophisticated quantitative and numerical techniques, notably, statistical models that take into account considerable data of all sorts (lists of places that may be involved identified by zip code, each with its own social and geophysical characteristics, stories of remarkable events, the nature and quality of buildings, descriptions of the populations, exposure to damages and their possible costs as a function of types of catastrophes, and more). These models are partly common to the different insurers, but each adds to them and enriches them with in-house models and with particular and specific knowledge. When only very partial series are available, or even no series at all, qualiquantitative models are put together. In all cases, tables are used and filled with a series of rubrics identical to those of the statistical models, and the usual listing, regrouping, and scoring operations, based on collective work, lead to numerical evaluations. As in the case of the rating of R&D projects or therapeutic molecules, the more singular the events are, the more the work of comparing is long, complicated, and...necessary. The final construction is like buildings erected on quicksand, shored up with various reinforcements, grids, and crossed elements, each of which is fragile, but that, linked to one another, produce rigidity and robustness that, in the end, manage to rise and stand, at least for a while. The more unprecedented the act of God, the more bound up it is in a story that is uncertain, in Knight's terms, and the greater the obstinacy agencies show in qualculating.

The authors show how in all cases, whether or not centers of big data are available, qualculating communities of experts form, trying to reach agreement as to the results of the qualculation and hence the premiums; agreement is sought not only between insurers and insured, but also between insurers and reinsurers. Unlike markets for wines and works of art, here, there is no need to dream up inexpressible subjective realities such as quality or reputation to explain how evaluations and qualifications are made. Yet in all cases, whether it be wines, contemporary art pieces, acts of God, or research and innovation projects, following the evaluating agencies, describing their qualculative practices, the instruments they use, and the communities they form is enough to understand how, in the end, an event that is by its very nature unique and singular becomes qualculable, that is to say comparable, commensurable, and subject to being given a score. The good is then profiled to turn into a commodity that can become the object of a bilateral transaction and for which, as we will see in Chapter 6 on affixing a price, a price can be given.

In this section, I have mostly considered the qualculative equipment of agencies on the supply side. The agencies involved in consumption also have specialized qualculating capacities. In the next section, we will observe the power dynamics between different agencies, and I will demonstrate that consumption is not fully controlled by the supply side.

POWER DYNAMICS BETWEEN AGENCIES

The rapid overview of qualculative agencies at work in market agencements leads to two observations. The first highlights how many agencies intervene, the second how many modes of qualculation they develop. Agencies face off in attempts to impose their qualculations and thereby the qualification of commercial goods and their modes of passiva(c)tion.

No model of qualculation is inherently superior to any other. Superiority is achieved over the course of the many confrontations between agencies that put them to the test. Superiority is always temporary, because the list of involved agencies changes, and with it, the composition of their equipment and the modalities of their qualculations also change. The qualculative power of an agency is only relational. Its definition depends on the definition of the qualculation. Its power is all the greater if the agency is in a position to a) take a high (but finite) number of entities into account; b) explore a rich and varied set of relations between these entities so as to establish bases for comparison and end up with groups of entities that are considered similar; and c) elaborate competitive procedures and algorithms in order to rank these entities (ordinal numbering).

Market agencements constitute a space in which this qualculative confrontation can take place. The trade-off is that in these commercial arenas, certain agencies come to occupy dominant positions and to weigh heavily on the ways in which goods get qualified. Market agencements are not spaces in which agents are on an equal footing. Many agencies are without any means of qualculation and thus in very weak positions, dominated by agencies that qualculate their decisions for them and impose their mark on the design of the goods that are exchanged. The inequality and the relations of domination that structure market agencements are direct consequences of the unequal distribution of qualculation powers and thus of the asymmetries in levels of equipment.

Let us return to the supermarket and the emblematic encounter it organizes between the goods for sale and the shoppers. A whole slew of agencies preparing the transaction is part of the scene. Each has qualculative capacities it draws on to frame and realize the transaction. Consumers are never alone, never isolated. They are distributed. As we have seen, their evaluations involve brands and all sorts of precalculated information provided by the supermarket and its setup. These include packaging with data about the product's composition, its origin, its labels, but also the shelving and the shelf labels, the labyrinth of aisles that propose and impose certain groupings, proximity relationships, price and quality hierarchies. Evaluations include situations, like a demonstration where the client becomes like the pedestrians being captured by the street vendors of London—or information systems—like the guidepost in the wine section that points out the vintages. Prostheses, which are designed, set up, and tested by supply-side agencies, are instruments that equip consumers and take part in the constitution of their qualculative agency. They do not, however, come to the store unprepared and destitute. Before even going into the supermarket, shoppers make shopping lists and read magazines and online consumer guides to orient their evaluations. Sometimes they even have tested the goods they are buying or share evaluations with family and friends. Furthermore, they are part of prescriptive relationships that intensify their thought processes and actions. In other words, supermarket customers are at the heart of a qualculative device that quite obviously does not exactly belong to them. As this emblematic confrontation shows, qualculative agents cannot be described as distinctly equipped entities; that is to say, one cannot claim that the equipment and tools could be divided into as many distinct families as there are different groups of agents involved. Certainly, agents come to the store with their own equipment, depending on whether they are, say, consumers or market professionals. They nevertheless also share a metrological infrastructure on which they draw as needed, depending on the circumstances.

Granted, when customers amble around a supermarket, they are surrounded by multiple devices that assist them in qualifying, classifying, and making hierarchies of the goods on offer, but these devices have mainly been designed, tested, and implemented without their having been directly involved in their design: buyers evaluate goods, but they use calculation tools that have been more or less explicitly offered or even imposed. As they inspect the shelves, read labels, guides, or instruction manuals, the customer continues a calculation that was started and framed by qualification professionals. Shoppers qualculate heteronomously.

This notion of heteronomous qualculation is important. In commercial arenas, it would be exceptional to have a face-off between some agencies that qualculate and others that do not. Indeed, to make their qualculations, some agencies depend heavily on the equipment designed and implemented by the very agencies they are facing in the marketplace. It is as though in a chess game, one of the players gradually colonized his opponent's brain so that the latter, while continuing what he experienced as his game, ended up being played more than playing. A particularly striking example of this transition from an autonomous to a heteronomous position is the one Pierre Bourdieu studies in his remarkable analysis of the real-estate market.[42] He describes how the meeting between the seller and the potential buyer becomes a showdown in which the former tries to impose his own calculation tools on the latter, often successfully. The buyers arrive with a series of criteria for choosing an apartment: location, proximity to public transportation and schools, number of rooms, price, but in the end, they adopt the criteria proposed by the seller. After the meeting, the buyers adopt the tools the seller presented in order to optimize the managing of their budget and to evaluate the qualities of the properties being offered.

One of the strategies implemented to lead an agent to qualculate in a predictable way involves organizing experiments during which they are cut off from all other equipment. This strategy has long been in use in the food industry, as well as in sectors such as perfume, in which the goods are primarily addressed to senses with which a human body is "naturally" equipped in order to evaluate. How can a person be made into a mere nose, induced to evaluate fragrances on offer positively? How can a customer who buys a ready-made meal or sits down at a restaurant table be reduced to the association of sensations that lead him to a positive appreciation of the food served to him? To answer these questions, full-scale tests are organized in order to identify the agencements that get through to the bodies and minds of the people targeted by limiting mediations and by preventing recourse to other qualculative resources.[43]

With the development of the neurosciences, these strategies are poised to become frighteningly effective. Whereas work on sensations and their expression used to draw on a method close to bricolage, there is now, in a much bolder way, a real program to equip the brain. The challenge is to "cleanse" test consumers so they become essentially a brain that is hooked up, controllable, and concentrated on the qualculation of the sensations their bodies transmit in such a way that the qualculative chain (which has to recognize and score the qualities of the goods submitted to it) is not distracted by fortuitous emotions, fits of conscience, or collateral misgivings that might make the qualculation deviate in unpredictable directions.

Many university laboratories are working hard to find a viable answer to this challenge; before imagining the devices that would reproduce what happens in the lab on commercial sites, they seek to determine the conditions under which neurosubjects emerge. Yes, it does seem possible to achieve this short circuit by choosing the right prostheses. After all, we have all seen the emblematic success of Stephen Hawking, affected by that terrible disease amyotrophic lateral sclerosis, which paralyzes the body while leaving cerebral capacities intact.[44] This pathology achieves what all neuromarketing experts are striving for—that is to say, the creation of a chimera, or a cyborg, if you prefer, made of a human brain hooked up to equipment that feels with and for him, that thinks with and for him, and that floods him with data that he has only to appropriate in order to finish the qualculation. Neurosciences are trying to extend what Stephen Hawking (with all his human and nonhuman assistants) showed—namely, that a human person reduced to a brain can be enhanced into an agency that qualculates the laws of physics and the universe.[45] Since their aim is much more modest, there is no reason to think they will not succeed. It is not a matter of equipping a qualculative agency to reconcile quantum physics with general relativity, but more simply and prosaically of designing an agency that, given a choice between two ready-made meals, predictably opts for the one that, after a long series of tests, has been designed so as to affect his brain as powerfully as possible.

In a study worth reading, STS scholar Steve Woolgar and his colleagues show how these neuromarketers reach their goal of stripping the human agent of everything that might lead him away from being the feeling brain they want him to be.[46] Granted, the laboratory device that makes this possible is still a little cumbersome and complicated. But one should never despair of technology! Ways will no doubt be found to transpose and transport this sociotechnical environment and to multiply and disseminate these new qualculative agencies. Perhaps hooked-up, assisted brains will eventually shop at the neighborhood supermarket or wait for a delivery to arrive at the front door.[47]

Dissymmetries do not always develop in the same direction, and their hold is never complete or irreversible. Jean Lave and her colleagues have shown that there are very simple behaviors of resistance that allow the consumer to at least partially escape the qualculative powers of the suppliers. Even if a human agent does not explicitly have recourse to arithmetic while shopping, that does not mean they do not qualculate.[48] A very widespread device, for instance, involves allocating various amounts to different categories of purchases: all agencies qualculate, more and more intensely. Furthermore, if we stick to considering only the relations between the agencies involved in a bilateral transaction, then either the buyer or the seller is in the position to dominate qualculation. Only a case-by-case analysis of the relations can determine whether there is autonomy or heteronomy. In certain cases, an institutional customer purchasing a complex product from an investment bank (let's say, a strategy for fiscal optimization or a contract covering exchange-rate risks) will have no visibility as to the real structure of the product or the way the bank charges and covers it; they will qualculate the product with the seller's instruments. In other cases, a multinational corporation's financial department will appeal to several banks, creating competition between funders, and will impose its own qualculation instruments without understanding the global strategy of the banking sector.

The relation of autonomy or heteronomy between qualculative agencies is obviously subject to variations, since it is actualized over the course of qualification trials. An agency can alternate between different equipment, change qualculation instruments during a transaction, modify its equipment to become more powerful, or, on the contrary, it can decide to adopt another agency's tools. Let us not forget that an agency's equipment can include tools and procedures for revising the very evaluations it has itself produced. This is frequent in the case of heavily equipped agencies such as financial institutions that have the means to put different qualculation tools in competition with one another. It is no less frequent, however, when the qualculation equipment is light: shifts are easier and situation reversals are more frequent and... spectacular.

In this connection, it is appropriate to remember the useful distinction between a planned buy and an impulse buy in a supermarket. In the former, the customer has a greater autonomy, relying on equipment (such as lists, information gleaned on the web, friends' advice) that is prepared ahead of time and depends less on the store's equipment. The latter corresponds instead to a heteronomous position: the consumer, strolling without any particular intention, is taken in by the calculating device created by marketing experts; the consumer becomes, as it were, an annex of this arrangement. Recent research on electronic commerce indicates that web users tend to adopt the first type of behavior, but that supply agencies like Amazon react in such a way as to flip them into heteronomy. As sociologist Christian Licoppe concludes: "The practices of the 'connected' consumer are neither determined in advance (as in the logic of planned purchasing) nor manipulated by the market environment, even with the consumer's consent (as in the logic of impulse buying). The conduct of one's acts of consumption oscillates between flexible guidance and opportunistic flexibility."[49] Whatever the case, a consumer can always (in principle) change provider, walk out of the supermarket, and check out the competition. This possibility obviously depends on the circumstances and in particular on the strategies deployed by the various competing sellers. As will be seen in Chapter 6, in sectors where an overwhelming majority of sellers are heavily equipped, consumers and users have no choice but to accept the state of being dominated.

OUTSOURCING QUALCULATIVE CAPACITIES

In order to increase its qualculating power, an agency can choose to incorporate or use the qualculations made by other agencies.

Let us return to the simple case of the encounter between consumer and seller within the framework of a commercial device at the moment when the bilateral transaction is concluded. A customer who walks into a supermarket is not facing an isolated qualculative agency, but rather a formidable association of agencies that have had the time and the means to coordinate their efforts and their qualculations in such a way as to make them almost unassailable. How could I, in front of shelves full of goods, redo a qualculation whose first operations were launched on faraway sites to which I have no access and were then taken up again a thousand times in other places, transformed, amended, tested, to elaborate a history of which there is sometimes a trace on the packaging, covered in data and analysis results and proudly flaunting a quality label? How could I be in any position to produce my own evaluation of this enigmatic, mysterious product? The only solution is to be prepared for the confrontation. I may first mobilize all the information and data qualculated by other agencies that are better equipped than I, such as consumer groups, internet sites with user reviews, evaluations provided by a network of friends, guides, and so on. I can also refer to my own experiences and prior purchases. The use of cell phones in supermarkets is more and more common as people turn to them to get an opinion from a friend in real time or check a site on the web for comparative reviews. The commercial force deployed by the supermarket is likely to anticipate my questions and to mobilize other results, evaluations, and qualculations immediately, depending on the questions or objections I may raise. What is at stake in this confrontation of forces is the number of connections an agency has established or can establish. This observation echoes one of the main results of social-network analysis: the more central an agent, the greater his influence. The isolated agent who can count only on himself, that is to say, on almost nothing, is barred from qualculation. To understand how such a situation came about, we should return to the definition of qualculation and its conditions of possibility. To make a good nonqualculable, it is enough, for instance, to prevent closure of the list of entities to be considered, or to facilitate the proliferation of relations between these entities, or to paralyze any attempt at classification. This would be a simple, but costly strategy that would aim at leading the dominated agency astray, into a labyrinth of relations from which there is no exit, thus reducing its agency to impotence, limiting it to its own somatic resources.

Since I refer to the autonomy and heteronomy of qualculation capabilities or to their cross-mobilization, I would like to underline that each agency integrates (at least to a certain extent) the evaluations (or elements of evaluation) made by other agencies into its own evaluations. The integration is maximal when one of them is condemned to heteronomy. It is partial, in varying degrees, in the opposite case. Furthermore, since agencies enter into alliances and subcontracting relations, these relations establish a qualculation space in which each agency shares its equipment with others, little by little, and necessarily takes their qualculations into account. We will come back to this question later.

These strategic interdependences are easy to identify in the reality of commercial activities. Consumer groups organize tests to compare and rank this or that family of goods, tests that mirror at least some of the characteristics and evaluations declared by the producers and resellers, who also integrate elements into their evaluations in anticipation of consumer groups' tests. These crossed anticipations, leading in some cases to consensual descriptions of the qualculated goods, can be found in all sectors of market agencements. They are common practice in financial activities (the very notion of speculation and the tools it uses imply such anticipations) and in the competition between agencies over market share. Economic theory has long since picked up on these crossed anticipations through game theory. However, the analysis can still be broadened by looking beyond the sellers and buyers to the multiple agencies involved upstream and downstream, with their diversity of equipment for shaping and framing anticipations. And let's not forget agencies in what might be called collateral positions, such as governments and legal institutions.

RELATIONSHIP DYNAMICS IN QUALCULATION

The power dynamics between agencies are not set in stone. To reverse an asymmetry between qualculative powers and flip the power relations, agencies can acquire new equipment, fight to establish devices that increase their autonomy, seek to establish connections and alliances with other agencies, or if necessary, take on the design of new qualculation equipment.

Management studies scholar Peter Karnøe followed the construction of a nuclear plant in southern England over the course of eight years (2007 to 2015). During this period, the government changed the framework for evaluation, and therefore the qualculation tools, three times in order to build new alliances and maintain the balance of power.[50] In the first evaluation, the hypothesis was that the price of natural gas and taxes on carbon emissions would grow: a simple calculation—based on the LCOE (leveled cost of electricity), the cost divided by the annual production over the life of the plant—showed that no public funding for the plant was necessary. Both Labour and the Conservatives supported the project. A few years later, however, the government defined a new framework when it faced the objections leveled by those who considered the observed decline in gas prices and the collapse of the market for carbon emission permits to be long-term phenomena. Critics held that nuclear electricity would therefore turn out to be more expensive than competing sources of energy. In that moment, the government no longer emphasized the absence of public funding as a criterion for evaluation, but insisted instead on supply security and the promotion of noncarbon technologies. The government then offered to guarantee a price that would protect the plant owner from a price drop in alternative energies. The opposition denounced the return to a policy of public subsidy and made an issue of the irrational and risky nature of predictions and commitments over more than half a century. So the government changed the evaluation framework and tools yet again. At this point, it insisted that the capacity to provide electricity no matter the circumstances or historical contingencies, the ability to "keep the lights on" while creating twenty-five thousand jobs, was the real stake of the plant. In 2020, as I write this, the story is far from over. Objections to the reactor vessels have now entered the debate. Steel, which had not had a place in the evaluation matrix, has become one of the main actors: uncontrolled migrations of carbon are seriously compromising the plant's security. And as the final straw, even within EDF, the French state company to whom the program was entrusted, there are voices denouncing inept decision making by the general management, which had the company take on a ruinous project. EDF's financial director has resigned.

From a story full of twists and surprises, Karnøe extracts a few essential lessons. First, he observes that the evaluation depends entirely on the frameworks that guide it and the tools that are used. That is not, however, the main point. According to him, the successive transformations of the evaluation frameworks show that the dynamics of the power balance between agencies cannot be dissociated from the implementation of the qualculation tools that they design and choose. These evaluation frameworks should not be considered simple rhetorical artifices. One of their very real properties is indeed that they account for the balance of power and contribute to its recomposition by creating space for new coalitions.

The geopolitical significance of qualculative powers is perhaps most visible in the financial world. One of the specific characteristics of this activity is indeed to make possible important changes in the relative size of actors; these changes can seem surprising, compared with other more industrial or more patrimonial forms of capitalism. This observation encourages us to relativize the relevance of a tradition inscribed throughout the social sciences that tends to consider different resources or types of capital available to agents as the breeding ground for power relations and domination. This type of approach is ill adapted to the analysis of market agencements, since, as we saw, the existence of capital, or the value of capital, depends on the qualculation equipment used. What is at stake for domination is not, then, the appropriation of capital, but rather of the qualculating equipment; in particular, what is at stake is the equipment that frames and supports *capitalization* processes—that is to say, the equipment that authorizes the assertion "this is capital" and that imposes the measure of it. Without accounting tools transforming an activity, or an entity into an asset whose value is decreed to be equal to the sum of the actualized revenues it produces, neither capital nor accumulation would exist.[51] The asymmetries produced by the unequal distribution of this accumulation would therefore not exist, either. Capital, as a resource and as a value, is a result of the capacity to impose the calculation of its value, not vice versa. This explains that the measure of capital can be a good substitute for the measure of power only in situations of status quo, or, if you prefer, of solid agreement on the modes of calculation.

Taking notice of qualculation equipment in commercial activities highlights why inequalities cannot be accounted for solely on the basis of information and information asymmetry. Information does not exist independently of its production and shaping. In certain markets, the problem is not access to information, but rather access to control over the design and implementation of all the tools and devices that allow observations to be made, observations to be transformed into data, and information fed into the qualculating practices that result in decision making.

Relations of domination that permeate and structure markets are inscribed in the relations of qualculation. This point of view is not new. However, it has become inescapable. Indeed, it is more and more difficult to pretend that commercial transactions take place between equals when the means for the qualculations through which goods are evaluated have become objects of experimentation and subjects of debates that render visible the asymmetries they harbor, as is the case in financial markets or mass distribution. One can and must therefore include in the analysis the increasingly numerous programs that tend toward providing new tools for agencies whose qualculative power is weak, or that tend toward increasing the qualculative power of the strongest, or, indeed, that tend toward changing the very rules of the game by introducing skills that require new criteria or new formulas, disqualifying the old ones. Recourse to wide debates, such as the one organized in France in 2013 around energy transition, aims to mobilize the most diverse skills and expertise and thus to widen the market agencements *until they are able to integrate new* qualculative agencies and to contradict those who had had a monopoly on evaluation operations. The design of new qualculation equipment has become a full-fledged activity. It constitutes a strategic stake in engineering market agencements, and it mobilizes wide communities of experts and specialists whose activity should be studied...and assessed.

QUALCULATION DEVICES ARE THE EQUIPMENT OF A HABITUS

The dominant never have as strong a hold as when the dominated have the impression they are the authors of their own choices. This is Bourdieu's notion of symbolic violence, a powerful contribution to the analysis of an apparently paradoxical situation. The operator that makes sense of this paradox is the "habitus," a set of durable and transposable dispositions that creates an "autonomy" that is only the illusory consequence of a situation of heteronomy. The habitus explains why and how agents generate choices that are merely the consequences of causal chains that escape them. Does this explanation still hold when one includes qualculation equipment in the analysis, the mostly extrasomatic equipment that Bourdieu only barely takes into account? Indeed it does! If we agree to extend the notion of habitus to qualculation instruments, I believe it is easier to explain why and how certain evaluating practices endure, even as they transform.

Take the case of Amazon's recommendation engine. I will illustrate with an anecdote from my personal experience.

You may also like. Back in 2015, on January 11, I received an email: "You liked Thomas Piketty, *Capital in the Twenty-First Century*, you may also like the latest Houellebecq novel, *Submission*, since those who bought Piketty also bought *Submission*." Since John Dewey, we have known that qualculation operations, which by classifying and ordering goods lead to their evaluation, are in some sense open investigations requiring recourse to tools and equipment. This message sent via Amazon's recommendation system is a sign that an investigation did indeed take place, that it was led on my behalf with tools more powerful than any available to me.

If I had double-clicked on Houellebecq without thinking, ordered, and the next minute received the book on my Kindle, I would have appropriated Amazon's qualculations. The choice is mine, I double-click when nothing forces me to do so, and yet this choice is not mine, it is presented by Amazon: "You may also like." My habitus, which allows me to react rapidly to a new situation, decides for me, but it is a habitus that is structured in an evolving way by Amazon and its algorithms. If I am cut off from Amazon, I will make different choices; if there is a habitus, it is indeed a habitus in the process of being reprogrammed.[52]

I did not in fact double-click. The equipment Amazon makes available to me and that I use so often has become an extension of my own body and my own mind. Yet it is not the only equipment on which, and with which, I can count. Other sociocognitive prostheses are also available to me, such as the ones I have mentioned in this chapter, that can be activated at any time. First there is my own experience as a reader. I had liked Houellebecq's *Whatever*. I found the following novels less convincing. The real break came when, in a rage, I threw *Platform* into a wastebasket in the hotel in Halifax where I was attending a sociology conference. The style, or rather the absence of style, and the nihilist sociology of the author got the better of my patience. Never again Houellebecq! My evaluation was confirmed by reading critics who said in a more elaborate and better-argued fashion what I had felt. Amazon's algorithms might qualculate for me, but they would never get me to change my mind. An agency can only very rarely be reduced to a single piece of equipment. It operates at the intersection of a multitude of tools and prostheses.

The investigation can always take a new twist, start out in new directions, no less structured. In other words, my habitus is (partly) open to being reprogrammed (which Amazon takes full advantage of) in a thousand different ways. Not only is a habitus less rigid than sociology has portrayed it to be; it is even more pliant once it is attached to a qualculative apparatus that is itself a programmable infrastructure.[53] The more the equipment that is available to me (and that avails itself of me) proliferates, becomes more complex, fragmented, and segmented, the more the extrasomatic resources become instrumental, the more that reprogramming, because it is always about reprogramming, becomes hard to follow, predict, and control. An agency's autonomy, which of course does not mean its independence, since the equipment is there and qualculates, depends on the range and complexity of the equipment available to it. Caving in to a friend's insistence, I did finally read the Houellebecq novel I had not bought. I did not like it.

What we learn from Amazon's recommendations is that a habitus can be shaped from the outside, so to speak. Granted, habituses are present, structured, and activated by encounters, but in the face of an event, a question, a solicitation, or an unexpected problem, a whole investigation and reconfiguration becomes necessary. Habituses, like habits, change; they adapt to novel situations in order to generate answers to new questions. It is this restructuring that Amazon's engines provoke, participate in, and seek to orchestrate. I was surprised and intrigued by the connection with Piketty. And if I did read *Submission*, it is because I lent a more attentive ear, without sharing his opinion, to the friend who had told me a thousand times how much he thought of the author. Without Amazon and its equipment, without its constant and energetic reminders that constantly put back on the table the unending task of social ranking that happens classically through the ranking of goods ("Like other readers . . . you might like Houellebecq"),[54] I would have done the same for this one as for the prior books by this author I had ignored, my attitude sustained by my daughter's disdain for him. Amazon's suggestions appearing on my computer screen trouble me, unsettle me, move me to rethink and requalculate "my" choices, but most importantly, push me to solicit other sociocognitive prostheses, to recombine them and make them evolve. After my own investigation, I am no longer quite the same. I have learned that I do not put Piketty and Houellebecq in the same category, that I do not consider them similar authors. I had never thought this through before. Quite frankly, I would never have thought to make an association between the two, to consider them companions. The first warranted discussion, even if I do not find his methods for evaluating capital very convincing. The other, in my mind, deserved only...the wastebasket. The very dynamics of the work involved in refining my evaluations show that there is no strict and mechanical determination of their content. Each qualculation is a new experience. And at the end of the experience framed by Amazon's algorithms, I have changed. I have learned things. My evaluation of Houellebecq has been confirmed, whereas before it had no doubt been a bit shaky; second, it is not because I read Piketty that I should read Houellebecq; and finally, an unexpected result—I know better why, having read Piketty, I didn't really like it, contrary to what Amazon asserts ("You liked Piketty...you may also like Houellebecq"). I see certain traits they have in common that I had not noticed, such as a similar way of considering the world as something that escapes us and a set of cultural or political structures to which we must submit or against which we must fight. I am more aware of the fact that submission and radicalism are just two sides of the same feeling of powerlessness and that this book, the one you are reading, is a very modest way of imagining another way.

After this experience in the form of an investigation, I do not qualculate in quite the same way. If I were not a distributed agency, this process that makes me change continuously would not have the same vigor and would not have the same effects. I would adhere more intimately, and more completely to my choices and decisions. A qualculative agency does not internalize anything definitively. Its equipment escapes the simple geography of territories and borders. It constitutes a common space of shared and structured infrastructures that act, make act, and are acted in return, transforming and redistributing themselves with the events they participate in framing. The Amazon recommendation engine is part of me while being outside me. No doubt my habitus has always been somewhat permeable, but with centers of big data and the proliferation of algorithms, this permeability can no longer be ignored, and that calls for deeper analyses of its dynamics.

After my reading of *Submission*, I continue to be touched by Amazon's suggestions and qualculations, but I now evaluate them differently. New message: "You may also like Bernard Maris," the Bernard Maris (an economist himself) who wrote a book proclaiming that Houellebecq is one of our best economists. This time I trash the mail immediately, trashing the offer of qualification. The powerful equipment I share with Amazon has been repositioned with respect to my other equipment. My reevaluation of Piketty, via Houellebecq and Amazon, has contributed to reconfiguring my qualculation equipment, which includes Amazon's algorithms, but does not submit to them. The qualculation provoked by an unexpected suggestion has certainly contributed to my reprofiling, but it also led to the reprofiling of the goods I evaluate. Since I did not order *Submission* on Amazon, my friend having lent it to me, I contribute to distending the connections between Houellebecq and Piketty; I contribute, obviously in a very tenuous and often temporary way, to undoing what other Amazon clients have done. The algorithm that did not convince me registers the refusal of these scores and continues its operations unruffled. In Amazon's big relational database, *Submission* is not quite the same book, and if other customers qualculate the way I do, it won't be the same book at all anymore. Its position in the network of associations having changed, its characteristics will have changed. Goods and agencies codefine each other over the course of qualculation tests. Oh, of course these transformations are usually minor! However, the evolution is continuous. The mutations, so many restructurings, are possible because the agencies are distributed and equipped, but also and especially because the goods themselves are engaged in passiva(c) tion and qualification processes set into motion by the evaluation operations.

I have told you this story to show you how processes such as Amazon's can reprogram a habitus. This experience put me in a position from which I think about my preferences in a way that was shaped by a particular framework where I would be led to follow the calculations of a slew of other buyers I will never know until I decided to buy a book I might not have know about otherwise—changing while remaining faithful to oneself, staying faithful to oneself while accepting changes, as Tancredi advised in Lampedusa's *The Leopard*.

Each visit to the site is like leading an investigation in close collaboration with Amazon to determine who I resemble and from whom I am distinct. No fixed reference or criterion seems to have been established a priori. For example, it would be amusing and quite incongruous if Amazon posted to my screen the following information: "Michel Callon, all those who have the same revenue you do and are, like you, petit-bourgeois intellectuals, liked Y. Why not you? Try the experience!" This does not, of course, mean that revenue and "social" positions are irrelevant, but only that through a series of decisions, they are constantly being worked over, associated and reassociated with other variables. Social positions are a result, not a starting point. It is the goods that put us into relation, and in return, through the choices we make, we put goods into relation with one another.

I have lingered on this example because Amazon's systems are so well known. The empirical fact that this one company is wiping out all other qualculative spaces, including classic forms such as supermarkets and shopping carts, is not trivial. But the same analysis could be applied to any relations between any agencies fighting over the evaluation and qualification of any goods. Over the course of the multiple confrontations organized by the market agencements (whether they take place in research centers around the definition of innovation projects, financial institutions to attribute loans, in judicial courts, industrial property institutions, design departments, supermarkets, marketing departments, sales sites online, or factories), power relations are established between qualculative agencies. From these, scores and profiles emerge that will determine how goods that may one day be involved in commercial transactions are qualified.

The work involved in establishing inventories, collecting, connecting, and classifying is taking over market agencements. That is no doubt why qualculation equipment attracts more and more attention and generates violent controversies. The role it plays in orienting commercial activities, in determining which problems or stakes are taken into account and how the different agencies involved participate, makes this one of the most urgent and important matters there are. How should scientific activity and its contribution to economic activity be evaluated? How should the externalities that degrade the environment, cause global warming, and threaten the health of populations be qualculated? Most importantly, how should all these effects be identified and measured? These are the problems and concerns that constantly call the framing of qualculating agencies back into question. I will come back to these matters in Chapter 7, devoted to the dynamics of agencements. However, until we grasp how markets work by diving into the heart of qualculation devices, where agencies and goods and their relations are configured and reconfigured, there is no point in denouncing domination, violence, or the hold of capitalist markets.

CHAPTER FOUR

Organizing Market Encounters

When competitive dancers showcase a successful alignment of steps on center stage, the spectators watch in amazement, forgetting the years of grueling classes, the long and boring rehearsals, the painful first meetings that took place between the partners, and the fastidious training to fine-tune the performance for the show. Indeed, everything is done so that all of these things will get overlooked. Agencies and goods align at the moment of a commercial transaction in much the same way that dancers' bodies come together on competition day. When I finally acquire a new tablet to whose charms I have succumbed, or when I receive a new pharmaceutical treatment for an illness that is reputed to be incurable, it is the culmination of a very similar story.

We tend to remain unaware of the numerous attempts, experiments, reversals, and rehearsals that lead goods or services to correspond so closely to what we are expecting. And indeed, why would we care about these processes? Yet the tablet and the medication, for which I am prepared to pay the full price because my pleasure or life depends on them, are only the provisional end point of a long series of prior encounters. Long before they reached me, they were being prepared, framed, and progressively shaped through encounters taking place at myriad different sites. How many researchers and engineers, experts in industrial property, seasoned financiers, marketers and salespeople, normalization experts, and consumer representatives will have cooperated on the same project, either willingly or under duress, before the consent to pay is obtained and the transfer of property in return for monetary payment takes place? How many different agencies will have met, in different times and places, to obtain the final and improbable alignment between a singular offer and a singular demand? A market agencement can be seen as a device that incessantly organizes the collective labor of producing encounters and progressive transformations in order to lead to this specific event: a good is offered by an agent to another agent, who accepts to pay in order to obtain it.[1]

The organization of each of these encounters is not, of course, left to chance. According to the logic of market agencements, the good must participate in a set of activities whose sole end is to reach successful bilateral transactions. Whether far upstream or close to the moment of commercial transaction, each encounter may take a variety of forms. Let me turn from dance to the oft-evoked metaphor of marriage, which can be useful to highlight how diverse the observed configurations can be. Regarding the union of two beings, matches can be more or less authoritatively imposed by a third party, as in family-arranged marriages, by what in the commercial world is called a prescriber. Alternatively, the match emerges from social networks that favor marriages within a given milieu, without the individuals involved having any sense of losing their freedom of choice. Finally, and this solution is directly connected to the rise of dating platforms, a match can be the outcome of signaling and active research that further increase the sense that deliberate choices are being made. In all three cases, matrimonial matches are prepared and framed; the modalities of framing vary, but the fact that the matches must be framed does not. What varies from one modality to another is the degree to which the search for a partner is made explicit. With platforms and their equipment, searching reaches its maximum.[2]

The same holds for all commercial transactions. Organizing preparatory meetings is, nowadays, a full-fledged activity that consumes time and resources. It is itself the concern of specialized activities that do not necessarily flaunt their ultimate aim. However, the existence of such activity is not new. It can be found in all commercial activities in more or less elaborate forms where the aim is to align supply and demand. As the logics of innovation and singularization increase their footprint, the alignment of supplies and demands poses an ever-renewed challenge. It has led to the growing increase of specialized technical activities: as the crowd of agencies that intervenes grows bigger, they require more formal and qualculative tools.

Organizing multiple encounters requires framing in the most concrete and literal sense of the term. Paths have to be traced, gateways imposed, long detours organized, all while preventing sudden changes of course. To describe how these encounters are organized, I will invoke the interface market model, the simplest model, to consider its limits as well as the limits of its expansion. It is important to note that an encounter involves more than simply establishing relationships; it explores and tests out matches. This observation leads us to the idea of a platform as a way of referring to the entire set of devices that create the conditions for matches and then to the idea of an *exploratorium*, to underline the fact that the matches made by platforms are the result of a whole set of investigations and mutual transformations that lead to the progressive alignment of offers, goods, and supplies.

ENCOUNTERS CREATE VALUE

The interface market model does not broach the question of how to organize and structure encounters. The model distinguishes only between two main families of agents: one on the supply side, the other on the demand side—two blocks that are put into relation and articulated by goods acting as platforms. According to the model, the market works because it organizes a confrontation between existing supplies and demands. Nothing is said of the concrete modalities of these encounters or, to pick up on Weber's felicitous formula, of the physical assemblages that frame and localize them in time and space. And nothing is said of the interdependent relationships forged in these meetings.

The rift between theories of the market and the study of commercial practices has deepened in part because of the stylized interface market model, with the importance this gives to abstract notions of supply and demand, and the absence of any questions about the genesis of the goods that structure them.[3] Both academics and decision makers interested in theories of the market and in the general conditions for confronting supply and demand erase the existence of commercial practices. In their view, such practices exist only to bring about the making of connections, which themselves have no significant impact on the functioning of the markets. Commercial practices are to the market as scaffolding is to the erection of a building: they are there in order to make something exist but have no impact on its content. But of commercial practices the interface model has nothing to say, other than that some are eventually more appropriate or efficient than others, depending on the circumstances.

There do exist a number of remarkable ethnographic studies, as well as abundant reflections by the professionals whose job it is to organize, choreograph, and ensure the success of the encounters. Until recently, however, these studies only very rarely, if ever, proposed contributions to theories of the market. The ambition was often to get as far away as possible from such theories and to contest their legitimacy, with good reason. Professionals know that the notions of supply and demand have little use. For them, there are practical problems that need to be solved: first, to capture potential clients and to materially shape their demand, and then to transform potential clients into real clients who agree to pay. Anthropologists or sociologists who are attentive to how the commercial devices designed and set up by professionals actually work draw the same conclusion: market theory describes a virtual world that has, at best, no relation whatsoever to the reality of commercial relationships. At worst, it makes consumers believe they have demands and that what is offered to them really takes them into account.[4] Supply and demand: these notions, which are essential for a general abstract description of the way interface markets function and which some consider useful for the regulation of economic activities, lose all relevance when it comes to commercial matching.[5] One of the objectives of this chapter is to show how, in order to understand markets, it is possible and even necessary to fill the gap in theory that is opening up.

This project does not start from a blank slate. Reducing supply and demand to aggregates and their meeting to the point where two curves intersect was of some relevance when it was a matter of conceptualizing price formation but is insufficient to account for market dynamics. That is why economists and sociologists have attempted to provide a more realistic account of the ways supplies and demands come to meet without abandoning the idea of a clear separation between them. The following will provide a quick summary of these contributions. This will allow me to probe the notion of platform in the following section.

COMMERCIAL MATCHES AND THE THEORY OF FRICTIONAL MARKETS

Let us start with Alvin Roth's study of matchmaking. We will then consider studies that prolong and expand Roth's economic theory: Peter Diamond, Dale

Mortensen, and Christopher Pissarides's contributions on frictional markets.[6]

For several decades, Roth has developed both theoretical and practical analyses of what he calls "market design," that is, the designing of markets, a process that can be followed all the way to implementation. When there exist a large number of potential supplies and demands, many obstacles can stand in the way of establishing a relationship between them. For instance, how can one ensure that an unemployed person with certain skills meets the employer who needs precisely those skills? Marketplaces, as seen by Roth and his followers, are complex machines that organize matches between existing supplies and demands, but fine-tuning them requires a great deal of attention. Roth explains that for the machine to work properly, the first requirement is that the volume of supplies and demands that can express themselves be sufficiently high for each agent to have a chance at a real choice, such that agreements that can satisfy both parties are conceivable. If the number of agents is too high, however, blockages are likely. In order to avoid these, the speed of transactions has to be set at an appropriate level. Markets must also provide a climate of security and relative comfort for the agents so they are not encouraged to opt for an alternative means of organizing matches! Furthermore, adds Roth, such a machine can be designed and implemented only through experimentation that progressively tests procedures and devices. If the latter are not well conceived, markets will fail to fulfill one of their main roles—namely, to organize the matches between supplies and demands and thus to contribute to everyone's satisfaction.

Roth and his colleagues have become masters of technical engineering. Some of their designs are striking. Roth, for example, contributed to designing and setting up the labor market for new medical school graduates whose first position is important, both for them and for hospitals. The graduates want to be chosen by the establishments that will give the biggest boost to their careers, while the hospitals want to be chosen by doctors whose profiles correspond to their most immediate needs. In order to avoid chaos, procedures conceived by Roth and his colleagues were put into operation. Students apply to a selection of hospitals and are interviewed. After the interviews, hospitals and students each establish their own rankings to indicate their preferences. Then a mechanism based on an algorithm produces a list of matches that takes crossed preferences into account.

With procedures such as these, there is vast scope to employ algorithms capable of efficiently establishing relations between a multitude of different supplies and demands and to set up centralized clearinghouses that provide real-time accounts of the matches made. These procedures can even be implemented in noncommercial areas. Roth has, for instance, worked on organ donation. Certain organs, such as kidneys, raise complicated problems, given that a) there are far fewer kidneys available than recipients; b) donors and recipients are not always compatible; c) long-distance organ transportation should be avoided; and d) a minimal concern for equity requires that the candidates who have been on the list the longest can legitimately expect to be served first. It took more than ten years of experimentation to reach a more or less satisfying solution, which should give us an idea of the complexity of the problems and the solutions that are imagined! Compared with the organization of organ donations, the labor market for doctors seems delightfully simple.

Questions of efficiency and morality are obviously entangled. As Fabian Muniesa brilliantly showed, this entanglement is just as present in any matching device that establishes waiting lists, priorities, and compromises. Problems of equity and social justice are at the heart of algorithms, including the ones that automate quotes for stock market assets.[7] Indeed, the implementation of these kinds of devices outside the commercial realm shows that framing matches is not in itself specifically commercial (in the sense I give to the adjective; see note 3 above). As I will show in Chapter 7, each of the four first framings, taken separately, may be equally found in noncommercial operations. It is the way they are threaded together with the fifth one (price formulation), and nothing else, that constitutes market agencements as such.

Matchmaking engineering appears to confirm that supplies and demands preexist, yet it makes significant progress when it affirms that they are irreducibly diverse. The practical work of building matching systems opens the door to perspectives that will allow economists to go even further in refining the interface market model. At this juncture, I need to bring in the work on frictional markets.

Let's recall Peter Diamond's acceptance speech for the Nobel Prize in Economics in 2010: "We have all visited several stores to check prices and/or to find the right item or the right size. Similarly, it can take time and effort for a worker to find a suitable job with suitable pay and for employers to receive and evaluate applications for job openings. Search theory explores the workings of markets once facts such as these are incorporated into the analysis."

For Diamond and his colleagues, there is nothing straightforward about the meeting of a multitude of different supplies and demands with different profiles. A market is basically a device that organizes these encounters. That organization consumes energy and resources. The theory of frictional markets, however, goes further than Roth, claiming that a meeting does not involve a mere match. A company and a supplier, an apartment owner and a rental candidate, two future spouses, an employee and an employer, a buyer and a product—it takes time for all these pairs to form. Associating, which requires mutual adjustments and adaptations, carries value for the agents. If the association breaks or fails, this value disappears. "Search" is a good term to refer to all the efforts that precede and accompany the encounter: collecting information, attempting self-presentation, and progressing through trial and error. Indeed, it is not a matter of simply mechanically matching agents who are already there, but rather a matter of an investigation that ends with the coprofiling of goods and agents and opens onto a successful bilateral transaction. On this point, Diamond and his colleagues really do add something significant to Roth's analysis: this work of investigation and the investments in time and resources it requires depend on the state of the market and in return, impacts the market. Whereas according to Roth they are outsourced and managed by an external agency, investigating is part of the market and its functioning. Drawing consequences from their observations, Diamond shows that prices at equilibrium are unique because they are established in the context of a bilateral monopoly where the surplus value created by the establishment of the relationship is shared by the two parties, in proportions, of course, that vary as a function of the power relations. Diamond's finding affirms the primary and foundational character of bilateral relations that I have put at the heart of the analysis of market agencements.

The theory of frictional markets, initially elaborated for labor markets, applies to all categories of markets because all of them face the problems of organizing encounters that produce value. This is certainly the case for financial markets, whether one considers the stock markets, or companies looking for financing, or banks looking for projects to finance. The approach equally applies to markets for the most ordinary goods. A study by Christian Broda and David Weinstein of millions of bar-coded products sold in the United States shows that most goods are caught up in shorter and shorter cycles of creation and destruction. This phenomenon considerably increases the weight of prospection activities and their constant renewal, as well as the importance of the bilateral monopolies linked to the value produced by matches. Frictional market theory is becoming ever more relevant.

If one had to choose an emblematic example of frictional markets, I would choose platforms such as Meetic that offer their services to people "looking for a serious and lasting match." Started in France, but later acquired by the American Match Group, Meetic presents itself as a site "that will introduce you to single people with whom you share affinities." To establish a profile, candidates are encouraged to fill out a questionnaire in the form of a personality test. Meetic's algorithms then calculate distances between profiles to allow those who have signed up to make reasoned choices about their first meeting. Meetic also offers support to help already paired couples evaluate the quality of their relationship. This engineering has all the characteristic elements of a frictional market: heterogeneous agents, search for partners via, notably, profiling, matching, and bilateral relations, and value created by a match that is shared among the protagonists. It is indeed a device that allows singular relations to emerge on a massive scale, each couple living a unique story.[8] Because it was him, because it was me. It is the classic essay on friendship by Montaigne and La Boétie,[9] revised by algorithms.

The paradoxical character of this example will not have escaped the reader. Although one has to pay to use the platform, the main aim of the meetings Meetic organizes is not to reach a commercial transaction! For my purposes here, this does not matter. Alfred Galichon, an economist who specializes in financial markets, uses tools for analyzing frictional markets both in derivatives exchanges and among people in search of partnership.[10] The framing of meetings with the objective of executing bilateral transactions can conclude with gifts or commercial exchange;[11] as I noted previously, it is the last two framings (attachment and price formulation) that determine which of these is happening.

One could say this framing organizes the meeting of soul mates. As Meetic shows, the search for a soul mate consumes more and more time and energy and requires sustained attention. Platform goods, in their primitive rusticity, cannot provide this level of articulation.[12] More complex platforms are required for the interface market to become a vast device that matches supplies and demands.[13] The important variable revealed in these studies is of course the teeming multitude of heterogeneous supplies and demands, which are different from one another, in search of themselves and others and which can become aware of what they are in quest of only after a long series of investigations and inquiries. In setting off to discover the other, each sets off toward self-discovery and sets the markets into motion. The platforms are the instrument of this exploration; they provide the required infrastructure.

SOCIAL NETWORKS

Economic sociology has also contributed to the analysis of how supplies and demands are matched by emphasizing the role of rules and the institutions that establish these relationships. The best summary of its contribution, however, is to be found in its notion of a network. Agents are not atoms with freedom of choice and movement. They are caught in bundles of relations that shape their affinities, adjust their profiles, and in the end, constitute the paths through which matches can be organized. Mark Granovetter's famous investigation of job searches shows as much.[14] Not only do social networks put into circulation the information that allows agents to adjust their expectations—the morphology of networks plays a determining role in the conclusion of the transaction: an agent in search of an employer or employee has more chance of finding what he is looking for by following the weak and rare links that move him away from the people with whom he has the narrowest and densest connections. What is important here is neither the result (the importance of the famous weak links) nor the difficulties inherent in the analysis of networks (that is, which relations should be taken into account and how one does an inventory of them). What Granovetter demonstrated and what has guided countless studies of social networks is that one has to start from pre-existing relations to explain how matches come about.[15] It makes little difference whether these relationships are friendships or professional connections or whether they are links established on platforms. The shared observation is that, as Meetic put it on the first of its web pages, "meetings never happen by chance," even if those involved are (sometimes, but not always) convinced they do. The network does not determine the match mechanically; it simply makes more likely (and more fruitful) certain encounters while excluding others.

Social-network studies, alongside those by Roth, Diamond, and their colleagues, confirm the limits of the interface market models and provide instruments for moving beyond them. Interface markets postulate the absence of any connections between supply agents and demand agents, other than those provided by platform goods. The sociology of networks, as well as the economics of matching and frictional markets, which contest this central hypothesis, have contributed to the foundations of a theory of market agencements. These studies start from the observation that heterogeneous supplies and demands exist and then face the problem of their matching—that is to say, the question of how to institute bilateral transactions (or if you prefer, bilateral monopolies) that will allow each agent to meet the agent who is offering what suits him best. In order for these matches to take place, they must be prepared and framed. No matches are conceivable without specific investments, the mobilization of costly resources, and platforms to frame and organize these meetings. Nor are they possible without the social relations that open possible paths for them.

Markets need platforms with features that are infinitely more complex than those offered by goods acting as platforms. Platforms are both technical and social. On a sophisticated platform, aggregated supply and demand represented by synthetic curves gives way to the multitude of singular supplies and demands that set out in search of one another. The aggregates, as we will see in a moment, sometimes exist. However, in order to exist, they must have been patiently constructed through the production of data, records, and statistical calculations. The aggregates do give a picture of successfully organized matches, but they do not explain them.

All of the studies I have discussed are a decisive step toward a new model of markets. Yet despite their contributions, they run up against a key difficulty that we still have to overcome. Although they recognize and affirm that profiles are diverse, there is no serious consideration of the mechanisms of coprofiling of supplies and demand, without which meetings and matches would be extremely improbable. Organizing a meeting is not enough to put a supply in a relationship with a demand. If the transaction is to have a chance of being consummated, there must be agreement as to the content of the service offered and the qualities of the good. It is not a given that a fit will be found between supply and demand. Achieving fit is one of the tasks of organizing matches.

Agents' identities, the goods they offer or demand, evolve throughout the search for the soul mate. Obviously, organizing fit must include the transformation of agents' profiles, or to put it another way, their expectations, proposals, or preferences. This coevolution allows the match to be made. I understand that it is difficult for an economist or a sociologist from whatever school to imagine agents with variable geometries. However, to any reader who has been convinced by the argument in the previous chapter, it will be easy to imagine agencies that compose, decompose, and recompose themselves, making and unmaking themselves in response to circumstances and occasions. Appropriate devices are required to set this process in motion, accompany it, and provide it with felicitous conditions. Everything encourages us to take a closer look at how encountering platforms function.

ENCOUNTERING PLATFORMS AND THEIR NETWORKS

If supplies and demands were independent of one another, if there were no common mechanism in their definitions, the chances of them leading to a transaction would be very low. Markets would collapse on themselves. How, then, does this surprising alchemy work such that some offer others precisely what they seem to expect, thus leading to individual matches and, if all goes well, to completed bilateral transactions?

Highlighting the role platforms play in putting agencies and goods into relation with one another is a first step. However, one has to go further and ask about the conditions for the success of these relations. From this perspective, the economics of matchmaking and frictional market theory and the sociology of social relations are not much help. They consider that the problem to be solved is that of matching skills or qualities that are already clearly established and whose genesis is not taken into account. The process leading to the existence of souls that one day, perhaps, will discover they are mates is left out of the analysis completely.

In order to understand the mechanisms through which candidates for matches sometimes end up finding what they are looking for or what they are incited to look for, one has to look at the adjustments that can lead to matches. These are of two main complementary sorts. The first adjustment corresponds to the innumerable training sessions and rehearsals of sport dancers preparing for the final competition. In market agencements, preparatory meetings on multiple sites take place, putting agents and goods into relation at different stages of their elaboration. But that is not enough. In what follows, I will suggest that an agencement can be described as a network of interacting platforms that elaborate the adjustments that will, in fine, incrementally, through continuous transformations, allow for the bilateral commercial transaction. Once we focus our attention on this collective organization, we will have to examine how on each platform, investigation, and exploration lead to the desired adjustments.

On each site where agencies and goods are successively put into relation, there are platforms that organize encounters and give new impetus to the qualification process. One step at a time, through iterations, reversals, and regular transformations, goods are profiled, and so are the different agencies involved. I will now turn to a description of these encounters and of the different devices that frame them. I start with the most studied sites in this process, those corresponding to the different activities surrounding the bilateral transaction itself. I will then turn to less explored sites, upstream in the process (design activities) or downstream (consumer spheres). Finally, I will return to the notion of platform.

There has been a spectacular evolution of the sites where commercial meetings are organized, from the fairs and markets of the Middle Ages to websites, via the invention and development of department stores and supermarkets. I will, of course, not attempt to summarize this history.[16] A convenient way to bring out the common traits of the devices that organize and singularize encounters between sellers and buyers is to consider the effects of the arrival of the internet and cloud services, which, by making explicit the practices they lead to, puts older devices in a new light while hinting at future evolutions.

The internet offensive has first provoked reactions from malls. If they want to survive as meeting devices, they will have to reinvent themselves. Since 2009, with the rise of online commerce, their sales in France have constantly decreased, partly because the internet, the cloud, and the advances in software delivery allow for easier, faster price comparisons and a better coprofiling of supply and demand. The impact of electronic commerce is already significant, since in 2015, it represented more than 7 percent of retail sales in France, some fifty billion euros, and its annual growth rate was in double digits.[17] However, as many studies have shown, the worst is never certain: the online universe is not simply a substitute for traditional modes of purchase. In 2013, 70 percent of transactions in stores were preceded by an internet search. Conversely, many internet purchases are made after a store visit. The current evolution seems to lead to a hybridization of the two devices and to new ways of organizing matches. Relying on the marketing studies that tend to show that thanks to the work of salespeople and the buyer's feeling of having invested a great deal in searching for the good that suits him,[18] a store has a hundred times more chance than does an internet site of transforming a visit into a purchase, malls have actively thought about new forms of meetings they can promote and new configurations to be imagined.[19] (There is, of course, no guarantee that the balanced developments I have just described will continue. At the time that I am working on the English edition of this book, the COVID-19 pandemic seems to have given a decisive, yet perhaps temporary advantage to e-commerce. But nothing definitive can be said about the future evolution. For example, the ecological footprint of the cloud may very well compromise its future.[20] In any case, the objective of this book is not to venture into this field of predictions, but to make the market mechanisms visible and intelligible.)

The answer that has been found offers a glimpse of radically new meeting devices: "Theatricalizing the supply and transforming shopping into a genuine life experience; bigger shopping centers easier to model; interior and exterior architecture more marked by its geographical environment; freedom of design for brands; wide circulation spaces with natural light and high ceilings; evocative sensorial universes; a mixture of stores periodically renewed; ephemeral shops to better follow and surprise the customers and incite them to on-the-spot decisions; commercial and cultural events; bespoke shopping; varied food options; spaces for relaxation and children's play; unlimited Wi-Fi; advertisement screens and game screens."[21] At the same time, there is another evolution, that of so-called "atmospheric" marketing, which theorizes this new conception of matches, underlining the importance of the milieu, the ecological bubble that protects and enfolds the customer, nourishing his sensations, and the fact of a hedonistic existence, preparing and staging encounters as exceptional and individually tailored events.[22] There are several things in these reconfigurations—notably, attention to affects and emotions in order to attach customers.[23] I will come back to this in the following chapter. However, there is also, and this is relevant in this section, an original way of putting supplies into relation with demands.

In commercial bubbles (one shouldn't talk about shopping malls anymore), it is easier to track the potential customer the way one tracks whales in danger in the vast ocean: with beacons. Brands are tracking customers. At the Printemps Haussmann department store, those who are still only visitors are geolocalized with an error margin of only two or three meters, thanks to the beacons in their phones—not so different from what the London pitchers had invented! In both cases, it is a matter of extracting the customer from the flow and the anonymous mass, to divert him, to prepare his capture. The means are vastly more sophisticated, but from the point of view of commerce, the aim is essentially the same—to make an improbable meeting happen.

This following or tracking is not limited to commercial sites in the strict sense. The latter are extended, delocalized in time and space, redefined, and dispersed. Franck Cochoy talks of "equipped serendipity" to refer to the set of devices that favor nonprogrammed meetings while providing agencies with the means to provoke them and to endow them with a significance likely to initiate a decision process.[24] 2-D bar codes and commercial applications for smartphones, geolocalizing software, and instantaneous marketing systems are all examples of the digitalizing of mobile consumption.[25] Are you interested in fabric at the Saint-Pierre market in Paris? You can be alerted to new arrivals by text message before anyone else not also connected in this way. Such technologies, which issue targeted alerts, set consumers and markets into motion and animate them, to pick up on Cochoy's great expression.[26] Equipped serendipity also includes the targeted advertisements that escort surfers over the course of their peregrinations on the web or the information sent to followers in real time on social media. Not only is the circulation of agents and of information made compatible and mutually reinforcing—the motives for interest and purchases are intensified and diversified. This favors the teasing that pushes toward an encounter and is the preamble to commercial commitment. These practices have given rise to matters of concern over the rise of a surveillance society, an economy of attention, and the invasive impact of geolocalization.[27] I will address some of these at the end of this chapter. However, the general argument of this book is that such opposition drives dynamism in market agencements and will lead to the instauration of new framing devices.

Equipped serendipity might become one of the prevailing modes of organizing meetings. It solves one of the inherent tensions in market agencements. On the one hand, a potential customer is invited to circulate; his eyes are opened, he is detached from his familiar environment, his habits, his prejudices. This being put into circulation, warming the mind, and sharpening curiosity does not happen only on the periphery of commercial bubbles. It also applies within. Aéroville, just outside Paris at the intersection of several highways, and the flow of potential customers they carry, pushes dramatization to the extreme. It does not simply incite consumption directly; rather, it puts on a show, offering a change of scene, organizing "unexpected shopping" as the website of this mall of a new type proclaims. This is done by producing events and setting people into motion within the bubble—organizing a sort of voyage through the labyrinth of a mall. Those who travel consume. The tourism industry has taken that lesson to heart. Gigantic cruise ships, floating cities crisscrossing the oceans, jumbo jets ferrying senior citizens who can barely walk and young people itching to go in order for them all to meet at sites that could well have done without their visit, all these transform the planet into a commercial bubble of which Aéroville is a model. However, and this is the other side of the paradox, incessant circulation should not lead to losing track of the customer, who must be constantly watched so as to be secured and brought to meet the offer that is destined for him. He has to be seized as he goes by, captured, held, but not for too long, so that the parade can go on, a bit like one of those dances in which one changes partner every time the gong sounds.

It is interesting to note that old practices are integrated and redefined in these devices. For instance, a sign used by a shopkeeper to alert the public to his shop became a company name and then, by metonymy, a chain of stores. Proudly displayed on the mall's website, it is now a means of communication and capture. The virtual web and the web woven by commercial bubbles merge and meld to accelerate and channel the wanderings while multiplying encounters.

Since Galileo, we have known that all motion is relative. The rule also applies to commercial activities. One can put either goods or customers into circulation. Customer travel requires highways and cars, planes and landing strips, fiber-optic networks, ultrapowerful computers with giant memories of several thousand petabytes, but also good old brick-and-mortar buildings—in other words, the heavy infrastructure that enables the commercial bubble Aéroville to exist. The well-named Aéroville seizes the customer in his plane and plunges him into a niche where everything is conditioned, including the air, to promote meetings and flashes. To ensure that goods travel faster than by word of mouth, print advertising was invented, and then multimedia ads, to Tupperware parties,[28] and recently, to what is called social media marketing. Such marketing promotes the circulation in social media of goods that are ready for commercialization, goods that have been specially designed to make themselves known and provoke debate.[29] A new population of fans, enlightened amateurs, and profane experts is being constituted, and it multiplies individual encounters between goods and agencies.

The rise of advanced sociotechnical practices such as atmospheric marketing, social media marketing, equipped serendipity, and market matching (as studied by Roth or in frictional markets), with their sophisticated electronic equipment, invites us, looking back as we are learning to do, to take a fresh look at older market agencements. In particular, it encourages us to look at the intermediation devices that have become invisible to us because we are so used to them. Although these sites are widespread, generally accessible, and relatively easy to study, they remain underexplored from the perspective of what their analysis can bring to the theory of market agencements.[30]

Let me give a few examples from recent ethnographic studies: malls and other shopping centers; supermarkets, with their parking lots, their aisles, and their pitchers, their specialty sections, their shelves and refrigerated racks, their shopping carts and squads of professionals mobilized to design, organize, frame, and maintain these encounters.[31] I might also mention undertakers, who connect with hospitals to channel the uninterrupted flow of corpses they offer to take care of for bereaved families;[32] the street vendors or the gamblers in withdrawal we met in the Introduction;[33] shopping streets or shopping galleries; covered markets; flea markets; the markets in Provence;[34] electronic auction markets;[35] shop signs; advertisements; storefronts; business cards handed to potential customers; cold calls; mailings;[36] internet sites;

lingerie parties; the Yellow Pages; guides; consumer magazines; and more. All these devices have been the subject or deserve to be the subject of detailed analyses for a sociology of market agencements. They can all be considered as both the results and the stakes of sets of practices and actions that aim to materially organize a confrontation between agencies and goods.

In order to suggest how general my framing is and how diverse its concrete modalities are, I want to turn away for a while from the encounters that directly precede a market transaction and set off for sites that are further upstream in time and space. Let us turn to the process of designing goods. For instance, let us look at biotech start-ups in search of new therapies whose development and evaluations are expensive. As they look for financing to develop their molecules, how can they make contact with interested investors? The same question arises for potential investors who are excited, rather than discouraged, by risk: Where can they find good investment opportunities? This matching is no easier than finding one's soul mate. The investor needs good reason to be interested in this or that start-up, whereas the start-ups need to find investors with whom they can establish productive partnerships. One of the devices that has been imagined in order to facilitate and prepare these matches is directly inspired by dating platforms. In both cases, the vocabulary is identical, only, since time is money, this is called "speed dating." Lafayette, a French bistro in the middle of Manhattan, organizes these meet-ups between a few dozen French biotechs, financial analysts, and journalists. The start-ups' objective is to make themselves known and especially to introduce their products as one introduces a person with services to offer: an artificial heart, patches, or a DNA test. The atmosphere is friendly, like a music lounge, says a journalist who participated in these meetings. In a relaxed atmosphere, a sort of commercial bubble, each start-up candidate practices the next morning's pitch: ten-minute timed presentations, face to face, with forty investors. The meeting is organized by brokers, matchmakers with fat Rolodexes who open the doors to big money. The slightest sign of interest is enough for valuations to leap upward, creating value. In these meetings, the "pitch" is vital, and it must cover a certain number of points: a description of the technology's potential, the revolutionary impact it can have on the market, and so on. Talk of pitchers is as relevant here as in the streets of London. It is not enough to meet investors; there must also be a presentation of the business, a profiling of the good.

In short—they pitch. As in London, at the Lafayette, everything hinges on a few minutes. Some investors stand up in the middle of a presentation to show their lack of interest, a public sign of rejection. The meetings (several hundred in 2014) are orchestrated by software and take place in miniscule boxes, like a prison visiting area. A bell rings when the time is up. Next! The device is hardly convivial, but it is very efficient: not a place for sentiment. Next! Fifteen meetings a day for each of the candidates, whether they are searching for capital or placing it. Without the platform and the speed dating, how would a small French company meet this strange investor who vacations every year in France and declares, "I woke up one morning and thought, what is going on in France?" How could this marriage between such singular profiles have taken place without the speed dating and the entire device that organizes it? Liliana Doganova confirms that all this is required. She followed organized meetings in the context of large conferences to match investors (generally Big Pharmas) and start-ups: same software, same scheduling, same bells, same cavalier way of getting rid of a candidate judged to be uninteresting. Doganova explains that here the matchmakers are called "finders."

With regard to financing—that is to say, the search and allocation of money—there are other examples worth mentioning. First, crowdfunding platforms, internet sites that allow entrepreneurs to appeal to a large number of web users in order to finance a project. These circuits can support projects to create companies, films, or personal loans. They are quite popular. In 2013, three billion dollars was raised in the United States.[37] It is worth emphasizing one of the characteristics of these platforms that materialize through the creation of websites that organize meetings. (One of the most famous at the time of writing is Kickstarter.) When a bank or a venture capital fund decides to finance a start-up or the production of a film, it has no direct proof that the consumers or users will be interested in the product or the film. Indeed, those responsible for the project cannot be sure of that either! The fact that people seem convinced enough to accept giving, lending, or investing money bears witness to the potential interest of the project. Not only does the crowdfunding platform make matches—it also establishes a sort of short circuit, aligning upstream and downstream, and it directly contributes to keeping track of the ultimate aim of the framing it operates—that is, to end up with goods that will be paid for. It creates an encountering site well upstream and at the same time ensures a connection downstream. What the profiling platform does is double: it bears on both the financier (who invests money) and the (potential) customer interested in the content of the project.[38] The platform also plays a leveraging role in the financing, since once it has been chosen, the project will find extra funding more easily.[39]

Of course, these initiatives warrant some commentary. Under what conditions are they viable? How should their activities be regulated? How can the information asymmetry, between underinformed lenders and unscrupulous borrowers, be reduced? What is their future? These questions, while obviously important, are not those I am interested in here. What counts for my purposes is the way the meetings these platforms organize are structured in a sector of market agencements that is far from the final (aimed-at) transaction and yet is articulated with it. This type of device provides a solution to the central problem of organizing meetings, like the computerized systems of financial markets that organize the face-off between buyers and sellers.

The preceding examples illustrate both the central character and the remarkable proliferation of encountering platforms. We should also mention similar structuring that is appearing in fundamental research, accompanying the rise of heavy equipment and interdisciplinary collaboration (whether in theoretical physics or in biology) and opening the way to extensions of market agencements, as in the explosion of biomedicine. Seen from Mars, a market agencement would look like a railroad network composed of a maze of tracks, marshaling yards, switches and switching centers, and roundhouses, configuring and reconfiguring trains while conveying packages and travelers, whatever their points of departure and arrival. There are those who would like to describe markets as though these devices had no impact on their functioning, their efficiency, and the quality of services rendered! A railroad company that took no interest in this infrastructure would be a pretty shoddy outfit!

To explain the growing grip meeting platforms have on the market and their increasing power to structure commercial activities, it is enough to recall that the ultimate aim of an agencement is the constantly renewed institution of bilateral transactions. In other words, market energy comes from the race to innovate products. A commercial transaction can be analyzed as an innovation, be it great or small, more or less minor. However, as we now know, innovation is a collective activity, built out of cooperation, back-and-forth movements, and iterations that in the end establish a connection between, on the one hand, very abstract and fundamental knowledge and, on the other hand, goods that respond to very concrete demands. The question this raises is how to organize meetings and collaborations between dispersed agencies that do not know each other and whose profiles are still hazy and far from explicit. All the studies show that the exploration, which happens through a great number of sites and has to result in a final bilateral transaction, is made easier by platforms and the networks they constitute. These are devices that organize things in such a way that many actors with different skills, expectations, and logics cooperate in very concrete ways around determined projects. Each platform is an encountering place for agents who, a few moments earlier, were often only strangers to one another and who will go back to being so after having explored their profiles and matched up long enough to go a little way together.[40] Goods in gestation circulate from platform to platform, coordinating the myriad of agencies that intervene at different phases of their qualification process. What some call innovation networks are in fact networks of platforms where the final good is prepared.

The notion of platform has many advantages in helping describe and analyze the organization of meetings within market agencements. It can be equated with a device constituted not only of material elements, but also of rules, texts, and incorporated skills that are caught up in a bundle of interdependences. Much is at stake in their design and their organization, not least of which is the definition of intellectual property. Of course, we cannot consider all these questions here; they are matters for market agencement engineering. In the following section, I will look at the way platforms make the entities who meet act. In other words, I will try to answer the following question: What does the verb "to meet (each other)" mean? As we will see, encountering platforms are devices for mutual exploration, what I suggest we call, after the interactive science museum in San Francisco, *exploratoriums*.[41]

PLATFORMS AS EXPLORATORIUMS

Once an encounter happens—everything is in the same place at the same time—two distinct layers separate: a before and an after, a here and an elsewhere. A space-time is sketched. This is not the simple crossing of two bodies, immutable, although mobile, impelled by their own inertia. The ballistics of the meetings that platforms organize and produce is more complicated. It requires the active participation of the agencies involved. Agents are not standing around waiting for a collision to occur. They search, test, try, negotiate before settling on an agreement. The meeting lasts; it unfolds in time and space. It is a process over the course of which identities change, and with them the qualification of the goods. A platform is not a static structure that simply adjusts the trajectories of bodies in motion. It is a dynamic device. It acts and makes act, accompanying the agencies and goods in their mutual transformations and adaptations. A platform is an exploratorium.

Let us come back to Amazon, which does seem to concentrate all the properties of encountering platforms. Having led me by its qualculators to read Houellebecq (in the previous chapter), Amazon insists and makes a new suggestion: Virginie Despentes. I end up ordering *Vernon Subutex*, her latest book, because I find a rather good review. Not only do I allow my identity to be reprogrammed, contaminated by those who, having chosen *Submission*, also chose *Vernon Subutex*, I also increase the intensity of the links and similarities between the two books and their two authors, whose identities are thus transformed. From the intertextuality to which I contribute and that is materialized in the form of relations established in Amazon's database, new convergences emerge that modify the signification of the works and the authors' personalities. Neither Amazon's customers, nor the books, nor their authors come out of this operation without having been affected: by crossing paths, each of their trajectories has been inflected and sent off in new directions. It is indeed a coprofiling, which will in fact be institutionally confirmed a little later, to my great surprise: Despentes would become a member of the Goncourt Academy, which had recognized Houellebecq with its Prix Goncourt a few years earlier. Yet despite the linkages made by Amazon and the Academy, to me, the two authors could not be more different. Both attack the moral order, but Houellebecq features spineless characters overwhelmed by a life they sadly but passively enjoy as their days wane. In contrast, Virginie Despentes makes us hear revolting voices overflowing with energy, imposing their order or acting to impose it. The style of the former is flat and resigned, while that of the latter is full of outbursts and force. At the time, I got the feeling I was in the minority with my view. This led me to reflect quietly upon my own tastes.

This example makes the structuring logic of these inflections explicit, a logic that is discovered only by moving forward. When I arrive on Amazon's website and before the messages and suggestions show up, I cannot imagine their content. And since the event—that of my meeting with other books and other readers—cannot be described, no probability, objective or subjective, can be assigned to it ex ante. This unlikely meeting, however, is carefully framed, as is proved by the relational structuration of entities that the database gathers and calculates. The meeting platform frenetically produces unexpected events for me. Unexpected, but programmed! Or rather, unexpected because programmed.

When I pass through Amazon's site, I am caught up in this work on myself and my choices, whether I like it or not. (And why wouldn't I like it?) Leaving me to decide what I want, however, Amazon takes on the role of a discreet MC and does not seek to exert any pressure on me that might incite me not to return. Like a gambler at a gambling machine, I am encouraged to renew the encounter again and again.

All encountering platforms play both sides at once: they make meetings happen while organizing alignments. That is why their description inevitably mixes the two dimensions that are nonetheless worth distinguishing analytically. In the words of its designers, Aéroville is a sort of giant behavioral psychology laboratory where multiple variables can be studied and acted on in order to profile and reprofile agents and goods in situ. Data are gathered, processed backstage by powerful calculators, and returned, carrying associations and suggestions for customers, orienting their steps, and modifying their ways of seeing (themselves).

Customer relationship marketing (CRM) is an example of a platform that organizes large-scale exploration activities that oversee the structuring of fruitful meetings.[42] A few years ago, Tesco, the largest British distribution group, present on all continents, launched a Clubcard, which it offered to its customers. The aim was, in Tesco's words, to begin "an ongoing dialogue with each of its customers." The card is a strategic piece in an assemblage that includes call centers, websites, software, and printing facilities and that stimulates productive exchanges between agencies and the goods on offer. It is at the heart of a device that aims to transform occasional meetings into long sequences of gatherings and thus, to construct a future for what might otherwise be only an initial contact, never renewed. These cards (thirteen million were active at the beginning of the 2010s) are powerful tools that not only make it possible to track each customer's purchases, but also help look for explanations for those purchases. According to Tesco, they make it possible to a) create a dialogue to establish what the customer wants; b) reward and thank the customer for his purchases; and c) suggest new products for him to try.

Tesco managers realized, for instance, that sales of flowers and wine increase dramatically just before summer vacation. Analysis of the data from the cards rapidly provided an explanation. As children finish the school year and will leave their teachers, parents thank the latter (yes, some parents do express their gratitude!) by offering a small present. These small presents, as they add up, generate nonnegligible flows of sales and profits. Tesco therefore decided to stock up shops at the end of school so that families could find what they were looking for. Is Tesco following its customers? In a sense, it is. Are the customers following Tesco? In a sense, they are. Customers obviously buy or do not buy flowers or give or do not give presents. Tesco just makes their lives and choices easier. However, by showcasing aisles full of flowers and wine and adding a sign suggesting that parents think of their little darlings' teachers, Tesco pushes the customer toward *those* choices, which become *their* choices.[43]

Tesco's exploration is even subtler than this example seems to indicate. The analysis of the data connected to each customer allows it to constitute profiles and classify consumers in homogeneous families grouped by the same purchases. The basic idea is to consider that a customer *is* what he buys. This associationist definition of identity opens the way to psychological tests that Tesco uses without hesitation, the better to explore the universe of goods and consumers so as to gradually constitute consumer families that share the same choices and the same evaluations. For each customer that the databases have assigned to a particular family, it is possible, through a simple statistical calculation, to identify the goods he has not yet bought, but is likely to want to acquire: "You bought X, like most people in your family who also bought Y. Do you want to try Y, too?" It may be goldfish and walking boots, rather than Despentes and Houellebecq, as certain relational marketing databases show.[44] The calculations that are made reveal norms and statistical variances and then transform them into social norms, each gap being presented to the customer as the opportunity, by closing the gap, to get closer to the norm that defines, for his family and not others, what it is to be a "good" consumer. This process of association is never over. Its strength lies precisely in the fact that it continuously takes into account developments and feedbacks. The Clubcard is a powerful exploration device.

Consumer magazines, available in the stores, play on these definitions and produce, with all the required goods, a thousand and one ways to be a grill master or organic chef. Fulfill yourselves—become what you are! The movement is accentuated by handing out coupons to customers. They are of three types: those that reinforce preexisting choices (reward discounts on the goods usually purchased), those that offer discounts on products bought by customers in the same family, and those that incite to buy new products. Loyalty cards obviously do much more than build loyalty! By allowing Tesco to explore its customers' world, to try their hearts and plumb their minds, CRM systems incite shoppers to explore the offers made to them. Loyalty cards are platforms. First, they conform to the definition of platform goods in the interface market model: they articulate supplies and demands. Then, they fulfill the function of meeting platforms: the chip allows cross-referencing and matching. Finally, they permit the dynamic organization of relations and the coprofiling this dynamism triggers. CRM experts are clear-sighted when they say "it is so important to have a system that can not only change with your customers, but is also capable of learning and adapting its actions so as to make predictive calculations based on past, present, and future behavior.... Analyses not only observe customers' practices, they learn at the same time as the customers do."[45]

Tesco has built a genuine exploratorium that produces an attentive supplier constantly inquiring into demands, as well as reasonable customers who are invited to think, express themselves, chose, and make fully informed decisions. Encounters are adjusted, and products transform themselves. Like Amazon's bookstore, agencies evolve and recompose. The organized joint explorations lead to the mystery and miracle of alignment. That such felicitous conditions (I offer what you ask for) can be obtained is explained by the fact that Tesco devotes vast resources and colossal instruments to explain them. If the meeting is successful, it is because the agencies are all asking a single question—namely, "How can we make this a success?"—and mobilize considerable resources to find the right answers.

Obviously, the exploration is asymmetrical, at least in this example. Granted, Tesco cannot be considered a panopticon that spies on its customers' every gesture and every thought. It is not a panopticon whose contemporary avatar is Big Brother. The asymmetry is subtler. Tesco presents as a sort of subcontractor, advisor, or well-informed coach who whispers in its customers' ears: "I am not here to tell you what to do, but to help you make your own choices in a reasonable and reasoned way."[46]

It is easy to apply this analysis to commercial sites where commercial transactions actually take place. Commercial bubbles such as Aéroville are, as we saw, sites of very structured experiences and investigations. However, the exploration dynamic I have just introduced applies to meeting platforms along the full length of the agencement. Some are far upstream, in the design and development phases. In speed dates organized for start-ups and investors to meet, or in the preliminary steps and rehearsals that follow, what is at stake is not only the meeting—trajectories intersecting in such a place at such a time—but also and especially the alignment of supplies and demands. These activities can be described as exploration activities that lead to the coprofiling of goods and agencies. These activities begin in labs, continue in financial markets, design departments, marketing offices, normalization or intellectual property institutions, all the way to sales sites or consumer groups, and this is obviously only an indicative list. After a thousand and one twists and interactions, the good is delivered. The exploration process is just another name for the innovation process.

Each platform can be described as an exploratorium, contributing to the singularization of goods and agencies. (Think of the specific matches worked out on Meetic.) The exploratoriums of a market agencement are thus powerful structuring instruments for bilateral transactions. The most striking way to show you how this works is to move from a general discussion of market agencements to a case study. I'd like to turn to the health care sector, which is increasingly animated by a whole series of meeting and exploratory platforms, each of which contributes, through a play of cleverly orchestrated interdependences, to singularizing commercial transactions in an extreme and repeated fashion. Notions such as personalized medicine and "translational" medicine underline how deep this movement has gone in the pharmaceutical industry.[47] The first expression underlines the growing importance of processes that align treatments and patient profiles, whereas the second insists on the necessity of coordinating research, on the one hand, and the design and implementation of treatments, on the other—from the bench to the bed, as the saying goes. These two explicit requirements lay the groundwork for the singularized medicine that my colleagues Peter Keating and Alberto Cambrosio described so well in their authoritative history of oncology.[48] They analyze a fifty-year evolution to show how the therapies conceived to treat cancer have been progressively transformed. In the 1950s, therapy aimed at killing (with moderate success) the cancerous cells without killing the patients, which was not always easy.[49] Fifty years later, the strategy has been completely reversed. It is no longer a matter of killing anything or anyone, but instead of intervening in the biological processes that govern the proliferation of cancerous cells. This strategy is inscribed in a new domain of actions and knowledges called "biomedicine."

Biomedicine involves intensive fundamental research to identify what are called "pathways," that is, the series of cascades of biochemical reactions that drive cells to proliferate. Research aims to figure out at what moment and at what biological sites intervention can be the easiest and the most efficient. Once the molecular target has been selected, one has to figure out whether or not it has been reached. Confirmation can be obtained only if certain biomarkers present in the cells illuminate the target. It turns out, however, that these biomarkers (which depend on the type of cancer being treated) exist only in certain patients. The aim and the nature of therapeutic trials change with this requirement. It is no longer a matter of verifying that cancerous cells, and only cancerous cells, are eliminated by molecules administered to patients. The trials aim to elaborate optimal strategies for intervening. The first aim is to identify the combinations of molecules to be administered and the sites to be reached; the next objective is to determine the profiles of patients to whom these treatments can apply.

The beginning of the investigation takes place in fundamental research laboratories, where neither the regimen (that is, the combination of molecules, treatments, and modes of administration) nor the patients who may benefit from it are known. When the process starts, no one knows exactly what *this* cancer is or who a patient suffering from *this* cancer is. The cancer is discovered as research unfolds and as the clinical trials align the regimen with the person. In the end, if felicitous conditions obtain, a biomarked patient is produced, and an efficient regimen for *this* biomarked patient is defined, both having been coprofiled and adjusted through successive transformations.

This is a process of singularization. It does not end with matching. Once set in motion, the interventions produce new problems that in turn call for new explorations. At no moment does the clinical trial give way to the therapy per se; the clinical trial as a full-blown research practice continues. It is part of the therapy.

The only aim of this process is to appropriate, make explicit, and define profiles, adjust them to one another, and match them such that a quasi-miraculous alignment is found between molecules, regimen, protocols, patient profiles, and doctor profiles. In short, an individualized therapy is a good that can become the object of a bilateral transaction: a treatment, administered by a hospital, whose price will be determined for the patient.

In a way, the entire pharmaceutical industry is organized like a giant platform built up from secondary platforms. To be successful in putting together a therapeutic match is even more complicated than organizing a meeting of soul mates who would like to share their lives, at least for a time: feelings fit together more easily than DNA sequences. It requires a profound transformation and requalification of patients (through biomarkers), but also the elaboration of regimens that kill oncogenes, suppress proteins, and block chain reactions by acting on biological pathways teeming with muddled entities. The quest, the exploration, is never over. The Breast International Group (BIG) is a sprawling platform that includes dozens of independent collaborative groups, each with its data centers, its affiliated investigation networks, its hospitals, its laboratories, its pharmaceutical companies (Roche, for example), its patient associations. BIG organizes clinical trials and under pressure from scientists adopts charters of scientific independence. (Roche does not have access to the databases and to intermediate analyses; the statisticians present their analyses to an independent oversight committee; rules are drafted to determine the conditions under which industrial property is attributed.) If the famous linear model of innovation were applied to describe interactions between research and commercial activities, it would simply extend the interface market model to scientific and technical research. It would describe the passage from abstract general knowledge to practical implementation as a series of successive, well-delineated steps contributing to the elaboration of the end treatment. But the interface model must give way in the face of the complexity of biomedical platforms and their entanglement. The final steps, the three phases of clinical trials where therapies are tested,[50] which prolong the linear model, are disappearing. They are being replaced by the new organization of matches between regimens and patients flagged by biomarkers. Instead of eliminating rogue cells, the objective of treatment is to intervene in a chain of reactions within the living body, to interrupt them, divert them, and reorient them in a direction more favorable to life. Development still happens in phases, because there has to be a way to proceed, but the phases are aimed at organizing coprofiling trials to increase the precision and relevance of the matching process. Everything is in motion, whereas in the previous organization of treatment, everything was fixed, the better to observe the impact on patients, who were also fixed and undifferentiated.

Matching is never definitive. It suggests a vanishing point, never reached, where there would be a constant accompaniment, continuously evaluated and reconfigured as a function of observed effects, taking into account the patient's expectations and his way of existing in each moment. Other work in a similar vein has highlighted the growing extension of the process of mutual adaptation of regimens and the patients to whom they apply. I am thinking here of Andrew Lakoff's and Philippe Pignarre's studies of psychiatry[51] or Vololona Rabeharisoa's study of rare diseases.[52]

The story of Bernard Desforges shows just how far these dynamic adjustments can go. Desforges was forty-nine, suffering from metastatic lung cancer, when the doctors gave him ten months to live. When he learned that his cancerous cells presented a genetic alteration that provokes an uncontrolled tumoral growth, a targeted therapy (Erlotinib, made by Roche) was prescribed for him in the UK. He then had a complete sequencing of his mutations and biomarkers performed, this time in the United States. Other targets became apparent. A second targeted therapy (Crizotinib, from Pfizer) was set up. It was followed by an immunotherapy aimed at reprogramming the immune system, in Germany. This extreme case shows that matches follow one another, linking up into a route that takes no account of borders, where partners, molecules, pathologies, and with them the patient's identity change and adjust to one another. This is clearly an expensive adventure that involves only a single individual and temporary therapeutic effects. Nevertheless, the extreme nature of the example illustrates the pursuit of intensive singularization, an exploratory logic that stops at nothing; like life, it is pursued indefinitely.[53]

Matching requires a lot of work upstream. Fixed, stable platforms are a distant memory, as is the relatively straightforward problem of matching a multitude of heterogeneous supplies and demands. Exploration, which was absent from the model of interface markets, since that was entirely and instantaneously supported by platform goods and was reduced to its final steps in matchmaking and frictional markets or in the network markets of sociologists, now appears indistinguishable from the market as a whole. The market is a sprawling exploratory enterprise devoted to organizing an unpredictable and unpredicted match between supplies, goods, and demands, which are all themselves unknown a priori! This is why the notion of market agencement should be preferred over the idea of a market.

If one agrees to call the set of devices that allows the joint investigation of goods and agencies and continuously produces their singularization an exploratorium, it is easy to show that this notion applies to all market agencements. Granted, the architecture and the modes of functioning of the exploratorium change from one agencement to another, but their existence remains. Amazon's website is an exploratorium. Having passed through it, the *volumen* (book) is no longer the same, any more than the *regimen* (treatment) is identical after clinical trials; a different reader and a different patient, as well as a different medicine and a different author, emerge from these events. Meetic is an exploratorium, and so are the platforms that offer sexual services for payment.[54] As are the labor markets,[55] the art and wine markets,[56] speed dating at the Lafayette bistro, or the atmospheric bubbles of the new malls. A systematic inventory of exploratoriums would reveal their generality and their diversity, whether they are simple or complex, stable or evolving. It would encompass the platform good of interface markets, which provokes and organizes meetings simply by being exposed, proclaiming, "Here is what I am; here is who is supplying me; and here is the demand to which I can respond," via its different spokespeople, manuals, comparative tests, reviews, or prescribers, but also the biomedical industry, which is itself an exploratorium full of mazes and labyrinths whose layout is constantly upset and modified. Those who enter an exploratorium thinking they are X come out as Y. Those who thought they were going to meet A end up meeting B. Those who thought the point of the trip was cancer find themselves at the bedside of a patient with myopathy. Market agencements are comparable to a bildungsroman in which the plot can be reoriented as it progresses. If we wish to hold on to what deserves to be preserved in the way of how markets function, we must not forget this point.

Whether the coprofiling is done downstream or begins very early and operates all along a network of platforms, ever more massive recourse to centers of big data and mathematical and statistical processing is involved in defining profiles and following their continuous transformations and deformations in order to ensure successful meetings. The accumulation of heterogeneous data recorded as they are produced, as well as constant work on their associations and relations, brings out singularities and makes it possible to delve into them. To target mechanisms, the biomedical practices Cambrosio and Keating describe accumulate data that has to be processed so as to uncover correlations that can provide profiles. The accumulation and interpretation are endless because the further forward the exploration moves, the more it produces information. If they want to move to a next phase or decide to reorient or stop a trial, those responsible for the exploration are condemned to lean on abundant, but irremediably incomplete data. There is no end to the investigation. There is no stable, definitive, well-known state; there are only intermediary states and information. Treating a patient is processing information. In biomedicine, this requirement has led to original statistical methods that attempt to analyze how much a handful of extra data points change established relationships. Profiling and singularizing feed on an important stock of data that are patiently accumulated and continuously updated by taking into account the new data produced by the ongoing exploration. In oncology, the tension that any exploratorium faces is managed by data-monitoring committees whose mission is to constantly study, analyze, and interpret intermediary information in order to make temporary decisions that will affect patients' quality of life in ways that are hard to predict and that will also therefore require the patients' participation.

The data produced and processed by exploratoriums oriented toward the intensive singularizing of agents and goods are not necessarily the result of direct meetings. To know *what* a consumer *is* and *what he wants* does not require being physically close. The traces each of us leaves online, traces that are signatures of a sort, have become a way for each of us to express what we are. They provide information and give indications of our behavior. Having ascertained to whom they are to be attributed, it remains only to record them, sort them, classify them, and learn to read and decipher them. These traces can be interpreted as proxies for traditional subjective notions such as opinions, value judgments (I like this product for such and such a reason), or decisions (actual purchase choices). But from a pragmatic point of view, recordings of these traces must simply be seen as making it possible to capture the organizing pattern of an agent's actions. We know what comes next. Each agent is characterized by a set of data (relating to different sectors of his activities and personality), and analyzing correlations makes it possible to put together profiles that can be grouped into classes whose proximity can easily be calculated—it just requires defining distance in a multidimensional space. An individual is a network of correlations. The challenge is no longer to analyze the reasons that move him to act or to take a position. Rather, it is to describe his behavior by identifying new data. The data constellation exhausts all that can be said on the subject. Profiling applies to all sorts of agencies, whether they are searching for a partner, a book to read, a great vintage, or a work of art to buy.

Sandrine Cassini, Chloé Hecketsweiler, and Anne Michel offer an overview of the sectors that have been profoundly affected by coprofiling platforms that continuously adjust matches. There are those we have already observed: health and targeted therapies; marketing, advertisement, and commercial practices; the labor market and hiring patterns. There are yet others to be considered: the insurance sector, with targeted contracts; financial markets that work toward ever more refined matching of lenders and borrowers; the energy sector, tracking consumption (with so-called intelligent sensors and smart meters) so as to allow for optimized offers; agriculture, with the growing part played by meteorological data determining where and what to plant, treat, and harvest. Each farmer is now profiled to have the right product available where and when he knows he will need it. The activities of producing, storing, and processing data to establish profiles (of goods, supplies, and demands) are booming. Data warehouses, equipped with machines and computers able to absorb and manage astronomical masses of data, are needed; ever more sophisticated algorithms are required to calculate, and recalculate, targets.[57]

A particularly transparent definition of singularization is at stake behind all these calculations: working on big numbers is key to personalizing what is put on offer. Singularization is extracted so that it stands out against the background of relations and the classifications they permit. Singularization is refined in direct proportion to the increasing numbers of relations — that is to say, physical or virtual meetings. The faster that data are accumulated, the faster that singular profiles can transform. A sort of vanishing point appears: if one were able to take a full inventory of all the data that define a good or an agency, then one could establish its irreducible uniqueness in practice. Paradoxically, however, it is precisely at that point that the entity's commensurability would be at its maximum. Uniqueness is the result of an infinite increase in relations.[58] We are going to exploit this observation in describing the role exploration platforms play in what can be called *mass singularization*.

SINGULAR MULTITUDES

Looking into matches and the role played by exploration platforms (the exploratoriums) makes it possible to understand why singularization and massification, far from being in opposition, are on the contrary the results of a single process. One way of highlighting the originality of this movement is to turn back to marketing practices, since marketing has always faced the problem of reaching many individuals at once.

With the rise of relational marketing, the ways of analyzing and characterizing a clientele, segmenting it, and making a match between supplies and demands has changed profoundly. For a long time, the strategy was to make more and more subtle classifications, relying on criteria external to the individuals (socioprofessional categories, for starters, then home addresses, religious practices, and so on). The hypothesis, sustained by a perspective solidly anchored in sociology, was that social class is primary, that it transcends the individuals of which it is composed, and that it can be the basis for predicting and possibly explaining behavior. Tell me which class you belong to, and I will tell you who you are (what you will buy). This proposition was for obvious logical reasons completely reversible. With the accumulation of large amounts of heterogeneous data and in a sort of subtle series of cross-fades, classification was progressively pushed toward higher resolution. At the limit, we get closer to the paradoxical situation in which the individual becomes a class of his own. We then discover that the notion of class was only a cognitive prosthesis that compensated for the weakness of available data. To dissolve the paradox, we need only reverse the reasoning and attend to individual differences (or similarities), working with variables that are no longer considered external, but rather attached to the individuals whose behavior they describe. These variables take on different values depending on the individuals; this allows for classes and sets to be reconstructed, starting this time from individuals. (The class is the terminus ad quem, instead of being the terminus a quo.) The method used by relational marketing does not abolish classification. It underlines that not only are classifications always at stake (we already knew that), they also evolve apace with the analysis of the data that contribute to performing them. Marketers have simply gone along with a more general movement, one that affects both the analysis of large numbers and the relations between individuals and multitudes. The segmentation remains; however, it runs in the opposite direction.

The first consequence of this approach is that it problematizes what we call an individual or a person. The example of the new oncology illustrates this point. Where there once was a patient who was an organism composed of organs contained in a somatic envelope and echoing the traditional conception of the (indivisible) individual, there is now a sort of deconstructed individual, transformed into a site where a cascade of complex biological pathways lead to the proliferation of sick cells, and one has to try to intervene to contain the cascade. In the clinical trials of yesteryear, the tests on patients came after tests on animals, which were already defined as integrated, indivisible organisms. In the new way of conceiving of things, clinical trials come after trials in test tubes. Thanks to singularization, the individual and the person seem dismembered, decomposed, transformed into biological sequences. Similarly, the profiling that is constantly revisited by meeting platforms such as Meetic can be analyzed as an enterprise that constantly revisits the problematization of identities: Who are you? The platform responds to this question with a series of evolving answers (the profiles); multiplicity and the transformations it implies dismember the initial identities. Breakdowns, decompositions, and recompositions transform people into complex and changing assemblages with what we might call variable ontologies. The phenomenon is accentuated by the fact that platforms are proliferating and spreading to new sectors of activity. When I go on Amazon's site, I am profiled in a certain way; when I consult a doctor at the Salpêtrière hospital about a myopathy that worries me, I come out of it, a few weeks later, in the form of a list of all the genetic mutations responsible for my pains; when I get a loan from my bank, I find an image and scores I did not expect reflected back at me. Who am I? The only thing I can answer is that I am a multiple, torn being, seen through a kaleidoscope, ceaselessly in motion. I could not claim at any time that somewhere in Big Brother's headquarters or in the circumvolutions of my neocortex there exists a pilot who controls the whole thing. My cogito gives way to our *cogitamus*. My tastes are the tastes of others, and so on. *I* is another, but especially *I* is disassembled the better to consume or produce. Individuals are somehow dismembered from below, whereas at the same time, new associations emerge, engendering new classes that redefine, so to speak from above, their identity and profile.[59] And if the individual is divided up, it is not due to chance or growing chaos. On the contrary, it is due to the proliferation of regularities, structurations, all sorts of classifications that cross over and reconfigure one another. Individuals are fragmented and distributed, beings are problematized, and all this happens in a hyperordered manner.[60]

The second consequence is that these platforms establish an original relation between the qualitative and the quantitative. Profiling involves grasping the singularity of a being. The further the profiling activity progresses, the more it intensifies and accentuates that singularity—that is to say, what makes an individual, human being or thing, qualitatively different from the others.[61] Having been put through the grinder, reconfigured by Amazon's platform or by the analysis of my genetic mutations on Généthon's sequencing platform, I have become a different being, one whose literary or genetic signature has been modified and made explicit. However, and here lies the paradox, but here also the paradox dissolves: these profilings that are intensified and multiplied require that a multitude of dimensions and variables be constantly correlated and compared. As children, we all played the game of connecting dots on a piece of paper to gradually see emerge the silhouette of a well-known character such as Scrooge McDuck or Gladstone Gander. Profiles produced by platforms detach themselves gradually from multiple disconnected points in much the same way. The commercial life game is even more complicated than the children's game. In relational databases, the number of points continually increases, even as the sought-after profiles change. To make singularities emerge from an inchoate multitude requires ever more and more complex numerical calculations. More qualities always call for more quantities.

The third consequence relates to aggregation mechanisms. In order to singularize alignments, platforms increase their number. Thus, Meetic organizes personalized meetings at scale. From the point of view of those who experience them, each meeting is a unique adventure; from the point of view of those responsible for the platform, however, it is only one of the many included in the set of all successful meetings. The platform aggregates while singularizing and separating. Similarly, if Tesco, Amazon, Big Pharmas, or capital risk funds increase the volume of their sales, it is because they adjust and singularize each good on offer. Multitude and singularity are thus the two by-products of a single process. Furthermore, thanks to the platform, they compose a set that holds together.[62] In elaborating a targeted regimen, Roche constructs a population and a market of patients that has its own coherence and that ensures a certain business volume for the company. David Riesman spoke of a "lonely crowd" to characterize contemporary societies.[63] According to him, the individual no longer follows tradition or seeks the source of his commitments in himself. He is caught up in mass consumption and the conformism it produces. With market agencements and their meeting platforms, Riesman's expression, although suggestive, becomes irrelevant. It is hard to pretend that consumption is an autonomous sphere in which consumers are condemned to be nothing but mere consumers who have no other obsession than to observe each other. Market platforms break that autonomy by interposing themselves between consumers, even as they connect them to each other. It is not easy to find an expression to render this strange collective dynamic. "Singular multitude" is probably the best, even if it does not make explicit the connection between the entities that compose this multitude. We will see this more clearly in the following section, when I consider the case of television.

Whatever the case, making explicit the role that meeting platforms play makes it possible to get a new perspective on the famous curves that, in interface markets, are supposed to represent supply and demand in a (so-called) aggregate form. From the point of view of market agencements, the aggregation of supplies and demands cannot be reduced to a simple arithmetical operation adding up distinct transactions. It is produced by platforms that, even as they connect qualities and quantities, set up devices to observe, collect, and process data. This means that in a very concrete sense, the famous law of supply and demand is not exterior to the agencies engaged in transactions. To put it in a more technical language, supplies and demands are endogenous variables, since their levels depend on successful meetings and realignments—that is to say, on the performances of the platforms that carry these out. Aggregations are in the hands of agencies (whether on the supply side or the demand side) not because the numbers can be manipulated, not because they could be kept confidential, but because aggregation operations are material operations that are blended into the very functioning of the platforms. Give me the platform (Meetic, Amazon, Roche), and I will give you the supply and demand curves. Any sum totted up by an outside observer would be mere speculation, as would be the hypothesis that there exists a point of intersection of these curves and that it marks the market price. If a company wants to avoid losing the monopoly on aggregation (and therefore on the organizing of meetings), it has only to keep the data produced by its platforms (at least partly) secret. A striking example of such a configuration is given by Tim Mitchell in *Carbon Democracy*.[64] He shows in great detail how the large Anglo-American oil companies managed to prevent all attempts at aggregation for several decades, thereby rendering the notions of supply and demand unusable, which gave the companies greater room to maneuver in manipulating prices. This illustration is all the more eloquent because it concerns a good (crude oil) of which it might have been thought that it was one of those standardized products one dreams of when speaking of aggregate supplies and demands. The struggle to aggregate meeting sites, as we will see in Chapter 6, is part of the struggle for control over determining prices.

MATTERS OF CONCERN

The history of commercial activities comprises a long series of innovations developed by economic actors that respond to the incessantly recurring problem of how to organize market encounters. Auctions in all their various formats—trade fairs, stock markets, shopping malls, electronic platforms—are some of the most important solutions. It is only quite recently, however, that meeting devices have become, as we saw in this chapter, objects for reflection and discussion in themselves, both for those interested in the theoretical analysis of commercial activities and for the professionals involved in commercial practices.

Framed meetings play such a central role in the alignment of supplies and demands, in the determination of goods' qualities, and in the definition of agencies' identities that they raise serious concerns and provoke intense debates. Which meeting platforms? What organization for these platforms? Although many solutions can be imagined, all of them can be contested because the organizational, moral, and political stakes are so high.

Without being exhaustive, I will survey these matters of concern, if only to underline the fact that alternatives exist.

WE ARE ALL BEING TRACKED!

Coprofiling, through the targeting of consumers it implies, seems to some to be a tracking exercise, a relentless manhunt that it is hard to escape. Big Brother does not just watch us. Insinuating himself into our private lives, he acts on us, transforms us, and directs our conduct without our even realizing it. The fact that traces are exploited (and it is, indeed, a matter of exploitation) is considered dangerous for private life, all the more dangerous because the interconnections between databases increase.[65] This concern does not lead toward denouncing profiling as reductive, but rather, on the contrary, to decrying the overly developed realism of such profiles. I am the one concerned, I am the one being tracked. Leave me alone! Stop this unbearable harassing! The further you refine the analysis of my behavior, the more you enter my inner world, entering into what constitutes my personality. The strength of this concern is an implicit admission: yes, what the databases grasp, in the end, after such accumulation and cross-referencing, is indeed something that could be me, that will end up being me, will force me to be me, and that is why this tracking seems so dangerous to me. Hence the demands for devices that would oppose and contain the tracking. Those who visit malls equipped with devices that allow for following potential customers can refuse this equipment. The right to be forgotten is being claimed loud and clear.

WE ARE NOT WHAT YOU SAY WE ARE!

A less brutal challenge is to denounce meeting and exploitation platforms for being reductionist. Profiling in order to set up matches leads to selecting and making explicit certain traits, organizing them into sets, and relegating to obscurity other aspects or dimensions that I may consider more important than those that were chosen. "I am not who you say I am," or "You don't have the right to reduce me to a few variables or, worse, to a few numbers." The account of a human being cannot be restricted to its behavior.

This objection can take very different forms. When Amazon sends me a message saying, "You liked Piketty, you should like Houellebecq," I can ignore it without feeling obliged to object. That is the *exit* strategy that Albert Hirschman studied: the consumer, and this is his strength, can exit the market, punishing the seller who did not manage to understand him in this way.[66] I can also move one step further toward activism by publishing an editorial or writing on my blog to say that Amazon is going off the rails, or rather that the readers calculated by Amazon are going off the rails: no, Houellebecq is not an economist, no matter what Bernard Maris and lots of Amazon customers say. Then again, if I find that this suggestion is the straw that breaks the camel's back, I might chose to join broader movements contesting the algorithms that are reducing us to our profiles despite ourselves and pushing us to act like sheep. This protest is not limited to a particular social milieu. Intellectuals, academics in the humanities, political parties, people like you and me who are tired of being infantilized can all join in. It can be linked to other causes, such as criticism of the kind of targeted advertisement on the internet, that, when I look up a word, offers me garden machines I don't need anymore. All these causes can be cumulated and can respond to each other to contest the organized tracking that reduces human beings to a handful of numbers, scores, or associations they want nothing to do with.

The case of health care occupies a privileged position among the causes for mobilization. Biomedicine, profiling patients and therapies, singularizing treatments, and recourse to biomarkers raise worrying questions. Some say no to the human person being reduced to genetic mechanisms, notably, in the case of illnesses that are deemed mental and especially by insurers who use this to calculate premiums. Others, seeing the promise of new treatments in all this, celebrate "geneticization" and clamor for more of it. Indeed, this worry may give way to another. What if the risk were that of reducing the human person or any situation to a collection of ever larger and more eclectic data? Reductionism is not what it used to be. It no longer is about (over)simplifying by limiting the number of variables considered. On the contrary, it now sallies forth in the glittering garb of the science of the complex:

Complex systems made up of interconnected networks, interactions between heterogeneous elements, and embracing several spatial and temporal scales are now prevalent. Biological systems are a striking example: multiscale (from molecular networks to organ organization), consisting of heterogeneous subsystems (e.g., genetic and metabolic networks) and nonlinear interactions and feedbacks, making their behavior difficult to understand using conventional reductionist approaches. These models can be used in urban planning (transport and distribution networks) as well as in biomedical domains (tumor growth, epidemic management), or in cosmetics and bioproduction.[67]

This is no longer the vulgar reductionism that a term such as "geneticization" suggests, the idea that a handful of well-chosen variables are enough to conjure a world. It is a complex reductionism that takes into account many entities, interactions, levels, and retroactions in order to better grasp and profile behaviors. Those who mock this hyperbolically positivist ambition of soaking up reality by multiplying observations and numbers may find their derision pointless. The algorithms are crunching imperturbably; the question is not so much to know how they grind, but how they should grind. The concern has shifted. Some quite rightly fear they will no longer exist except as avatars, unwittingly captive to invisible databases.

The reader knows that I could give many more examples. I could evoke the case of researchers reduced to indices that are unanimously decried and just as unanimously used, notably by those organizations, public agencies, or companies in search of laboratories with which to establish contracts. And when one who finances research projects and researchers wants to wed, they can free themselves of these reductive indices and appeal to enormous bibliometric databases that make it possible to profile supplies and demands precisely. The solution to the aporia of reductionism is not to calculate less, but to calculate more. For those who are sensitive to this matter of concern, the challenge is to invent new tools, and not to give up on calculation.[68]

Should we fear that with platforms, people are reduced to profiles, that beings made of flesh, emotions, and passions are reduced to flattened silhouettes, and that the flavor and meaning of the human person will be lost? This is, of course, an open question. It may be that with market agencements and the intensification of singularized alignments, people, rather than being the measure of all things, will be measured by them.

THE STRUGGLE FOR DATA

One way to oppose the wrongdoing of reductionism (whether the reductionism is simple or complex) without contesting the method it promotes is to demand that the data it feeds on be controlled. For instance, some see in the growing trend of producing selfies not just a sort of autism or narcissism, but rather a brutal and popular way of reclaiming the power to do one's own profiling.

An emerging contention is that the data that make it possible to calculate profiles should be controlled by individuals. Since these data are destined to define identities, expectations, needs, and behavior, why should we accept that their definition, collection, and processing lie in the hands of those who use it to pull in a profit? As Gilles Bastin rightly says, "Our capacity to trust them to represent the world in which we want to live... probably depends on the outcome of this struggle."[69]

This is the position taken by the Conseil d'État in France in its report on digital technology and fundamental rights (September 9, 2014).[70] Regarding platforms that highlight certain profiles of work (and therefore agencies), the Conseil d'État suggests imposing that they take into account certain criteria that promote cultural diversity, for instance, through positive discrimination regarding certain French or European products. Thus, when a request is submitted to a search engine, some results might appear on screen in a special dedicated window, separate from the other results.

Identical demands have been made on flourishing biobanks. These platforms collect and maintain "immense collections of samples of human tissue, blood, urine, plasma, or cell lines, collected in hospitals and kept in optimal conditions to be available for free to scientists, whether they work for the public sector or pharmaceutical companies."[71] Like most centers of big data, these biobanks are a tool for bespoke medicine that can adapt therapies to genetic profiles. The biobank set up by the European Union in Graz, Austria, holds more than six million samples. It is, however, only one element in a network of platforms containing two hundred million samples coordinated by the Biobanking and Biomolecular Resources Research Infrastructure. Like traditional banks, these banks of a new type develop their own trades (there are now master's degrees in biobank management) because the collecting has to be organized, delicate property problems have to be solved, and everything must be properly preserved, cataloged, identified, traceable, barcoded. These banks of a new type (which, like traditional banks, accumulate and produce benefits, in this case both monetary and therapeutic) also contribute to making the very idea of personhood problematic. Bodies arrive dismembered, fragmented, decomposed. They are then reconfigured via assemblages and comparisons in such a way that pathological profiles and adapted therapies emerge. Patients' groups also chime into the discussion. These biobanks do nevertheless contribute to freeing medicine from the constraints of "real" bodies, insofar as they make it possible to imagine sorts of avatars of human beings or laboratory animals "in order to test the medicines of the future," as Joëlle Stolz says, "without risk or misgivings." Both biobanks and platforms such as Meetic can imagine the debates that arise from such a situation. The debates are all the more contentious because the problems are not only questions that might too easily be called ethical. The stakes are also financial and monetary. There are no limits to the markets onto which profiling may open.

IS THIS THE END OF THE COLLECTIVE?

Is it possible that intensive singularization, particularly in the form of profiling, undermines the very foundations of social life?

Contemplating Netflix's success, Olivier Schrameck, when he was president of the French Conseil supérieur de l'audiovisuel (CSA), voiced the fear that television will become a consumer good that is tailored to the spectator's projected personality, based on his past tastes, socioprofessional characteristics, or buying habits. Television would thus be like a "silo" system, encouraging "confinement," "prolonging private space," rather than "a window that confronts the spectators with new realities." Operators such as Netflix, he adds, "follow an individual logic, different from ours, which is collective.... Customized television threatens the model we defend, that of an audiovisual offering that provides social cohesion, favoring diversity and cultural pluralism."[72] In his diatribe, the president of the CSA took aim at television for becoming a machine that shreds the collective through the excessive singularizing of what it offers.

Is this actually the case? Playing the individualization card, will televisual platforms necessarily destroy social connections and the collectives they weave? Will they necessarily create the "serial" groups Sartre spoke of in the *Critique of Dialectical Reason*, rather than fusional groups?[73]

It is not inevitable for things to evolve that way. In fact, it is unlikely they will. Nothing stands in the way of, or rather, I should say, everything points toward the possibility that singular multitudes will be taken up into collectives. Platforms, televisual or otherwise, produce both multitudes and singularities at once. The contradiction can be overcome and has in fact at least partially *been* overcome with the simultaneous development of two new and complementary forms of television show.[74] One is television on demand, which we can call nonlinear. It allows the spectator to watch series, films, and documentaries in a desynchronized way; the internet, fiber-optic cable, and data storage make this possible. Playing the singularization game, streaming allows for detailed tailoring of services and profiles.[75] A second, called "event television," broadcasts live reporting: sports, reality TV, continuous news channels, and breaking news. Event television, leaning on a mass audience, extends and orchestrates collective mobilizations. The huge demonstrations in France on January 11, 2015, provide a striking illustration of this. Each individual participating in the demonstration abolished his or her identity to make way for a single collective identity, expressed and shared as "Je suis Charlie."[76] Anonymous and invisible though the spectators in front of their screens may be, they also participate in the demonstration. Event-driven viewing, aided and amplified by live streaming and handheld footage, increases the scale of the gathering, of the indistinct mass. A journalist from BFM TV, serving as a live mediator, made the connection between the two crowds, the one in the streets and the one in living rooms, merging them into one. This multitude, whose image and reality blend into each other, is held by the screen that provides its image and reflects it back to the multitude. The multitude can take on any name: some will say it is the nation resisting, others that it is the people rising up, still others that this is the exclusion of the *banlieues*, and so on. It is a controversial matter, figuring out what the collective is, but there is no question that the collective is there. I am "black, blanc, beur";[77] I am Zidane;[78] I am Charlie. In both cases, the mechanism is the same. Televisual platforms give life to singular multitudes.[79] Event television pulls together, aggregates, and collects singular profiles, synchronizes what has been dissociated in time and space by nonlinear television, thus making real what anthropologists have often emphasized—namely, that there is a cadence to social life. By showing that the two movements, one toward individualization, and one toward aggregation, cannot be dissociated from one another, television gives a conspicuous, large-scale illustration of the combination of singularization and aggregation at work in matching platforms.

Many, like Schrameck, have clamored that singularization and coprofiling kill the collective and undo the social fabric. Many others, on the contrary, rejoice that platforms allow individuals to resist and avoid being drowned in undifferentiated masses in which they are alienated. Each camp hears only half the story. Like television, market agencements, by adjusting supplies and demands, create collectives galore; at the same time, they promote singular beings. The political choice, which remains to be organized, is not between the individual and the collective, but between different configurations of singular multitudes.[80]

CHAPTER FIVE

Affectio Mercatus: Attachments and Detachments

Here are some passiva(c)ted goods ready to share their existence with new-comers; here are some agencies, capable of evaluating these goods; here are agencies and goods in encounters that have been organized to coprofile them in order to make a match. These successive formattings do not necessarily mean the match will become a transaction. Each of us has experienced it a thousand times: we may highly value a good, yet not be ready to acquire it in exchange for cash: "It's too expensive, or not expensive enough; I don't really need it; I have other priorities"; and so on.

Consider again the case of platforms such as the French dating sites Meetic or Adopteunmec, which organize the search for a companion. The match is doomed unless it concludes with the partners committing to an adventure they agree to pursue to its end, whether it be intense or superficial, brief or long last-ing. Alignment and matching is one thing, attachment quite another. Attach-ment describes the (successful) process of reconfiguring an agency such that having been transformed and wanting to persevere in a new way of being, it has only one option left—namely, to appropriate the good and pay to obtain it.

How the price gets affixed will be the subject of the following chapter. For now, I am interested in the strange process that leads to the action aptly described by the phrase "to consume." To consume is to lead an action to a degree of total consummation, its definitive accomplishment. As in poker, one has to pay to see, one has to take action and not stall on the way.

To push agencies to take the plunge requires powerful forces. Common sense has it right when it speaks of consumers' insatiable desires, commercial frenzies, industrial greed, or the legitimate ambition to be a millionaire celebrated by Emmanuel Macron. Speculative fever carries traders to great heights before leaving them, a little later, waiting in humiliation, their lips curled in an ironic smile, for the movers to come for their cardboard boxes, strewn like wrecks on the sidewalk next to them. And then there is the entrepreneur's taste for risk, but also the pride in work well done or the pleasure in listening to beautiful music and tasting good wine.

Until now, we have kept at a distance from the heat of passions and emotions, of everything that provokes, encourages, or facilitates movement or attraction, of everything that moves goods and agencies, precipitates them toward each other, and concludes with irresistible attachments. It would be a serious mistake to ignore that world. It is time to fill this lacuna and to add an element to the scene. I suggest we call it *affectio mercatus*. It is neither the hidden side of the market nor its dark side or even an underground world from which it draws resources and vigor. *Affectio mercatus* is at the heart of the market. It is a source that animates and agitates us as agents; it communicates energy and inclines us; it shapes our preferences, nourishes our expectations, stimulates our infatuations, and leads us to the point where some of us are ready to pay in order to attach ourselves to the goods we covet that others only want to be rid of.

Why speak of *affectio mercatus*? Because the expression resonates with *affectio societatis*. *Affectio societatis* refers to the set of motives, feelings, passions, and moods that lead people to gather together in a business or a non-profit organization, to adopt the aims and participate in the collective action it organizes. Similarly, *affectio mercatus* refers to the set of mechanisms that push agencies to engage in a collective action that concludes, at some point, with a bilateral transfer in return for monetary compensation.

Make no mistake! The forces that lead to attachment and symmetrically, for the sellers, to detachment are not simply already there, pent up in some huge reservoir, waiting to be tapped. Need or desire does not exist as a general resource. It exists only in relation to such and such an object. Entrepreneurial risk, speculative fever, a taste for good wine—none of these are given. They are all shaped by education, practice, apprenticeship, imitation. *Affectio mercatus* is a mode of framing that is on par with the pass(act)ivation of goods, the qualculation equipment of agencies, and the organization of encounters.

Like these framings and in their lineage, it shapes, interrupts, and channels market activities. *Affectio* and *affection* are in fact not very far from the French term *affectation*, which in that language refers to being assigned a position or being earmarked for a purpose.

Drawing upon the word's usage in French, I would like to give the term "affectation" a second meaning and use it to refer to the actions that lead an agency to be *affected* by the goods on offer. The platforms we visited in the previous chapter could then be considered as devices that tend to produce a double affectation: the first affectation (1) assigns goods to agencies; the second affectation (2) reaches and touches agencies to such an extent that some attach to these goods and others detach from them. This chapter depends upon the reader mastering this distinction, which is drawn from French, but does not exist in English.[1]

Anyone who has studied commercial activities has thought about *affectio mercatus* in one way or another. We must therefore start from the considerable work that has been done on the subject. In the first section, limiting myself essentially to economics and to economic sociology, I offer a reading that underlines their contributions and identifies some of the questions still open. I will then concentrate on a crucial aspect of *affectio mercatus*—namely, on the attachment and detachment mechanisms that explain why some agencies are ready to pay and others to sell. I will also examine the devices that implement attachment and detachment.

SEARCHING FOR *AFFECTIO MERCATUS*

In the canonical version of the interface market model, understanding the force that impels agents to engage in commercial transactions has been simplified to such an extent that it often ends up being completely ignored. How can we give a detailed and convincing account of the fact that some consumers become attached to certain goods (be they simple material objects or services) such that they will consent to pay for them? As the reader will have guessed, if one wants to give an account of these mechanisms in their complexity and to grasp the energies that set them in motion, the notion of supply and demand comes up short. Indeed, the problem has not escaped economists, sociologists, and anthropologists who study commercial activities. That is why some of them have made such efforts to enrich the interface market model, without, however, going so far as to explicitly recognize the role the goods themselves play in all the excitement. In the following, I will offer a cursory summary of this body of work, its important contributions, and the questions that remain.

ECONOMIC ANALYSIS

The mystery of universal attraction was first explained through quite simple motives. The consumer seeks to acquire certain goods and is ready to devote part of his resources or his wealth to this quest because he is impelled by the irrepressible needs these goods promise to satisfy. These needs may be more or less natural, primary or sophisticated, more or less dependent on the consumer's activities and lifestyles. Depending on the psychosociological theories invoked, they are needs that can be described as desires, mimetic fever, or a mere search for ostentation. More neutral and descriptive notions have also been forged in order to group these forces of attraction and account for their efficacy under a single term that is easy to understand. Take, for example, widely used expressions such as "use value" or "utility." Their main function is to reduce the whole diversity of relationships and inclinations between human agents and goods to one fuzzy category. The same goes for producers. To account for their participation in the customer's questing, there is talk of greed, the desire of enrichment, will to power, an entrepreneurial bent, and the need for job satisfaction, all of which are fulfilled by the naked pursuit of profit and/or the pursuit of client satisfaction.

Given the complexity of the problem, economists first tried to rid themselves of having to discover the inner motivations for acting. Indeed, as Joseph Schumpeter underlines, there is no need to plumb hearts and minds in order to understand how (interface) markets work and ensure their efficiency. The motivations or passions that guide agents, leading them to their decisions, do not matter. When Newton was asked about the nature of the gravitational force whose effects he observed, he answered, "Hypotheses non fingo"—I do not make, or feign, hypotheses. The same goes for the universal attraction in the space of interface markets. All that counts are the supplies and demands, which, like the forces of Newtonian mechanics accelerating stars, accelerate agents toward one another. Moreover, the presence of goods, which appear like promises made without any hypothesis as to their origin, appears to guarantee that these forces do not hurl agents toward impossible targets. Nobody can deny that motives and motivations are necessary. However, in this way of thinking, they do not need to be taken into account in the functioning of the market. It suffices that they feed decisions, which are the only variables that need to be taken into consideration. Schumpeter recalls that economists went to great lengths to be rid of the notion of utility and its hedonist overtones and to replace it with notions such as preferences, which simply observe the choices made. If they failed somewhat, it is because it is difficult to freeze commercial mechanisms and reduce agents to cold decision makers when they are obviously creatures moved by their passions, sometimes falling into addictive behavior, often losing themselves in speculative conduct or taking incomprehensible risks. Can one really consider these passionate modes of behavior as disturbances, when they are at the heart of the ways markets function? Is it not vain or even inefficient to attempt to purge them?

Economic theory, in its different guises, quite quickly perceived the difficulties that flow from the (epistemological) will to separate decisions from motivations. Emotions, passions, and mental dispositions inevitably interfere with the content of decisions. That is why there is so much talk of the *criteria* for decisions as a way of putting emotions at a distance while recognizing their role. Whether they are regrets to be minimized, risks or losses to avoid, precautions to be taken, future generations to care for, all criteria, whatever they are, connect back to motives, feelings, or values held by the deciders. The word does not matter much, but there is some instance that defines and imposes a hierarchy on the relevant information, what must be taken into account; there is some instance that organizes and processes information to prepare for the decision. My sense is that economists are more and more aware that if one wants to make progress in the analysis of markets and in understanding agents' decisions, it is essential to put the question of the sources and motives for action back at the center of the analysis. A similar inclination explains the recent spectacular rise in behaviorist economics. Its method is not actually new. It ties back into those of the great ancestors—notably, Adam Smith.

The importance of affective states, without which the commercial machine could not work, became apparent very early, at the same moment as the notion of market was invented as an abstract concept that made it possible to describe the organization of commercial exchanges. Adam Smith's work is emblematic in this respect, because he shows that it is impossible to conceive of markets that are not rooted in emotions. Take away the emotional environment, and markets would collapse. The market is a superstructure resting on an infrastructure composed of feelings and states of mind.

When Smith makes the pursuit of interest the wellspring of commercial engagement, he hurries to add that agents in competition for (rare) goods must be regulated by forces that incite restraint and measure in order to avoid a destructive war of all against all. His well-known solution rests on a double device. Agents are passionate beings. What controls them, what avoids them being pitted against one another by their passions, is that they can share pain and emotions.[2] This sympathy is guaranteed by the presence of an impartial spectator, whether real or virtual, whose position anyone can and must adopt. Taking on the manner of seeing and of listening to the voice of this impartial spectator engenders sympathy,[3] which ensures that the calculation of interests will be contained, thereby avoiding the overflowing effects to which the forces that put it in motion might lead. Anthropologist Julia Elyachar has brilliantly taken up this method in her analysis of the evil eye, the avatar of the impartial spectator that imposes moderation on those who carry out projects for microcompanies around Cairo.[4]

The mechanisms Smith imagined are a remarkable illustration of one of the most common ways of explaining how commercial institutions can be viable—namely, via an argument that invokes, in one way or another, antagonistic forces whose effects cancel each other out. If selfishness provides the impetus for action and guides it, the antidote is a good dose of altruism. Likewise, to correct the blind pursuit of interest requires a good dose of disinterestedness. Such reasoning makes it absolutely clear that the institution of commerce is rooted in the world of passions, which can be divided into two categories. There are the passions centered on the agents, which lead them to take into account the effects their decisions will have on themselves, and then there are the passions that directly affect their relations with other agents. Smith shows that the market is viable only if these two types of passions coexist in balance: those of selfish agents worried only about themselves and those of agents full of empathy who do not hesitate to put themselves in the other's shoes. In his stimulating analysis of the relationship between the theater and the market in the Elizabethan era, Jean-Christophe Agnew adds that interest

MARKETS IN THE MAKING

often gains the upper hand in this constant struggle because sympathy wears out quite quickly, just as the spectator in the theater is returned to the ordinariness of daily life when the curtain comes down and the lights go back on.[5]

The mechanism Smith suggests is unusually elegant. For a long time, it provided the framework for analyzing the role of passions in commercial activities. Nevertheless, the formulation he chose has serious weaknesses. It grants a great deal to the impartial spectator and the moral sense he inspires. Yet impartial spectators are like the ghosts haunting Scottish castles: in the end, they terrify only credulous children into behaving well! No doubt that is why it became necessary to replace the idea of empathy with that of trust, guaranteed by solid institutions.[6] Kenneth Arrow has provided a foundational insight into the centrality of this disposition in market functionality: according to him, without trust, without the lubrication it provides, markets could not survive themselves.[7] If interested action, unbridled and opportunistic, is not severely regulated, it rushes to its own destruction because the supports it needs disappear, one by one. No viable and sustainable pursuit of profit is possible without a confident atmosphere that ensures a favorable environment, and it follows that there is no social optimum. The price to pay for continuous market action, for keeping the temptation of fraud and plundering at bay, is moderation, as well as a certain loyalty and honesty. There are many much-studied mechanisms that produce agents' disposition to inspire confidence and trust each other. Trust can come from repeated interactions the agents want to prolong. It can be guaranteed by belonging to a group whose members are known each other, are interdependent, and share the same norms. Or it can be encouraged by the existence of devices and ad hoc procedures (for example, warrantees, labels, or an innovation such as blockchain, which logs transactions). Whatever its origin, trust's only function is to contain the markets, avoiding overflowing effects and the catastrophes that might result from them. It is as though since Smith, the theorists who have most made markets rest only on the satisfaction of individual interests or on the free range of passions, oblivious of others, feel compelled to imagine devices in order to attenuate and prevent the deleterious effects of these emotions. There is no attempt to deny the existence of passions, since without them, markets could not exist. Rather, for markets to be viable, each passion has to be controlled by a counterpassion, which keeps it from overflowing.

The anthropology on which these analyses rest is rather banal. It is the avatar of a very old tradition that looks for the play of antagonistic forces—good and evil, Eros and Thanatos, vice and virtue—both in human nature and in institutions. What matters to my argument is the admission that passions are integral to market activities, since the viability of those actions would be unintelligible without them. If one wants to give an account of an agent's decisions, it is no longer possible to overlook their frames of mind, their emotions, or their moods, which frame and feed the process that leads to those decisions. The question is shifting. It is no longer "What decisions do agents make?" but "Why do they decide what they decide?" To answer this question, the analyst has to venture into new territory, the territory covered by behavioral and cognitive studies that are more and more often carried out with recourse to experimental setups.

Studies that focus on trust mark the beginning of a gradual reorientation of economic analysis. The importance of trust lies in the fact that it enables actors to make decisions in a complex and uncertain universe. It is not only a mental and affective disposition that influences behavior. It is also a form of knowledge and a way of grasping reality. In the face of unknown risks, the rational behavior might be to abstain from acting. If, however, I trust an agent or an institution offering to collaborate or transmit information, then I can decide to commit to a course of action that I might otherwise have hesitated to undertake. Once trust matters, there is no reason to stop there, since it is only one of the mental dispositions that can affect my decisions. Once the door is ajar, one has to accept that it can be opened completely, letting in all of the passions and emotions insofar as they affect decision mechanisms in one way or another. This is no doubt why economists' studies of emotions and affect have increased so dramatically in the last few years.

Anger, fear, risk aversion, envy, jealousy, happiness, urgency, surprise, frustration, or guilt—why not ask how an array of emotions affects decisions, making them unpredictable and destabilizing preference hierarchies? Venerable empathy, which had been somewhat forgotten, but which is perhaps another name for altruistic feelings, the care for others, has been explored systematically in the last few years through studies that show that under certain conditions, agents can manifest forms of disinterest, whereas they might well have chosen to follow their own interests.[8] Why not consider that every decision is made on the basis of emotions? This does not prevent it from being reasonable or rational.[9] The great forefathers were not afraid to ask the same questions and . . . to suggest the same answers. Vilfredo Pareto, with his theory of derivations, asserts that rationality is not opposed to the devastating forces of passion, but that it instead channels them by diverting them from their untamed course: if reasons escape reason, they are nevertheless its principal matter. Max Weber went in the same direction when analyzing the role of the Protestant ethic in the spirit of capitalism: "The impulse to acquisition, pursuit of gain, of money, of the greatest possible amount of money, has in itself nothing to do with capitalism. . . . Capitalism may even be identical with the restraint, or at least a rational tempering, of this irrational impulse."[10] Albert O. Hirschman's thesis is not far off: interests and the decisions that calculate them, sustained by competitive markets, are merely derived, but civilized expressions of passions.[11]

Passions cannot be reduced to a force that pushes agents to act from the inside by giving meaning to their actions. They also allow for agents to understand the situations in which they find themselves and to react appropriately. An analyst who takes passions into consideration is led to take an interest in these chains of actions and reactions. In order to study them, one will tend to privilege theories of behavior and their frequent recourse to laboratory experiments. Indeed, affects can rarely be studied in the wild. Rendering them observable requires specific equipment and protocols. Emotions, and this is essential for our purposes, are linked to devices in which they participate and outside of which they lose all meaning. Affects and their effects cannot be separated from the material and discursive contexts in which and through which they are expressed. The conclusions and generalizations drawn from experiments are valid, in a rigorous sense, only if the same environment is reproduced in reality.

From the research in experimental psychology on emotions and their role in market dynamics, studies of addiction deserve a special mention. These studies start from a daring hypothesis put forward by neoclassical theory: addiction is a particular form of consumption, and the question whether it is or is not a pathological behavior is not to be solved by economics. For economics, it is enough to say that it obeys the hedonistic principle. The user consumes ever-increasing quantities to increase his pleasure.[12] There is therefore no difference between an addictive substance and any other good. What is essential, as far as the collective well-being is concerned, is that the markets in which these goods are exchanged function decently. The state intervenes only if consumers are poorly informed about the long-term effects of consuming these substances or if external negativities generated by the consumption (for instance, traffic accidents or the destruction of family structures) become unbearable. This model seems like a caricature. It nevertheless captures important aspects of the issue. Many studies have shown, for example, that consumption responds at least partially to price variations (it diminishes when prices increase) and that it is also sensitive to information campaigns. Although they rely on these studies, behavioral economists nonetheless underline their limits and give an interpretation that is a refutation of neoclassical basic assumptions. They assert that a) consumers of addictive substances disavow their own behavior, describing past actions as mistakes, as the result of decisions that, to some extent, were not their own; b) in their lucid moments, they tie their own hands and inflict sometimes unpleasant treatments on themselves in order to avoid relapses;[13] and c) to avoid relapses, addicts who have stopped enter therapies that act on their behavior without new information being necessary. Yet if one were to remain within the neoclassical framework, one would have to assume that an agent informed by his own experience cannot constantly make the same mistakes. In the neoclassical world, an agent would avoid imposing a priori constraints on himself because to do so would be to forgo future alternative choices, and he would have no reason to spend in order to control himself because he would find all the energy necessary to correct his mistakes within himself.

If one wants to explain observed behaviors, there is no method other than experimentation. According to those who lead these experiments, investigations using the neurosciences show that in addiction, the pleasure principle is not the central force. Becoming dependent is linked to learning systems being perturbed by consumption. According to behaviorists, the malfunction is due to the existence of two decision-making circuits.[14] The first corresponds to decisions made urgently, the second to decisions that follow long deliberation. The first are visceral, the second reasoned. This does not mean that decisions made urgently are systematically irrational, but they do become so when it is a matter of consuming addictive substances. These bypass the long circuit and lead to massively overestimating immediate pleasure in relation to future unpleasantness. One could thus classify every substance and every good in one of two families. Addictive substances are those that, because of their intrinsic properties, upset the capacity for producing correct hedonistic predictions because they exaggerate the anticipated benefits of their consumption. If I may refer back to Chapter 2, what behaviorists draw from the neurosciences is that the inherent force of appropriately passiva(c)ted addictive substances is to pacify those who consume them while inducing them to keep on consuming.

An addictive good is like any other good, but its capacity to act produces enduring attachments. This result, as we will see, is of prime importance because it breaks with the model of interface markets and admits the role played by goods in the structuring and dynamics of market activities. The lesson worth retaining is this: if agents get attached, are captured by goods, it is at least in part because the goods are made to be...captivating.

SOCIOLOGY AND ANTHROPOLOGY

For a long time, sociology and economic anthropology repeatedly pointed out that the science of economics was unrealistic in its analyses of agents' decisions, including the decision to buy or sell. These disciplines accumulated proof that agents only very rarely calculate. Most of the time, agents are moved by their tastes, drives, prejudices, desire to show off, or simply by the advice and counseling of friends or experts they trust. Sociology postulates that such forces might animate and agitate agents' inner worlds, but their origin and sustenance lies outside. The forces are anchored in the social and cultural universe in which agents are plunged. After passing through complicated trajectories related to social positions or social relations, the emotions and cognition of agents are shaped to make them act. The general argument was honed on a classic case: How can suicide be explained? Obviously, by affective or psychological states such as melancholia or depression acting as immediate, proximate causes. If this instance did not exist, the process that leads to ending one's days would not begin. However, having recognized that role, Émile Durkheim immediately adds that this mental and affective state, for instance, melancholia, is produced by currents, in this case, suicidogenic currents in multiple forms, that are shaped in society conceived as a whole and that, once formed, affect each individual and push him to act in a certain direction. The metaphor of a wave is perhaps preferable to that of (suicidogenic) currents: one could say that emotions join together like a body of water caught up in a wave created far out at sea.

Durkheim's analysis has continuously inspired sociological thinking. The force of the analysis lies in the fact that it applies to events and sentiments that seem to be the most intimate, the most individual—not only suicide, but also the grief linked to mourning, artistic emotion, or the rush of the senses induced by a collective spectacle. These different emotions, these affective universes, offer an obvious social dimension, sanctioned by rites and customs, that make certain gestures and postures compulsory in such circumstances. Passions not only grab hold of the mind; they move bodies and shape their very behavior. The more the interior the action seems, the more it is in fact exterior, articulated, and translated through the body and its emotions. Countless studies have extended this line of research to further the elucidation of mechanisms that affect agents and to explain how relational structures share the ways of feeling, being touched, being moved, thereby leading to certain types of decisions. Norbert Elias, for instance, shows how emotions can be produced by the relational structure of a network: the longer the chains, the more agents are incited to calculate, whereas the more the relations are dense and closed, the more they rely on trust.[15] Michel Crozier transforms this observation into a methodological resource. He maintains that sociological inquiry must start from affects or feelings and reach out toward the social relations themselves, as well as to the strategies deployed by agents. (For example, he shows how the jealousy that maintenance workers feel in relation to production workers leads them to withhold crucial pieces of information.)[16] Are emotions at the heart of professional activities in certain trades? What would a sales agent be without minimal enthusiasm for the products he offers? What would a manager be if he were not able to communicate to his collaborators the desire to reclaim by force ill-gotten gains from the competition? What would a health care professional be if he were incapable of expressing, at least superficially, some sympathy or compassion in the face of someone's suffering and distress? In the service sector, affects are everywhere, and manifesting them is part of the work itself. To a certain extent, all work requires managing or mastering the expression of emotions. Sociologist Arlie Hochschild refers to a form of labor called "emotional work," which leads to the idea that there are certain devices that enable this type of work, orient it, and facilitate its expression. In *The Managed Heart*, she shows that airline agents are trained to manage both passengers' fear of turbulence and their own anger at grumpy or rude guests. She also illustrates the process by which collectors are trained to curb their compassion or sympathy for debtors.[17] These analyses—and I could give many more references—all contribute to showing that without *affectio mercatus*, without the palette of emotions that make agents act and without the devices that lead them to decide to buy or sell, market activities would not survive.[18] There is in fact also room for affects with the opposite sign, ones that distance agents from commercial activities and draw them instead toward indignation or resistance or to pursue projects for alternative marketplaces that favor other ways of seeing, feeling, and knowing.

Pierre Bourdieu, the person who most convincingly and successfully developed this theoretical perspective, pushed this way of reasoning to its extreme. In putting the dispositions of agents at the center of his analysis, he showed that the multiple and diverse currents that affect agents do not touch everyone in the same way. If one admits that distinct social positions exist, and that there are relations of domination between them, it follows that the modes of what I am calling affectation will be different depending on the positions occupied as well as on the relations between these positions. Most importantly, it follows that their very affective content will reflect these relations in one way or another. When a subordinate is paralyzed with shyness in front of his hierarchical superior or filled with shame when he senses he has broken the rules, when a consumer from the working classes manifests a preference for food that "sticks to the ribs," he is expressing how the situation and positions in which he finds himself affect him. Meaning, emotions, behavior, and social position are intertwined.

When this analysis is applied to market activities, it denies any active role to the goods that are the object of commercial transactions. Goods are taken to be inert things, surfaces on which social relations and the affects they produce are projected in the form of taste and distaste.[19] For those who refuse to believe that things participate in decision making, certain goods whose description resists all objective and consensual analysis provide particularly privileged objects of study. Thus, the wine market is to economic sociology what drosophila are for genetics. What are the forces that lead a consumer to select one wine over another? Systematic studies track the physical-chemical qualities of wine in a vain attempt to make intelligible connections with the qualities that are perceived by consumers. It seems impossible to establish the relationship. The appreciation of wine is almost entirely in the hands of consumers, or rather, in those of the intermediaries who, as we will see, advise them. Appreciation, however, owes practically nothing to the objective properties of the beverage. Sociology dives into this gap because it seems to show and prove one of its central theses. Given that one cannot identify stable connections between the inherent characteristics of the good and the ways it is appreciated or evaluated by economic agents, whoever they may be, means that these connections don't exist. Taste must explain the decisions! Tastes and distastes are, by construction, detached from the objects that serve as screens onto which these tastes are projected. The social explains how tastes are formed, oppose one another, and differentiate themselves. No maxim is falser than the famous aphorism "De gustibus non est disputandum," "In matters of taste, there can be no dispute." To the contrary, tastes are entirely a matter of debate and controversy! They are exclusively linked to the desire to distinguish oneself; to overpower someone else or to submit to his judgment; to construct oneself or to be assigned a social identity and a place in the hierarchy of positions. For the same wine, an entire palette of opinions is formed that reflects, reveals, and expresses social differences and relations of domination. It does not much matter what is in the bottle, so long as it contributes to the production and reproduction of positions. Inebriation and addictions catch economists' attention when they account for decision making but fall off the radar for sociologists of consumption. A sociologist who looks into a bottle of Romanée-Conti or a bottle of supermarket plonk sees only the phantasmatic shadows of the social. Taste and its regimes codify aesthetic norms and vary depending on the era and on the milieu. They are in perpetual transformation, nourished by the strategies of agents struggling to improve their social positions.

Sociology's contributions are essential. These studies enrich and extend the economic analysis of the role affects play in decision making and in agents' commitments, showing the centrality of *affectio mercatus* in market dynamics. Some of them emphasize the role devices play in the shaping of agents' dispositions. These contributions should not, however, stop us from noting their limitations. When it comes to recognizing the role played by the goods themselves in the production of affects, sociology has no chops. Economists have never forgotten the participation of goods, if only by invoking notions such as that of utility or functionality, and with the work of behaviorist economics on addictive substances, they have come to insist on its importance more and more. Sociology, in contrast, has shown that agents act as full-fledged social beings when they make the most personal and individual decisions (to end their days, to buy such and such a product at this place and time). In doing so, however, sociology has inevitably lost interest in material things, in the way they are arranged to channel and orient courses of actions.

In the following chapter, which is devoted to price formation, I will come back to these analyses and their limits in greater detail. For the moment, I will simply summarize what the economic and sociological work I have just presented contributes to the model I am developing here. These studies agree in emphasizing the part played by affects in the process that leads agents to commit to a commercial transaction. There is no market without *affectio mercatus*. When they explore the emotions put in play in commercial activities, economists underline the part they play in decision making, as well as in the viability of these activities. They also insist on the role played by the products or goods in setting off these affects and sustaining them, thereby participating in the cognitive processes and sometimes, when their addictive power is great, profoundly structuring these processes. The sociology of market activities tends to highlight the collective character of the processes that feed and shape the *affectio mercatus*. It also introduces the idea that there are devices that can be described as organizational or institutional and that frame these processes, which economists ignore, even if they get mentioned in studies of trust. In sum, what should be retained is that to solve the enigma of how market transactions get established—this improbable meeting over the course of which an agent detaches from a particular good in favor of another agent who decides to attach to it—one has to recognize the importance of the devices that nourish and frame affects. These devices can be considered sociotechnical because they combine material and human elements; they allow goods to assert their qualities and to participate in the attachment process. The following two sections are devoted to the analysis of attachment devices.

HOW GOODS GET ATTACHED AND DETACHED

If we want to understand the role that goods play in the decisions agents make when they engage in a commercial transaction, we must give up on the idea that it is possible to separate the intrinsic (or objective) qualities of goods from their extrinsic (or subjective) qualities. We can no longer try to distinguish between what goods really are and really allow one to do, on the one hand, and what agents think they are or think they allow one to do, on the other. This opposition, which is very difficult to shake, is anchored in a sort of primal scene: the meeting of an object and a subject who preexist independently of one another. A car moves, circulates, transports; it endows its driver with a kind of autonomy. Each of these qualities is unquestionably associated with the vehicle in question. They are the basis of the user's appreciation of the car, an appreciation that may be informed by advice, opinions, or information collected from magazines, but that will at least in part rest on these intrinsic qualities.

Those who follow this approach usually add that not all goods are so easily characterized. In actuality, goods lie on a continuum between those whose functionalities or qualities are immediately and unambiguously clear to their acquirers and those whose characteristics are not so clear, are more uncertain and more difficult to express and to which potential users can more easily attribute their own meanings. For example, through its formulation and its presentation, the Baygon spray I use to eliminate insects invites me to make a frank observation of its efficiency. It is enough to take a quick look at the dead ants and spiders on the ground. The self-evidence of what Baygon *does* and *is* cannot be found in a bottle of Romanée-Conti or a flacon of Frédéric Malle perfume. When I spray Baygon, I get rid of insects that are infringing on my life; when I drink a glass of Romanée-Conti or make a gift of a bottle of Frédéric Malle, I can't help thinking that I am entering into a world where symbolic values do matter more than physical properties. In these two extreme cases, many insist that the divide between intrinsic and extrinsic qualities be maintained. Yes, when you contemplate Baygon's effect, you may be accused of polluting the atmosphere, or worse, of threatening biodiversity: an individual user can become an enemy of the earth. In the same vein, when I was a mere twenty years old, I happily asserted, with as much arrogance as I could muster, that preferring a good Burgundy to a bottle of supermarket wine was pure snobbery! Yet as I became more seasoned, and each bottle I drank gave rise to different appreciations depending on the company in which they were consumed, I could not turn around and deny that the chemical properties of wine continued to matter.

Facing these commonly shared observations, some say that what impels agents toward goods is always a mixture of objective factors (yes, this particular wine is an original chemical substance) and subjective factors (yes, it can be differently appraised in different situations). In this view, a good is a nexus of properties, some of which are objective, while others are subjective. One always buys and sells the symbolic as much as the physical, no matter what one says and no matter what one does. They are compelled by the idea that the human brain constructs more or less exact representations of the outside world from the perceptions that inform it, blending subjectivity and objectivity. If there is sometimes agreement between people, it is simply because all these perceptions have been strictly framed. Thus, we can predict that nothing makes agreement necessary other than learning and discipline.

In no uncertain terms, this is not my conclusion. This multifactorial analysis, which understands decision making to be the result of a variable combination of objective and subjective factors, might serve to explain, ex post, why this or that choice was made. It will have a hard time, however, giving an account of the process that leads to this outcome, because it ignores the mechanisms through which the good and the agent interact, leading some qualities, which are difficult to categorize ex ante as objective or subjective, to express themselves and become explanatory factors in the end, but only in the end. If one stays faithful to the primal scene in which two beings who are intrinsically strangers to one another meet, it would be impossible to find a solution to the enigma of the successful transaction using a multifactorial analysis.

I have sketched a way out of this impasse in the previous chapters. The market meeting does not take place between two beings who belong to different worlds and are destined to remain, whatever happens, exterior to one another. It is a shared adventure that is deployed in many sites, over the course of which the coprofiling of goods and agencies takes shape like a seamless cloth. These multiple and incessant interactions weave a web of relations that establish continuity between agencies and goods. They produce attachments.[20]

In order to analyze and understand the process of attachment that percolates through market agencements, it is time to devote a few additional lines to the notion of affect. I have used words almost interchangeably that refer to a set of phenomena within which it is difficult to make sharp distinctions. When I refer to the lure of profit or entrepreneurial taste, I would tend to use the word "passion"; when I talk of trust, the term that comes to mind is rather "sentiment," "belief," or even "sensation"; and when I watch a gambler hypnotized by the slot machine in front of him gradually spending a month's salary in two days, I wonder whether he is not subject to drives that deprive him of all judgment. If I wanted to give a name to the forces that project agents into the future, I could equally evoke the word "humors" to underline the permanence of certain dispositions or desires. All of these terms might be appropriate. However, given that they are commonly used in uncontrolled ways, there is a potentially troublesome drawback to using them insofar as they are associated with the idea of an interior, subjective world that exists separately from the outside, objective world. As will be clear by now, I want to banish this hypothesis because it prevents us from having an adequate understanding of how various encounters and the explorations to which they give rise participate in the transformation and conjoined profiling of goods and agents. In short, the hypothesis prevents us from understanding how goods act on agents to the point that the latter consent to pay and possibly to enter negotiations about price. This is why to refer to this action I prefer the rarer term "affect," which has the advantage of leaving open the great division between objective world and subjective world and yet suggesting a set of actions that regularly subvert this great divide. In order to be even clearer, I will speak interchangeably of "affect" and "affectation." It turns out that affect and the action of affecting are related to the notion of *affectation* in French that I brought up earlier; they establish a connection between the two different significations of this term as it is used in the French language.[21] The first commonly refers to a good being assigned to an agent (this is what the organization of meetings tends to obtain); the second, rarer, makes reference to the action through which an entity is modified and transformed. Because it lasts and serves as a crucible for a whole series of engagements, relation building, actions, and reactions, the act of encountering (affectation 1) transforms goods and agencies (affectation 2). The transformations that take place in affectation 2 cannot be dissociated from the meeting that happens in affectation 1. After these terminological clarifications, we still need to understand how this operates.

The notion of affect (affectation 2) has the advantage of being inscribed in an intellectual tradition that brings original answers to the questions of the origins of attachment (and detachment) and of the mechanism by which it occurs. Notably, it emphasizes the role of the body in the way agents and their environment are articulated, which is crucial for understanding both how market agencements and mechanisms of attachment function. Pragmatist psychology managed to capture this tradition and express it in terms well adapted to the analysis of commercial transactions. To be affected by something or someone (affectation 2) "corresponds to the subject becoming aware of corporeal modifications triggered by apprehending certain objects or facts."[22] To be convinced of this, "it is enough to imagine an emotion and to make a thought experiment consisting in subtracting all bodily feelings from it; there is nothing left but a cold and neutral intellectual state."[23] Emotion is a corporeal relation to the other. The result is that the affected agent becomes aware of this articulation with the world and of its effects on him. The entwinement of body and spirit refutes Cartesianism and the short-circuit it establishes between the world and thought. It allows us to understand how a meeting organized with goods, affectation 1, must affect agents, affectation 2, in order to lead to a commercial transaction. The word "affect" does justice to the action of things and beings on the agent.[24]

The dynamics of attachment always begin with a question, with something troubling the agent: he is perturbed by what he is faced with, by what is being offered to him. A seller runs through his pitch—think back to the street vendors; an advertisement upsets conventional wisdom; a start-up offers an original molecule. When everything is running smoothly, when things and actions are repeated again and again in an identical way, the question of attachment will not arise: the devices for trust will suffice to guarantee the transaction. The goods are there; they have uses, values, qualities. They are acquired or not out of habit. In the face of a new event, however, in a new situation that is not reducible to any known situation, the agent must figure out a response. He has to face questions as elementary and fundamental as "What will this good do to me?" "Will this profile on Meetic suit me to such an extent that I will not be able to do without it, that it will hold onto me as tightly as I will hold onto it?" "Is this new treatment profiled for me, will it become part of my life, become the regimen I adopt?" In order to reclaim some serenity, a certain equilibrium, the agent has to investigate and experiment. And if the good does (sometimes) end up being indispensable, it is because the agent gradually becomes attached to it over the course of the investigation. The inevitable tension between the agent and the good is resolved only by their simultaneous transformation and adaptation. And it is over the course of this process, which takes the form of an investigation saturated with affectation 2, that the agent elaborates a discourse on the motives of his attachment.

A central part in this exploration is verbalizing—putting into words. Consider the example of a meal where the wine on offer becomes the subject of a conversation among the guests. What should they think of this bottle? The collective investigation (a prototype of all the investigations of the same type at larger scales) takes the form of a conversation that makes reference to the label, the color, that invites tasting and commenting and generates comments that are in turn commented on. Opinions and debates follow each other, answering to one another, are interrupted by all sorts of tests and demonstrations. The wine, its bouquet, the length of its finish express themselves, little by little, as they are expressed by each participant in the conversation. Sometimes a way of seeing, feeling, speaking that is local, but of course feeds on prior conversations or readings, manages to be established. At the end of this exchange, which is a test both for the guests and for the wine, it is no longer the same wine that is drunk, and the guests who drink it are not the same either. Everyone has changed, at least to a certain extent. A community of wine enthusiasts has taken shape. The words that come to the amateurs' minds are important in the dynamic of these changes and in their expression. But one should not forget the wine, which, by affecting their bodies, participates actively in this putting into words, loosening tongues and getting the guests to speak. Our bodies resonate and our minds reason; that is, in sum, what William James tells us. It is obvious that goods count in the shaping and expression of attachments because they act on bodies that learn to be affected by them. If agents are capable of such reflexivity ("I really like what I like"), it is because the process of attachment is also a process of expression over the course of which they learn what they are and what they are becoming and, symmetrically, over the course of which things and goods express what they are or what they can be and what they can make others do (the term in French is *faire faire*). It is not the case that there exist, on the one hand, things and the world, and on the other hand, representations and words to speak of them. Words and things are interwoven, like macramé. The exchange of goods cannot be dissociated from the exchange of words.

Borrowed from Antoine Hennion, who has made a decisive contribution to this current of analysis, the preceding illustration summarizes what recent work devoted to the attachment process has taught us.[25] Yes, as Franck Cochoy emphasizes, things matter—they are concerns, they affect agents, and they incite investigation. The agents are affected, however, only if they have learned or have been taught to be affected. Verbal exchanges, which articulate precepts and concepts, play a central role in this learning. Attachment is a matter of conversation, and like the latter, it is a matter of know-how.

Luckily, the attachment process is a structured process that can be organized from the moment goods trouble agents through to the investigations this provokes. Over the course of these investigations, affects are produced, identities transformed and connected, durable connections made, and solid associations between goods and agents established. This requires designing and implementing devices that give goods and agents the time and space to surprise and be surprised. The requirement of devices becomes all the more pressing as the singularization of products becomes more important and implies more intensive innovation. In order to be accepted and integrated in social life, goods forcefully demand pliable frameworks within which to unfold and deploy so as to produce emotions and affect agents rendered curious, receptive, and attentive.[26]

Sociologist Emmanuel Kessous's research provides a good illustration of devices that function in attachment, as well as of the tight connections they must weave between affectation 1 and affectation 2.[27] On the dating platform he studies, candidates are first required to engage with profiling operations that allow users to evaluate and classify the different participants. Next comes a period of bilateral relations, which, after a number of twists and turns, end up becoming concrete in the form of a relationship that will be a fleeting affair for some or possibly, as the protagonists hope, could last a lifetime. Nothing is given at the start; everything must be acquired. Attachment is gradual, built up through successive trials. It progresses with each step of the investigation that the protagonists lead as they set off to discover, or rather I should say to invent, not only themselves and others, but also the type of relationship they will cement. This investigation would be impossible if it were not framed, channeled, and structured by the platform, its technologies, its algorithms, its categories. This sociotechnical platform constitutes an almost pure form of attachment device. The investigation provokes surprise, generates speech, organizes trials, stages bodies that express themselves, first through photographs and words, then eventually through physical meetings.

What happens on dating platforms has its equivalents in the analog world. Take Jacques Séguéla, the man behind advertising campaigns for Citroën and the campaign for Carte Noire coffee, "a coffee named desire." When he invited Nicolas Sarkozy and Carla Bruni to a dinner he had organized, his modus operandi was like a platform analogous to that of Meetic. The same operations took place (profiling, self-presentation, conversations that swerved into the intimate register), which led to a lasting affair ("Carla and me, it's serious," Sarkozy famously said), although it could have ended with a shorter encounter. Séguéla does not work with multitudes, which makes his matchmaking role harder and more uncertain, but the stakes are the same: manufacturing attachments and consequently setting up a device that prepares and performs attachments.[28]

There is a common perception among purists that dating platforms are contaminated by commercial models. Yet as I am arguing here, the supposed opposition and incompatibility between an impersonal commercial world and the world of emotions, passions, and attachments does not exist. Once participants have been profiled and the possibility of making connections has been organized, they do not have to institute a new space to reengage in authentic relationships. Dating platforms demonstrate that attachments have a role to play in the dynamics of commercial transactions: without attachments and the devices that produce them, supply and demand remain abstract, disembodied notions. Kessous irrefutably shows that contrary to what a long critical tradition has sustained, the market does not exclude personal relations. As economic sociologist Viviana Zelizer has magnificently shown, not only does the market enrich and color preexisting relations, it also constantly creates new ones, which it multiplies and nourishes. In a striking shortcut, Cochoy synthesizes this movement by putting forward two complementary notions—collection and selection. Understood as both actions and as results, these notions account for the fact that markets make relations between agents and goods proliferate, which generates collection, while attempting to rarify them through successive selection.[29]

In this analysis, the bodies of things and people play a privileged part in the constitution and expression of affects and in the transformative process of attachment. Some will ask whether such an analysis can be transposed to market agencements, which, as we have seen, are peopled by qualculative agencies, equipped and matched, and which therefore are never or only exceptionally in direct contact with things. The example of Meetic (or of Séguéla the matchmaker) allows this question to be answered in the affirmative. Yes, agencies have bodies. To accommodate this observation, I would like to introduce the classical notion of a *sensorium*, which refers to the entire set of modalities of perception through which an organism experiences and interprets its environment. In the case of unequipped human beings, the sensorium designates the perceptions provided by the five senses, perceptions that affect the subject and lead it, through verbalization, to give meaning to the things that it encounters that move it. Yet the idea of a sensorium can easily be applied to qualculative agencies. Through their equipment, they also feel, perceive, and express themselves. Newton got it right when he introduced the idea that time and space are the *sensorium dei*. He thus reconciled his view of space-time as a fixed and independent reality with the existence of an omniscient and eternal God without having to worry about their respective places. Space and time, he said, are God's equipment. They ensure his presence in the world without drowning him in the world, and at each point in space and time, they allow him to perceive what is happening and be affected by it. In fact, Newton speaks of space as "affection."[30] Agencies (starting with God himself) are equipped, and their equipment is the sensorium. In general, distributed equipment constitutes the flesh, spirit, and soul of agencies.

Consider a company and its bookkeeping, some of which is founded on double-entry methods, a widely disseminated instrument that captures, processes, and interprets data and structures the affects of the company as agency. We say that BP or Total are *affected* by the oil crisis, plummeting prices, or Saudi Arabia's strategy in making American fracking nonviable. The processes of affecting qualculative agencies, these assemblages of human bodies and other materials capable of perceiving, verbalizing, asking about the decisions to be made, capable of attaching or detaching, are similar to those of human beings totally stripped down, those naked bodies disarmed. What changes is the composition of the sensorium. Users of the platform on the French dating site Adopteunmec (the name means "adopt a guy") are obviously not placed in a to face-to-face encounter the way Nicolas Sarkozy and Carla Bruni were during the famous meal that started their union and their mutual attachment. The person who engages on the platform is a sort of cyborg; it is only much later that they will stare into the eyes of the person selected after a first evaluation, a first scoring. Meanwhile, the platform of space-time where qualculations are made is their sensorium, as it collects and formats information, makes associations, syntheses, classifications, and hierarchies. In fact, if one thinks about it, a relationship between a human body and an object of attachment that involves no pomp or finery is quite the exception. Around Séguéla's table laid for dinner there is much equipment.

This analysis shows that attachment is inscribed in a process that is an extension of the previous framings I have presented. Attachments require a pass(act)ivated good (here, this good is put into relation with another being); they require qualculative agencies that evaluate profiles; and they also require more and more intimate meetings, which allow for adjustments and matches and which, at the same time, prepare for attachment. As I have insisted, to be effective, affectation 2 can never be completely dissociated from affectation 1.

Companies have understood the value of this connection very well, especially on digital platforms. To avoid any cooling off, messages are sent within a millisecond of a customer's arrival on a site so as to reorient them toward other purchases before their possible departure. This is called retargeting. A manager explained to me that this rerouting requires no fewer than eight hundred employees, most of whom are mathematicians, and several hundred million euros in funding. This is no longer a matter of the alchemy of feelings, but rather of algebra. Passions, emotions, and affects are carried in and channeled by algorithms that circulate them in networks. I will now turn my attention toward attachment devices that are closely intertwined with the devices that handle the encounters of qualculative agencies.

One last word before we leave this section. There is, a priori, no guarantee that explorations and investigations, with all of the hesitations, uncertainties, and incomprehension they produce, will end each time with an attachment of goods and agencies. When Séguéla invites Sarkozy and Bruni, there is no way of knowing in advance whether they will leave together when the last *digestif* has been drunk or at least leave having exchanged cell phone numbers. All that is known is that Séguéla has skill and many trump cards in hand. The same goes in market agencements and commercial transactions. There is always a risk that no deal will be concluded. The same problem has been appearing for so long, however, that people have learned to put together solutions that produce acceptable results, year in, year out. Social technologies have been designed, tested, and transformed so as to favor successful attachments. They are embodied in know-how, recipes, procedures, and tools that get the job done. The mystery will never be dissipated. No one knows or will ever know the answer to the enigma of the market, because no definitive answer exists. Solutions are constantly being reinvented. What we have, then, are devices imagined and cobbled together that work. It is time to examine some of them.

THREE ATTACHMENT DEVICES FOR ENGAGING GOODS

I am going to suggest that we programmatically distinguish three types of attachment devices: devices for *listening and dialoguing*, devices for *coproducing*, and devices for *addicting*. The importance of the goods in the attachment process and the way they participate in it vary from one family to the other. Listening devices leave little room for goods, which are present only as a backdrop. They provide the dialogue with a few of the references required to make sense of what's happening on a theatrical stage. These devices aim at convincing potential customers that the good on offer corresponds precisely to what they want and expect and that they should therefore attach themselves to it. With coproduction devices, consumers are involved in the design and production of the goods that are destined for them. These devices put the agents in direct contact with the good and favor attachment because they organize interactions and mutual adaptations: "This good is for you, since you designed it." With addiction devices, things are endowed with maximal hold on agents' bodies. In this family of devices, goods are designed to create dependency (or rather a certain degree of dependency), which dissuades agents from freeing themselves and thus quasi-mechanically ensures attachment.

In practice, attachment devices are a combination of all three types. Successful attachment requires that an agent somehow recognize that what is being offered corresponds to what they want. An agreement can be obtained, however, only if the consumers were involved at some point in the good's design process, either directly or indirectly. Finally, to prevent the attachment from dissipating before the transaction takes place means establishing a certain dependency with bodies and minds. In the following, I will give a stylized description of these three families of devices, with a few examples to show how they function. I will then briefly discuss the detachment mechanisms without which no market transaction would be conceivable. Sellers must also go through a transformation and accept being detached from goods in which they have invested themselves.

DIALOGUE: HERE'S WHAT YOU NEED!

For the seller, the simplest way to begin the attachment process is to convince potential consumers that the good on offer corresponds exactly to what they need, that it brings an answer to the problems they have or should have.

The function of this type of device is to gradually ascertain what customers expect, hope for, or want by getting them to articulate it themselves. To reach that point, the conversation takes the form of a dialogue similar to the *chjam'è rispondi* Corsican songs, which take the form of a succession of improvised questions and answers. If the dialogue is properly directed, and if all goes well, it can lead to an agreement ("Here is what you need" answered by a "Yes, this is the good I want") and to the promise of a successful attachment.

The simplest way to get a customer to recognize that he really wants the good on offer is to organize a face-to-face meeting between the seller and the customer. They can then enter into dialogue. Whether a grocer, butcher, hardware vendor, or salesman who travels abroad, any seller will tell you that learning to manage this type of conversation, both with regular customers and with newcomers, is essential to success. The conversation is sustained by the presence of goods. Laid out in the stall or appearing in the form of catalogs, flyers, or videos, they are available to be appreciated, scrutinized, or touched. At any moment, when reticence surfaces or an objection appears, returning to the goods can help overcome the difficulty and allow the attachment to progress.

Pitchers are masters of this art, which is as difficult as it is ancient. In his work on very small and medium companies, sociologist Alexandre Mallard tells the story of how a vendor crisscrossing the countryside in his van in the Vendée understood there was no point in waiting for customers in the marketplace.[31] He tracks them down at home, one by one. Two honks on the horn announce his arrival. "It's me, it's you, I am coming for you, Madame! Look at this fish, it's your favorite. I am at your service, here to help, here to solve your problems." The conversation continues from one visit to the next, always like the *chjam'è rispondi*, chiming and responding. Such a conversation, in which the seller, the customer, and the merchandise meet in the flesh, can also be adapted to industry. Sociologist Liz McFall makes this point when she tells the story of the life insurance market in the UK. As she recounts, experienced agents had to be sent to each home to present the product while being attentive to suspicious clients. The agents succeeded beyond the industry's wildest expectations. They became intimate friends, confidants, for this mass of poor people, renewing limited-time contracts week after week—not an isolated pitcher, but hundreds of salesmen in dialogue with a multitude of customers treated as unique people.[32]

The internet is a great, low-cost platform for launching and keeping up these personalized conversations in which customers on a large scale make explicit what they expect and appreciate. Sociologist Kevin Mellet identifies three strategies. The first turns to the internet as a vector for contagion to create buzz. The second seeks to reach and convince opinion leaders or prescribers who will come to act as relays and spread the exchanges to their followers. Finally, the third strategy is to use tools such as Facebook to animate the network of those who declare themselves as your friends, starting a "real" dialogue with them, without intermediaries.[33]

These strategies participate in a more general movement toward research on consumers, their practices, their aspirations, or their problems.[34] This research is not disinterested. It aims to convey consumers' diverse and sometimes contradictory words to companies; it is led by a myriad of players who try to make the customers speak so as to better capture them. Many complementary methods are used, including statistical analysis (for instance, using data related to socioprofessional categories), collecting the data picked up by the sales force, face-to-face interviews with customers, and in situ observation of practices, focus groups, or neighborhood meetings where products are displayed for comment. Anything goes. There is no limit on the imagination. These investigations allow for endless back-and-forth. They establish not one, but several truths, all temporary and changing. They play a central role in the design of advertising campaigns, in the conversations they feed and that feed them.

Research on consumers does not lose sight of the goods themselves. It implicates these goods in the conversation to varying degrees. In the food industry, there are tastings; in showrooms, real consumers are invited to see, touch, smell, react, say, and thus give a live commentary on the force of their attachments. Success, however, is not guaranteed. Before they are definitively certified and measured by the flow of money, there is something uncertain and fragile about attachments.

The reversible, temporary, and partial nature of attachments is not necessarily a flaw. Of course, one needs attached consumers, but they should not be too attached, otherwise markets would fall into repetitive routines and would soon fall asleep for good. What matters is that the conversation not falter. A conversation requires upkeep. One has to rekindle the relation to the consumer, honk twice, begin research afresh. For instance, loyalty cards make this possible by maintaining contact and updating the data.[35]

As both McFall and Mallard show, keeping up a conversation from the supply side, or actually, several parallel conversations, requires a great deal of energy and resources. It requires an impeccable organization, one capable of mobilizing multitudes of experts and professionals inside and outside the company, sometimes in real time, in order to coordinate, process the data, and brief agents sent out "on the ground." In his work on call centers, Mallard observes that even if conversations are carefully prepared and framed, they sometimes slip out of control because the profiling of the interlocutors and their matching have not been well adjusted or because the organization of the conversations suffers from a poor allocation of resources, which increases the waiting time before the conversation begins.[36]

Those who design and put goods on offer must also be prepared to detach from them. Of course, there is no ambiguity. All of the protagonists know that this exchange of words will conclude with a commercial transaction. It is thus an interesting conversation, and it is not easy to manage, especially when the entire organization needs to be taught how to begin a dialogue that has no other purpose than to attach, *to get*, the customer.[37] Offering help, showing attention or empathy, without forgetting that one is there to further commerce is indeed something that has to be learned. There are theater classes that teach the skill. Mallard describes how, over the course of a telephone conversation between a customer and the employee of a call center, the latter alternates with mastery between personalized speaking and exchanges that show that there are two roles, that of the seller and that of the customer. (In one moment, "My name is Dominique. How can I help you?" In the next, "Orange reminds you, dear Mr. Callon, that your cable contract cannot be terminated free of charge before the end of November.")[38] This role playing can go awry at any point. The seller moves ahead on a knife's edge. Too much familiarity or not enough, and the conversation is off to a bad start. All the more because the customer is on the alert: they know that after a cascade of intermediaries have intervened, they risk being *had* by the discussion, by Dominique or by anonymous slogans or advertisements.

At any moment, the conversation could veer into lies, bad faith, dirty tricks, cynicism, cheating, or fraud. It could also slip into a noncommercial register.[39] Skillfully navigating between these two pitfalls (developing arguments that could turn out to be fallacious and failing to complete the transaction) requires a great deal of know-how. In such a dialogue, what is at stake is neither the sincerity of the seller nor the credulity of the customer, but effectively framing passions and affects. When the conversation is adroitly steered, no one is fooled, no one believes it, and yet everyone believes it, because everyone knows that an objective, definite truth is out of reach. The French terms put it well—a pitcher is a *bonimenteur,* one who lies well.[40] Not everyone is up to the job of lying well. It is infinitely more difficult than telling the truth.[41]

COPRODUCTION: YOUR TURN!

Conversation cannot be circumvented. Silent relations cannot lead to attachments. However, if conversations are cut off from their object, the goods and things, or if they do not get close enough to them and remain mere verbal exchanges, they fast lose all (commercial) interest and soon ring hollow. Those who design *conversation devices* are keenly aware of this connection. In order to facilitate and reinforce the production of attachments, they contrive to give goods ever more chances to intervene and express themselves.

What if the goods themselves were the main actors in exchanges? And what better way to manage this than by inviting consumers into the design and production process? The more closely I am associated with the manufacturing of the good that is destined for me and the earlier I can intervene in the discussion around its qualities and its shaping, the greater the chance I will become sincerely and lastingly attached to it in the end.[42]

The organization of innovation processes attests to the efficiency of devices that aim to involve customers in the innovation process to ensure success. Eric von Hippel calls this the "democratization of innovation," underscoring that the design of new products is opening up.[43] Although the term "democratization" may be excessive, since access to design processes remains very selective, it does point to the increasing involvement of users. Exposure to goods helps those for whom they are intended learn what they want. For instance, in the case of therapy development, involving patient groups to attach to the treatments and molecules they have helped test is a phenomenon that will not disappear anytime soon. Sociologist Vololona Rabeharisoa cites the example of a small group of patients suffering from an extremely rare blood disease who work in close contact with a few researchers and doctors to test a promising substance.[44] Likewise, in their history of treatments against cancer, STS scholars Alberto Cambrosio and Peter Keating document how patients are involved in intermediary decisions (such as whether to continue the trial or not) and are thereby led, little by little, to become dependent upon the very treatments they are helping develop.[45] Countless studies show that this type of organization is spreading, notably in the service sector. New concepts are invented to describe it. There is talk of a new regime of innovation[46] or of the *prosumer* and of *consomma(c)tion*, two neologisms that contract the two words "consumer" and "producer." Management scientist Henry Chesbrough successfully introduced the notion of *openness*, pointing to the multiple agents liable to be involved in the design and production of new products.[47] It would in fact be more precise to speak of the openness of products themselves: over the course of their qualification, they are profiled in such a way as to solicit reactions from a wide range of relevant agents.

According to art historian Svetlana Alpers, Rembrandt anticipated this movement. In an attempt to live from his art and rid himself of his patrons' influence, he undertook to build a market for his work.[48] Not only was

Rembrandt an entrepreneur, making his studio into a production unit and his students into collaborators committed to a collective project, he also imagined a series of innovative setups, singularizing transactions even as he increased their number. Each painting that left the studio was extended in the form of new works, each original, but slightly different from the previous ones, notably through a detail or two discussed with the patrons. Art historians have referred to these as "multiple originals." Furthermore, his paintings had ongoing careers. Rembrandt retained the right to recall a painting, if necessary through repurchasing, in order to touch it up. Numerous notarized documents specify how touch-ups were decided and carried out. A painting was not a unique accomplishment, frozen for all of time. For instance, even as it was being produced, *The Conspiracy of Claudius Civilis* was conceived of as a work in progress, the first of a long series of variations and transformations in which those who successfully acquired the painting would be involved. Through a process of extreme singularization and carefully maintained openness, the paintings were thus transformed into so many open-ended sites of creation. Amateurs and clients were invited to these sites, and as they participated at some stage in the qualification of the painting, they became attached to it. As commercial passiva(c)tion dictates, it remained only for Rembrandt to ensure that this evolving work would be attributed to him. He did this with consummate mastery. As Alpers explains, Rembrandt was "an entrepreneur of the self."

Openness is increasingly becoming a crucial quality of goods. It is a powerful force of affectation and attachment in that it goes so far as to include, often explicitly, the possibility or even the necessity of adaptations and requalifications after the commercial transaction has been completed. Tinkerers prefer materials that allow them to improvise and to...tinker; similarly, it seems that the most dedicated coders clamor to praise Linux, Android, Firefox, and all the open systems and software, rather than Apple and its locked systems. In an excellent self-analysis, management scientist Hans Kjellberg convincingly documented how a "collector's item" car (by definition open to requalification), once acquired, and even as it is itself transformed, entered his life, transforming his relations with those close to him, his friends, and his children, redefining his modes of life.[49] The transfer of property, the crucial moment of attachment, reinforces itself. The thing *has* the consumer as much as the consumer *has* the thing.

Marketing has not failed to notice the development of openness.[50] It has multiplied ways of soliciting consumers, leading them to interact more directly with goods and opening the possibilities of requalification.

The simplest, most rudimentary mechanism is the invention of self-service retail spaces, which organize a face-off between consumers and products.[51] As Cochoy has amply demonstrated, this arrangement sets up a consumer who has no choice but to be forced to choose for himself. The consumer is constituted as a "free" subject (a freedom that is, of course, highly constrained), who, like any free subject, hesitates and formulates questions for himself, but eventually reaches a decision to which and through which he feels committed. This is not a matter of a simple conversation of self with self. In other words, it is still a conversation between self and the professionals who have organized the presentation of the goods. Tailored with inscriptions and messages, the products on the shelf, and indeed the shelving itself, speak to the consumer, attract attention, suggest further investigations and explorations: the products are loquacious, expressive through the simple fact of being there, squeezed up against one another, collected and selected. As the consumer passes in front of the shelves, the framings change, alternating and blending into each other; the shopping cart, a crucial invention, operates as a form of memory, displaying what has been chosen and perhaps leading the consumer to reconsider the choices in front of their eyes. Things hail the consumer, forcing the consumer to take them into account.[52]

The brand phenomenon has allowed marketing to go much further in putting the consumer to work. Take the case of American Apparel and the campaign it launched in the 1990s to establish its place in the clothing market, as analyzed by sociologist Carolin Gerlitz. The brand created its style.[53] Its first step was to approach customers, inquiring into their behavior. American Apparel's gamble was to enter into people's intimate sphere. The company launched a campaign of photographs that closed in on the body, scrutinizing faults, beads of sweat, or burgeoning cellulite and unhesitatingly evoking sexuality. By defending a different exploration, American Apparel distinguished itself from its competitors, which distanced themselves from real bodies and dissimulated what they considered imperfections, making pants float and showing the flaps of checkered shirts flying in the wind. The brand stuck to the body with clothes that stuck to the skin, showing, rather than coating—

figure-fitting clothing made from supple and elastic material. It established the terms of an original conversation that would take place with things: T-shirts, shirts, tights, and pants, these are the things that speak and are spoken of. It might have failed, yet it succeeded. A certain identity emerged in contrast to existing identities, with its own social spaces and urban sites, such as East London. The brand and its aesthetic were anchored in groups whose identities it helped forge. Meanwhile, and this is what is interesting, the American Apparel style progressively became a tool for participatory creation. In fact, users spontaneously associated certain practices with the brand, although the brand did nothing to fashion them. (This universe can be explored by searching the web with "American Apparel" as the keyword.) Ideas, identities, quirky and different practices were connected as though the brand had become a platform. It became a common noun that designated a way of being and dressing, stimulating imaginations and suggestions that then needed only to be collated. Not only did the conversation around the existing goods offered by the company spread; what is more, there emerged from all sides novel associations likely to lead to new products. The brand became an arrangement for participatory creation, putting a vast number of agents to work on a volunteer basis. In some cases, a machine such as this one can become extremely productive. Gerlitz cites the example of Dove, which mobilized a whole range of intervening parties, putting groups of women to work by organizing forums and sites and orchestrating a vast movement around the questioning of beauty norms, especially those spread by the media. The brand thus managed to take part in the elaboration of new practices and new meanings around beauty. After such collective and highly mediatized work, which resembles a social movement, consumers are all the more likely to become attached, since the good is itself attached to the new practices, stakes, and preoccupations that they share. The product has been opened, unfolded; it has been enriched, transformed, inserted into a new network of associations. All of this is accomplished by the brand, which is to marketing what collaborative platforms are to new product design. The brand attaches, and one becomes attached to it. It becomes a collective force that performs the opening of goods and pushes them into maximal entwinement with ethical, political, or cultural preoccupations, which it in turn transforms. It is not (only), as has so often been said, a device for producing trust. To echo Gerlitz, the brand manages value flows from opposite directions. As the good becomes multivalent, its economic value increases.

ADDICTION: PAY TO GET EVEN MORE ATTACHED!

Starting and maintaining a dialogue is good. It is even better to orient the dialogue toward the codesign and coproduction of goods, which provides those for whom they are destined with margins of maneuver to experience and express what they want. As the affectation process proceeds from one device to another, things weigh more and more. But the most effective approach for attaching people is to manage the dialogue so that goods condition behavior directly, become indispensable to the customers, and throw them into a state of dependence that they cannot dream of leaving.

Devices that seek to addict the user are not new. In their unnerving simplicity, they are sometimes stunningly efficient. A few years ago, Lucky Strike put cigarettes on the market with a mentholated tablet in the filter. When the tablet heated up and the smoker pressed the "on" button, the taste of the cigarette changed. Apparently, adolescents loved them. To use their expression, they would "blow the tab" as fast as possible. This little device had two effects. The first was to bring a taste that had been ascertained to bring a pleasant sensation to the young smoker, inciting him to breathe in deeply. To swallow smoke so young is to take a serious step toward long-term addiction and also, as a possible secondary effect, lung cancer. Inciting the adolescent to "blow the tab" is a more secure and radical commercial strategy of attachment than all the slogans and advertisements put together.

In order to understand the mechanisms of addiction as the same mechanisms that attach users to goods (defined in this model of markets as having completed the decisive step toward establishing a bilateral transaction with consent to pay), let us return to Las Vegas with anthropologist Natasha Schüll.[54] In Nevada, gambling has become a full-blown economic and commercial activity with an industrial organization that is exclusively and massively oriented toward the production of addictive behavior and the accumulation of the immense commercial benefits it produces. To explain this economic success, it would be too easy to appeal to *panem et circenses* (bread and games), a human nature that needs to have its guilty weaknesses flattered. Turning to such an explanation would seriously underestimate the colossal investments in brain power and in dollars required to actualize these inclinations and to transform more and more occasional gamblers in search of distraction into dependent, immersed, drowned gamblers who seek only to cut themselves off from the world around them. So much research and experimentation is necessary to organize this dependency and to ensure that it brings maximum profits to the casino that reducing addiction to a face-off between a solo gambler and a screen is blindness. In silent conversation with this gambler are machines, high-tech innovations, armies of architects, psychologists, and marketers, other casinos competing for the most competitive algorithms, mathematicians aiming to establish the laws of chance so that it really is true chance (which is not as easy as it seems), battalions of lawyers and elected officials debating the morality or lack thereof of such practices, and governments eagerly amassing the taxes flowing into state coffers.

Schüll describes the design and functioning of these addiction devices with surgical precision. First, a long, labyrinthine path attracts the customer to Las Vegas (low-cost plane tickets, price-reduced hotel rooms) and leads him without much thought to the heart of the casino, into what gamblers call the "zone," a closed space of a few square feet, an island in the ocean of the some hundred thousand square feet of the gaming room where all of the variables (temperature, light, colors, sounds, and smells) have been calculated and tested to provoke emotion. The gambler is then facing *his* machine, designed to take the measure of their propensity for addictive practices and, if possible, to reinforce them. The goal is to increase the speed of bets, to not interrupt the gambler while he is winning (so he continues to place the winnings), to avoid wasting the gambler's time cashing in on his gains or searching for more money (for instance, by transforming credit cards into betting instruments), to settle him for as long as possible—he must leave his seat only to satisfy physiological needs such as to go to the toilet or to eat. Everything is controlled: what one hears (integrating background noise), what one sees, what one feels. Comfort is curated in the smallest details, such as those seats, which subtly vibrate depending on what is happening. If attachment and addiction are successful, it is because the service is designed with the active participation of consumers through the dialogue and coproduction practices the casinos have set up. The machines are an environment in and of themselves; they capture gamblers emotionally and retain them.[55]

In great detail, Schüll shows how essential elements of affectation are integrated into the slot machine's software and its microprocessors. For example, the reels give the impression they are set off by the push of a button, as though the player were mechanically spinning the reels, when actually it is the number generator, constantly at work, that changes the draw every millisecond. The gambler is only selecting what is generated at the moment he pushes the button. Having lost, if he leaves his seat and sees the following player win, he might, so he tells himself, regret it, thinking he might have pocketed the gains had he stayed and played another few rounds. This incites the player to continue. Another way of creating the same feeling ("If I go on, I will win") is to make the winning configuration appear next to the losing one that previously fell to the gambler.

The machine is programmed in such a way as to decide the rate at which funds are committed. Depending on the player's usual strategies (duly recorded through data tracking and constantly recalculated), it can favor infrequent, big wins or, on the contrary, more limited and more frequent gains. However, eating away at gamblers' money in small doses seems to be the surest way for the casino to pull in the profits. The continuous flux of small wins inexorably leads the gambler into the addiction zone, creating the illusion of false wins as the losses slowly accumulate.

The machine massively intervenes in the way the gambler feels his losses and wins. Affect is in the industry's hands, with its computer experts, architects, designers, or experimental psychologists who, as one of them explains, work toward making the gambler functionally autistic: "You are the machine and the machine is you. Take leave of people." This is attachment reaching its pinnacle. The machine is directly connected to mental states. The gambler is in the mousetrap. Innovations follow one another so that the gambler will give up any thought of calculating and finally let the machine play in his stead—twenty parallel poker games, or a hundred, if the gambler so wishes. The autoplay function confirms that what is left is only a programmed cyborg. The gambler does not even watch the cards anymore, only the counter that displays losses and wins. And soon he won't even have to go to the machine anymore—the machine will come to him or, better, he will carry it with him. It will offer him what he likes and what he can no longer do without so as to carry him ever further from the world around him. He will have "blown the tab" for good.[56]

Addiction devices are spreading in a number of sectors and taking on greater importance. Indeed, many have observed that certain innovations in the gambling industry, such as biometric recognition or software dedicated to tracking fraudulent collusions, have been adapted in other sectors: airports, trading floors, insurance, banks, and the homeland security industry. One of the sectors where addiction devices have long played a central role is in food. In that case, what are shuffled are not card combinations, but rather combinations of sugar, fat, and salt calculated by mathematical models and validated by taste tests.[57] Then there are the dependency mechanisms that bind users through their body to their cell phones, screens, video games, and medicines, not to mention the traditional substances, tobacco and alcohol. In fact, the very notion of addiction has become a central category for marketing: the designers of the Blackpills application, which "creates, produces and diffuses short clips, engaged and radical, aimed at young adults and their cell phones," make no bones about their objective to offer series that are "raw and addictive."[58]

For the Romans, the word "addiction" referred to the state of a free man reduced to slavery because of debt. Echoing this etymology, we should go further and evoke the force and pervasiveness of the addiction devices linked to money and in particular to credit activities.[59] One of the most lucrative populations for lenders is that of the impecunious, living on the edge of the poverty level. They are the main customers for revolving loans, small sums borrowed over short periods at astronomical rates (300 percent APR). Well managed, this population can be made loyal, one loan after another, generating considerable revenue. How can this be achieved? To answer this question, sociologist Joe Deville analyzed Wonga's success in the UK. Despite higher interest rates, Wonga surpassed the competition for several years, managing to durably attach its customers, who are poor and always in need of money.[60] Deville explains that Wonga never renegotiates contracts and refuses to extend existing loans. The rules of the game are that one has to have paid back the previous loan to get a new one. Just as the casino seeks out a gambler who pushes the button as many times as possible to renew the bet, the stakes for Wonga are gradually to establish the contours of a population that always lacks money but pays back the loans on time. No sugar, no salt or fat to lure and render dependent. Instead, there is a questionnaire and thirty criteria to fill out in five minutes online. Backstage, complicated calculations are made based on the mass of accumulated data in order to define behavioral profiles and identify, as the activities develop, those that correspond to the company's target: the right borrower for this business model is poor and punctual. The Wonga customer learns to live with permanent debt that is repaid without fuss. He is dependent on the money lent by Wonga, and this dependence depends only on him, his behavior. If he stops paying back, he is free, but impoverished. Credit can be constructed like a slot machine that lends coins instead of swallowing them and that has learned, via questionnaires and algorithms, to carefully select a customer who will not be able to detach. The sequences are the same, with small sums that slowly generate large revenues and customers who behave properly so as to stay in the game: poor people who, because they are poor, are good candidates for repeat requests, poor people to whom the possibility of repetition is promised if they behave appropriately—in short, people who play the game and behave as they should. These, explains Deville, are the stakes of the relations Wonga establishes with its customers and to which it responds by setting up its calculation platforms and algorithms.

José Ossandon further confirms how efficient these addiction devices are in his work on the growth of credit cards provided to their customers by the large distribution companies in Mexico.[61] Cards that serve as means of payment can also be used to obtain cash and contract miniloans at very high interest rates. Their holders can lend these cards to family members or friends. The companies that emit these devices run nonnegligible, but statistically manageable risks. Like Wonga, their aim is to enact consumers that behave in accordance with their business model—that is, those who repay on time and to whom one can renew loans. This case is particularly interesting because it attests to a phenomenon of growing importance: the emergence and development of private monies, in this case, shared by the holders and users of the card, on one side, and, on the other side, those who emit the cards. Ossandon convincingly shows that these monies take hold of those who use them, gradually creating dependency. A credit card is a self-reinforcing device that attaches by making dependent: the more you use it, the more you will use it again.

MORE AND MORE ATTACHING ATTACHMENTS?

Successful attachments imply some form of conversation, coproduction of goods, and addiction. For example, in Las Vegas, those who design the gambling space regularly take tours of the floor to interview their gamblers. They organize focus groups, and working closely with the gamblers, they polish the ergonomics of the "zone."[62] No addiction device can do without conversation and coconception or coconception rooted in conversation. No doubt the inverse also holds. Without recourse to coconception or to mechanisms that create dependencies, attachments would be so fragile as to be imperiled, along with the profits they generate. Nevertheless, the combinations that allow for a great diversity in the commercial strategies are infinite. They play on the more or less partial and ephemeral nature of attaching.[63]

My sense is that addiction devices aiming to trigger durable dependent behaviors are increasingly important in the production of commercial attachments in what is usually called capitalist markets. In this case, addiction and profit seem closely linked and dependent on one another. Addiction is therefore becoming a central category in the social sciences, even if it is historically contingent.[64] Anthropologist Paul Rabinow considers addiction a starting point for thinking about today's *anthropos*.[65] Engineering addiction and addictive practices makes explicit and weaves together on a whole new scale the stuff that contemporary man is made from. The range and degrees of addiction extend every day, each good finding the agencies it will take and each agency the goods on which it will depend.[66]

I cannot draw these remarks to a close without evoking the question of detachments. It is as important on the supply side as on the demand side to manage affects that make the agents act. I have already raised this issue in the case of listening and coproduction devices. With addiction devices, however, this issue of detachment takes on a whole new dimension and becomes a constant source of worry. As Schüll's interviews with designers and engineers show, they also find pleasure in the gaming industry. There is pleasure in tracking and above all in capturing the gambler, snatching him from the clutches of competitors without ruining him: the customer must live. The greater the hold machines have and the more gamblers' dependency increases, the more those on the supply side exult. They also exult when they win a court case brought by a state that accuses them of not truly respecting the laws of chance in the way they decide upon losing configurations. We would need a Hannah Arendt to account for the banality of evil in a situation where responsibility is put on those whom the device aims to make less responsible in an economy of affects in which exultation is exchanged for dependency with consent. In order to avoid public opprobrium, the gambling industry finances both treatment centers for dependent gamblers and research to identify those gamblers most likely to fall into irreversible dependency—just as mobile phone providers hire psychologists to explain to parents how to manage their children and their mobiles. Likewise, the food industry employs battalions of dieticians to convince consumers not to overconsume the products they offer, and public powers set up commissions for the overindebted to wean them off credit. Market attachment produces concerns that will haunt us for quite a while and will make market agencements subject to debate.

The challenge that market agencements must meet in constantly renewed ways is to lead someone all the way to the point that they consent to pay to acquire it. Without taking into account the world of passions, it would be impossible to understand how this challenge can be met: the *affectio mercatus* stimulates trust, but also, even more fundamentally, it agitates, heats, perks up, as marketers would say, and pushes agents to consider that they cannot do without the good being offered. To explain how these connections are made, we saw that one has to give up the convenient hypothesis according to which goods and agents are exterior to one another and instead put their conjoined evolution at the center of the analysis. It is over the course of this evolution and the explorations it provokes that a bundle of interdependencies are eventually woven that attach the good to the one for whom it was destined. The agent is affected by the good (*affecté par*) at the same time as they are assigned to it (*affecté à*). This double movement requires that agencies and goods be simultaneously engaged; the various modalities of this engagement led me to distinguish three families of attachment devices.

No matter the type of device, the practical framing of affects is a permanent invention. There is neither a best way nor a universal solution: it all depends on the good and the agents involved. This explains why success is never guaranteed and why, when it seems to have been achieved, it often turns out to be incomplete and temporary. Through the framings they impose, devices provoke reactions and protest. Attachment, as the word says, is not far from the act of taking hold, which can generate resistance.

Thus, the devices conceived to attach consumers are subject to constant criticism. For instance: "Advertisement is full of lies and degradation;

algorithms with their data and databases are reductive and produce a travesty of reality and real needs. The coproduction of goods is an illusion and participation a mirage: Who can claim that all consumers are heard? Who would dare assert that what they say or ask for is really taken into account? There are countless solicitations that are ignored, repressed, or forgotten." As for the actual addiction, it provokes flashes of lucidity, indignant protests, and calls for resistance against the risks of enslavement and decay. In fact, each attachment strategy can be used by agents as a resource to denounce the limits of others. For instance: "Why was I never told about this good on which I am now dependent? Why was I not explicitly involved in its design?" Or again: "Why settle for organizing an amiable conversation about this substance, as though there were nothing special to say about the risk of addiction?" In the face of these ever more complex and problematic movements brought about by the multiplication of attachment devices, the control of the delicate chemistry and the subtle logistics of affectations become a strategic stake.

CHAPTER SIX

Price Formulation

Hic Rhodus, hic salta![1] We have arrived at the decisive moment. Let us imagine that goods have been pass(act)ivated, qualculative agencies equipped, meeting sites distributed, regulated, and arranged. Furthermore, let us imagine that attachment, detachment, and consent to pay have been obtained through the skillful promotion and management of affects. All that is left is to craft a price.

Crafting prices does not interrupt the continuity of the previous framings. It is inscribed in the long and tortuous process through which goods and agencies are singularized. Recall Las Vegas and its slot machines. First, chance had to be domesticated, produced on demand in the discrete form of an association of figures on separate reels, moved by complex algorithms and set off at the simple push of a button. Gamblers had to seat themselves facing this organized production of random configurations flashing onto a digital screen as though coming from nowhere. Future gamblers had to be nudged toward the airports from which cheap flights take off to the gambling capital, then guided to the machines that would assist them in their calculations and decisions. An atmosphere had to be created, a succession of screens orchestrated, so as to lead these gamblers to gradually forget the outside world, all for the pleasure of continuing to play. Carried away by this force, abandoning themselves to it, the gamblers had only one thing to do: pay, then press a button so the motion would go on and they could remain playthings of chance.

What all of the slot machine designers in the world have learned is that once consent to pay has been obtained, there are a thousand ways to obtain the payment of a *certain* sum. Some gamblers prefer to win big or lose big and cut the trip short. Others prefer a long, slow process of falling asleep: they press the button often, repeat the liberating gesture many times, win a bit, lose a bit, to make it last, enjoy for as long as possible the state of weightlessness whose pleasures and charms Michel Butor described so well in his novel *La modification*.[2]

Is the price a gambler pays really determined by comparing supply and demand? One can say this, of course, but the explanation comes up rather short. When he finds himself in a situation where he is face to face with the machine, the gambler has been acted on as much as he has acted. Over the course of this journey, the constitution of supply and demand have become so entangled that it would be useless to try to introduce a sharp distinction between them. Moreover, and this is why the gambling situation is so interesting, price is an essential component of this service. It is a strategic variable that determines its quality, not the reverse. By choosing a price level (such a stake, at such a rhythm), the gambler sets the conditions for the experience to be a success, in that he sets the conditions that will make him quiver or founder. The price thus participates forcefully in the qualification of the good. It is a quality of the good. It does not measure the good's value.

In this chapter, I will argue that what is obvious in the case of the gambling industries is true for other commercial sectors. Pricing does not come after the goods' qualification; rather, the pricing process feeds and prolongs that qualification. To underline this reversal, I suggest we think in terms of *price formulation*. This notion emphasizes the fact that a price is not determined at some moment at which supply and demand are supposed to meet. It is the result of a process that often begins very early, when a good is still only a vague idea in a design studio or a research lab. It also highlights that establishing the price is a strategic variable around which power relations are formed and through which the establishment of bilateral monopolies is at stake.

This chapter should serve as an introduction to the analysis of price formulation in market agencements, a task that requires a particular theoretical effort. Few studies are actually useful to me, other than a growing set of empirical studies made in the last few years, which will provide precious help. This analysis also requires making some inroads into the black box of how agents calculate prices, which is not always easy to grasp and explain. We must follow agencies in their work as they design and implement the different formulations that allow them to establish prices and to ensure these prices will be accepted.

Since the inversions with respect to traditional approaches are most manifest in this chapter, I will begin by giving a detailed picture of the usual explanations of pricing. This will lead me to draw attention to the concept of a *discriminating monopoly*, a concept that will be useful for showing how prices participate both in establishing (singularized) bilateral transactions and in multiplying them. The notion of price formulation that I am introducing provides a new analysis of the relations of domination that cut across commercial activities.

THEORIES OF PRICING IN INTERFACE MARKETS

Theories of pricing are generally conceived of for markets whose architecture is presumed to resemble the interface market model—that is, markets with disjoined supplies and demands, platform goods, and competition for those goods. These theories usually combine two opposing approaches. The first can be related to standard microeconomics, which considers that markets constitute a machinery whose principal virtue is that it eliminates power relations in favor of a collective calculation that reaches an optimal compromise on prices by taking into account the position and expectation of each agent. The second approach, developed mainly by the new economic sociology, contests this hypothesis and endeavors to show that pricing depends on the structure of social relations and the balance of power it imposes. Despite their divergences, both methods consider that price levels are determined by markets and the way they function.

STANDARD MICROECONOMICS

According to standard microeconomics, prices are or should be jointly calculated by agents and the markets. To clarify this point, we should start from the bilateral transaction, the reference situation that the invention of interface markets tends to use as a starting point, if only to immediately push it into the background.[3]

In a bilateral transaction, which consists of a seller S, a buyer B, and a good at stake in the transaction, all the possible calculations are made by the agents. The necessary calculating skills are elementary, but very strict. It must be the case, and it suffices, that S knows the price (Ps) above which he will accept to sell and that B knows the price (Pb) above which he will refuse to buy.[4] The transaction will have a strong chance of success if $Ps \leq Pb$ since in that case, whichever price is finally chosen, everyone will be a winner. Let's define G as $Pb - Ps$. If $G = Pb - Ps$ is > 0, there exist many possible prices between Ps and Pb. Each of these prices corresponds to a certain sharing of G between the two agents. Which price is finally agreed upon depends on negotiation, on the bargaining between the two agents and, therefore on the power relations, which include, notably, but not solely, rhetorical skills, blackmail, better information, power positions, custom, manipulation of cognitive mechanisms (such as the framing of the negotiation by the first price mentioned), and more. Thus, in a bilateral transaction, pricing is a result of some combination of calculating activities and the balance of power.[5]

Those who defend interface markets cannot but deny the centrality of the bilateral transaction. Indeed, it is easy to understand that by increasing the number of agents (that is to say, of buyers and sellers), one increases the probability of seeing different values for Ps and Pb proliferate. Because the interface market intensifies the degree of competition, it is thus charged with progressively wiping out what comes down to power relations and their negotiation in establishing prices: at any moment, the bilateral negotiation can be interrupted and reframed by a third party, whether buyer or seller. Speaking phenomenologically, one can say that the stronger the pressure exerted by the market, the lower the chance that bargaining among agents can become established: it is the market that bargains. With the establishment of the interface market, which makes it possible to confront distinct and independent blocks, calculation is generalized and extended. The calculation ensured by markets, which can be compared to a giant price calculating machine, is added to the calculation ensured by agents. This moves us from the combination *price = calculation by B and by S + power relations* to the combination *price = calculation by B and S + calculation by the market.*

One of the ambitions of microeconomic theory is to study in detail the conditions under which information (notably about goods) is organized and revealed and circulates such that the market can take on the role it should play in discovering prices. The ideal is that the intervention of calculating agents (affixing Ps and Pb) will be reduced to its minimal, but strategic and morally just expression.

The war declared on the ever-possible prominence of bilateral transactions never ends because agents overflow with malice and inventiveness in order to impose these transactions as the rule. That is no doubt one of the reasons why economic theory has taken an increasing interest in the intermediary configurations that I propose to call *paucilateral*, configurations in which there are only a small number of agents and take place between the multilateral and the bilateral ones—that is, between situations of strong competition and situations that can be described as monopoly/monopsony. Inaugurated by Cournot's duopoly theory[6] and extended by game theory, this approach makes it possible to understand how agents organize in order to formulate prices and how the strategies followed can lead them closer to or further from the price levels obtained in a situation of strong competition.

This analysis can be extended. Economist William Baumol and his academic and industrial allies redefined the very notion of bilateral transactions through the theory of contestable markets. Under certain conditions, this theory makes it possible to show that a situation of bilateral transaction (say, a monopoly) can be considered equivalent to a situation of multilateral relations: prices are calculated as though there were many buyers and sellers, since if the agents engaged in the transaction abuse their monopoly position, legions of agents will unfailingly appear, attracted by the lure of profit, thus reestablishing the calculating power of the markets.[7]

ECONOMIC SOCIOLOGY

Economic sociology has not shown much interest in the question of pricing. When it has, it has generally been to underline that situations in which prices determined through a simple confrontation between supplies and demands, external to one another, constitute an exception. Indeed, beyond the face-off between sellers and customers lurks the invisible and complicated web of social relations, a web that formats their meetings and imposes its logic. In economic sociology, to understand how prices are formed means starting from a very general hypothesis called *embedding* that asserts that agents are never isolated. Rather, they are always connected to one another. Following Jens Beckert's interesting article on this subject, one can distinguish four different forms of embedding and therefore four different sociological interpretations of price formation mechanisms.[8]

A first conception of embedding is developed by those according to whom markets can be likened to webs of social relations between agents. Prices depend on the play and strategy of influence, power, or mimesis structured by these social networks.[9] They are determined by the structure of the relations established between agents.

In his study devoted to open-outcry auction stock markets,[10] sociologist Wayne Baker shows the direct impact of network structure on price formation and price levels. His investigation of the stock option markets starts from an observation that goes against what standard economic theory asserts. According to the latter, bigger markets are supposed to be more competitive than smaller ones, and greater competition should attenuate price volatility. However, in Baker's study, the opposite happens: in the market with the most actors (seventy-one, on average, per observation) there is high volatility, whereas on the smaller one (twenty-seven actors on average, per observation) volatility is low.

Baker explains this phenomenon by showing that the quoted values of options depend on the number of participants. When it is low, everyone interacts with everyone, which favors uniformity in evaluations and stabilizes prices. When participation increases, the communication networks stretch out and fragment. Different agents do not compare either the information they have or their evaluations, so prices spread and are more volatile.

Social-network research calls into question the oversimplified relationship between an increase in the number of agents and the intensity of competition. It underlines that supposedly independent agents are actually connected and that these interrelations impose their logic. The importance of networks is a question that economic sociology has explored very systematically. Mark Granovetter's foundational work shows that in the case of the labor market, the networks and their morphology determine the relations between supplies and demands and thereby influence salary levels.[11] In a now-classic study devoted to big corporate law firms, Brian Uzzi and Ryon Lancaster discovered, through a sophisticated statistical analysis, that the stronger and more numerous the connections between firms and clients, the lower the prices of legal services.[12] Looking at producer markets, Harrison White proved that to affix their prices and their production volumes, as well as to maximize revenues, companies observe their competitors' behavior through their own clients. The strategies companies follow to set their prices are then determined by the structure of their closest relationships, corresponding to what are called niche markets.[13] Once again, the network acts, but here it is reduced to its local dimension.

Turning to social networks in order to study markets is widespread, and there are numerous other examples I could cite. From the sociologist's (or economist's) point of view, the reference structure is still the bilateral transaction—that is the point from which all of these studies begin. However, instead of attending to the competitive pressure generated by agents as a function of their number, sociologists introduce an intermediary variable that changes the shape and effects of this pressure. They abandon an unrealistic hypothesis according to which an undifferentiated population of more or less numerous agents chooses either to cooperate or to act alone. The scene is instead one in which the population is structured by interconnections, exchanges, and power relations. It is these networked interdependencies, and not merely the number of participants, that account for the intensity and the nature of competitive pressure and its effects on prices. The network structure prevails, tempering demographic pressure by shaping the circulation of information. Nevertheless, whether one counts agents or considers the networks they form, in both cases, the bilateral transaction serves as the firm point of departure for the analysis of prices.

Through a second concept of embedding introduced by sociologists, markets can be seen as specific force fields.[14] The very notion of a market, with the unrealistic hypothesis that there would exist autonomous and separate supplies and demands, is a pure fiction. In reality, as Pierre Bourdieu asserts, prices do not adjust automatically. They are the result of the power relations associated with the positions occupied by agents in the economic field.[15] Dominant agents are well aware of this: from their point of view, the fiction of competitive markets, which some intellectual or political authorities (such as official committees and think tanks advising decision makers or regulatory agencies fighting unfair monopolies) aim to establish at all costs in order to neutralize power relations, is a very real threat.[16] What would a company in a monopoly situation have to gain from the implementation of rules that rigorously open the markets to competition? Its interest would be, on the contrary, to maintain the spontaneous tendency of real markets to paralyze competition. Hence, for instance, multinational companies deploy strategies in order to impose *numerus clausus* ("closed number," limiting those involved, for example, in cartels or in situations of collusion) so as to ensure that prices are essentially determined by the balance of power.

The description of markets that these sociological analyses offer is, on the factual level, close to the one provided by industrial economics as it developed in the 1970s, with notions of market structure and monopoly power, linked, for instance, to the erection of barriers to entry or to the development of economies of scale or of scope.[17] Economic agents are in a permanent struggle to occupy and keep dominant positions, opposing by all possible means the advent of a wider competition that would challenge their incomes.

A third conception of embeddedness considers markets to be institutions shaped by rules, conventions, or norms. The organization of competition and its management can be regulated in such a way as to eliminate or attenuate the risks of impediments to competition, such as those that result from collusion and price agreements. Regulation can impose quality standards or a minimum wage, define intellectual property rights, or determine how externalities are taken into account, which is the case when environmental or labor safety laws are enacted. The list goes on: regulation can define classifications and appellations contrôlées (in France, controlled product designations) that aim to make the qualities of goods increasingly visible and less ambiguous; there can be legislation concerning taxes and excises, as well as on the modes of calculating or levying them; an agency can affix key interest rates. Whether public powers or private agents initiate their elaboration, all of these regulations have an impact, direct or indirect, on price levels. Once they are stabilized and regularly implemented, as in the cases of taxes, environmental rules, or collective wage agreements, they can become routinized, some subsets of which can be taken care of by algorithms and integrated software in the pricing procedures.[18]

Finally, there is a very wide and very loose vision of embeddedness. A fourth way of explaining price levels is to make them depend (at least in part) on agents' sets of values and therefore on the global cultural determinations that shape their preferences. These determinations may go so far as to push some agents to refuse the commodification of certain goods for reasons often described as ethical.

In sum, no matter how it defines embeddedness, economic sociology refuses to believe in the possibility of commercial transactions that totally escape power relations. Sheer numbers do not change anything. When two agents are face to face, even if they are surrounded by a multitude of disconnected agents who transform the market into a pure calculating machine, the invisible, but decisive crowd of social relations slips in. They take the form of networks, fields, regulation systems, or cultural determinations. These relations, which bring all their weight to bear on the encounter, preexist and format it in irreversible ways. In a way, economic sociology is only a footnote to Weber's famous assertion: "Money prices are the product of conflicts of interests and of compromises; they thus result from power constellations."[19]

CONTRIBUTIONS AND LIMITS

The microeconomic approach rightly emphasizes that pricing can and must give rise to a *distributed* (calculation) process, which is indistinguishable from the market. When there are many agents, the market, thus conceived, resembles a squad of very simple robots (they are only asked to establish thresholds), collectively performing better than a small number of complex robots, which would be quite incapable of facing up to the difficulty of the operations required. The market as a whole has more developed cognitive capacities than those of two agents engaged in a bilateral transaction. Without entering into the debate about the efficiency or efficacy of competitive markets, points I will return to in Chapter 8, what should be noted is that in this model, prices are formed in a calculation space peopled by numerous and different agents who are localized in a multitude of dispersed sites and who each contribute, *nolens volens*, to the formation of observable prices. This is the main lesson of economic theory.

Sociology, in its sometimes fratricidal struggle against microeconomic theory, underlines that neither agents nor markets are free in their calculations. Granted, the process that leads to affixing prices is distributed, but it is embedded in, managed, and oriented by networks of interdependencies, norms, or power relations that determine the result. Pricing is a collective movement that mobilizes a multitude of agents connected to one another as though, on the site where the transaction takes place and at the moment it is concluded, a throng of other sites weighed in on its outcome. Regulations, relations of domination, cultural impregnations, constraints relayed by networks of relations—all of these collective structurings of commercial action explain why *Ps* and *Pb* and the modes of sharing *G* cannot be pushed outside the framework of the market and must therefore be *internalized* in market functioning.

In these models, the practices leading to what is called price formation are distributed and internalized. These are two essential results that I will try to capture in the notion of price formulation. This will be possible, however, only by taking positions that are the completely in reverse of the work that has just been presented. The preceding analyses postulate that prices are dependent variables determined, in one case, by the conjoined play of individual preferences and competition, in the other by social relations or social structures. The most extreme and least theoretical form this method takes is the statistical analysis of the different parameters that explain price levels. What happens in a commercial transaction and in fact in each bilateral transaction is determined by a general context, by a constellation of factors that can be grasped through a set of variables that can account for the price in a particular place, at a particular moment, as long as the variables are appropriately chosen. The practices and strategies for pricing that different agents deploy are bracketed out, since it is postulated that these practices do no more than take note of, shape, and transmit the influence of contextual or structural forces.

In the model of market agencements that I am presenting, these practices are on the contrary absolutely central to the analysis. Prices are not mere dependent variables that arrive at the end of the road. They are at the heart of the mechanisms that organize the conjoined transformation of goods and agencies and prepare their singularization. Before introducing the notion of price formulation that makes this reversal possible, I invite the reader to devote a few minutes to research on wine markets, one of the best attempts at compromise between the methods of economics and sociology. What I seek to show with this example is that the distinction between the objective dimension and the symbolic dimension of goods to which this compromise leads nevertheless fails to take into account the reality captured by market agencements.

THE PRICE OF FINE WINES: WHY IT'S IMPOSSIBLE TO DISTINGUISH THE SYMBOLIC FROM THE MATERIAL DIMENSIONS OF GOODS

The market for high-end wines is one of economic sociology's favorite topics. For sociologists, as indeed for economists, it is a huge challenge to explain how prices are formed for this market. In these models, the sensory qualities of the wines cannot be the only factors that explain prices. First, because experts very often disagree with one another and regularly revise their judgments as the wine ages.[20] Second, because the differences in observed prices are not due to the objective properties of the goods or to asymmetric distribution of information about these properties. As Jens Beckert explains, two bottles of wine may be sold at prices that range from a few euros to more than three hundred euros, despite the fact that the chemical characteristics of their content are very similar and despite the fact that data on them are widely available.[21]

Beckert rightly points to the myriad intermediaries who itemize, compare, establish hierarchies of, and evaluate what they deem to be the intrinsic qualities of the wine, thus contributing to how their prices are established. Jumbled together, they include experts, distributors, journalists, amateur wine clubs, organizers of wine tastings, and of course, influential wine critics who produce buying guides such as Parker's or Hachette's. All of these intermediaries, equipped with measuring instruments and evaluation protocols, put into words, conceive elements of language, develop categories, and circulate discourses that are addressed almost exclusively to those who have the resources and cultural codes that give access to the social game of evaluation. Beckert explains that the essential difference between the six-euro bottle and the bottle at 120 euros is generated by this intermediary milieu and the social rankings it enacts. The proof of this is to be found in sales statistics: those who are richly endowed with cultural and economic capital buy the 120-euro bottles; those who are poorly endowed pick up the six-euro bottles.

Certain sociologists or economists easily move from this peculiar observation to the idea that it is possible to draw an analytic distinction between two types of markets. In the first type of market, the quality of the goods can be measured by their material characteristics, which can be easily objectified, are difficult to contest, and around whose appreciation social agreement coalesces. Consumers take the properties of these goods as givens. Beckert suggests referring to these as *standards markets*. In the second type of market, products put in play qualities that are aesthetic or related to taste, moral content, or elements of social status. In these cases, the qualities are subject to controversial judgments; assessments diverge. Real markets, adds Beckert, mix these two components in varying proportions. Everything does have a material value (let us call this a functional and objective value),[22] as well as a value that sociologists like to call symbolic—that is, subjective and socially constituted. Logically, therefore, the value that prices measure must be a composite value that combines these two components. Economic theory helps to understand how the objective component is constituted. To explain real prices, however, one cannot forget to take the symbolic dimension into account, since through a complex and sophisticated interaction of intermediaries, it weighs in on prices, producing and reproducing status differences both among producers and among consumers. The more intermediaries, the more diversified and professionalized they are, the more important the symbolic component becomes.

The distinction between objective and symbolic characteristics makes it possible to explain how pricing mechanisms contribute to perpetuating relationships of domination between economic agents. Developing the symbolic qualities of a wine is costly. Indeed, it requires important investments, among other things, in technology (eliminating pesticides, hand picking the grapes, micro-oxygenation, new oak barrels), in choosing small, well-situated plots, in differentiated access to networks of critics and methods of commercialization, or in the choice and control over marketing tools. These investments, the way they are chosen and implemented, provide fodder for the host of intermediaries who collectively contribute to evaluating wines and establishing a hierarchy among them. Prices, adds Beckert, are indexed to these hierarchies and by the same token become themselves powerful tools of social discrimination. At the top of the scale, one finds producers with sufficient resources to invest in the symbolic dimension and the networks of intermediaries that feed it, courting consumers who are financially and culturally capable of entering the collective evaluation game: the "good" wines go to them. At the bottom of the scale, one finds the producers who simply produce hectoliters and consumers condemned to wines cheaper in price because these have been judged by poorly qualified intermediaries or, worse, are not even worth talking about. The impecunious drinker is mystified. The wine he is drinking is not chemically or biologically different; it is symbolically devalued. Like Siegfried when he accepts the cup containing the potion that will make him forget Brunhild, members of lower classes may think they are drinking wine, but actually they must be drinking to forget how dominated they are! And as they empty their glasses, they are accepting this domination.

Should we preserve this idea of a symbolic dimension of goods, which provides an elegant explanation for how prices are established and how they participate in power relations? Beckert answers in the affirmative. According to him, this is all the more important because in our affluent societies, functional needs (linked to the usefulness of goods and to their objective characteristics) have basically been satisfied: the way goods are appreciated is increasingly connected to their symbolic dimension. Beckert encourages us to learn to decipher the wine market or the art market in such a way as to pay attention to distinguishing material and symbolic values in order to be better equipped for understanding the markets of the future.

Beckert's interpretation ultimately rests on the hypothesis that for any good, it is possible to draw a distinction between intrinsic (material) qualities and external (social or symbolic) qualities. The former are the outcome of material operations that happen before the good is put on the market, while the latter result from symbolic operations that are constitutive of market functioning. Wine is a chemical and biological substance that comes to be seasoned and pepped up with properties that, having been produced by the milieu of intermediaries mentioned above, do not originate in the wine itself, but in the social milieu through which it circulates and in the innumerable stories told about it. Symbolic qualities are to objective qualities what dressing is to salad.[23]

This way of looking at things does not correspond to the reality that is captured by the model of market agencements. Over the course of the previous chapters, we have established that goods are processes, sociotechnical assemblages that are formed and transformed throughout their careers. This is why it should be impossible to think of wine at any point in its career in terms merely of chemical or biological characteristics that would constitute a substrate to which sociocultural or symbolic characteristics might later be added, like successive layers deposited by a 3-D printer. The choice of site, the style in which the vineyard is organized, the history of the land and the region, the conditions of exposure to sunshine, the decision to use oak barrels or not, the modalities of ageing of the wine, the design of the labels, the shape of the bottle, and the circuits through which it is commercialized—none of these are external to the wine. These elements are not there simply to feed the machine that produces social distinctions. They constitute the weft and the substance of "wine" as a product, not so much because they determine its objective properties (for instance, this much exposure to sun producing this number of degrees of alcohol), but simply because their association composes a dense nexus of qualities that defines the product (see Chapter 2), just as so-called chemical qualities do.

Determining the price of the wine is only one step in this qualification process, a profiling process that leads to a finely calibrated adjustment between a good and its buyer. The notion of symbolic value is perhaps only a prosthesis invented to explain the gap between what is supposed to be the real value of the good and its observed price, a bit like the furring that carpenters insert to fill the space between furniture and the walls on which it is fixed. The price, however, is neither the consequence nor the measure of the value of a good. It participates in the formulation of this value, which, as I have shown in the two previous chapters, has no end point. Price is a cause of value, but only one of its numerous causes. The consumer buys the price, just as he buys the exposure to sunshine, the region, of the style of wine making. Turning things around like this frees us from the pressing and insoluble problem that we inherited from classical political economics—namely, the question of connecting price and value.[24] However laudable it may be, any attempt to reach a compromise between economic and sociological explanations of price formation is bound to be unsuccessful because it fails to acknowledge that the qualification of goods is a process. The only possible strategy for escaping from that dead end is to put pricing practices at the center of one's analysis. Introducing the notion of price formulation aims to do precisely that.

PRICE FORMULATION

PRICES ARE ALWAYS QUALCULATED FROM OTHER PRICES

To introduce the notion of formulation (and the associated notion of a formula), the simplest approach is to start from an obvious observation: a concrete price is always established on the basis of at least one other price—that is to say, it is only one element in a series of prices that come before and after it. I have known as much since primary school, since we learned the famous rule according to which *sale price = cost price + profit margin*. This rule refers to another operation that makes it possible to establish the cost price from the purchase price and the different costs involved in obtaining the final good and making it available to customers. A little later in my schooling, we were also taught that these operations are false or are as arbitrary as any other convention. (How can one know what the real cost price is? How can one establish precisely what the production costs are?)[25]

To say that one cannot know precisely what an objective cost is or could be does not, however, prevent economic agents from spending their time calculating prices and especially calculating them from other prices, which are themselves calculated from other prices. This goes on without it being possible to define either a starting point or an end point. In fact, as economists Gerald Faulhaber and William Baumol noted, the *marking up* technique[26] remains the simplest, most widespread, and most efficient rule used by supply-side agents to set prices. What is important to my argument right now is not to assess whether this technique is correct or adequate, but to observe that it is used.[27] Note also that even if cost price is a myth, any company that forgoes precise knowledge of the cost price of its services endangers itself.[28] One can therefore, paraphrasing economist Piero Sraffa, say of prices what he suggested to say about commodities: they are always made on the backs of other prices.[29]

Let us agree to call price formulation the set of operations that, from a series of existing prices (Pi), provide the price (Pj) at which a given transaction takes place: $Pj = f(Pi)$.[30] Formulating the price includes the work of elaborating and testing the formula $f(xi)$.[31] The formulation implies choosing the values of Pi that are to be taken into account. It mixes qualitative (nonnumerical) operations and quantitative (numerical) operations—that is why we call these operations qualculations—but also physical characteristics, aesthetic properties, and of course other prices. Formulation obviously requires a unit of accounting. One of the absolutely essential tasks of the sociology of market agencements is to identify these formulas, their formation, and the strategies to which they give rise, as well as their classification and evolution and the moral, technical, and political controversies they provoke. We will have to refine, extend, or even amend this notion of formulation, but it has the advantage of making accessible to observation and analysis the complex operations that are either supposed to take place in agents' brains or to be the result of anonymous mechanisms. Furthermore, it makes it possible to give a realistic account of the empirical results that are already available while taking on the *distribution* and *internalization* requirements that any theory of prices must satisfy.

WORKING OUT FORMULAS

Before going further into the analysis of price formulation, I will start from an example: the banal example of animal flesh being transformed into a commodity to which a price is assigned. This example will allow me to highlight the material and equipped nature of the work involved in formulation and to identify some of its main characteristics. An attentive examination of the long and tortuous process of the pass(act)ivation of the animal and the transformations it undergoes shows that price formulation is intimately linked to this process, so well described by sociologist Guilhem Anzalone, from whom I borrow the following stylized presentation.[32]

Anzalone's analysis centers on the trajectory followed by the meat production process,[33] from an animal frolicking in a field or moping in a stall to the display case in which flesh, transformed into meat, placed in a container wrapped in cellophane with the proper labeling, awaits a customer who will not shy away from paying the asking price. There are multiple steps along this trajectory, which he analyzes as a stepwise process of deanimalizing, composed of a succession of transformations and (re)qualifications (Chapter 2). Once the beast has been slaughtered, first the skin, guts, head, feet, and spine have to be removed to produce half carcasses. Thus requalified, the animal is ready for a second series of transformations, which, once the muscles have been separated from their membranes, fat, and connected bones, make it possible to group types of meat, which are then vacuum packed. The meat is then "cut," which means cut into slices to be sold in retail. The last qualification is the presentation in a supermarket of *pieces* whose characterization has been completed with new variables, such as acidity and color, which put the final touch on the qualification of the good offered to the customer. Between the flesh, full of promise, that a trained eye can imagine under the skin of a calf still suckling its mother and the containers lined up in the refrigerated display case, everything has changed and nothing has changed. The same miracle always takes place: operations follow one another, combining the evaluation exercises we met in Chapter 3 into a long series. The result is a kind of transubstantiation.

The progressive framings, through separation, dismemberment, and successive cuts, shape entities that start to exist by themselves, detached from their temporary environments to appear ultimately in the form of pieces on display in cellophane. The framings organize the rankings, which establish distinctions between pieces on the basis of multiple variables, both qualitative and quantitative, such as color, part of the animal, texture, and so on. These variables suggest a hierarchy of pieces that can be complex and that can vary according to the criteria and qualities that are taken into consideration. This continuous scoring[34] work is done at each of the qualification sites by duly equipped intermediaries and professionals in the sector who evaluate the meat as they transform it. At each of these steps and on the basis of a selection of scores and the ordinal scales they offer, intermediate prices, Pi, are qualculated with the help of specially conceived formulas. These prices flow together and combine with one another as the transformation process moves forward until a final formula is reached. Summarizing all the others, the final formula provides the Pj posted in the supermarket.

The following illustrations concern only the part furthest downstream in this chain to give some idea of the complexity of these formulations.

In the final steps of the process, everything moves forward from the purchase price affixed by the distribution company at the end of the global negotiation process with suppliers. This is the result of applying a series of operations that starts from a general rate and integrates invoice discount and quarterly and end-of-year discounts to produce a purchase price said to be "triple net"—in other words, Pi. To these first formulations are added those that are the result of negotiations between the corporate "meat manager" and different suppliers who, if the negotiations are successful, will be added to the catalog of referenced suppliers. Through these discussions, led on the basis of the Pi from the previous step, the maximal prices $(Pi + 1)$ are reached and communicated to the floor managers of different stores in the form of market-price lists. These managers can negotiate the prices down directly with their own suppliers. Finally it is the floor managers who must put the different pieces of cut meat into trays, but also, and this is not so easy, who must decide how to present the trays and assign a display price to each of them. How do they go about this?

The margins of maneuver are nonnegligible. The decisions and choices the floor managers make are not directly dictated by anyone. They can, for instance, while upholding the framework agreements, set up special promotional offers, as long as they take into account those that are decided at the corporate level so as to avoid contradictions between stores. They can also renegotiate prices with the suppliers. However, their range of action goes beyond these few variables; in France, they intervene between the moment when the ready-to-cut meat arrives on location, piled up in "caddytainers," large metal crates with multiple shelves on wheels in which the merchandise is stored, and the moment of shelf placement. Consider a floor manager facing one of these caddytainers, which contains five ready-to-cut hindquarters that have to be transformed, unhesitatingly, into a series of labeled trays, each label proclaiming the final price. No human brain, not even the best trained, would be able to perform such a formulation without the help of assistants. The first prosthesis on which the floor manager relies is the caddytainer itself. Indeed, it summarizes and extends the long job of dismembering and evaluating that has been done upstream from the supermarket. The crate itself allows for rapid inspection by grouping together pieces that are qualified as similar: one can imagine how the floor manager would react if suddenly a bouncing, lowing heifer were delivered instead! The second prosthesis on which and with which the floor manager can count is a calculation sheet.

The calculation sheet traces out the three main steps through which the hindquarters will go. The first three-line table describes the product on arrival as a function of its weight, price per kilo, and total price. The following table represents the transformation effected by the dismemberment (the carving) of the rears as a function of the categories of pieces put up for sale. This table specifies the proportion and weight of meat sold in each category, as well as the sale price per kilo, which allows the software to calculate the sales revenue imputable to each piece and the total sales revenue from the five hindquarters. The last part of the sheet provides a synthesis similar to the operating account the (corporate) meat manager constructs: it relates the purchase and sale amounts in order to obtain the mass and the margin rate. To construct this sheet, the floor manager uses elements from the different sources previously identified: the purchase price per kilo of the ready-to-cut meat taken from the weekly price sheet suppliers provide, the total weight of the caddytainer, its distribution as a function of the different pieces and the expected yield, the sales price of the pieces as determined by the meat manager for the previous range of dates. It also includes the cost of packaging and losses,[35] so-called market data—that is to say, the numbers known to everybody, which can be found, for instance, in industry publications. Finally, the floor manager can also take into account the prices posted by competitors. At the end of this complicated qualculation, the $Pi + 2$ prices, given by a formula that, as we see, combines and integrates the series of prices Pi, $Pi + 1$, and so on associated with each of the intermediary qualifications, are labeled on each tray. Granted, this is far from the elegant simplicity of the marking-up technique I mentioned above because these formulations are likely to take on sophisticated mathematical forms. The difference, however, is not in the nature of operations, but only in their degree of complexity.

This illustration, borrowed from retail, highlights the scale of investments required to formulate prices. The notion of formulation, which has the advantage of referring simultaneously to qualculative practices and their results, underlines that these are powerfully structured and regulated activities. Pricing practices take on forms (that is why it is relevant to speak of formulas) whose general properties are suggested by the example of meat.[36]

a) The first observation that an empirical examination of pricing activities encourages is that material devices play an important part.[37] The operations involved in these activities are not purely abstract. No population of human brains, however brilliant, is capable of formulating prices without outside help. They need caddytainers, Excel spreadsheets, graphs, display cases, and instruments to measure acidity and colorimetry, not to mention accounting and management software, knives, and instruments that make it possible to measure, notably, how tender the meat is, as well as all the devices mobilized upstream from distribution.

b) Prices are the result of qualitative and quantitative operations simply by virtue of the fact that they are articulated through the evaluating activities that were presented in Chapter 3. At each of the steps in the qualification process, the meat passes through the equipped hands of agencies that collect, group, class, and put it into hierarchies, pursuing and extending the gradual, reasoned dismembering of the beast. At step (i), the identification and hierarchy of the pieces (which can take the shape of an index assigned to a piece summarizing its ranking) provide the elements from which the Pi prices, corresponding to this stage of qualification, are formulated. At this point, it should be emphasized that the $Pi-1$ associated with the pieces reevaluated over the course of step (i) are akin to any of the other qualities of the said pieces: the hierarchy at (i) takes the $Pi-1$ values into account without necessarily being constrained by them. To put this more formally: the observed successive spreads, between Pi, $Pi-1$, $Pi-2$, etc., do not add up to produce Pi, since they never apply to the same pieces—the initial piece is progressively requalified and therefore transformed. Pj (the price quoted to clients) is a function of the series of

Pi values and through them of the requalification and transformation process. As I wrote up front in the Introduction, the price is only one among all the other qualities that is debatable and open to controversy. Anzalone, who describes this long and complex process in detail, sums it up perfectly: "A product's evaluation and its price formation are grafted onto the process of its description."[38]

c) A third observation is that via the formulas that establish them, prices establish relations between different evaluation and pricing sites, making them interdependent. Both the structuring of the agencement and the tracing of its borders are a result of the incessant work of constructing relations effected by the different formulas that cross and intersect, making a maze of connections that define the agencement's contours and constitution. The network of formulas imposes a dynamic on the affixing of prices. It gives rise to multiple exchanges back and forth between the different sites, as well as to iterations, adjustments, and incessant trials and errors. The graft to which Anzalone refers, which means that pricing and qualifying are two entangled processes, starts well upstream from the supermarket stands and well upstream from the slaughterhouses. Prepared for the commercial chain that will lead it to the meat aisle in a supermarket, the cow is a composite being, engaged in several parallel existences from the moment it is born. Its first capers begin to sketch out its sale. When a breeder looks at his herd, he guesses and evaluates the future carcasses that will one day parade in front of the eyes of a "qualitician"—in France, this is the name for a technician in charge of determining quality—who has to decide on the fate of each animal in thirty seconds. Will the shape and thickness of their muscles and their level of fattening allow some of them to move from the status of labelable to prelabeled beasts and later, if the butcher gods are favorable, to that of labeled beef? The animal never ceases to be a real cow, bellowing and quite alive, but its owner raises it so that it is already prepared for what it will become: a dead cow, assemblages of pieces and slices that, after many evaluations, transformations, and formulations, will have to convince customers in a supermarket or a luxury butcher shop; it is a cow whose price flits across its flanks like the retroprojected shadow of slaughterhouse payment schedules or the Excel spreadsheets of floor managers in Romorantin, a small town in the center of France. From the moment of their conception, the animals are simultaneously embedded in several metrological networks, several chains of measuring measures, which, underlining some qualities and amplifying them, make these animals exist both as cows whose characteristics can be found in any encyclopedia and as commodities dispersed in market-price lists. The breeder is not breeding any old cow, but a species that one might call commoditized or commodifiable cattle, the way one speaks of a Normande or Friesian cow. In fact, there are as many profiles of commodifiable cattle as there are possible profiles of their commercial qualities. The number of these new species is not infinite, however, because an ox cannot be eviscerated, cannot be dismembered, cannot be cut up in any old way, even in a purely commercial logic, even if the knife is wielded by the most avid for the immediate profit of capitalists.

Transformed as it moves forward, carried toward its certain destiny, the cow takes on value as it changes state. This commercial destiny lies in an ontological multiplicity that leads to the formulation of the prices at which the final transactions are offered and concluded.[39] As the cow circulates, it leaves behind a trail of formulating agents. The question being posed is not "What is an animal with such and such characteristics worth?" but rather "What qualities should the animal be given, if it is going to be offered at such and such a price?" The formulation has the double property of maintaining the distributed character of calculations and integrating, internalizing, and summarizing them. Although they are distant, all the different sites are present in the final formulation, which connects and brings them together.

As a concept, formulation highlights markets' formidable qualculative power. The usual vision, which takes into account only the relations between supplies and demands, seriously underestimates what makes market agencements so strong—namely, their capacity to organize singular transactions, to aggregate them, and to include pricing in the continual work of adjustment. Supplies and demands matter in the work of formulating prices, but this work does not boil down to observing a ready-made confrontation. Pricing, in the way it has effects on all the sites involved and notably on the process of designing goods and qualifying them, acts from within on the definition of what constitutes supplies and demands and on the qualities of goods offered for sale. In no sense does it measure a state of relations between supplies and demands to which price might be considered external.

PRICE FORMULATION SINGULARIZES GOODS

Until recently, it was difficult to conceive of prices as simple qualities participating in the singularization of goods. What used to seem absurd now seems obvious. Bespoke, personalized pricing has become common practice, which finally makes explicit that price is never completely external to the good, but that it is in fact one of its essential characteristics. This is accentuated by the widespread development of a particular pricing practice—namely, *yield management*. Indeed, yield management provides a remarkable illustration of the practices involved in price formulation.

How is the price determined on the ticket I buy for a Paris-Marseille trip? The answer to this question is not straightforward.[40] The first observation is that since the dawn of railways, prices have always been calculated with the help of formulas. The second is that these formulas have evolved profoundly over time as power relations have changed. The history of this formulation is the painful break from what once seemed obvious: that price should depend on distance traveled. This break unfolded in three stages.

The first price formulation goes back to the 1920s and 1930s. It is very simple, even simpler than marking up. The price (Pj) was a function of the distance (D) between the departure point and the arrival point and a price (Pi) that depended on the cost of a kilometer traveled. One should add that this price per kilometer took on different values depending on the class in which the customer traveled. When the formulas appeared, Pi was calculated from the index of coal prices (a) and the index of salaries (b), with a formula of the type $ax + b$.

The second formulation was marginal cost pricing. It appeared as rail transport lost its monopoly, given the increased competition from road transportation. This idea, tried out in socialist economies and introduced in France by Maurice Allais, was to imagine how an efficient market reflects the costs and takes them into account in price formation. All of Allais's students at the École des Mines in Paris, of whom I was one, remember his famous parable of the passenger at Calais. The question posed was close to the one that interests me here: How much does it cost to have a passenger board the train for Paris at Calais? Allais rightly observed that the existing formula did not bring an acceptable answer to that question. The cost of an extra passenger depends on his order of arrival and depends on the number of passengers who show up. If the train is not full, the additional passengers cost practically nothing, as long as seats are available, but when it is full, the answer is no longer the same! An extra car will have to be added, and then, if the number of passengers continues to increase, a second train will have to be programmed, and finally, if the number of extra trains grows beyond a certain threshold, one will have to consider doubling the tracks. Without going into detailed calculations based on the notion of marginal development cost, it is easy to understand the practical translation of this observation. It leads to taxing certain tickets in order to reduce spikes in demand by inciting those travelers most sensitive to price variations and whose schedules are the most flexible to travel at off-peak hours. This is the principle behind the decision to create a tricolor calendar (blue, white, red) to fill the trains at off-peak hours with senior passengers. The new formula was $Pj = A + D \times C \times \vartheta(t)$, where D is the distance between the departure city and the arrival city, A a fixed extra tax, C a constant corresponding to the price per kilometer, t a departure time, and ϑ a parameter that varies with the schedule.

The third formulation, however, abandons any reference to distance. One can imagine how counterintuitive it may have been for the SNCF, the Société nationale des chemins de fer français, France's national railway, to explain to a potential passenger that the price they were going to be charged had nothing to do with how far they were traveling! Is the fact that it costs me more to drive my car from Paris to Nice than from Paris to Bourg-la-Reine in its southern suburbs only an illusion? The SNCF's answer is yes, and not without good reason. The SNCF explains that the tricolor calendar, which maintains a connection with the distance, is too rigid and does not discriminate enough. The formula is too crude. Since at any given moment, different lines do not have the same occupancy rate, it is absurd to price them in the same way.

The SNCF understood then that an elegant way to hear Allais's lesson was to consider that purchasing a ticket must be associated with reserving a seat. The verb "to travel," taken in isolation, does not mean much and says nothing precise about the service rendered; the good is only poorly qualified. What counts is how one travels. The SNCF decided that for the passenger, traveling is not being transported. Traveling means sitting in an assigned a seat. This seat is more or less comfortable; it is available in this or that train, at this time or that; it can be reserved more or less ahead of time; the reservation can or cannot be changed; it can or cannot be canceled without incurring penalties and allowing the customer to opt for another train. Since every seat is different from all the other seats, it is normal and legitimate to pursue this process by attributing a singular price to the seat. It just has to be qualculated. After a fact-finding mission that took them to the United States (by plane), the yield management that the sales agents of the SNCF decided to implement was designed using this approach.

Yield management—selling the right product to the right customer at the right moment and at the right price, the price being simply a quality—is a transposition into practice of the model of discriminating monopolies.[41] I suggest we now take a detour through this model.

DISCRIMINATING MONOPOLY AS A REFERENCE SITUATION

A company in a monopoly situation is by definition alone. It has room to maneuver to affix both prices and the quantities offered for sale, although it must adapt to a constraint: the price and the quantity produced must be adjusted to customers' demand. In the case of a pure monopoly, this constraint corresponds to an intuition based on the self-evident character of the law of supply and demand. If the company decides to increase the volume of its production, it will have to lower the sales price (which is supposed to be unique) so that the demand can absorb the added production. Assuming the company seeks to maximize revenue, we see that beyond a certain threshold and given the diminishing price, the increase in quantity will not bring in additional revenue. This threshold depends on the elasticity of the relationship between demand and price: the less the demand is sensitive to price level, the more the monopoly can increase its income.

To make this analysis compatible with the model of market agencements, we have only to free ourselves from the hypothesis that goods are identical and price is unique. Pricing has to be considered the ultimate phase in the singularization of goods. The reference situation is not one in which a given homogeneous good is supplied to an undifferentiated clientele, but rather one where multiple goods are on offer, proposed at different prices to a population of customers who are themselves different. Every monopoly is considered akin to an assemblage of bilateral monopolies, each corresponding to a unique

transaction established between a supply and a demand whose singularization is ensured, at the very least, by a specific price being established.

In the case of a *perfectly* discriminating monopoly, each consumer is identified and characterized by their capacity to pay for the good or service they are
offered. Economist Étienne Wasmer thus presents this as the case of a monopoly "that would know at the exact moment when you buy a coffee at the only
machine in the cafeteria that is working, how much you are really prepared to
pay for the mokaccino. The monopoly...will then take all the surplus for each
customer."[42] The main difference with classical situations of pure monopoly
or pure competition is that the prices (of what we used to consider the same
good) are not unique, but are instead adapted to each customer. The mokaccino on offer for this customer at this moment in this place is obviously different from the mokaccino on offer elsewhere at another moment to another
customer, even if the beverages are comparable.

Between a pure monopoly that knows only a block of demand and is a limit
configuration of interface markets and the purely discriminating monopoly
that knows only singularities and tips into the world of market agencements,
there are a number of intermediary configurations. For instance, blocks of
consumers can correspond to a segmentation of the clientele: for each unit
sold at the same price to the same type of buyer, the price varies according to
the type of buyer as qualified by age, occupation, and so on. What is significant in the analysis I am putting forward is that beyond the description of
these imperfections, the reference situation is no longer pure competition or
its antithesis, pure monopoly. The reference is now the purely discriminating
monopoly—that is to say, an agency that offers only singularized goods for
sale at different prices.

In the case of a discriminating monopoly, the company has to endow itself
with powerful equipment in order to observe the customers (to determine
their *Pb*) and effect infinitely more complicated calculations than those of a
pure monopoly or companies in situations of oligopoly.[43] One can no longer
say that prices are the result of the meeting of supplies and demands except in
a metaphorical manner. Prices are calculated on a case-by-case basis. In order
to explain how they are determined, the only available strategy is to carry out
an ethnography of pricing to show how in market agencements and over the
course of the bilateral transactions they frame each agency operates its own

qualculations, taking into account (and internalizing) the (distributed) qualculations realized at other sites by other agencies. Yield management (also called revenue management) is a good starting point for such investigations, which should also pay attention to the knowledge and instruments that are designed, tested, and implemented by pricing professionals.

YIELD MANAGEMENT

A discriminating monopoly is not a fanciful invention. Yield management is its most accomplished practical translation. Until recently, it seemed unrealistic to consider that one could have instantaneous access to the Pb of customers. With the arrival of centers of big data that enable the data to be collected and the development of data-processing tools, this is now conceivable. In conjunction with the hypotheses and contributions of behavioral psychology, big data makes it possible to establish profiles and manage the long, costly procedures by trial and error that used to be necessary to reach the Pb.

Yield management has given rise to intense research and experimentation. Management scientist Andrew Boyd's book gives a good presentation of this work.[44] He starts by noting that with the resources of big data and the internet, it is time to introduce a bit of science and technology into pricing activities. The market, and with it the law of supply and demand, says Boyd, does not determine much. Prices are established as a result of struggles between agents who try to impose their own qualculations. In this struggle, equipment counts—in both senses of the term. It makes the difference, and, Boyd adds, if suppliers want to optimize their revenues, they have to wrap their heads around the fact that each transaction is a bilateral transaction that requires singular goods offered at prices that are established in a singular way. Supply does not confront *one* demand, but rather a multitude of different potential demands; it can satisfy these only if it disaggregates itself into a multitude of singular offers.

The book presents the formulas and the calculations that allow both for this exploration and for the optimization of revenues. Yield management is a practical application of the theory of discriminating monopolies. It does not simply play on prices, but instead makes prices one of the many qualities that allow goods to be singularized and makes it possible to construct the market as a sum of bilateral monopolies. Which good, for whom, and at what price?

These are the questions the supplier must ask, knowing that the answer must take into account a series of constraints and, notably, the fact that the singularization of goods must not lead to an upheaval in design and production activities that would lead to an unreasonable increase in costs.

Boyd explains that yield management was imagined by airline companies during the upheaval provoked in the 1980s by deregulation policies that rekindled competition. To face these conditions, they revived the process of singularization, concentrating on what they controlled—namely, how the seats offered to passengers would be qualified. Their personalization, like that of the SNCF seats, can be achieved by attaching characteristics such as the possibility of changing the reservation or not, choosing a position in the aircraft, reserving far ahead of time, selecting the date and time of the flight, and so on. Customers are profiled. This singularization seems slight, but it can be successfully carried out only through a complete overhaul of both sales networks and techniques and the ways reservations are handled. Heavy computational infrastructures, sophisticated algorithms, and data-collecting devices are set up in order to singularize seats and formulate their prices. The material component of these innovations becomes visible when one accepts the idea that a seat is not simply a piece of furniture with armrests and a back. The seat on which the passenger sits includes the systems for reservations and price formulations. These systems have had at least as great an impact on the transformation-requalification process as the invention of assembly-line production in the automobile industry of the 1930s. Before these disruptive inventions, the continuous updating of reservations was a real conundrum, with complicated heavy mechanical systems that depended on constantly sorting perforated cards.

Having started in the airline industry, this movement then scattered everywhere, notably into ground transportation such as the railways. More and more companies put scientific pricing into practice. As yield management experts put it, a hotel is just a plane without wings. Thanks to wisely placed sensors, the price of a bottle of Coca-Cola for spectators at an American football game can vary with the temperature of the moment, the hypothesis being that the hotter it is, the more fans are willing to pay for refreshments.

Personalization through pricing is not new, but for a long time, it remained invisible. Boyd describes amusing situations in which the discounts given confidentially to certain customers gave rise to leaks that severely embarrassed producers. Singularizing through pricing was done, but in a clandestine and artisanal fashion. Scientific pricing rationalizes this practice, which becomes a full-fledged object for research and development. Price formulation is henceforth an industry with its platforms, its professional associations, its institutes and training seminars, its university teaching, its conferences, and its particular know-how spiced with a grain of cynicism.[45]

Inspired by yield management work, most online businesses have recruited entire teams to work on price formulation. These experts process both internal data (the number of items in stock, the age of products) and external data, collecting the prices of hundreds of references on dozens of sites several times a day. They are thus able to follow changes in the supply and in the qualification of the goods on offer, a requalification that includes adjusting the price. The formulas, in the form of algorithms, determine at each moment the price that will maximize margins. In these formulas, elements such as the weather, the hour of the day, whether or not the web surfer has been to a price comparison site, the approach of school holidays, what is on television that evening, or the content of the literary supplements of big newspapers are all variables that may be taken into account. More individual data, such as the brand of the computer (Mac users are presumed to have more money), can also be taken into account in the formulation. The increasing part played by pricing technicians, notably in e-commerce, translates into permanently changing prices. Prices are now dynamic. *Que choisir*—a consumer magazine in France—followed the evolution of a GoPro Hero 4 black edition between January 15, 2015, and February 15, 2015.[46] On each of the four online sellers observed, the prices varied from one day to the next by 100 euros, and at one point, the spread between the prices offered by the different sellers reached 150 euros. This volatility of prices, comparable to that of financial markets, and their multiplicity are not mysterious if one accepts that prices are one among many qualities that play a crucial part in the singularization process. The price can even depend on whether or not the customer is looking into the different prices on offer through a search engine—that is, on the specific behavior and expectations of a particular consumer. On the supplier's side, it is less a matter of knowing whether the prices offered by the competition are different than it is of knowing whether the web user cares! Can one imagine a higher-precision bespoke service than a service that takes into account the customer's preoccupations and least-public behavior?[47]

I could give many more examples. Yield management and the science of price formulation are everywhere. What should be emphasized, however, is that pricing plane or train tickets is one of the simplest cases. Without leaving the transportation sector, to understand how complex certain formulations have become, consider a longer time frame. Personalizing seats is then no longer reducible to the logistics of reservations. In the long term, it will depend on the configurations of aircraft. Architecture and design have contributed to this movement through their own evolution over a number of years. They now make interior layouts more flexible and more easily diversified, consistently aiming at enabling price discrimination. Each of the sites that participates in the design and implementation of these innovations thus becomes party to the formulation of prices, whose complexity grows.

One can go even further in exploring the role played by pricing over the course of goods' transformation and singularization. Just as machining, wire drawing, and stamping techniques can be applied to different materials in different industrial sectors, as the spread of yield management shows, price formulation techniques can be equally applied to the sale of plane or train seats, hotel reservations, or the sale of electronic products. If they are full-fledged contributors to the production process of goods, it is because they intervene materially in this process.[48] They are devices that act on goods by transforming them. (This is why a seat on the TGV is qualculated differently by yield management than a seat on a local train qualculated by the tricolor system.) This observation is obvious for industrial procedures, whose technical conception takes the calculation of costs into account, notably through the methods of value analysis, but it is no less true when one considers final consumption. In the latter case, the price has a tangible material existence (bar codes, labels, various inscriptions) that visibly affects the good, much like tattoos or scarifications transform a body and change its expression.[49] If one turns one's attention to the materiality of prices and its role in the qualification of goods, Catherine Grandclément's descriptions of supermarkets come to appear as the revelation of something that, like Edgar Allan Poe's purloined letter, had become invisible by being too visible.[50] Try the experiment yourself: go into a Walmart Supercenter one day when, as the expression goes, prices are slashed, and you will be as disoriented as a French visitor in the streets of Hong Kong. There is a proliferation of tags, labels, streamers, multicolored banners, discount coupons, crossed-out prices, and formulas calculating the savings to be grabbed. The customer wanders among price qualculations as much as among the goods on offer, in a strange palace of mirrors in which the prices on display infinitely diffract and multiply, connecting to one another, coloring the goods with new nuances, and finally becoming one with them; the label invites the customer to enter into this maze and to find his own way to the goods that await him, the ones that have been specially designed for him.

Taking the price as a singular quality into account is not new, even if, until recently, it was both hard to manipulate and hard for those who watch markets from the outside to understand and to acknowledge. Pricing professionals have long known how to do this, as the technique of line pricing used by five-and-dime stores shows. In that instance, the customer simply decides to buy the price before they decide which item to buy at that price.

PRICE FORMULATION AND TRANSACTION VOLUME

An airline company that practices yield management personalizes each of the seats it offers to its clientele and therefore faces off against a set of demands that are singular, that together add up in the company's accounts. How is the best possible combination of prices to be selected? There is no one best way. A company can calculate fares that optimize a variable it considers relevant (for instance, the ratio of margin to sales volume), the constraints on investment it imposes on itself (fleet composition—number and models of planes, interior layout, total payroll, and so on), or the constraints that are imposed on it (the architecture of air routes, the location of the hub, and more), as well as the offers expected from the competition. Whatever the objectives, a priori, the calculation can be only indicative; the single realistic procedure is progressive trial and error.

The ever-greater singularization of services can lead to an extraordinary complexity of calculations that require numerous iterations before leading to a result that can be considered satisfactory. The complexity is even greater well upstream from the process of the qualification of goods, at the beginning of singularizing the product and with it the qualculation of intermediary price, as in the case for pharmaceutical products. As a consequence, the calculation of the aggregate value of the variables considered as strategic by a pharmaceutical company (traditionally, they consider sales volume, return on investment, ecological footprint, and more) is not obtained directly from the quantities sold, since each good has different characteristics. The calculation must endeavor to assess as systematically and precisely as possible how much each good sold contributes to the achievement of the company's overall objectives. Quantities and qualities become inseparable: in a situation of extreme price discrimination, a singular configuration of qualities can correspond only to a single good and a single customer.[51]

In sum, the discriminating monopoly model is precious because it makes it possible to understand how the modalities of affixing prices (price formulation) participate concretely in the process of qualifying and singularizing goods while keeping open the possibility of multiplying and summing bilateral transactions. Whether the supplier concentrates on a particular service or chooses to serve a great number of clients, price formulation follows the same logic. From one configuration to the other, the only change is in the number of transactions that complicate the qualculation. To do full justice to the dynamic of market agencements, the model must be expanded: it is not sufficient to say that the same product is offered at different prices to different clients. Rather, what is on offer are products that are each different from one another, whose singularization may have begun well upstream, and that have stayed connected to each other throughout the production process, often through technological interdependencies. Singularization and massification are not opposed to one another. They are mutually reinforcing.

In the model of interface markets, where platform goods compete with each other, the aggregation of transactions does not raise any particular difficulties. Since prices apply to the same products, the calculation of the relation between price and quantity is (relatively) simple.[52] In the model of market agencements, one cannot talk about the supply curve, the demand curve, or their intersection since the characteristics of the good vary with the volume offered by the supplier. The situation that serves as a reference to understanding these agencements is the confrontation between discriminating monopolies, each of them offering each of its customers a particular good and a particular price.

This configuration is not unique to the most advanced market organizations. It is very common and does not threaten the viability and continuity of market agencements. Economist Alan Kirman demonstrated this brilliantly in his famous study of the Marseille fish market.[53]

Fish markets are classic objects for economics, first, because they are very old, but also because of the wide diversity of their forms of organization (auctions by ascending or descending price or over the counter). Kirman chose to study Marseille's markets because there were detailed data on the transactions. He was able to analyze information pertaining to each individual transaction—237,162 in total—over a three-year period that recorded the identities of buyer and seller, the category of fish, the weight of the lot, the sale price, and the temporal position of the transaction in the daily series of transactions of each seller. There were also other characteristics that make Marseille a particularly interesting object of study. It is a large market, and its organization is original: more than five hundred buyers and forty-five sellers meet in the wholesale market in Saumaty, even if not all are present every day.[54] More than one hundred and thirty types of fish are sold. Moreover, prices are not posted ahead of time, and no one knows how much stock is for sale when the market opens. Finally, all sales take place over the counter—that is to say, bilaterally. There is little negotiation, little bargaining, and the prices given by each seller are to be considered as "Take it or leave it." Kirman's analysis yields surprising results. A high proportion of buyers are faithful to their sellers. Furthermore, in a single day, the same vendor may offer different prices to different customers, and the consecutive prices for a single type of fish for different buyers can vary by up to 30 percent. Moreover, faithful customers are systematically charged the highest prices. It is enough to make Air France or EDF pale with envy!

Overall, Kirman shows that the Marseille market is a realistic model of competition between discriminating monopolies.[55] The lesson is all the more relevant because buyers and sellers are invited to conclude their transaction within a rigid spatiotemporal framework within earshot of one another. One might have imagined that the usual modalities of competition would prevail in such conditions. Not so. Instead of the perfect competition of neoclassical markets that one might have expected, one discovers the perfect competition of market agencements. The data Kirman analyzed prove beyond any possible doubt what one suspected—namely, that while short of being natural and spontaneous, an organization that rests on competition between discriminating monopolies is commonplace and perfectly viable.

Air France, Amazon, and EDF are not the only ones to play the discriminating monopoly card. It is a general practice. That is why I am arguing that this can and should serve as the reference model for understanding how agencies elaborate price qualculations that reconcile the singularity of goods with the multiplication of bilateral transactions in a satisfying way.[56]

WHY PRICE COMPETITION AND NONPRICE COMPETITION IS A FALSE DISTINCTION

Consider the case of mobile telephone service providers when a new operator, Free, entered the French market in 1999 with an aggressive commercial strategy. Let us look at this from the perspective of a customer of Orange, the main French telecom operator. The contract he has with the historic operator corresponds to a classic bilateral transaction—that is to say, a successfully singularized service: the user's attachment to his telephone and the actions it allows convinced him to consent to pay the monthly amount required.[57] This outcome is the culmination of a series of framings that led to the transfer of rights in return for payment: first the market attachment (which triggers the consent to pay), then the accepted formulation of a price (the subscription fee, which frequently implies a multiyear subscription), and finally payments, which fulfill the transaction.[58] Free arrived on the scene and offered lower prices while barely modifying services. The offer was based on a simple finding: the user's attachment to the mobile telephone—and the courses of action the device allows—is largely irreversible. Furthermore, this situation was achieved by a slew of French operators (SFR, Bouygues, Orange, and ... Free), but it is not controlled by any of them. The telephone is a platform, and the operator is only one of its many contributors. Of course, the telephone would be nothing without the cell towers and without the quality of communications supported and ensured by the different operators, but it also would be nothing without the web, the Apple Store, Google Play, the innumerable apps and services to which it gives access, or the geolocalization satellites. The plan that describes the good that an operator is offering is but one element in a complex and evolving device[59] that would have no value in the customer's eyes if that device were to falter or disappear. One can say that the plan opens up a new step in perpetuating the singularization process. Following this strategy, the new operator piggybacks on a vast number of past investments that make the success of the plan possible, yet without having to fight or pay for them. By slashing prices, Free does not challenge the singularization process as a whole. It is not offering the exact same plan at a lower price. Rather, it offers a plan that is more singularized *because* it is cheaper. There is no guarantee that this singularization strategy will work, of course. It works only if this new quality (the price) makes it possible to capture customers and attach them durably by detaching them from other operators and by getting them to fulfill the terms of contract.

Am I going against common sense or betraying a taste for paradox by saying that Free participates in intensifying singularization, rather than engaging in a classical standardization strategy? After a period of intensive innovation and nonprice competition, is there not a move, as is often the case, to a period of price competition? No, because this distinction, which has been overused, only superficially captures the process in question. With or without Free's slashed prices, the mobile telephone remains a highly singularized good. Given its insertion in a sociotechnical device that is constantly evolving, it leads its user into a conjoined movement that openly reconfigures identities. What is called price competition is only the tip of the iceberg: its conditions of possibility depend entirely on the powerful movement of singularization that carries it. By opting for Free, I reconfirm my attachment to a mobile phone, one of whose qualities has been modified in a way that suits me: its price. A long series of continuous investments is necessary to make price a discriminant quality.[60] Free does not herald the reign of desingularization (or standardization), but rather a continuation of the intensification of singularization and its consolidation. It is because the customer is *already* attached and has *already* been led to the point at which he consents to pay that, helped by many comparative reviews and assistant calculators, he can succumb to comparing prices and making a decision on that basis.

In any case, when price as a quality becomes a crucial variable on a trajectory of singularization, a new episode in the struggle to capture clients often begins. The formulations that Free proposes provoke counterformulations that attempt to reorient the singularization process, endeavoring to reduce price to the status of one among many other qualities. More and more plans with different prices and different services appear. Comparison tools, with their multicriteria tables, proliferate. The mobile phone is a constantly evolving good whose applications and uses are diversifying and feeding into singularization strategies.

To better understand the logic of this dynamic, one need only recall the double meaning of the word *affectation* in French.[61] At the moment when I am *affected* by (*affecté par*) the position of the needle showing that my gas tank is almost empty as I am driving on the highway, I find myself *assigned* to (*affecté à*) one of the gas stations whose prices are displayed on my navigation software app. Likewise, it is because I am *affected* by the estrangement of one of my old friends who moved to Toulouse, and because I feel the need to visit him, that I find myself *assigned* to (*affecté à*) airline transportation and that I come across the service offered by Air France or EasyJet. As all those who have studied situations of *sociotechnical lock-in* have clearly seen, in such circumstances, I am not really free to refuse the mobile phone, airline transportation, or fuel. This same story of attachment devices and the conjoined evolution of the profiles of goods and agencies continues to unfold. At a certain point, this leaves price the only discriminating quality left in play and the potential customer an agency that has been progressively configured in such a way as to be sensitive only to price. If, having been thus formatted, I choose Free, Carrefour, and EasyJet, I can rejoice in having gotten a good deal, in having made a good calculation. This movement—which makes price into a quality that, in affecting me (*m'affecté par*), assigns me to (*m'affecte à*) EasyJet, Carrefour or Free—could not be prolonged if it did not maintain and extend the affectations/assignments that preceded it and that made me unable to do without the cell phone, the car, or the plane. Thus, the result of intensive singularization through prices is not that the consumer is finally led to enter the realm of rational calculation, but that he let himself be carried by the *affectio mercatus* that leads him, in this case, to consider price a crucial characteristic. The price competition is nothing but one particular and (very often) transitional modality of the competition over qualities.

HOW PRICE BECOMES A TOOL FOR RANKING

The price of a kilo of sirloin can vary in a ratio of one to two, depending on the vendor and the location. This is an enigma that requires explanation. Some will postulate that differences in quality account for the difference in price.

Others will suggest that one butcher is twice the thief. Yet others will argue that some consumers accept the higher price because it distinguishes them from the others. Neither the inquiries and investigations to support one thesis or another nor their answers matter much to me. What interests me is that the prices, which emerge from the series of rankings produced by instruments of evaluation, are themselves in turn powerful and extraordinarily simple tools for ranking goods, sellers, or buyers. These tools are all the more powerful because they can be applied across all commercial goods.

With prices, comparison does not necessarily remain within a single class of products that were circumscribed by the underlying price formulations. Through prices, it becomes possible to compare and rank goods that had not been compared and ranked before. Not only can we say that this bottle of a great vintage represents a day's work at minimum wage; one can also say that its relative position in the class of bottles of wine is comparable to the relative position of an Audi Q5 in the class of SUVs. One ends up producing scales, which paves the way to constructing hierarchized classifications of people. For instance, out of these rankings, a class of consumers might emerge who buy great vintages and high-end SUVs and who vacation on fabulous exclusive islands. The existence of what Bourdieu calls *structural homology* can be explained as the more or less stable outcomes of this complex process of classification, which is already a classic object of analysis within sociology.[62]

The effects of these rankings cannot be considered as isolated phenomena. They are the last step in a series of operations through which price formulation is performed. The price, which is but one particular quality of the good, is transformed into an autonomous variable that engenders social classifications. This reversal, neglected by the market interface model, is at the heart of market agencements. In order to explain how this reversal happens, it is worth devoting a few lines to the conceptual distinction that describes the dual nature of measuring, expressed in French by the terms *mesure mesurée* and *mesure mesurante*.

To illustrate this distinction, let me refer to the well-known case of what is called intellectual quotient or IQ. First the notion of intelligence had to be defined (by experts) as a set of dimensions and subdimensions that were supposed to capture the underlying trait. In a second step, scales for each of these dimensions or subdimensions were constituted. Next, each scale was qualified, and finally, hierarchized classes were produced. So defined, the quotient allowed us to begin speaking of levels of intelligence. Finally, tests were designed to organize the exploration, quantification, and hierarchization of this intelligence, resulting in the expression of IQ through numbers (for example: 100, 120, 140 . . .) that correspond to the underlying process of constructing this way of capturing intelligence—*mesure mesurée*. From there follows the process of deploying the measurement as a tool—*mesure mesurante*—during which the qualculation behind the IQ (that is, the choice of dimensions, proxies, tests, and so on) could be simply black-boxed. IQ can now be used as an alleged neutral instrument measuring a reality that can consequently be seen as objective.

It is like using any kind of yardstick. When I say: "The length of this table is one meter," I don't care how meter as a unit has been defined and how the tool I have in my hands has been produced. What matters for me is simply the statement "The length is one meter," even though it could be alternatively be stated as "The length is thirty-nine inches." The same is true with IQ. What is measured by IQ is simply one definition of "intelligence." From an analytically construed term, intelligence manages to become an objective and indisputable entity. Instead of being the outcome of IQ testing (designed as a *mesure mesurée*), intelligence becomes what is measured by IQ (conceived of as a *mesure mesurante*). This (classic) reversal allows us to understand why this specific tool can be interpreted as an instrument of (social) classification and stratification: people can be grouped according to their intelligence as measured by the tests. This tool contributes to structuring social life: it transforms the definition (the assembled components that make up this definition of intelligence) into an objective attribute (the intelligence of the tested persons). The effects engendered by such tools cannot be denied or dismissed; instead, they must be carefully described and analyzed.

All metrological operations can be subject to this type of reversal, but prices are particularly susceptible. Having been fed by a long series of classifications (processes of price formulation), they can in turn be transformed into a tool for ranking that can be applied to goods themselves. The scoring systems used in consumer lending provide a striking illustration of this mechanism, with its different stages. Lenders (for example, banks) typically design products (loans) that differ by such qualities as, for example, the amount, duration, rate of interest, or insurance premiums. The prices of the loans whose formulation combines these characteristics are, as for any other good, nothing but a specific quality. Recall for a moment how price discriminates seats in planes or in trains: loans are just like seats or hotel rooms—they are part of a process that ends with them becoming singular. And like seats and hotel rooms, loan products are in search of clients, only in this case, the clients are borrowers.

In Anglo-Saxon countries (the United States and Britain), organizing encounters between singularized loan products and potential borrowers was made possible by information intermediaries called credit bureaus, which date back to the nineteenth century. In the beginning, credit bureaus collected information on business operators in view of transmitting it to possible transaction partners.[63] A trading entity could consult these bureaus to find out whether this or that counterpart had a reputation for paying their bills. Later, small, local bureaus emerged that did this work for households. Today, consumer credit bureaus equipped with electronic databases continue to gather publicly available information on individuals and banks, establishing synthetic documents that report on things such as outstanding loan amounts and legal proceedings incurred and keeping a record of all those who have requested access to these documents in the last two years. In this system, the information about individual market participants is a commodity. Institutions that underwrite loans, employers, insurance agencies, public administrations, and more broadly, any organism that can justify a business interest in this information, such as a landlord, can all have access to this information.

As Martha Poon has documented, what is known publicly in the United States as a FICO score is a trademarked product, developed on the back of the previously competitive underlying information commodity (the credit record at the bureau), that has had far more utility to lenders in their own financial product development than rich, unfiltered credit files. The American FICO score does not consider income level, employment situation, civil status, age, or address, even though those variables are central to the scores developed in other places, such as France.[64] Marketing materials tell us that FICO is calculated based on payment history (35 percent), level of outstanding commitments (30 percent), recent credit history (15 percent), type of loans held (10 percent), and new loans (10 percent), and it summarizes all of this information in the form of a number on a scale that lies between 300 and 850. Scores sold in a competitive marketplace for information, but all provided by FICO on a common scale, radically transformed US credit by permitting a mass market for credit cards to emerge in which credit was itself a product detached from banking relationships or retail transactions. Instead of waiting for people to approach them to borrow, using FICO, lenders were actively able to issue unsolicited credit card offers by dipping into the bureaus like a dating service to find or match people to whom they wish to create a credit attachment. A matching platform, FICO is an exploratorium device similar to those presented in Chapter 4. When a match is fulfilled, what has been achieved is the establishment of a singular relationship between a packaged product (including its price) and a unique borrower, a relationship that is made possible through the FICO intermediary.

What must be clear is that the lenders are not especially interested in the borrowers as individuals. In order to manage credit as a mass-production process, what matters are the summary scores in the same way that for people looking for soul mates, what matters up front are profiles. The business of lenders is to underwrite product offerings that are adapted to the different score groups and that are simultaneously attractive to the collection of individuals who correspond to that score group. Once the transaction is complete, the aggregate product must also allow lenders to achieve the business objectives they are pursuing (for example, optimizing income, minimizing the risks of nonpayment, and so on). The definition of the qualities of loans is always in the hands of the lenders. There is a vast variety of possible configurations, or in the language of this book, loan profiles. Yet they can all be aligned on a seemingly seamless continuum, from loans with many options for high amounts of capital with lower interest rates to loans with fewer options for lower sums with higher interest rates. We all intuitively understand that the former are usually designed for higher scores and the latter, which under uncapped interest rates are just as lucrative a business, for lower scores.[65]

Although the topic feels well understood, the clarifications I am making are essential. They shed light on the too often unrecognized reversal mechanism that is the core of this section. Like IQs, the FICO score can be considered in two different ways. First, it is a way of producing measurement (*mesure mesurée*). Indeed, from the different dimensions and subdimensions that Fair, Isaac selects and quantifies, FICO scores define a space that makes it possible to create loans, qualified in part by their level of score. A class of loans corresponds to a given range of FICO values and therefore allows the market to group together types of loans with similar characteristics (amounts, interest rate, duration, and so on), even if they are not originated by the same lender. FICO then acts to project its measurement (*mesure mesurante*): outside the mechanics of loan production, the FICO score can be used to characterize and rank people on a linear scale. The FICO score, an index calculated from multiple qualities found in credit data and specific to the credit system, is now seen as a unidimensional scale. From a tool designed to aptly synthetize credit data for the design of mass credit products, it has been readily transformed into an instrument that classifies and hierarchizes human beings.

Once this reversal has taken place, it is obviously tempting to seek out the meaning that lies behind this unidimensional ranking. In the case of IQs, the interpretation seems simple. IQ (as a *mesure mesurée*) measures the intelligence of the people to whom the tests are applied. These people can therefore be ranked according to a single quality: their level of intelligence as measured by the tests. In the case of the FICO index, figuring out what the reduction to a single dimension could mean has collapsed back to the nineteenth-century character trait called "creditworthiness," as if the name for this somewhat arbitrary numerical aggregation of heterogeneous characteristics were timeless.

Though as endlessly debated, the meaning of the FICO score is far from obvious. First, since its aim is the qualification of the goods on offer (loans), the FICO score is not bound to take into account any of the sociographic data usually selected to qualify people, such as socioprofessional categories, income, lifestyles, and so on. To characterize borrowers more directly, lenders must supplement the calculation of the score by returning to the raw credit file data. Once they have succeeded in attracting and attaching a client base, lenders can also gather additional information and can therefore elaborate sociological or psychological descriptions of their clientele and use them for their own purposes, particularly to gain an advantage over their competitors.[66]

Needless to say, it is mainly social scientists who are engaging in this work of repurposing FICO scores to directly classify agents. For example, economic sociologists Marion Fourcade and Kieran Healy have convincingly shown that the Weberian notion of *life chance*, the probability that someone's life will turn out in a particular way, could be correlated with FICO scores and therefore with the types of loans sold by lenders and particularly with their prices.

Once this result is obtained, the sociological analysis can then be pursued and arrive at statements such as the following: by using the FICO score, lenders offer to populations living in difficult conditions loans whose characteristics, and in particular prices, only worsen these conditions.[67]

As I said before, my purpose here is not to discuss the robustness or the relevance of this type of statement. It is simply to highlight the reversal mechanism that on the basis of an index leads to the qualification of the people with whom it is associated. Instead of being considered as a definition (always perfectible or modifiable) of intelligence, IQ is used as a tool to discriminate people who find themselves classified according to what is now considered to be their intelligence. The *mesure mesurante* takes precedence over the *mesure mesurée*. This movement, in the case of FICO scores, is all the more effective since its definition is a commercial black box, which is not the case with IQ. A FICO score becomes part of an environment that imposes itself and is discursively imposed as an indisputable reality on customers. It is easy to understand why the social sciences are so interested in this kind of configuration, especially as scoring practices calculated through proprietary systems become more widespread.

I have discussed the dual property of measurement systems at length because it is a mechanism that paves the way to the notion of quality, singular without an *s*. But why discuss the notion of quality at this point? Above all because this notion is constantly invoked by agents themselves to explain price differences between products considered as belonging to the same family, as for example when one speaks of the quality/price ratio.[68] Quality is considered to be measured, in a practical way, by price: quality is what the price is supposed to measure. This alleged one-to-one correspondence obviously leaves room for controversies and contradictory appraisals. But whatever it may be, what is assumed to exist as a hidden attribute of goods, named quality, is what prices should discover or express. Prices can now be seen as an intermediate variable between goods and consumers. They, too, transform a good's ranking into a ranking of people.[69]

FORMULATIONS ARE EVERYWHERE

The activity of price formulation is a fairly recent subject of study. Nevertheless, there is very detailed work on the role played by those known in France as engineer-economists.[70] In many countries, their contribution has been (and still is) decisive in sectors such as electricity, telecommunications, and transportation. The numerous controversies their formulas have given rise to are well documented.[71] The same goes for financial markets and for the markets for insurance and reinsurance, which have long since become choice sites for formulas.[72] Studies by Sandrine Barrey have shown, against all expectation, that very elaborate formulas are conceived and used in distribution sectors where prices are strictly regulated.[73] In a very innovative book, François Vatin widens the analysis to a great range of lines of business.[74] Several authors make direct reference to the notions of formulas and formulations in order to show how prices are calculated—for example, in the case of financing company projects or setting unemployment compensation for part-time workers in the entertainment industry.[75]

It is worth noting that this formulation work is present in unexpected areas. For example, we are starting to have access to the secrets of the art market and the market for great vintages.[76] Juan Pablo Pardo-Guerra's work on auction-house companies is one illustration. Having followed the sale of famous works, he makes the qualculations that precede the auction itself explicit, notably underlining the importance of producing and distributing catalogs of the items for sale, which, according to him, are powerful tools in price formulation.[77]

Consider this entry in the catalog for a 2006 auction at Christie's in London: "Lot 18, sale number 1619." It corresponds to a charcoal drawing attributed to Michelangelo. The catalog gives a brief description of the work. It gives its dimensions (248 × 176 mm), then notes that it is a representation of a man's head and torso (looking downward), as well as a study of the left shoulder and two studies of the right shoulder. The entry specifies that this work first belonged to the artist's family in Florence, that it then moved into the hands of John Malcom of Poltalloch (1805–1893), who passed it on to his son, who bequeathed it to his cousin, who then sold it to its current owner at Sotheby's in London on November 24, 1976. Through the references this biography establishes, it contributes, according to the process we saw in Chapter 2, to the good's qualification and particularly to its authentication. The catalog does not just describe these qualities: it establishes the work's relation to other elements, positing associations. For instance, it notes family resemblances with other works.

It briefly evokes the literature devoted to Michelangelo—notably, what covers this sort of study. It gives an exhaustive list of exhibitions in which the drawing has been shown. Detailed connections are made to other Michelangelo works such as the *Pietà* in Saint Peter's and the Christ in his *Last Judgment*. Overall, the catalog operates simultaneously as both a purveyor and an analyst of associations. It offers a precise picture of all the qualities the work possesses by virtue of the relations it is in, which are, as Pardo-Guerra underlines, retraced (and produced) by the catalog's narrative.

Through the operations of classification and ordering that it authorizes, the work of cataloging corresponds to the evaluations described in Chapter 3. But it also goes beyond that. It also integrates a host of prices (Pi), which enable the qualculation of the price (Pj), which Christie estimates. These prices were paid in previous sales or were estimated by experts at different moments of the work's life. They also include the prices (paid or estimated) of comparable works of Michelangelo's or painters close to him. As in the case of the pieces of meat followed by Anzalone, it is impossible to distinguish the operations that determine value from those that affix the price. Value no more precedes the price than the price serves to establish the good's value. The formulation and the different prices it combines emerge through the operations of association, classification, and ranking from which they cannot be abstracted. Conversely, the evaluation uses the price as one of the criteria, one of the qualities, on which to base its qualculation. Until one understands that the price is one among many qualities, the mechanisms of how it is affixed (of its triangulation, to use Pardo-Guerra's suggestive term) remain mysterious and resist analysis.

We can now see why the entry for lot 18 runs to no fewer than fifty pages, mixing price, quantitative material measures, expert reports, references to historical databases, photographs, historical context, and more. Without this descriptive inventory, the drawing would be reduced to a light sheet, weightless, and as alone as the young women from Brittany who, at the beginning of the last century, stepped off the train in the Montparnasse station. It would be as far from operational as a fighter plane whose documentation, weighing more than the plane itself, has been lost. Auction-house companies and their catalogs constitute an infrastructure whose finality is to animate the networks of associations, linkages, and evaluations that affix prices. Like the consumers we will meet shortly who negotiate the formula for the price of natural gas backed up by a *Que choisir* campaign, the client who participates in a public auction can, of course, depending on the resources available to him, negotiate the price offered by Christie's or other bidders. In market agencements, however, the struggle is over the formulation of prices, and not over the prices themselves.[78]

I cannot give an inventory of the studies that show how few areas escape this immense reflection on the practices of pricing. Furthermore, a new wave of complex mathematical formulations that migrate and disseminate has been brought on by the spread of yield management. However, to validate the hypothesis according to which prices—all prices—are formulated, I must push beyond the best-studied cases, in which the work of formulation appears in an explicit, asserted, and argued manner. I must show that it also holds for the very numerous transactions in which formulas seem to be absent and where they are essentially qualitative. In order to make this point, I turn again to Jane Guyer and her study of the Yorubas' commercial activities. (See Chapter 2.)

Appealing to the triple distinction between nominal, ordinal, and numerical scales with which the reader is now familiar, Guyer describes the process that begins with words, which serve to designate things, and that ends with numbers (prices) associated with these things. This grid of analysis allows her to follow the price-affixing mechanisms in face-to-face situations. In this case, as she tells it, the agencies who meet face a considerable task since they have to construct the framework for their interaction (how to proceed in order to organize an exchange that begins with an exchange of words) while identifying the benchmarks and reference points that will allow them to reach a price acceptable to both parties. This job is all the more important and indispensable because the transaction takes place at the margins, in border zones where no one can claim that norms or shared institutions exist, in places where, to obtain goods, there is always a hesitation between armed force, theft, brutal extortion, and gentle commerce and the switch from one regime to another sometimes comes unexpectedly. This situation is all the more interesting because the agents are not only face to face, but, furthermore, very poorly equipped, and they have only one ambition (namely, to exchange goods for payment), and a single preoccupation (namely, to affix their price). If it can be shown that prices are formulated in this case, that would constitute a decisive step toward a price theory adapted to market agencements.

Guyer shows that agents affix prices by skillfully combining three scales.

In one place, for instance, the Yorubas use the word *ackie* to refer to a good that corresponds to a weight of gold whose worth is 480 cauris. (A cauri is a shell used as money.) In this remarkable case, the word used to refer to a good is its price, which is the simplest way to affix the price. The strategy used corresponds exactly to the line-pricing strategy mentioned earlier ("Everything for one euro"): what is bought is a price as much as a good, and the price is therefore simply one of the good's qualities. Translations do not end there, because moving from one dialect to another, one can play with words in an even more subtle way by varying values. For instance, a good that here is called *ackie*, is called *soa*, or *gro*, or even *mithqual* elsewhere, these terms designating either different gold weights, going from 0.05 to 0.15 ounces, or equally different numbers of cauris, from 480 to 1,200.[79] In this case, the formula that, through successive translations, establishes a relation of identity between words operates a conversion from a price system associated with another place (j) by providing the Pj corresponding to the original Pi.[80] A series of equivalences is thus established, making commensurable what was not and offering several solutions to the insoluble problem of the monetary measure of exchanged goods. The chain is endless. These measures are in turn translated into different ethnic numbering systems in base twelve. For example, the *mithqual* is equivalent to twelve hundred, as defined by Muslims, and to twelve times eighty, in the Bambara numerical system.[81] To put it starkly, it is as though, for instance, the word "hundred" that we use daily without there being ambiguity did not have the same value everywhere, even though it was understood everywhere, corresponding to the numbers "hundred" or "eighty" in our numbering system, depending on place and interlocutors. This new translation extends the job of conversion and complicates price formulation.

Conversions from one scale to another are nothing other than sophisticated translations that play, so to speak, on ambiguities and semantic polyvalence, notably associated with numbers, as well as with words: language and its games prepare the exchange and serve the formulation. It is not the case that there are, on one side, the evaluations, and on the other, the prices, or on one side, qualitative practices that determine values, and on the other, quantitative ones measuring these values. The same thing, the same word, simultaneously points in both directions. Words and things weave a network of significations that allow transitions, always fragile and open to challenge, from qualitative to quantitative. Guyer explains that one can, for instance, agree that thirty ignames are the same thing as fifty ignames and that for 1,100 CFA, one can get the same thing as for 750, as little as is the case in sales in which all the items between eleven and nineteen euros are sold at a single price of ten euros. In other cases, equivalences are postulated with goods to which a price has already been assigned. To move from a numerical scale (sums of money) to an ordinal scale (that structures intervals between thresholds) and vice versa, there are unlimited translations and therefore formulations. The calculation, both determinate and modular, that regulates the combination of scales in a supple and flexible manner leaves significant room for improvisation.

Guyer introduces the idea of "trope" in order to describe how correlations are regularly established between scales that in principle are unrelated to one another, giving rise to improvisation and innovation. A trope is a figure through which a word or an expression is diverted from its literal meaning, as are the words "ackie," "cauri," or "hundred." It prepares the way for conversion operations. Each scale, whether it be ordinal, nominal, or numerical, has its own tropes through which it can be correlated with the two other scales: worlds that are a priori incommensurable can thereby communicate; beings can be matched with numbers or ranks. The tropes that transform Pi into Pj are elementary operators of the formulation. They provide pathways for conversions without determining them mechanically. The implementation of these conversion translations requires great ingenuity and high-level skills such as great proficiency in languages, words, kinship relations, or, and clearly this is not an exhaustive list, numbering and measuring systems. These skills are not uniformly distributed. Those who have them or have access to them have an undeniable advantage.

Guyer is no doubt touching on the most fundamental and universal forms of price formulation, those that are embedded in languages themselves, in their tropes and scales.

THE POWER OF FORMULAS

Everyone qualculates, but when it comes to establishing prices, the capacity for designing, discussing, and imposing formulas is unequally distributed. This is as true for the Yorubas as it is in the City of London. We can talk about the power of a formula and therefore of the power of formulating work in the same way that we speak of the calculating power of a computer or a group of statisticians. This power depends upon the capacity to connect a large number of variables, forces, sites, and temporal horizons and to compose with them a figure that is rendered indisputable.

In his remarkable study of the world cotton market, anthropologist Koray Çalişkan observes the existence of both multiple local prices, such as those established on the İzmir Exchange or over the course of a bilateral negotiation between a small Egyptian cotton producer and a trading company, and prices that are described as global, such as those affixed by the New York Board of Trade. (Global prices are themselves multiple because they apply to different types of financial derivatives.) All of these prices lead to the proliferation and singularization of different categories of cotton—most notably, different because they are deliverable in different places at different times.[82] These prices, whether they be local or global, are connected through the multiple formulas put to use by agents at multiple sites distant from one another at the moment of bilateral transactions. A formula adopted at site Sj to determine a price can establish a connection with a site Si by integrating Pi, the price at this other site, into the calculation of Pj, the price of the good that is the object of a bilateral transaction at Sj. Several formulations can thus enter into competition at site Sj, depending upon the choice of other sites, Si, that they take into account, as well as the choice of coefficients that connect the various corresponding values of Pi.

Çalişkan's work is extremely important because he had no qualms about leading his investigation throughout the different categories of sites where cotton prices are formulated. After training as a trader, he followed how prices are affixed in the market for derivatives. He shared the life of Turkish farmers in his native language and then, having learned Arabic, shared the life of Egyptian peasants. He witnessed transactions between famers and trading companies. He took part in the process of establishing cotton quotations in several regional exchanges in the Middle East and followed the pricing strategies of professional employer organizations. One major finding emerged from his investigation. Over the course of a transaction, whatever it is, the advantage goes to the agency that has the capacity to connect and analyze the largest number of sites and prices, including past or future prices, in places as far flung as Izmir and New York, Cairo and Beijing, but also in the lower Nile Delta, the Adana region, India, Uzbekistan, Burkina Faso, and even the territories occupied by ISIS. How many sites and prices can you take into account to formulate your own price? The little Egyptian producer will always lose at this game; he is no match against those who master the art of formulation. It is not enough to refer here to information asymmetry, even if access to data is, of course, strategic. It is more precise to speak of dissymmetries in the capacities to formulate. These are comparable to the asymmetry between IBM's Deep Blue and chess master Kasparov or Google's DeepMind and Go professional Lee Se-Dol. It would do these two champions no good to make a full inventory of all the combinations since their poor brains, despite a few billion connections, would be quite unable to process it all. The dissymmetries are even greater when Kasparov and Lee Se-Dol are replaced by ordinary players, who do not have the calculating power of the computers but have also never had a chance to improve their skills and their virtuosity through exposure to better players.[83]

Power is lodged not only in the multiplicity of variables and sites taken into account, as well as in the sophistication of the algorithms entrusted with the qualculations, but also in the choice of which sites and variables to exclude. A classic strategy for controlling the existing balance of power by framing it is to impose that certain effects of an activity be ignored—for instance, by making it impossible (or very costly) to formulate a price for them. Chemical pollution that has effects on health or the environment, the release of greenhouse gases that contribute to global warming, and the dissemination of modified genes that contaminate neighboring crops are all events that may not be integrated into the usual price formulation. This exclusion contributes to denying the existence of the agencies who suffer these effects and therefore to destroying their capacity to participate in the price formulation. Exclusion is just as patent when no price is put on the activities that benefit other agencies, such as those of university researchers who further the fundamental knowledge a company will later use. The agency that is able to become the master of the formulation by simultaneously imposing the list of sites that should be taken into account and those that should be ignored has a decisive advantage in the struggles over prices.

The formulation of a price at a given site on the occasion of a bilateral transaction connects this site to all the sites the formula integrates and combines.

The Egyptian peasant who tries to negotiate with his interlocutor is actually facing the qualculative agencement that the interlocutor can mobilize. The formula does not establish the market price, but a price that holds locally and applies only to the bilateral transaction happening in the moment. The power relation that is then established between the partners depends on the number of allies—sites and formulas—on which the proposed formula depends. The formula collects in a certain place at a certain time and for a given transaction the market agencement that it takes into account. This agencement is thus recruited alongside the agencies in the negotiation of formulas and prices. The main effect of globalization—which comes about as a great number of sites around the planet are put into relation with one another—can therefore be that it increases local asymmetries between agencies involved in bilateral transactions. This sway appears most clearly in the case of consumer credit. Interest rates and the amounts that can be borrowed at a given rate, as well as guarantees and schedules, are affixed by formulas that are essentially determined by the supply, a supply that integrates a long series of intermediary variables linked to the global market. This does not mean that lenders can do as they please! Some of the prices (Pi) that they take into account are imposed on them, such as the key interest rates set by central banks. The formula, however, escapes the borrower entirely. They have nothing to say either about the choice of variables, the determination of their value, or their combination. What applies to credit applies to a lesser extent to the price of energy or transportation. For those goods and services, the consumer is strongly incited to establish a relation between his revenues and his expenses in a budget evaluation that determines his choices and orients his decisions.[84]

Given the financialization of the economy, agents are more and more deeply immersed in a space of price qualculation whose instruments, whether they are imposed by suppliers, offered by organizations charged with defending them, or made available by their bank (which offers budget management software on its website), transform them into budget managers.[85] This situation doesn't affect only those with the tightest budgets. For the rich, the budget question is also an obligatory passage point. The only difference, and it is a significant one, is that the wealthy can recruit heavily equipped assistants to help them out.

The modalities of domination are played out in the interdependent relations woven by the formulas. That is why it seems appropriate to speak of a formula's grip. The formula weaves a network. Its strength is measured by its capacity to associate and exclude or to lose the agency that becomes its prey in a labyrinth of qualculations. Gripping is an action; it is the result of a story; it is involved in a relational process that leads to "certain actors, individuals or groups taking control of the experiences of the social world."[86] The act of release (*déprise*), which is the unraveling and reknitting of the connections made by formulas, should be considered from the same angle. Equality in formulating power can absolutely not be considered a benchmark situation that should serve as a promise of normal balanced functioning, despite the fact that to some, it might be kept as a moral objective that should be reached at all costs. It is only one possibility among many, one that is difficult to achieve and that should be analyzed as such.

CONFRONTING FORMULAS

When an agency or a group of agencies weighs in on price, they do so by imposing not the result of a calculation, but the formula that will determine the calculation. That is why one cannot establish a direct link between the intensity of competition and price levels. Sociologist Thomas Reverdy explains how in the European electricity market, the intensification of competition, which had been expected to lower prices, acted on the formulas for price calculation to unleash a spectacular price increase. There is no reason why competition would have mechanical effects on the space of formulations, a space that lies between the relative levels of supply and demand and pricing.[87] Analysis must then consider the competition between formulas and the mutation and selection mechanisms of the formulas that it implies.

MAKING FORMULAS INDISPUTABLE

How can the dynamics of the confrontations between formulas be described? In order to answer that question, I suggest considering two sets of contrasting configurations: those in which the existing formulas are private and unchallenged and those where they are made public (in part) and discussed. One of the interesting questions is how one moves from one of these situations to the other.

There are several strategies available to those who want to shield formulas from dispute. The first and most efficient involves leaving the agency that benefits from the service free to affix the price it will pay. That is what happens in Las Vegas, where the gambler chooses the size and rate of his bets. He closes the deal and agrees to it by pushing the button. When the price established by the formula is the main quality of the good, the formulation is not a matter of concern. When I enter a shop in which everything is for sale for five euros, I cannot be shocked that I do not find a bottle of Calon-Ségur at that price! Here again, Las Vegas is incredibly efficient. A gambler has no reason to question the validity of the price since what counts for him is to be taken in by the rhythm of the rollers that move and stop and that he then makes move again by pressing the button and paying! The anesthesia of the critical faculties is all the more effective because the sensations are similar no matter what price is paid. There is a double trigger for the indisputable grip. It first takes hold because the price is not imposed but chosen. Second, once chosen, the price is forgotten. The gambler is caught up in rhythmic time, and if he pays, it is to preserve this grip, like the customers in Émile Zola's *The Ladies' Paradise*, caught up in the shopping frenzy. To hell with the formulas, as long as one can pay!

Another strategy, also widespread and well proven, involves designing formulas that assign a zero price to goods, which are then said to be free. When I pick up a copy of the newspapers piled at the entrance of the metro in the morning to occupy me during my ride, I am unlikely to experience an irrepressible onslaught of revolt or indignation, any more than I am likely to have such a feeling when I click on the site freely suggested by Google or Yahoo. Of course, in a more lucid moment, I may rail against these devices, which spare me from having to shell out money by imposing unsolicited advertisements on my attention.[88] I may even, as often happens, decide not to read the ad that appears on my screen by closing my eyes so as not to see it and by making it disappear as fast as possible. However, the result is nevertheless there: I know that a skillful formula, which can be found in any publication devoted to two-sided markets, lets me off of paying, but at 7:00 a.m., on the threshold of a difficult day, I have no desire to dispute it. And indeed, what would be the point of my exclaiming to the public at large, as one sometimes does so as to avoid being indebted to someone who wants to make a gift, "I absolutely insist on paying!" It is a matter of buying a zero price, not accepting a present! And that remains true even if nothing compels me to pick up the newspaper and even if, were I really in the mood to complain, I created a consumer rights group.

A third possible strategy is dissimulation with a good dose of denial. One of the agents declares, "I do not have a formula; there is nothing to discuss." One may be in good faith in denying that one uses a formula—that is to say, that one performs a series of operations to reach a price. Yet prices do not drop out of the sky. Even in the extreme case studied by Guyer, formulas are mobilized, made up through recourse to tropes, rule-bound sequences of translations, word associations, and ordinal scales. Here, however, either the agent does not want to enter into a discussion about them because they seem self-evident (he is simply "passing on the costs") or he decides simply to deny their existence.

To understand how common such practices are, we can turn to political scientist Katayoun Shafiee's fascinating work. She was lucky to have access to all the archives of the Iranian state and Aramco (BP's ancestor) and to find all the formulas the company's back office used at the beginning of the nineteenth century to negotiate the royalties it paid to the Persian government.[89] These could not be more quantitative or more explicit. An external observer who knew nothing of these calculations, such as the Iranian government itself, might have the feeling that prices were determined in a purely arbitrary manner, whereas in fact, it was a matter of a carefully calculated arbitrary manner as all arbitraries are and, moreover, in a purely mathematical form: in this case, the power relation was used to hide a particularly sophisticated qualculation that allowed Aramco not only to affix its prices, but also to be in a position to justify them if they were challenged—for instance, by providing details about costs. One of the most frequent rhetorical forms associated with such denials refers to the laws of the market: prices are what they are because the markets calculate them. This strategy has not disappeared. In sectors such as the pharmaceutical industry, where formulations are both central and explicit, practices are kept largely secret despite the pressure of government powers or patient groups.[90]

DEBATING FORMULATIONS

Existing formulations are always likely to be challenged and eventually transformed. New ones imposing unprecedented modalities of qualculation thus emerge, associated with new relations of domination.

One way of identifying controversial situations is to consider a telltale sign—terminological innovations and the debates to which they give rise. Let us take the exemplary case of fictitious commodities as defined by Polanyi.

According to him, certain things or goods resist commodification because they are available and accessible without having to be produced. As we saw in Chapter 2, his objection cannot be made from the perspective of market agencements: labor, land, or money, if appropriately transformed, qualified, and singularized, can enter bilateral commercial transactions without any particular difficulties.

In these singularization processes, price formulation plays an important role. It is the object of conflicts, which frequently take the form of terminological quarrels. As with the Yorubas, words, the meanings they are charged with, and the formulas they refer to run the show.

Labor is an exemplary case. Each term used to refer to its price corresponds to types of contracts and therefore to formulas that frame the qualculations to be performed. One way of questioning the formulation is to question the words chosen. One can speak in a technical manner about the price (or cost) of labor or of the labor force, but when collective agreements are negotiated, only salaries are discussed. The idea of salary can be interpreted as a set of specifications that the formula determining the price of labor has to respect; the etymology says as much, since it seems the word comes from the salt ration and the monetary payment Roman workers were given to buy their salt. There is the idea of a payment that enables living (and, indeed, the formula very often includes some indexation of prices that measure the cost of living) and also compensates for a harm. (Work is suffering, fatigue, wear, drudgery; it is a challenge, a kind of abuse for which workers must be indemnified.) The salary relation, as Robert Castel masterfully showed,[91] is synonymous with affiliation and attachment; it is a promise of stability and security, fulfilled notably by distributing compensation smoothly through time, as is shown so clearly by the (explicit and complicated) formulas used in the calculation of the unemployment benefits for part-time entertainment industry employees in France. (They are called *intermittents du spectacle*.)[92] As many economists recommend with good reason, this commitment can go so far as to include provisions that an employer who fires an employee must contribute a certain sum to a fund that finances an allowance, which thus enters into the formulation of the price of labor.[93] It is hard to imagine any formulation more complex, more sophisticated, and more qualiquantitative than the one that establishes the salary of an employee.

Given how varied the range of words is, one could extend the terminological analysis. There is talk not only of "salaries," but also of "indemnities," "honoraria," "remuneration," "payoff wages," "emoluments," or "compensation."[94] Each of these terms refers to a specific way of formulating (and qualculating) the price of the labor force while simultaneously qualifying it. Thus, certain formulas make it possible to have limited commitments, such as honoraria, or the zero-hour contract in the UK, in which an employer is not obliged to provide any working hours to an employee. Others, on the contrary, imply regular work.

In choosing one term over another, one opts for a particular formula. Violent struggles often lurk behind words, as is shown, at the time of writing, by the confrontation between those who claim that Uber drivers are employees and those who, on the contrary, want to preserve their status as independent workers. Uber fuels this dispute. It could have folded the cost of labor into the price of the ride, but separated them by design, which is precisely what the dispute is about. Terminological quarrels are the harbingers of conflicts over the modalities of price formulation.

The reader will have no trouble extending this analysis to the other two categories of fictitious commodities. The formulations of land's prices differ according to the nature of relations as qualified between users and owners. Consider, for example, the case of sharecropping versus leasing for agricultural land. As for the price of money, there is an explosion of more and more exotic notions: fixed or variable rates, actuarial or face-interest rates, effective annual interest rates, and key interest rates, not to mention usury rates. The case of money provides the most formulated prices and the richest terminology. There again, words express underlying struggles, which become explicit as they enter public space.

Furthermore, to make formulas explicit and open to debate, a direct discussion of their content makes it possible to move to the next level. Price formulation establishes a list of elements that enter into the qualculation. At the same time, it marks the border between what is taken into account and what is pushed to the outside. Challenges to formulas can rest on the ways these choices are made. Critique of a formula produces a dynamic that leads to the emergence of new formulas. It is no longer a matter of entering into discussion through terminology, which acts as if terms and conditions are to be respected, but of diving into the black box in order to understand what the price is and should be made of.

Take the case of the markets for natural gas. Given the strategic nature of providing energy and the almost total control providers have over price formulation, this becomes, at least in democratic regimes, a full-blown political matter. It makes sense, then, as a first step, to make the formulation public in order to organize a debate. That goal is not easily reached because companies are loath to have their accounts spread out under the public eye in order to negotiate their formulas.[95]

State intervention can orchestrate a debate around formulas. In France, the price of natural gas is given by an almost public formula that is constantly negotiated:[96] since it was set up, it has been incessantly reformulated. In 2009, at the request of GDF Suez, the main French gas provider, renamed Engie in 2015, it was decreed that a subformula that makes it possible to calculate Engie's supply costs and to integrate them into the price calculation would be included in the formula. As I write these lines, the subformula takes into account changes in the euro/dollar exchange rate (long-term supply contracts for natural gas are in dollars), an average of the mean monthly rate for domestic fuel, an average of the mean monthly price of Brent crude oil.... It is not easy to reach a compromise on these kinds of formulas and on each of the variables they include. For instance, one has to reach an agreement on what an average of averages of averages is! And this is only one among many episodes since the gas supply has evolved by reducing the share of long-term contracts. In the last ten years, the formula has constantly been contested and modified as prices and the balance of power between formulators varied.

Consumers broke into the very closed circle of formulators in 2014 via *Que choisir* which, under the slogan "Gaz moins cher ensemble," "Cheaper gas together," launched a campaign to solicit offers from gas providers for more favorable legal conditions for consumers. The initiative was denounced by unions for making the price formulation into the very object of negotiation. They saw this as supporting dominant economic models and the dogma of free competition. UFC-Que Choisir—the consumer group that publishes the magazine—responded by saying "one chooses neither a company, nor free competition, but the best offer." If there is competition, the consumer group might have added, it is not the competition of interface markets, but of market agencements. What is at stake is the qualification of goods, which includes price formulation. A show of strength by marching in the streets or blocking public transportation is not enough when qualification is at stake; one has to give oneself the resources and equipment that are required to demonstrate and evaluate the respective merits of different competing formulations. In order to earn the right to participate in the struggle for formulation, UFC-Que Choisir has 130 employees, a 30-million-euro budget (95 percent of which comes from the sales of its magazines), member-readers it can mobilize to carry out studies, and the means to carry out its own consumer experiments: this is the price to be paid for a seat at the table where prices are discovered and set—in other words, of weighing in on the process of price formulation.

In the health care and medical treatment sectors, patient groups have thrown themselves into the fight to formulate. The struggle is never as intense and conflict ridden as in the case of affixing the prices of genetic therapies for rare diseases. On the supply side, the variables taken into account in the proposed formulas systematically include the considerable amounts spent on research and development. In 2012, the pharmaceutical company Roche declared 8.4 billion dollars of research and development for Solaris, a medication aimed at a few hundred patients suffering from very rare forms of anemia or renal pathologies. The formula also takes into account the cost of alternative treatments, the benefits for patients (benefits are evaluated as a function of extended life expectancy, improved quality of life, and deaths avoided), the effects on the costs borne by social security organizations, and more. All of these criteria are subject to fierce discussion by patient groups, who cannot remain indifferent to the calculation Roche suggests, given that the annual cost per patient is 440,000 dollars and the sales generated by this medication are of the order of a billion dollars. One of the solutions patients have suggested is to cap prices in order to account for the uncertainty about risks (such as side effects) or the long-term efficacy of the medication. Another suggestion is to regulate the way prices evolve such that they move in relation to observed results.[97]

HOW PROBLEMS CAN INCITE DEMANDS FOR REFORMULATION

Various forces impel discussions about pricing formulas and call for their transformation. These discussions are generally linked to the expression of concerns and preoccupations generated by the existing formulas that lead to them being questioned and to new formulas emerging. Formulas obviously raise a great variety of concrete problems. As a partial illustration, I will here evoke those that are linked to inclusion, exclusion, and their systemic effects.

INEQUALITY BY EXCLUSION, INEQUALITY BY INCLUSION

A formula includes, but at the same time, it is a device that excludes. It establishes a framework and places outside the frame a set of elements that are not taken into account. The most direct mechanism, as already noted, involves simply ignoring certain groups affected by the commercial transaction. Neighbors suffering from chemical pollution or populations affected by climate change due to greenhouse gas emissions are condemned to inexistence by the governing formulas. Some have requested that those formulas be changed, that electricity or pesticides be sold at prices that include those damages. Others have demanded that the price of coffee integrate the suffering of producers in the Global South.

Beyond calling for what has not been counted to be taken into account, one can identify and denounce a more profound mechanism that combines discrimination and forms of exclusion.[98] The formula not only ignores what is beyond the limit it traces. Like checkpoints that turn back immigrants on the grounds they do not have the required qualifications, the formula indirectly controls access to some types of commercial transactions.

Take again the case of the credit sector.[99] The way loan prices are diversely formulated provides one of the best illustrations of this subtle mechanism. In the United States, as a standardized information commodity widely used by banks, FICO has undoubtedly permitted radical inclusion in credit markets. Through its own way for formulating prices, it installs a qualification of products based on a particular evaluation of risk that can qualify "the poor" for loans and actually target them at a high interest rate, as opposed to the previous situation of completely excluding economically marginalized people from the credit markets.[100]

But this unprecedented access to credit produces two interdependent effects. First, through the reversal described in a previous section ("How Price Becomes a Tool for Ranking"), prices allow for the emergence of a hierarchy among product lines that can then be seen by agents themselves or by social scientists as maintaining and reinforcing powerful pecuniary inequalities.

While in 1965 the poor paid more for goods and were excluded from credit, by 2008, poorer people had access to credit for which they paid more than wealthier people. By widening the credit market, the commoditization of FICO scores contributes through inclusion to maintaining existing inequalities.[101] This corroborates what one of my Corsican friends, who tries to get by on 750 euros a month, told me: "When you are poor, you pay more for everything."[102] This mechanism operates on a large number of purchases in daily life. The more discriminating monopolies resort to sophisticated yield-management tools and in particular to scoring and associated price formulations that contribute to the singularization process of goods, the more they feed pecuniary discriminations that are often felt as inequalities.

But that's not the whole story. This process of discrimination is coupled with mechanisms that can be interpreted as leading to *quasi-exclusion*. Here again, because of its complexity, the credit sector is a textbook case. The credit sector can be described as a set of tiered markets, with revolving credit card issuance from banks driven by FICO scores being only one tier among many. As we can observe, when people in search of loans do not get access to bank credit, they are left with no choice but to turn to alternative markets. This mechanism is all the more effective since candidates for alternative types of loans, even if they have to pay extortionate interest rates and bear the formulations that set them, often see such products as preferable to not having access to credit at all. Thus, borrowers who are living on the edge of FICO markets run from bank loans to payday lenders and sometimes return back to banks.

In any case, it turns out that some potential borrowers find themselves de facto excluded from the bank credit market. But given the fact that for political reasons, a complete exclusion is hardly viable, it is more appropriate to name it a quasi-exclusion that ejects some people toward other markets that are often more disadvantageous for them from a financial point of view. A hierarchy of different marketplaces for credit has been established with which people are meticulously "matched." Even if unwillingly, the consumer finance sector is a powerful contributor to enacting tools and practices that participate in the structuring of social life: they both include and exclude.

This coupled mechanism, strongly associated with price formulation, of discrimination and quasi-exclusion is now found in education, health care, and the insurance sector, and it is more and more contested. Discrimination and exclusion are contested, for example, in the case of medical treatments that impoverished populations cannot afford; they are contested when insurers refuse to insure; they are also contested when the right to put oneself in debt is claimed on the basis of the fact that the experience of debt produces a responsible man who knows how to count while reminding individuals that they need one another.[103] When it highly discriminates and finally excludes, the formula is likely to become the target of protests that push for it to be made explicit, analyzed, and perhaps reformulated.

A third mechanism for discriminating and excluding combines the two previous ones: the formula can exclude by assigning a nil price to a thing, an event, or a practice, thereby condemning it to inexistence. We have already seen several such situations. When Monsanto inserts a gene into a seed in hopes of creating a plant that will be resistant to the herbicide Roundup, which it originated, it does not have to integrate the long and costly research done by Rosalind Franklin, which helped Jim Watson and Francis Crick discover the double helix. And who could fault the company? When I pick up a copy of the free commuter newspaper *20 minutes* at the entrance to the metro station, I am not necessarily aware of the fact that through that gesture, along with the two or three million other people who do the same thing, I weigh in on the pricing formulation that the Ouest-France company negotiates with advertisers. Formulating prices in such a way that some are nil makes it possible to isolate them from discussion. In the medium and long terms, however, it is not rare for concerns and objections to be expressed. Who has not heard alarms at the plundering of fundamental science by private interests? Who has not fulminated against the omnipresence of intrusive advertising systems that degrade political messaging and make the survival of the press even more difficult because they must now charge a fee to remain independent?

Nil prices are a problem. I am aware that some theoretical models explain and justify these formulations. However, beyond the fact that their foundations are often fragile, what matters here is that such models do not adequately address the concerns these formulations provoke. It is never self-evident that a price should be nil. For that to be the case, there must be certain forms of activity organization, revenue distribution, and resource management, and these forms cannot be designed without taking into account the debates they produce. For instance, services that are available for free on the web imply nonnegligible access costs for users, including the necessary material and paying internet access providers; they also imply that data have been provided for free by the user to companies that then sell it.[104] As sociologists Joëlle Farchy, Cécile Méadel, and Guillaume Sire show, the formulation of the different prices of a multisided platform that organizes and coordinates the activities of many different players (for example, a streaming music service) turns out to be extremely complex. It requires skillful tinkering that mobilizes elements of economic theory in order to justify compensating for nil prices with nonnil prices (this is called a cross externality) in an attempt to integrate social justice considerations while taking into account the always limited and costly possibilities of measuring activities and contents.[105] All of the tinkering required inevitably arouses concern and protests.

A prominent example is the internet: should it be available to everyone for free? This is a challenging question that has even the best experts deeply perplexed. After years of discussion, controversy, and intense lobbying, the Federal Communications Commission (FCC), which regulates communications in the United States, came to a decision. On Thursday, February 26, 2015, by a vote of three to two, the commissioners approved a three-hundred-page document setting strict rules and giving the internet the status of a public good.[106] The ruling stipulates that "all data should be treated in the same manner, whatever their destination and points of departure." Internet access providers must charge for the connection, but not for the data provided; they must not distinguish between data that come from an established site and data from a local sports club.

In a conflict on this scale, involving a merciless clash between telecommunication operators and internet giants, economic models and theories may provide reference points. They can present solutions as reasonable or efficient. They cannot, however, impose the choice of solutions. It makes sense to talk of a public good—that is to say, a good that must be made available to the public at a nil price, only after a public debate. This is a general rule: one cannot discuss the nature of a public (or common) good without including its essential qualities, its price, and the formulation through which that price will be determined. As we have seen, pricing formulations powerfully contribute to the organization of the market agencement.

Through the mechanisms of discrimination and exclusion they provoke, formulations feed movements that challenge them and push for their transformation. The instabilities that can result are a further source of concern.

Prices are always formulated from other prices. If reference prices begin to fluctuate, if the amplitude of the fluctuations is beyond expectations, compounding or multiplying, rather than cancelling one another out, prices and formulas can explode. This, in turn, can lead to effects that create chain reactions. If these impacts are not clearly circumscribed and limited, such as when the wheat price increases the price of bread,[107] they are what are called *systemic effects*. Financial products provide the best possible example of such explosions. For example, derivatives can be constituted by formulas that connect the price of assets that have been chosen in such a way that their variations should be independent of one another. According to some observers, the 2008 crisis was at least in part due to the fact that many of those assets were not supposed to be correlated. In other words, assets that were supposed to vary independently of one another progressively became correlated with each other, each of them being affected, contrary to expectations, by the movements of the others. Correlation contributed to the amplification of initial fluctuations. The case is interesting because it shows that the notion of formulation is quite useful for understanding such phenomena. Agencies manufacture prices from other prices, and through the choices they make, they contribute to the creation of price movements. Donald MacKenzie, for instance, observes that applying certain (Gaussian) laws of probability to the formulation of option pricing (derived from other prices) led to amplifying price fluctuations and produced panic behavior. He further shows that the power of these systemic effects intensifies with products such as collateralized debt obligations, or CDOs, which allow for redistributing risks linked, for instance, to property loans. As these products became widespread, they produced correlations between underlying assets that had initially been uncorrelated.[108]

The devastating effects produced by formulations that contribute to bank failures such as that of Lehman Brothers or to the bankruptcies of nations, as was the case with Iceland, make visible the qualculations that previously remained within limited and almost private circles. This opens their content up to discussion. However limited and belated they may be, the increased awareness and protests that ensue lead to new framings by imposing certain rules on the formulas.

WHAT ABOUT MORALITY?

Whether it is the terminological quarrels they provoke, the list of elements they do or do not take into account, the way they justify certain nil prices, or the untimely overflowing they provoke, formulations are at the heart of controversies that can be described as moral and political issues. What is at stake is not (or no longer) simply to contest a price ("It is too high; it deprives the poor; it is unfair"), but to enter into and possibly dispute the way the price is qualculated. The central question—"How has this price been composed and what is it composed of?"—prepares the way for an altogether different question. To use a category developed by Luc Boltanksi and Laurent Thévenot, it concerns the justification not of the price, but of the formula used, of the choices it imposes, and the effects it produces.[109] Each formula institutes its own world, a world fraught with moral and political issues.[110]

As Guillaume Yon and Alexandre Mallard have shown concerning marginal-cost electricity pricing, moral preoccupations permeate the way in which these prices are calculated.[111] For instance, price equalization was one of the first questions that surfaced as production and distribution networks were developed in the late 1940s. Should those customers who are far from production sites be charged more, or should everyone be charged the same price, regardless of the transportation costs of the electricity? The equalization that was adopted in the end is the result of a long history of fervent discussions over different formulas.[112] Maximal tension was reached when Marcel Boiteux, then the CEO of EDF, pleaded for pricing that takes into account the costs that users make the production bear. According to this doctrine, transportation costs should be imputed to the client. The FNCCR (Fédération nationale des collectivités concédantes et régies),[113] however, opposed this calculation and managed to impose the principle of a single price throughout the national territory. This principle was finally written into article 2 of the law modernizing public service on February 10, 2000. If EDF agreed in the end to total equalization of domestic services between city and country, it is, of course, because the balance of power was not in its favor. However, to carry the day, the FNCCR did more than simply defend the interests of the populations it represents. It spoke the language of formulas, challenging the idea that transportation costs for energy should be taken into account and invoking the fact that users are equal citizens who should not be penalized for living farther away from reactors. Had the formula Boiteux proposed not individualized a *Pi* associated with the cost of transportation, this line of argumentation and the reformulation to which it led would have been pointless.

Since any price is the product of a formula, it is in the formula itself—in its conception, its constitution, and its implementation—that morality and politics are to be found, because it is there that values, demands, or cultural norms are lodged. Fabian Muniesa's work on affixing prices at the moment when the Paris Stock Exchange was automated confirms that the discussion of formulas, the questions they raise, and the solutions they suggest frame the ethical questions and shape the answers provided. Moral questions arise because a formula must be chosen that can be implemented by the computer in order to set opening and closing market prices in such a way as to avoid disadvantaging anyone; moral questions arise because algorithms have to be written in such a way as to treat supply and demand fairly. Should sale offers or requests that are not transmitted at the same moment be considered equivalent from the point of view of their processing? And, if so, what is the relevant time interval? Once the closing prices have been set, what should be done with the offers or requests that remain unfulfilled when the principle of first in, first out allows the matter to be settled by auction? Writing the algorithm forces these questions of justice to be explicitly raised (or as is commonly said, "formulated") and answered.[114]

Moral concerns are lodged in the labor of formulation and are most pressing when the formulas tend toward being explicit and therefore subject to controversy. As Jane Guyer explains, certain prices are considered normal, while others are considered unfair. She adds that such a judgment is not made in the name of moral values that seek, for instance, to temper the cold and cruel realism of capitalist market economics. Rather, they are judgments of the way in which prices are calculated. According to her, a moral price is a correctly calculated price, which is say one whose formula can be justified.[115] The justification is not external to the formula. It is, in part, dependent on it, on the way it is composed, just as a lawyer must respect the rules of the law to plead his client's case effectively or as a composer must bow, at least in part, to the rules of musical composition in order to reach an audience. Morality does not contain and limit the calculation. Rather, it is present in the formulation; it is contained within the qualculation.[116] Such morality as there is present is to be traced to the heart of the market agencements, in each of their framings and in particular in price formulation. We cannot pretend that markets, held to be immoral or amoral (that is, outside the world of morality), need a soul and a heart so they can offer human beings an acceptable and fair world in which one might thrive.[117] You do not make markets moral; you open up to debate the process through which their framings are designed.

There is much to study so that it becomes possible to describe the labor involved in price formulation, to understand how formulas are elaborated and sometimes contested, to explain how they transform, how they enter into competition with one another, and how they come to impose themselves. Before taking on such a project, it seems reasonable to outline the different possible configurations, if only to impose some order on the observation of practices so as to better perceive their dynamics. Unfortunately, there is a severe dearth of empirical material. For instance, and simply to suggest some of the paths that should be explored, one can think of criteria such as the number of formulations in competition with one another, the private or public character of the formulations (which can vary within a single agencement from one site to another), the diversity of prosthetic prices (Pi) used and/or suggested, the difference in qualculative skills required by the different formulations and their distribution, or the balance, for each, between numerical and nonnumerical variables. The formulation's degree of controversy is also an important dimension, because it can determine the pressure to make the formula public and explicit.

Among the questions that arise, a particularly sensitive one I want to briefly evoke is the possibility that market agencements will generally evolve toward ever more explicit and debatable formulations.

Several mechanisms favor such an evolution. The first is linked to the increasing importance of pricing in the process of singularizing transactions. When the bilateral transaction is the general rule, sellers have to justify the prices they set. They must convince each client that the transaction in which they are engaging is not a banal monopoly situation or simply a matter of the balance of power. The idea in interface markets, that if it is organized well, competition leads to pricing that is somehow optimal, cannot be relied on in the case of market agencements. The only strategy to show that the price is not arbitrary is to link it to all the investments and all the actions that, by singularizing it, have led to the fit between it and its recipient. In other words, sellers are incited to make their formulas as explicit as possible in order to be able, if necessary, to engage in negotiation with the client on that basis. This constraint of making the formula that qualculates the price explicit and (relatively) public leads to decomposing it into constitutive elements. "Tell me how your price was composed, and of what, and I will tell you whether I accept it," rather than "Tell me whether or not it was formed at the end of a well-organized competitive process."

Such presentations, orchestrated to prove that prices are not arbitrary, are not a new phenomenon. They surface whenever anger is brewing. Consider as an illustration the famous advertisement campaign designed by François Missoffe, a French minister of agriculture in the 1960s, under the slogan "Suivez le bœuf!"—"Follow the beef!" Posters all over France showed the diagram you might see in a butcher shop outlining the different cuts of meat on a steer. But instead of naming each cut (shanks, flanks, or loin), the image gave a breakdown of the price of the meat, highlighting the costs of production, slicing, transportation, distribution, and so on. It was a demonstration that aimed to answer the questions increasingly on consumers' minds. In the energy or transportation markets, one often sees graphic stylizations showing how a 100-euro bill (representing the cost of gas at the pump) can, like Missoffe's ox, be cut into several pieces, each of which represents one of the costs that enters into the price of gas and explains how it is established. In yield management, making the elements of a price explicit is specified as one of the tasks of formulation, which thus falls largely into the public domain. The requirement to be explicit appears to be increasingly and irreversibly accepted as legitimate. It will be all the easier to satisfy when the costs associated with the organization and framing of singularized transactions (costs that can be described as a particular category of transaction costs) are significant enough to call for dedicated accounting practices.[118] To respond to the question raised, future sellers will be able to tell their clients how the price formulation takes these data into account. The formula then becomes a tool for demonstrating that the price was qualculated with tact and measure (to borrow a charming expression invoked by the French National Medical Council) or in a fair and reasonable way (as patient groups claim medication should be), thus making it possible to convince the client by showing how the price is constituted.

The second mechanism that contributes to formulas increasingly becoming explicit is linked to the impressive expansion of the community of formulation workers. Price formulation used to be an artisanal activity, and in some singular cases, such as those of the Yorubas or the pitchers on London's streets, a skill based on practice and experience. Craftsmanship has progressively given way to an almost industrial organization. As I mentioned earlier, courses, professional groups, conferences, and journals dedicated to it have proliferated. I should also underline the increasing involvement—notably in the telecommunications, energy, and transportation sectors—of professional economists, who, at least in France. extend and amplify the pioneering work of engineer-economists. These professionals refine the design of formulas by introducing sophisticated tools derived from things such as game theory (notably for auctions) or theoretical physics (notably for financial products).

When the formulations are not made explicit, when they privilege qualitative variables and remain mostly private, observers find themselves in a difficult situation. Market agencements are opaque. Long and difficult studies will be required to throw some light on their practices, render their formulations more explicit, and at least in certain cases, more quantitative and less private. As Jane Guyer has proved, sociology and anthropology should provide significant contributions to the fieldwork these studies will require. But very frequently, social scientists are rather less effective than lawyers, journalists, or activists to force companies to unveil parts of commercial secrets.

Public authorities also contribute to the work of making formulas more explicit. They indeed regulate, no longer by controlling prices, but instead by intervening in subtle ways in their formulation. They can simply impose a few variables (such as taking into account the cost of pollution or the inclusion of social security obligations) or certain coefficients or certain thresholds framing the formulas without getting into the details of their content, details that remain essentially a private matter. Policies regulating competition contribute, in their own way, to introducing price formulation into the public space.

Consumer groups, and more generally organizations from civil society, are also beginning to participate actively in the work of formulation.

A favorable environment is required to make formulas explicit and to subject them to debate. However, we should harbor no illusions. Price formulation plays such an important part in the competition between agencies that despite the forces pushing for formulas to be made explicit and subject to debate, there is no reason to believe they can completely and definitively escape the attraction of private spaces and become fully public objects. The aim should not be to reach total transparency. The work involved in formulation has an irreducibly opaque quality, and full explicitness makes no sense. The aim should be, more modestly, to reach a fecund equilibrium between the forces that tend to shield formulas from being discussed and those that, on the contrary, expose them to such discussion.

CHAPTER SEVEN
How Do Market Agencements Evolve?

In the social sciences, few philosophical concepts have met with as much success as the notion of *dispositif*. This surprising adventure begins with Michel Foucault's work. Although the notion is present throughout his writings, the most precise and detailed definition appears in an oft-quoted 1977 interview:

> What I'm trying to pick out with this term is, firstly, a thoroughly heterogeneous ensemble consisting of discourses, institutions, architectural forms, regulatory decisions, laws, administrative measures, scientific statements, philosophical, moral and philanthropic propositions—in short, the said as much as the unsaid. Such are the elements of the apparatus [*dispositif*]. The apparatus itself is the system of relations that can be established between these elements.... I understand by the term 'apparatus' a sort of shall we say—formation which has as its major function at a given historical moment that of responding to an *urgent need*. The apparatus thus has a dominant strategic function.... I said that the apparatus is essentially of a *strategic* nature, which means assuming that it is a matter of a certain manipulation of relations of forces, either developing them in a particular direction, blocking them, stabilizing them, utilizing them, etc. The apparatus is thus always inscribed in a play of power, but it is also always linked to certain limits of knowledge that arise from it but, to an equal degree, condition it. This is what the apparatus consists in: strategies of relations of forces supporting, and supported by, types of knowledge.[1]

As Giorgio Agamben suggests, this definition can be summarized in three points: a) it involves a heterogeneous set of elements, the *dispositif* in itself being the network that connects these elements; b) given its strategic dimension, the *dispositif* is inscribed in power relations; c) as such, it is the result of the intersection between power and knowledge relations.[2] Thus defined, the *dispositif* has a general character that allows for approaching prisons, the police, religion, and yes, markets in the same terms. It contributes to the study of the mechanisms through which living beings (notably, human beings) are caught up in webs of constraints that are often born of successive historical sedimentations and that make emerge and format new forms of subjectivity (such as that of *homo economicus*) and new modalities of action associated with these subjectivities (such as the pursuit of profit or maximal satisfaction), all of which do not have universal value, but appear at a given moment as a historical singularity. As Foucault will later underline, these constraints apply not only to the governed, but also to those who govern. Although Agamben is fairly silent on this point, it should be added that discourses play a significant role in constituting *dispositifs* and rendering them explicit. Discourses determine the borders of *dispositifs* and enunciate their truth while at the same time being one of their constitutive elements. They are neither inside nor outside, neither infrastructure nor superstructure. No *dispositifs* without discourse; no discourse without *dispositifs*. Discourses give access to *dispositifs*, but as Paul Veyne rightly emphasizes, "one cannot separate the modality of accession from that to which it offers access."[3]

As can be seen in Foucault's definition, one of the reasons to turn to the notion of *dispositif* is that it frees thought from a view of the social that establishes strict distinctions between spheres, fields, subsystems, separate and distinct institutions. It is, of course, out of the question to contest that differences exist. There are recognizable dissimilarities between a legal ruling, a scientific theory, a moral principle, a convention, an industrial machine, and an enzyme, and when one walks into a church (whether or not there are moneychangers in the temple), one knows it is not a supermarket. It is, rather, a matter of maintaining that one can never move directly from one principle to another, one proposition to another, one generation of machines to another, or one commodity to another without a detour that involves and mobilizes a set of elements external to the relevant sphere of activity. That is the meaning of the term "heterogeneity." No doubt Foucault would add that these detours are not fortuitous, but are instead determined by models, by regularities, that constitute the *dispositifs* and networks he describes. There is, for instance, a certain way of using instruments to develop a theory, to test a machine to make it more efficient, or to manage a company to ensure its sustainability, and so on. In other words, the notion of *dispositif* makes it possible to capture reproduction and innovation in a single movement without having recourse to such notions as structures, institutions, or fields; those notions do impose regularities, but they make it difficult to explain how regularities sometimes give way to novelty. The notion of *dispositif* makes singularities comprehensible: every observable event, such as the elaboration of a new scientific proposition or the institution of a new bilateral transaction, is a *concatenatio causarum*, an intertwining of creative uprisings and repetitive behaviors, of movements of revolt or resistance and acts of obedience. The *dispositif* is like a machine that is designed to manufacture homogeneous objects from heterogeneous ingredients.

The advantage of the notion of *dispositif*, as Foucault defines it, is that it prioritizes detailed analyses of observable material and discursive practices that we now know must be described, whether in science, law, economics, or other fields, as the putting into relation of separate dissimilar elements in order to face the problems that arise, one by one. A *dispositif* is sufficiently flexible and variable (reconfigurable) to explain creation, innovation, and change mechanisms and sufficiently rigid to identify what, in these dynamics, involves repetition and reproduction.

WHY THE TERM MARKET "AGENCEMENTS" AND NOT "DISPOSITIFS"?

Given all this, why would I choose the term "market agencements," rather than "market *dispositifs*"? The main reason is because the way the notion of *dispositif* has been understood and used has linked it with hypotheses and positions that are rarely made explicit or debated, but that have deeply altered its meaning.

The first difficulty is linked to the distinction that is implicitly accepted, although rarely acknowledged, between living beings and the *dispositifs* (as defined above) in which these living beings are caught and formatted. There are signs of this propensity to repeat the great divide. One of them is the emphasis Foucault puts on the strategic part the social sciences play in the *dispositifs* he studied. At the heart of the Foucauldian *dispositif* is a requirement that justifies its raison d'être, which is, in the words of Agamben, to "manage, govern, control, and orient—in a way that purports to be useful—the behaviors, gestures and opinions of living beings."[4] The *dispositif*'s main function is to dispose of man. Seen from this perspective, it shapes man's dispositions, which implies that the human and nonhuman components can be separated within the *dispositif* without challenging its internal economy. The dissymmetry introduced between different types of scientific knowledge is striking: nonhuman technosciences are limited to being resources that can be mobilized without interfering with human subjectivities whereas humanities play a unique role in shaping and enacting the latter. To put it crudely: studying quarks does not bring anything substantial to the project of constituting human dispositions whereas the very purpose of psychology, psychoanalysis, sociology, or economics is to contribute to this subjectification. Life sciences, however, occupy an intermediary position. Granted, they work to identify and objectify new entities (genes, antibodies, viruses) that extend the scope of available resources, but at the same time, they profoundly renew what we know about human identities as well as the tools to intervene with, and to reshape, them. That is why many extremely interesting and original studies have used a Foucauldian perspective to analyze findings from genetics, biotechnologies,[5] or pharmaceutical psychiatry.[6] One can go further in proposing a more refined analysis of the part molecules play in the construction of identity, further reducing the gap between *dispositif* and disposition.[7] By making the association between humans and nonhumans (whether animated or inanimate entities) into the hallmark of *dispositifs*, the sociology of translation (or actor-network theory) made it possible to get away from this distinction altogether. In order to underline the change, in this new perspective, *dispositifs* are renamed "assemblages" or "arrangements," or, indeed "agencements."

The second reason to choose the term "agencement" follows in part from the first. Although it comes from an interpretation of the notion of *dispositif* that I have criticized for being reductionist, it is potentially included in and even strongly suggested by that definition. Indeed, asserting the bipolar nature of a *dispositif* (the network of heterogeneous elements that enter into the disposition of human beings, which the latter have at their disposal) opens the way to making the assemblage of heterogeneous elements that constitutes the *dispositif* into a variable result of purely combinatory practices. It is as if the relation between the human and nonhuman elements of the *dispositif* were not reciprocally constitutive relations: the *dispositif* and its network of constraints then give way to an assemblage, like a game of LEGO.

This drift has been all the more marked with the translation of the term *dispositif* into English, which has raised innumerable problems. "Device" and "apparatus," the two favored terms, have the disadvantage of evoking the material and mechanical world of technical artifacts. They accentuate the distinction between the human and the nonhuman, two poles that Foucault is intent on joining, even though he tends to separate them. And if that were not enough, this questionable translation has been reinforced by the translation of "agencement," a notion deliberately introduced by Deleuze and Guattari to refine and enrich Foucault's analysis.[8] Whereas "agencement" evokes an arrangement's capacity to act, the translators opted for the notion of assemblage, which accentuates, rather than erases the limits of the notion of *dispositif*. (They might have imagined a neologism, *agencing* for instance, which has the advantage of suggesting that an agencement is an agency considered both in its capacity to act and its constitution.) Foucault, who has had a greater influence on the Anglo-Saxon social sciences than on studies within France, has certainly suffered from these treacherous translations, but the social sciences have also suffered from them. Agencement has boomeranged back to the French social sciences in the guise of "assemblage" (whose only virtue is that it is both an English and a French word) or even as "arrangement." These two notions risk erasing what is innovative in *dispositif* and especially in agencement, as Deleuze defines it, revisiting Foucault.

The initial victims of this drift in meaning understood the problem. The difficulties Anglo-Saxon colleagues faced and the ways they tried to overcome them are interesting for my purposes. Take the example of Manuel De Landa's book, which aims, among other things, to clarify Deleuze's and Foucault's contributions.[9] De Landa insists on the fact that the different elements that make up an assemblage (human or nonhuman) have their own lives and existences. In other words, according to him, the relations between the elements that make up an assemblage are in no way necessary (organic); they are historically contingent. From the perspective of the social sciences, this formulation, which insists on the particular ontology of assemblages, leads to the following propositions: a) every *social* entity is made up of heterogeneous elements (materials, humans, texts, and so on); b) each of these elements has its own dynamic, which unfolds in a space and according to a temporality to which it is attached; c) the entity composed of these elements evolves and transforms depending on the interactions of its elements: the effects of these interactions do not follow from any simple causality and are largely contingent; d) an element can be extracted from a given assemblage and introduced into another *dispositif*, where it will enter into new interactions, producing different effects; e) distinguishing between entities that would be intrinsically macro or micro makes no sense since an element can be included in one assemblage, but once detached from that assemblage, it can be considered as an entity that, in turn, includes a whole series of elements and therefore constitutes a world of its own.

To illustrate this, let us take the example of a city. A city can be described as bringing together populations, industrial activities, a network of roads, organizations, public policies, political movements, regulations, unemployed youth, advertising slogans, and so on. The populations are inscribed in cycles of existence that play out over several years, whereas the time frame for some companies may be limited to a few months. It is hard to anticipate how the city will evolve, given how complex and unpredictable the interactions are between populations, economic activities, evolution of the electoral system, and so on. It is clear that there is value in describing the city as an assemblage, if only because it allows for greater realism in the analysis. However, at the same time, one can understand the skepticism this approach can provoke. By insisting too much on the constitutive complexity of assemblages, one risks abandoning too easily any hope of reaching realistic simplifications that require that one make a choice, determining the most significant variables, rather than simply celebrating the world's complexity. Yet how far should one go, for instance, in decomposing the assemblage into its constitutive elements, given that each of them is itself an assemblage, *all the way down*? The description of the city becomes as monstrous as the city itself. It might even be that the description contributes to rendering it even more monstrous than it is. What is true for cities is true for markets and the assemblages from which they are constituted.

AN AGENCEMENT ACTS

To escape this impasse requires coming back to one of the questions Foucault and Deleuze raised about the sources and modalities of action. The notion of agencement brings an answer to this question more explicitly than the notions of *dispositif*, assemblage, or arrangement ever could. An agencement cannot be reduced to a complicated configuration of elements associated with each other in a particular way; it is also and especially what acts. In his own definition of the notion of agencement, as well as in his commentary on Foucault's work, notably on *Discipline and Punish*, Deleuze emphasizes that agencement allows one to move beyond the opposition between expression and content, between material forms and formalized functions as introduced by structuralism and "vulgar" Marxism.[10] For instance, material forms such as the prison or the hospital, whose resemblances have often been noted, fulfill different functions: in one case, to punish, in the other, to heal, which are, of course, not exactly the same thing. Deleuze takes up the diagram Foucault proposed in order to refer to the entanglement of what has generally been called the assemblage (or the arrangement, or even the *dispositif*) and the modes of action that it deploys and structures. The diagram profiles a certain mode of action for the agencement. The panopticon and its diagram are useful in each situation in which a task or conduct has to be imposed on multiple individuals. Starting from this observation and in order to clarify a terminology fraught with a number of ambiguities, I suggest we restrict the notion of agencement to the combination arrangement plus specific action and that we qualify agencement in such a way as to designate the type of specific action in play. Thus, we can speak of technical, political, or scientific agencements, each one giving shape, through the framings it organizes, to a certain mode of collective action — that is, a coordinated action around a strategic goal such as a bilateral transaction, in the case of market agencements.

A market agencement is any agencement that in practice solves the problem of attaching a good to an agency in exchange for monetary payment. In other words, its function is to institute bilateral commercial transactions. This specificity of the collective action (or function) is obtained through a series of interdependent framings that I have described in the previous chapters. These framings produce strong constraints, weaving power relations that orient the action and make it a market action by structuring the elementary operations of which it is composed.

The analysis this book offers is compatible with the general definition of an assemblage. Here one finds the heterogeneous elements, the entanglement of discourses and material entities, the possibility for each of these elements to follow its own trajectory, to enter into other assemblages, and to be analyzed, in turn, as an assemblage. Teeming interactions and the absence of simple, univocal determinations are also to be found here. Pricing, for instance, is the result of formulations that link a large number of variables in a complex and evolving way. Greater precision and realism are possible when one describes market activities in terms of assemblages. However, if one stuck only to this description, it would be impossible to explain what collective action involves. These difficulties can easily be overcome if one reintroduces into the analysis what the term "assemblage" tends to remove. The question of framings is at the heart of my description of market agencements. I insisted, for example, on the asymmetry between goods (framed to act passively) and the agencies that evaluate them. I also described in detail the skills and equipment of qual-culating agencies, the courses of action implied by organizing meetings and the manufacturing of attachments, and the part formulas play in the prag-matics of pricing. This simple enumeration shows that the notion of arrange-ment (or of assemblage) is not enough if one wants to take collective action into account, a collective action that is endlessly put into words and is in no way anarchic or chaotic. In an assemblage, entities are, so to speak, left to their own devices. They act lawlessly, desperately, and irremediably, generat-ing untold turmoil. Market agencements, on the other hand, are structured by framings that format the courses of action, all the while being what is at stake in the action. This brings us back to Foucault's intuition, notably, the idea that action is driven by strategic aims—in this case, instituting bilateral transac-tions. The formulation and signification of these aims change over time, but they guide and give meaning to the action.

THERE ARE NO MARKET AGENCEMENTS
WITHOUT NONMARKET AGENCEMENTS

Let us take the example of personalized medicine in the pharmaceutical industry, which we have already examined in previous chapters. It involves agencements whose strategic goal is to design and offer personalized treat-ment (as medicine or a form of care), the elaboration of which requires a great number of varied agencies intervening at different moments in the process of qualifying and defining therapies. We saw that the expression "translational" medicine, coined by specialists in the field, is a good summary of one of the problems raised by the number of players, all very different from one another. The sites where therapies are elaborated, tested, and manufactured, in short, where they are qualified and requalified, include university laboratories, investment funds, hospitals, research and development departments, Big Pharmas and their strategic management, and patient groups. These sites are linked through various connections of varying strengths and different natures. The challenge for the market agencement is to favor relations between these sites in such a way as to mobilize skills without which new therapies would not see the light of day without losing sight of the fact that the endgame is to provide a service in exchange for a satisfactory monetary compensation. It is appropriate to speak of "translational" medicine, since the term underlines the need to establish continuity in the collective action of the market while favoring contributions to and enrichments of the design of treatments that are increasingly well adapted to patients.

In order to understand how the different framings contribute to feeding and structuring collective action in such a way as to institute bilateral commercial transactions—that is to say, to be open to contributions without losing sight of the final goal, it is useful to introduce two complementary notions, those of *alignment* and *articulation*. These notions will allow us to pull together certain of the observations detailed in the preceding chapters. With them, we can describe market agencements as multisite networks while accounting for their dynamism oriented toward the institution of bilateral transactions and the competition that supposes in view of creating attachments and imposing prices on the transactions.

ALIGNMENT

Let us take the case of biotech companies in search of potential investors and their collaborations with big pharmaceutical laboratories. One of the sites for such searches is biotech conferences, where meetings are organized between candidates who might eventually cooperate. As we have seen, these meetings formally correspond to encountering, one of the five framings that prepare a market transaction. In her research, sociologist Liliana Doganova has further shown that they also provide a chance for biotech companies to:

a) ensure that everything has been done to verify the nontoxicity of the molecules (passiva(c)tion), b) evaluate the qualities of the treatment, c) convince a big pharmaceutical company they are worthy of attachment, and d) prepare the price formulation. In other words, within a perfectly circumscribed spatiotemporal frame, the other four framings that contribute to realizing the end bilateral transaction with patients are aligned and prepared. Of course, nothing is definitively settled in that place at that time. In other places and at other moments—that is to say, on other sites—the evaluations will be made again, new meetings will be organized, and so on. However, between these sites, the need to take into account the necessary alignment of the five framings, or to put it simply, the goal of reaching a bilateral transaction, will have been taken into account. The translation implies that "translational" medicine is thus initiated and pursued at each site of the market agencement, from beginning to end, from the bench top to the patient's bed. The final goal, to align the framings, remains in focus at each moment.

The medical example helps show that alignment can be obtained in a thousand different ways. In the case of therapeutic innovation, one has thus moved from the pipeline model to the translation model. The pipeline model, which remains the most widespread, points to the obstacle course a molecule must follow, progressively and sequentially, from the laboratory site to the hospital site. At each step, the molecule is requalified. After in vitro tests, one moves to animal testing, then to evaluating the therapeutic potential and then the nontoxicity of the molecule on human beings, all to verify that it treats patients in a satisfactory way. There are few steps backward, few sites involved. With the translational model, there are many steps back, many iterations and feedback loops, and the number of sites increases.[11] Aligning framings when there are numerous sites is a complicated task, one that requires more finesse and subtlety, as well as more discipline, than when there are only a few sites and agencies. With the proliferation of groups and stakes, the management and organization of translational medicine is an ongoing challenge.

This challenge is all the greater because the translation model takes the lead in a growing proportion of commercial activities. Because of the adjustments it implies, the singularization of goods, which starts very early in research and development departments, requires ever more agencies, interactions, and iterations. The inventory of sites in play that have to be aligned is not limited to the traditional phases of design, manufacture, and distribution. These distinctions blur. For instance, sites linked to consumption cannot be kept away from the process of goods' qualification and the preparation of the commercial transaction. Any subscriber to *Que choisir* and any internet user who answers a satisfaction survey, any member of a fan club or user group, any patient belonging to a patient group, is involved in the alignment process.

The final achievement of alignment comes about with price formulation. By establishing relations between the different evaluations, intermediary and prosthetic prices, price formulation establishes a connection between all of the sites involved in the collective action. It plays a crucial role in the orientation of the agencement toward market action. Economic theory's intuition that prices sum up the way the market works is not wrong. It's not that they convey all available information—who could verify such a claim? Prices simply say that a whole set of operations that took place during the qualification of the good on the various sites through which it passed has been taken into account, but in a way that is obviously open to discussion and controversy. Prices take hold of that story and summarize it in such a way that it can continue—that is to say, in order to give the good a chance to pursue its career by changing hands once the transaction has been completed. Alignment, like the formulation itself, is a *coup de force* that can be subverted and reversed.

One of the most striking illustrations of the conflicts and controversies that alignment provokes involves the modes in which market agencements mobilize academic research. Many estimate that too strict an alignment puts science itself in peril, threatening its capacity to open new avenues of research and to serve the general interest. Should the cost of the fundamental research that makes possible its development and manufacture be included in the cost of medicine, accepting by the same token that fundamental research be submitted to market forces? Or should fundamental science be financed independently (for instance, through taxes) so as to allow it to explore new paths and produce knowledge that can be used for free by any economic agent and whose cost of production does not appear in the price of medicine? However much of a caricature, this alternative shows the link between pricing and alignment. The two therapeutic models evoked earlier, the pipeline model and translation, illustrate the tension. In the first case, the sequential alignment can accommodate divergent academic research, as long as the possibility that a handful of molecules makes it to the end of the pipeline is preserved. In the second case, the dynamics of iterations and other loops gives impetus to academic research, which is thereby more closely aligned with Big Pharmas and the demands of patients, given the links with start-ups, patient groups, and consortiums of university laboratories. Price formulation becomes more conflictual, notably with the controversial and complicated qualculation of academic contributions.

ARTICULATION

An agencement cannot be reduced to a list of sites connected to one another, protected by a border that could be considered to separate what is internal to the agencement and what is external. Foucault and Deleuze underline this point, Foucault when he speaks of networks, Deleuze when he evokes lines of flight. An agencement (whether market, political, technical, artistic, or religious) cannot be compared to Europe's Schengen Area, with its free circulation within its borders and its controls over exchanges with the outside. It can function and be extended only if it is vascularized—that is to say, enriched with continuous contributions and therefore open to other sites and agencements. This requirement of openness guarantees the agencement's capacity for innovation, for renewing and extending bilateral transactions.

Even when the alignment of the different sites and activities that contribute to the commercial action is carried to its extreme, we should not forget that each site and activity is also caught up, at the same time, in other collective actions, in other types of agencements. As we have seen, openness to the outside is one of the essential characteristics of assemblages, and it is a characteristic shared by agencements. In sum, the same activities can be multiframed. For example, a university scientist who, in the framework of a financed contract, works on a project in collaboration with a company's production engineers or salespeople is part of a market agencement, yet his activity is also involved in agencements that can be called scientific insofar as they participate in a collective action that produces statements that can be contested, disproved, or validated by colleagues. Furthermore, the same research activity may be simultaneously oriented toward altruistic relations—such as when the scientist receives gifts for the research or transmits materials or lines of code to a colleague or a partner—or toward ethical preoccupations, as when he hesitates to develop certain lines of research for moral reasons. Consumers, too, can be multiframed: they can buy a package from a telecom provider as a gift for someone, or if they are handy, divert bandwidth to construct a private surveillance apparatus. Likewise, an engineer who perfects a cogenerator and aims to optimize its economic viability does not thereby give up concern for work well done; he may be involved with communities of experts who value the efficiency of the machines they design. As we saw in Chapter 6, it can even be that company economists, whose task is to maximize returns on investments, introduce political concerns into the price formulations they suggest. These tensions are the rule, not the exception. They have been described a thousand times by the sociology of professions, moral and political sociology, and the sociology of organizations. Research in these fields provides repeated reminders that a single logic of action cannot, on its own, account for the richness and complexity of practices. The notion of agencement proves necessary in order to understand distributed and strategically oriented collective action, as well as the active role of the material environment. It does not erase these tensions. Rather, it leads to modifying the interpretations invoked to account for them.

An academic researcher involved in an industrial project is not required to reconcile demands imposed from the outside (nor does he impose such a requirement on himself). His activities are formatted by the different agencements in which he is a player: the objects on which he works, and therefore the work itself, are framed by the multiple, distributed collective actions with which they are associated. When he studies a cellular mechanism for blocking the growth of cancerous tumors, the object he manipulates and that he analyzes is profiled simultaneously by the search for a medical treatment that a creditworthy client will not be able to do without and by the production of statements that can withstand scientific critique and objections. The same analysis can be applied to all of the agencies involved in a market agencement. The formula that an economist-engineer develops can take into account, in its very expression, the capture of a client and the search for social justice, as in the case of establishing electricity prices. These few examples, which should be subject to systematic analyses, show that in each of these sites, a market agencement is articulated year in and year out with other types of agencements (technical, scientific, ethical) and that this articulation is at stake in the very modalities of framing—that is to say, in the form given to cellular mechanisms in biology, mobile telephones, cogeneration, or price formulation.

The work that goes into this shaping is itself an object worthy of research; such research might, for instance, identify the conditions under which one agencement locally wins out over the others with which it is articulated. For my purposes in this chapter, suffice it to emphasize that a market agencement is always intertwined with other types of agencements. Given the growing multiplicity of sites it connects, a market agencement may give the illusion that the market is everywhere. However, this is indeed an illusion, since it is grappling with other modes of agencement within each of those sites. A market agencement does not develop within a territory, but instead according to a topography or geometry reminiscent of fractals.

Each site that participates in the alignment of the activities of a market agencement is traversed by one or several borders. Jane Guyer talks of margins to refer to these articulations that traverse each site, adding that gains are made only at the margins. Increases in values are fed by the collision of differences in evaluation.[12]

TRANSACTION-FREE ZONES

On the one hand, the agencement closes in on itself and its strategic aim of instituting bilateral market transactions. On the other hand, it opens onto other types of agencement that provide the resources and energy it needs. Here again, we find the tension generated by familiar oppositions, just as commercial and noncommercial activities are known to complement and nourish each other. Yet there is an essential difference. In the case of market agencements, rather than being established between spheres, fields, or worlds that remain exterior to one another, complementarity is obtained locally, site by site. This raises the question of the overall architecture and the organization of activities. How are alignment and articulation made compatible, despite the fact they tend to be in opposition at any given site?

There is, as far as I know, no satisfying answer to this question. To give a hint at a plausible solution, let's turn to Carliss Baldwin and her concept of a transaction-free zone, which, as the name implies, is a zone in which commercial transactions do not occur.[13]

To illustrate this notion, the easiest way is to consider an example, say, a center for scientific research that wishes to participate in both industrial and academic life. This double affiliation leads it to participate in communities of experts and in the advancement of knowledge while also becoming part of the commercial world and its activities. Its involvement in economic life may be sporadic and minimal, similar to a laboratory for fundamental research that simply buys equipment or recruits researchers and technicians on the job market. Its involvement may also be constant and substantial, similar to labs that cooperate with a powerful partnering firm on a regular basis. Whichever balance is chosen, the problem and the solution are the same: they have to organize in such a way as to remain compatible with both market agencements and scientific agencements.

Such compromises are by no means impossible. Over the last one hundred and fifty years, scientists and industrial players have progressively learned to develop forms of organization that favor this double game. A frequent solution for the links between research centers and industry is a matrix organization, crossing technological and innovation projects. The first organization ensures the articulation with scientific activities, the second with industrial activities. All that remains is to organize the crossovers. (This requires a lot of know-how and finesse!) Those who loudly clamor that the values and norms of science cannot be reconciled with those of the markets have been proven wrong. The adjustments are made daily and easily through the choice of objects and subjects of research.

One might also cite the case of coders who organize in order to design and produce (so-called) free software, which can be used at no cost by other expert communities and can simultaneously be taken up, with a few contractual arrangements, by commercial entrepreneurs. Or one could cite the example of groups that start by offering services for free and then, once the basic products have been tested, enrich, complete, and transform them into commercial goods. Research centers, expert communities, and nonprofit organizations—all of these are cases of transaction-free zones that are inscribed in commercial alignment strategies while preserving an articulation with other types of agencements.

Establishing transaction-free zones is not a new strategy. Depending on the state of development of market agencements and depending on the type of agencements that have to be articulated, they take on various evolving forms. Baldwin suggests an interesting parallel. Observing that the legal status of limited liability companies, only two centuries old, was precisely aimed at creating spaces that would be protected from the market while being caught up in it, she draws a distinction between "encapsulated" and "unencapsulated" transaction-free zones. An incorporated company (a company that is registered and has legal personhood) is encapsulated within borders that ensure a large measure of autonomy, as well as the possibility of being free, internally, from all bilateral transactions. An open-source community is unencapsulated.[14] In both cases, we have transaction-free zones.

A transaction-free zone does not directly depend on its shareholders. (If a shareholder is in debt, the firm is not affected, and, conversely, the shareholders are liable only within the limits of the shares they hold.) The only requirement a free zone of this type faces is that of its own survival and its own financing, which is made possible through its articulation with commercial activities. In this case, the form of organization is generally what economists call "hierarchical." It is designed to ensure, insofar as possible, the unity of action of the collective that is the incorporated firm. By analogy, and to designate the free zones that ensure a living environment for expert communities cooperating to elaborate goods that will then also enter commercial transactions, one can speak of "unencapsulated firms," since these communities have neither legal personhood nor national affiliations.[15]

The establishment of free zones maintains the vascularization of market agencements while contributing to the pursuit of commercial collective action. Of course, questions of costs, technical coherence, and moral preferences come into play, but only as secondary considerations, in order to draw the borders more precisely.[16] The existence and constitution of free zones arise from a higher imperative: no commercial transactions without openings toward the activities that nourish and renew them.

The constitution of unencapsulated free zones, zones that are free from all internal commercial transactions and that are not companies, is becoming common with the development of market agencements that include and mobilize a growing number of heterogeneous sites, which each provide occasions for articulations with other noncommercial agencements. The activities connected to exploiting and commercializing products derived from blood provide a striking example of this. As Philippe Steiner has convincingly showed, blood donation mixes and articulates activities that prohibit any commercial transaction (one gives blood) with others that are involved in commercializing derivative products (such as plasmas).[17] However, as an illustration, I will refer instead to sociologist Anissa Pomiès's work devoted to the emergence of a new market concerning "specialty" coffees because this example brings out free zones' role outside the technological sectors in which they are usually considered.[18]

A few years ago, the observation that coffee bars serve mediocre coffee led to initiatives to enhance the value of the product. This involved setting up world championships for baristas, those who make and serve coffee, and defining a set of rules to frame the way espressos and cappuccinos are made. A barista who wants a shot at the podium needs to tell the story of the coffee selected (origin, production conditions, taste qualities), choose certain materials, follow a set of rules (grinding specifications, infusion time), offer balanced coffee (neither too bitter nor too acidic), obtain a certain texture for the frothed milk and enhance it with original patterns, and ensure the quality of service by following standards of hygiene and manners. Coffee, thus requalified in four dimensions (narrative, technical, sensorial, and service), bears no resemblance to a standardized product such as the espresso served in Parisian brasseries—robusta, overroasted, bitter, and so on. These competitions frame a qualification that suggests and opens numerous options: the choice of coffee bean, modes of roasting, quantity used, water temperature, color of the crema, and so on. Baristas who follow the formalized procedure set up by the championships in their own coffee shops can subtly adapt to the client and be in a position to argue that it is good coffee. This movement deepens singularization and the tight coprofiling it requires.

The championships—there are in fact several, each of which has a slightly different definition of a good coffee's qualities—exclude any commercial transaction: the coffee made is not sold, and at no point in the preparation is price mentioned—no cost calculation. Money does not count! All the efforts converge to qualify a coffee without a price. These championships are transaction-free zones such as Baldwin describes, which of course exclude neither hierarchies nor power relations: they call on specialized judges and head judges, promulgate rules and charters, demand docile submission from baristas, and crown it all with a score on which the final ranking is based. This score is later used on commercial sites as one of the variables taken into account in price formulation. A barista who has participated in the championships or watched them on television, another who has talked to colleagues or taken classes to prepare for them, can qualculate the price asked of his client by referring to the scores that "impartial" judges have given to different profiles of espressos or cappuccinos. The formula that is finally chosen can, again using scores produced outside commercial sites, take into account the evaluations made by other transaction-free zones, such as roasting championships, classes, or clubs. The multiple and heterogeneous articulation gives dynamism to the whole. The communities of amateurs that take shape and gravitate around free zones can verify that the qualifications elaborated there have some connection to the average consumer. As for the market agencements, they are nourished by the participation of free zones in the network.

Transaction-free zones reconcile the contradictory requirements of articulation and alignment. They frame, prepare, and vascularize, interrupting the work of alignment without thereby excluding it. The very dynamism of market agencements is at stake; this reconciliation impacts their capacity to renew themselves, transform themselves, and make novel transactions and new forms of activity emerge. Commercial and noncommercial activities are complementary, not substitutes for one another. The complementarity takes different forms and is expressed in various ways. Anthropologist Anna Tsing provides the illustration of one possible configuration in her amazing book devoted to the career of the matsutake mushroom, which is harvested by communities of gatherers in Oregon, then is transferred into Japanese commercial circuits in order to satisfy customers who stop at nothing to get hold of it; the mushroom is sometimes transformed into gifts and is constantly observed by scientific communities.[19] To characterize this configuration, Tsing uses notions such as "patch," which refers to the different communities through which the mushroom travels, or "recycling" to describe the metamorphoses of the matsutake as it moves from one continent to another against the backdrop of capitalism in ruins. To feed, perpetuate, and extend itself, this ruined capitalism captures activities that take place well beyond its borders, in a world in which everyone is trying to survive in their own way, including by shamelessly pillaging natural resources. One could generalize from Tsing's analysis and show how, from the perspective of market agencies, research laboratories, communities of geeks, or free software advocates get exploited and how they react against this influence. This tension is at the heart of market agencements.

Tsing's terminology is well suited to situations in which the commercial and noncommercial activities show strong exteriority. However, to give a fully general description of the different configurations, which are more and more often characterized by a high level of entanglement, I prefer recourse to the notion of "free zone." The complementary notions of alignment and articulation also seem more correct and relevant to the model of market agencements. Depending on the configuration, the lifestyles differ (some free zones favor relations of solidarity, others hierarchical relations), and so do the dynamic of concerns and confrontations (some play on cooperation, others on contestation).[20]

THE DYNAMICS OF CONCERNS

Market agencements are machineries whose aim is to find regular and satisfying solutions to the strategic problem of instituting and multiplying commercial bilateral transactions. The thesis developed in this book is that the result is obtained by deploying a (distributed) collective action structured by a series of five framings and that it takes the form of a multisited network that organizes their alignment and their articulations. These networks can be described as innovation networks in competition with one another.

Agencements are in constant motion. They are animated by forces. Some of these forces tend to reinforce and reproduce existing framings, whereas others tend, on the contrary, to transform them. Whether they are positive or negative, whether they overthrow or consolidate existing arrangements, these forces are at the heart of agencements. To understand how they function, one needs to introduce a notion with which the reader is by now familiar: the source of concern or problems. As we have seen throughout this book, framings produce matters of concern. None of the framings is so perfect as to avoid overflowing. Entities that participate in different courses of action always at least partially escape the predictable and disciplined behavior one would like to impose on them. They cause trouble, which reaches other entities and pushes them to (re)act.

A wonderful illustration of this process linking actions and reactions can be found in La Fontaine's famous fable "The Cobbler and the Financier"—not unrelated to the subject of this book.[21]

A cobbler sang from morn till night;
'Twas sweet and marvellous to hear

. . . .

His neighbour, on the other hand
With gold in plenty at command
But little sang, and slumber'd less —
A financier of great success.
If e'er he dozed, at break of day
The cobbler's song drove sleep away
And much he wish'd that Heaven had made
Sleep a commodity of trade
In market sold, like food and drink.

La Fontaine sets the scene between two agencies whose activities enter into conflict with one another. The cobbler is a permanent problem, a source of constant concern for his rich neighbor. The latter, used to buying and selling everything, would like to transform sleep into a commodity and enter into a bilateral commercial transaction with the cobbler. This dream is not impossible (as the French term for "slumlord" shows: "marchands de sommeil" are literally sleep merchants). However, the fable's financier lives in a world in which sleep is not yet a commodity. He therefore chooses to go see his neighbor and inquire what troubles him. He quickly learns that the poor cobbler's constant worry, his main existential problem, is how to procure his daily bread. This is not a chance to be missed. The financier immediately says to the cobbler:

These hundred pounds I hand you here
Will make you happy as a king.
Go, spend them with a frugal heed;
They'll long supply your every need.

Freed from daily torment, the cobbler rejoices. He goes home and hides the silver there. "And," as La Fontaine puts it, "with it laid his joy aside. / No more of song, no more of sleep, / But cares, suspicions in their stead." Unable to stand it any longer, he rushes back to the financier, begging him to take back his money and to return his songs and his sleep.

This edifying fable brings together all the elements one needs to understand the dynamics of agencements. There is an action carried out by the cobbler: he sings at the top of his voice. There is an overflowing that constitutes a problem for his neighbor, bothering and worrying him until his life is so upset that he can no longer sleep. This unbearable overflowing pushes him to act. Action, like life, never begins—it continues. The financier, a connoisseur of the human soul (how could he not be, when he has made a fortune?), does not believe in the stories told according to which human beings are moved only by self-interest, and it is always possible to obtain what one wants for money by upping the stakes. (How much do you want to be quiet?) He knows that the action is directed toward solving problems, and as a good investigator, he interrogates the cobbler in order to discover his main source of concern and worry. He realizes that he will indeed have to pay—not for him to stop singing, but to calm the hunger that drives him. By giving the cobbler money, he ruins his life and cuts him off. Exchanging problems and matters of concern, translating them from one to another and sometimes going so far as to pay in order to create, maintain, and orient this movement—this is the basic module, the simple sequence of distributed collective action. The framed action overflows, it creates trouble that reframes it and reorients it in new directions. The cobbler used to sing and sleep; thanks to the financier, who frees him from hunger, he no longer sings or sleeps, and the story starts again.

All framings overflow. The financier's motives are not important. The only thing that counts are the concerns he faces and for which he needs a solution. Market agencements go through the same process. Like all agencements, they produce problems, worries, matters of concern. This mode of functioning is neither pathological nor abnormal. It is inherent in agencements, and it is a result of the form collective action takes. In the case of market agencements, in order to produce bilateral transactions and the singularization of goods that doing so requires, this collective action is structured by the five framings. In order to move ahead, it must maintain these framings at all cost, the only solution often being to reconfigure them in order to somehow absorb the overflowings and contestations they provoke. The way a market agencement functions cannot be separated from the dynamic of the matters of concern it raises and from which they overflow or of the ensuing attempts at reframing. Each agencement thus follows a singular trajectory. Each story can, however, be analyzed with the same tools: they derive from the same conceptual framework and make it possible to track the play of forces that organizes around the framings and the problems they raise.

Each framing is the source of possible overflowings of matters of concern, which affect and divert the action in unexpected directions. If one wants to describe the way a market agencement functions, the method is therefore obvious: one first has to run through the framings in a careful empirical exploration of the overflowings and the problems they raise and then observe the actions that respond in order to eliminate or reframe the problems. Even though regularities do often appear, due to similarities in framing *dispositifs*, it would make no sense to attempt to establish an exhaustive inventory of these confrontations since circumstances play a determining role in their emergence. The following illustrations supplement what has already been said in the preceding chapters. They are presented only in order to give an overall view of this approach and the way in which it makes it possible to unify a framework of analysis.

The overflowings that have been studied the most are those linked to the first market framing, the one concerning goods and their passiva(c)tion. No doubt this is because these issues become more and more visible as commercial activities, which include the domestication of ever more beings, prove to be problematic. The inventory of matters of concern provoked by passiva(c)tion grows longer every day, as does the list of protest movements to draw attention to these matters: chemical substances attacking the environment, threatening health; buried carbon, ceaselessly extracted and spewed into the atmosphere as carbon dioxide, provoking global warming; transgenic organisms that may alter both plant and animal equilibria in the long term; human labor, subjected to machines or ordered to be creative, but not excessively so; animals that are subjugated or transformed into meat; financial derivatives that induce systemic crises; agricultural land sold to property developers. The latter, property rights, call for reshaping existing framings in order to respond to the problems that arise. In the coming years, they will no doubt be at the heart of many claims: it is a question raised by the massive irruption of problems generated by the passiva(c)tion of living beings, but also by the growing importance of free zones, which crystalize novel demands and call for collective property rights to be set up. This might be similar to GNU, the free software system launched by Richard Stallman in 1983, copyleft, or Creative Commons.[22]

These big questions, which make the headlines in the media and international conferences, should not make us forget the many overflowings generated by the way the qualification of useful everyday goods is evolving. Despite being less visible, this change can be analyzed in the same terms. For instance, Frank Azimont and Luis Araujo show how food, whose primary function might be to feed, is gradually requalified into foodstuffs with new functions: the foodstuffs not only feed, they can claim to be good for one's health—what they call "functional goods."[23] This transformation and reframing, which modify the programs of action of which the good is capable, are the result of taking into account the untimely overflowings of foodstuffs that, granted, are nourishing, but that stand accused of having negative impacts on consumers' health. Consumer groups raise a health question whose solution has been inscribed in the good. This opens the way for an extension of existing commercial transactions to constitute a market juxtaposed to the preceding one that it will perhaps one day replace. The turmoil is appeased, the consumer can sleep soundly again, although always in a way that can be disrupted. Are the experts correct who assert that the food is good for one's health? Are they paid by big agribusinesses that finance their work? Passiva(c)tion is never irrevocable. It is never guaranteed. Indeed, as we saw in Chapter 2, very often, the ways it is obtained can be attacked indirectly, leading to property rights being challenged, as is the case with genetically modified broccoli or when people question the ownership of so-called "individual" data.

Formatting qualculating agencies (Chapter 3) is also the source of serious concern. The concern can be about the very modalities of qualculation and the choice of tools and instruments used. Indeed, in light of such concerns, there have been proposals to impose modifications: counting and accounting for the firm's actions in a different way, no longer allowing shareholder value to be the dominant criterion of action, or encouraging new accounting tools—for instance, by modifying the legal status of corporations.[24] Simpler suggestions ask that it be made possible for patient groups, nonprofit organizations, or consumer groups to take part in commercial activities from which they are often excluded and to institute new modes of qualculation. These exercises are becoming increasingly complicated because they increase the number of qualculating agencies. The diversity of evaluation tools this diversity produces can lead to frontal oppositions and situations of open conflict.

To continue this overview, we should look at how the organization of encounters (Chapter 4), through the drastic framings it imposes, provoke reactions that focus on contesting the choices made and on challenging the massive exclusions they sometimes produce, leaving vulnerable populations on the sidelines. An increasing number of algorithms, rankings, and classifications are judged to be partial and simplistic. They also have an increasingly strong grip on the establishment of reputations, conformism, or hierarchies, as well as on the competition among agents and on the profiling of our future behavior through the instauration of digital infrastructures that are programmable.[25] As a result, both the use of algorithms and the modes of qualculation they impose are being challenged. The next step would be to show how attachment devices (Chapter 5) engender critique. Advertising is deemed deceptive or alienating or is mocked. Branding policies and their ambitions to shape consumers' cultural universes are accused of mystifying and manipulating, promoting the reign of image and appearance. Devices that have users participate in the definition of goods are denounced as strategies for excluding or anesthetizing critical faculties. Recourse to addictive practices can be incriminated for being cynical and immoral.[26] Finally, to complete an overview, one should review how price formulations (Chapter 6) and the injustices or abuses they nourish are contested, whether it be the pricing of labor, of energy, of food, or of transportation. This work should be extended by looking at the mechanisms of reframing that in some cases make it possible to absorb the challenge and find solutions. It is clear, however, that these analyses cannot be done at an abstract, general level. They make sense only in relation to a particular agencement or a particular area since they must take account of the specificity of both the framings and the matters of concern.

Emphasizing the dynamics of framings-overflowings highlights how many diverse trajectories a given agencement can follow. It makes no sense to talk of *an* alternative. There are potentially an infinite number of alternatives. Which ones are actualized depends on the modalities of the different framings, the manner in which the overflowings they provoke are experienced, the way the demands for reframings are expressed, and the nature of the power relations established over the course of these clashes. As Franck Cochoy has rightly noted, it should furthermore be underlined that market agencements not only raise the question of the matters of concern they generate—they also raise the question of how to articulate these matters and of their hierarchy.[27]

In general, the different forces around framings and their reconfiguration are not independent of one another. First, some framing devices are found in many market agencements: for example, accounting instruments, property rights, tools for qualculating externalities, meeting algorithms, and so on. Alliances and convergences can therefore be observed with the composition, coordination, and aggregation of local initiatives from site to site, framing to framing. This sometimes leads to the emergence of widely shared movements or the expression of preoccupations and solutions that have a certain generalized status. However, there are also many divergences, and the convergences are often ephemeral and called into question by circumstances. For instance, in their book devoted to contested markets, Philippe Steiner and Marie Trespeuch observe that the response to one matter of concern often creates others that are just as serious, the new configuration producing new fragilities as it seeks to alleviate others.[28]

This should not induce extreme relativism. All configurations do not have equal merit. Evaluating them requires discussions and confrontation. I will give a few examples in the following chapter, and I will take a more systematic look at the question of how market agencements and moral and political agencements are articulated in a later book. First, I would like to turn to two stylized examples in order to show how attention to framings-overflowings makes it possible to highlight different ways of functioning and therefore contrasting dynamics.

In the first case, funerals, there are multiple and heterogeneous forces at work, and the sources of concern that are taken into account are very diverse. Over the long term, a few centuries, the configuration of the market agencements involved in funerals has been profoundly transformed under the pressure of framing and reframing operations. In the second case, housing construction, the power relations have been remarkably stable, at least for the past decades, despite constant attempts at destabilization. The status quo is preserved by maintaining and reinforcing qualculating equipment that allows the agencies in place to impose a certain way of defining and imputing costs. In both cases, the agencements' dynamics are shaped by how the balance of power evolves around the framings and overflowings.

TRAJECTORY 1: FUNERALS

As Pascale Trompette has shown, the economization of funerals is an old story.[29] Under the ancien régime, the church played a central role in orchestrating this process by establishing detailed fees depending on the services. A priest sitting with a body through the night was paid three pounds, and the payment by the faithful was understood to be an offering. The church then redistributed the profits to take care of the funerals of the poor. The French Revolution challenged the church's role. Rather than being considered a purveyor of solutions, its involvement came to be seen as a problem. As undertakers came on the scene, guaranteed a monopoly by local authorities, commercial transactions gradually replaced offerings. This commercial activity was nevertheless framed in such a way as to ensure, through the constitution of a genuine free zone, that services were free for the poor: the contract with municipalities stipulated that companies had to bear the funeral costs of the needy.

This double framing—noncommercial for the poorest deceased, commercial for the others—creates a specific problem, namely, the problem of how free services should be financed. To handle this, undertakers began increasing the singularization of services. Different classes of funerals were introduced. Personalization and coprofiling entered into the catalogs. Each class has a corresponding basket of services-goods, brought together in a graduated and ordered table where precise descriptions are given of types of coffins, draperies, chandeliers, hearses, and so on. These tables further distinguish the services provided inside the church and those outside. These tools open the way for a formulation that indexes prices on the class of funeral and generate a surplus to finance the poor. The agencement organizes the redistribution of profits—the requirement of free zones that, in this case, articulate commercial activities with social solidarity—to respond to the requirement that the impecunious be looked after. Some do not hesitate to call this economy moral because it endorses the distinction between what is considered superfluous and what is held to be essential, between the ostentatious and the necessary. It is an economy that lacks neither realism nor cynicism: the vanity of some relieves the poverty of others. The border between the two circumscribes a space within which competition can take place for the singularization-differentiation of services.

This profitable competitive activity progressively incites new agencies (some of which are actually called "funeral agencies" in French, "agences de funérailles") to enter the business, concentrating on the organization of ceremonies and on the sale of what is perceived as superfluous, thus endangering the redistributive morality. Beyond this ongoing concern, a further challenge gradually presents companies with an unexpected problem. Death occurs more and more frequently in hospitals or institutions that care for the elderly, rendering the families' involvement less direct and less pressing. New agencies (hospitals and so on) enter the scene while others, such as the church, slip into the background. The framings that used to create the relations between supplies and demands and affect family members of the deceased so as to lead them to engage in the bilateral commercial transaction become less relevant and efficient. The competition to capture bodies (and their families) has gone through a series of reconfigurations, mainly related to the devices that organize matches and the associated attachment devices. The reconfiguration operates in several registers. Legal: there are contracts with municipalities and conventions with hospitals. Spatial: funeral parlors are mostly located inside or near hospitals and become sort of secondary extensions of the hopspital, housing the dead and gathering the families. Often, in fact, the scene of staff in white coats moving between the hospital and the funerary room establishes compelling continuity between the two, even when the staff belongs to the funeral home. The funerary room lays the ground for singularizing services organized around the coffin, its presentation, and the entire setup that goes with it. The coprofiling happens through the choices of the coffin, the flowers, the tomb, the ceremony. It allows for demands to be articulated and an ever-greater individualization of the service to be set up. The market agencement is at its most commercial when it renders competition invisible, sliding the body in one continuous motion from the bed in which death caught it to the room and the coffin where it starts its second career with the undertaker who will distinguish it from the others. Yet there is in fact competition here. The offer, the good, and the supply are so tightly bound and entwined that the other forces are rendered almost invisible, at least for a while.

In order to make their services profitable, companies must regularly process a great number of bodies and coffins: this is what makes this device possible. The device holds the entire market agencement together by narrowly aligning the framings and rigidly circumscribing its articulation with the hospital world. Its function is similar to the one that manages and commercializes airplane seats, except that singularized seats are replaced by coffins, by the varieties of wood from which they are made, and by the varying profusion of flowers and processions. The discriminating monopoly collects the consumer surplus, which of course increases profits, but also allows for financing the burials of the poor.

As I have said, no framing is definitive because each invariably provokes new matters of concern. Recently, small companies that had not enough financial resources to enter the market started denouncing undertakers' de facto monopoly, rightly explaining that funeral parlors operate as devices to exclude not the bodies, but those service providers who wish to take charge of them in exchange for money. The dynamic resumes. New problems call for new solutions, which have yet to be invented.

Pascale Trompette retraces the evolution of the funeral market over the long term, illustrating the wellsprings of dynamics in market agencements, showing how such agencements function. She shows how futile it would be to limit the list of agencies involved to those who provide services and those who benefit from them: public powers, religious authorities, and hospital structures are part of the story and indeed play crucial roles. A further lesson is that this story is articulated by successive framings. The development of devices that ensure qualculation and evaluate the services on offer are at the heart of the story. However, the successive devices for the passiva(c)tion of the service are even more central. Where there was once a short circuit that began with the deceased being detached from their family contexts and immediately (re)attached to the church and the communion of saints,[30] there is now a much longer circuit that after a series of successive attachments transforms an elderly person living in an assisted living facility into a patient hooked up to tubes that are finally unplugged, then into a body lying in a funeral parlor where the family comes (or does not come) to say goodbye before it is shut into a coffin that will be burned in a crematorium; the collection of the ashes are the final moment of this odyssey. How could one hope to penetrate and understand the dynamics of these markets without focusing the analysis on retracing the history of these framings and without drawing the connections between these transformations and the concerns they have produced at different moments in their development, as well as the successive responses to these concerns? The competition that drives market agencements is won or lost on the mastery of these framings and their transformations. As one can see, it concerns the ever more active singularization of services. Each company seeks to respond to the problems raised by reconfiguring the devices more convincingly than the competitors and by offering new services with an even higher degree of individualization. The invention of funeral parlors and the alignment they produce between service passiva(c)tion, qualculation, matching, attachment, and price-formulation devices is not extraneous to the analysis of agencements and their free zones. On the contrary, it is their very substance.

TRAJECTORY 2: HOUSING

The trajectory of the French funeral market is characterized by a profound transformation of framing devices, as well as by a great proliferation of agencies and a spectacular evolution of services. This development is all the more remarkable because the way a society cares for its dead does not lend itself to rapid change. Yet in less than a century, the careers of the deceased have been deeply shaken up and have adapted to the growing reach of commercial transactions: in a sector in which one might have expected only slow and laborious changes, market agencements' capacity for innovation has turned out to be particularly efficient. Such a capacity for renewal, opening, and adaptation is not the general rule. Other trajectories and other dynamics can be observed. The housing market—not the one for the final resting place of the dead, but the one for homes for the living—is a good example of a sector that has resisted new technologies and new products for decades, despite their being available and promising.

In order to understand how market agencements manage to close in on themselves, to maintain existing alignments and framings, to limit any new articulations that imperil their equilibrium, to rarify the agencies and sites involved, and to contain the expressions of concerns, let us move to England and follow Heather Lovell and Susan Smith in their analysis.[31] They ask a simple question: Why has the housing market not been transformed by the technique that involves assembling elements prefabricated elsewhere at a building site? The usual answer is that this technology has not spread because the cost of prefabricated elements remains significantly higher (about 10 percent more than the cost of traditional building). However simple and obvious this answer may be, it is also less than satisfying. Whatever the sector, there has been so much invested in existing technologies, so much research done, and so much feedback from experience that they are always superior to technologies that, having never been developed on a large scale, remain expensive! If this were the right explanation, it should then apply to almost all fields of activity, and existing technologies should only very rarely be replaced by emerging technologies.

A significant number of studies, however, demonstrate the opposite, and it is easy to account for this supposed anomaly. Emerging technologies can at first take hold in niche markets and then become more competitive as they spread. Taking the long view, entities such as financial markets or public authorities can decide to support new technologies that they view as promising, and so on. These different explanations start from the fact that cost is neither the only nor the most important criterion. The determining element is the existence of groups with enough resources, driven by interests and anticipations that push them to support a new technology rather than the existing one. One might consider this analysis to be sociological, insofar as it emphasizes the power relations between actors with diverging logics. It has the advantage of being able to account for both blocked and open situations: if the balance shifts, the dynamic is likewise reversed.

Whether precedence is given to the economic explanation or the sociological one or indeed to one that combines them (showing, for instance, how certain actors can manage losses or impose unbearable ones on their competitors), what is generally overlooked in the emergence of new technologies is the role of calculation instruments. In their investigation, Lowell and Smith correct for this blind spot by taking the framings as their point of departure. Asking how costs are calculated, they ascertain that the calculating codes are imposed by traditional building techniques. For example, experts in the field are unanimous in their opinion that in the subsector of prefabricated construction, delivery schedules are kept more closely and there are fewer defects, whereas, in traditional masonry, delays grow and defects multiply. However, these events are not taken into account in the calculations and evaluations that are generally made. This is the case, notably, for the costs that might be associated with defects and delays and that in fact are not integrated into the calculations at all: this exclusion obviously penalizes the prefabricated option. In other words, these failures of the traditional framings are ignored, although they inflict real nuisances on some of the agents—most notably, clients. The calculation instruments render these matters of concern invisible, deny their existence, and ultimately maintain and reinforce the status quo. It is indeed a matter of costs, but it plays out in the choice and design of the instruments that allow for their calculation. It is indeed a matter of power relations, but it plays out in the way in which framing devices (here, calculation codes) treat concerns by ignoring and eliminating them. The situation is secured, with a remarkable economy of means, simply by controlling the qualculation instruments.

One could easily generalize this analysis. In order to understand why some market agencements follow certain trajectories rather than others, why in some cases configurations develop and transform (in the case of funerals), while, in others, the forces of reproduction are stronger than the forces of transformation (in the case of housing), or again, why the trajectories change over time, moving from blocked to unblocked situations, one should start from the framing dynamics, the overflowings, and the matters of concern they produce, as well as from the reactions and reframings they elicit. This dynamic is saturated with balances of power, which are established and actualized through the design and implementation of framing devices, whether it be the modalities of passiva(c)tion, the choice of qualculation instruments, the organization of matches, the production of attachments, or price formulation.[32]

It might seem that there would be no practical consequences to reversing the perspective. In the case of construction, isn't the main thing to show that it is a matter of both costs and power relations? The answer is no. Consider the types of intervention (for instance, by public authorities) that could encourage the unlocking of the agencement.

By explaining things through arguments about costs, in this case the non-maturity of alternative technologies, one can favor the emergence of the latter by creating protected spaces where first trials can be carried out and where the new technologies can progressively take on the old as they mature. The sociology of interests could push for work on symbolic resources (launching campaigns to show that prefabricated is not synonymous with poor quality) or organizational and financial resources (by facilitating initial investments that are important for the prefabricated sector). In both cases, exploring matters of concern is left aside to make way for political resolve of the most traditional sort.

The market agencement perspective provides new targets. It brings out the importance of calculating equipment and pricing formulas and orients possible new interventions toward modifying these devices with the avowed aim of tackling the hidden problems, which exist despite not being explicit. The logic of possible political interventions is to put together powerful alliances in order to impose or generate small changes that may produce considerable effects—for example, penalizing late deliveries or defects. If the aim is to reconcile mass construction with singularization, it should be added in this particular case that the unlocking of the sector would be facilitated if other actions were undertaken at the same time to weigh on other framings (*affectio mercatus*, organization of encounters) in order to assert the superiority of prefabrication over traditional building.

The dynamics of market agencements are organized by the tension between framings and overflowings. They are inscribed in framing devices and in the reconfiguration of these devices. Depending on the forces that intervene and on the balance established among them, the dynamic varies, leading in some cases to lock-ins, and in others to lock-outs. One can imagine weighing in on these dynamics and the effects they produce, on the way that they take matters of concern into account or fail to do so. There is therefore room for engineering, and in particular, for political engineering, which broaches the matter of evaluating different possible configurations. The question is, What is a good market agencement? In the next chapter, I will see how we might begin to answer this question. My aim will not be to get to the bottom of the issue, but rather to stake out some points of reference for work I will develop later.

CHAPTER EIGHT

The Role of Theorization
in Transforming Markets

In the preceding chapters, I have examined those carefully calibrated devices that orient and structure commercial activities in order to demonstrate the infinite variety of configurations and arrangements that can provide concrete answers to these fundamental questions.

Among the many imaginable configurations, can we establish a hierarchy? Could we favor the establishment of those that for one reason or another are considered either the best or the least harmful? The analysis of market agencements would not be worth anyone's time if it did not provide some answer to this question. My intention is to give those who want to intervene in the design and functioning of markets some grasp on solving the problems they raise and mastering the effects they produce.

In this final chapter, I will not discuss the procedures or devices that must be designed and implemented for preferences to be expressed and ordered. My aim is decisive, yet modest. I will contemplate a basic question: How the concerns voiced by stakeholders can play a role in the processes through which they evolve. In the previous chapters, I suggested how each of the five framing devices may lead agents to raise concerns, to elaborate and express propositions to address these concerns, and to generate solutions. Through this dynamic, new framing devices can sometimes emerge. This is how market agencements are capable of being transformed and of evolving.

To understand how this evolution happens, the sequencing that organizes the progressive switching from one framing device to another deserves to be precisely analyzed. Put in a nutshell, we have to understand how the expression of concern and propositions, whether formulated by agents directly involved in market agencements or by distant observers such as academics, politicians, or philosophers sometimes lead to progressive changes in framing devices and agencements. To put it in a more general way, my aim is to clarify how analyses and claims can be translated into practice in the choice and institution of specific market agencements. For reasons I have discussed elsewhere, I will mainly focus on how economic theories, be they highly formalized or not, contribute or can contribute to the evolution and transformation of market arrangements.[1] Once this is done, it will be possible in a later work to investigate the evolutionary process itself and in particular to identify how reasoned interventions can lead under certain conditions to sought-after results.

In order to describe, situate, and assess the impact of these possible interferences,[2] it is provisionally useful to represent the dynamics of agencements as a series of open cycles that lead to one another and whose basic cell is represented in Figure 1.

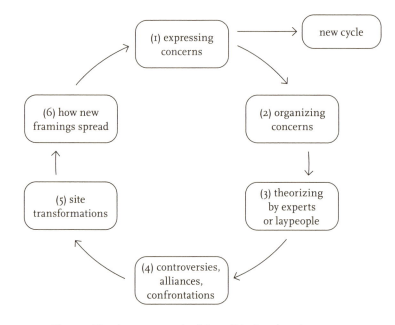

Figure 1: The elementary cycle of the political engineering
of market agencements (first representation).

The initial configuration and the corresponding framings lead to a series of worries or concerns being expressed (1). These concerns enter into relation with one another, creating allies or antagonists, and sometimes contribute to the emergence of more general concerns, such as those expressed in slogans for a better food, an end to bullshit work, and so on (2).[3] In a second phase, responses or solutions are elaborated in the form of arguments, scenarios, programs, models, or theories (3), which give rise to controversies, some of which remain local, whereas others seek to create wider audiences gathered around more general problems (4). Next comes the time of experimentation, with the implementation of solutions and compromises that were elaborated over the course of phase 3. New sites take shape (5), and new framings are set up (6). In turn, these give rise to new concerns, which launch a whole new cycle. The first phase (1 + 2) is that of concern, the second (3 + 4) that of designing new framings, and the third (5 + 6) is about enacting them.

Whatever transformations take place, one of the most blatant outcomes of such cycles is to bring forth novel, practical answers to basic questions: Which goods will be produced, by whom, for whom, and at what prices? Those questions are at the core of what can be called the politics of market agencements because they are directly related to the organization of social life. Second, because the possible answers are multiple and in principle open to debate, from this perspective, the intermediate work of rendering explicit and theorizing plays a crucial role because it contributes to unraveling and to arguing the different positions and propositions at stake. No political position in relation to market agencement can do without some form of argued and documented thought that connects expectations, hopes, or claims with actions that should be undertaken in order to satisfy them. In this chapter, my ambition is to set up an inquiry by presenting three cases—financial markets, global warming, and the place of genetically modified plants in commercial activities—that highlight the need for a suitable articulation between theoretical work with the internal dynamics of market agencements. This work must not be dissociated from the analysis of framings and the problems they induce, nor should it lose sight of the aim of finding answers (that is, novel framings) that respond to the observed overflowings. I should note that in what follows, I will not be proceeding with a deep examination of the ways in which economic theories contribute to the constitution of economic reality. That will be for a second volume, itself a necessary step before broaching the broader question of the politics of market agencements.

The choice of these three examples will allow me to highlight the limits of Figure 1 and to propose a new representation. Contrary to what the figure suggests, theorizing work is pervasive and takes place during each phase of the cycle. It cannot be restricted to a well circumscribed step in a process. First, theory participates in shaping the concern, then it directly contributes to designing new framings, and finally it helps the new framings become viable. In order to respond to these requirements, theorizing work must develop beyond the circle of recognized experts, and those who do this work must not hesitate to engage in experimental activity; in doing so, theory moves from technical engineering to technical and political engineering. What I will try to suggest in the following lines is that theorizing work, whatever its degree of abstraction or formalization, whatever its value orientation, is an unescapable obligatory passage point. No more, no less.

THEORY AS CONTRIBUTION TO THE EXPRESSION OF CONCERNS: REOPENING THE DEBATE ABOUT FINANCIAL MARKETS AND THEIR DESIGN

What is a "good" financial market?

The formulation of this question is interesting only if it is assumed that there are several possible answers. Engaging with the question requires us to abandon the idea that there is one best way, a single conception of what a good financial market is. Yet this condition is not sufficient. It is also necessary to be able to propose an analytical framework that makes it possible to grasp and express the diversity of options while indicating the obstacles to action.

In this section, I will show why the classical model of efficient capital markets can lead only to a dead end in such a conversation. On the other hand, the market agencements model provides all the elements to express and explain the concerns to be taken into account, as well as to design and implement the forms of organization that provide appropriate responses to these concerns.

What is a "good" financial market? There are as many potential answers to this question as there are possible definitions of "good." The answers depend on the objectives assigned to financial markets. I will take economist Alfred

Galichon's formulation, which seems to be a good summary of mainstream economic theory, as my point of departure. It makes the quest for the definition of good into its main preoccupation.[4]

According to Galichon, the first objective of financial markets is to distribute funds so as to ensure that economic activities are financed. The second objective is to guarantee the savings of economic agents. This definition has the advantage of being quite realistic. It does not privilege investments in any way (because indeed, not all credits are devoted to financing investments). It also underlines that a variety of agents and sites are involved in financial markets, from an individual trying to finance the purchase of a car, an apartment, or daily living requirements to a multinational company launching a takeover bid on a competitor. This definition suggests other possible definitions. One could, for instance, without abandoning Galichon's framework, add the requirement that access to credit should be ensured for all agents, that households with small revenues should have their savings protected, and so on.[5] I will return to this point. For now, let us accept this minimal definition of what these markets are for. It makes it possible to introduce and discuss two notions that are often invoked to asses the quality of markets in general and of financial markets in particular: effectiveness and efficiency.

A (financial) market is deemed effective if it allows the set objectives to be reached. It is considered efficient if it does so with an optimal allocation of resources—that is to say, as economically as possible. Given the complexity of this program, the task of elaborating and implementing it, which is both moral and political, is generally left to enlightened experts. It is essentially left to economists. In this approach to market agencements, which is of the order of technical engineering, experts dispense with collecting and collating the concerns raised by the way existing markets function. They see no need to consult the different agents involved, since the two notions, efficiency and effectiveness, are supposed to capture and summarize all legitimate aspirations and between them define the qualities of a good market. Experts take on phases 1 and 2, those of concern (Figure 1). They are the ones who set objectives for the markets, impose criteria for their functioning, and on that basis determine its best configurations. If experts feel legitimate, it is because the objectives and the associated rules seem indisputable. Once objectives have been defined, all that remains is to implement them.

In the following lines, I am particularly interested in the problems raised by efficiency, first because it is a morally and politically sensitive question, but also because it has a more general scope beyond financial markets. Given their structure, however, these remain an important site for testing the realism of efficiency.

Under what conditions is a market efficient? The answer to this question is given by so-called neoclassical economists. It relies on the hypothesis that agents make decisions on the basis of posted prices. It then adds that these decisions are optimal when the prices synthesize and summarize all of the available information, and notably, when they consider the possible consequences of their decisions. Two conditions must be fulfilled to test the hypothesis: the first concerns the cognitive capacities of the agents, who must be able to carry out sometimes complex calculations; the second is connected to the availability of information and in particular to the precise meaning of the expression "complete information." Examining these two conditions is one of the fundamental concerns of the rational expectations hypothesis (REH).

Expressed in ordinary language, the REH can be summarized in one simple proposition. In order for prices to play the part they should, it suffices that agents (whether on the supply side or on the demand side) have available all necessary information to anticipate the consequences of the decision they may or will make and that furthermore they be convinced that all the other agents involved, either on the supply side or on the demand side, have the same information available and are equally convinced that all agents are in this situation. Each agent behaves in the most rational way possible when he knows all that he has to know in order to make decisions on the basis of evaluating their consequences. If it is fulfilled, this condition guarantees that the market, which synthesizes all these calculations in pricing, functions as a device that allows every agent to reach their objectives and ensures that the result is obtained with the greatest economy of means.

What about financial markets? The first thing one observes is that agents increasingly have recourse to cognitive prostheses. Without them, they would not be able to gather the information they need, nor would they be able to make the calculations involved in pricing. If financial markets are the most heavily equipped of all markets, it is because the need for such instrumentation was acutely felt. As Galichon puts it, when subjected daily to a deluge of information and news, a human being in the financial markets who was "reduced" to their mere brain and body would be rapidly be overwhelmed.[6] Without prostheses, they would not survive. If they refused assistance, the agent would be condemned to sink either into routine, applying the same generic recipes to every situation, or into mimesis, copying other agents' behaviors. In both cases, they give up being rational—that is to say, they give up on calculating their decisions on the basis of information, since the information is available in principle, but they are unable to process it. This is why, Galichon explains, there is a frenzied race to overequip agents: computers, models, simulations, ever more powerful algorithms. Nothing is too good, nothing too expensive, when aiming for efficiency.

That human beings feel the need to equip themselves is perfectly compatible with the REH. Given the emphasis a theory based on this hypothesis places on calculation capacities and demands for information, it also provides a strong incentive to invest in the cognitive prostheses whose set of specifications it also contributes to defining. In that, it is no different from other economic theories. The real raison d'être of economics is neither to describe reality nor to put forward verifiable predictions, but rather to identify the conditions under which reality could conform to what economists say it is and thereby to contribute to the design of devices that could be set up in order for agents to behave as economists say they do or wish they did.[7] Financial markets illustrate this thesis perfectly.

So far, so good. There would be nothing to get worked up about if it weren't for the fact that given their accumulation and dissemination, these cognitive prostheses, which aim to make people so rational that machines sometimes end up purely and simply substituting for human beings, end up creating more problems than they solve. It can happen that prostheses that were supposed to bring real markets closer to the (efficient) ones described and wished for by the REH instead move them away from the ideal! This slippage is due to the fact that all agents end up adopting the same tools, which, as they spread, constitute the basic equipment of financial markets. When each agent uses the same algorithms, processes the same information, and makes the same calculations at the same time as all the other agents, markets flip into mimesis—the sworn enemy of rational behavior—and indeed into the blindest kind of mimesis, fed by machines with no limits.

The worst part is still to come! Some agents who are aware of the dangers brought about by the mimetic amplification produced by their prostheses and the problems they produce try to take a stand against these dangers.[8] The most obvious strategy is to resist the movement toward standardizing equipment and standardized financial products. As sociologist Vincent Lépinay has shown, depending on the resources that can be mobilized, entities strive to develop in-house software, dedicated tools, or unique financial products in order to durably win over the clients they want to attach.[9] Different agents tend to construct their own universes and render them opaque to the competition. Each is intent on constructing a singular informational bubble that protects them and in which they can be isolated because the others have only partial access. This fragmentation is accentuated by increasing numbers of bespoke techniques and a proliferation of financial products and also by the fact that many transactions take place in "gray" markets, far from any observation or control. Here, then, is the paradox. The overly equipped way in which financial agents function generates strategies that oscillate between two opposite poles: systematic mimesis and runaway markets, or extreme fragmentation and implosion. In both cases, the required conditions for efficiency are undermined.

More and more studies push forward the analysis of these mechanisms and confirm the important role that the singularization of products plays in the dynamic of financial markets. I will give two illustrations of this point.

The first example is the fits of irrationality that regularly descend on financial markets. These movements have always been difficult for economists to explain, notably economists who, like proponents of the REH, contend that markets establish the right prices. These prices are "discovered," as they see it, through an organized confrontation between multiple agents who recalculate their decisions as new information appears. Price is the end point of a continuous, gradual process made up series of experiments in trial and error.

If these markets functioned as the REH says, price adjustments would take the form of fluctuations with limited amplitudes and with opposite variations converging continuously toward a provisional equilibrium point. Yet when there is a crisis, precisely the reverse happens. There are continuously upward or downward movements, with growing amplitudes over time. To explain this anomaly, one might invoke psychology, a possibility I will address later. Before diving into the depths of human mind, however the simplest thing to look at is the evaluating tools the agents are using.[10]

Roman Frydman and Michael Goldberg, who might be considered mainstream economists, have replaced the pure minds of the REH with a population of heavily equipped agencies involved in a true division of labor. They focus on agencies such as Bloomberg Terminals that collect, process, present, and diffuse data in the form of a news stream that can be personalized. Frydman and Goldberg obviously do not use my terminology, but what they essentially claim is that each agent makes qualculations using both fundamental data such as GNP or unemployment rates and circumstantial information such as the state of geopolitical relations or appraisals of the promising character of emerging technologies.

Backed up by statistics, they show that with a very simple model that distinguishes only two families of qualculating agencies, one can easily account for the succession of periods when price movements are amplified and periods of adjustment with small fluctuations. The first family of agencies uses frameworks of evaluation that privilege short time frames and that select information related to current circumstances; the second family widens the time frame and opts for evaluating tools that take into account fundamentals and sustainable movements of the economy. Frydman and Goldberg thus contrast short-term thinkers and long-term thinkers. When carried by the long-termists, a movement lasts. The tools of the short-termists, profiled as they are to focus on the successions of the most immediate changes, mechanically lead to feeding the movement: the more prices go up, the more demand rises, and, conversely, the further prices go down, the further demand sinks. We do not have to go into the details of these models or discuss, for instance, what is meant by "fundamental" and "nonfundamental data." (One can make pragmatic distinctions.) Let us simply recognize that we can easily account for the dynamics of observed crises with a great economy of means: it is enough to postulate the existence of two populations equipped with instruments that select and calculate information differently.

What is key in this explanation is the emphasis on the devices for collecting and processing information. It is not the agents who are short-termists or long-termists, but rather the coupling formed with their instruments.[11] These couplings are not always balanced. Sometimes the tools supplant those who use them, imposing their mimetic logic without meeting any pushback! In his work on the spread of the Black-Sholes model, which continuously calculates the value of certain financial products,[12] science studies scholar Donald Mac-Kenzie has shown that several of the technical characteristics of these models, such as recourse to Gaussian probabilities,[13] sustain and amplify rising or falling movements, rather than managing them and activating restoring forces.[14] The trend toward runaway prices is all the more inevitable because algorithms are often relevant only on the condition that their number of users is limited, whereas in practice, everyone ends up using them. There are a number of reasons why these diabolical couplings are formed and spread. It would be interesting to identify the reasons. They are related to the initial training that agents receive, the culture of the organizations that employ them, and their prior experiences, but also to the commercial strategies of the companies that develop these instruments.[15]

My second example is the systemic crises that propagate from a local source of instability throughout financial markets and even go so far as to unsettle whole parts of the economy. Donald MacKenzie's work shows that if one wants to account for this in a direct and elegant way, the best strategy is to start with qualculating equipment and more specifically the equipment associated with the evaluation of innovative financial products.[16] The case study that is particularly emblematic involves products designed to cover the risks related to loans (risks of default when the borrower cannot pay or risks of prepayment when the borrower pays back early, which can affect how much the lender makes). In order to measure these risks, agents elaborate scores comparable to the calculation of the FICO index discussed in Chapter 6. Once the score is attributed, loans are grouped into families, from the surest (AAA) to the most risky (BBB). In the case of mortgages, a specialized company (called a special-purpose vehicle) is set up to buy back credits and resell them as shares (this is called an ABS, asset-backed security). When a buyer acquires them, he must be paid an interest rate that is higher in proportion to the higher risk as measured by the scoring tools. With (industrial) loans, the step of creating an intermediary company is generally skipped: the transaction between the credit holder and the buyer, who covers the risks, includes an insurance component calculated on the basis of the scores. It is called a credit default swap, or CDS, which can be understood as a particular type of insurance contract.

However—and this is why the example is useful for my purposes—one of the crucial problems raised by these securities is evaluating the systemic risks they induce: that is, when companies or individuals default, producing a chain reaction of failure. After investigating the tools used by different agents, MacKenzie reached a conclusion that will not surprise the reader. As expected, there is no consensus on the tools used to make these evaluations. To simplify, MacKenzie suggests grouping the tools into two families that lead to radically different appreciations of the systemic risk. What is most surprising is that the two evaluation devices coexist and clash, sometimes in ferocious opposition, within a single organization. The same products are considered by some experts to carry inevitable crises, whereas according to others, they are relatively safe. This tension does not derive from the psychological orientation that one might think would influence the choice of tools, but simply from organizational traditions and different disciplinary backgrounds. What happens to an ABS or a CDS let loose in economic space? There is no single answer, and there is no chance there will be. Rooted in the choice of different qualculation devices, a controversy rages. In the midst of this controversy, all hope vanishes of establishing any control over these capricious products, which pit the most seasoned experts against one another. All of the elements for a chain reaction are present: the proliferation of innovative products feeds the proliferation of more and more sophisticated evaluation tools, which select and process information differently and which tend toward ever more disagreement. Regulators are paralyzed by the absence of agreement on risk evaluation. Potential systemic effects can develop unimpeded under the eyes of experts who are divided, condemned to appearing irresolute. As the reader will have understood, unless innovative products are forbidden, no regulation can directly ensure a unification of tools and hence make it possible to curb the financial chaos their diversity mechanically produces.[17] The situation is really not very different from the one that prevails on the tobacco market or the market for crop-protection products. Monsanto and Philip Morris International have long known that the best way to keep the field open for their products (and hence for their products' potentially devastating effects) is to divide the experts by encouraging the proliferation of evaluating tools that produce contradictory results. As seen in Chapter 2, products, whatever they are, come into the world more or less toxic. Without a consensus on evaluation tools, that battle for passiva(c)tion is indeed lost before it starts, and with it, the possibility of stabilizing sustainable market agencements. Financial markets, when they speak about junk products, do not escape these difficulties.

Frydman and Goldberg's study of self-perpetuating price movements and MacKenzie's analysis explaining how certain risk metrics encourage systemic effects highlight equipment's central role in the (dys)function of financial markets. This role can only grow as financial production intensifies under the boom in computation, big data, and algorithms, making this equipment even more complex. Under these conditions, efficiency is an increasingly impossible ideal to reach, since every new attempt to approach it actually contributes to moving further away from the stated objective.

Can we imagine other explanations that would preserve the possibility of approaching efficiency? Are there alternative approaches that provide counter-examples to the framework presented in this book?

Of course! Instead of pursuing the effects of accounting equipment and product innovation, as I have done, others have chosen to plumb the depths of the human mind. Those researchers prefer the obscure and as yet mysterious world of psychology and mental mechanisms to the open space of tools and equipment, which is relatively easy to explore, directly open to the investigator, and includes the agent as one of its constitutive elements. The stakes of such research are high, since it is a matter of identifying objects on which to intervene in the hopes of opening a pathway to efficiency.

Some economists have bravely ventured into the terrain of the mind. Either deliberately or through negligence, they ignore equipment and prostheses, plumbing hearts and minds in search of hidden variables that would explain observed behavior. One of these variables, indeed, the best known, makes it easy, too easy, perhaps, to explain the observed movements. Their answer is risk aversion, which is said to affect agents with varying intensity. Risks combine uncertainty with possible losses. When risks are high and aversion is strong, prices tend to collapse; on the contrary, prices shoot up when risks are limited and agents are willing to take them on. Other equally simple explanations can be imagined that are also linked to psychology. For instance, some have put forward the hypothesis that agents are extremely sensitive to the particular circumstances in which they make decisions. When I am on the highway at nightfall, I cross some drivers who have turned on their lights. The more their number grows, the more I convince myself to fol-low suit. It is easy to understand why as more drivers turn on their lights, the movement is amplified and accelerated, leading to a situation in which all lights are on.[18] The same goes on in financial markets. Above certain thresh-olds, mimesis becomes the rational behavior. Everyone becomes a short-termist, and prices spiral out of control. There is no need anymore to bring up instruments or equipment in order to account for collective behavior. It does not make a difference whether the human agent is the driver of a car with headlights on a dark highway, a passenger on the *Titanic* realizing suddenly there are fewer places in the lifeboats than passengers, or an assistant trader aghast as he watches prices dive on his screen. Only psychology matters. Mimesis reigns.

It is not easy to refute such interpretations founded on agents' psychol-ogy with recourse to hidden variables such as risk aversion or interpretations that postulate the existence of an irrepressible propensity, mimesis. Intrin-sically, they are neither more nor less plausible than explanations that high-light equipment and products. And yet a choice must be made between these interpretations, first because they are mutually incompatible, but also, and especially, because the choice of explanation determines what should be done in order to identify and make exist what will be considered a "good" market. Should one be satisfied with acting on agents' psychology by inciting them somehow to take the "rational" decisions that will lead to what is optimum? Or should one in fact take into account equipment and products and their effects in order to act on their formatting and to find acceptable solutions to the prob-lems they produce? Framing minds or practices: the question is a serious one. The fate of the concept of efficiency and hence the stakes and modalities of theorizing work depend on the way this question gets answered.

I do not think the choice is arbitrary. The history of science teaches us that the relative value of two explanatory systems cannot be reduced to their logical coherence or their capacity to explain or predict observable events. Once these two requirements have been satisfied, value depends on a system's capacity to bring to light new problems, reveal original questions, and open up avenues of research. The research strategy that involves continuously complicating psycho-logical models in order to account for what is observed makes me think of the gambit of those historical figures who wanted, at all costs, to save the theories to which they were (viscerally) attached through recourse to as many ad hoc hypotheses as necessary. Tycho Brahe, who wanted to account for observations that seemed to refute the Ptolemaic cosmology sanctioned by the Catholic Church, masterfully used this strategy: by adding epicycles to planet trajectories, he managed to reconcile empirical observations and official dogma, thus staving off the Copernican Revolution and Kepler's solution. Historians of science recognize that Tycho Brahe's construction was impeccable, give or take a few details, both logically *and* in its capacity to explain and predict. However, in the world of scientific research, what determines a theory's success once it is consistent with the data is its capacity to suggest fruitful developments, to take up new challenges. Tycho Brahe failed, despite the support of princes and the formidable power of his cutting-edge observatory. His system was judged to be too cumbersome, too closed in on itself, with no opening on new perspectives, forcing experts to rehash to same old arguments and to go around in circles, like the planets and the sun around the earth.

When it comes to the study of financial markets, history seems to be repeating itself. The efforts of those experts who defend the REH are laudable, their theoretical constructions are often admirable. But I cannot help but feel that they are the Tycho Brahes of economics, turned toward the discipline's past, rather than toward its future. By introducing as often as is necessary novel variables such as risk aversion or propensity to mimesis, one can (as with epicycles) easily account for what is observed because doing so makes it possible to account for (almost) anything. The intellectual price to pay is that one maintains the interface market as the conceptual basis and chooses to be blind to the increasing richness and effectiveness of market agencements. I consider this price much too high!

What can I say other than may the best position win! Rather than run the risk of losing myself in the depths of the human soul, without any hope of return, I prefer to pursue the investigation of the framings outlined in this book and the problems they raise, which theory must clearly cover if it hopes to be of any use. As studies of the financial markets have come out showing with ever-growing precision and detail the multitude of agents involved, as well as the diversity and complexity of their qualculating practices, choosing this strategy more generally seems to me all the more important. Despite their efforts to complicate the usual representations, Frydman and Goldberg fall short of reality. Anthropologist Horatio Ortiz and economic historian Sabine Montagne, who have interacted with the financial markets for many years, underline what a mistake it is to reduce the list of agents to the usual suspects.[19] For example, if one considers only the asset management sector, one has to include investment funds; insurance companies; brokers; analysts; companies such as Bloomberg that collect, sort, and transform data into widely distributed news; investment banks and a significant part of the banking system; scoring agencies, which often force companies to adopt certain behavior; but also small savers, more and more of whom come from the middle class; companies' financial services; sovereign wealth funds; high net worth individuals; and even foundations, whose funds are collected by financial companies. This list also includes all of the agents drawn from different sectors across the economy to whom the funds in question are allocated. These crowds, whose existence has long been ignored, do not come empty-handed. They are equipped with qualculation tools and equipment that cannot be reduced to any simple model. They design and offer products and evaluations of these products that do not fit into any single framework. They may be single individuals or, on the contrary, institutions committing their own funds and striving to maximize revenues on their capital. They may be patient groups, such as the French Association against Myopathy, throwing themselves into the industrial development of new treatments without the goal of increasing shareholder value.[20] I welcome these crowds, the problems they formulate, and the challenges they raise! I prefer them to the improbable beings, also more and more numerous, but less and less convincing, that some experts pull out of human brains the way magicians pull rabbits from empty hats. I would like us to cherish these crowds, to listen to them: if we are willing to lend an ear, they can tell us which worries should be taken into account, provided they are not separated from innovation strategies and equipment.

We could, we should, push further in considering each of the framings I have presented, following the qualification process of financial products (which are constantly being renewed, so intense is the innovation) or launching studies of agencies and their ever-evolving algorithmic and computer equipment, which in turn incessantly produces classification, ranking, and scoring systems. We should pay attention to the organization of encounters and matches (think of ways auctions are automatized or the ways personalized products are distributed), and we should take inventory of the attachment or addiction mechanisms that make some products indispensable to some agencies, such as the consumer loans discussed in Chapter 6. Finally, we should be doing ethnographies of price formulation, which, in the case of a certain number of products such as derivatives, takes the crystal-clear form of an abstract mathematical formula that is complex and reconfigurable. All of these studies would make it seem even more unrealistic for experts, hanging on to their ideal for the market, to avoid starting from the concerns and problems agents face; it would make it difficult for those experts to decide, without a tremor, to choose their models as sole sources of inspiration. It is not within anyone's power, least of all mine, to disqualify the notion of efficiency. It is unquestionably a fine moral notion; it is fascinating. Its practical usefulness, however, is doubtful. One can say of efficiency what Xenophanes of Colophon once said of truth: "No man has known it, nor will he know it; neither of the gods nor yet of all the things of which I speak. And even if by chance he were to utter the perfect truth, he would himself not know it; for all is but a woven web of guesses."[21] If efficiency exists, perhaps it can be reached only by chance, without anyone knowing it has been reached. One might as well say that it does not exist.

Giving up on efficiency and the outdated conception of theoretical work it supposes while turning to an attentive engineering of framings and the multiple concerns that need to be taken into account introduces a new way of conceiving of the relationship between commercial activities and politics. Theoretical work can provide a powerful contribution to the definition of a "good" market, on the condition that we turn away from universal abstract models contrived by experts in search of technical solutions. Theory should start with agencements, their equipment, the framings, and the overflows they provoke. Theory should be elaborated on the basis of the concerns generated by the agencements that are already in place. Their identification, their expression, and their inventory require collective work that goes beyond a narrow circle of experts.[22] This has to be done before one can begin elaborating solutions and designing new framings (phase 2 in Figure 1). On this renewed basis, how can theorization develop? I will try to provide some elements of an answer to this question by examining different economic responses to the challenges of climate change.

The industrial development of the last three centuries is responsible for the accumulation of greenhouse gases that have led to climate change and in the long run threaten the existence of entire populations. Controversial for several decades, this finding is now shared by all the experts in this area, even if some points of disagreement remain. It is generally recognized that markets greatly contributed to climate change for the simple reason that the cost of the damage produced by sending carbon dioxide into the atmosphere has not been taken into account until recently.[23] Neither companies, nor households, nor states were previously incited to control and limit these emissions. Global warming proceeded without any force hindering its momentum. Standard economic theory, as we know, has given a name to this sort of failure. It's called a "negative externality."

Let us return to Figure 1 and to the loop that, like a cross-fade, describes the passage from one configuration of market agencement to another. As far as climate change is concerned, which stage of the cycle are we in?

The process of addressing market failure is clearly further along on the issues of climate change than it is in financial markets. The market failures that are still being debated in the case of the financial industry and whose causes remain controversial are more clearly substantiated in the case of the economic activities that produce greenhouse gases. Numerical data, acceptable metrics, and credible models explain the effects and make it possible to anticipate future movements. The matter under discussion is no longer the analysis of existing markets and the mechanisms that explain their failures—this is no longer contested—but instead the analysis of the configuration necessary to foil these failures. In sum, the concerns (1 + 2) from the figure are there, and their expression, visibility, and legitimacy are largely givens. Since they are the natural point of departure for the work of theorization, the stakes of this work are very different from the work required in the case of financial markets. Whereas the latter are a privileged site through which to explore the relation between theorization and the expression of concerns, the fight against climate change is a textbook case for understanding how the work of theorization, when it takes the organization of commercial activities as its object, can contribute to the discovery and elaboration of solutions to concerns that are already expressed.[24]

Various worries and concerns over climate are certainly visible and audible, but there is no guarantee that they are compatible with one another. There are indeed many groups that are directly concerned with global climate change: first, the scientists and experts who chose it as an object of study and investigation and who have worked hard to have it recognized in public space; the public powers mobilized by these experts and by the international organizations that contributed to supporting and organizing their work; but also populations in danger, such as the inhabitants of islands under threat by rising ocean levels or fishermen affected by the variations in oceanic acidity.[25] One should also consider political parties, corporations, nonprofit organizations, countries whose interests are affected in one way or another by global warming—that is to say, the emission into the atmosphere of the carbon buried in the bowels of the earth. These concerns are manifested in different ways. Oil-based states or multinational companies intent on valorizing fossil fuels do not conceive the same fears and do not imagine the same actions as scientists who are deeply worried about the fate of future generations. To complicate things further, one should add the groups that are only indirectly concerned, but whose actions may have impacts on the release of carbon into the atmosphere. This includes, for example, companies engaged in the development of renewable energies, but also urban planners and architects who design and develop modes of transportation, those responsible for employment policies fighting unemployment, and so on.

The proliferation of concerns that are connected or that can be connected to the question of climate change produces a complicated and changing geopolitics. Under such conditions, how is one to decide which commercial devices to set up? Only by establishing a hierarchy of the concerns to be addressed and excluding those considered to be detrimental to the action one wishes to undertake. In the current situation, ongoing concerns tend to feed proposals that range between two extreme and conflicting options: either minimizing and eventually making greenhouse gas emissions disappear by leaving the carbon underground or, on the contrary, fighting for the right to continue emitting without any particular constraints. Making this choice supposes that procedures and devices exist that can be properly described as political whose objective would be to make acceptable selections among the protagonists. Absent these devices, I would prefer to put forward the (reassuring) hypothesis that a strong majority has voiced a preference for the first option and consider how one could imagine the (re)framings that would adequately respond to the requirements that follow from this choice.[26] I am simply suggesting that all we have to do to regain a margin of freedom is to change our compass and set aside the standing notion of an efficient market.

One can clearly enunciate the objective being imposed (rather than shared)—namely, to leave as much carbon as possible buried in the earth. However, it is in no way obvious how to respond. How can commercial activities contribute to the pursuit of this objective? In order to show the difficulties that await us and to highlight the dead ends to which we are led through reasoning and propositions that abstain from thinking in terms of market agencements, it is convenient to begin by following the work of economists who share our preoccupations, but forbear questioning the usual visions of the market.

In the face of impending catastrophe, in the face of an economy that produces as many bads as goods, it would be unseemly for economists to duck out—they, the very experts who repeated for ages that the market is the best possible solution, despite its failures. And they have not ducked out. No doubt, that is why many of them have been involved in political battles and have taken on the habits of social engineers in greater numbers than ever before. Through intellectual laziness or misguided persuasion, some economists continue to think that they are not there to imagine lukewarm compromises, that it is enough to want pure and perfect markets, that the best of all possible worlds can exist, and that it is their mission to make it exist! But these are only a weak minority. There are many who have converted to what one might call, inspired by the notion of realpolitik, a realistic economic policy: one that takes into account power balances and the irreversible effects produced by history and accepts that one has to work within those constraints. These economists are a precious resource. It is to these people, and only these people, that I devote the following discussion, since their attention to the world, such as it is, does not make them forget that their raison d'être is to help us imagine configurations that might satisfy the greatest number of people, ensure the common good, and insofar as possible, reduce waste. As they recognize, lucidity condemns one to understand that such an objective is largely unrealistic. But that is no reason, they will add, to lose sight of the normative aim that is embodied notably in the idea of markets. Let us go along with these economists for at least a little while, although to position the theorizing work of market agencements, I will have to abandon them along the way, rejecting the idea that the goal is to minimize the difference from an ideal model. To the contrary, it is my position that the most satisfying strategy to apply in order to frame the process of economization might be to start with the worst of all possible worlds and to set as the goal getting as far away from the worst as possible.

Economic theory has provided three devices to help face market failures and the climate change they induce. The state can decide to impose constricting regulations in an authoritative way, enacting norms that cannot be broken and setting thresholds for greenhouse gas emissions. The second device one can conceive of involves setting maximal quantities for a given industry or a given country: quotas are set for free or auctioned, and a market for emission permits, which set the price of carbon, is organized in such a way as to respect the set thresholds. The third way is through taxation: political powers can decide on the price or prices of carbon and make greenhouse gas emitters pay as a function of how much they emit. Policy makers can choose to impose norms, to intervene on quantities and then let prices establish themselves, or they can act directly on prices in such a way as to limit quantities.

All three solutions combine politics and economics in a different way. The first gives absolute priority to political action. It requires strong and legitimate governments, nation-states, or international organizations to impose behavior aimed at ensuring that the common good is achieved and that they are capable of doing so in an authoritative way against the coalitions of interests that oppose them. Economists tend to think this is the least good solution, because it inevitably leads to generalized waste. If the political solution is worse than the ill it claims to cure, what is left is homeopathy—treating the evil with evil, the deregulation of the economy with more economy, market failures with more markets—but it has to be a homeopathy that does not limit itself to infinitesimally weak dilutions. Politics is not absent from the second and third strategies. Whether it be for emission permits or taxes, it is clear that a legitimate power is required to define them, impose them, set them up, and monitor them. Nevertheless, these necessary interferences seem lighter than those required by pure and simple regulation, at least on paper. On paper, it is in fact impossible to decide which form of economization is the most efficient: markets for permits or for taxes. They are equally effective, say the economists, and produce the same effects in that they allow for "internalizing the externalities"—that is, making those who produce the damage pay for it.

The difficulties begin as soon as one leaves the white paper or the blackboard. One is then quickly faced with oil and chemical oligarchs who play with prices, lobbyists who fight to avoid taxes or to increase them, and sovereign states that refuse to have their industrial policy dictated by others. One also runs up against insoluble metrological problems; one hesitates as to the quantitative targets to set or the price levels to be determined. And to make things worse, one finds oneself thrown into an ongoing story from which it is almost impossible to escape: Kyoto opted for intervening on quantities and setting up emission permits that were soon contested; Europe, following Kyoto, went for the chaotic constitution of a market that still does not function well; the United States and China balked, talking out of both sides of their mouths; Scandinavian countries set up a tax system.

What to do? With the exception of a few fundamentalist libertarians who refuse all compromise ("the market, nothing but the market"), professional economists generally opt for some combination of the different solutions, evaluating the quality of the combination by appealing to efficient markets that define the best possible solution as their reference model. They call this "the first best." Since the first best is out of reach, however, realistic economic policy aims to identify a second best. Then, if that, too, seems unrealistic, a third best, and so on, until they reach some arrangement that takes all the constraints into account. Of course, the further one moves from the model, the less markets are efficient and effective. The economist assures us that the recommended configuration is nevertheless the closest possible to the first best.

The idea that one might have to give up on the first best option to be realistic is not new. As early as 1956, two articles were published introducing the notion of second best. One author was Marcel Boiteux, then the head of France's electrical utility, EDF, as well as a famous economist. He tackled the problem of electricity pricing by a public company with a total monopoly on production and distribution. This monopoly was the result of a political decision, which it was unthinkable to contest at the time. Mainstream economic theory indicates that in such a situation, the optimal allocation of resources (Pareto optimum, or first best) requires marginal-cost pricing, pricing of the last kilowatt-hour produced and distributed.[27] However, Boiteux explained that if EDF were to adopt that rule, it could not reach budget equilibrium and would set itself up for structural deficit. Indeed, given that increasing returns are characteristic of the production and distribution of electricity, the marginal cost is far below the mean cost. Therefore the pricing that economic theory prescribes would automatically lead to deficits. One way of absorbing those deficits would have been recourse to a levy, that is to say, a tax, a solution that is the best one possible, at least according to some economic theories. Boiteux, however, clearly sensed that public opinion would be against it. Having taxpayers finance a monopoly is not very popular. He opted instead for a pricing policy that allowed for the deficit to be eliminated by charging the most dependent customers more per kilowatt-hour. Those who could not conceive of reducing their consumption as prices rise (typically, certain industries) would be charged more. To the marginal-cost rule, a condition that could not be fulfilled, Boiteux added a rule of budgetary equilibrium. The proposed arrangement stays as close as possible to the first best (insofar as it implies only a small pricing adjustment for a limited category of consumers), but it is, of course, only a second best. To the first constraint, which might be described as sociological (not to resort to taxation in order to avoid alienating public opinion), he added a second, which was a matter of social justice and could be described as moral. Indeed, the second condition stipulates that the isolated farmer lost in the French countryside not be penalized and that he be charged the same as Parisians in chic neighborhoods, even if hooking that farmer up to the grid turns out to be very expensive. (See Chapter 6.) One slides, then, from second best to third best, and one could keep going, if necessary. Only the first step hurts! Boiteux invented a form of political engineering that makes it possible to conceive of more and more complex and heterogeneous market agencements. Such arrangements are devised to rationalize the use of production factors, ensure equal treatment, send signals of good management, and attest to the monopoly's independence.[28] These compromises move away from efficient markets while minimizing the fact that this is what they are doing.

A second publication from 1956, one by Richard Lipsey and Kelvin Lancaster, also considered the matters of choosing arrangements and the right distance from first best.[29] These authors imagined the theoretical conditions required for efficient markets were not fulfilled and then said that the second-best solution (necessarily less good that the first best, which is why it is called second best) cannot simply be obtained by ensuring the presence of all the other conditions the model prescribes. On the contrary, according to them, the second-best scenario may require that all the other conditions also be absent; the optimal arrangement (that is, the second best) may have only a distant resemblance to the efficient market (first best). It is a bit like a chef who has intended to bake an apple pie, only to discover that he has no apples. Customers would not be very happy that he offers a dessert that brings together all the ingredients of an apple pie, except the apples! In such an emergency situation, the best strategy is for the chef simply to apologize and serve the chocolate cake he makes so well, even if it is not quite as good as his apple pie. Chocolate cake is a second best. What Lipsey and Lancaster discovered is that one should learn to be satisfied with a chocolate cake one knows how to make, rather than hankering, at all costs, after an apple pie that cannot be made. However, and this is where economics turns out to be a little more complex than pastry, when you opt for second best, you have to be able to explain why you have chosen this configuration. In other words, you must find arguments that prove, one way or another, that you have not strayed too far from first best.

This approach, largely elaborated and led by economists, is generally followed in the case of the economization of carbon emissions. Since the world in which global warming is taking place has a history, and since that history cannot be rewritten; since the world is full of unequal agents who reason differently from one another, form opposite expectations, and attempt to have their choices prevail by imagining sophisticated strategies to paralyze their competitors or their customers; since future events are clouded in uncertainty, making prices volatile and unstable—in short, since the world is the way it is—arrangements must be imagined that take the world as it is into account as efficiently as possible. This brings us to the idea of a list of market configurations. Each configuration will be associated with elements and variables; as these are gradually taken into account, there will be justification for moving further and further from the optimum, since new constraints are continually being integrated.

Let us come back to carbon. Imagine the best of all possible configurations, the first best. The economists say it can be reached only if there is a global planner who has all the information and a complete arsenal of economic policy instruments. Thus armed and backed by flawless international agreements, the planner would be able to decentralize the demanding policies required in that situation by relying only on accurate price signals. However, at the beginning of the twenty-first century, no serious expert would dare claim that in a world devastated by wars and conflicts, it is possible to imagine a purely economic solution, whether it be a universal tax or a market for permits. States will never delegate their authority to a supranational authority. At best, the first best can only be a reference, useful, but out of reach. Therefore we have to fall back on an arrangement that may be imperfect, but satisfactory, and we must trace its contours, sort through the constraints, accepting some, avoiding others. Depending on how that line is drawn, one ends up with a number of different solutions that can be ranked as a function of their distance from the reference model.

The most optimistic economists think that one way of getting around the obstacle of national sovereignties would be to set up international institutions that can wield carrots and sticks and that could impose a unique universal price for carbon while avoiding all noncompelling voluntary commitments. This is a position that traces the contours of what might be a second best. It is held, however, by only a small minority. The large majority of economists have given up on moving beyond the constraints that the proponents of a second-best solution still consider negotiable. States will be there for a long time to come. That is why most economists resign themselves, with a heavy heart, to imagining a third best. Indeed, they have made a long list as they establish an inventory of the constraints that preclude mandatory voluntary commitments and a single carbon price. Some constraints can be described as sociological: the weight of public opinion; the diverging interests of sovereign states; the moves of pressure groups to obtain the exemptions they are sure to get; the regulations of international commerce; the existence of multiple *dispositifs* that are difficult to dismantle; the problem of determining quota levels and their allocation; grandfather clauses[30] and the aspirations of developing countries; the development of a reliable and credible way of measuring carbon. Other, more obtrusive economists are concerned with the obstacles any imaginable process of economization will run up against, which are related to the fact that even if the preceding constraints were lifted, it is impossible to coordinate agents' expectations and therefore impossible to incite them to leave carbon in the ground. So many radical uncertainties weigh on future events around global climate change and the cost of the ensuing damages, as well as around the state of resources and the strategic interactions between agents, that expectations, even regulated by financial markets or insurance markets, are doomed to produce instability and chaos. The boat that must be piloted to a safe harbor is heavily laden. It is not fitted out to be second best. Therefore, realistic economists, no longer believing in a pure form (taxes or markets), yet still guided by their concern for the best possible, advocate for arrangements that combine the different tools: regulation, taxes, and permit markets. Falling back on third best increases the distance from the model, despite the ever-present concern that we not to move too far away from the ideal.

A plethora of configurations are suggested as third best. To illustrate this, let us consider a stylized model involving four groups of actors with diverging interests: the monopoly of oil-producing countries; a planner speaking for the consumer countries that are considered virtuous (they want to avoid warming); nonvirtuous consumer countries that are only weakly committed to ecology and are focused on their own development; finally, public opinion (notably in the so-called virtuous countries) that looks suspiciously on transfers from the rich to the poor.[31] Imagine that in this world, which intends to be as close as possible to the real world, the virtuous countries decided to impose a tax on carbon ("tax" here is a generic term that can cover the additional price for emission permits as determined by a market). The predictable reaction of the producers' monopoly would be to compensate for falling demand by lowering the price of oil, which would incite greater consumption by nonvirtuous countries. Thus, at first, when the tax was instituted, the stock of carbon in the atmosphere would increase faster than it would have without such an intervention. This example illustrates how complex the chain reactions are likely to be. The inventory of these chain reactions leads to proposing arrangements that should combine a) a commitment, compulsory if possible, among virtuous countries to maximum emission thresholds; b) a commitment to set up a minimum level of internal carbon tax; c) an international market allowing for the exchange of national quotas between participating countries (on the Kyoto model); d) managing the unpredictable reactions of fossil fuel markets (rapidly imposing high prices for carbon and ensuring their rise in the medium term so as to discourage rapid extraction and the irreversible increase of the greenhouse gas stock);

e) redistribution of the carbon tax toward nonvirtuous countries to help them favor the right technologies; and f) a pedagogical effort to make public opinion understand the logic of this redistribution. There are also other elements important for the constitution of a carbon economy to be a successful case of economization: elaborating and implementing a good measuring system; rigorous surveillance devices in order to detect opportunistic behavior; the likely need to institute several carbon prices, depending on the industries involved; and national and international institutions whose mission is to set up these arrangements and ensure they function well and are sustainable.

This simple list, which applies only for this very simple and highly stylized model, gives a sense of the complexity of the arrangements that correspond to third best. The complexity is such that it makes it very difficult to demonstrate, even qualitatively or in an indicative manner, that the proposed solutions would not trample the efficiency criterion. The more economic theory adopts the realistic economic policy approach, the more difficult it becomes to verify its normative aim. By dint of compromises, one ends up with propositions for which there is no evidence that they might bring true solutions. My pessimistic conclusion explains why some rather discouraged economists settle for invoking a fourth best as a last resort. Giving up on any idea of central coordination—in other words, a common house or a common world that would impose their moral and political requirements—they opt for a concoction of local initiatives still inspired by the vague and distant concern for efficiency, and they bet that the confluence of little streams generated in this way will gradually lead to a strong current in the right direction. Thus, they opt for the multiplication of local carbon markets wherever possible, either regional, national, or sectorial; communication between these different markets; creation of short-term financial markets managed as much as possible to avoid runaway speculation; border taxes; taxes at the source; pressure on producing countries; local and solidarity-based economies; and so on. Anything goes. And they pretend to believe, to reassure themselves, that this accumulation of measures will in the end converge in such a way as to produce acceptable results. We don't have any apples, we don't have any chocolate...let's be satisfied with leftovers and make them sweet.

This last approach is clearly an attractive way to keep sight of the planet's fate, to show care for future generations, to be attentive to constraints and power relations without abandoning all hope of efficiency. It is also clear how hopeless it is. I do not mean to decry patching together a fourth best! Far from it. However, economization conceived of as a series of disclaimers makes this approach unconvincing and uninspiring. Yet from one global conference to another, governments and other players have ended up adopting this strategy, which inevitably leads in small steps toward a catastrophe we do not want to see, since we turn our backs on it, eyes riveted on an ideal world we are growing inexorably further from. The only remaining alternative is a choice between slow and gradual resignation, on the one hand, and a brutal and authoritarian global solution, on the other.

To escape this trap, I can see no other practical solution than to invert the direction of the process of economization. We should stop using a sole criterion—that of an optimum to be reached—to evaluate the actions to be undertaken, and we should certainly stop evaluating actions as a function of a unique value, whether it be called "efficiency," "a fight against waste," or "saving the planet and its inhabitants." I see no other solution than to turn things around 180 degrees, to position ourselves no longer in relation to an unreachable good, but rather in relation to evil or evils that concern us, trouble us, worry us. In other words, we should start with matters of concern; we should consider their diversity and establish by trial and error which are likely to mitigate emissions of greenhouses gases. Instead of choosing the best possible situation as an attractor when one knows it cannot be realized, we should choose to fight off the worst situations, which will come about, for sure, if we do nothing.

The general principle I am proposing gives a direction to the process of economization, but it does not determine any particular trajectory, mainly because the concerns linked directly to climate change are linked to other matters of concern that reinforce these matters of concern or on the contrary undermine them in the way elements of a network can oppose one another. Aggregations around common interests and coalitions are likely to take shape, adopting distinct causes, translating them into one another, and ensuring their convergence. Some, for instance, have long fought for energy transition, and not only because they were worried by climate change! There are countless forces in each particular time and place that could participate in forming alliances, even if climate change is not their main concern: those who design and produce solar panels or wind turbines; experts in home automation and insulation; automobile companies that promote electric vehicles; citizens fighting for more sober consumption; urban planners and architects who advocate for more compact cities and public transportation that guzzles less gas; political parties strategizing to keep their seats by fishing for ecological votes; citizens mobilized against the deterioration of their life conditions; financial experts in search of new products. This is where political strategy gets involved. If we, you and I, are worried about climate change, the only question to address to potential allies is the following: Does the cause you defend contribute or not to conserving fossil fuels?

It used to be said that the markets could build the common good from individual selfishness, provided a few well-thought-out regulations were put in place. The proposition should be reversed. In order to ward off the common evil that you and I believe genuinely threatens us, would it not be simplest to work to coordinate actions that may indeed be diffuse, that indeed pursue different goods, but that added together push back the catastrophe you and I fear? Such a coalition can succeed only if it shows itself to be capable of weakening and paralyzing at the same time the forces that pull in the opposite direction. According to these, the real catastrophe is not brought about by wars, migrations, or the massive pauperization of entire populations, but by the disappearance of industries linked to the exploitation of fossil fuels or the arming of petrostates. They assert that without growth, unemployment would be ubiquitous and with unemployment, greater threats than climate change would appear. They hope and believe that traditional markets will find a way to solve the problems in the end and impose the necessary adjustments. There is therefore no possibility of an alternative modality of economization without doing the difficult work of sorting that is necessary to figure out one's choice of allies and opponents.

In the process of economization I'm presenting, which works the other way around from the one that currently predominates, we can engage with every initiative that we can, whatever the motivations and aims, that contributes to leaving carbon underground and to minimizing atmospheric emissions. These initiatives may come in the form of devices that profile *homo economicus*, calculating their decisions on the basis of their own interests, but with appropriate evaluation and accounting instruments (fiscal incentives, indices linked to share portfolios that contribute to decarbonizing industrial activities, internalization of externalities) and with new objects (green obligations for renewable energies).[32] They may also be binding laws or regulations making certain behavior compulsory and punishing violations severely. Those who wish to go further should imagine devices that favor altruistic and solidarity-based behavior, the localization of economic behavior known as short-circuiting,[33] sober consumption, and moral reflection on the future of our planet. And let us not forget what a huge effort in research and development, experimentation and investigation, is required in order to bring out new resources, new processes, and new products. Furthermore, what would this alliance be if it did not tackle, head on at the same time, the questions of worldwide inequalities, poverty, and the wars that are tearing our planet apart? Consider countries such as Sweden, where, at the time of writing, a tax of 117 euros is levied on each ton of carbon dioxide emitted into the atmosphere, where the regressive redistribution effects of environmental taxes have been compensated for by appropriate fiscal reform (because by taxing everyone, one sometimes penalizes the poorest), where clean technologies are developed, and where the aim to "leave for the next generation a society in which the main environmental problems will have been solved" has been written into the constitution. Such countries show that political engineering of market agencements is viable. Others are following, such as some Canadian provinces, Chile, and perhaps China, which uses climate policy as a means of government. Nonetheless, from one country to another, the configurations of the agencements will differ, and there is no reason to believe that framings will eventually be homogenized.

The social sciences may contribute, at least partly and in different ways, to this theorization. For example, there is work to be done in order to identify the forces, spread out and disseminated, that are moving in the right direction—that is, moving away from the evils to be avoided—although often without realizing they are doing so. The conception of acceptable criteria to appreciate the results obtained is another potential area of contribution. Economic theory—that is, a reconfigured economic theory—could also offer a powerful contribution to this evaluation by identifying the unexpected effects, by participating in the conception of new accounting instruments, by redefining efficiency in such a way as to take into account the innovation processes without which the worst will remain certain.[34] This is why economic theory and the economy could reinvent themselves at the same time on the basis of what exists today if they started from the numerous mobilizations that concerted political action can make converge. With some tinkering, recombining, local experimentation, and partial coordinations, we could move away from the worst of configurations, what we might agree to call the nth worst, to go to $n\text{-}1$ worst, then the $n\text{-}2$ worst. At each step, the economization proceeds, building on a political and material infrastructure that ensures solidity and stability. The more we ascend a steep path to get away from the worst situations, the more we contribute to finding satisfying solutions. In the modern scenario, we face a descent into hell that we are trying to fight or delay. In my approach, we face an ascent as we discover the good by getting further away from the evil that we see and want to flee.

Over the course of this step-by-step progressive inquiry, with the dose of Machiavellianism it implies, new framings will take shape, allowing the cycle of political engineering to move forward. It is clear that the goods on offer will no longer be the same, since they will have internalized, in their very qualification, the concerns linked directly or indirectly to global warming. We will no longer consume the same thing or in the same way. It is clear that the qualculation tools, and notably the accounting tools, will have changed. For instance, depending on whether they are counted as assets or provisions, including emission quotas in company accounting will produce very different impacts on their results and hence on the orientation of industrial strategies. It is clear that the modes of organizing meetings between the different agencies involved will have profoundly evolved, including not only the classical institutions such as the UN, the IPCC (Intergovernmental Panel on Climate Change), or the stakeholder conferences, with their rules and adjustment mechanisms, but also sites of metrological normalization, where the instruments of measure for emissions and their effects will be negotiated; there are also different auction devices. It is clear that the forms of *affectio mercatus* and the attachment devices will have been profoundly transformed with the rise of local solidarity markets. Finally, to crown the lot, price formulation will have been disrupted, taxes or new prosthetic prices will be included, such as those attributed to carbon in the markets for emission rights. Starting from the concerns, from their shaping and expression, one inevitably ends up linking together problems that disciplinary work has contributed to separating. In this conversation, we are reconnecting the relationship between production and consumption.

The resulting agencements cannot be described a priori since the details will be found in the process of moving forward: market organization means permanently conflictual invention! Here, I want only to underline that what is at stake in theorization, in the negotiations and power plays it implies, is the reconfiguration of framings that will play out over multiple sites and mobilize numerous different agencies. The notion of agencement makes it possible to think and describe this diversity, to verify that the addition of these little forces can lead to a united movement in the intended direction. Everything could help. Those who want to participate in this program to reduce carbon release into the atmosphere should not neglect anything. *Faire l'économie du pire* in both senses of the French expression: to minimize the worst, but also to organize this avoidance as robustly and efficiently as possible. In this movement, politics, morality, and economics are not like tectonic plates that drift and collide, creating hot spots where they make contact, provoking earthquakes and eruptions that disappear before surfacing elsewhere. Rather, political expressions, commercial transactions, and moral concerns are everywhere in agencements: in each framing, in each strategy for alignment or articulation. Borders are constantly redrawn locally. And if the work of theorization is so important and necessary, it is because as in the war games of military training, it makes it possible to provide at any moment a representation of the state of existing forces, current movements, and emerging trends, in turn making it possible to answer the simple question at the heart of action: What next?

No successful instance of reasoned political engineering that is oriented explicitly and willfully toward aims that certain agencies cherish and seek to reach (in this case, limiting climate change) can avoid playing the game of contending with existing forces. Although such a strategy could sometimes succeed (everything depends on circumstances), it would be vain to seek a political or moral agreement first (the earth is in danger, it should be saved, and with it, future generations) and only afterward deduce the commercial configurations best suited to this agreement. Theorization requires humility. It requires refusing moral or political grandiloquence. To attract attention, increase public awareness, and organize possible convergences, it may be appropriate to say that the planet is in peril or that our shared home is on fire. The warnings are of little use, however, in the design of market agencements. "Good" configurations can be found only by climbing up the slope: they are found by trial and error, a bit by chance. They appear to us "almost unnoticed, like a mist seeping gently beneath a closed door,"[35] on condition that we never lose sight of the only goal that unites us—namely, pulling away from the worst, with the support of all the forces that can facilitate this movement if the proper agencements are found. We could speak, by antithesis, of taking a distance from the *pessimum*, rather than searching for the *optimum*! There is no single configuration because there is no agreement on concerns and their articulation. Let us resign ourselves to admitting that there *can* be no agreement.

HOW MARKET AGENCEMENTS COEXIST: THE CASE OF GENETICALLY MODIFIED CROPS

If we think carefully about the cycle of political engineering of market agencements, we will be led to abandon the regulative idea of efficiency. This also invites us to attend to concerns—that is to say, to the formulation of new objectives for agencements. These are our first insights into the relations between economics and politics in markets. Once objectives have been expressed and their multiplicity and divergences observed, the perspective I have put forward opens onto the following question: What are the practical provisions that must be imagined in order to design agencements and their articulation with moral and political action?

Practical provisions, however, are not enough to carry the day. Sometimes—rather often, in fact—the divergences are such, the concerns are so contradictory, that the work of theorizing, even if it seeks to be humble and modest, fails to conceive of agencements that could hold these opposing forces together and align alternative framings. In such situations, states often turn out to be the central actors that, in the name of what they define as the common good, take on the mission of finding and ensuring modes of lasting coexistence for the different agencies. For this, recourse to theory is useful—indeed, indispensable. When the objectives being defended are irreconcilable and the power relations are such that no one will compromise, the question becomes how the different market agencements in competition with one another can be made to cohabit durably. This is the situation I want now to present in outline, to show how the political engineering of market agencements leads to the task of theorizing novel ambitions and objects. The recent history of agriculture and agribusiness and the place of genetically modified crops (GMCs) provides a striking illustration.

At first, at least in certain European countries, there were serious health and environmental concerns when GMCs were introduced. How could one be sure that these plants, which escape what is considered natural regulation, would not provoke deleterious effects on human health in the long run or, more generally, would not threaten the equilibrium of ecosystems? Such were the worries and concerns that prevailed at first. They led several states to forbid the use of GMCs. However, beyond these classical problems, other questions and issues quickly appeared, problems of a quite different nature. Behind the decision regarding GMCs, some saw a more profound choice between two ways of organizing and practicing agriculture, two ways of structuring agribusiness. On the one hand, there is an agriculture that considers itself respectful of natural cycles and that, when it uses techniques of crossbreeding and selection, is content to organize natural processes by intensifying and orienting them. This agriculture is committed to valorizing farmers' autonomy and skills and to supporting their mastery over the way their agricultural holdings are managed. On the other hand, there is an agriculture that relies on the massive use of invasive technologies, aiming to modify plants' genomes artificially in order to obtain plant species that can withstand drought, pesticides, or herbicides or that can produce medical treatments or improve nutritional content, and so on. Here, the farmer's role is to implement techniques that are defined from the outside. These forms of agriculture and agribusiness are organized in order to respond to such radically different preoccupations that they appear to the protagonists to be mutually incompatible. The main reason for this incompatibility—there are, of course, others—is linked to diverging conceptions of how to orient and organize research. In the first case, research gives priority to outdoor experimentation in field research stations. Its main operating mode is crossbreeding selections in open surroundings. This research, which more and more often calls on sophisticated techniques and advanced knowledge, depends on a close collaboration between farmers and scientists. It requires a form of industrial property (in France, the Certificat d'Obtention Végétale, COV, the certificate of plant variety protection) that favors its type of innovation. It leads to food products that are qualified as natural and presented as respecting ecological equilibrium, and it stimulates establishing what are called short distribution channels. In the second case, most of the research is in laboratories, mostly private, some public, and is confined to scientists. It is characterized by the near total absence of farmers, whose role is essentially to make use of seeds and techniques that are defined without them. This research requires massive investments that are controlled by powerful multinational companies. It relies on an intense collaboration between companies and academic circles. It protects its results through a vigorous intellectual property policy that ensures a de facto monopoly for a handful of seed producers acting globally, such as Monsanto or Syngenta. In this configuration, farmers' skills are radically transformed, and the end consumers are supposed to be interested only in prices and the functional qualities of the goods, without a thought for natural equilibria, social responsibility, or the living conditions of farmers.

These two ways of organizing economic activities (let us call them MA1 and MA2)[36] are totally incompatible, or at least that is how the proponents of what can be summarily described as "natural agriculture" see things. Granted, this black-and-white depiction of the situation is simplistic. By seeking compromise, intermediary strategies are developed. For instance, searching for a form of industrial intellectual property that while protecting laboratory research and the recourse to expensive cutting-edge technologies also preserves farmers' autonomy and margins of maneuver, guaranteeing that consumers would be offered a choice. As techniques evolve to organize a transition from pure transgenesis toward forms of assisted genetic selection, the search for a middle road may become easier. For the moment, however, there is a fierce confrontation between two models that consider themselves all the more impossible to reconcile because recent judicial rulings have increased multinational companies' grip on seed production by extending patentability to plant species themselves. (See Chapter 2.) In Europe, where for historical reasons this clash is particularly violent, the idea has taken hold that the only possible solution is not to let market forces and technique arbitrate between these two fundamentally opposing worlds, but instead to organize their coexistence. It is no longer a matter, as in preceding examples, of designing and implementing agencements that take well-identified concerns into account, but of conceiving of a kind political engineering we might call "conservatory" that provides safeguards so as to ensure that both forms of agencements, with their specific policies, are sustainable. This is a way of refusing to arbitrate between them, at least for a while. It is as though in the case of global warming one compromised between two modalities of economy, one in which greenhouse gases were ousted, the other in which they were tolerated. The comparison is not irrelevant: those who decry genetic agriculture assert that genetic dissemination is inevitable and threatens the entire planet.

It is as though secularism had migrated from the religious sphere to the economic sphere. Coexistence has become a legal obligation, both in European law and in its national transcriptions. Article 2 of the French law on GMOs of June 25, 2008, stipulates that "genetically organized organisms cannot be cultivated, commercialized, or used except in ways that respect the environment and public health, agricultural structures, local ecosystems, and the commercial sectors 'without genetically modified organisms,' and this with full transparency." It adds that "freedom to consume and produce with or without genetically modified organisms without harming the integrity of the environment and the specificity of traditional quality cultures is guaranteed respecting the precautionary principle, principles of prevention, information, *participation* and *responsibility*, inscribed in the Environmental Charter of 2004 and respecting European provisions" (my emphasis).

The technical engineering of markets, as it exists today, cannot fulfill such a set of requirements. The markets, by construction and whatever regulations are imagined, can do nothing about the way science is organized other than indirectly and therefore in a superficial and limited way, beyond the very crude and unrealistic and therefore unrealizable principles of separation of open academic research and closed private technological research.[37] Furthermore, they are quite incapable of fulfilling the requirements for participation and consultation specified by the law or of making room for the protection and development of certain forms of traditional activities and the territorial structurings these activities require. Although it should not disappear from our radars altogether, the notion of efficiency is even more difficult to mobilize than in the case of financial markets or global warming. In any case, no regulation would be strong enough to contain such powerfully antagonistic forces. Thus, what is at stake is a way to conceive of agencements that through the framings they impose and the configurations they favor ensure that both forms of commercial activity continue to be viable.

Let there be a commercial configuration, MA1 or MA2. Under what conditions can it exist in a sustainable way or even grow without threatening the existence of other agencements that are considered to be equally legitimate and as having to be preserved at all costs? It is the task of theorization to answer that question. As in the previous cases (financial markets and climate change), in order to identify possible answers, the simplest strategy is to start from the (rare) available theories that have studied the mechanisms through which certain commercial configurations eliminate others. They center on a notion that we have already encountered: sociotechnical lock-in.

According to theories of sociotechnical lock-in, markets lock themselves into models of functioning that end up limiting the choices available to agents. Three factors explain this movement. The first depends directly on the balance of power and the political dealings that extend from it. Certain agents—I'm thinking of the electronuclear sector in France in the 1970s and 1980s—can disqualify and eliminate sufficiently effectively and for sufficiently long the options that go against their interests or preferences. The effects linked to the accumulation of skills, knowledge, and know-how increasingly supplement the direct actions of these coalitions. When an option has access to research and mobilizes the scientific and technical milieu more and more exclusively, it ends up with a relative advantage that gives it a strong position in economic competition: the technologies and skills in which there has been heavy investment rapidly become more efficient than those that have been deserted, even if the latter, with investments of the same magnitude, might have been comparable. Evolutionary economists sum up this mechanism in a striking way when they say that a technology does not necessarily take over because it is the best, but rather that it is the best because it has taken over. This advantage grows over time, notably if it is shored up with solid property rights. Finally, complementarities between techniques, skills, and activities establish themselves, further increasing irreversibility and lock-ins. For example, Monsanto, which is perfecting transgenic corn that is glyphosate resistant and which at the same time offers glyphosate (Roundup) to farmers to eradicate weeds, ends up becoming inescapable. All in all, a world takes shape that leaves little room and little chance for alternative worlds. Sociotechnical lock-ins nip any project for the coexistence of different market agencements in the bud.

The problem is to imagine mechanisms that might prevent such lock-ins. For instance, in the case we are concerned with, the conflict between MA1 and MA2, what type of market agencements would have to be designed in order to respond to the legal injunctions and ensure the durable coexistence of genetic agriculture and natural agriculture? One can sense that if nothing were done, the dominant dynamic described by theories of sociotechnical lock-ins would lead to the gradual exclusion of MA1, which would be reduced to niche activities, to MA2's benefit. The balance of power between the two agencements and the nearly total exclusion it would eventually lead to derive essentially from the capacity that the firms that chose to implement MA2 have to mobilize immense technological resources. MA2 would gain control of the market without encountering any resistance because it would, early on, have had scientific and technical power vastly superior to that on which MA1 could rely.

In the medium term, however, MA2's victory is not yet a foregone conclusion, insofar as in some countries, and notably in the EU, resistance has organized. The resistance is essentially political around certain states aiming to mitigate MA2's dominance. In countries such as France, Austria, Germany, and the UK, the relations between MA1 and MA2 in agriculture have been structured by a distribution of strongholds upstream and downstream of the industrial sector. The actors of MA1 have only very limited access to research and development, whereas those of MA2 (mostly non-French) can mobilize considerable scientific and technical resources and consequently master the upstream of this economic sector. This is the case, first because historically, some of the most powerful companies come from the chemical sector, where they already had scientific and technical firepower, but also because this situation of asymmetry has been reinforced over the years. However, the balance of power is shifting. Meanwhile, the agencies of MA1 have not been inactive. They have skillfully established their downstream domination, alternating between intimidation practices, legal action, and political lobbying, leading political deciders to forbid GMOs and persuading consumers to take part in the fight. The institutional lock-in, as it takes shape downstream, leans in favor of MA1. The confrontation between these two movements is resolved in a sort of Yalta between upstream and downstream. It is, however, a fragile Yalta. However strong they are, the (political and ethical) institutional lock-ins are not as efficient or durable as those anchored in knowledge and know-how and in the rules and social networks of industrial property rights.

The question is therefore how to get out of this fragile and paralyzing equilibrium toward a coexistence that, to be durable, must be established both in the sector of scientific and technological research and in the sector of production and commercialization. (How can what is downstream do without what's upstream, or vice versa?) The theoretical answer is obvious: MA1 must be given broad access to technological resources, notably by facilitating cooperation with public research in field experimentation, and the regime of intellectual property rights must be transformed in such a way as to bring it closer to the one the COV inaugurated. Then, and symmetrically, MA2 must be given access to farmers' fields, but in such a way that the territorial distribution between different types of agriculture is strictly organized and controlled, notably by implementing devices for consultation, (environmental and health) monitoring and tracking, and ensuring larger-scale geographical segmentation, which favors reasoned mingling of different crop types.

This kind of political engineering is demanding. It must first imagine the appropriate framings for each of the MAs and then ensure their articulation. This requires numerous inventions. I will not give an inventory, but just mention a few as an illustration: qualculation instruments, which, in order to ensure the continuous integration of the produced data, must be coupled to the devices that measure and monitor potential externalities; the organization of commercial meetings that favor short circuits and lead to an attachment to a natural agriculture dynamic, but that also allow interested farmers to understand the specific qualities of transgenic seeds and to work to showcase their commercial value; price formulations that integrate what certain economists have called "preservation of identity costs," both farmers' identities and plants' identities, formulations that further take into account the costs of prevention, monitoring, and acquiring the knowledge necessary to improve control over contaminations, but also the cost of coordinating the different agents (linked to the way participatory decision devices work), as well as the costs of compensating for losses when contaminations do occur. To all of this, one should add the balanced management of public research activity and cooperation with private agencies.[38] Altogether, such political engineering, which remains largely to be invented, breaks with the usual models for commercial activity and market functioning. It is the only possible viable strategy if we are to respond to the set of requirements set out in Article 2 of the 2008 law and to make the qualification of goods (which goods, for whom, and at what prices?) one of the key issues for organizing economic activities. The notion of market agencement can nourish this brainstorming, whose goal is to establish compromises between aims that are equally respectable and legitimate. The notion of market agencements can help, first because it considers all the activities, from upstream to downstream, that contribute to establishing commercial transactions and also because it draws attention to the different framings and their materiality.

It goes without saying that this goal, whose legal status has been noted, is not shared by everyone. There is nothing exceptional about such an absence of consensus regarding the requirements that market agencements policy should fulfill. In this case, there is significant opposition to the idea that coexistence is a good thing. A very influential minority considers that once GMOs are planted, it will be impossible to avoid contaminations and the dissemination of transgenetic crops and thus impossible to stop their progression. Putting it aside for a subsequent book, I will not go into that debate here. Whatever the case, and whatever the conclusion, theoretical work cannot escape the difficult matter of how to establish the durable and viable coexistence of different agencements that are considered to be mutually incompatible. Not only does this work provide a chance to show and to prove that it is possible to impose binding political objectives on market agencements; it opens a radically new perspective. If it focuses on agencements and their framing devices, an adequate and finely calibrated organization of market activities contributes to making commitments and orientations effective in ways that mere regulatory measures never could.

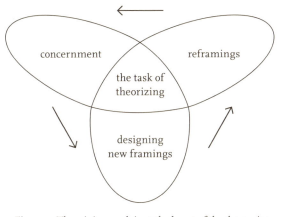

Figure 2: Theorizing work is at the heart of the dynamics and the politics of market agencements.

The only aim of this final chapter was to underline the central role of theorizing work once certain political or moral demands have been formulated. Contrary to what Figure 1 may have suggested, theorizing is neither a unique moment nor a time-bound activity in a sequential process—theorization is at the heart of the dynamics of the arrangements. (See Figure 2.) As we saw in the case of financial markets, it should be driven by the concerns that existing agencements raise. As the analysis of the contributions of market activities to the politics of fighting global warming suggested, theorizing must also help to conceive of framings that provide answers to the questions on the table, taking the existing power relations into account and imagining acceptable compromises among the multitude of concerns and proposals. Finally, theorization must venture to undertake the difficult task of proposing new framings and accept the challenges of implementing these. Even where, in extreme cases, no common solution is to be found, this may require inventing modalities for the coexistence of competing solutions and agencements. Agriculture is a case in point.

"The idea of another society has become almost impossible to think and indeed no one today has even the sketch of a new concept. We are condemned to live in the world we live in."[39] These are not the words of Margaret Thatcher, who memorably once asserted "There is no alternative!" These are the words of François Furet, the expert on revolutions. If Furet is partly correct, it is because he is talking about society. As Alain Touraine said forty years ago, society doesn't exist anymore, and so it is pointless to try to change it. But between the first and the second of Furet's sentences, there is a slippage that surreptitiously ruins his argument while opening up new perspectives. We live in a world of qualculative agencies and goods that constantly change and proliferate, that of agencements, whether they be market, political, or moral. No description can peg that world and reduce it to what we call society.[40] When we have barely caught a glimpse of it, it has already changed. And the possibility of interfering and acting on the trajectory lies in the multitude of small changes that feed this dynamic, of which I have tried to give a preliminary inventory, limited, granted, to market activities. Other worlds are possible, but they must be composed from elements and resources that lie far beyond those generally associated with the term "social." The aim of this book, which is reaching its end, is precisely to offer a more complete picture of market activities, one that accounts for their organization and functioning and that provides footholds for orienting their dynamics and development.

Notes

PREFACE TO THE ENGLISH EDITION

1. Karl Polanyi, *The Great Transformation: The Political and Economic Origins of Our Time* (Boston: Beacon Press, 1957), p. 252.

2. Ibid., p. 255.

3. Katharina Pistor, *The Code of Capital: How the Law Creates Wealth and Inequality* (Princeton: Princeton University Press, 2019).

INTRODUCTION: THE ENIGMA OF THE MARKET

1. My description of London "market pitchers" is based on the one given by Trevor Pinch: Trevor Pinch, "Performativity and Economic Demonstrations: Pitching Quality and Quantity," in Yannick Barthe, Madeleine Akrich, Fabian Muniesa, and Phillipe Mustar, eds., *Débordements: Mélanges offerts à Michel Callon* (Paris: Presses des Mines, 2010). For the account that follows, see pp. 372–76. As Pinch describes them, they are "a special form of seller found on many markets in the UK (and some places in Europe) who sell goods by an elaborate verbal spiel, accompanied by humor, antics and demonstrations. They are specialists in attracting a crowd of ordinary shoppers to their stall; they are not interested in single sales but want to make many sales of the same goods at the appropriate moment in their routines." For more on street vendors and hucksters, see Roman Le Velly, "Les démonstrateurs de foire: Des professionnels de l'interaction symbolique," *Ethnologie française* 37.1 (2007), pp. 143–51.

2. *Translator's note*: The French term *dispositif* is a crucial term for Callon. In different contexts, it might be translated as "arrangement," "setup," "apparatus," or "mechanism." However, in order to mark the fact that this is a quasi-technical term, it has been most consistently translated as "device." Indeed, as the argument throughout the book makes clear, this word choice is also a methodological choice, following Foucault. For

further explanation on the author's position regarding Foucault's use of *dispositif*, see Chapter 7.

3. The following is based on the descriptions and analyses proposed by Natasha Schüll in a book that opens up important original perspectives on the mechanisms of consumption and addiction: Natasha Schüll, *Addiction by Design: Machine Gambling in Las Vegas* (Princeton: Princeton University Press, 2012). I hope I have not betrayed the author's central argument, even though I have taken the liberty of adding fictional dialogues or personal comments and interpretations in some places.

4. *Translator's note: Agencement* might be translated as "arrangement" or "layout." It can refer to the way elements are laid out in space or the way they combine to create an effective whole. In order to preserve the insistence on the agency arrangements, the choice was made to import the term into English. The author fully elaborates its meaning in Chapter 7.

CHAPTER ONE: FROM INTERFACE MARKETS TO MARKET AGENCEMENTS

1. Committee on Oversight and Government Reform, Committee Hearings of the US House of Representatives, *The Financial Crisis and the Role of Federal Regulators*, 2008, https://www.gpo.gov/fdsys/pkg/CHRG-110hhrg55764/html/CHRG-110hhrg55764.htm.

2. Ibid.

3. Although some will find it excessive, there may be a grain of truth in Douglass North's famous claim: "It is a peculiar fact that the literature of economics and economic history contains so little discussion of the central institution that underlies neoclassical economics—the market." Douglass C. North, "Markets and Other Allocation Systems in History: The Challenge of Karl Polanyi," *Journal of European Economic History* 6 (1977), p. 710. This assessment can be equally applied to other schools of thought.

4. *Editor's note:* The author fully elaborates the meaning of the term "agencement" in Chapter 7. For a quick definition, see the translator's note 4 of the Introduction above.

5. Critique of the market economy frequently relies on the existence of other forms of organization of economic life and on the hypothesis that they are mutually exclusive. For instance, following Karl Polanyi and the anthropological work he inspired, one can invoke organizations that favor reciprocity (accounting for others, their expectations, and their needs) and that develop complementary and interdependent relations between the members of a collective; those that privilege domestic autarchy, with relationships of mutual assistance and sharing; or those characterized by a central authority such as a state, which dictates rules and norms imposed on all and regulates the

production and circulation of goods, as well as the redistribution of wealth. For a presentation of all these alternative forms and their possible (in)compatibility, see Jean-Michel Servet, "Le principe de réciprocité chez Karl Polanyi: Contribution à une définition de l'économie solidaire," *Revue Tiers Monde* 2 (2007), pp. 255-73.

6. For a compelling presentation of this argument, see Katharina Pistor, *The Code of Capital: How the Law Creates Wealth and Inequality* (Princeton: Princeton University Press, 2019). "Capitalism, it turns out, is more than just the exchange of goods in a market economy; it is a market economy in which some assets are placed on legal steroids" (p. 11).

7. Colette Depeyre and Hervé Dumez, "What Is a Market? A Wittgensteinian Exercise," *European Management Review* 5.4 (2010), pp. 225-31. According to Ludwig Wittgenstein, to capture the signification of a word, one must inquire into its usages.

8. Roger Guesnerie, *L'économie de marché* (Paris: Flammarion, 1996).

9. Clifford Geertz, "The Bazaar Economy," *American Economic Review* 8.2 (1978), pp. 28-32.

10. Michèle de La Pradelle, *Market Day in Provence* (Chicago: University of Chicago Press, 2006).

11. Mitchel Abolafia, *Making Markets: Opportunism and Restraint on Wall Street* (Cambridge, MA: Harvard University Press, 2001); Caitlin Zaloom, *Out of the Pits: Traders and Technology from Chicago to London* (Chicago: University of Chicago Press, 2006); Jean-Pierre Hassoun, "Trois interactions hétérodoxes sur les marchés à la criée du Matif: Rationalité locale et rationalité globale," *Politix* 13.52 (2000), pp. 99-119. The Matif is the French international financial futures market, which opened in 1986 and was absorbed in the merger of the Paris Bourse with Euronext NV to form Euronext Paris.

12. It is banal to say that the aim of a model is not to render reality, but to help the observer perceive its central features and to give means to act on it. The question is obviously to know how to identify and justify the variables or the characteristics deemed to be essential.

13. Guesnerie, *L'économie de marché*, p. 10.

14. Mark Granovetter, "Economic Action and Social Structure: The Problem of Embeddedness," *American Journal of Sociology* 91.3 (1985), pp. 481-510.

15. Some will appear in subsequent chapters.

16. The term "group" used by Allais is probably not the best choice. Maurice Allais, *Cours d'économie générale*, vol. 1 (Paris: École nationale supérieure des Mines, 1959), p. 71. It would no doubt be better to speak of *populations* of buyers and sellers.

17. In the following, the word "goods" refers to both material goods and services. (See Chapter 2.)

18. Jean-Charles Rochet and Jean Tirole, "Platform Competition in Two-Sided Markets," *Journal of the European Economic Association* 1.4 (2003), pp. 990–1029.

19. Datafication implies that *something* is made into data. Contrary to what the Latin etymology suggests, data are not given. As the social study of science has shown, they are the result of a process that is implied by the term data*fication*. It is worth noting that by focusing exclusively on how human beings are represented in big data, social scientists are missing the point of what data-driven systems do in markets. Big data is not about quantifying human life. See Martha Poon, "Corporate Capitalism and the Growing Power of Big Data: Review Essay," *Science, Technology and Human Values* 41.6 (2016), pp. 1088–1108.

20. Paul McNulty, "A Note on the History of Perfect Competition," *Journal of Political Economy* 75.4 (1967), p. 396.

21. Antoine-Augustin Cournot, *Recherche sur les principes mathématiques de la théorie des richesses* (Paris: Hachette, 1838), p. 55.

22. I could give many more references. "A market may be said to exist wherever there is competition, even if only unilateral, for opportunities of exchange among a plurality of potential parties." Max Weber, *Economy and Society: An Outline of Interpretive Sociology*, ed. Guenther Roth and Claus Wittich, trans. Ephraim Fischoff et al., 2 vols. (Berkeley: University of California Press, 1978), vol. 1, p. 635.

23. Allais, *Cours d'économie générale*, p. 71.

24. Integration is called vertical when the different stages of production and distribution of a certain type of good are grouped together under a single authority; integration is said to be horizontal when a company takes control of its competitors. In both cases, the intensity of competition diminishes for lack of combatants. Competition becomes imperfect.

25. It could just as well be called "imperfect monopoly."

26. Social networks existed well before the internet. In sociology, the notion designates groups of people between whom relations are established (kinship, friendship, or relations of communication, exchange, and so on). The structure of the networks, that is to say their morphology, explains certain behavior.

27. Among the many studies that develop these different approaches, references in economic sociology include Harrison White, *Markets from Networks: Socioeconomic Models of Production* (Princeton: Princeton University Press, 2001); Pierre Bourdieu,

The Social Structures of the Economy, trans. Chris Turner (Cambridge: Polity, 2005); Neil Fligstein, *The Architecture of Markets: An Economic Sociology of Twenty-First-Century Capitalist Societies* (Princeton: Princeton University Press, 2001); Robert Salais and Michael Storper, *Worlds of Production: The Action Frameworks of the Economy* (Cambridge, MA: Harvard University Press, 1997); Lucien Karpik, *Valuing the Unique: The Economics of Singularities* (Princeton: Princeton University Press, 2010).

28. See journals such as *Research Policy* or the *Journal of Evolutionary Economics* for interesting attempts to combine the neoclassical perspective (roughly characterized by the preeminence given to agents and their decisions) and the purely evolutionary perspective (which privileges the dynamics of products, skills, and techniques). Having been an editor of *Research Policy* for twenty years, I know that the evolutionary theory does not enjoy great prestige in the community of economists, who generally criticize it for not providing a robust analysis of agents' behavior. This (real) weakness is compensated for, however, by the rich analyses it devotes to goods and products and more specifically to their technological content and to their evolution.

29. Benjamin Coriat and Olivier Weinstein, "La construction sociale des marchés," *La Lettre de la regulation* 53 (September 2005), pp. 1–5. My emphasis.

30. This is the minimal definition given by economics textbooks: "The market is a notion used in economic theory to designate an institution through which buyers and sellers interact and engage in exchange." Karl Case, Ray Fair, and Sharon Oster, *Principles of Economics* (Cambridge: Pearson, 2009), p. 71. For a more elaborated analysis, see, for example, Douglass C. North, *Institutions, Institutional Change and Economic Performance* (Cambridge: Cambridge University Press, 1990). For an overview of the sociological approach, see Frank Dobbin, *The New Economic Sociology: A Reader* (Princeton: Princeton University Press, 2004).

31. For a synthesis, see Bruce G. Carruthers and Laura Ariovich, *Money and Credit: A Sociological Approach* (Cambridge: Polity, 2010).

32. Bill Maurer, "The Anthropology of Money," *Annual Review of Anthropology* 35 (2006), pp. 15–36. See also David Graeber, *Debt: The First 5,000 Years* (New York: Melville House, 2011), and Bill Maurer, "David Graeber's Wunderkammer, *Debt: The First 5,000 Years*," *Anthropological Forum* 23.1 (2013), pp. 79–93. One should equally note that barter has not disappeared in modern and contemporary economies and can coexist or interact with commercial activities and with the most sophisticated of monetary payments. Furthermore, where barter existed on a large scale, as in various African regions before colonization, the introduction of money did not oust it.

33. Adam Smith forcefully expresses the hypothesis of the founding nature of exchange: "The division of labour...is the necessary, though very slow and gradual consequence of a certain propensity in human nature...the propensity to truck, barter, and exchange one thing for another.... In a tribe of hunters or shepherds a particular person makes bows and arrows, for example, with more readiness and dexterity than any other. He frequently exchanges them for cattle or for venison with his companions; and he finds at last that he can in this manner get more cattle and venison, than if he himself went to the fields to catch them." Adam Smith, *The Wealth of Nations* (New York: Bantam Dell, 2003), pp. 22-24. Following Smith, the market has been improperly considered as a form of organization that sets up the meeting between several individuals who intend to exchange. As previously said, this conception is no longer accepted. What consumer would think that he or she would "exchange" a sum of money for a packet of washing powder? To speak of payment in view of acquiring a product conforms more closely to reality; moreover, it does not exclude that in certain circumstances, this payment be interpreted as a form of exchange. By dissociating exchange and commercial transaction, one avoids the thorny problem of the difference between market and non-market exchanges. On this point, see the illuminating comments of Ronan Le Velly, "Qu'est-ce qu'un échange marchand?: Proposition de trois définitions cumulatives pour l'analyse," in John Tolan, ed., *L'échange* (Paris: L'Harmattan, 2009), pp. 201-21. Jane Guyer reaches the same conclusion. After exploring all sorts of markets in Africa and in the West, she suggests considering that "the logic of models based on exchange no longer captures the complex that makes payments possible." Jane Guyer, *Legacies, Logics, Logistics: Essays in the Anthropology of the Platform Economy* (Chicago: University of Chicago Press, 2016), p. 113. These arrangements and the financial ingenuity they imply (as for instance when I buy a car through a leasing agreement) make the notion of exchange inappropriate, or in any case, inadequate. On the importance of the notion of payment, see Bill Maurer, "Payments: Form and Function of Value Transfer in Contemporary Societies," *Cambridge Journal of Anthropology* 30.2 (2012), p. 19. That payment is not exchange is an essential observation. In the text previously cited, Coriat and Weinstein underline, quite rightly, that an analysis of markets that takes monetary phenomena (and notably the fact that money is also a merchandise whose price is indexed on its capacity to make credit possible) into account must perforce be very different from an analysis that reduces money to its instrumental role. On this point, see Chapter 2.

34. Guesnerie, *L'économie de marché*, p. 22.

35. It seems we owe the definition of a commercial transaction as the legal trans-

fer of property to John Roger Commons. According to him, the transfer concerns not goods, but property rights. John R. Commons, *Institutional Economics* (Madison: University of Wisconsin Press, 1934).

36. There are numerous different descriptions of the institutional arrangements of markets. What one can call "institutionalist" theories, for instance, provide long lists of rules that make it possible to grasp both what is common and what is variable in commercial institutions. Other theories (for example, those developed by the Austrian school around authors such as Friedrich Hayek) stick to what they consider essential: they consider that the market and its organization naturally derive from the initiatives of a multitude of isolated and autonomous agents engaged in competition that ensures the emergence and success of configurations and norms that turn out to be the most efficient and the most robust. For an elaboration of these conceptions, see Philip Mirowski, *Never Let a Serious Crisis Go to Waste: How Neoliberalism Survived the Financial Meltdown* (London: Verso, 2013). Those who consider that firm and commercial activities can be likened to a nexus of contracts develop a similar point of view. As they see it, the market does not exist a priori; as for Hayek, it is an always temporary and disputed achievement that depends on the state of the balance of power between (naturally calculating) agents and on the negotiations they enter to reach agreements and contractualized compromises. See, for example, for a recent update, Éric Brousseau and Jean-Michel Glachant. *The Economics of Contracts: Theories and Applications* (Cambridge: Cambridge University Press, 2002).

37. Harrison White, "Where Do Markets Come From?," *American Journal of Sociology* 87 (1981), pp. 517–47. As Philippe Steiner quite rightly underlines, White actually makes a distinction between two models, that of the arena and that of producer markets, which are in fact two variants of interface markets: in both, goods are considered as platform goods. Philippe Steiner, "Le marché selon la sociologie économique," *Revue européenne des sciences sociales* 43.132 (2005), pp. 31–64.

38. Viviana Zelizer, "Fine Tuning the Zelizer View," *Economy and Society* 29.3 (2000), pp. 383–89.

39. Among other things, the rules define and oversee the modalities of competition, the modalities for attribution and transfer of property rights, the organization of money, the terms and conditions under which contracts may be concluded, the definitions of the prerogatives of buyers and sellers, and more.

40. Trevor Pinch and Richard Swedberg, eds., *Living in a Material World: Economic Sociology Meets Science and Technology Studies* (Cambridge, MA: MIT Press, 2008).

41. I borrow this suggestive formulation from Luc Boltanski, *On Critique: A Sociology of Emancipation* (Cambridge: Polity, 2011), p. 75.

42. Quoted in Richard Swedberg. *Max Weber and the Idea of Economic Sociology* (Princeton: Princeton University Press, 2000), p. 120.

43. The expression refers to a group of multidisciplinary works that study the relations between science, technology, and societies.

44. Donald MacKenzie, *Material Markets: How Economic Agents Are Constructed* (Oxford: Oxford University Press, 2009); Donald MacKenzie and Jean-Pierre Pardo-Guerra, "Insurgent Capitalism: Island, Bricolage and the Re-Making of Finance," *Economy and Society* 43 (2014), p. 156.

45. See Chapter 7. I borrow the term "legal coding" from Pistor, *The Code of Capital*.

46. When I say *this* good, I refer to the particular good that is the object of the transaction. This remark is very important in relation to mass markets. The Volkswagen Golf I buy is different in some aspect from those bought by customers before or after me, even if it is the same model. Each transaction is irreducibly singular. This point, broached from various angles in the different chapters of this book, will ultimately be clarified with the generalization of the concept of discriminating monopoly, in Chapter 6, the chapter devoted to the establishment of prices.

47. Joseph Schumpeter, *History of Economic Analysis*, rev. ed. (Oxford: Oxford University Press, 1996), p. 1151.

48. Chamberlin had it right when he spoke of monopolistic competition, and not of imperfect competition. The most correct expression would no doubt be "competitive monopoly" (in fact, he uses the term "competing monopolies"), making monopoly the configuration that can serve as a benchmark to reveal the mechanisms of competition. See Edward H. Chamberlin, "The Product as an Economic Variable," *Quarterly Journal of Economics* 67.1 (1953), pp. 1–29.

49. The list of the means through which a monopoly situation can be obtained is almost infinite and is constantly being revised: industrial and commercial secrets, regulation, industrial property, political lobbying, brands, control over commercial circuits and sites, research-and-development capacities, siphoning of skills, and so on. At this stage of the analysis, the nature of the means mobilized does not matter.

50. The question of the effects of competition on firms' innovation strategies has led to numerous conjectures and empirical analyses, but no clear conclusions have emerged. The terms of the question shift when one adopts the framework of market agencements.

51. My definition of innovation has nothing to do with those usually used, from

Joseph Schumpeter to Clayton Christensen. Clayton M. Christensen, *The Innovator's Dilemma* (Cambridge, MA: Harvard Business School Press, 1997). For me, innovation refers to the simple addition of a new bilateral transaction. One of the best syntheses of the vast literature on different types of innovation is, in my opinion, the one William Abernathy and Kim Clark put forward some time ago: William Abernathy and Kim Clark, "Innovation: Mapping the Winds of Creative Destruction," *Research Policy* 14.1 (1985), pp. 3–22. Although they don't use the term, the authors show that a product can be made singular in a thousand different ways (technical characteristics, production or commercialization methods, sale location, price, and so on).

52. Indeed, such cases are referred to as "ruinous competition."

53. Pascal Le Masson, Benoît Weil, and Armand Hatchuel, *Strategic Management of Innovation and Design* (Cambridge: Cambridge University Press, 2010).

54. See note 52 above.

55. AMAPs are the French equivalent of the community supported agriculture (CSA) movement in North America.

56. Claire Lamine and Juliette Rouchier, "D'une charte l'autre: Le processus de révision de la charte des AMAP comme indicateur d'une institution qui se renforce," *Revue de la régulation* 20 (2016), http://journals.openedition.org/regulation/11966.

57. Etymology confirms this interpretation: *pro-ducere* is to lead forward. Marx concurs when he asserts that "the product only gets its 'last finish' in their consumption.... A railway on which no trains run, hence which is not used up, not consumed, is a railway only δυνάμει [potentially], and not in reality." Karl Marx, *Grundrisse: Foundations of the Critique of Political Economy*, trans. Martin Nicolaus (1857; New York: Penguin, 1993), p. 91. One could translate this affirmation into the language of market agencements thus: "Consumption does not interrupt the qualification process of the product; it extends it by contributing to it."

58. Chamberlin, "The Product as an Economic Variable." There does not necessarily have to be a general agreement as to the qualities of a good for a market to exist. If all goes well, the market agencement will allow the profiles of buyer, seller, and product to be adjusted simultaneously through its functioning.

59. For a formal presentation of these two types of network, see Michel Callon, "Can Methods for Analysing Large Numbers Organize a Productive Dialogue with the Actors They Study?," *European Management Review* 3.1 (2006), pp. 7–16, and Michel Callon, "From Science as an Economic Activity to Socioeconomics of Scientific Research: The Dynamics of Emergent and Consolidated Techno-Economic Networks, in Philip

Mirowski and Esther-Mirjam Sent, eds., *Science Bought and Sold: Essays in the Economics of Science* (Chicago: University of Chicago Press, 2002), pp. 277-317.

60. The literature already contains hundreds of references to studies that argue for this requalification. Let me point to the ones that examine communities of experts engaged in activities linked to the conception of goods: Ash Amin and Patrick Cohendet, *Architectures of Knowledge: Firms, Capabilities and Communities* (Oxford: Oxford University Press, 2004); Ash Amin and Joanne Roberts, eds., *Community, Economic Creativity and Organization* (Oxford: Oxford University Press, 2008). On the democratization of innovation, Eric von Hippel, *Democratizing Innovation* (Cambridge, MA: MIT Press, 2004). On open innovations, Henry William Chesbrough, *Open Innovation: The New Imperative for Creating and Profiting from Technology* (Boston: Harvard Business School Press, 2003). The sociology of innovation deserves a special mention: see especially Le Masson, Weil, and Hatchuel, *Strategic Management of Innovation and Design.* Also a special mention for evolutionary economics: Pierre-Benoît Joly, Arie Rip, and Michel Callon, "Reinventing Innovation," in Maarten J. Arentsen, Wouter Van Rossum, and Albert E. Steenge, eds., *Governance of Innovation: Firms, Clusters and Institutions in a Changing Setting* (Camberley: Edward Elgar, 2010), pp. 19-32. It is worth noting that work in economics increasingly integrates early phases into the market, especially the phase where ideas are created. See Patrick Cohendet, Jean-François Harvey, and Laurent Simon, "Managing Creativity in the Firm: The Fuzzy Front End of Innovation and Dynamic Capabilities," in Thierry Burger-Helmchen, ed., *The Economics of Creativity: Ideas, Firms and Markets* (London: Routledge, 2013), pp. 131-50.

61. Max Weber uses the word *Vergesellschaftung*, translated in English as "consociation" and in French by "sociation." See Weber, *Economy and Society.*

62. Smith, *Wealth of Nations*, pp. 22-23.

63. Giovanni B. Dagnino, *Handbook of Research on Competitive Strategy* (Cheltenham: Edward Elgar, 2012). For a recent and original illustration of this point, see Franck Cochoy's study of metallic skis, in which he successfully links competition to the material characteristics of goods: Franck Cochoy, *Une histoire du ski: Aluminium, gens de glisse et "coopétition"* (Paris: REF.2C editions, 2015).

64. This term refers to an analytical approach initiated and developed by Erving Goffman and then enriched by Bruno Latour, who emphasized the role of objects and materialities. Erving Goffman, *Frame Analysis: An Essay on the Organization of Experience* (Cambridge, MA: Harvard University Press, 1974); Bruno Latour, "On Interobjectivity," *Mind, Culture and Activity* 3 (1996), pp. 228-45.

65. For more precise definition of the term "passiva(c)tion," see Chapter 2. The word has been chosen to highlight that a good must simultaneously respond to two imperatives, between which it must find an equilibrium. On the one side, activation—the good must be capable of eliciting and contributing to new courses of action. On the other side, what could be called "passification"—the good must be amenable to control and must remain predictable.

66. Michel Callon, Fabian Muniesa, and Yuval Millo, "Market Devices," *Sociological Review* 55.2 (2007), pp. 1-12.

67. Nicolas Dodier and Janine Barbot, "La force des dispositifs," *Annales HSS* 2 (2016), pp. 421-48.

CHAPTER TWO: THE PROCESS OF MAKING GOODS MOBILE AND ALIENABLE

1. Lawyers sometimes refer to this great divide as the *summa divisio*. Rights can include the capacity to make decisions about the goods to be produced, about the people to recruit, or about the way goods can be accessed, the profits they generate, and their use. Obligations can specify the responsibilities associated with objects and their use. These rights and obligations vary in time and from one community to another.

2. For a detailed discussion of property rights, their dynamics and their diversity, see, for example, Bruce G. Carruthers and Laura Ariovich, "The Sociology of Property Rights," *Annual Review of Sociology* 30.1 (August 2004), pp. 23-46; Katharina Pistor, *The Code of Capital: How the Law Creates Wealth and Inequality* (Princeton: Princeton University Press, 2019).

3. In 1967, Jean-Paul Sartre said that when he read an important work, he chewed it for a long time to break it down into its constituent elements, each of which had to be taken into consideration. See *Sartre et de Beauvoir*, documentary film by Max Cacopardo, 1967, http://www.film-documentaire.fr/4DACTION/w_fiche_film/56295_1. The same applies to anthropological studies based on in-depth field investigations: they must be chewed to extract the conceptual and empirical tools embedded in them that are used by anthropologists to figure out answers to the problems they have chosen to solve. For readers interested in an overall appreciation of the contributions and limits of economic anthropology, see Koray Çalışkan and Michel Callon, "Economization, Part 1: Shifting Attention from the Economy toward Processes of Economization," *Economy and Society* 38.3 (2009), pp. 369-98.

4. For an analysis of these mechanisms, see Philippe Steiner and Marie Trespeuch,

eds., *Marchés contestés: Quand le marché rencontre la morale* (Toulouse: Presses universitaires du Mirail, 2015).

5. Pierre Bourdieu takes up this opposition, endorsing the distinction between gifts and commodities. See Pierre Bourdieu, *Outline of a Theory of Practice*, trans. Richard Nice (Cambridge: Cambridge University Press), pp. 171–73.

6. Paul Bohannan, "Some Principles of Exchange and Investment among the Tiv," *American Anthropologist* 57.1 (1955), pp. 60–70.

7. Maurice Bloch and Jonathan Parry, "Introduction: Money and the Morality of Exchange," in Maurice Bloch and Jonathan Parry, eds., *Money and the Morality of Exchange* (Cambridge: Cambridge University Press, 1989), pp. 1–32.

8. Philippe Descola, *Beyond Nature and Culture* (Chicago: University of Chicago Press, 2013).

9. Jane Guyer, *Marginal Gains: Monetary Transactions in Atlantic Africa* (Chicago: University of Chicago Press, 2004).

10. Philippe Steiner, "Don de sang et don d'organes: Le marché des marchandises fictives," *Revue Française de Sociologie* 42.2 (2001), pp. 357–74.

11. Arjun Appadurai, "Introduction: Commodities and the Politics of Value," in Arjun Appadurai, ed., *The Social Life of Things: Commodities in Cultural Perspectives* (Cambridge: Cambridge University Press, 1988), pp. 3–6; Igor Kopytoff, "The Cultural Biography of Things: Commoditization as Process," ibid., pp. 64–92.

12. Romain Garcier, "Disperser, confiner ou recycler?," *L'espace géographique* 43.3 (2014), pp. 265–83.

13. Annette Weiner, *Inalienable Possessions: The Paradox of Keeping-While-Giving* (Berkeley: University of California Press, 1992); Maurice Godelier, *The Enigma of the Gift* (Cambridge: Polity, 1999).

14. In one case, the exclusion is spatial (spheres of circulation); in the other case, it is temporal (a succession of different states).

15. Bruno Latour, *Reassembling the Social: An Introduction to Actor-Network Theory* (Oxford: Oxford University Press, 2005).

16. Webb Keane, "Semiotics and the Social Analysis of Material Things," *Language and Communication* 23 (2003), pp. 409–25.

17. Nicholas Thomas, *Entangled Objects: Exchange, Material Culture, and Colonialism in the Pacific* (Cambridge, MA: Harvard University Press, 1991).

18. Gilbert Simondon, *On the Mode of Existence of Technical Objects*, trans. Cecile Malaspina and John Rogove (Minneapolis: Univocal, 2016).

19. Martin Kornberger et. al., *Thinking Infrastructures* (Bradford: Emerald Group, 2019).

20. Lisa Gitelman, *Always Already New: Media, History, and the Data of Culture* (Cambridge, MA: MIT Press, 2006); Lisa Gitelman, "Souvenir Foils: On the Status of Print at the Origin of Recorded Sound," in Lisa Gitelman and Geoffrey B. Pingree, eds., *New Media, 1740–1915* (Cambridge, MA: MIT Press, 2003), p. 271.

21. There is an immense literature devoted to the role of objects and the environment in framing courses of action. Here are some of the foundational publications: Edwin Hutchins, *Cognition in the Wild* (Cambridge, MA: MIT Press, 1995); Edwin Hutchins, "How a Cockpit Remembers Its Speeds," *Cognitive Science* 19.3 (1995), pp. 265-88; Donald A. Norman, *Things That Make Us Smart* (Reading: Addison-Wesley, 1993). On the basic notion of affordance, see James J. Gibson, *The Ecological Approach to Visual Perception: Classic Edition* (East Sussex: Psychology Press, 2014), chapter 8; Lucy A. Suchman, *Plans and Situated Actions: The Problem of Human-Machine Communication* (Cambridge: Cambridge University Press, 1987). The most insightful economists have found the classic notion of usage less than satisfactory for quite some time, arguing that goods prompt and take part in courses of action. For instance, Ronald Coase perfectly expresses the need for this change of perspective when dealing with commercial transactions: "What are traded on the market are not, as is often supposed by economists, physical entities, but the rights to perform certain actions." Ronald Coase, "The Institutional Structure of Production," *American Economic Review* 82.4 (1992), p. 717. More than a century earlier, Marx takes a similar view in the first chapter of *Zur Kritik der politischen Ökonomie*: "As a use value, the goods have a *causal* effect. Wheat, for example, *acts* as a foodstuff. A machine replaces work in certain circumstances. This effect of the goods, through which they alone are use value, the object of consumption, can be called their service, the service that they render as use value." (My emphasis, my translation from German.)

22. Suchman, *Plans and Situated Actions*, pp. 118-31.

23. Madeleine Akrich, "The Description of Technical Objects," in Wiebe E. Bijker and John Law, eds., *Shaping Technology / Building Society: Studies in Sociotechnical Change* (Cambridge, MA: MIT Press, 1992), pp. 205-24. "Designers...define actors with specific tastes, competences, motives, aspirations, political prejudices.... A large part of the work of innovators is that of inscribing this vision of the world in the technical content of the new object. I will call the end product of this work a script" (p. 208).

24. Michel Callon, "An Essay on Framing and Overflowing: Economic Externalities

Revisited by Sociology," in Michel Callon, ed., *The Laws of the Markets* (Oxford: Black-well, 1998), pp. 244–69.

25. On this joint learning process, see Alexis C. Madrigal, "Inside Waymo's Secret World of Training Self-Driving Cars," *Atlantic*, August 23, 2017, https://www.the atlantic.com/technology/archive/2017/08/inside-waymos-secret-testing-and-simulation -facilities/537648/.

26. I hesitated for a long time between using an existing word, "passivation," and creating a neologism, "passiva(c)tion." I went with the first option in a text published in French in 2013, Michel Callon, "Qu'est-ce qu'un agencement marchand?," in *Sociologie des agencements marchands: Textes choisis* (Paris: Presse des Mines, 2013), pp. 325–440. I quickly realized that the term "passivation" was taken up by my few readers or listeners in its usual sense: to make something be unable to act and to reduce it to a purely instrumental role. Indeed, in physical chemistry, passivation refers to a material becoming "passive," that is, less affected (less corroded) by the environment. Admittedly, they understood that investments are necessary to achieve this result. But they overlooked the other part of the story: to be transformed into commodities, things must be made *active*. It is the reason why I prefer to stick to the word "passiva(c)tion." If some readers are by chance convinced by my analysis, but are not (yet) ready to use this ugly term, I humbly suggest they adopt the term "passivation," but warn their readers that they are using it with the more ample meaning I give to "passiva(c)tion." I thank you in advance for your cooperation!

27. Charles Aubry and Charles Rau, *Cours de droit civil français, d'après l'ouvrage allemant de C. S. Zachariae*, 3rd ed., vol. 2, no. 162 (Paris: Cosse, 1863), quoted in Florence Bellivier and Laurence Boudouard-Brunet, "Les ressources génétiques et les concepts juridiques de patrimoine," in Catherine Labrusse-Riou, ed., *Le droit saisi par la biologie: Des juristes au laboratoire* (Paris: LGDJ, 1996), p. 179.

28. Maurice Godelier, *The Enigma of the Gift* (Chicago: University of Chicago Press, 1999); Godelier, *The Making of Great Men: Male Domination and Power among the New Guinea Baruya* (Cambridge: Cambridge University Press, 1986). As I said above, it's not my purpose to discuss Godelier's thesis on the organization of Baruya society. I only pinpoint the existence of the more general practice of keeping while giving. On the distinction between great men and big men, see Maurice Godelier, *Big Men and Great Men: Personifications of Power in Melanesia* (Cambridge: Cambridge University Press, 2009). For a critical discussion, see Marilyn Strathern, *The Gender of the Gift: Problems with Women and Problems with Society in Melanesia* (Berkeley: University of California Press, 1990).

29. Elinor Ostrom, *Governing the Commons: The Evolution of Institutions for Collective Actions* (Cambridge: Cambridge University Press, 1991). For an in-depth discussion, see also Marie Cornu, Fabienne Orsi, and Judith Rochfeld, eds., *Dictionnaire des biens communs* (Paris: Presses Universitaires de France, 2017); Fabienne Orsi, "Réhabiliter la propriété comme *bundle of rights*," *Revue internationale de droit économique* 28.3 (2014), pp. 371–85.

30. The term "dismemberment" (*démembrement*), used in French to indicate this separation of rights, says explicitly that the thing is part of the person who puts it into circulation.

31. A widespread practice, usufruct is a system in which one party uses the property of another without owning, but while bearing certain obligations to the property as spelled out in a contract. Separating usufruct and bare ownership allows the donor (for instance, the parents) to continue to use the good while having transmitted it (for instance, to their children). What matters to me in this example is the possible (and effective) separation of the two rights. The distinction applies to property assets (for example, an apartment) but also to movable assets: a stock portfolio can be given in a way that separates the two rights. In this case, the one who has usufruct is authorized to sell shares to optimize management on condition they are replaced by other equivalent ones.

32. For an updated and annotated English edition, see Marcel Mauss, *The Gift: Expanded Edition*, trans. Jane I. Guyer (Chicago: University of Chicago Press, 2016). In his brilliant *Introduction to the Work of Marcel Mauss*, Claude Lévi-Strauss's slightly condescending critique ultimately ends up replacing one magic force with another that is just as magical, but supposedly more fundamental: the propensity to exchange that impels the receiver to offer a countergift to the giver ("the primary, fundamental phenomenon is exchange itself") is indeed just as mysterious as the presence of *hau* in the thing! Claude Lévi-Strauss, *Introduction to the Work of Marcel Mauss*, trans. Felicity Baker (London: Routledge and Kegan Paul, 1987), p. 47. Marshall Sahlins puts forward a more radical and materialist critique: the *hau* does not refer to a spirit, but to the profit generated by the given things, which, as such, must be returned to the giver. Marshall Sahlins, *Stone Age Economics* (Chicago: Aldine Atherton, 1972). In the name of (Western) science, Lévi-Strauss rejects indigenous explanations. Sahlins respects them, and although he modifies the interpretation, he keeps the idea that is essential for what I want to articulate: the thing, after it has changed hands, has not really cut the connections that link it to its first giver.

33. Cattle also are marked with a branding iron. Branding and earmarking have a common origin going back at least as far as Sisyphus. To discourage his neighbor Autolycus, who stole his cattle and even managed to sell them back to him after repainting them a different color, Sisyphus had the idea of engraving his monogram under the hooves of his animals, which allowed them to be traced on the roads leading to Autolycus's stable, confounding the thief. Franck Cochoy, *Une histoire du ski: Aluminium, gens de glisse et "coopétition"* (Paris: REF.2C editions, 2015).

34. If I were focusing on the gift, I would have to make an inventory of these practices. See Michel Callon and John Law, "Introduction: Absence-Presence, Circulation, and Encountering in Complex Space," *Environment and Planning D: Society and Space* 22 (2004), pp. 3–11.

35. Thomas, *Entangled Objects*, p. 39.

36. Paoli liberated Corsica from Genoa's domination and set up, for a short period, democratic institutions partly designed by Jean-Jacques Rousseau.

37. Don Corleone gives a fabulous illustration of this practice in Francis Ford Coppola's *The Godfather*. Bonasera asks Don Corleone for help in taking revenge on the man who raped his daughter. When the Godfather accepts, Bonasera inquires: "How much shall I pay you for this service?" Don Corleone: "Bonasera, Bonasera! What have I ever done to make you treat me so disrespectfully? If you'd come to me in friendship, then this scum that ruined your daughter would be suffering that very day. And if by chance an honest man like yourself should make enemies, then they would become my enemies. And then they will fear you.... Some day, and that day may never come, I'll call you upon to do a service for me. But, uh, until that day, accept this justice as a gift on my daughter's wedding day." As Fabian Muniesa, from whom I borrow this illustration, observes, Mauss could not have said it better. Fabian Muniesa, "Attachment and Detachment in the Economy," in Peter Redman, ed., *Attachment: Sociology and Social World* (Manchester: Manchester University Press, 2008), pp. 112–41. Without the Godfather's speech, the service (assassinating the rapist) would have tipped into commercial logic.

38. One of the letter's characteristics is to have been written by Paoli; the accompanying note can even be transferred, since it adds to the qualification and its authenticity.

39. Readers familiar with the economics of conventions, and in particular with the foundational work of the late François Eymard-Duvernay, will no doubt have picked up on the difference between his terminology and mine. Eymard-Duverney uses the notion of attachment to signify that the good (and notably the service) keeps the trace of A, the person who puts it into circulation. François Eymard-Duvernay, "L'entreprise

comme dispositif de coordination: Modèles d'entreprises, qualifications du produit, qualifications du travail," PhD diss., Paris 10, 1994. As the double-possible status of an autographed letter shows, it seems to me preferable to appeal to the general concept of disentanglement in order to be able later to distinguish between the disentanglements that keep the good's attachment to A (marking) from those that detach it from A (unmarking). In the first case, the relation to A is *presence*, in the second case it is *reference*. On the ontological status of these two modes of existence, I refer the reader to Bruno Latour's foundational work, *An Inquiry into Modes of Existence: An Anthropology of the Moderns* (Cambridge, MA: Harvard University Press, 2013).

40. The rule is so general that Michel Serres speaks of "quasi-objects" to designate things that, like the rugby ball that jumps from three-quarter back to three-quarter back to land in the winger's hands, keep no trace of their history. It is also amusing to note that the winger who runs toward the opposing team's in-goal area has been unmarked, just like the ball he carries in his hands!

41. Joel Podolny has shown that goods' qualifications are powerfully affected by the status of the agents who offer them for sale and that the commercial brand (*marque*) is one of the privileged supports of this narrativizing. (On the role of brands, see Chapter 5.) Joel Podolny, *Status Signals: A Sociological Study of Market Competition* (Princeton: Princeton University Press, 2010).

42. Traceability can attribute extra qualities to the good, which can then travel with these qualities and yet be detached from its designers and developers. It also makes it easier to solve problems of responsibility once rights have been commuted. It should be analyzed as a continuation, and not a suspension, of the process of disentanglement with detachment. This practice is not new. Although it may have been known under different names, in all cases, the same process of detaching without loss of reference is in operation.

43. Ronan Le Velly, "Fair Trade and Mainstreaming," in Laura T. Raynolds and Elizabeth A. Bennett, eds., *Handbook of Research on Fair Trade* (Cheltenham: Edward Elgar, 2015), pp. 265–80.

44. This story is now well documented: Michel Foucault, "Authorship: What Is an Author?," *Screen* 20.1 (1979), pp. 13–34; Carla Hesse, *Publishing and Cultural Politics in Revolutionary Paris, 1789–1810* (Berkeley: University of California Press, 1991). On the topic of science, see Mario Biagoli and Peter Galison, eds., *Scientific Authorship: Credit and Intellectual Property in Science* (London: Routledge, 2014).

45. The shift from the term *auto*mobile to the term *self*-driving car nicely shows the ongoing redistribution of competencies and identities between the car and its "driver."

46. Christopher Tozzi, *For Fun and Profit: A History of the Free and Open Source Software Revolution* (Cambridge, MA: MIT Press, 2017).

47. See Orsi, "Réhabiliter la propriété comme *bundle of rights.*" I brought up this evolution when I underlined the growing importance of the bundles-of-property-rights approach in legal theory.

48. Fabien Girard and Christine Noiville, "Propriété industrielle et biotechnologies végétales: La *Nova Atlantis.* À propos de la recommandation du Haut Conseil des Biotechnologies," *Revue internationale de droit économique* 28.1 (2014), pp. 59–109.

49. The problems raised become even more complicated with the arrival of new plant breeding techniques (NPBT), for instance, the use of enzymes (CRISPR-associated protein 9 or transcription-activator-like effector nucleases: TALENs) to rapidly modify the genome of plant or animal cells.

50. It should be remembered that some patients brought legal proceedings against pharmaceutical companies that, having used their diseased cells to develop treatments, then offered to sell the treatments back to those patients without in any way sharing the profits. Marie-Angèle Hermitte, "L'affaire Moore ou la diabolique notion de propriété: L'homme en danger de science," *Le Monde diplomatique*, December 1988, pp. 20–21. These appropriation problems are exacerbated by the development of practices of the quantified self, which increase the quantity of personal or intimate data, especially in the domain of health.

51. The reality of this labor and the specific investments it requires are generally disregarded, notably by anthropologists. Maurice Godelier, whose crucial contributions to economic anthropology cannot be overemphasized, distinguishes three categories of objects. There are objects that can be transformed into commodities (alienable and alienated); there are those that may be given (alienated), but that keep an attachment to their donor (and are therefore inalienable). Finally, there are those of a sacred order: they are inalienable and not alienated and are transmitted down the generations. Each society, Godelier adds, defines what is for sale and what is not and thereby defines its own identity. Margaret Jane Radin follows the same logic in her classic article, "Market-Inalienability," *Harvard Law Review* 100.8 (1987), pp. 1849–1937. Both of these analyses are limited in the same way—namely, they make moral and cultural values the ultimate arbitrators of the transformation of things into commodities without allowing that the materiality of the things has any say in the decisions.

52. Karl Polanyi, *The Great Transformation* (Boston: Beacon, 1957), p. 72.

53. Philippe Steiner, "Les marchés agroalimentaires sont-ils des 'marchés spéci-

aux'?," http://ses.ens-lyon.fr/fichiers/Articles/ac20.pdf. The fictitious qualification is unconvincing insofar as its only function is to make it easier to denounce commodification when it is judged to be excessive. Goods are processes, and there is no reason to reduce the production merely to the industrial manufacturing.

54. Pistor, *The Code of Capital*, p. 1.

55. Slave markets have recently been documented in Libya and Sudan. See Free the Slaves, "Our Model of Freedom: Slavery Today," https://www.freetheslaves.net/our -model-for-freedom/slavery-today. They have also been revived in Kuwait through apps that connect people who trade domestic workers. See Owen Pinnell and Jess Kelly, "Slave Markets Found on Instagram and Other Apps," BBC News, October 31, 2019, https:// www.bbc.com/news/av/technology-50240012/maids-for-sale-how-silicon-valley-enables -online-slave-markets.

56. This does not prevent controversy. As Viviana Zelizer has shown, studying divorce procedures, it is not always easy, even for the most seasoned judges, to decide whether favors granted by companions when they lived together should be analyzed as gifts or as salaries. On this subject, which is particularly illuminating for the analysis of market activities, see also Philippe Combessie, "L'argent en milieu 'libertin': Entre mise en scène et occultation. Jeux de séduction et mobilité sociale au féminin," *Terrains/ Théorie* 1.1 (2015), https://www.researchgate.net/publication/282197589_L'argent_en_ milieu_libertin_entre_mise_en_scene_et_occultation. He shows the strategies that allow women in particular situations to remain at an equal distance from prostitution and "disinterested" relations.

57. William Reddy, *The Rise of Market Culture: The Textile Industry and French Society, 1750–1900* (Cambridge: Cambridge University Press, 1984).

58. Yves-Marie Abraham, "Le travail, marchandise fictive?: Cent ans de marchandisation de la main d'œuvre mexicaine aux Etats-Unis," *Revue Interventions économiques* 38, 2008, online since 12/1/2008, accessed 03/22/2017, https://journals.openedition. org/interventionseconomiques/360.

59. Laurent Thévenot, "Rules and Implements: Investments in Forms," *Social Science Information / Information sur les sciences sociales* 23.11 (1984), pp. 1–45.

60. Martha Lampland, *The Value of Labor: The Science of Commodification in Hungary, 1920–1956* (Chicago: University of Chicago Press, 2016).

61. Pierre-Michel Menger, *The Economics of Creativity: Art and Achievement under Uncertainty* (Cambridge, MA: Harvard University Press, 2014).

62. Luc Boltanski and Eve Chiapello, *New Spirit of Capitalism* (London: Verso, 2018).

63. Olivier Godechot, "Financialization Is Marketization!: A Study of the Respective Impacts of Various Dimensions of Financialization on the Increase in Global Inequality," *MaxPo Discussion Paper* 15.3 (2015), https://econpapers.repec.org/paper/zbwmaxpod/153.htm.

64. Writing a genealogy of money presupposes an agreement on what the word "money" means, which is far from obvious and may sooner or later produce anachronisms. The search for origins often leads to narratives that give pride of place to progress, which, in the case of money, means endorsing its growing abstraction.

65. Bill Maurer, "The Anthropology of Money," *Annual Review of Anthropology* 35.1 (2006), pp. 15-36.

66. As we will point out later, those different functions are not given once and for all—they are the outcome of innovations that have been progressively stabilized and disseminated through trial and error. Moreover, they don't exhaust the possibilities of what money may do.

67. As, for example, in a period of very high inflation.

68. Karl Polanyi came close to defending this thesis, which was taken up in a radical form by David Graeber in *Debt: The First 5,000 Years* (New York: Melville House, 2011). In a review of Graeber's book, Bill Maurer notes: "As Graeber explains, however, pure barter as such never existed. The myth of barter is a handy story for explaining the origins of money in terms that warrant market theories of price and commodity exchange. But, historically and ethnographically, it does not hold water. None of this is news to anthropologists." He adds, "Money is not developed out of barter, to solve the problem of the double coincidence of wants." Bill Maurer, "David Graeber's Wunderkammer, *Debt: The First 5,000 Years*," *Anthropological Forum* 23.1, pp. 79-93. "The history of non-metallic and the so-called primitive money…decenters the classic focus on exchange, placing emphasis more on social payments like marriage gifts, tax" and "allows us to ask questions about how powerful people in any given society establish the standards through which value is configured and assessed." Bill Maurer, "Primitive and Nonmetallic Money," in Stefano Battilossi, Youssef Cassis, and Kazuhiko Yago, eds., *Handbook of the History of Money and Currency* (Singapore: Springer, 2018), p. 16. This reversal has considerable consequences. The existence of money supposes a rich network of social relations and institutions, whereas barter does not. As a means of payment and store of value, money establishes a strong social relation that disappears when it is considered as a means of exchange. See Jane I. Guyer, *Legacies, Logics, Logistics: Essays in the Anthropology of the Platform Economy* (Chicago: University of Chicago Press, 2016).

69. On the emergence and the increasing importance of the store-of-value function, see in particular Massimo Amato and Luca Fantacci, *The End of Finance* (Oxford: Polity, 2011) and Guyer's commentary in Guyer, *Legacies, Logics, Logistics*, p. 224.

70. There are very few studies of how the very nature of materials can influence the different actions they may foster. See, however, Jean Denis and David Pontille, "Material Ordering and the Care of Things," *Science, Technology and Human Values* 40.3 (2015), pp. 338–67; Cochoy, *Une histoire du ski*; Bernadette Bensaude-Vincent, *Éloge du mixte: Matériaux nouveaux et philosophie ancienne* (Paris: Hachette-littératures, 1998).

71. In the vocabulary of economics (a high degree of) liquidity refers to an amount that is immediately available, which can take the form of coins and notes, bank assets, or financial assets. Liquid assets are less subject to the risk of capital loss. Another property that is essential should also be mentioned: fungibility—that is, substitutability. Under certain conditions of standardization, one kilo of silver can be replaced by another kilo of silver, a one-euro coin by another one-euro coin, and so on. Easy substitutability facilitates the transformation of money into a commodity.

72. Some authors prefer to use the term "infrastructure" to refer to the assemblages that allow money to function as money. For describing the process of passiva(c)tion, the notion of associated milieu is more appropriate. Both have in common their relative invisibility.

73. If we agree to call a very low degree of liquidity "viscosity," then one could say that a stamp collection is less viscous than a Rembrandt.

74. This explains why there have often been attempts to link the existence of money closely to that of the state or a powerful central administration, both of which can play an important role in the constitution of its associated milieu. The main contribution of the state is undoubtedly to promote the gradual emergence of a money that is accepted in the territory it governs and is consequently likely to be more easily engaged into a process of commoditization.

75. For example the short message service (SMS) can be utilized for money services.

76. The French word, *actif,* has the advantage of underlining the active nature of assets, as do the Italian or Spanish terms, *attività* and *activo.*

77. For a well-documented and convincing analysis, see Jacques Melitz, "The Polanyi School of Anthropology on Money: An Economist's View," *American Anthropologist* 72.5 (1970), pp. 1020–40.

78. Depending of your interlocutor, this classification can be extended and refined.

The underlying idea is that any monetary "system" is an assemblage of different kinds of money.

79. As noticed by Perry Mehrling, the specialization is very frequently hierarchized. See Perry Mehrling, "The Inherent Hierarchy of Money," in Lance Taylor, Armon Rezai, and Thomas Michl, eds., *Social Fairness and Economics: Economic Essays in the Spirit of Duncan Foley* (New York: Routledge, 2013), pp. 392-404. I thank Martha Poon for this reference. I would like to reinforce that this hierarchy is not inherent in money, but the outcome of the institutional and constitutional distribution of powers.

80. The United States instituted both of these types of regulation at different times: the first with the Volcker Rule in 2010 and the second with the Glass-Steagall Act in 1933. The Basel III agreements also aim to regulate banks' liquidities, as well as their recourse to financial instruments. These various measures are intended to provide a framework for money creation—that is, the ability of commodity money to generate money.

81. But Polanyi's distinction between general-purpose money and special-purpose money is empirically wrong. All monies are special-purpose monies. See Melitz, "The Polanyi School of Anthropology on Money."

82. In financial markets, some money supplies must be reserved exclusively for certain usages (for instance, home acquisition) in order to be convertible into goods (for instance, in the form of a loan).

83. Natasha Schüll, *Addiction by Design: Machine Gambling in Las Vegas* (Princeton: Princeton University Press, 2012), p. 226.

84. Bruce Carruthers and Arthur Stinchcombe, "The Social Structure of Liquidity: Flexibility in Markets, States, and Organizations," in Arthur Stinchcombe, ed., *When Formality Works: Authority and Abstraction in Law and Organizations* (Chicago: University Chicago Press, 2001), pp. 109-39.

85. Viviana Zelizer, "The Social Meaning of Money: Special Monies," *American Journal of Sociology* 95.2 (1989), pp. 342-77; Viviana Zelizer, *Economic Lives: How Culture Shapes the Economy* (Princeton: Princeton University Press, 2011). Particular norms regulating monies are associated with these specialized uses. Jeanne Lazarus, "À la recherche des normes contemporaines de l'argent: Éléments pour l'analyse de la promotion de l'éducation financière," *Terrains/Théories* 1 (2015). See also Supriya Singh, *Marriage Money: The Social Shaping of Money in Marriage and Banking* (Sydney: Allen and Unwin Academic, 1997). Singh shows the frameworks that regulate the uses of different forms of money: deposits, loan accounts, checking accounts, short-term savings, automatic payments.

86. For an empirical illustration of this diversity, see Akos Rona-Tas and Alya Guseva, *Plastic Money: Constructing Markets for Credit Cards in Eight Post-Communist Countries* (Stanford: Stanford University Press, 2014). Unfortunately, the authors give too much sway to the notion of "country" instead of analyzing the associated milieu of the cards, which can include, among other things, data structures and other technological infrastructures.

87. A local exchange trading system (LETS) organizes the exchange of products or services within a closed group, generally constituted as an association. The money used is a specific and local currency (means of payment) that generally forbids savings (store of value) and the speculation and interest that go with it.

88. Jean-Michel Servet, *Une économie sans argent: Les systèmes d'échange local (SEL)* (Paris: Seuil, 1999); Jérôme Blanc, *Les monnaies parallèles: Unité et diversité du fait monétaire* (Paris: L'Harmattan, 2000); Jérôme Blanc, ed., *Monnaies sociales: Exclusion et liens financiers, rapport 2005–2006* (Paris: Economica, 2006). For a recent update, see Peter North, "Alternative Currencies: Diverse Experiments," in J. K. Gibson-Graham and Kelly Dombrovski. eds., *The Handbook of Diverse Economies* (Cheltenham: Edward Elgar, 2020), pp. 230-37.

89. For an illustration of this, see José Ossandon, "'My Story Has No String Attached': Credit Cards, Market Devices and a Stone Guest," in Franck Cochoy, Joe Deville, and Liz McFall, eds., *Markets and the Art of Attachment* (London: Routledge, 2017), pp. 132-46.

90. In this case, it is likely that the state will play an essential role.

91. Consider Facebook's moves to develop a cryptocurrency that the company claims will bring about wider financial inclusion. Initially called "libra" (a single stablecoin), then "'libra 2.0" (a multicurrency stablecoin), the project has just been rebranded under the name "diem" (an e-commerce payment system with a libra token) and placed in the hands of an association in which Facebook will participate only through the membership of a subsidiary that exists to build the company's digital wallet (Novi). These rapid transformations over an eighteen-month period are a clear signal that private monies are steeped in controversies. See Timothy J. Massad, "Facebook's Libra 2.0: Why You Might Like It Even If We Can't Trust Facebook," *Brookings*, June 22, 2020, https://www.brookings.edu/research/facebooks-libra-2-0.

92. Conversion is always problematic and subject to controversy. As I reread this manuscript, François Fillon, a candidate in the French presidential election, has just revealed that his son used the salary he paid him as a temporary parliamentary assistant

to reimburse the pocket money his father had given him...or rather, had paid him in advance. For a sharp analysis of these matters see Bill Maurer, *How Would You Like to Pay?: How Technology Is Changing the Future of Money* (Durham: Duke University Press, 2015).

93. Consider the devices that, in the case of the Catholic religion and in Islam, allow interest rates to be reconciled with religious beliefs and moralities. The Catholic Church used to condemn the principle of interest rates that risk shackling debtors and only finally accepted it in the precise case in which the lender risks not being paid back. (More precisely, interests were authorized by the Scholastics to compensate for a loss endured, the loss of an anticipated profit, the risk of losing loaned capital, or an uncertain profit.) Similarly, Islam considers that the practice of usury (*rîba*) constitutes a very grave sin. In both cases, solutions were imagined that in practice function like loans with interest: the lender can, for instance, become his debtor's associate, sharing the gains. Protestants showed greater flexibility: Calvin considered it normal that money be productive, just like any other commodity. On these financial practices and their links with theological debates, see Giacomo Todeschini's seminal book, *I mercanti e il tempio : La società cristiana e il circolo virtuoso della ricchezza fra Medioevo ed étà moderna* (Bologna: Il Mulino, 2002.) See also Pierre Jeannin, *Marchands d'Europe: Pratiques et savoirs à l'epoque moderne* (Paris: Éditions Rue d'Ulm, 2002) and Reinhold C. Mueller, *The Venetian Money Market: Banks, Panics, and the Public Debt* (Baltimore: John Hopkins University Press, 1997).

94. According to some authors, the practice of forward sales goes back to antiquity. In *Marchands d'Europe*, Pierre Jeannin highlights the role played by two major financial innovations, the bill of exchange and then the discounting of commercial paper, which, according to him, are the two pillars of so-called modern finance. Financial instruments or products are contracts negotiated in capital markets. Besides classic stocks and bonds, there are instruments with exotic names that allow for facing particular risks connected to asset values: futures, options, and warrants can cover for the risks linked to stocks; structured products such as the famous asset-backed securities or collateralized debt obligations are designed to protect against several economic risks.

95. The English language uses the more neutral term "share" for this product, which is a security representing a fraction of capital and giving the right to certain benefits.

96. On this process of transformation, see Madeleine Akrich et al., "The Key to Success in Innovation Part I: The Art of Interessement," and "The Key to Success in

Innovation Part II: The Art of Choosing Good Spokespersons," *International Journal of Innovation Management* 6.2 (June 2002), pp. 187–206 and 207–25, respectively.

97. Yuval Millo, "Making Things Deliverable: The Origins of Index-Based Derivatives," in Michel Callon, Yuval Millo, and Fabian Muniesa, eds., *Market Devices* (Hoboken: Wiley-Blackwell, 2007), pp. 196–214.

98. The underlying asset is an asset on which the derivative's price is based. It can be financial (stocks, bonds, treasury bonds, futures, foreign currencies, stock indexes...) or physical (raw agricultural products or minerals...).

99. The CFTC is an independent federal agency created in the United States in 1974 that regulates the markets for options and futures.

100. Quoted in Martha Poon, "For Financial Certainty, Try Machine Gambling," review of Natasha Dow Schüll, *Addiction by Design: Machine Gambling in Las Vegas*, *Journal of Cultural Economy* 7.4 (2014), p. 523. See also Martha Poon, "Can Anthropology Save Finance?," *Journal of Cultural Economy* 7.1 (2014), pp. 121–26. On the unattended effects of probabilities on the derivatives pricing in financial markets, see Elie Ayache, *The Blank Swan: The End of Probability* (Hoboken: Wiley, 2010).

101. Donald MacKenzie, *An Engine, Not a Camera: How Financial Models Shape Markets* (Cambridge, MA: MIT Press, 2006).

102. Maurer, "The Anthropology of Money."

103. One could also refer to the case of scientific knowledge and its commodification. Michel Callon, "Is Science a Public Good?," *Science, Technology and Human Values* 19.4 (1994), pp. 395–424.

104. Jean-Baptiste Fressoz, *L'apocalypse joyeuse* (Paris: Seuil, 2012).

105. The story of the market passiva(c)tion of red meat is obviously more complex than this vignette allows, once you add refrigerated transportation, land use, and more. For a thorough account of the American history of meat production, see Joshua Specht, *Red Meat Republic: A Hoof-to-Table History of How Beef Changed America* (Princeton: Princeton University Press, 2019).

106. Claude Milhaud, *L'autre hécatombe: Enquête sur la perte de 1 140 000 chevaux et mulets* (Paris: Belin, 2017).

107. Procedures such as authorizations for the commercialization of medical treatments, or the creation of agencies such as ANSES (the Agence nationale de sécurité sanitaire de l'alimentation, de l'environnement et du travail), or INERIS (the Institut national de l'environnement industriel et des risques), contribute to this passiva(c)tion. The latter includes not only control and surveillance agencies, but also all research and

experimentation activities aimed at preventing untimely overflowings (*débordements*). Here, one should mention the part, by now well studied, played by different certification or labeling procedures that guarantee that the passiva(c)tion was obtained according to governing rules.

108. The notion was invented by Jean Bustarret, director of INRA, the Institut national de la recherche agronomique.

109. Overflow disorders are not limited to the aspects that concern health and the environment. From this perspective, the case of genetically modified plants is very illuminating: unpredictable and problematic effects are first and foremost socioeconomic. (See Chapter 8.) Max Weber, underlining that market competition is supposed to be peaceful, had perhaps not imagined that it would be goods, even more than people, that would transform into the ferment of conflict and sometimes incite to violence.

110. In what are called material goods, the human presence is very real (for instance, in the form of inscriptions that note the origin: produced by Columbian Indians, or the artisanal production of Camembert, which is molded by professionals using a ladle). Services, however, are distinguished by different types of assemblages between humans and nonhumans. On this conception of services, see Jean Gadrey, "The Characterization of Goods and Services: An Alternative Approach," *Review of Income and Wealth* 46.3 (2000), pp. 369–87. The purchase of a service by B is the purchase from an organization of the right of usage for a specific period of a sociotechnical capacity held by A that allows B to undertake certain courses of action, which, as in the case of material goods, are more or less precisely qualified.

111. Granted, technical objects should not break down or malfunction, but controlling them is generally less problematic than controlling as yet undomesticated living beings.

112. Drawing on the analytical framework developed by Viviana Zelizer, Kimberly Kay Hoang shows how in the hostess bars of Ho Chi Minh City, services (notably sexual services) are skillfully framed and formatted. The hostess is free to refuse a request she considers inappropriate. At the same time, however, she must be capable of improvising so that her delivery contributes, in a perfectly consensual and programmed way, to the negotiation of industrial contracts between the clients to whom she provides "assistance": "No hostesses, no contracts," admits a businessman. Kimberly Kay Hoang, *Dealing in Desire: Asian Ascendancy, Western Decline, and the Hidden Currencies of Global Sex Work* (Berkeley: University of California Press, 2015). Vietnamese bars are complex devices that establish a subtle equilibrium between framings and overflowings. The

hostesses interviewed by the author freely admit it when they describe the competencies they must master in order to satisfy the clients (with widely varying profiles and expectations) and facilitate transactions, emphasizing the appeal of their work because it frees them from traditional subjection to employers. Jean Gadrey offers an interesting classification of service providers by making a distinction between three logics. In the first, human and technical skills that constitute the service are accompanied by an intervention on the beneficiary's account, as in the case of a consultant or a garage; in the second, these skills are made available to the beneficiary, as in providing electricity or a car rental; in the third, the beneficiary participates in the delivery of the service, which takes the form of a show, as in the case of a cruise on the Seine or a visit to Euro Disney. Gadrey, "The Characterization of Goods and Services." The hostess bars in Ho Chi Minh City mix the first and the third models: the hostesses put on a show (as do the entertainers at Euro Disney), and they prepare industrial transactions, like any consultant from Arthur Andersen. One can imagine that domestication will take different forms, depending on the logics at play. Jean Gadrey, personal communication. On services and their growing place in market activity, see Stephen Vargo and Robert Lush, "Evolving to a New Dominant Logic for Marketing," *Journal of Marketing* 68.1 (2004), pp. 1-17; Faïz Gallouj and Faridah Djellal, eds., *The Handbook of Innovation and Services: A Multidisciplinary Perspective* (Cheltenham: Edward Elgar, 2010).

113. These computational devices work through experimental initiatives, which are still in trial-and-error mode: for example, the elaboration of so-called intelligent algorithms, notably with recourse to "deep learning," a sort of automatic learning that attempts to structure data as it is acquired in such a way as to make decisions that are adapted to circumstances.

114. While there are a booming number of studies describing the worrying commodification of everything, including individual data, parts of human bodies, scientific knowledge, and so on, they usually do not challenge traditional conceptions of markets.

115. See, for instance, Fressoz, *L'apocalypse joyeuse.*

116. Sue Danielson and Will Kymlicka, *Zoopolis: A Political Theory of Animal Rights* (Oxford: Oxford University Press, 2013). The qualification of animals and of the relations they can sustain with human beings requires investigation; this can lead to the recognition of rights they had been denied. Éric Baratay tells the story, for example, of Islero, the famous bull who met the no less famous Manolete on August 28, 1947. He was first accused of being a coward (*manso*) by the aficionados because he refused to fight, but was requalified as farsighted, a heavy handicap when you have to face the

founder of modern bullfighting. Éric Baratay, *Biographies animales: Des vies retrouvées* (Paris: Seuil, 2017). It turns out that Islero was no exception. All bulls are afflicted with eyesight that puts them at a great disadvantage in front of toreros. To establish equal rights, and if one really wanted to continue these fights to the death, one would have to either choose myopic matadors and deprive them of their glasses or invent corrective lenses specially for bulls.

117. See, for instance, Emanuele Coccia, *The Life of Plants: A Metaphysics of Mixture* (Cambridge: Polity, 2018).

118. The problems generated by the different framings correspond to what Bruno Latour has called "matters of concern." Latour, *Reassembling the Social*, pp. 87-120. I use notions such as worries, problems, and concerns interchangeably to give an account of the effects of this process of "concern."

119. The term "datafication" vividly illustrates what I mean when I propose the neologism "passiva(c)tion." As everyone knows today, datafication is never given. Rather, it is a process that can be described as a specific case of passiva(c)tion. For an overview, see, for example, Ulises A. Mejias and Nick Couldry, "Datafication," *Internet Policy Review* 8.4 (November 29, 2019), https://policyreview.info/concepts/datafication.

120. Frédéric Lordon and André Orléan, "Genèse de l'état et genèse de la monnaie: Le modèle de la *potentia multitudinis*," in Yves Citton and Frédéric Lordon, eds., *Spinoza et les science sociales* (Paris: Éditions Amsterdam, 2007), pp. 127-70.

121. On this point, see Michel Aglietta and André Orléan, *La violence de la monnaie* (Paris: Presses universitaires de France, 1982). In this book, deeply inspired by the Girardian theory of violence, the authors rightly emphasize the ambivalence of money that, given the way it functions, produces both fragmentation and centralization.

122. Marion Fourcade, "Cents and Sensibility: Economic Valuation and the Nature of 'Nature,'" *American Journal of Sociology* 116.6 (2011), pp. 1721-77.

123. John Law, "What's Wrong with a One-World World," *Distinktion: Journal of Social Theory* 16.1 (2015), pp. 126-39; HeterogeneitiesDOTnet, http://www.heterogeneities.net /publications/Law2011WhatsWrongWithAOneWorldWorld.pdf, pp. 1-2.

CHAPTER THREE: AGENCIES AND THEIR QUALCULATIVE EQUIPMENT

1. I will remind the reader again that in this model, goods encompass both material entities and services.

2. I use the notion of evaluation to refer to the different operations of qualculation presented in this chapter. What some propose to call valuation includes the evaluation

and the processes of attachment studied in Chapter 5 and sometimes even the price formulation analyzed in Chapter 6. John Dewey rightly insisted on the fact that one should
pay attention to the process by which values are instituted and constituted (valuation),
rather than to the instituted values.

3. Economists call these goods "experience goods"; only with use do they reveal
their qualities.

4. There are cases where devices have progressively lead to an extreme standardization of goods that previously drew their reputation from their place of origin. For
example, in the now well-documented case of Bordeaux and Tuscany wines, the appella-
tion "d'origine contrôlée" is considered indecipherable by some American drinkers and
has been replaced in international markets by stringent technical norms of production
such as those established by Robert Parker. (See the documentary *Mondovino* [2004],
directed by Jonathan Nossiter.) It is worth noting that Burgundy wines are not particularly appreciated by North American consumers. If I may dare give my point of view,
they are missing out.

5. It is obviously a question of framed uncertainty: the course of an event like a World
Cup final obeys very strict, even ritualized rules. As stringently framed commercial situations become more frequent and more sought after, for some people, the surprise provoked by unexpected variation in goods can indeed lead to more anxiety than pleasure.

6. There is an increasingly rich literature in disability studies that argues for the
importance of disabled bodies in innovative processes. See, for example, Mara Mills,
"Hearing Aids and the History of Electronics Miniaturization," IEEE Annals of the History of Computing 33.2 (2011), pp. 24-45, https://ieeexplore.ieee.org/document/5771310.
For a similar exploration in science and technology studies, see also Michel Callon, "Dis-
abled Persons from All Countries, Unite!," in Bruno Latour, ed., Making Things Pub-
lic: Atmospheres of Democracy (Cambridge, MA: MIT Press, 2005). Myriam Winance,
"Trying Out the Wheelchair: The Mutual Shaping of People and Devices through
Adjustment," *STHV* 31.1 (2006), pp. 52-72; Ingunn Moser and John Law, "'Making
Voices': New Media Technologies, Disabilities, and Articulation," in Gunnar Liestøl,
Andrew Morrison, and Terje Rasmussen, eds., *Digital Media Revisited: Theoretical and
Conceptual Innovation in Digital Domains* (Cambridge, MA: MIT Press, 2003), pp. 491-
520; Michel Callon, "Economic Markets and the Rise of Interactive Agencements: From
Prosthetic Agencies to 'Habilitated' Agencies," in Trevor Pinch and Richard Swedberg,
eds., *Living in a Material World: Economic Sociology Meets Science and Technology Studies*
(Cambridge, MA: MIT Press, 2008), pp. 29-56.

7. Philippe Pignarre, *Le grand secret de l'industrie pharmaceutique* (Paris: La Découverte, 2003). Philip Mirowski, *Science-Mart: Privatizing American Science* (Cambridge, MA: Harvard University Press, 2014).

8. The list of cognitive biases gets longer every day: selective attention, excessive optimism, aversion to losses, comfort-zone behavior (tendency not to revise choices), propensity to favor conformist behavior and imitate others, and more.

9. For a general presentation, see Richard Thaler and Cass Sunstein, *Nudge: Improving Decisions about Health, Wealth, and Happiness* (New York: Penguin Books, 2009).

10. *The Ghost and Mrs. Muir* is a 1947 romantic-fantasy film starring Gene Tierney and Rex Harrison and directed by Joseph L. Mankiewicz. It was also a TV comedy series starring Hope Lange, which ran from 1968 to 1970. Mrs. Muir discovers that the seaside house she's rented is haunted by an old Captain Daniel Gregg. Gregg at first resists this intrusion, but he develops a ghostly love for his Mrs. Muir.

11. For a synthetic presentation of judgment devices, see Lucien Karpik, *Valuing the Unique: The Economics of Singularities*, trans. Nora Scott (Princeton: Princeton University Press, 2010).

12. What follows is the result of work done in collaboration with Fabian Muniesa. Michel Callon and Fabian Muniesa, "Markets as Collective Calculative Devices," *Organization Studies* 26.8 (2005), pp. 1229–50.

13. Nowhere is this definition more appropriate than with database manipulation. When we say that data-driven algorithms calculate, it is worth noting that they do not do so in a strictly mathematical way. In the search for patterns, forms of big data must be put in relation to one another depending on the objective that is at stake. I thank Martha Poon for pointing this out.

14. For a recent update, see Franck Cochoy, "The Cultivation of Market Behaviors and Economic Decisions: Calculation, Qualculation, and Calqulation Revisited," in Frederick F. Wherry and Ian Woodward, *The Oxford Handbook of Consumption* (Oxford: Oxford University Press, 2019), https://www.oxfordhandbooks.com/view/10.1093/oxfordhb/9780190695583.001.0001/oxfordhb-9780190695583-e-13. A quick Google search suggests the term has been taken up in the literature. However, those who insist on keeping both of the original terms might reserve "judgment" for evaluating operations that are more qualitative (with few numbers) and "calculation" for those with many numbers. The point is that calculation is not, by its very nature, different from judgment.

15. Jane Guyer, *Marginal Gains: Monetary Transactions in Atlantic Africa* (Chicago: University of Chicago Press, 2004).

16. For a detailed presentation of Guyer's book, see Michel Callon, "Il n'y a d'économie qu'aux marges," *Le Libellio d'AEGIS* 4.2 (2008), pp. 1–18.

17. Naming things implicitly sets up a distance. If I say "barley" and "wheat," I identify two different goods from the point of view of economic theory. I could just as well have said "cereal," and in that case, there would only be one good that I could contrast with other goods, such as vegetables or prepared foods. Yet there again, no essentialism is possible. Designation operations are inextricably qualculation operations.

18. Émile Benveniste, *Le vocabulaire des institutions indo-européennes* (Paris: Minuit, 1993).

19. "Caddytainers" are large crates with shelves and wheels in which goods are stored in French supermarkets. We will run into them again in Chapter 6, which is on price formulation.

20. I have retained the word "calculation," since it is the one Benveniste explores and uses, but the definition he gives is actually the definition of qualculation.

21. The supermarket shopping cart is an interesting space of calculation. It constitutes a perfect example of a device that allows for goods to be organized in a single space so that several forms of verification and estimation become possible. For many goods, prices are not normally admitted in this space (they stay connected to the shelves), and the consumer's qualculation can therefore be oriented toward nonarithmetical modalities. Franck Cochoy, "Le calqul économique du consommateur: Ce qui s'échange autour d'un chariot," *L'Année sociologique* 61.1 (2011), pp. 71–101.

22. This idea of an invitation resonates with the notion of "affordance": double-entry bookkeeping suggests certain types of action while at the same time making it possible to achieve those actions. See James J. Gibson, *The Ecological Approach to Visual Perception* (Abingdon: Psychology Press, 1979).

23. Max Weber, *Economy and Society: An Outline of Interpretive Sociology*, ed. Guenther Roth and Claus Wittich, trans. Ephraim Fischoff et al., 2 vols. (Berkeley: University of California Press, 1978), vol. 1, p. 90.

24. Ève Chiapello, "Accounting and the Birth of the Notion of Capitalism," *Critical Perspectives on Accounting* 18.3 (2007), pp. 263–96.

25. The literature on this subject is vast. One can get some idea of the different positions by consulting the following: Raymond de Roover, "The Development of Accounting Prior to Luca Pacioli According to the Account Books of Medieval Merchants," in Ananias C. Littletown and Basil S. Yamey, eds., *Studies in the History of Accounting* (London: Sweet and Maxwell, 1956), pp. 114–74; Basil S. Yamey, *Essays on the History of Accounting*

(New York: Arno Press, 1978); Bruce G. Carruthers and Wendy Espeland, "Accounting for Rationality: Double-Entry Bookkeeping and the Rhetoric of Economic Rationality," *American Journal of Sociology* 97.1 (1991), pp. 31–69; John F. Padgett and Walter W. Powell, *The Emergence of Organizations and Markets* (Princeton: Princeton University Press, 2012). For a recent version, which no doubt gives too much importance to double-entry bookkeeping, see Jane J. Gleeson-White, *Double Entry: How the Merchants of Venice Created Modern Finance* (New York: W. W. Norton, 2013).

26. The notion of calculative practices that Peter Miller proposes also offers a way around the instrumental understanding of calculation: see Peter Miller, "Governing by Numbers: Why Calculative Practices Matter," *Social Research* 68.2 (2001), pp. 379–96. This qualculative agency has the advantage, I suggest, of more clearly taking into account the variety of modalities of action to which the practices give rise and in particular the possibility that some calculations are made with strategic aims.

27. Katy Mason, Hans Kjellberg, and Johan Hagberg, *Marketing Performativity: Theories, Practices and Devices* (New York: Routledge, 2018).

28. More generally, the practice of benchmarking, which involves comparing and ranking the performances of companies or competing products (and which reaches well beyond commercial activities), attests to the growing influence of qualculations and their tools. Isabelle Bruno and Emmanuel Didier, *Benchmarking: L'état sous pression statistique* (Paris: La Découverte, 2013).

29. To evaluate R&D and innovation projects, current techniques, such as the valuation of options, are directly borrowed from methods for evaluating portfolios of financial assets.

30. Philip Mirowski and Robert Van Horn, "The Contract Research Organization and the Commercialization of Scientific Research," *Social Studies of Science* 35.4 (2005), pp. 503–48.

31. Liliana Doganova and Marie Eyquem-Renault, "What Do Business Models Do?: Narratives, Calculation and Market Exploration," *Research Policy* 38.10 (2009), pp. 1559–70.

32. Frank Knight, *Risk, Uncertainty and Profit* (Cambridge: Riverside Press, 1921).

33. Marion Fourcade and Rakesh Khurana, "From Social Control to Financial Economics: The Linked Ecologies of Economics and Business in Twentieth Century America," *Theory and Society* 42.2 (2013), pp. 121–59.

34. The LBO is a financial operation that involves buying out a (troubled) company by taking on debt to banking organizations, which preserves the profit earning of the

company's own capital. The debt is generally paid back through a rigorous (and often brutal) lowering of costs, which makes it possible to draw on the cash flow.

35. Jérôme Haas, "Normes comptables internationales: Pour 'compter juste,' nous devons retrouver l'horizon de long terme," *Le Monde*, April 23, 2013, https://www.lemonde .fr/economie/article/2013/04/22/normes-comptables-internationales-pour-compter-juste -nous-devons-retrouver-l-horizon-de-long-terme_3163967_3234.html.

36. Alex Preda, "Les hommes de la Bourse et leurs instruments merveilleux: Technologies de transmission des cours et origines de l'organisation des marchés modernes," *Réseaux* 21.122 (2003), pp. 137–66.

37. Preda notably shows that tickers and their curves are behind "chartism," which involves predicting the probability of certain future evolutions as a function of the (past) shape of curves. France, having only belatedly adopted this technology, stayed away from this know-how, at least for some time. Since visualized recordings of price variations were not available to them, experts in France threw their energies into theoretical speculations, culminating with Louis Bachelier and his hypothesis about random variations, a theory that is dominant today because it fits with the notion of efficient markets. (The efficient market hypothesis implies that at any given moment, prices integrate all the available information, preventing anyone from predicting how they will evolve, condemning traders to use probability distributions.)

38. Daniel Beunza and Raghu Garud, "Calculators, Lemmings or Frame-Makers?: The Intermediary Role of Securities Analysts," in Michel Callon, Yuval Millo, and Fabian Muniesa, eds., *Market Devices* (Malden: Blackwell / Sociological Review, 2007), pp. 13–39.

39. Alexandra Ouroussoff, *Wall Street at War: The Secret Struggle for the Global Economy* (Cambridge: Polity, 2010).

40. Michel Feher, *Rated Agencies: Investee Politics in a Speculative Age* (New York: Zone Books, 2018).

41. Paula Jarzabkowski, Rebecca Bednarek, and Paul Spee, *Making a Market for Acts of God: The Practice of Risk-Trading in the Global Reinsurance Industry* (Oxford: Oxford University Press, 2015).

42. Pierre Bourdieu, *Les structures sociales de l'économie* (Paris: Éditions du Seuil, 2000).

43. Fabian Muniesa and Anne-Sophie Trébuchet-Breitwiller, "Becoming a Measuring Instrument: An Ethnography of Perfume Consumer Testing," *Journal of Cultural Economy* 3.3 (November 2010), pp. 321–37.

44. Hélène Mialet, *Hawking Incorporated: Stephen Hawking and the Anthropology of the Knowing Subject* (Chicago: University of Chicago Press, 2012).

45. Ibid.

46. Tanja Schneider and Steve Woolgar, "Technologies of Ironic Revelation: Enacting Consumers in Neuromarkets," *Consumption, Markets and Culture* 15.2 (2012), pp. 169–89.

47. Of course, one should not take the optimistic predictions of neuromarketing at face value. As Franck Cochoy notes, "Once one lets the person who has been formatted in a lab to function in the medical imagery register out into nature, all the connections that were suspended for a moment will move back into place and therefore replay cognition in a different register from that of neurosciences. The drama of marketing founded on cognitive sciences has always been that it is restricted to the person being manipulated in the lab. We don't have much idea how much he is related to a person in normal life," personal communication. Franck Cochoy is no doubt right. See also Natasha Dow Schüll and Caitlin Zaloom, "The Shortsighted Brain: Neuroeconomics and the Governance of Choice in Time," *Social Studies of Science* 41.4 (2011), pp. 515–38. I remain a little less optimistic than Cochoy. It is not impossible that through forcing, transformations, and heavy equipment, it would be possible to make a distant relative of neuroscience's brain live out in the open: one should never discount an outcome based on optimism alone.

48. Jean Lave, "The Dialectic of Arithmetic in Grocery Shopping," in Jean Lave, Michael Murtaugh, Olivia de La Rocha, and Barbara Rogoff, eds., *Everyday Cognition: Its Development in Social Context* (Cambridge, MA: Harvard University Press, 1984), pp. 67–94.

49. Christian Licoppe, Anne-Sylvie Pharabod, and Houssem Assadi, "Contribution à une sociologie des échanges marchands sur Internet," *Réseaux* 116.6 (2002), pp. 97–140.

50. In his study of the Hinkley Point nuclear power plant, Peter Karnøe uses the notion of frameworks for evaluation proposed by Beunza and Garud in "Calculators, Lemmings or Frame-Makers?" Peter Karnøe, "Framing the Deal for Hinkley Point in the UK: Performing Political Valuation of Economic Reality for New Nuclear Power," (forthcoming).

51. Fabian Muniesa et al., *Capitalization: A Cultural Guide* (Paris: Presses des Mines, 2017).

52. Thanks to Kindle, Amazon has access to my ways of reading (for example, the

passages I select and comment on, the books I abandon halfway through), which it can compare to other readers' ways of reading.

53. Computer scientist Seda Gürses and colleagues have introduced the idea of the programmable infrastructure to draw attention to the specific changes that computation brings when integrated into other types of infrastructures, including market forms. As they argue, what is being called "technology transformation" is an attempt by global tech corporations to make all types of infrastructure programmable. The increased programmability of the human habitus is an endpoint of this endeavor.

54. The message from Amazon I got today is less ambitious. It reads: "Readers who liked Piketty also liked Houellebecq."

CHAPTER FOUR: ORGANIZING MARKET ENCOUNTERS

1. The word "encountering" (or "encounter") should be understood in its broadest sense. It can be, for instance, meeting, matching, or dating. An encounter implies a contact. It may lead to a relationship that is terminated, without a future. But it can also give rise to a common lasting investigation, which is the form that will be privileged in this chapter.

Market agencements organize the possibility of encounters between different entities, agencies, or process-goods, at different stages of their transformation and qualification. These encounters are usually multiple and occur in different places and at different times. As we will see in this chapter, they do not only concern classic interactions between producers and consumers.

2. Dating platforms share a number of traits with commercial coordination. In fact, the commercial metaphor has often been used to describe the search for partners or spouses. One used to say of a young woman that she was "on the market" to signify that a spouse was to be found; it was also said, but more rarely, of young men! Michael Pollak used this metaphor very subtly to describe the mechanisms through which homosexuals managed to meet and conclude "deals" at a time when homosexuality was subject to violent public opprobrium. Michael Pollak, "L'homosexualité masculine, ou: Le bonheur dans le ghetto?," *Communications* 35.1 (1982), pp. 37–55.

3. Commercial activities, in common parlance, include all activities devoted to the establishment of transfers of ownership through monetary payments. They are most often carried out by professional agencies (marketers, logisticians, computer specialists, and so on) who remain invisible and are usually neglected by traditional market theories.

4. The situation has changed over the last few years. See, notably, Luis Araujo, John Finch, and Hans Kjellberg, eds., *Reconnecting Marketing to Markets* (Oxford: Oxford University Press, 2010); Detlev Zwick and Julien Cayla, *Inside Marketing: Practices, Ideologies, Devices* (Oxford: Oxford University Press, 2011).

5. As Weber so nicely puts it when he closely associates markets with commercial practices, to a large extent, even though the consumer has to be in a position to buy, his wants are "awakened" and "directed" by the entrepreneur. Max Weber, *Economy and Society: An Outline of Interpretive Sociology*, ed. Guenther Roth and Claus Wittich, trans. Ephraim Fischoff et al., 2 vols. (Berkeley: University of California Press, 1978), vol. 1, p. 92. Now, before waking the consumer, one makes him dream: "I dreamed it—Sony made it!"

6. The importance of this work for economic theory was highlighted with the awarding of two Nobel prizes, one in 2012 to Roth, and the other in 2010 to Diamond, Mortensen, and Pissarides. For a description of Roth's work for the general public, see Alvin Roth, "The Art of Designing Markets," *Harvard Business Review* (2007), pp. 1–8. (For more details, see marketdesigner.blogspot.fr.) On frictional markets, see the excellent presentation by Étienne Wasmer, "Le prix Nobel 2010: Les marchés frictionnels," *Revue d'économie politique* 121.5 (2011), pp. 637–66.

7. Fabian Muniesa, "Un robot walrasien: Cotation électronique et justesse de la découverte des prix," *Politix* 13.52 (2000), pp. 121–54.

8. Franck Cochoy, personal communication, drew my attention to a delicious and erotic reference on matching. In *Les bijoux indiscrets*, Diderot illustrates the myth of lovers looking for their other half through the image of geometrically shaped sexes searching for their exact counterpart. Denis Diderot, *Les bijoux indiscrets*, chapter 18, "Des voyageurs," pp. 35–36 in the electronic version found at https://www.ebooksgratuits.com/blackmask/diderot_bijoux_indiscrets.pdf

9. Michel de Montaigne, "Of Friendship," in *The Complete Essays of Montaigne*, trans. Donald M. Frame (Stanford: Stanford University Press, 1965), book 1, chapter 28, pp. 135–44.

10. Pierre-André Chiappori, Alfred Galichon, and Bernard Salini, "The Roommate Problem Is More Stable than You Think," *CESifo Working Paper Series* 4676 (2014). Arnaud Dupuy and Alfred Galichon, "Personality Traits and the Marriage Market," Maastricht School of Management, *Working Paper* 41 (2012).

11. Philippe Steiner, *La transplantation d'organes: Un commerce nouveau entre les êtres humains* (Paris: Gallimard, 2010), pp. 194–231.

12. Roth proposes to distinguish between two types of marketplaces: those that

offer homogeneous products and those that require fine-tuning the matchmaking between similar, but heterogeneous supplies and demands.

13. The market interface model, by its very definition, cannot integrate the even more complex platforms that organize the coprofiling of goods and agents (see below) and that rely in particular on an entire digital infrastructure that allows the (increasingly) rapid and fluid renewal of bilateral transactions.

14. Mark Granovetter, *Getting a Job: A Study of Contacts and Careers* (Chicago: University of Chicago Press, 1995).

15. For a presentation of the analysis of social networks, see the following excellent synthesis: Emmanuel Lazega and Tom A. B. Snijders, *Multilevel Network Analysis for the Social Sciences: Theory, Methods and Applications* (New York: Springer, 2016).

16. On salons, see, for instance, Guillaume Favre and Julien Brailly, "La recette de la mondialisation: Sociologie du travail d'un organisateur de salons," *Sociologie du travail* 58.2 (2016), pp. 138–59.

17. In 2020, during the COVID-19 pandemic, it reached 10 percent of retail sales, increasing to 105 billion euros. Fevad (Fédération e-commerce et vente à distance), "La Fevad publie les chiffres-clés du e-commerce en 2020," https://www.fevad.com /chiffres-cles-du-e-commerce-en-2020.

18. It is clear that after having decided to wander through the shopping mall, I have the impression I have made a great deal more effort in the search (I didn't come for nothing!) than if I had simply gone through a series of double clicks from my chair.

19. This information is taken from Valérie Segon, "De nouveaux concepts pour théâtraliser l'offre," *Le Monde*, December 3, 2013, p. 12.

20. Another example of twists and turns due to COVID-19: in France, where for political reasons, small bookshops have maintained a significant place, the pandemic has been an opportunity to mobilize support for their activity and considerably enrich the services they offer.

21. Segon, "De nouveaux concepts pour théâtraliser l'offre."

22. Catherine Grandclément, "Climatiser le marché: Les contributions des marketings de l'ambiance et de l'atmosphère," *ethnographiques.org: Revue en ligne des science humaines et sociales*, no. 6, November 6, 2004, https://www.ethnographiques.org/2004 /Grandclement.

23. Anne Schmidt and Christoph Conrad, eds., *Bodies and Affects in Market Societies* (Tübingen: Mohr Siebeck, 2016).

24. Franck Cochoy, "From Strategy to Equipped Serendipity: Lessons from Ezio, the

Black Angel of Florence," in Rita M. Denny and Patricia L. Sunderland, eds., *Handbook of Anthropology in Business* (Walnut Creek: Left Coast Press, 2014), pp. 683–84.

25. "Serendipity" refers to the fact of discovering something by chance. Here, it is used to underline that the mobile phones guide the potential customer's wanderings in such a way as to lead him to the (meeting) point he had no idea of previously. To paraphrase Pasteur, one might say that chance meetings favor the customers who have been prepared for them—by their smartphones.

26. See Franck Cochoy, *Une histoire du marketing: Discipliner l'économie de marché* (Paris: La Découverte, 1999).

27. Shoshana Zuboff, *The Age of Surveillance Capitalism: The Fight for a Human Future at the New Frontier of Power* (New York: PublicAffairs, 2019); Yves Citton, *The Ecology of Attention* (Cambridge: Polity, 2016); Martha Poon, personal communication: "Indeed, only 35 precent of mobile device users worldwide reported that they are willing to share location data to get more personalized advertising, according to the location services company HERE Technologies in August 2019." See eMarketer, "Location-Based Advertising Is Becoming More Costly," https://www.emarketer.com/content/location-based-advertising-is-becoming-more-costly.

28. Alison Clarke, *Tupperware: The Promise of Plastic in 1950s America* (Washington, DC: Smithsonian Books, 2001).

29. In 2013, online advertisement was 20 percent of advertising revenue. The analysis of data left on the web by consumers allows for targeted advertising. *Le Monde,* "Éco et Entreprise" supplement, April 3, 2013, p. 4.

30. When it comes to the algorithms used by companies to process digitalized customer data with a view to proposing encounters that may lead to commercial transactions, the paradox is symmetrical: everyone knows they exist, many have a fairly precise idea of how they work, yet few are able to get into the very heart of the black box, so strategic is the trade secret. See, for example, Frank Pasquale, *The Black Box Society: The Secret Algorithms That Control Money and Information* (Cambridge, MA: Harvard University Press, 2015).

31. Sandrine Barrey, Franck Cochoy, and Sophie Dubuisson, "Designer, packager et merchandiser: Trois professionnels pour une même scène marchande," *Sociologie du Travail* 42.3 (2000), pp. 457–82; Catherine Grandclément, "Vendre sans vendeurs: Sociologie des dispositifs d'achalandage en supermarché," PhD diss., École des Mines de Paris, 2008; Catherine Grandclément, "Le libre-service à ses origines: Mettre au travail ou construire le consommateur?," *Entreprises et Histoire* 64.3 (2011), pp. 64–75.

32. Pascale Trompette, *Le marché des défunts* (Paris: Presses de Sciences Po, 2008);

Pascale Trompette, "Une économie de la captation: Les dynamiques concurrentielles au sein du marché funéraire," *Revue française de sociologie* 46.2 (2005), pp. 233–64; Pascale Trompette and Olivier Boissin, "Entre les vivants et les morts: Les pompes funèbres aux portes du marché," *Sociologie du Travail* 42.3 (2000), pp. 483–504.

33. Trevor Pinch, "Performativity and Economic Demonstrations: Pitching Quality and Quantity," in Yannick Barthe et al., eds., *Débordements: Mélanges offerts à Michel Callon* (Paris: Presses des Mines, 2010), pp. 369–80; Natasha Schüll, *Addiction by Design: Machine Gambling in Las Vegas* (Princeton: Princeton University Press, 2012); Roman Le Velly, "Les démonstrateurs de foire: Des professionnels de l'interaction symbolique," *Ethnologie française* 37.1 (2007), pp. 143–51.

34. Michèle de La Pradelle, *Market Day in Provence* (Chicago: University of Chicago Press, 2006).

35. Marie-France Garcia, "The Social Construction of a Perfect Market: The Strawberry Auction at Fontaines-en-Sologne," in Donald MacKenzie, Fabian Muniesa, and Lucia Siu, *Do Economists Make Markets?: On the Performativity of Economics* (Princeton: Princeton University Press, 2007), pp. 20–54.

36. On all these, see Alexandre Mallard, *Petit dans le marché: Une sociologie de la très petite entreprise* (Paris: Presses des Mines, 2011).

37. Bogdan Filip Popescu, *Crowdfunding à la française* (Paris: Presses des Mines, 2015).

38. For reasons that are easy to understand, these platforms cannot replace (global) financial markets, with their central banks, their different currencies, their hierarchies, their risk-hedging tools, and so on. What is important in this example is the idea that there is nothing that prevents innovative new devices from combining financing and stakeholder engagement in ways that might be generalized. (See Chapter 7.)

39. Economists have coined the term "network externalities" to describe this process: the wider the network, the greater the number of agents who may become interested in the project.

40. Ash Amin, *Lands of Strangers* (Cambridge: Polity, 2012).

41. The Exploratorium, a museum of science, technology, and arts in San Francisco, has been called "a mad scientist's penny arcade, a scientific funhouse, and an experimental laboratory all rolled into one" that "offers visitors a variety of ways...to explore and understand the world around them" (Wikipedia).

42. As defined by practitioners, CRM is a technique based on client relationships and customer loyalty. Using customer data and feedback, companies develop long-term relationships and brand awareness. CRM varies greatly from the traditional transactional

marketing approach, which focuses on increasing individual sales numbers. It is based on various devices aimed at collecting and analyzing individual data.

43. Anthony Beckett, "Governing the Consumer: Technologies of Consumption," *Consumption, Markets and Culture* 15.1 (2012), pp. 1-18. I recommend this journal as a source for those readers who are interested in marketing techniques and the part they play in the organization of market agencements.

44. Sami Coll, *Surveiller et récompenser: Les cartes de fidélité qui nous gouvernent* (Geneva: Seismo, 2012). The book emphasizes surveillance and does not give enough attention to the explorations these cards allow.

45. Marsha Zorn, "Why Predictive Analytics Usurp CRM as Key to Sales Success," private email, February 16, 2016.

46. The same can be said of Amazon. To reduce it to a surveillance system is a political error that overlooks the reasons for its commercial success. Big Brother was never an exploratorium. In view of the multiplication of systems for collecting and processing individual data in sectors other than the market one, the matters of concern raised by their joint implementation and linkages are bound to multiply. These matters of concern cannot be captured by the old notion of surveillance. Rather, they are associated with the emergence of issues revolving around, among others, the construction of identity, privacy, individual rights, and intellectual property.

47. David Jones, Alberto Cambrosio, and Andrei Mogoutov, "Detection and Characterization of Translational Research in Cancer and Cardiovascular Medicine," *Journal of Translational Medicine* 57.9 (2011), pp. 9-57.

48. Peter Keating and Alberto Cambrosio, *Cancer on Trial: Oncology as a New Style of Practice* (Chicago: University of Chicago Press, 2012). Keating and Cambrosio have drawn attention to the relevance of the notion of platform for describing the movement of innovations, notably in medicine.

49. This ambiguity was inscribed in the first moments of discovery. It was doctors charged with picking up and performing autopsies on the corpses of soldiers killed by gas in World War I who identified its strange therapeutic properties.

50. Phase 1 follows the preclinical phase aims to evaluate tolerance and the absence of undesirable side effects; phase 2 starts to study efficacy and dosage; phase 3 studies effectiveness, properly speaking.

51. Andrew Lakoff, *Pharmaceutical Reason: Knowledge and Value in Global Psychiatry* (Cambridge: Cambridge University Press, 2006); Philippe Pignarre, *Le grand secret de l'industrie pharmaceutique* (Paris: Découverte, 2003).

52. Vololona Rabeharisoa et al., "From 'Politics of Numbers' to 'Politics of Singu-larisation': Patients' Activism and Engagement in Research on Rare Diseases in France and Portugal," *BioSocieties* 9.2 (2014), pp. 194–217.

53. Pascale Santi, "Cancer: Favoriser l'accès aux thérapies ciblées," *Le Monde*, "Sci-ences et Médecine" supplement, February 4, 2015, p. 2.

54. Lynne Pettinger, "Market Moralities in the Field of Commercial Sex," *Journal of Cultural Economy* 6.2 (2013), pp. 184–99. The article shows how the platform pro-poses evaluation systems that facilitate the singularizing of services, notably by allow-ing exchanges on the basis of behavior considered to be morally "good": morality is not exterior to the service, but instead incorporated in its qualification.

55. See, for example, François Eymard-Duvernay and Emmanuelle Marchal, *Le juge-ment des compétences sur le marché du travail: Façons de recruter* (Paris: Métailié, 1997).

56. See, for example, Pierre François, *Le monde de la musique ancienne: Sociologie économique d'une innovation esthétique* (Paris: Economica, 2005); Pierre-Michel Menger, *La profession de comédien: Formation, activités et carrières dans la démultiplication de soi* (Paris: La Documentation Française, 1997); Vincent Cardon, "Produire l'évidence: Le travail d'appariement et de recrutement dans le monde du cinéma," *Sociologie du Tra-vail* 58.2 (2016), pp. 160–80.

57. Sandrine Cassini, "Bataille géante autour du magot des données," *Le Monde*, "Éco et Entreprise" supplement, October 14, 2013, p. 20.

58. This applied sociology is related to an old intuition in the social sciences and more precisely in Georg Simmel's theory of social circles, which influenced the analy-sis of social networks: "The development of the public mind shows itself by the fact that a sufficient number of circles is present which have form and organization. Their num-ber is sufficient in the sense that they give an individual of many gifts the opportunity to pursue each of his interests in association with others." Georg Simmel, *Conflict and the Web of Group Affiliations*, trans. Kurt H. Wolff and Reinhard Bendix (1922; Glencoe: Free Press, 1955). Quoted in Charles Kadushin, *Introduction to Social Networks: Theo-ries, Concepts, and Findings* (New York: Oxford University Press, 2012), p. 46. Profiling is exploring the universe of social circles.

59. For a visualization of these relations, see Bruno Latour et al., "The Whole Is Always Smaller Than Its Parts—A Digital Test of Gabriel Tardes' Monads," *British Jour-nal of Sociology* 63.4 (2012), pp. 590–615.

60. In *Incorporated!*, an exhibition in Rennes in 2016, Ed Atkins gave a forceful description of this development: "In one of these films, *Safe Conduct*," he "shows a man

who, caught up in the mechanisms of security checks in an airport, responds to them so well that he ends up dismembered and putting his guts through the X-ray machine." Emmanuelle Lequeux, "Quand l'art donne corps à l'économie," *Le Monde*, November 29, 2016, p. 21. See also La Criée Centre D'Art Contemporain-F, "Exhibition: 5th edition Les Ateliers de Rennes—Biennial of Contemporary Art. Incorporated!," https://www .la-criee.org/en/incorporated-2.

61. Singularization is the strategic aim of market agencements. (See Chapter 7.) It prepares, facilitates, and accompanies the completion of commercial transactions. This framing, like the other four, is ambivalent: it adjusts and constrains. Singularization (whether intense or not) is always part of an exercise of power.

62. The multitude is not a matter of sheer numbers. The notion refers to an open crowd, a rich grouping of people in a variable geometry composed of diverse identities, all of whom recognize themselves, at least for a moment, as sharing a common affect.

63. David Riesman, *The Lonely Crowd; A Study of the Changing American Character* (New Haven: Yale University Press, 1950).

64. Timothy Mitchell, *Carbon Democracy: Political Power in the Age of Oil* (London: Verso, 2013).

65. For an American encapsulation of this position, see, for example, Julia Angewin, *Dragnet Nation: A Quest for Privacy, Security, and Freedom in a World of Relentless Surveillance* (New York: Times Books, 2014).

66. Albert O. Hirschman, *Exit, Voice, and Loyalty; Responses to Decline in Firms, Organizations, and States* (Cambridge, MA: Harvard University Press, 1970).

67. Private mail. Excerpt from an invitation to a meeting organized in 2013 by X-Biotech (an alumni association of École Polytechnique). Translated from the French.

68. Isabelle Bruno, Emmanuel Didier, and Julien Prévieux, *Statactivisme: Comment lutter avec des nombres* (Paris: La Découverte/Zones, 2014).

69. Gilles Bastin, "Big Data vous regarde!," *Le Monde*, "Le Monde des livres" supplement, April 18, 2014, p. 2. See also Bruno, Didier, and Prévieux, *Statactivisme*.

70. The Conseil d'État is the French counterpart of the Supreme Court in the United States.

71. Joëlle Stolz, "Biobanques: Le patient recomposé," *Le Monde*, "Science et Médecine" supplement, June 18, 2014, p. 4.

72. Olivier Schrameck, quoted in Alexandre Piquard, "Télévision: Les algorithmes, qui analysent les usages, suscitent un grand débat" *Le Monde*, September 13, 2014. Indeed, Netflix explicitly makes such a claim: "For us a central point is the algorithm,

artificial intelligence.... The platform is a meeting site for people and shows." Netflix's suggestion motor, like Amazon's, promises to offer a personalized selection of series and films, depending on what has been watched previously, the characteristics of the work watched, and the consumption habits of millions of other users. These are of course suggestions that some users will find problematic or will refuse.

73. In Sartre's conception, serial groups are groups in which "individuals are oriented toward the same goals by their response to existing conditions and structures in the environment, which are the collective legacy of human actions and decisions in the past." Wikipedia, s.v. "Seriality (Gender Studies)."

74. Alexis Delcambre, "La fin de la télévision à la papa," *Le Monde*, "Éco et Entreprise" supplement, September 14-15, 2014, p. 3.

75. For the classic article, which examines some 76,897 microgenres available on Netflix, see Alexis C. Madrigal, "How Netflix Reverse-Engineered Hollywood," *Atlantic*, January 2, 2014, https://www.theatlantic.com/technology/archive/2014/01/how-netflix-reverse-engineered-hollywood/282679. (Martha Poon, personal communication.)

76. "Je suis Charlie"—"I am Charlie"—was the omnipresent slogan by which people and institutions signaled solidarity with those assassinated in the offices of the satirical magazine *Charlie Hebdo* by Islamic terrorists on January 5, 2015.

77. After France's victory in the football World Championship of 1998, the team was celebrated as "black, blanc, beur" (black, white, Arab), playing on "bleu, blanc, rouge" (blue, white, red), which refers to the tricolor national flag. In the ensuing euphoria, "black, blanc, beur" seemed to have become a rallying cry, calling French people to support a stronger racial integration and to take responsibility for immigration.

78. Zinedine Zidane is a very popular French football player and a Muslim of Algerian Kabyle descent.

79. Another illustration of this form of television is the French Téléthon, very different from the US one. Some have even called the show, which is organized each year by the French association against muscular dystrophy, "the fourteenth of July in winter," in reference to the French national holiday.

80. This concept of a multitude is close to Spinoza's: "Inasmuch as men are led, as we have said, more by passion than reason, it follows, that a multitude comes together, and wishes to be guided, as it were, by one mind, not at the suggestion of reason, but of some common passion." Benedict de Spinoza, *A Political Treatise*, in *The Chief Works of Benedict de Spinoza, Vol. 1*, trans. R. H. M. Elwes, chapter 6, article 1, https://oll.libertyfund

.org/title/elwes-the-chief-works-of-benedict-de-spinoza-vol-1#lf1321-01_label_388. Affect binds the group; market agencements contribute to the process of producing affect.

CHAPTER FIVE: *AFFECTIO MERCATUS*: ATTACHMENTS AND DETACHMENTS

1. For a further explanation, see note 21 below.

2. Emma Rothschild, *Economic Sentiments: Adam Smith, Condorcet, and the Enlightenment* (Cambridge, MA: Harvard University Press, 2002).

3. "Whenever I endeavor to examine my own conduct—whenever I try to pass sentence on it, and either to approve or condemn it—it's evident that, in all such cases, I divide myself, as it were, into two persons.... One is the spectator, whose sentiments with regard to my own conduct I endeavor to enter into by placing myself in his situation and considering how it would appear to me when seen from that particular point of view. The second is the agent, the person whom I properly call 'myself,' the person about whose conduct I as spectator was endeavoring to form some opinion. The first is the judge, the second the person judged of." Adam Smith, *The Theory of Moral Sentiments* (Cambridge: Cambridge University Press, 2002), p. 131.

4. Julia Elyachar, *Markets of Dispossession: NGOs, Economic Development, and the State in Cairo* (Durham: Duke University Press, 2005).

5. Jean-Christophe Agnew, *Worlds Apart: The Market and the Theater in Anglo-American Thought, 1550–1750* (Cambridge: Cambridge University Press, 1986).

6. To be thorough here, recall that competition, as Albert O. Hirschman puts it, is itself a robust device for containing passions and reducing them to a calculation of interests. Kenneth Arrow is clear that neither empathy nor competitive mechanisms are enough. There must be other, opposing passions.

7. Kenneth Arrow, *The Limits of Organization* (New York: Norton, 1974). Although a tad repetitive and full of platitudes, the literature on the notion of trust is vast. Sociologists such as Niklas Luhmann consider trust to be one of the pillars of collective life. As for economic theory, a good synthesis was given by Diego Gambetta: *Trust: Making and Breaking Cooperative Relations* (Oxford: Blackwell, 1988). For economic history, a useful source is Francesca Trivellato, *The Familiarity of Strangers: The Sephardic Diaspora, Livorno, and Cross-Cultural Trade in the Early Modern Period* (New Haven: Yale University Press, 2009).

8. Philippe Steiner, *Donner: Une histoire de l'altruisme* (Paris: Presses universitaires de France, 2016).

9. On these points, see the useful synthesis by Emmanuel Petit, *Économie des émo-*

tions (Paris: La Découverte, 2015), and Bruno Latour and Vincent-Antonin Lepinay, *The Science of Passionate Interests: An Introduction to Gabriel Tarde's Economic Anthropology* (Chicago: University of Chicago Press, 2010).

10. Max Weber, *The Protestant Ethic and the Spirit of Capitalism*, trans. Talcott Parsons (New York: Scribner's, 1950), p. 17.

11. Albert O. Hirschman, *The Passions and the Interests: Political Arguments for Capitalism before Its Triumph* (Princeton: Princeton University Press, 1977).

12. Gary Becker and Kevin Murphy, "A Theory of Rational Addiction," *Journal of Political Economy* 96 (1988), pp. 675–700; Gary Becker and George Stigler, "De gustibus non est disputandum," *American Economic Review* 67 (1977), pp. 76–90.

13. Jon Elster, *Ulysses and the Sirens: Studies in Rationality and Irrationality* (Cambridge: Cambridge University Press, 1985).

14. Peter Diamond and Hannu Vartiainen, eds., *Behavioral Economics and Its Applications* (Princeton: Princeton University Press, 2007). The assertions of behaviorists are controversial. What interests me here, however, is not so much to evaluate their solidity (indeed, I would be quite incapable of doing so!), but rather to take note that there is research that explicitly aims for an empirical analysis of how goods act on and with people.

15. Norbert Elias, *The Civilizing Process: Sociogenetic and Psychogenetic Investigations*, rev. ed., trans. Edmund Jephcott (Oxford: Blackwell, 2000).

16. Michel Crozier, *The Bureaucratic Phenomenon* (Chicago: University of Chicago Press, 1964).

17. Arlie Hochschild, *The Managed Heart: The Commercialization of Human Feeling* (Berkeley: University of California Press, 1983). As the number of service jobs increases, so does the amount of emotional work being done.

18. See, for instance, Alexandra Bidet, *L'engagement dans le travail: Qu'est-ce que le vrai boulot?* (Paris: Presses universitaires de France, 2015).

19. For an incisive critique of these approaches, see Antoine Hennion, *The Passion for Music: A Sociology of Mediation* (Surrey: Ashgate, 2015). On the notion of a regime of taste, see Zeynep Arsel and Jonathan Bean, "Taste Regimes and Market-Mediated Practice," *Journal of Consumer Research* 39.5 (2013), pp. 899–917.

20. For the case of precious goods, see Anne-Sophie Trébuchet-Breitwiller, "Le travail du précieux: Une anthropologie économique des produits de luxe à travers les exemples de parfum et de vin," PhD diss., École des mines de Paris, 2011.

21. *Translator's note*: The French verb *être affecté* can have the same meaning as its literal translation in English: "to be affected." One can, for instance, "être affecté par"

(be affected *by*) climate change, emotions, marketing strategies, or books. However, "être affecté à" means to be assigned to—for example to be assigned *to* a job, a group, a position, or a task. The term *affectation* refers to the fact of being *affecté* (affected), but since it does not mark the preposition (*par* or *à*, by or to) it evokes both possible meanings. It thus allows the author to make the point that the two functions can be distinguished analytically and yet cannot be dissociated.

22. Jean-Hugues Déchaux, "Intégrer l'émotion à l'analyse sociologique de l'action," *Terrains/Théories* 2 (2015), http://journals.openedition.org/teth/208.

23. Ibid.

24. A third meaning of the word "affectation" is commonly recognized in English. It is said of someone that their behavior is "affected" when it seems like they are acting out a part. An affectation is also the capacity to present a different image of oneself. This practice is commonplace in market activities, notably in branding strategies discussed below.

25. Antoine Hennion, "Those Things That Hold Us Together: Taste and Sociology," *Cultural Sociology* 1.1 (2007), pp. 97–114; Antoine Hennion, "Pragmatics of Taste," in Mark D. Jacobs and Nancy Weiss Hanrahan, eds., *The Blackwell Companion to the Sociology of Culture* (Oxford: Blackwell, 2004), pp. 131–44; Antoine Hennion, "Attachments, You Say...?: How a Concept Collectively Emerges in One Research Group," *Journal of Cultural Economy* 10.1 (2017), pp. 112-12; Antoine Hennion, "From ANT to pragmatism: A Journey with Bruno Latour at the CSI," in "Recomposing the Humanities—with Bruno Latour," special issue, *New Literary History* 47.2/3 (2016), pp. 289-308; Antoine Hennion, "Paying Attention: What Is Tasting Wine About?," in Ariane Berthoin Antal, Michael Hutter, and David Stark, eds., *Moments of Valuation: Exploring Sites of Dissonance* (Oxford: Oxford University Press, 2015), pp. 37–56.

26. On the strategic role of curiosity, see Franck Cochoy, *On Curiosity: The Art of Market Seduction* (Manchester: Mattering Press, 2016).

27. Emmanuel Kessous, "From Market Relations to Romantic Ties: The Tests of Internet Dating," in Franck Cochoy, Joe Deville, and Liz McFall, eds., *Markets and the Arts of Attachment* (London: Routledge, 2017), pp. 147–61.

28. "They both arrived, and I said to them: 'Listen, we're going to have a match for fun, you have fifteen minutes to seduce each other.' She started and he picked up the ball, and it became true. I saw that they were both losing control at some point because they were saying 'I can't do this anymore, this isn't a game any more, this is life,'" Séguéla reported. "Nicolas Sarkozy et Carla Bruni: Jacques Séguéla révèle de croustillants détails sur leur rencontre, *Nonstop People*, August 16, 2020, http://www.non

-stop-people.com/actu/politique/nicolas-sarkozy-et-carla-bruni-jacques-seguela-revele-de
-croustillants-details-sur.

29. Franck Cochoy, "From Social Ties to Socioeconomic Attachments: A Matter of Selection and Collection," in Cochoy, Deville, and McFall, eds., *Markets and the Arts of Attachment*, pp. 22–37. On the role collections play in enriching goods and agents, see also Luc Boltanski and Arnaud Esquerre, *Enrichissement: Une critique de la marchandise* (Paris: Gallimard, 2017).

30. "Space is an affection of being in so far as it is being." Isaac Newton, in A. Rupert Hall and Marie Boas Hall, eds., *Unpublished Scientific Papers of Isaac Newton: A Selection from the Portsmouth Collection in the University Library* (Cambridge: Cambridge University Press, 1962), p. 136, quoted in Steffen Ducheyne, "Isaac Newton on Space and Time: Metaphysician or Not?," *Philosophica* 67.1 (2001), pp. 77–111.

31. Alexandre Mallard, *Petit dans le marché: Une sociologie de la très petite entreprise* (Paris: Presses de l'École des Mines, 2011), p 121.

32. Devices of personalized conversation are at the heart of contemporary markets. There are a thousand ways to address each consumer as though one knew everything about the person and what that individual expects. The simplest method is to address the person by name, as the producer of mineral water who offers bottles engraved with first names well understood. Marsha Zorn, an expert in customer relational marketing (CRM), shrewdly remarks, "Isn't it great to hear yourself called by your first name when you walk into your favorite restaurant? Isn't it nice that you are served your favorite beverage before you even open your mouth?"

33. Such practices are invading all domains and are particularly developed in the creative sectors, notably in music. Andrew Leyshon and his colleagues describe a new economic model in the music industry. Creation is associated with collective events that exploit fans' enthusiasm and lead to a real "commerce of affects." This powerful mobilization of consumer attachment devices is not simply conversational. Fans can be involved so that the creation has a collective aspect and the devices then transform into coproduction of the type I analyze below. Andrew Leysho et al., "Leveraging Affect: Mobilizing Enthusiasm and the Co-Production of the Musical Economy," in Brian J. Hracs, Michael Seman, and Tarek E. Virani, eds., *The Production and Consumption of Music in the Digital Age* (Abingdon-on-Thames: Routledge, 2016), pp. 248–62.

34. Tomas Ariztia, "Manufacturing the Consumer's Truth: The Uses of Consumer Research in Advertising Inquiry," in Cochoy, Deville, and McFall, eds., *Markets and the Arts of Attachment*, pp. 38–54.

35. See the Tesco example in the previous chapter.

36. Alexandre Mallard, "You Are a Star Consumer, Please Hold the Line: CRM and the Sociotechnical Inscription of Market Attachment," in Cochoy, Deville, and McFall, eds., *Markets and the Arts of Attachment*, pp. 89-107.

37. Joe Deville and Liz McFall, "The Market Will Have You: The Arts of Market Attachment in a Digital Economy," in Cochoy, Deville, and McFall, eds., *Markets and the Arts of Attachment*, pp. 108-31.

38. Alexandre Mallard, "Cadrer et encadrer la vente: Réflexion sur l'avenir des relations interpersonnelles dans une société d'organisations commerciales," in Franck Cochoy, ed., *Du lien marchand: Essai(s) de sociologie économique relationniste* (Toulouse: Presses universitaires du Mirail, 2012), pp. 81-106.

39. For a subtle analysis of these switches, see Lucien Karpik, *French Lawyers: A Study in Collective Action, 1274–1974* (Oxford: Oxford University Press, 1999).

40. On the notion of honest commerce as a legal formulation of this truth regime, see Roland Canu and Franck Cochoy, "La loi de 1905 sur la répression des fraudes: Un levier décisif pour l'engagement politique des questions de consommation?," *Sciences de la société* 62 (2004), pp. 69-91. You, dear reader, may think that this praise of rhetoric is typically French. I concede that we love *bonimenteurs*. But I remain convinced that every salesperson is a *bonimenteur*, and every buyer is sensitive to *bonimenteurs*.

41. In marketing, it is often repeated that buyers are liars. No one is more of a liar than I am! On the (notably discursive) devices that engage agents, see Robert-Vincent Joule and Jean-Léon Beauvois, *Petit traité de manipulation à l'usage des honnêtes gens* (Fontaine: Presses universitaires de Grenoble, 2002).

42. Madeleine Akrich, Michel Callon, and Bruno Latour, "The Key to Success in Innovation," *International Journal of Innovation Management* 6.2 (2002), pp. 187-225.

43. Eric von Hippel, *Democratizing Innovation* (Cambridge, MA: MIT Press, 2004).

44. Vololona Rabehariso et al., "From 'Politics of Numbers' to 'Politics of Singularisation'," *Biosocieties* (2014), pp. 194-217.

45. Peter Keating and Alberto Cambrosio, *Cancer on Trial: Oncology as a New Style of Practice* (Chicago: University of Chicago Press, 2012).

46. Pierre-Benoît Joly, Arie Rip, and Michel Callon, "Reinventing Innovation," in Maarten J. Arentsen, Wouter Van Rossum, and Albert E. Steenge, eds., *Governance of Innovation: Firms, Clusters and Institutions in a Changing Setting* (Camberley: Edward Elgar, 2010), pp. 19-32.

47. Henry Chesbrough, *Open Innovation: The New Imperative for Creating and Prof-*

NOTES

474

iting from Technology (Boston: Harvard Business School Publishing, 2003). For a more recent presentation, see Joel West, Ammon Salter, Wim Vanhaverbeke, and Henry Chesbrough, "Open Innovation: The Next Decade," *Research Policy* 43 (2014), pp. 805-11.

48. Svetlana Alpers, *Rembrandt's Enterprise: The Studio and the Market* (Chicago: University of Chicago Press, 1988). For an interesting perspective, see Charlotte Guichard, "Du *'nouveau connaisseurship'* à l'histoire de l'art: Original et autographie en peinture," *Annales: Histoires, Sciences Sociales* 6 (2010), pp. 1387-1401.

49. Hans Kjellberg, "Acquiring Associations: On the Unexpected Social Consequences of Possessive Relations," in Cochoy, Deville, and McFall, eds., *Markets and the Arts of Attachment*, pp. 162-79.

50. Luis Araujo, John Finch, and Hans Kjellberg, eds., *Reconnecting Marketing to Markets* (Oxford: Oxford University Press, 2010); Roderick Brodie, Linda Hollebeek, and Jodie Conduit, eds., *Customer Engagement: Contemporary Issues and Challenges* (Abingdon-on-Thames: Routledge, 2015).

51. Hans Kjellberg and Claes-Fredrik Helgesson, "The Mode of Exchange and Shaping of Markets: Distributor Influence in the Swedish Post-War Food Industry," *Industrial Marketing Management* 36 (2007), pp. 861-78; Franck Cochoy, "La captation des publics entre dispositifs et dispositions, ou le petit chaperon rouge revisité," in Franck Cochoy, ed., *La captation des publics* (Toulouse: Presses universitaires du Mirail, 2004), pp. 11-68.

52. Franck Cochoy, "Calculation, qualculation, calqulation: Shopping Cart Arithmetic, Equipped Cognition and the Cluster Consumer," in "Market Forms and Marketing Practices," special issue, *Marketing Theory* 1 (2008), pp. 15-44.

53. Carolin Gerlitz, "Interfacing Attachments: The Multivalence of Brands," in Cochoy, Deville, and McFall, eds., *Markets and the Arts of Attachment*, pp. 72-88.

54. The following passages summarize and reflect as closely as possible some of the descriptions and analyses presented in Natasha Schüll, *Addiction by Design: Machine Gambling in Las Vegas* (Princeton: Princeton University Press, 2012).

55. Nigel Thrift, "Re-inventing Invention: New Tendencies in Capitalist Commodification," *Economy and Society* 35.2 (2006), pp. 279-306.

56. It should be emphasized that the manipulation of the gamblers is repeated in a manipulation of the manipulators. Casino operators are the target for those who promise ever more competitive addiction devices. It would be more accurate to talk of "addiction chains" that derive from and feed one another.

57. That recently led some restaurants to offer caviar with ketchup!

58. Alexis Delcambre, "Blackpills mise sur 'l'addiction' aux videos sur mobile.'" *Le*

Monde, March 29, 2017, https://www.lemonde.fr/actualite-medias/article/2017/03/29/blackpills-mise-sur-l-addiction-aux-videos-sur-mobile_5102319_3236.html.

59. A Roman citizen who could not pay his debts and became his creditor's slave was called a *nexus*, a word designating "he who is attached, bound." Addiction is no doubt the purest expression of attachment.

60. Deville and McFall, "The Market Will Have You."

61. José Ossandon, "'My Story Has No String Attached': Credit Cards, Market Devices and a Stone Guest," in Cochoy, Deville, and McFall, eds., *Markets and the Arts of Attachment*, pp. 132–46.

62. This explains why with gambling, addiction devices vary widely from one country to the next. In Japan, in the pachinko rooms, the seclusion zone Schüll describes does not exist. The gambler has to struggle constantly against the deafening noise of the machines, the way Western pinball players do. Creating dependence is essentially an experimental matter. I thank Franck Cochoy for drawing my attention to this point.

63. For an illustration of this diversity in the case of telecommunications, see Emmanuel Kessous and Alexandre Mallard, eds., *La fabrique de la vente: Le travail commercial dans les télécommunications* (Paris: Presses des Mines, 2014).

64. The qualification of addiction as a medical category is very controversial. Here, I am simply using the term in its lay meaning: the inability to stop doing or consuming something, even if harmful.

65. Paul Rabinow, *Essays on the Anthropology of Reason* (Princeton: Princeton University Press, 1996).

66. The notion of addiction has become a full-fledged economic category with the regulation of certain markets (tobacco, alcohol, gambling, food, and so on). In a report dated October 4, 2016, Terra Nova, a think tank close to the French Socialist Party, suggests creating an authority to regulate cannabis along the lines of the authority for regulating online gaming set up after the May 12, 2010, vote that legalized gambling. The report asserts that "the question of cannabis is analogous to that of connected gaming, consumers having similar behavior patterns." The establishment of a regulated market aims in both cases to dry up the criminal commercial activities and to manage a public health problem that criminal policies cannot handle. As to the creation of administrative authority, its aim is to prevent the state from falling into fiscal addiction by becoming too dependent (financially) on those who are dependent on cannabis!

1. "Here is Rhodes, jump here!" This locution appears in *Aesop's Fables* and was recycled by Hegel and Marx. It means that the situation forbids any shilly-shallying, that the action at stake is to be executed. In this book, the reality test is indeed to explain how prices are determined in actual commercial arrangements.

2. Michel Butor, *La modification* (Paris: Éditions de minuit, 1957). Available in English as *Second Thoughts*, trans. Jean Stewart (1958) and later as *A Change of Heart* (1959) and *Changing Track* (2017, revised translation). In it, the protagonist gradually suspends taking a decisive, life-changing action.

3. See the classic presentation of a barter situation with two agents in Alfred Marshall, *Principles of Economics*, 8th ed. (London: Macmillan, 1920), p. 464.

4. Economists call *Pb* the "reserve price."

5. How agents discover *Ps* and *Pb* is itself a question. In the bilateral transaction, one has to consider the possibility that finding these two prices is also at stake in the power relations between agents. There is therefore a whole range of configurations in the process of determining the transaction price, and they vary according to the relative importance of calculation and power relations.

6. Antoine Augustin Cournot, *Researches into the Mathematical Principles of the Theory of Wealth*, trans. Nathaniel T. Bacon (1897; New York: Macmillan, 1927).

7. William J. Baumol, John C. Panzar, and Robert D. Willig, *Contestable Markets and the Theory of Industry Structure* (New York: Harcourt Brace Jovanovich, 1982). The notion of *workable competition* put forward by John M. Clark a few decades earlier is quite similar to that of contestable markets. See Hervé Dumez and Alain Jeunemaître, "The Unlikely Encounter between Economics and a Market: The Case of the Cement Industry," in Michel Callon, ed., *The Laws of the Markets* (Oxford: Blackwell, 1998), pp. 222-43. These studies question the very notion of competition and the way it is complexly linked to the number of agents in play. This leads to two ways of verifying that competition exists. In the first case, the hypothesis is that the correct organization of the interface market, that is to say, the number of agents involved, is a sufficient indicator. In the second case, one goes to the essential: you have to show that the price is well calculated and that the part that depends on power relations has been eliminated.

8. Jens Beckert, "Where Do Prices Come From?: Sociological Approaches to Price Formation," *Socio-Economic Review* 9.4 (2011), pp. 757-86.

9. The study of social networks is an area of research that has developed considerably over the last three decades. See, notably for economic sociology, Mark Granovetter,

"Economic Action and Social Structure: The Problem of Embeddedness," *American Journal of Sociology* 91.3 (1985), pp. 481-510; Wayne Baker, "The Social Structure of a National Securities Market," *American Journal of Sociology* 89 (1984), pp. 775-811; Joel Podolny, "A Status-Based Model of Market Competition," *American Journal of Sociology* 98.4 (1993), pp. 829-72; Brian Uzzi and Ryan Lancaster, "Embeddedness and Price Formation in the Corporate Law Market," *American Sociological Review* 69.3 (2004), pp. 319-44; Harrison White, "Where Do Markets Come From?," *American Journal of Sociology* 87 (1981), pp. 517-47. Certain authors do not hesitate to move from one model of networks to another or to combine them. White, for instance, considers that in certain market configurations, producers lose interest in consumer preferences, simply observing how consumers react to the prices offered by competitors, whereas in other configurations, he highlights the role of the networks of relations between buyers and sellers.

10. Baker, "The Social Structure of a National Securities Market."

11. Mark Granovetter, *Getting a Job: A Study of Contacts and Careers* (Chicago: University of Chicago Press, 1995).

12. Ryon Lancaster and Brian Uzzi, "Legally Charged: Embeddedness and Profit in Large Law Firm Legal Billings," *Sociological Focus* 45.1 (2012), pp. 1-22.

13. White, "Where Do Markets Come From?"

14. Pierre Bourdieu, *The Social Structures of the Economy*, trans. Chris Turner (Cambridge: Polity Press, 2005); Neil Fligstein, *The Architecture of Markets: An Economic Sociology of Twenty-First-Century Capitalist Societies* (Princeton: Princeton University Press, 2001).

15. Bourdieu, *The Social Structures of the Economy*.

16. Tim Mitchell shows that multinational oil companies managed to impose their antimarket policy successfully for several decades. Timothy Mitchell, *Carbon Democracy: Political Power in the Age of Oil* (London: Verso, 2013).

17. Joe Bain, *Industrial Organizations* (New York: Wiley, 1968).

18. Mark Zbaracki and Mark Bergen, "When Truces Collapse: A Longitudinal Study of Price-Adjustment Routines," *Organization Science* 21.5 (2010), pp. 955-97; Shantanu Dutta, Mark Zbaracki, and Mark Bergen, "Pricing Process as Capability: A Resource-Based Perspective," *Strategic Management Journal* 24.7 (2003), pp. 615-30.

19. Max Weber, *Economy and Society: An Outline of Interpretive Sociology*, ed. Guenther Roth and Claus Wittich, trans. Ephraim Fischoff et al., 2 vols. (Berkeley: University of California Press, 1978), vol. 1, p. 108.

20. For a demonstration of how Bordeaux wines mature, see Orley Ashenfelter,

David Ashmore, and Robert LaLonde, "Wine Vintage Quality and the Weather," *Chance* 8.4 (1995), pp. 7–14. The authors' analysis and the controversy it provoked are presented in Étienne Wasmer, *Principes de microéconomie: Méthodes empiriques et théories modernes* (London: Pearson, 2010).

21. Jens Beckert, Jörg Rössel, and Patrick Schenk, "Wine as a Cultural Product: Symbolic Capital and Price Formation in the Wine Field," *Sociological Perspectives* 60.1 (2017), pp. 206–22.

22. There can, of course, be uncertainties as to these objective qualities, some of which will be discovered only with use. This explains the existence of devices aimed at reducing these uncertainties. For example, testimonials from prior purchasers and users are increasingly solicited and make it possible to provide answers to the questions that candidate buyers are asking about the product. It is nonetheless supposed that the qualities are intrinsically, materially attached to the good.

23. This analysis is in line with the interface market model, which is based on the same opposition between objective and subjective properties.

24. Marx, who did so much to shore up an objective definition of value, frees himself from this question in book 3 of *Capital* with his ingenious theory of production prices.

25. Claude Riveline, *Évaluation des coûts: Éléments d'une théorie de la gestion* (Paris: Presses des Mines, 2005).

26. This technique involves the seller calculating the price by adding the gross margin to all the costs incurred.

27. Gerald R. Faulhaber and William J. Baumol, "Economists as Innovators: Practical Products of Theoretical Research," *Journal of Economic Literature* 26.2 (1988), pp. 577–600.

28. Éric Brousseau, Pascal Petit, and Denis Phan, *La mutation des télécommunications des industries et des marchés* (Paris: ENSPTT-Economica, 1996).

29. During the famous "two Cambridges" controversy between economists such as Joan Robinson and Piero Sraffa at the University of Cambridge in England and economists such as Paul Samuelson and Robert Solow at the Massachusetts Institute of Technology, in Cambridge, Massachusetts. Piero Sraffa put forward the idea that in order to solve the problem of the macroeconomic aggregation of the factors of production (capital and labor), an empirically based strategy should start from the production process of commodities and from the observation that a commodity is always produced from commodities of previous generations. Piero Sraffa, *Production*

of Commodities by Means of Commodities: Prelude to a Critique of Economic Theory (Cambridge: CUP Archive, 1975). For a recent technical and political updating, see David Rezza Baqaee and Emmanuel Farhi, "JEEA-FBBVA Lecture 2018: The Microeconomic Foundations of Aggregate Production Functions," *Journal of the European Economic Association* 17.5 (October 2019), pp. 1337–92, https://academic.oup.com/jeea/article-abstract/17/5/1337/5585840?redirectedFrom=fulltext.

30. The symbol f( ) must be taken in its literal sense, a "function of." This (elementary) symbolism does not mean that the formula must be mathematical. The following sentence is a formula: "The price depends on the cost of energy, the productivity of the most recent machines, the salary and social security costs of employees, weather forecasts, and the result of the referendum the government has called."

31. Price formulation is a process whose outcome is a formula that determines a price. The term "formula" is to be taken in its very rich and polysemic meaning. One speaks, for example, of mathematical formulas as well as chemical formulas or any combination of ingredients that are arranged to produce a new entity, which, once stabilized, enforces an equilibrium between a set of heterogeneous forces. For a useful definition of "form," see Eduardo Kohn, *How Forests Think: Toward an Anthropology Beyond the Human* (Oakland: University of California Press, 2013). The term "formulation" encompasses material elements. For example, a form designates in French a wooden block used to mold a shoe. And when one makes reference to Formula 1, whether one is referring to car races or very cheap French hotels, one is referring to arrangements in which material components (rooms, cars, and so on) play a prominent role.

32. Guilhem Anzalone, "Comment transformer un produit en marchandise et lui attribuer un prix: Le traitement de la viande dans la grande distribution," *Sociologie du travail* 51.1 (2009), pp. 64–77. I will stick closely to Anzalone's text, pointing out what in his analysis contributes to understanding the formulation process.

33. It is worth noting that this is not a description of standard American meat production. It is about butchered meat, as opposed to frozen packages of industrially packaged meat, where the parts of many animals are put together.

34. On classifying and scoring operations, see Chapter 3.

35. Losses are due to goods being either thrown out or stolen.

36. On the notion of form, see note 31.

37. On the importance of material dimensions, see note 31.

38. Anzalone, "Comment transformer un produit," p. 69. The formalisms (Pi, $Pi-1$, $Pi-2$, and so on) as well as the resort to the concept of formula, are mine.

39. On the notion of ontological multiplicity, see Annemarie Mol, *The Body Multiple: Ontology in Medical Practice* (Durham: Duke University Press, 2000).

40. For a detailed presentation of this story, see Jean Finez, "La construction des prix à la SNCF, une socio-histoire de la tarification: De la péréquation au *yield management* (1938–2012)," *Revue française de sociologie* 1.55 (2014), pp. 5–39.

41. The relationship between yield management and the discriminating monopoly model deserves further investigation. It seems that Jules Dupuit, a French engineer who introduced the notion of *consumer surplus* in the 1850s, was one of those who initiated the discriminating monopoly model. The consumer surplus corresponds to the difference between the price (*Pb*) that the consumer is ready to pay and the unique price that the seller would determine in order to ensure a sales volume he judges to be satisfactory. Dupuit used it, among other things, to justify tolls on waterways and the creation of different classes for rail transport. The maddening amplification of data in the ad-based economy of the internet has fostered the dissemination and implementation of the discriminating monopoly model.

42. Wasmer, *Principes de microéconomie*, p. 346.

43. In this case, companies can settle for playing with two variables: quantities and prices (possibly taking into account their cross elasticity). In the case of a discriminating monopoly, each good corresponds to a different price, and therefore the optimization calculations are infinitely more complex. It would remain to describe and explain this convergence between the implementation of the model, the availability of appropriate computational tools, and the existence of vast databases from which to drive the computation. It seems reasonable to expect that singularization processes be linked to constant interactions between both lines of evolution as proved by the development of firms such as Amazon or Google. For a brilliant and influential analysis of how Amazon has progressively established a powerful discriminating monopoly, see Lina M. Khan, "Amazon's Antitrust Paradox," *Yale Law Journal* 126.3 (2017), p. 96.

44. E. Andrew Boyd, *The Future of Pricing: How Airline Ticket Pricing Has Inspired a Revolution* (New York: Palgrave Macmillan, 2007).

45. As, for instance, INFORMS, the Institute for Operation Research and the Management Sciences.

46. "Enquête: La rentabilité coûte que coûte," *Que choisir*, no. 536, May 2015, pp. 16–23.

47. Recourse to qualculating algorithms in real time to affix prices leads in fact to the paralysis of competition through prices, as Ariel Ezrachi and Maurice Stucke's

empirical study very convincingly shows: Ariel Ezrachi and Maurice Stucke, *Virtual Competition: The Promise and Perils of the Algorithm-Driven Economy* (Cambridge, MA: Harvard University Press, 2016). They show, notably, that when companies use the same pricing algorithms, from the classical point of view, it looks as though they were agreeing on prices (collusion).

48. Fabian Muniesa, "Market Technologies and the Pragmatics of Prices," *Economy and Society* 36.3 (2007), pp. 377–95.

49. This is the literal and most prevalent form of affixing a price to a good: assigning the price to a label, "affixed" either on the good or on a digital strip, and the easiest way to play on the price, and only on the price, in order to requalify the good, is to change the labels and what they display (in French: "faire valser les étiquettes," "to make the labels dance").

50. Catherine Grandclément, "Vendre sans vendeurs: Sociologie des dispositifs d'achalandage en supermarché," PhD diss., École des Mines de Paris, 2008.

51. Within mainstream economics, a perfectly discriminating price is obtained when it corresponds to the maximum amount that the customer concerned is willing to pay to acquire it. The problem is obviously that one cannot access this amount, *Pb*, directly. It is all the more difficult to identify since the encounter with the client and the joint exploration involved will lead to a possible agreement only at the end of the actual price formulation work.

52. In the last instance (although its particular form depends on the number of agents involved), the calculation rests on the famous so-called law of supply and demand, a law that holds that "when people want more of a good than is currently being produced, its price will rise. This higher price increases producers' profits and provides an incentive for existing firms to expand production and for new firms to enter the industry. Conversely if an industry is producing a good for which there is no market or a good that people no longer want in the same quantity, the result will be excess supply and the price of that good will fall. This outcome reduces profits or creates losses, providing an incentive for some existing firms to cut back on production and for others to go out of business." Karl Case, Ray Fair, and Sharon Oster, *Principles of Economics* (Cambridge: Pearson, 2009), p. 759. It is generally added that this spontaneous price-affixing mechanism leads to an optimal allocation of resources. This inference, which I will discuss in the last chapter in the case of financial markets, does not need to be considered here. The only thing I am interested in here is the explanation of how prices are affixed that is provided.

53. Alan Kirman, "Market Organization and Individual Behavior: Evidence from Fish Markets," in James E. Rauch and Alessandra Casella, eds., *Networks and Markets* (New York: Russell Sage Foundation, 2001), pp. 155-210.

54. During the period covered by Kirman's study, the market was open every day from 2:00 a.m. to 6:00 a.m.

55. This observation is my own. In his text, Kirman does not refer explicitly to the concept of discriminating monopoly.

56. Kirman identifies an unexpected result: when the economist aggregates supplies and demands, the prices—even aggregated—follow the classical law of supply and demand. The Marseille fish market may well be efficient! I can understand why he finds this result significant, but in the context of an analysis of market agencements, it does not have any particular significance. That the law of supply and demand be respected at the aggregate level is not a necessity. Indeed, an agencement may lead to different aggregate results, depending on the strategies developed by the agencies. What matters to me here is that competitive monopolism is found in traditional markets, which demonstrates its viability.

57. The bilateral transaction, when it is concluded, implies that attachment has been obtained, or in other words, that the good's singularization has been successful.

58. Service transactions increasingly include a subscription for a given time span. This provides a good illustration of how two framings (attachment and price formulation) can be entangled.

59. This is the associated milieu discussed in Chapter 2.

60. Chamberlin's examples include things such as the salesperson and the color of the car. See Edward Hastings Chamberlin, *The Theory of Monopolistic Competition: A Reorientation of the Theory of Value*, 6th ed. (London: Oxford University Press, 1948), p. 56.

61. See Chapter 5, note 21.

62. Pierre Bourdieu, *Distinction*, trans. Richard Nice (Cambridge, MA: Harvard University Press, 1984).

63. Martha Poon, "Score Cards as Devices for Consumer Credit: The Case of Fair, Isaac & Company Incorporated," in Michel Callon, Yuval Millo, and Fabian Muniesa, eds., *Market Devices* (Hoboken: Wiley-Blackwell, 2007), pp. 284-306.

64. In France, scoring is an important part of loan management, but the scores do not circulate outside the organization that produces them because prevented by strong data protection laws (la CNIL), they are not calculated by entities such as bureaus or sold as commercial goods.

65. The customers who have either missed the occasional repayment or can pay back only very slowly become profitable customers because they pay a great deal of interest over time while repaying little capital. As we saw in the previous chapter, they are also good candidates for relationships of attachment through addiction. It is important to note that the achievement of FICO was never that it predicted defaults accurately, because the default rate is a property of the products (singularized loans) conceived and proposed by lenders, not of people. Indeed, as Martha Poon points out (personal communication), if you apply arduous terms in your product design, you will increase the rate of default at any score level!

66. If, for example, a lender realizes that the people interested in its loans are overwhelmingly located in rural areas, it can undertake more systematic prospecting while adapting its products more finely to the target group as respecified. Risk managers can also participate in this exploration by trying to establish possible correlations between types of loans, all marked by FICO scores, and their specific default risks.

67. The lower the score, the higher the price of loans and the more life conditions are deteriorated for borrowers, whose material situation is already difficult. Via the FICO score and the price formulation that flows from it, the past weighs even more heavily on the borrower's shoulders. See Marion Fourcade and Kieran Healy, "Classification Situations: Life-Chances in the Neoliberal Era," *Accounting, Organization and Society* 38 (2013), pp. 559-72.

68. In the interface market model, assessing quality plays a central role. See Harold Hotelling, "Stability in Competition," *Economic Journal* 39.153 (1929), pp. 41-57, and Lucien Karpik, "L'économie de la qualité," *Revue Française de Sociologie* 30 (1989), pp. 187-210.

69. I hope the reader has understood that quality is a material result of elaborate qualification processes and not a hidden variable lying in wait that the formulation must discover. This observation should lead us to revise the existing analyses of uncertainty concerning goods and their qualities. It follows that when instituted by price differences, quality is neither an intrinsic property of goods that can give rise to information asymmetries nor a socially constructed property unconnected to the goods themselves.

70. The French term *ingénieur-économiste* underlines the fact that until recently, French economists were mostly graduates of engineering schools such as the École Polytechnique, the École des Ponts, the École des Mines, and so on, where they were trained in mathematics and physics. See Theodore M. Porter, *Trust in Numbers: The Pursuit of Objectivity in Science and Public Life* (Princeton: Princeton University Press,

1995); Marion Fourcade, *Economists and Societies: Discipline and Profession in the United States, Britain and France, 1890s to 1990s* (Princeton: Princeton University Press, 2009).

71. Valery Yakubovich, Mark Granovetter, and Patrick McGuire, "Electric Charges: The Social Construction of Rate Systems," *Theory and Society* 34 (2005), pp. 579–612; Gabrielle Hecht, *The Radiance of France: Nuclear Power and National Identity after World War II* (Cambridge, MA: MIT Press, 1998); Guillaume Yon, "Théorie économique, réalité industrielle et intérêt général: La recherche de l'optimum à Électricité de France (1946–1965)," PhD diss., École des Mines de Paris, 2016; Tom Hughes, "The Electrification of America: The System Builders," *Technology and Culture* 20.1 (1979), pp. 124–62; Thomas Reverdy, *La construction politique du prix de l'énergie* (Paris: Presses de Sciences Po, 2014); Alexandra Bidet, "Dessiner le marché, démultiplier le calcul: Les rationalisations materielle et formelle dans la téléphonie au tournant des années 1980," *Revue française de socio-économie* 1.5 (2010), pp. 165–83.

72. Donald MacKenzie, *An Engine, Not a Camera: How Financial Models Shape Markets* (Cambridge, MA: MIT Press, 2006); Vincent Lépinay, *Codes of Finance: Engineering Derivatives in a Global Bank* (Princeton: Princeton University Press, 2014); Porter, *Trust in Numbers*.

73. Sandrine Barrey, "Formation et calcul des prix: Le travail de tarification dans la grande distribution (The Work of Setting Prices in Hypermarket Chains)," *Sociologie du Travail* 48.2 (2006), pp. 142–58.

74. François Vatin, ed., *Évaluer et valoriser: Une sociologie économique de la mesure* (Toulouse: Presses universitaires du Mirail, 2009).

75. Martin Giraudeau's article on this subject is itself an important contribution to the sociology of formulas and price formulation: Martin Giraudeau, "Formuler le projet d'entreprise," in Vatin, ed., *Évaluer et valoriser*, pp. 137–54.

76. On wine markets see, for example, the website of the American Association of Wine Economists, https://www.wine-economics.org, and its *Journal of Wine Economics*, https://www.wine-economics.org/journal; also the blog *Priceonomics*, https://priceonomics.com. Of course, one should track the ways these studies are used and transposed in the relevant sectors. In general, a good strategy for accessing formulation practices, especially when they protect themselves from external eyes, is through the innumerable sites, associations, and publications run by pricing professionals.

77. Juan Pablo Pardo-Guerra, "How Much for the Michelangelo?: Valuation, Commoditization and Finitism in the Secondary Art Market," *Cultural Sociology* 5.2 (2011), pp. 207–23.

78. A historical analysis of the formulas for qualculating the price of works of art and the confrontation to which they give rise would be enlightening. There is interesting information concerning the primary art market (galleries offering works that have not yet entered market circuits) in Olav Velthuis's book that shows that the standard formula includes the prices of comparable works or works by the same artist and gives significant weight to the material dimensions of pieces. Velthuis adds that dealers rely on pricing scripts that function like a formula over the course of the many decisions they make: Olav Velthuis, *Talking Prices: Symbolic Meanings of Prices on the Market for Contemporary Art* (Princeton: Princeton University Press, 2005). Svetlana Alpers shows how Rembrandt was able to break free from dominant formulations that indexed the prices of paintings on the number of hours necessary for their completion. Svetlana Alpers, *Rembrandt's Enterprise: The Studio and the Market* (Chicago: University of Chicago Press, 1988). A precious historical literature is devoted to contracts linking artists to their patrons, contracts that generally specify the price formulation.

79. Jane Guyer, *Marginal Gains: Monetary Transactions in Atlantic Africa* (Chicago: University of Chicago Press, 2004), p. 54.

80. Ibid.

81. Ibid.

82. Koray Çalişkan, *Market Threads: How Cotton Farmers and Traders Create a Global Commodity* (Princeton: Princeton University Press, 2010).

83. In his analysis of traders' pay, Olivier Godechot shows the effects of these asymmetries on the affixing of prices. If someone in a position of responsibility wants to drive up the level of his bonuses, he has only to threaten to leave with his entire team, which would deprive the bank of a large part of its qualculative skills. Olivier Godechot, *Wages, Bonuses and Appropriation of Profit in the Financial Industry* (Abingdon: Routledge, 2017).

84. Weber rightly underlines the role of budget calculations when he distinguishes between firms and budgetary units, which include what is now called household economics. Weber, *Economy and Society*, vol. 1, pp. 98–99. See also, Bourdieu, *The Social Structures of the Economy*.

85. Hélène Ducourant, "Du crédit à la consommation à la consommation de crédits: Autonomisation d'une activité économique," PhD diss., Lille 1, 2009; Jeanne Lazarus, "Prévoir la défaillance de crédit: L'ambition du scoring," *Raisons politiques* 4.48 (2012), pp. 103–18. In France, at least, government authorities play an essential role in regulating this qualculation space. There are procedures that aim to manage overindebtedness, forcing banks to include the poor and to detect fragile customers, setting

up places for budget advice, organizing classes on financial education, and defining "reference budgets" for households. Pierre Concialdi, "Les budgets de référence: Un nouveau repère dans le débat public sur la pauvreté," *La Revue de l'Ires* 3.82 (2014), pp. 3–36.

86. Francis Chateauraynaud, "L'emprise comme expérience: Enquêtes pragmatiques et théories du pouvoir," *SociologieS*, February 23, 2015, https://journals.openedition .org/sociologies/4931.

87. Reverdy shows how the New Organization of Market in Electricity (NOME) law, voted on in 2010 after intense negotiations among François Fillon's government, the European Commission, the administration, the electric utility company EDF, and its competitors, established three distinct formulas: a regulated price for individuals, a market price for those who wish it, and the ARENH (Accès régulé à l'électricité nucléaire historique) price, which gives EDF access to its electricity at nuclear prices. See Reverdy, *La construction politique du prix de l'énergie*, and Thomas Reverdy and Daniel Breslau, "Making an Exception: Market Design and the Politics of Reregulation in the French Electricity Sector," *Economy and Society* 48.2 (2019), pp. 197–220.

88. It is in order to take these possible concerns into account that some companies offer to block advertisements.

89. Katayoun Shafiee, "Cracking Petroleum with Politics: Anglo-Persian Oil and the Socio-Technical Transformation of Iran, 1901–1945, PhD diss., New York University, 2010; Katayoun Shafiee, "A Petro-Formula and Its World: Calculating Profits, Labour and Production in the Assembling of Anglo-Iranian Oil," *Economy and Society* 41.4 (2012), pp. 585–614.

90. Vololona Rabeharisoa and Liliana Doganova, "Making Rareness Count: Testing and Pricing Orphan Drugs," *Working Papers Series* 16-CSI-03 (2016), https://hal-mines -paristech.archives-ouvertes.fr/hal-01379153.

91. Robert Castel, *From Manual Workers to Wage Laborers: Transformation of the Social Question* (New Brunswick: Transaction, 2003).

92. In the study he devotes to this subject, Mathieu Grégoire provides the chronological series of formulas and counterformulas suggested by the protagonists in order to set the daily compensation of these workers. Mathieu Grégoire, "Attribuer une valeur au hors-emploi: L'intermittence du spectacle," in François Vatin, ed., *Évaluer et valoriser*, pp. 93–114. The formula being used at the moment he published his text and that is entirely quantitative and mathematical can be described as follows: the payment, indexed to the minimum wage, is a linear combination of the referenced annual salary,

the number of hours worked, and a fixed part. Furthermore, it is conceived to guarantee a minimal level, itself a function of the minimum wage per day, that grows in relation to the annual salary and number of days worked. Who said one could not fall in love with a growth rate? In any case, one can fight tooth and nail for a formula and its composition, as shown by the struggles that for several years, starting in 2014, pitted the *"intermittents"* against the Socialist government.

93. Symmetrically, a bonus, possibly passed on to salaries, could be given to companies that do not let workers go.

94. The idea of compensation is interesting. To compensate indicates the idea of an indemnity that aims at reestablishing a broken equilibrium. In the case of work, it underlines that all labor is suffering and effort and that the price paid does not include profit, but simply registers the costs, the time spent, and the efforts provided. This is a configuration that, taken to the limit (the formula can be considered to be a markup without a profit margin), tips it into nonmarket activities. See, for instance, Klaus Hoeyer, "Tradable Body Parts?: How Bones and Recycled Prosthetic Devices Acquire a Price without Forming a Market," *Biosocieties* 4 (2009), pp. 239–56.

95. Economic theory has very effectively contributed to the design of devices, notably contractual ones, that incite companies to reveal their costs and the way they calculate prices.

96. See Ministère de l'Économie des Finances et de la Relance, "Le prix du gaz et de l'électricité," economie.gouv.fr/facileco/prix-gaz-et-lelectricite.

97. On this subject, see Nicolas Touchot and Mathias Flume, "The Payers' Perspective on Gene Therapies," *Nature Biotechnology* 33.9 (2015), pp. 11–13.

98. In the following, "discriminating" should not been taken in its legal signification, as when one speaks of antidiscriminatory laws. "Discriminating" means simply differentiating, performing distinctions.

99. The presentation that follows is largely inspired by unpublished work by Martha Poon and the long conversation I had with her. Without Martha, I think I would have made the mistake of not seeing how inclusion and exclusion are closely related.

100. Credit markets in France have not been as radically inclusive as in the United States because they don't have the passa(c)tivated, market-ready, common score upon which to build credit products that can in turn be passa(c)tivated and sold onto the secondary markets. Martha Poon, personal communication.

101. For the account of how this expansion of credit happened in subprime mortgage lending, see Martha Poon, "From New Deal Institutions to Capital Markets: Commercial

Consumer Risk Scores and the Making of Subprime Mortgage Finance," *Accounting, Organizations and Society* 34.5 (July 2009), pp. 654-74.

102. For the same argument, but in 225 pages, see the classic book by David Caplovitz, *The Poor Pay More: Consumer Practices of Low-Income Families* (New York: Free Press, 1968).

103. The point is that few are genuinely excluded from all credit markets, broadly defined, which is why US outstanding consumer credit exceeded $14 trillion in 2019. See above.

104. The term "digital labor" refers to the activity done for free by those who leave traces on the web by providing requested data or simply by visiting sites. This labor is invisible. The word "labor" implies that it is work, and it is unpaid. Although the expression is suggestive, it is also problematic. It would be better, playing on the double meaning of the word "digital" (one types with fingers and exchanges digital data) to speak of digital activities that in certain cases can be considered labor. What is important, for my purposes, is that the fact that no compensation is offered for this activity is a sign of a problem that has not been discussed, a persistent ambiguity. Is it an activity that is simply fun? Is there a sort of tacit contract between the one who leaves traces and the operator who uses those traces to come back to the user with new services? The answer depends on the particular circumstances in which this activity takes place. "When it is free, you are the product!" remains a striking formulation of a certain protest by users that confirms that concerns about services for free or nil prices are justified.

105. Joëlle Farchy, Cécile Méadel, and Guillaume Sire, *La gratuité à quel prix?: Circulation et échange de biens sur Internet* (Paris: Presses des Mines, 2015).

106. Martin Untersinger, *Le Monde*, "Éco & Entreprises" supplement, February 28, 2015, p. 8. What is established by one text can be undone by another, as the decisions of the Trump administration in 2017 demonstrate.

107. Economists sometimes call these effects "pecuniary externalities."

108. Those interested in this subject should consult Donald MacKenzie's publications: Donald MacKenzie and Yuval Millo, "Constructing a Market, Performing Theory: The Historical Sociology of a Financial Derivative," *American Journal of Sociology* 109.1 (2003), pp. 107-45; Donald MacKenzie, "The Credit Crisis as a Problem in the Sociology of Knowledge," *American Journal of Sociology* 116.6 (2011), pp. 1778-841; Donald MacKenzie, "Knowledge Production in Financial Markets: Credit Default Swaps, the ABX and the Subprime Crisis," *Economy and Society* 41.3 (2012), pp. 335-59; See also Christian Walter and Jacques Lévy Véhel, *Les marchés fractals:*

Efficience, ruptures et tendances sur les marchés financiers (Paris: Presses universitaires de France, 2002).

109. Luc Boltanksi and Laurent Thévenot, *On Justification: Economies of Worth* (Princeton: Princeton University Press, 2006).

110. Donald MacKenzie, "An Equation and Its Worlds: Bricolage, Exemplars, Disunity and Performativity in Financial Economics," *Social Studies of Science* 33.6 (2003), pp. 831–68.

111. Guillaume Yon, "L'économicité propre à EDF: Sur la formule de tarification de l'électricité au coût marginal (1948–1958)," PhD diss., Lille, 2012; Guillaume Yon and Alexandre Mallard, "The Moral Life of Formulas: The Construction of Marginal Cost Pricing of Electricity in Postwar France," presented at the "Embeddedness and Beyond: Do Sociological Theories Meet Economic Realities?" conference, Moscow, October 25–28, 2012.

112. François-Mathieu Poupeau, "La fabrique d'une solidarité nationale: État et élus ruraux dans l'adoption d'une péréquation des tarifs de l'électricité en France," *Revue française de science politique* 57.5 (2007), pp. 599–628.

113. This is a French national association of local and regional authorities. It roughly translates as the National Federation of Granting and Regulating Authorities.

114. Fabian Muniesa, "Un robot walrasien: Cotation électronique et justesse de la découverte des prix," *Politix* 13.52 (2000), pp. 121–54. Algorithms are becoming a major subject of concern. More and more virulent controversies surround the way they are shaped and the choices they make. Their design and implementation are major stakes for market agencements.

115. Jane Guyer, *Legacies, Logics, Logistics: Essays in the Anthropology of the Platform Economy* (Chicago: University of Chicago Press, 2016), pp. 211–19.

116. This explains why moral relativism is not possible concerning price formulation. The formulas transform morality into something qualculable, as is seen when the salary levels of Chinese workers are denounced as *too* low, or the pay of CEOs of large corporations is decried for being *too* high. Moral qualculation is an old story. The *lex mercatoria* that defined the rules and principles for commerce in Europe in the Middle Ages, for instance, condemned any transaction in which the price was more than 50 percent above the common price—in other words, fair price < 1.5 times the average price.

117. The notion of moral economy, an expression used by E. P. Thompson (Edward P. Thompson, "The Moral Economy of the English Crowd in the Eighteenth Century," *Past & Present* 50 [1971], pp. 36–76) and much criticized, is not applicable to market

agencements. The latter cannot be held to be moral, immoral, or amoral. Moral questions infiltrate each of their framings, notably in the activities of price formulation. For a given agencement, the mechanisms through which goods are pass(act)ivated may be held by some to be immoral, while others consider them legitimate. The same goes for the four other framings. And at no point can the answers provided, local and fluctuating, be added up in such a way as to characterize the agencement as a whole.

118. Transaction costs include all the costs necessary for organizing market transactions. According to some economists, these must be minimized in order for the market to be the most advantageous mode of coordination. Transaction costs become a key investment for market agencements, which are strategically oriented toward instituting, and multiplying (costly) bilateral transactions. By the same token, they must be carefully evaluated and taken into account insofar as it is no longer a matter of simply minimizing them, but rather of optimizing them. Whereas it is hard to explain why agents would spend time calculating transaction costs in the interface market model (which seriously diminishes the model's power of explanation), these costs take on such an important strategic value in market agencements that agents cannot omit qualculating them with the greatest care.

CHAPTER SEVEN: HOW DO MARKET AGENCEMENTS EVOLVE?

1. This quotation is from Giorgio Agamben, *"What Is an Apparatus?" and Other Essays* (Stanford: Stanford University Press, 2009), p. 2. The full text can be found in Michel Foucault, *Power/Knowledge: Selected Interviews and Other Writings 1972–1977*, ed. Colin Gordon, trans. Colin Gordon et al. (New York: Pantheon Books, 1980), pp. 194–228. The quote is on pp. 194-95 and 196. Agamben has slightly modified the translation.

2. Agamben, *"What Is an Apparatus,"* p. 3.

3. Paul Veyne, *Foucault: His Thought, His Character* (Cambridge: Polity, 2010), p. 50.

4. Agamben, *What Is an Apparatus?*, p. 12

5. Nikolas Rose, *The Politics of Life Itself: Biomedicine, Power, and Subjectivity in the Twenty-First Century* (Princeton: Princeton University Press, 2006); Paul Rabinow, *Essays on the Anthropology of Reason* (Princeton: Princeton University Press, 1996).

6. Andrew Lakoff, *Pharmaceutical Reason: Knowledge and Value in Global Psychiatry* (Cambridge: Cambridge University Press, 2005).

7. Peter Keating and Alberto Cambrosio, *Cancer on Trial: Oncology as a New Style of Practice* (Chicago: University of Chicago Press, 2012); Vololona Rabeharisoa et al., "From 'Politics of Numbers' to 'Politics of Singularisation': Patients' Activism and

Engagement in Research on Rare Diseases in France and Portugal," *BioSocieties* 9.2 (2014), pp. 194–217; Daniel Navon and Gil Eyal, "Looping Genomes: Diagnostic Change and the Genetic Makeup of the Autism Population," *American Journal of Sociology* 21.5 (2016), pp. 1416–71.

8. Gilles Deleuze and Félix Guattari, *Kafka: Toward a Minor Literature*, trans. Dana Polan (Minneapolis: University of Minnesota Press, 1986).

9. Manuel De Landa, *A New Philosophy of Society: Assemblage Theory and Social Complexity* (London: Continuum, 2006).

10. Gilles Deleuze, "What Is a *Dispositif?*," in Timothy J. Armstrong, ed., *Michel Foucault, Philosopher: Essays Translated from the French and German* (New York: Routledge, 1991), pp. 159–68.

11. On this model, see Madeleine Akrich et al., "The Key to Success in Innovation Part I: The Art of Interessement," and "The Key to Success in Innovation Part II: The Art of Choosing Good Spokespersons," *International Journal of Innovation Management* 6.2 (June 2002), pp. 187–206 and 207–225, respectively.

12. Jane Guyer, *Marginal Gains: Monetary Transactions in Atlantic Africa* (Chicago: University of Chicago Press, 2004).

13. Carliss Y. Baldwin, "Where Do Transactions Come From?: Modularity, Transactions and the Boundaries of Firms," *Industrial and Corporate Change* 17.1 (2008), pp. 155–95.

14. This does not prevent it from setting up a quasi-market with profit centers.

15. I am not sure that it is appropriate still to speak of firms. It would be better to save this term for incorporated free zones. Indeed, the word "firm" refers to the capacity for holding to a collective contractual obligation that is authorized and required by the status of legal personhood (*firma* refers to the commitment and signature). A community is never held to this type of commitment.

16. The existence and development of noncommercial zones, enclaves within the market sphere, are usually explained by invoking the calculation of the organizational costs of transactions (in some cases it may, for instance, be cheaper to choose hierarchy, rather than a commercial transaction), technological constraints (an organization maintains control over highly interdependent technical operations), or institutional constraints (connected, for instance, to values such as solidarity and reciprocity or to dominant rules). These different explanations do not mention what is central from the perspective of market agencements—namely, the necessary invention of organizational compromises between alignment and articulation.

17. Philippe Steiner, "Don de sang et don d'organes: Le marché des marchandises fictives," *Revue française de sociologie* 42.2 (2001), pp. 357–74.

18. Anissa Pomiès, "The Role of Expertise in a Taste Regime Creation and in Market Shaping: An Ethnography of Coffee Contests," PhD diss., ESCP Business School, 2015.

19. Anna Lowenhaupt Tsing, *The Mushroom at the End of the World: On the Possibility of Life in Capitalist Ruins* (Princeton: Princeton University Press, 2015).

20. See, for instance, the work of Michel Lallement, *L'âge du faire: Hacking, travail, anarchie* (Paris: Seuil, 2015).

21. Jean de La Fontaine, "The Cobbler and the Financier," in *The Fables of La Fontaine*, ed. J. M. W. Gibbs, trans. Elizur Wright (London: George Bell and Sons, 1892), pp. 178–79.

22. Copyleft is a general method for making a program (or any other work) and all its extended or modified versions free. Creative Commons is a nonprofit organization whose aim is to offer an alternative legal solution to those who wish to free their works from intellectual property rights judged to be too constraining.

23. Frank Azimont and Luis Araujo, "Credible Qualification: The Case of Functional Foods," in Susi Geiger et al., eds., *Concerned Markets: Economic Ordering for Multiple Values* (Cheltenham: Edward Elgar, 2014), pp. 129–52.

24. As Blanche Ségrestin and Armand Hatchuel have argued, this requires revising the legal status of companies in such a way as to clarify the conditions under which control and management can be dissociated. Shareholders' right of control should not be, as it is today, essentially a right to manage the company in their own interest! In the United States as of 2017, more than fifty-five hundred companies had taken up public benefit corporation status, which allows companies to associate the search for profit with a public-interest mission without fear of being challenged in court by their shareholders.

25. See Chapter 3, note 53 on programmable infrastructures.

26. On the debates around certain addictive commercial practices, see Philippe Steiner and Marie Trespeuch, "Maîtriser les passions, construire l'intérêt," *Revue française de sociologie* 1 (2013), pp. 115–80.

27. Franck Cochoy, "Facing the Future: Beyond 'Interested' Markets and 'Contested' Markets," in Geiger et al., eds., *Concerned Markets*, pp. 238–56.

28. Philippe Steiner and Marie Trespeuch, *Marchés contestés: Quand le marché rencontre la morale* (Toulouse: Presses universitaires du Midi, 2015). The ban on transforming corneas into commodities (to prevent the poor from selling their bodies) rarifies their availability and thereby worsens conditions for the visually impaired.

29. Pascale Trompette, *Le marché des défunts* (Paris: Presses de Sciences Po, 2008). For a summary of her work, see Pascale Trompette, "A History of the French Funeral Market," *Economic Sociology: The European Electronic Newsletter* 16.1 (2014), pp. 34-36. This article is the main reference in English for Trompette's work on funeral markets.

30. The communion of saints is, for Christians, the union of all the faithful, dead and alive, united through belonging to Christ in a sort of collective solidarity throughout time and space.

31. Heather Lovell and Susan J. Smith, "Agencement in Housing Markets: The Case of the UK Construction Industry," *GeoForum* 41 (2010), pp. 457-68.

32. Evolutionary economics has greatly contributed to revealing and making explicit lock-in and lock-out phenomena. There is now an abundant literature on the subject. Although the analyses offered do not explicitly mention framing devices, they do actually revolve around them and can thus be considered essential contributions to the analysis of market agencements.

CHAPTER EIGHT: THE ROLE OF THEORIZATION IN TRANSFORMING MARKETS

1. Michel Callon, "What Does It Mean to Say That Economics Is Performative?," in Donald MacKenzie, Fabian Muniesa, and Lucia Siu, eds., *How Economists Make Markets: The Performativity of Economics* (Princeton: Princeton University Press, 2007), pp. 311-57.

2. On the notion of interference, see John Law and John Urry, "Enacting the Social," *Economy and Society* 33.3 (2004), pp. 390-410; John Law, "Economics as Interference," in Paul du Gay and Michael Pryke, eds., *Cultural Economy: Cultural Analysis and Commercial Life* (London: Sage, 2002), pp. 21-38. The notion of interference suggests that the theoretical work is situated in a force field and that therefore its effects are limited, localized, and problematic.

3. On metaconcerns, see "The Dynamics of Concerns" in Chapter 7.

4. Alfred Galichon, "Est-il vraiment important que les marchés soient efficients?," *Revue Banque hors-série* (2011), pp. 10-16.

5. Or more vaguely, one could say that financial activities should serve society, rather than the reverse, without specifying which objectives should be reached or how that should be determined.

6. Galichon, "Est-il vraiment important que les marchés soient efficients?," pp. 10-16.

7. Michel Callon, "Introduction: The Embeddedness of Economic Markets in Eco-

nomics," Michel Callon, ed., *The Laws of the Markets* (Oxford: Blackwell, 1998), pp. 1-57; Fabian Muniesa and Michel Callon, "La performativité des sciences économiques," in François Vatin and Philippe Steiner, eds., *Traité de sociologie économique* (Paris: Presses universitaires de France, 2009); Koray Çalişkan and Michel Callon, "Economization, Part 1: Shifting Attention from the Economy towards Processes of Economization," *Economy and Society* 38.3 (2009), pp. 369-98.

8. The mimesis can lead either to self-feeding crises that the agents cannot escape or, sooner or later, to a drastic cutback of the collected profits.

9. Vincent Lépinay, *Codes of Finance: Engineering Derivatives in a Global Bank* (Princeton: Princeton University Press, 2014).

10. Roman Frydman and Michael Goldberg, *Beyond Mechanical Markets: Asset Price Swings, Risk, and the Role of the State* (Princeton: Princeton University Press, 2011).

11. This conception of the relationship between tools and agencies was presented and justified in Chapter 3.

12. Donald MacKenzie, *An Engine, Not a Camera: How Financial Models Shape Markets* (Cambridge, MA: MIT Press, 2006). The Black-Scholes model makes it possible to calculate an option's price as a function of the price variations of the underlying assets. At its heart, is a rather simple partial differential equation borrowed from statistical physics.

13. These characteristics seem to be consistent with the rational expectation hypothesis.

14. This is why many financial market specialists argue for adopting other probabilistic models, such as Lévy distributions or nonprobabilistic distributions such as Mandelbrot fractals. For further discussion of these questions and notably of the improvements on the Black-Scholes model, see MacKenzie's remarkable *An Engine, Not a Camera.*

15. As André Orléan underlines, the expectations that feed these movements relate to the evolution of the market and not to so-called fundamentals of the economy. To complete his description, one might add that these expectations are largely realized by and embodied in instruments that can be described and whose history and evolution one can trace. I do not think he would disagree. See André Orléan, *L'empire de la valeur: Refonder l'économie* (Paris: Seuil, 2015).

16. Donald MacKenzie, "The Credit Crisis as a Problem in the Sociology of Knowledge," *American Journal of Sociology* 116.6 (2011), pp. 1778-1841.

17. As Martha Poon has shown with FICO, common regulation can be a force in

pushing populations to commit to a certain tool. It was adopted universally in the United States, not as a tool of risk management, but as a tool for avoiding the fines associated with the enforcement of equal-opportunity laws. Nonetheless, FICO tamed the chaos of local underwriting to allow nationally pooled loan structures to emerge twenty years later. The unifying factor for markets was not the adoption of the economists' notion of risk, but rather federal laws. See Martha Poon, "Statistically Discriminating without Discrimination," *CRESC Working Paper Series London School of Economics*, London, 2013. Regulation can unify markets *indirectly*, and it does so in the United States all the time. Has this irreversibility and locking in made it difficult for new tools to emerge? It's hard to say.

18. For a clear and pedagogical presentation of self-reinforcing mechanisms, see Jean-Pierre Dupuy, *La panique* (Paris: Les Empêcheurs de penser en rond, 2003).

19. Sabine Montagne and Horatio Ortiz, "Sociologie de l'agence financière: Enjeux et perspectives," *Sociétés contemporaines* 4.92 (2013), pp. 7–33.

20. Sociologist Olivier Godechot refers to "rationality bazaars" to underline that on trading floors alone, at least three forms of qualculating equipment cohabit: those derived from technical analysis (see Chapter 3), those that use so-called fundamental economic variables, and those that use algorithms and probability distributions. Each agent calculates differently from other agents on the basis of information that is itself different. Power relations are woven around this equipment, and positional hierarchies take shape. It is easy to imagine what the bazaar looks like when one moves off the trading floor! See Olivier Godechot, "Le bazar de la rationalité: Vers une sociologie des formes concrètes de raisonnement," *Politix 52* (2000), pp. 17–56.

21. Quoted in Karl Popper, *The World of Parmenides: Essays on the Presocratic Enlightment* (London: Routledge, 1998), p. 46.

22. Regarding financial markets, some of Robert Schiller's propositions point in this direction, notably when he calls for new actors, beyond experts, to be invited to design and create new financial markets, Robert Schiller, *Macro-Markets: Creating Institutions for Managing Society's Largest Economic Risks* (Oxford: Oxford University Press, 1993).

23. I should immediately add that the results from planned economies are just as grim!

24. It should be noted, however, that there is a growing interconnection between the concerns as they are now starting to take shape in relation to the financial markets and those that are already widely expressed in relation to climate change. The purpose

of the current chapter is not to enter into the intertwining of concerns and the elaborated responses. This will be the subject of the second volume I consider to devote to market agencements. Through a set of judiciously selected cases, the current chapter simply shows the role played by the work of theorizing at each stage in the cycle of transformation.

25. A single population can also be affected both positively and negatively, as Nastassja Martin shows. Nastassja Martin, *Les âmes sauvages: Face à l'Occident, la résistance d'un peuple d'Alaska* (Paris: La Découverte, 2016).

26. One could, of course, chose the second option and attempt to conceive sustainable solutions and devices so as to save the industries that live on fossil fuels and the states that feed on them. Those who take part in the political engineering of market agencements should publish a declaration of interests beforehand!

27. In economics, marginal-cost pricing is the term used to designate the practice of setting the price of a product to equal the extra cost of producing an extra unit of output.

28. Guillaume Yon, "Théorie économique, réalité industrielle et intérêt général: La recherche de l'optimum à Électricité de France (1946-1965)," PhD diss., École des Mines de Paris, 2016.

29. Richard Lipsey and Kelvin Lancaster, "The General Theory of the Second Best," *Review of Economics Studies* 24.1 (1956-57), pp. 11-32.

30. So-called grandfather clauses involve not modifying capacities that have historically been acquired and are still current. In this case, it is a matter of not wiping out the past.

31. Roger Guesnerie, "Pour une politique climatique globale," in Philippe Askenazy and Daniel Cohen, eds., *5 crises: 11 nouvelles questions d'économie contemporaine* (Paris: Albin Michel, 2013), pp. 637-97.

32. See Mats Anderson, Patrick Bolton, and Frédéric Samana, "Hedging Climate Risk," *Financial Analysts Journal* 72.3 (2016), pp. 13-32.

33. See, for example, Richard Douthwaite, *Short Circuit: Strengthening Local Economies for Security in an Unstable World* (Dublin: Lilliput Press, 1996); expanded online edition, June 2003, https://www.feasta.org/documents/shortcircuit/Short_Circuit.pdf.

34. On what this redefinition of economics as a discipline could and should be, see Antonin Pottier's work: Antonin Pottier, *Comment les économistes réchauffent la planète* (Paris: Seuil, 2016). The author insists on the fact that one cannot continue to privilege only economic growth. The preservation of life and biodiversity must be taken into account.

35. Pope Francis, *Laudato Si'*, http://www.vatican.va/content/francesco/en/encyclicals/documents/papa-francesco_20150524_enciclica-laudato-si.html.

36. MA is short for "market agencement."

37. Michel Callon, "Is Science a Public Good?," *Science, Technology and Human Values* 19.4 (1994), pp. 395–424.

38. On all these points, see Michel Callon, "How to Design Alternative Markets: The Case of Genetically Modified / Non-Genetically Modified Coexistence," in Gerda Roelvink, Kevin St. Martin, and J. K. Gibson-Graham, eds., *Making Other Worlds Possible: Performing Diverse Economies* (Minneapolis: University of Minnesota Press, 2015), pp. 322–48.

39. François Furet, *Le passé d'une illusion: Essai sur l'idée communiste au XXe siècle* (Paris: Livre de poche, 2003), pp. 808–809.

40. Bruno Latour, *Reassembling the Social: An Introduction to Actor-Network-Theory* (Oxford: Oxford University Press, 2007).

Index

encountering (third framing), 59, 363, 378; market-oriented passiva(c)tion (first framing), 18, 57-58, 101, 376; noncommercial operations, 206; and overflowings, 80, 373, 375, 376, 378-79, 386; price formulation (fifth framing), 59; purpose of, 57-60; qualification-singularization (second framing), 58-59; types of, 57, 206. *See also* affectio mercatus; Price formulation.

Franklin, Rosalind, 345.

Free (telecommunications company), 319-21.

Free zones, 370-73, 376, 380.

French Association against Myopathy, 401.

French Conseil supérieur de l'audiovisuel, 241.

French National Medical Council, 352.

French Revolution, 380.

French Rugby Federation, 84.

Frictional markets, 204, 206-208, 210, 216, 229. *See also* match making.

Friedman, Milton, 33, 179, 182-83.

Frydman, Roman, 395, 398, 400.

Fugger (banking family), 171.

Functional goods, 377.

Funerals, 379, 380-83, 385.

Furet, François, 426.

Futures, 129-30.

GADREY, JEAN, 140.

Galichon, Alfred, 208, 390-91, 392-93.

Gambling, 23-24, 123-24, 130-31, 262, 278-81, 283-84, 287-88; price of, 29, 288, 337; singularization of, 27-29; space for, 283; "zone," 24-27, 279, 283.

Game theory, 40, 192, 291, 352.

Garcier, Romain, 70.

Garud, Raghu, 181-82.

GDF Suez (Engie), 341.

Geertz, Clifford, 34.

Gene therapy, 138.

Généthon, 234.

Genetically modified organisms, 136, 138, 389, 419, 421, 423, 425. *See also* agriculture; transgenesis.

Geolocalization, of customers, 214.

Gerlitz, Carolin, 276, 277.

Gift, The (Mauss), 84.

Gitelman, Lisa, 76.

GlaxoSmithKline, 176.

Global warming, *see* Climate change.

Glyphosate, 422.

GMCs, *see* Genetically modified crops.

GMOs, *see* Genetically modified organisms.

GNU, 376.

Godelier, Maurice, 70, 82, 83, 85, 444 n.51.

Goldberg, Michael, 395, 398, 400.

Goncourt Academy, 221.

Goods: commodification of, 65; commodification-resistant, 67-69, 73, 104, 339; devices for characterizing, 152-54, 157; qualification of, 53-54, 58; singularization of, 59, 315; transformation of, 315. *See also* Density; Inalienable possessions; Sphere of exchange.

Goods, evaluating: nominal, ordinal, and numerical scales, 330.

GoPro, 314.

Grandclément, Catherine, 315.

Granovetter, Mark, 35, 209, 292.

Great Transformation, The (Polanyi), 45.

Greenhouse gas emissions, 79, 334, 376, 389, 404; economization of, 409-16; and market failures, 403-406; market for, 144; and optimum-based approaches, 409-13; policy instruments, 406-7, 411-12, 415, 416; quotas, 406-407, 416; regulating, 406-407; taxes on, 193, 406-407, 411-12, 415; worst-case avoidance, 413-18. *See also* Energy transition.

Greenspan, Alan, 31-32.

Guattari, Félix, 359.

Guesnerie, Roger, 34-35.

INDEX

Weiner, Annette, 70, 72–73, 82.
Weinstein, David, 208.
Weinstein, Olivier, 42.
Whatever (Houellebecq), 196.
White, Harrison, 45, 292.
Williamson, Oliver, 33.
Wine markets, 156–57, 257–58, 297–99.
Wolfe, Tom, 122.
Wonga, 281–82.
Woolgar, Steve, 189.
Work, unit of, 109.

XENOPHANES OF COLOPHON, 402.
X-linked severe combined
    immunodeficiency, 138–39.

YELLOW PAGES, 217.
Yield management, 308, 310, 312–16,
    330, 344, 351.
Yon, Guillaume, 348.
Yoruba people, 182, 330, 331, 339.

ZELIZER, VIVIANA, 45, 85, 86, 124,
    266, 445 n.56.
Zola, Émile, 122, 337.

ZONE BOOKS *NEAR FUTURES* SERIES

Edited by Wendy Brown and Michel Feher

Reckoning with the epochal nature of the turn that capitalism has taken in the last three decades, the editors of *Near Futures* seek to assemble a series of books that will illuminate its manifold implications—with regard to the production of value and values, the missions or disorientations of social and political institutions, the yearnings, reasoning, and conduct expected of individuals. However, the purpose of this project is not only to take stock of what neoliberal reforms and the dictates of finance have wrought. *Near Futures* also purports to chart some of the new conflicts and forms of activism elicited by the advent of our brave new world.

Near Futures series design by Julie Fry
Typesetting by Meighan Gale
Printed and bound by Maple Press